A HISTORY OF THE FEDERAL RESERVE

ALLAN H. MELTZER

A HISTORY OF THE

# Federal Reserve

VOLUME II, BOOK TWO, 1970–1986

THE UNIVERSITY OF CHICAGO PRESS • CHICAGO AND LONDON

The University of Chicago Press, Chicago 60637
The University of Chicago Press, Ltd., London

Paperback edition 2014
Printed in the United States of America

23 22 21 20 19 18 17 16 15 14    2 3 4 5 6

ISBN-13: 978-0-226-51994-4 (cloth)
ISBN-13: 978-0-226-21351-4 (paper)
ISBN-13: 978-0-226-51996-8 (e-book)
DOI: 10.7208/chicago/9780226519968.001.0001

Library of Congress Cataloging-in-Publication Data

Meltzer, Allan H.
A history of the Federal Reserve / Allan H. Meltzer
p. cm.
Includes bibliographical references and index.
Contents: v. 1. 1913–1951 —
ISBN 0-226-51999-6 (v. 1 : alk. paper)
1. Federal Reserve banks. 2. Board of Governors of the Federal Reserve System (U.S.) I. Title.

HG2563.M383 2003
332.1′1′0973—dc21

2002072007

∞ This paper meets the requirements of ANSI/NISO Z39.48-1992 (Permanence of Paper).

CONTENTS

A HISTORY OF THE FEDERAL RESERVE

FIVE

# International Monetary Problems, 1964–71

A worldwide system of flexible rates would, I very much fear, be a continuous invitation to economic warfare as countries maneuvered their rates against each other—or more charitably, influenced their own rates to reflect in each case the immediate interest of the country concerned. There then would be no widely recognized established rate levels, and no presumption of any obligation to maintain rate stability. . . . "I doubt that forward markets could ever as a practical matter get started in any currencies—except perhaps at discounts so large as to make the nominal markets meaningless"
—Robert V. Roosa, in Friedman and Roosa, 1967, 50–52.

Robert Roosa, the person most directly responsible for international economic policy in the first half of the 1960s as Treasury Undersecretary, believed flexible exchange rates were impractical and unworkable. Markets could not be relied on to determine exchange rates. Only some version of a pegged exchange rate system, even if encumbered by controls, could be made to work satisfactorily. A principal reason was that all major countries had adopted full employment as their principal policy goal.[1] That idea dominated international monetary policy in the 1960s.

The United States adopted two major pieces of economic legislation affecting economic policy in the 1940s, one domestic (the Employment Act) and one international. The Bretton Woods Agreement, in practice, became an international dollar standard. United States policy was responsible for maintaining the dollar price of gold at $35 an ounce. This objective required monetary policy either to accept the inflation rate or price level

1. The other person in the debate, Milton Friedman, argued the opposite. An unemployment goal would be easier to achieve if exchange rates were flexible.

consistent with the $35 gold price or to pursue a domestic employment goal by adopting controls and restrictions on trade or capital movements. Roosa chose capital controls.

The domestic and foreign objectives were often in conflict. Several administrations and the Federal Reserve gave most attention to the domestic effects of its policy. The Federal Reserve regarded the balance of payments and the exchange rate as mainly administration problems. Administrations chose to maintain high employment and to reduce the unemployment rate as much as possible. Policy did not totally ignore the balance of payments problem, as it was known, but government was reluctant to accept an increase in the unemployment rate, however temporary, to achieve an international policy objective. It relied instead on (1) a growing number of controls on capital movements to reduce the number of dollars going abroad, and (2) policy adjustments in countries receiving dollars to maintain existing exchange rates. During the 1960s, particularly after 1965, the United States did not have a long-run policy. It met each crisis with a short-run bandage.

Negotiators of the Bretton Woods Agreement spent much effort on preventing a return of deflation. They did not expect or plan for inflation. As Eichengreen (2004, 7) notes, the two principal negotiating countries had different objectives. The United States wanted a system that would maintain stability; the British wanted more policy flexibility. All of the concern about deflationary policy focused on avoiding repetition of United States policy in the 1920s. The principal surplus countries in the 1960s, Germany and Japan, were reluctant to appreciate, just as the United States had been in the 1920s.

In practice, U.S. inflation became the principal source of problems after 1965. Foreign governments complained repeatedly about the inflationary impact on them arising from their dollar receipts. It forced them to choose between allowing their prices to increase, increasing controls on capital movements, and revaluing their exchange rates. They didn't want to do any of the three; in particular, they did not want to take any action that would reduce their exports and employment. They wanted the United States to solve the problem without slowing its growth enough to slow their growth and employment more than marginally.

The Bretton Woods system had a short life, both because member countries' objectives and policy were dominated by maintaining full employment and because the agreement in practice had a flaw.[2] Countries

2. McKinnon (1993, 603, table 2) lists the formal and informal rules of the Bretton Woods system.

other than the United States did not have to inflate or deflate. They could revalue or devalue their currencies against gold and the dollar when their exchange rates were misaligned. In practice the system's operating rules did not permit the United States to devalue, and both Roosa and President Kennedy opposed devaluation. The general belief was that if the United States devalued against gold, other countries would follow by keeping their dollar exchange rate fixed.[3] Even so, devaluation would have increased the nominal value of the gold stock, solving the so-called liquidity problem that concerned policymakers in the 1960s.

Trapped between the unwillingness of countries to revalue their currencies in response to export surpluses and higher rates of growth on the one hand and the inability or unwillingness of the United States to devalue on the other, the System stumbled from crisis to crisis in the late 1960s. At the outset, in recognition of its historic position, the British pound was a reserve currency, akin to the dollar. However, Britain was, more than most, on an employment standard—determined to pursue Keynesian policies of demand growth to maintain full employment. A series of crises ending in devaluation in 1967 greatly reduced the pound's role as a reserve currency.

Between December 1965 and August 1971, when the United States unilaterally stopped selling gold, foreign official institutions (mainly central banks) accumulated $28 billion in dollar claims, an 18 percent compound annual rate of increase (Board of Governors, 1976, 934; 1981, 346).[4] Most countries held these balances in U.S. Treasury bills.

France was an exception. The French government complained that the United States had a unique position. Its citizens could acquire assets and goods abroad, making payments in their own currency. Other countries had to hold the dollar as part of reserves; the United States received seigniorage. This complaint was a restatement of French complaints about the gold exchange standard in the 1920s; France (and others) could not do what the United States could do. Excess supplies of French francs required French disinflation or devaluation; excess supplies of U.S. dollars required France (and others) to inflate or revalue. The United States had to pay the interest cost only on the dollar assets that others accumulated.[5]

3. Devaluation would have required congressional legislation. The delay would have disrupted currency markets.

4. This compares to a 5 percent compound rate in the preceding six years. By the time of the breakdown, the Canadian dollar had left the system. Switzerland and Austria had revalued, and West Germany had floated the mark in spring 1971. On the role of excessive U.S. monetary expansion, see Darby et al. (1983), Bordo (1993), and Eichengreen (2000). For a contrary view, see Cooper (1993, 106).

5. Bordo, Simard, and White (1995) reviews the French position. See also Solomon (1982).

**Table 5.1** United States Monetary Gold Stock and Liquid Liabilities to Foreigners (in $ billions)

| YEAR | MONETARY GOLD | LIQUID LIABILITIES TO FOREIGNERS |
|---|---|---|
| 1960 | 17.8 | 21.0 |
| 1965 | 13.8 | 29.1 |
| 1966 | 13.2 | 29.9 |
| 1967 | 12.0 | 33.3 |
| 1968 | 10.9 | 33.8 |
| 1969 | 11.8 | 41.7 |
| 1970 | 11.1 | 43.3 |

Source: Adapted from Schwartz (1987, Table 14.3, 341).

Stepping back from the many discussions and policy actions to look at the system's evolution shows a steady increase in liquid dollar liabilities to foreigners and the nearly steady decline in the U.S. monetary gold stock available to convert the remaining dollar liabilities into gold. Claims against the stock passed the U.S. gold stock in 1960. By 1965, the claims were more than twice the stock, by 1968 more than three times. Legislation in 1965 first removed gold reserve requirements against bank reserves and in 1968 against currency. This made the entire gold stock available. These actions that were intended to show willingness to support the fixed gold price also called attention to the gold outflow and the ineffectiveness of U.S. policy. Table 5.1 shows these data.

By 1970, liquid liabilities to foreigners were four times as large as the available gold stock. Although the U.S. gold stock stopped falling in 1968 after an embargo was in place, claims or potential claims continued to rise. In the first nine months of 1971, claims rose an additional $21 billion. There was no sign that claims would slow, and no prospect that they would reverse. By 1969 the breakdown of the system would not surprise U.S. policy officials. They did not know when it would occur, but they expected it would. And they understood that any large claim to convert dollar liabilities into gold was likely to trigger a run that could exhaust the remaining stock.

Discussion of these problems went on for several years. Presidents and high officials promised repeatedly to maintain the $35 dollar per ounce gold price, but they did not say how they expected to do so. Officials spoke repeatedly about the three problems of the international monetary system—liquidity, adjustment, and confidence. In practice, they resolved the liquidity problem by producing the special drawing right (SDR) in 1968, a substitute form of international currency to supplement gold and dollars in settlements between central banks. This was a solution to the so-called Triffin problem, discussed in chapter 2, making the international monetary system less dependent on the supply of U.S. dollars. By the time countries agreed on this solution, international reserves were rising rapidly. The SDR did not have much effect or much influence on subsequent events.

The problem that policymakers failed to solve, and rarely discussed, was the adjustment problem—how to get more flexibility in exchange rates.[6] In the 1920s, the unresolved problem of the fixed exchange rate system was the absence of an adjustment mechanism acceptable to the participants. Then, the pound was overvalued, the franc undervalued. Britain would not deflate; France and the United States would not inflate. The system broke down, but the policymakers learned nothing. In the 1960s, the dollar was overvalued. The United States would not deflate or disinflate; the Europeans and Japanese disliked inflation.[7] Again, countries would not adjust exchange rates. The Bretton Woods system ended in the same way; the fixed rate system collapsed.

In the 1920s, the nearly universal system of fixed exchange rates lasted from about 1925–27 to 1931, when Britain and several other countries left the gold standard. The Bretton Woods system lasted longer, but less than ten years—from the beginning of currency convertibility in January 1959 to March 1968, when the United States embargoed gold de facto. In the next few years, the system limped along until President Nixon made the gold embargo absolute in August 1971.[8]

The usual explanation of the failure of Bretton Woods invokes the impossibility of reconciling free capital movements and currency convertibility, fixed exchange rates and full employment. The conflict between fixed exchange rates and the full employment policies was the principal problem in the late 1960s. The choice was never a serious issue for the United States; the Johnson and Nixon administrations always chose em-

6. Robert Solomon, the principal Federal Reserve staff person in international negotiations, describes (Solomon, 1982, 187) the breakdown of the fixed exchange rate system as "inevitable" because of the absence of an adjustment mechanism for the overvalued dollar. Paul Volcker recognized the problem and the likely outcome on becoming Undersecretary for Monetary Affairs in 1969. For an early prediction, see Friedman (1953).

7. Volcker (2006, 17) described the official position. "I can assure you that it was certainly a cause for immediate removal from office—if you raised any question about the gold/dollar link or the exchange rate of the U.S. dollar."

8. Two incidents—the floating of the pound in fall 1931 and the floating of the mark in spring 1971—illustrate the change in beliefs and orientation. Despite depression and high unemployment rates, the New York Federal Reserve Bank responded to Britain's 1931 decision by first raising the buying rate on acceptances and soon after raising the discount rates from 1.5 to 3.5 percent in two steps; other central banks followed. In 1971, the Board did not consider any changes in the discount rate or other restrictive action to defend the currency out of concern for domestic employment.

ployment. The Federal Reserve retreated behind the institutional fact that the Treasury and the administration were responsible for international economic policy.

There are four possible solutions to the adjustment problem (Friedman, 1953): (1) devaluation against gold and major currencies, (2) deflation, (3) borrowing as long as foreigners would lend, and (4) imposing controls of various kinds. Some of these solutions could be achieved in different ways. For example, countries could revalue their currency relative to the dollar. Or, foreigners could inflate faster than the United States. In practice, the United States relied mainly on three and four, usually to a degree insufficient to solve the long-term problem.

The system might have continued if price adjustment had occurred promptly in response to domestic policy choices, differences in productivity growth, changes in the extent of capital mobility, and the like. Flexible prices would have adjusted domestic real wages and the real exchange rates, avoiding the domestic policy problem and the misalignment of the dollar exchange rate.[9] One factor strengthening wage and price downward rigidity was the growing belief that policymakers would not end inflation.

The Bretton Woods Agreement reflected the problems of the interwar gold exchange standard. The authors could not foresee the rapid postwar growth in Europe and Japan, the permanent change in their relative real output and productivity, and the need to adjust real exchange rates to the permanent changes that occurred.[10] The agreement recognized that adjustment to structural (i.e., permanent) changes would occur, but it left to each country to decide how and when to make the change. Countries were slow to recognize the need for appreciation, slower still to implement it.

Japan, West Germany, and France illustrate two extremes. The yen remained fixed at 360 to the dollar throughout the period. The Bank of Japan and the Japanese government accumulated dollar assets, mainly short-term instruments. Monetization of the dollar inflow increased Japan's money stock. Japan's price level rose more rapidly than the U.S. price level, especially in the early 1960s. The real exchange rate appreciated against the dollar by about 25 percent. Chart 5.1 shows the yen-dollar exchange rate adjusted for consumer price level changes.

9. Johnson (1970) makes this point. See also Aliber (1993). Bernstein (1996, 497) adds that in the years leading up to 1958, the IMF had to assure countries that a U.S. recession was not "the beginning of a great depression."

10. The authors also did not foresee the extent of the change in United States policy. After World War II, the U.S. worked to achieve lower tariffs and increased its lending to recovering and developing countries. Further, it took responsibility for maintaining political stability, adding to its foreign spending by keeping armed forces in several countries.

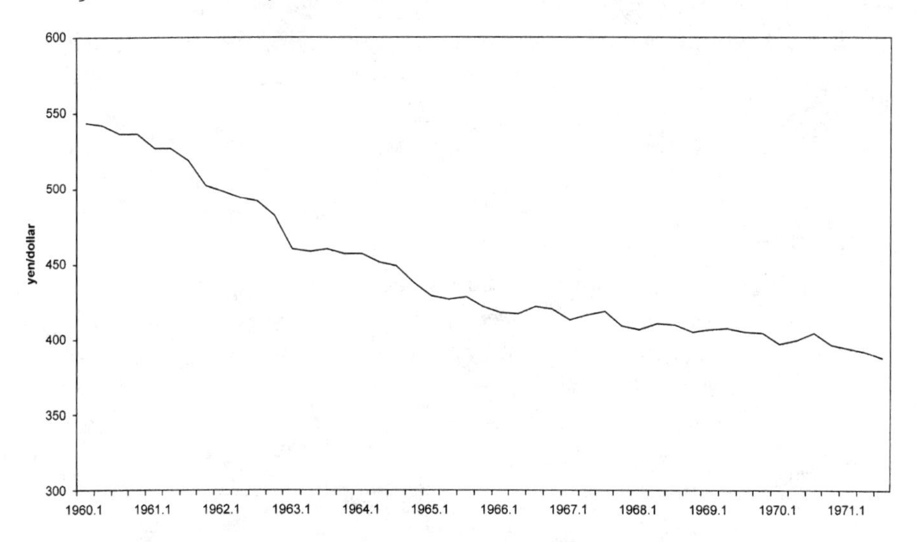


Chart 5.1. Yen-dollar real exchange rate, 1960:1–1971:3.

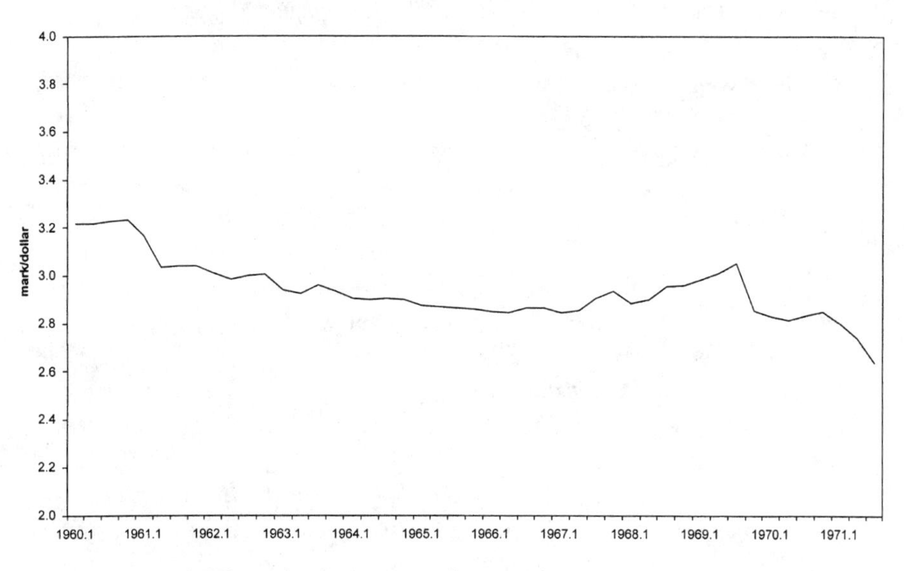


Chart 5.2. Mark-dollar real exchange rate, 1960:1–1971:3.

The West German government and the Bundesbank tried to limit domestic inflation. In 1961 and 1969, the government revalued the mark against the dollar; taken together, the mark appreciated by 12.5 percent. Inflation rates were similar for the period as a whole, so the real exchange rate appreciated much less than the yen-dollar exchange rate and much less than needed to reduce the persistent German payments surplus. Chart 5.2 shows these data.

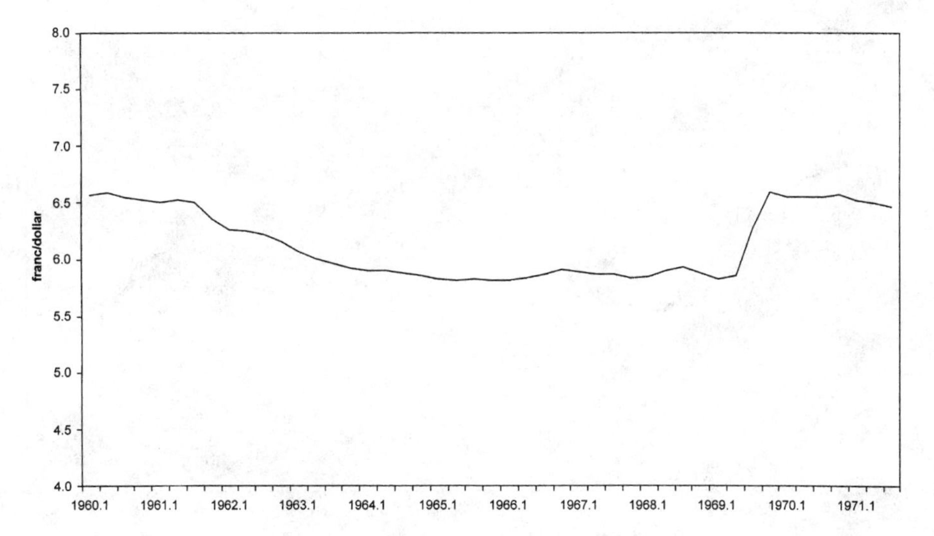


Chart 5.3. Franc-dollar real exchange rate, 1960:1–1971:3.

The French franc appreciated against the dollar during the early and mid-1960s (Chart 5.3). In 1969, France depreciated its exchange rate, restoring about the same real exchange rate as in 1960. Although France drew regularly on the U.S. gold stock, it did not permit its gold purchases to adjust its real exchange rate.

In contrast to the bilateral real exchange rates, the deflated price of gold shows a steady decline during the postwar years after 1949. By September 1959, the real price of gold had fallen back to the level reached in October 1929 (Chart 5.4). Price increases had fully offset the nominal revaluation of gold in January 1934. Between autumn 1959 and the closing of the gold window in 1971, the real price of gold declined an additional 3.3 percent to a level far below any price during Federal Reserve history to that time. No wonder many observers expressed concern about the scarcity of gold for transactions. A 50 percent increase in the nominal gold price, to $52.50 an ounce, would have restored the real price to the 1956 level and increased the 1965 U.S. gold reserves to more than $21 billion, more than enough to maintain the fixed exchange rate system for several years or longer.

An increase in the dollar price of gold would have increased international liquidity and adjusted the dollar to the permanent postwar changes. Political considerations—including concern about benefits to South Africa and the Soviet Union, but also beliefs about response by Europeans—ruled out that solution. An adjustable gold price, such as Fisher's compensated dollar, would have adjusted the dollar-gold price based on changes in an index of commodity prices. This would have solved the confidence prob-

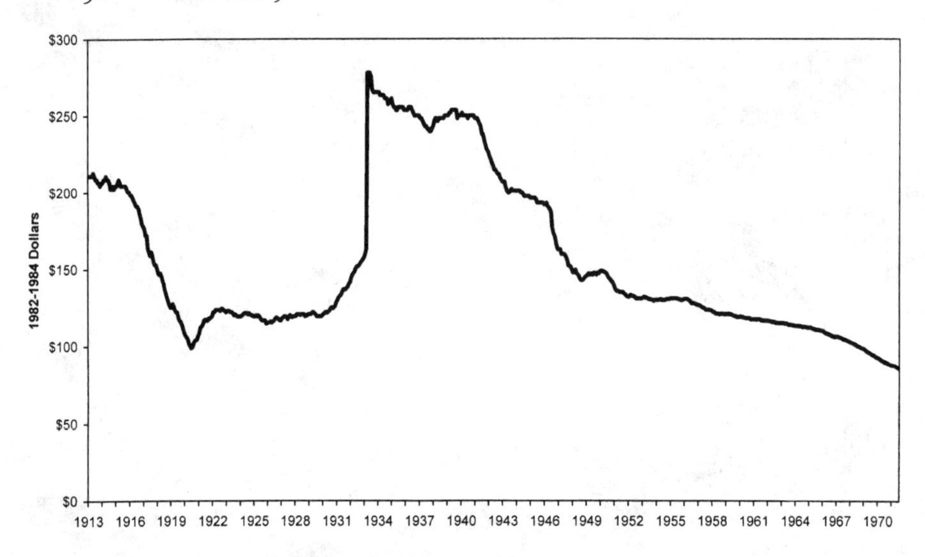


Chart 5.4. Real price of gold per troy ounce.

lem by keeping the system close to equilibrium and reduced adjustment and liquidity problems.

Bordo (1993) showed that during the short life of the Bretton Woods system, which he dates as 1959–70, developed economies experienced relatively high and stable growth and relatively stable prices compared to other international monetary systems. For these years, the mean inflation rate rose 3.9 percent in the countries that are now members of the G-7.[11] This is higher than the low inflation rate during the years of the classical gold standard, 1881–1913. Real per capita growth during these years was substantially higher than in any other period in Bordo's table (1993, 7). The relatively low standard deviation of the seven countries' inflation rates shows up again in the relatively modest mean change in the real exchange rate.

This good performance is subject to four qualifications, however. First, many countries prevented adjustment of prices, output, and the exchange rate by maintaining exchange controls. Second, real per capita growth rates depend on the spread of new technology, the reduction in trade barriers, the development and expansion of the European common market, and other forces. Third, pressures increased for price and real exchange rate changes that occurred after the Bretton Woods system ended. Fourth, the United States introduced several restrictions on capital movements, tied

11. United States, United Kingdom, West Germany, France, Japan, Canada, and Italy are the G-7 members.

**Table 5.2** Current Account and Liquidity Basis, 1961–70 (in $ millions)

| YEAR | CURRENT AACCOUNT | LIQUIDITY BASIS[a] |
|---|---|---|
| 1961 | 3821 | −2371 |
| 1962 | 3388 | −2204 |
| 1963 | 4414 | −2670 |
| 1964 | 6822 | −2800 |
| 1965 | 5431 | −1335 |
| 1966 | 3029 | −1357 |
| 1967 | 2584 | −3544 |
| 1968 | 611 | 171 |
| 1969 | 399 | −7012 |
| 1970 | 2340 | −4415 |

Source: Economic Report of the President, 1971, 1980.
[a]Change in liquid liabilities to foreign official holders and changes in official reserve assets. Chosen because it is widely used in official discussions.

foreign aid to dollar purchases, and required purchases of military and other goods and services in home markets. These are selective devaluations of the dollar that do not appear in the published exchange rate data. Some had a large welfare cost. Despite these qualifications, the exchange rate system worked comparatively well until the cumulative effect of U.S. expansive policies and declining real growth caused the breakdown (Darby and Lothian, et al., 1983; Schwartz, 1987a, chapter 14).

The experience of the 1920s and the 1960s taught a common lesson: fixed exchange rate systems rarely last long in the contemporary world.[12] Countries are unwilling to make their economies adjust to the exchange rate. The public is unwilling to accept the at times large temporary losses of employment required to maintain the international value of its money.

## PROPOSALS AND ACTIONS 1965–67

In 1964, the United States had its largest trade balance and current account surplus since 1947. The expanding world economy, low domestic inflation, and improvement in the terms of trade contributed to bring the balance of payments problem toward a satisfactory equilibrium. Unfortunately, the good news did not last. Table 5.2 shows current and capital account balances for the decade; the capital outflow in 1964 was the largest to that time.

The tone of official discussions mirrors the current account data in

12. Obstfeld and Rogoff (1995) show this for a large number of countries. It remains to be seen whether the European Monetary System will change that conclusion by introducing a common currency and making exit difficult.

Table 5.2. Optimism that the problem would be managed rose in 1964 and remained in 1965. A little extra push from new controls might be all that was needed. "Voluntary" controls on bank lending and foreign investment lowered the liquidity measure of the deficit for two years despite reductions in the current account surplus. After that the trade surplus began a precipitate decline and the growth of claims against gold (liquidity basis) reached levels far above previous values. The response to the 1967 British devaluation, rising domestic prices, and continued expenditures for the Vietnam War was a virtual embargo on gold; the two-tier system begun in 1968 ended gold sales to the public and ended the London gold pool. The Johnson and Nixon administrations continued the "voluntary" programs, strengthened them, made some mandatory, but did little to solve the long-term problem of an overvalued real exchange rate.

Reductions in the capital outflow in 1965 reflect the initial response to the so-called voluntary programs. The large fluctuations in outflow in 1968 to 1970 reflect a number of factors but especially the response to interest rate changes at home and abroad. These gave the appearance in 1968 that the outflow had reversed. The change was transitory, reflecting the effect of regulation Q on banks' decisions to repay euro-dollars in 1968 and borrow euro-dollars in 1969.

The initial effect of controls on lending or investing abroad was much stronger than its permanent effect. Banks and firms found ways to substitute. The interest equalization tax encouraged bank lending, so it became necessary to put a ceiling on bank loans. Banks could acquire euro-dollars, borrowing the dollars that flowed abroad and relending to their customers.

The main problem in the 1960s was not a U.S. current account deficit. Throughout the 1960s, the United States typically had a surplus on current account. The problem was that the trade and current account surpluses were not large enough to finance private investment abroad plus military, travel, and foreign aid spending abroad. As foreigners bought gold and accumulated dollars, concern rose that the gold price would not remain fixed or the dollar would not remain convertible into gold.

The Kennedy and Johnson administrations faced a choice—slow the outflow of dollars by reducing money growth or adjust the exchange rate system by devaluing. They chose instead to impose controls of various kinds. Each new crisis brought new controls. At first, they may have hoped that the problem was temporary, that the controls would get the system through a transition. This hope must have died by the late 1960s, but the Johnson economic and financial advisers never developed a lasting solution to the international problem.

Eichengreen (2000, 212) found no evidence that controls had a significant effect. As is often the case, markets circumvent controls and regulations. A main reason in this case was that the availability of substitutes undermined control programs. The public reacted negatively to controls, and officials were unwilling to introduce stronger measures that might have succeeded in prolonging the system. The records of the period suggest a growing sense of resignation, belief in the inevitability of a breakdown.

In December 1964, the Cabinet Committee on the Balance of Payments forecast the 1965 balance of payments deficit at slightly under $2 billion, the smallest deficit since 1958, about equal to the projected deficit for 1964.[13] The committee anticipated a decline in the trade surplus and further increases in bank loans and foreign investment. It recommended a balance of payments speech by the president reporting progress and extension of the interest equalization tax (IET) to bank loans.[14]

By late January, the committee had completed its recommendations. In addition to renewing the IET and extending the tax to bank loans with more than one year to maturity, the committee recommended a Federal Reserve–administered program to reduce the number of banks lending abroad, additional reductions in military spending abroad,[15] a 2 percent increase in the IET for shorter maturities declining to 1 percent on longer maturities, and "an attack on overseas investment in the developed countries" (memo, McGeorge Bundy to the president, Johnson Library, National Security File, Balance of Payments, January 22, 1965).

The Federal Reserve was responsible for the "voluntary" lending program with assistance from the Comptroller and the FDIC. In the first year, banks were asked not to lend more than 5 percent above the amount lent in 1964.[16] Loans to foreigners with maturity greater than one year became

13. The Cabinet Committee consisted of the Secretaries of State, Defense, Commerce, and Treasury (chair) plus the Chairman of the Board of Governors and others from the administration. The committee often met with the president to present its findings. The committee recognized that the policy of requiring U.S. exports to be shipped in U.S. flag carriers lost sales to competing suppliers.

14. Congress gave the president standing authority to apply the IET to bank lending abroad when it passed the IET.

15. The memo recognized the cost of some of its proposals for the military. For example, supplying oil from the United States to troops in Europe cost twice as much as buying it from the Middle East. Nevertheless, the committee favored the policy of spending at home to reduce the dollar outflow. These and other decisions show the emphasis on appearance and the neglect of effective actions.

16. The 5 percent ceiling included export finance, a step that seems counterproductive. The reporting and consultation requirements exposed banks to anti-trust violations. The government asked for a legal waiver of these requirements for two years. The Board recognized the problem posed by including export credit but feared creating a large loophole if it did not restrict such credits (Board Minutes, February 18, 1965, 6–7).

subject to the IET. At the Board, Governor Robertson was responsible for the program.

Initially, the investment program was also voluntary. Secretary of Commerce John Connor asked all companies to participate if they had investments of at least $10 million in developed countries at the end of 1964 or exports of at least $10 million in 1964. Companies were supposed to report quarterly on their assets and exports and to forecast for the following year. Participating firms were asked to reduce holding of short-term assets abroad to the 1963 level, to increase exports, repatriate export proceeds, and reduce the rate of investment. The goal was to reduce net outflow by 15 to 20 percent below the 1964 flow. Johnson (1966) concluded that the program had a modest effect.

The most controversial item among the proposed changes called for a tax on tourist travel. Opponents cited the regressivity of the tax, the reaction of foreign governments, and the effects on trade negotiations in progress at the time. The tax proposal reappeared several times but was not adopted. The most the administration did on this issue was to reduce tourists' duty-free allowance from $500 to $100.[17]

The effectiveness of controls varied with the opportunity or ability to substitute uncontrolled for controlled transactions. Tying military spending is inefficient, but substitution is limited. Tying foreign aid or military spending reduces the real value of the spending but may induce larger appropriations. Controls on private financial transactions are most easily circumvented.

Offsetting steps to reduce the balance of payments deficit and the gold outflow were decisions of the French and Spanish governments to convert excess dollar stocks into gold. The Treasury estimated that France would convert $300 million and Spain $210 million during 1965. In addition, France planned to convert its monthly flow dollar surplus of about $50 million. The Treasury estimated that Russian gold sales would decline that year. The net effect would be a sale of about $500 million in gold in 1965 (memo, Secretary Dillon to the president, Johnson Library, Francis Bator papers, Box 16, January 4, 1965). Actual gold outflow reached $1665 million that year, the largest outflow since 1960 and the largest percentage loss in the postwar years to that time. Part of the increased gold outflow went to pay $258 million for an increase in the U.S. IMF quota. In addition to the U.S. payment, countries bought gold from the U.S. stock to pay for

17. The report notes Chairman Martin's "promise . . . that if confidence can be sustained, U.S. domestic credit will be kept easy" (McGeorge Bundy to Johnson, Johnson Library, National Security File, Balance of Payments, January 22, 1965).

the portion of their increased quotas that had to be paid in gold. By year-end, the Treasury held only $13.8 billion, of which approximately $13 billion was held as required gold reserves for bank reserves and currency.

In his February 10 message to Congress, the president asked Congress to repeal the gold reserve requirement against bank reserves. Removing the gold requirement on reserves meant that monetary action was less restricted, and more of the gold stock was available for payment. This concerned several members of Congress, and some bankers wanted a letter from the president to Congress disavowing Congressman Patman's recommendations that would have reduced Federal Reserve independence. The president agreed, and Secretary Dillon testified in favor of continued independence (memo, Dillon to the president, Johnson Library WHCF Box 51, January 13, 1965). Patman accused the bankers of using "blackmail" to defeat his legislation (letter, Patman to president, Johnson Library, WHCF Box 51, January 15, 1965). On March 3, 1965, Congress approved the change. The gold reserve requirement for currency remained in effect until 1968.[18]

The Board discussed a new ruling that would restrict access to the discount window by banks that made foreign loans. Opinions differed. Governors Charles N. Shephardson and Mills preferred to reduce reserve growth (Board Minutes, January 19, 1965, 15–16). There was no agreement at the time. Later, the Board rejected the proposal to restrict discounting.

President Johnson's message extended Federal Reserve responsibility for voluntary compliance by non-banks and financial institutions, including insurance companies, pension funds, and investment companies. This was the first time that the System had responsibility for non-bank lending. Few, if any, savings and loan associations made foreign loans, so the program excluded them (ibid., February 18, 1965, 10).

Banks in the aggregate did not use the 5 percent limit in 1965. On December 3, the Board extended the program for another year and increased the 1966 lending limit to 109 percent of the December 1964 base. The Board's statement gave priority to loans supporting exports and for nonexport credits, and to loans to developing countries. The Board asked that the four percentage point increase in lending be spread evenly over the four quarters of 1966 (Board Minutes, December 3, 1965, Item 4). By February 1966, banks were $800 million below their ceiling.

In October 1966, Governor Robertson proposed that the voluntary pro-

18. Governor Mills opposed the change. He preferred to let the reserve banks hold deficient positions. Under the Federal Reserve Act, the Board could assess a fine against deficient reserve positions. The majority favored eliminating all gold reserve requirements and notified the Treasury to that effect (Board Minutes, January 4, 1965, 3–10).

gram be put on standby for 1967. Banks were $1.2 billion below the guideline. He regarded the guidelines as ineffective. Mitchell and Shephardson supported him, but Maisel said the voluntary program was ineffective and should be made mandatory. Brimmer and Daane argued that the Federal Reserve was part of an overall administration program. Dropping the lending program would increase pressure on the other parts. Chairman Martin favored suspension, but he did not think the administration would agree to it.

The decision authorized Robertson to make the case for suspension to the Cabinet Committee on the Balance of Payments (Board Minutes, October 19 and 20, 1966). The Board would not issue new guidelines but would continue to monitor data and reinstate the program if necessary or desirable.

The cabinet committee rejected the proposal for a standby program. It asked the Federal Reserve to recommend ways to restrict use of the $1.2 billion unused in 1966 and to give additional incentives for credits to finance exports and loans to developing countries. The 1967 guidelines, announced on December 12, 1966, followed the cabinet committee's suggestions (Board Minutes, December 12, 1966, Item 3).

The Commerce Department program was even less effective than the Board's. The administration chose to maintain the voluntary program but tightened the standards. Corporations were asked to repatriate earnings, borrow abroad, and bring home all dollar balances held abroad not needed for working capital (Fowler to the president, Fowler papers, Johnson Library, Box 52, October 12, 1965). Secretary Fowler wanted to tighten the program sufficiently to bring the balance of payments to full balance in 1966. By March 1966, he recognized that this would not happen. He proposed a new program—a tax of $6 per individual for each day spent abroad with a $100 deposit paid before an individual could leave the country. The tax would be $50 for travel in North America or the Caribbean.[19] Fowler estimated that the tax would yield between $585 million and $1.17 billion a year. The State and Commerce Departments opposed the tax, and it was not adopted.

In May, Secretary Fowler wrote to President Johnson advising him that

19. Fowler suggested an alternative, a progressive tax of one-tenth of one percent of adjusted gross income per day with a minimum of $6 and a maximum of $50 per day (Ball papers, Johnson Library, Lot 74 D272, March 18, 1966). The administration also wanted South Vietnam to invest surplus dollars in U.S. bonds and larger offset payments by West Germany. Secretary McNamara said that the Germans should be told "no money—no troops" (Cabinet Committee on Balance of Payments, Fowler papers, Johnson Library, Box 53, March 25, 1966). Germany paid $700 million in 1966.

despite the new controls, the payments deficit for 1966 would be at least as large as in 1965 and probably larger. "The fundamental problem can be summarized as follows: our trade surplus is shrinking; growth of our services surplus is being held back by the growing tourist deficit; together our surplus on goods and services combined will not be sufficiently large to compensate for the governmental dollar outflows . . . ; and private capital outflows" (memo, Fowler to the president, Johnson Library, Balance of Payments, Vol. 3, Box 2, May 10, 1966). The memo recommended again a tax on tourists, additional reductions in government military spending abroad, prepayment of debt owed by foreigners, and getting foreigners to commit to purchase long-term debt instead of more liquid short-term debt. No one proposed reductions in foreign aid. The administration worked to reduce private spending and to maintain its own spending.

Fowler then discussed some policy changes such as increased tax rates and tighter monetary policy (higher interest rates) if "it could be tolerated here" (ibid.). Also, the interest equalization tax could be extended to direct investment abroad in place of the voluntary program.

The Cabinet Committee on the Balance of Payments proposed a more restrictive, but still voluntary, program for business external investment. The committee asked for a reduction of $30 million in foreign investment. To offset the reduced cost of foreign travel, it asked, again, for more reduction in tourist expenditures abroad.

Fiscal and monetary policy changes aside, most of the proposals offered only one-time changes that would not permanently reduce the payments deficit. Like the earlier programs, the 1967 policy proposals responded to a perceived crisis but offered no permanent solution. Maintenance of employment dominated other goals. Restrictions, of course, relieved some pressure by selectively devaluing the dollar to overcome some specific problem.

Proposals for permanent solutions to the problem were not entirely absent. Milton Friedman testified several times in Congress and spoke publicly about the benefits of removing restrictions and allowing the dollar to float. James Tobin told President Kennedy that "devaluation was not unthinkable," but the president warned him not to mention the idea outside his office (Solomon, 1982, 61). Working Party 3 of the OECD included exchange rate changes as one means of adjusting to imbalances by both surplus and deficit countries (ibid., 60). Members of Congress, especially Henry Reuss (Wisconsin), urged more rapid and effective action. The frequent hearings he held gave public attention to proposals for exchange rate adjustment and expansion of world liquidity. And proposals for devaluation began to appear in the popular press (memo, Arthur Okun to the president, Johnson Library, Weekly Balance of Payments Report, August 6, 1966).[20]

Solomon gave three main reasons for rejecting exchange rate adjustment. First, the $35 gold price was "a basic underpinning of the system" (Solomon, 1982, 61). Multilateral floating had not occurred and many, like Robert Roosa, did not believe it could maintain an equilibrium exchange rate system. Second, the large stock of dollars held by central banks and governments meant that devaluation of the dollar would be costly to holders and more costly to those who had not drawn gold than to others. Critics said foreigners would no longer willingly hold dollars, so there would be major changes in the international system (ibid.). Third, the United States had a current account surplus in 1964–65. European countries rejected the idea of adding to that surplus by revaluing their currencies, despite the fact that a large part of the capital outflow was the cost of defending them.[21]

The costs of the Vietnam War contributed greatly to the problem. Budget director Charles Schultze told the president that in contrast to business capital investment and bank lending abroad, government outlays had increased substantially. For fiscal years 1966 and 1967, "expanded defense activities in Southeast Asia account for all [the] $657 million increase [in net dollar outflow abroad], and more" (memo, the Gold Budget, Johnson Library, WHCF, FI9, July 14, 1966).

Rising inflation and the perceived inability to solve the adjustment problem or to reduce the payments deficit heightened pessimism. Repeated problems with the pound added to the gloom. One of the Federal Reserve's senior staff stated his concern explicitly: "The long-run outlook for our balance of payments is dimmer now than it was a year ago, in my opinion, because of the gradually accelerating rise in U.S. industrial prices. The real news about the balance of payments is that there is no really good news to report" (FOMC Minutes, May 10, 1966, 33). Convinced that the nominal exchange rate could not depreciate and unwilling to reduce military spend-

20. Charles Coombs mentioned that proposals by European and American economists for wider exchange rate bands disturbed the market as a possible prelude to devaluation of the pound (FOMC Minutes, March 1, 1966, 27). Coombs and the New York bank always opposed parity changes.

21. France favored the devaluation of the dollar. Jacques Rueff proposed a doubling or tripling of the dollar price of gold (Solomon, 1982, 64). Chairman Martin, in a speech in June 1965, publicly rejected a return to a gold standard as an attempt to "turn back the clock of monetary history" (ibid., 81). In the first half of 1966, the Treasury sold $324 million of gold to France. Without these sales, the gold stock would have increased. Some in the State Department proposed ending gold sales to France ("selective non-convertibility") or ending gold sales entirely (memo, Fowler to the president, Johnson Library, Bator papers, Box 15, June 21, 1966, n. 6).

ing abroad or to disinflate or deflate to adjust the real exchange rate, policymakers saw exhortation and restriction as their only available course.

During the System's restrictive policy in 1966, banks borrowed from their foreign branches, importing euro-dollars.[22] At the Board's August 31 meeting, research director Daniel Brill reported that banks had imported $1 billion of deposits in the two months since mid-year. This reduced the payments deficit but permitted banks to expand domestic lending.

Governor Brimmer proposed making deposits in foreign branches subject to deposit reserve requirements. Maisel and Mitchell supported him, but the staff pointed out that in 1921 the Board had ruled that balances due to a bank's foreign branch "did not constitute a deposit liability against which reserves must be maintained" (Board Minutes, August 31, 1966, 5). The inflow had slowed by the time the Board reconsidered the issue in October, so the Board did not act.

Pressure on the pound increased in the fall. Transfers out of pounds into euro-dollars increased, reducing British reserves and weakening the exchange rate. The Federal Reserve wanted to avoid devaluation of the pound, so it considered whether new restrictions would help. A report by officers of the New York reserve bank concluded that "controls that may be imposed on head office borrowings from foreign branches are likely to be severely limited by a variety of opportunities to circumvent them and to reduce their actual impact" (Report of the Committee of Officers, Board Records, October 9, 1967, 11). The main drawback was a likely shift of foreign loans to domestic offices, adding to the capital outflow. The value of loans was much greater than the value of euro-dollar deposits channeled from foreign branches to home offices. The committee concluded that the most feasible way for the Bank of England to avoid the loss of reserves was to raise its interest rate. The Board took no action. Soon after, the officers committee urged the Board to use "moral suasion" to encourage the large New York banks to reduce their borrowing from foreign branches to help

22. Euro-dollar deposits were dollar liabilities of banks outside the United States. At the time, these deposits were not counted as part of the base for deposit insurance fees or, as discussed in the text, reserve requirements. They avoided regulation Q ceilings. At the end of 1966, $13 billion was outstanding (Report of Committee of Officers, Board Records, October 9, 1967, 1). The euro-dollar market grew rapidly after the United States imposed the interest equalization tax. The market was unregulated and operated mainly in London. Participants in the market bought and sold dollar-denominated assets that were a close substitute for deposits at U.S. banks in the United States. Some analysts saw the euro-dollar market as an escape mechanism by which the banking system could create money without holding reserves. The committee report did not make this error; it recognized that deposits were substitutes for deposits in U.S. banks. Private deposits could increase slightly from funds that might otherwise have been held as foreign official reserves (ibid., 7).

the pound. Suggestions of this kind, if implemented, called attention to the weakness of the pound, possibly encouraging speculation.

In October 1967, the Board began work on revisions to the 1968 voluntary program of credit restraint. Governor Robertson, who administered the program, proposed removing the exemption from the guidelines for Export-Import Bank financing. The Board agreed, but the Treasury did not, so the proposal died (Board Minutes, October 10 and 19, 1967).[23]

After Britain devalued the pound from $2.80 to $2.40 on November 18, the administration had two concerns.[24] First, if several other countries followed Britain, the benefits to Britain would be small and Britain's problem would continue. Second, pressure might shift to the dollar. In fact, there was a run on gold. In the first week after the devaluation, the London gold pool sold $578 million. France had quietly withdrawn from the gold pool in June 1967 but chose to announce its withdrawal on the Monday following the British devaluation. A hastily assembled meeting of the other members on November 25 reaffirmed their intention to remain in the pool and support the $35 per ounce price. The run slowed, but the gold loss for the month was $1.5 billion. By January, U.S. sales to cover these losses reached $1 billion (Johnson, 1971, 316–17).

The administration and the Federal Reserve looked for more stopgaps. In November, the Board's guidelines called for renewal of the ceiling at 109 percent of a bank's 1964 loans.

These guidelines did not remain in effect. Soon afterward, Chairman Martin proposed to ask banks with foreign branches to shift a substantial share of their loans to foreigners from domestic to foreign offices (Board Minutes, December 19, 1967, 8–9). Governor Robertson outlined a new "voluntary program" for 1968. The proposal cut banks' lending ceilings from 109 to 103 percent of their 1964 base; it called for ending all term credits (over one year) to Western Europe; and it asked banks to reduce short-term loans to Western Europe by 40 percent. Robertson estimated that these changes would reduce outflow by $300 to $500 million.[25]

23. Sherman (1983, 45) reported that long-term rates rose relative to short-term rates in 1967. He attributed the change to shifting demands for credit "because of growing expectations as the year progressed that interest rates were more likely to rise than decline in the future. . . . [T]he expanded growth in bank reserves, bank credit and money over the year as a whole moderated the rise in the overall interest rate structure despite the greatly increased demands for credit." Sherman said reserve growth was 10 percent. He did not recognize that the Federal Reserve's strong response to the 1966 slowdown induced anticipations of inflation. Instead of slowing the rise in long-term rates, policy induced it.

24. The next section discusses the British devaluation.

25. Until February 1968, banks could make equity investments in foreign banks. The Board voted to treat these investments as credits, thereby putting them under the credit

Governor Brimmer wanted a mandatory program in place of the voluntary program. The Board agreed to drop the word "voluntary" but not to introduce "mandatory." President Johnson invoked the Trading with the Enemy Act of 1917 to restrict capital flows to our allies. He announced the new program on January 1, 1968, as part of a balance of payments program that tightened corporate investment abroad and asked for repeal of the remaining gold reserve requirement against the note issue. The Board cooperated with the president's program by asking bank and non-bank financial institutions to provide a capital inflow of $400 million for banks and $100 million for non-banks during 1968.

Gardner Ackley told the president that the aim of the program "was to get through 1968 without an international financial crisis" (memo, Ackley to the president, Johnson Library, Box 53, December 23, 1967, 1). He warned, however, that "most of the improvement sought by the program is not long-term. It will continue only as long as we continue doing things that are distasteful" (ibid., 2). Ackley later added: "A good case can be made that we are only buying time with our program; that the fundamental difficulties will not go away but will only be repressed; that a crisis will only be postponed not avoided" (ibid., 2). He proposed as a long-term solution to demonetize gold "quickly and at one stroke" (ibid.) The United States would offer to convert dollar liabilities to gold. If the desired conversions exceeded the gold stock, each holder would get a proportional share. The United States would pledge to stabilize its exchange rate at the existing parity by buying and selling foreign currencies. "If it subsequently developed that we could not maintain the parity of the dollar . . . we would have to let the dollar 'float' or else . . . announce a change in its parity" (ibid., 3).

There is no evidence that the president responded. The new program of restrictions went into effect. Even more than the program it replaced, the new program showed the government's willingness to place its priorities and interests above the public's.[26] The new program did not require reduced lending by the Export-Import Bank. It exempted loans to Canada and developing countries. It failed repeatedly to meet its targets for reduc-

guidelines. The new regulation banned banks from making any equity investment in any corporation in Western Europe. A bank could open a branch abroad provided it remained within its overall credit ceiling (Board Minutes, February 7, 1968, 1–5).

26. At the October 1967 World Bank meetings, the United States supported a substantial increase in resources for the International Development Agency (IDA) of the World Bank. Bank rules restricted tying loans to domestic exports. At about this time Fred Borch, chairman of General Electric, wrote to Commerce Secretary Alexander Trowbridge complaining about the disproportionate burden placed on business, neglect of the long-term benefits of foreign investment, and the failure to restrict the public sector "where the deficit is created" (letter Borch to Trowbridge, Johnson Library, RG40, September 14, 1967).

tion in government spending abroad. This placed more of the burden of adjustment on private consumption, investment, and lending.[27]

The initial reaction to the new program was positive. In the first week, the London gold pool gained $5 million compared to net sales of U.S. gold in December. The administration resumed consideration of additional travel restrictions, though Congress was unlikely to adopt them in an election year. One proposal called for the president to impose them using the 1917 Trading with the Enemy Act. Secretary Fowler advised Johnson not to do that. He believed the market would interpret it as a step toward full exchange controls, setting off a run against the remaining gold stock. Further, he explained that international agreements permitted controls on capital movements. Travel restrictions would violate trade rules prohibiting controls on current transactions (memo, Fowler to the president, Johnson Library, Box 53, January 12, 1968).[28]

## PRESSURES ON THE POUND

As the Bretton Woods system developed, it had two reserve currencies, the dollar and the pound. London supplemented New York as a market in which countries held reserves. It was the weaker of the two, more subject to pressures for devaluation. Six years after restoring current account convertibility, Britain experienced a loss of gold and dollar reserves. The 1964 "crisis" was the first of several culminating in devaluation of the pound in November 1967.

Even more than in the United States, Keynesian policies for growth and high employment were the main goals of British economic policy. Lacking the large initial postwar gold reserves of the United States, it could not ignore the bursts of inflation and balance of payments problems to which

27. Chairman Martin reported that the administration had moved decisively toward capital controls. President Johnson's executive order announcing the 1968 program said that anyone subject to the jurisdiction of the United States who owned over 10 percent interest in a foreign business venture was prohibited from engaging in any transaction that transferred capital to a foreign country or national outside the United States (Board Minutes, December 29, 1967, 13–17). In August, Secretary Fowler acknowledged that tied exports under the U.S. aid programs (AID) replaced regular commercial exports (Fowler to the president, Johnson Library, WHCF, File FO4-1, August 8, 1967).

28. Paul Volcker, who served as a Treasury official in the early 1960s and again during the Nixon administration, designed some of the restrictions and controls. He summarized the experience: "I don't think anyone has satisfactorily answered the question of what was accomplished in terms of the ultimate balance of payments of the United States or in terms of the competition between national markets" (Volcker and Gyohten, 1992, 35). But he noted that controls encouraged development of foreign financial markets, reducing the importance of New York.

these policies contributed. Like the United States, Britain rejected relative deflation as a permanent adjustment.

Britain, represented by Lord Keynes, had done much to create the International Monetary Fund (IMF) as an institution to enhance international monetary cooperation. The first reaction was to treat the payments problem as temporary, borrow from the IMF and its trading partners, and avoid devaluation. In this respect, the policy repeated the mistakes of 1925 to 1931.

International cooperation failed in this case as in so many others. The British payments problem proved persistent, not temporary, so it required a permanent solution such as devaluation of the real exchange rate. Borrowing and restrictions on spending succeeded in changing the timing of the devaluation, and in that sense the various programs were successful for a time. But to the extent that spending restrictions and other measures slowed the economy or increased unemployment, they were followed by expansive measures and a renewed capital outflow.

As in the 1920s, the pound was overvalued against most currencies. This time the dollar was overvalued also. U.S. officials feared that devaluation of the pound exchange rate would shift pressure to the dollar, just as it had in 1931. And once again, France followed its own policies, cooperating with others at times but failing to do so when it served its purpose. Since one of the purposes was to force devaluation of the dollar against gold, it was often at odds with the United States and others.

Pressure against pound exchange rates rose before the 1964 election.[29] By September 1964, a month before the election, Britain had to borrow $500 million from the Bank for International Settlements and draw $200 million, to support the pound. The economy operated at a high level, so the new government of Harold Wilson tried to shift spending from imports toward home output. In a telegram to President Johnson, Wilson explained the government's program. The current budget deficit was worse than he anticipated before the election.[30] He had rejected both devaluation and higher interest rates, the latter "because of its restrictive effect on the economy and because of its impact on your own problems" (Department

29. Solomon (1982, 82–99) describes the problems and the actions taken. He participated in most of the meetings. This discussion supplements his with materials from administration and Federal Reserve records.

30. Wilson projected a £800 million deficit for the year. This number, like the $2.5 billion U.S. deficit at about this time seems small by current standards. The U.S. price level increased approximately 3.5 times between 1964 and 2003, but the nominal payments deficit increased twentyfold.

of State, Johnson Library, Central Files, FN (2UK, October 24, 1964)). Instead, he planned to rely at first mainly on non-monetary changes—a surtax on imports, a rebate (subsidy) for exports, and an incomes policy related to productivity.

The announcement did not include strict fiscal measures or higher interest rates. Under market pressure, the Bank of England raised its discount rate in late November and spent up to $1 billion to defend the exchange rate.

In late November the U.S. Treasury organized a $3 billion loan, $500 million from the United States and $2.5 billion from the central banks in Europe, Canada, and Japan. France participated but announced that this was the last time.[31] The U.S. commitment included a $250 million increase in the Federal Reserve swap or credit line. This time the Bank of England raised its lending rate from 5 to 7 percent. The Federal Reserve followed with a 0.5 percentage point increase. Renewed reserve drains followed brief periods of improved international payments. The British government tried credit controls, wage and price guidelines, and reduced spending with little lasting effect.

On March 27, 1965, Secretary Dillon expressed renewed concern about the pound. He did not expect the British to offer a fiscal budget in April stringent enough to strengthen international reserves. He told President Johnson that the French had launched a speculative attack and spread rumors that the British would devalue that weekend. Dillon suggested that the French wanted to "indirectly attack the dollar" (memo, Dillon to the president, Johnson Library, WHCF F04-1, Box 32–39, March 27, 1965).[32]

By early August, the Federal Reserve was back to planning what it would do if the British devalued. The plan was to buy long- and medium-term securities to prevent a disorderly dollar market. The FOMC, with Treasury support, would maintain bond prices close to pre-crisis levels. The members rejected smaller purchases at declining prices. The strength of System action would depend on the size of devaluation and the number of

31. Although the circumstances differed, this episode is in some respects a replay of the 1927 experience, when Britain was reluctant to raise interest rates and France was reluctant to lend its support (see Meltzer, 2003, 175–76). Soon after the loan, Prime Minister Wilson came to the United States seeking a longer-term credit. At the time, the United States favored a 25 percent increase in IMF quotas and would not ask for additional IMF credit for Britain.

32. Soon afterward, the French ambassador tried to ease tension by telling Horace Busby, one of the president's aides, that journalists in Washington and Paris promoted bad relations. He compared Chairman Martin's speech at Columbia University to statements by General de Gaulle. "The General does not know much about gold . . . what he has asked for . . . is not a return to the Gold Standard . . . [but] to look for a better standard then we now have" (memo, Busby to the president, Johnson Library, C081 FI9, June 10, 1965).

countries that followed Britain. Paul Volcker, the Treasury representative at the meeting, asked whether the Federal Reserve would want to tighten policy in the event of a large (15 percent) devaluation. He suggested that after the Federal Reserve protected the dealers, interest rates could be raised to support the dollar (memo, Young to Martin, Board Records, August 7, 1965). Chairman Martin discussed the proposal at the FOMC the following day. He recommended raising the ceiling on the amount the manager could buy to $2.5 billion between meetings (from $1.5) and to allow the manager to exercise discretion.

Planning continued after the threat of a crisis passed. A year later, September 1966, the staff reaffirmed the earlier proposal and decided that in the event of a major collapse the Federal Reserve would either ease policy generally or open the discount window. The Treasury would be responsible for supporting the government securities and agency markets (memo, Staff to FOMC, Board Records, September 1, 1966).

Higher interest rates in Germany and the United States, and a dockworkers strike in Britain, a new budget and rising wage rates renewed the run on the pound in May 1966. The U.S. Treasury bought £2 million to support the currency. European governments were not willing to support the pound further except for its reserve currency status; they would lend only to offset liquidation of reserve balances held by other countries in the London market (FOMC Minutes, June 7, 1966, 7–8).[33] The balances had accumulated during World War II.

Anti-inflation actions in the United States and West Germany raised market interest rates in 1966. Other countries followed to maintain their payments balances. In January 1967, Secretary Fowler met with the finance ministers of Germany, Britain, Italy, and France to coordinate lower interest rates. The meeting did not reach an explicit agreement, but the participants agreed to "cooperate in such a way as to enable interest rates in their respective countries to be lower than they would otherwise be" (Chequers trip, Johnson Library, Bator papers, Box 8, January 23, 1967). Germany reduced its rate following the meeting. The Federal Reserve did not lower the federal funds rate until March, but Treasury bill rates began to decline the week after the meeting.

By August the special manager, Charles Coombs, was both agitated and fearful. "He thought there was a clear danger of a breakdown of the international financial system within the next month or six weeks. He saw

33. The following is representative of prevailing attitudes: "The British stabilization program of July 1966 led to rising unemployment, which exceeded 2 percent of the labor force in the summer of 1967. . . . [T]his level of unemployment must have been politically onerous for the Wilson government" (Solomon, 1982, 93).

very little that the Group of Ten could do to stop it; their negotiations had reached an impasse. . . . The burden therefore fell directly on the Open Market Committee" (FOMC Minutes, August 23, 1966, 10). The FOMC authorized expansion of the swap lines.

In the next three weeks, the System added $1.7 billion to its swap lines, bringing the total to $4.5 billion. The largest change was $600 million additional for Britain, bringing its line to $1.35 billion. The FOMC increased twelve of its thirteen lines; France was the exception.

These efforts again postponed the devaluation but did not prevent it. On November 12, two British Treasury officials met in Washington with Secretary Fowler to warn him that devaluation was likely, perhaps that week. Only "assurance of substantial long-term credit" could change the outcome (memo, Fowler to the president, National Security File, Johnson Library, Gold Crisis, Box 54, November 12, 1967, 1). The British position had been hurt by a new war in the Middle East, the closing of the Suez Canal, and the withdrawal of Middle East deposits from London. They expected to lose much of their remaining (net) reserve of $800 million when they announced the latest trade data the following week. Overall, Britain's gold stock declined from 71 million ounces in 1964 to 37 million in 1967.

The immediate problem arose because the British government would not raise the Bank rate to the level of euro-dollar rates. Money flowed out of covered sterling deposits into euro-dollars, draining reserves. The Bank of England used several stopgaps that raised market rates without raising Bank rate. The outflow continued.

Market data suggested that Bank rate should have increased by one percentage point. After some delay, the Bank raised the rate by 0.5. This was not sufficient to stop reserve losses (Maisel diary, October 24, 1967, 1–3).

Fowler mentioned the advantage of ending the recurrent problem by devaluing the pound. He rejected that course. "The risks to us are just too great to take this gamble" (ibid., 2).[34] Pressure would shift to the dollar. France might follow Britain by devaluing to increase pressure on the U.S. to raise the gold price. There would be a run on the gold market.

Fowler tried to get agreement on another loan. International cooperation failed. The United States offered to buy $500 million in pounds with a guar-

34. More than two years earlier the State Department made its position clear. It opposed devaluation. "If they should make a big external move, they would wreck much more than the monetary system. Our foreign political and defense policies would be badly mangled" ("Some thoughts on the British Crisis," Department of State, Ball papers, Johnson Library, Lot 74 D272, July 28, 1965).

antee of exchange value, but the principal European central banks would not agree to a long-term loan, and the British would not accept additional short-term loans. The IMF directorate would not agree to a $3 billion dollar package as an alternative (Board Minutes, November 14, 1967, 4–9).[35]

Martin urged Fowler to try to persuade the IMF's managing director, Pierre-Paul Schweitzer, to change his mind. The most Schweitzer would offer was $1.4 billion.[36] That was not enough for the British. Unlike the 1920s, they wanted no more short-term credit or partial support. In a sign of the change in attitudes that had occurred, Britain preferred devaluation to repetitive crises. Governor Robertson opined that "funds advanced to the British and disbursed by them were likely in the end to represent additional drains on the U.S. gold stock. The decision regarding the position of the United States was for the administration rather than the System to make, but in his opinion the time for sterling devaluation was at hand" (FOMC Minutes, November 14, 1967, 28). Robertson recognized that a British devaluation would increase speculation against the dollar. "The United States was in a better position to deal with them [speculators] now than it might be one or two years hence" (ibid.).

Only Maisel supported Robertson. Brimmer took issue with them, claiming that the pound was not overvalued permanently. The measures to control spending and costs "appeared to be taking hold" (ibid., 33). He thought that the United States should help the British continue their program.[37] As often happens in decisions of this kind, there was less interest in facts than in being finished with the problem.

Four days later, on Saturday, November 18, 1967, Britain devalued the

35. Discussions in Washington, Basel, and Paris continued to the end. Chairman Martin added that he and Dewey Daane had sat through several meetings with the Treasury. They "had taken pains to make it clear that they could not in any way commit the System to participation in the guaranteed sterling proposal and that such participation would involve a change in the character of the System's operations to date" (Board Minutes, November 14, 1967, 13).

36. Martin later explained Schweitzer's reasoning. First, the $3 billion credit was so large it "would endanger the entire structure of the Fund if anything went wrong" (Board Minutes, November 14, 1967, 21). (How the IMF changed in the 1990s!) Also, the IMF did not believe Britain was a good credit, given its outstanding foreign debt (ibid., 22).

37. The Board's attorney, Howard Hackley, told the members that "there was no express authority in the Act for the Federal Reserve to extend credits to foreign banks" (FOMC Minutes, November 14, 1967, 34). However, there was a precedent in the 1925 loan to Britain when it returned to the gold standard. No money had been drawn, however. Hackley concluded that the program for longer-term assistance "would not involve greater legal questions than now existed" (ibid., 35). With this weak assurance, the FOMC voted unanimously to participate in the Treasury's purchase of covered pounds and increased the ceiling on purchases of forward foreign currencies.

pound from $2.80 to $2.40. As in 1931, this was a major break in the fixed exchange rate system. The system was now under increased pressure from gold losses. The Federal Reserve responded by raising the discount rate 0.5 to 4.5 percent to defend the dollar. The British government imposed new restrictions, and the Bank of England raised the discount rate to 8 percent. France let it be known that it had withdrawn from the gold pool in June. This increased the U.S. share of withdrawals from the gold pool.

## END OF THE GOLD POOL

Concerns that devaluation of the pound would increase pressure against the dollar and the gold pool proved correct. In the week following the British devaluation, the gold pool sold $578 million. Demand rose throughout the week, with nearly half the sales on Friday. In all, the pool members had agreed to provide a total of $1.37 billion to the pool. Less than 10 percent remained. For the month of November the pool sold $836 million; the U.S.'s direct share was 60 percent ($495 million), but it could be asked to reimburse other countries desiring to replace the gold they sold (FOMC Minutes, December 12, 1967, 3).

At a special meeting of the gold pool, in Frankfurt, with France absent, the members voted to continue their support of the pool, prevailing exchange rates, and the $35 gold price (ibid., November 12, 1967, 4–5, footnote 1).[38] Several members showed reluctance, but they agreed (Solomon, 1982, 96). And all countries except France agreed to increase swap lines again, this time by more than $2.5 billion to $7.08 billion. During the year, Norway, Denmark, and Mexico joined the swap network.

Attitudes started to change. A group of leading academic economists met as consultants to the Treasury in early December 1967. The dominant view was that the United States should not tighten monetary policy for balance of payments reasons, and many opposed additional exchange controls. "They felt a floating dollar . . . would be preferable" (Maisel diary, December 6, 1967, 1). Let other countries decide whether they wished to peg to the dollar or float. The group divided on the role of gold in the proposed system. This position followed the writings of a leading international economist, Gottfried Haberler. As early as 1965, Haberler (1965)

38. New York's report to the FOMC hints at the tension in relations with the British. New York agreed with the West German and Swiss position that the British could have avoided devaluation. "No unacceptable conditions would have been attached. The blunt fact was that the British Government made the decision to devalue on its own accord" (FOMC Minutes, November 27, 1967, 8). Later, pressed by Hugh Galusha (Minneapolis), Bruce MacLaury argued that devaluation was not necessary (ibid., 23). The United States made $500 million available ($100 from the Federal Reserve, the rest from the Treasury) in addition to the $1.35 billion swap line (ibid., 14).

urged a policy of "benign neglect." As head of President Nixon's task force, he urged the president-elect to ignore the balance of payments.

Uncertainty, indecision, and differences of opinion also arose among central bank governors. Hayes reported that the bankers could not reach agreement at the Basel meetings in early December. Several countries wanted to withdraw from the gold pool. They urged the United States to reduce capital investment in Europe and borrow from the IMF to support the gold price instead of relying on the gold pool (Maisel diary, December 12, 1967, 2). Discussions began to consider alternatives to the gold pool including a two-tier system with official sales restricted to other central banks and governments.

During fourth quarter 1967 and first quarter 1968, the United States gold reserve fell $2.3 billion, more than 18 percent of its stock in September 1967. The federal funds rate rose from 4.02 percent in the week following the U.K. devaluation to 5.40 in the last week of March 1968. Bond yields, however, showed little net change, and stock price indexes rose until mid-January, then declined slightly. These markets showed no sign that participants thought a major event had occurred.

President Johnson met with his advisers and some principal members of Congress on November 18. The president made another strong commitment to the tax surcharge and probed the congressional leadership about what it would take to get the surtax passed. He remained reluctant, but yielded on spending reductions. He told the participants, "If we don't act soon, we will wreck the Republic." And he issued a public statement again "unequivocally" reaffirming his commitment to the $35 gold price (Sterling Devaluation and the Need for a Tax Increase, Johnson Library, National Security File, November 18, 1967).

Early on the first trading day following the British devaluation, Monday, November 20, the trading desk implemented the plan agreed to earlier by placing bids for long-term bonds slightly below the market. The System bought $121 million of one- to five-year issues, $65 million of longer-term issues, and $427 million of bills. Stock prices fell nearly fifteen points in the first half hour (Annual Report, 1967, 268). After those initial reactions, markets stabilized, and there was no crisis. By the close on the following day, bond prices were above the prices at which the System bought (FOMC Minutes, November 27, 1967, 63).

Despite their failure to prevent devaluation, participants in the negotiations regarded the experience as "a strong reaffirmation of international financial cooperation" (FOMC Minutes, November 27, 1967, 29). Only France had gone its own way, acting in "an unfriendly and mischievous fashion" (FOMC Minutes, November 27, 1967, 31). But it had "little power to affect developments by means other than making press statements and leaking confidential information in an effort to embarrass the United States" (ibid.). These statements proved to be overly optimistic.

One of the anomalies of the gold pool was that the U.S. government supplied gold to match the demands of foreign citizens, but it was illegal for U.S. citizens to buy or hold gold. Contrary to claims about international cooperation, Solomon explained that if the U.S. failed to supply gold to the pool, the market price of gold would rise above $35 an ounce. Foreign central banks could then sell on the market and buy at the $35 price from the Treasury. "In fact, some central banks might be tempted to buy gold from the United States for the purpose of reselling it at the higher market price" (ibid., 30–31). Within a little more than three months, the two-price system became official policy.

To maintain fixed parities, the central banks agreed to sell their currencies for dollars in the forward market as required. This gave reassurance that they intended to maintain the exchange rate and moderated the effect of a dollar inflow on rates elsewhere. The amount of forward exchange market operations did not have to be shown on Federal Reserve statements. Also, the Federal Reserve agreed to a $1.5 billion temporary, additional increase in the swap line with eight participants. The main reason was concern that other countries might follow Britain by devaluing. Among developed countries, only New Zealand, Spain, and Denmark had done so. By the end of November, temporary increases brought the Federal Reserve's swap lines to $6.08 billion (FOMC Minutes, November 27, 1967, 57–58).

The outflow from the London gold pool continued and showed signs of increasing. Hayes (New York) reported that several members of the pool had discussed a temporary suspension of gold trading if another surge of demand occurred. Perhaps with an eye on the falling U.S. gold stock, Italy and Belgium announced that they would not stay in the gold pool indefinitely (ibid., December 12, 1967, 15). "There was a growing sense of disenchantment. Mr. [Karl] Blessing of the German Federal Bank, one of the country's most loyal friends in Europe, said that if the deficit in the U.S. balance of payments remained large the group's discussions might as well be brought to an end because they would be futile" (ibid., 17). The program that President Johnson announced on January 1, 1968, tried to satisfy European demands to slow U.S. investment in Europe.[39]

39. According to Martin, the president's new program convinced members of Congress that he had solved the problem, so they did not have to increase tax rates. This set off a new run on gold. Martin called the central bank governors and explained that the United States understood that its payments and budget deficits were "intolerable." "Steps are going to be taken

The FOMC did not discuss a more restrictive monetary policy. The economy was emerging from the 1966–67 slowdown, so the System did not consider the classical solution to a currency problem—higher interest rates and slower money growth. In fact, it didn't mention any change to give greater weight to its Bretton Woods obligation. Even repetition of Blessing's clear warning made no difference. They placed their hopes on the surtax and devoted their efforts to persuading Congress, especially a reluctant Chairman Mills of the Ways and Means Committee.

As pressures on the pound and the dollar continued, Coombs came to believe that the pound could not be maintained at $2.40. He wanted Britain to borrow at the IMF to repay its liabilities to the United States. At the Board, Solomon argued the opposite side. Events showed him to be right. By early 1969, the British had a large current account surplus from which they repaid many of their debts (Solomon, 1982, 99).

The United States had the bigger problem. Controls on foreign lending and investing and government purchases were insufficient in 1967 to offset costs associated with the Vietnam War. The payments deficit (liquidity basis) reached a $7 billion annual rate in the fourth quarter. The administration responded with the additional "temporary" controls announced in the president's message on January 1, 1968. The hope at the time was that over the longer term, Vietnam spending would decline and exports would increase enough to restore balance. The administration did not develop a long-run program, however.[40] It relied on wage and price guidelines to control production costs, mandatory guidelines to control overseas investment, and the panoply of short-term measures discussed earlier. When the president announced the program on New Year's Day, he said that it would bring the balance of payments close to equilibrium in 1968 by restricting $3 billion of outflows. Instead, the current account balance declined by $2 billion. By late January, the administration considered allocating an

---

as rapidly as possible to correct this" (extemporaneous remarks, Martin speeches, April 19, 1968, 3). The central bankers "agreed to continue in the pool operations" (ibid., 4).

40. Ackley's discussion of the administration's international economic policy explains that most of the policy actions originated in the Treasury.

> We generally loyally supported the Treasury view . . . to have exchange controls without really having them, to invent ways of enticing or persuading foreigners to hold dollars and not demand gold, and to keep patching things up . . . to save what was probably an unsaveable situation. . . . [W]e did get by without any serious trade restrictions. We did a lot of stupid things in the government account: we spent a hell of a lot of money to buy in ways that minimized the balance of payments strain; we shipped beer to Germany for our troops to drink over there. . . .
>
> [T]his is one of the areas where I, at least, believed that the scientific or professional involvement in the political process really involved some conflicts. (Hargrove and Morley, 1984, 265)

additional $500 million for the Export-Import Bank to encourage exports in 1968.

The president's program received a mixed response.[41] The gold outflow slowed, at first, but did not stop. At its February meeting, the bankers on the Federal Advisory Council told the Board that the program did not "come to grips with the basic problem" (Board Minutes, February 20, 1968, 30). They wanted "unmistakable evidence of fiscal restraint" (ibid.) and a determined effort to reduce inflation. Chairman Martin responded that "he was discouraged about the number of people who were expressing a non-cooperative attitude on the grounds that they expected the program to break down" (ibid., 30–31). He urged the bankers to reject the defeatist attitude and urge others to do the same.[42]

The president sent his advisers to brief foreign governments just ahead of his announcement. Coombs reported on European concerns. As usual, they wanted the capital outflow from the United States to end, but they feared that higher U.S. interest rates would cause them to increase their rates. They favored the tax surcharge as a way of avoiding tighter monetary policy (FOMC Minutes, January 9, 1968, 13). Robert Solomon reported, however, that at Working Party 3 late in January, the members expressed willingness to cooperate by expanding their economies as the United States adopted the surtax and other restrictive actions. "Even the French representative was anxious to have other continental European countries pursue expansionary domestic policies" (ibid., February 6, 1968, 15). President Johnson emphasized that he had maintained his commitment to European defense and had avoided trade restrictions. He asked for the

41. The president's advisers split on two other recommendations. One put a border tax on imports and rebated indirect (real estate, excise, etc.) taxes on exports. The second taxed tourist expenditures. Vice-president Hubert Humphrey argued that politically the administration could not put a mandatory tax on tourism and keep voluntary restraints on capital investment abroad (Department of State, Minutes Cabinet Committee on the Balance of Payments, December 21, 1967). The president rejected both proposals. "I don't like the 'border tax adjustment' at all. . . . It will stimulate speculation as a step toward devaluation. . . . It hits at an area that is not the root of the problem. . . . The tourist tax proposal is complicated—cumbersome—will obviously produce only limited results—advertises weakness to millions of people . . . inhibits international good will . . . certain to be used by the Republicans in an election year" (Dept. of State, telegram, President Johnson to Joseph Califano, December 23, 1967). The president proposed tax reduction for businesses that repatriated foreign capital and earnings. Taxation of foreign earnings was still under discussion in 2004.

42. Parts of the program violated rules of the General Agreement on Tariffs and Trade (GATT). By exempting Canada, Mexico, and Caribbean countries from new duties on tourist purchases, it violated the most favored nation clause that required equal treatment. Flat-rate duties on all tourists' purchases differed from the specific duties negotiated under GATT, also a violation (letter, Trade Negotiator William Roth, to Secretary Fowler, Department of State, March 8, 1968).

reaction abroad to the border tax proposal. The response was that foreign governments would not retaliate, if the tax was legal under GATT rules. The president decided not to propose the tax to Congress (Department of State, report of Nicholas Katzenbach and Frederick Deming to the president, January 7, 1968).

Martin tried to calm the markets. In a speech on February 14, he insisted that "the future evolution of the system can and should be based on the present price of gold" (Martin Speeches, February 14, 1968, 1). Devaluation against gold "would undoubtedly be accompanied by an equal change in terms of virtually all other currencies" (ibid., 8). Even if true, and there is much less certainty than his statement claims, the United States would have more gold to satisfy the claims against it. He called "man's enslavement to gold for monetary purposes" barbarous. The solution to international money problems, he said, was international cooperation and replacement of gold with SDRs. As usual, he made no mention of the need for realigning real exchange rates.

It was too late for soothing words and pledges. If the administration and the Federal Reserve wanted to maintain the fixed exchange rate system, they had either to find a way to devalue the dollar against other currencies or deflate. They were not ready for either choice, and they rarely mentioned the real exchange rate. Political opinions had started to change, however. A growing group in Congress favored an end to the fixed rate system. Senator Jacob Javits's statement in late February, calling for suspension of convertibility into gold, expressed this sentiment publicly (Eichengreen, 2000, 209).

The System's immediate concern was removing the last gold reserve requirement. Gold reserve requirements began in 1882, when Congress established a gold reserve (Krooss, 1969, v. 4, 3150). The opposition blamed the administration's inflationary policies and wanted to have an election issue. Congressman Patman introduced amendments that would have prevented gold sales to countries that permitted their citizens to own gold. This included most countries (letter, Fowler and Martin to Patman, Volcker papers, Department of the Treasury, February 20, 1968). A majority recognized that the Bretton Woods system could not continue unless the United States exchanged dollars for gold at a fixed price and, if they did not release the gold reserve, the end would come soon. On March 18, President Johnson signed the Act to Eliminate the Gold Reserve Against Federal Reserve Notes.[43] The bill passed the Senate with a two-vote margin.

43. Some Federal Reserve banks were below the 25 percent statutory gold requirement. On March 14, the Board and the reserve banks agreed to compute the requirement weekly

At the time, the Federal Reserve held only $3.5 million in free gold (FOMC Minutes, April 2, 1968, 30). The act severed the last tie of money to gold.

By March 5, the breakdown of the system seemed at hand. Coombs reported to the FOMC that the gold pool continued to lose "record breaking sums," that the Canadians had also lost "record breaking sums" trying to support the Canadian dollar, and the British "were not gaining on sterling" (Maisel diary, March 6, 1968, 14). The Canadians threatened to float. This raised concerns that the British and others would use this as a reason to float.

The United States' gold stock declined nearly $1.2 billion in March, 10 percent of its holdings at the end of February, almost all of it prior to closing the gold market. When the Board met on the morning of March 14, Governor Robertson announced that the United States had sold $350 million on the London market that day. Britain sold $250 million on the same day. Late that afternoon, the FOMC held a telephone meeting. Chairman Martin reported that, in a meeting with President Johnson and Secretary Fowler, they had accepted the British decision to suspend operations of the London gold pool (FOMC Minutes, March 14, 1968, 3). Participating central banks agreed to meet in Washington on March 16 and 17 to stop the run against the dollar and the pound. That was the end of the gold pool. Closing the gold market prevented further decline in aggregate official gold stocks.[44] The United States and other countries remained obligated to buy and sell gold to other members of the Bretton Woods system at the $35 price. Much of the gold sold on the London market went to private holders. Canada, West Germany, Switzerland, and others sold gold (net). The difference for these countries was that their reserves changed composition.

---

instead of daily, level the requirements of the reserve banks instead of permitting deficiencies at one or more banks, reallocate gold daily instead of monthly, and reduce the tax for gold reserve deficiencies from 0.5 to 0.1 percent for ratios from 20 to 25 percent. Once the legislation passed, none of these changes remained relevant. The Federal Reserve could then settle interdistrict transfers using securities instead of gold (Board Minutes, March 14, 1968, 7 and 23–24).

44. Canada also faced a serious reserve drain. Governor Louis Rasminsky told U.S. officials that Canada lost $1 billion of reserves out of $2.5 billion held at the end of February 1968 defending its par value. Rasminsky wanted a $1.5 billion short-term loan. The Federal Reserve agreed to increase the swap line by a maximum of $100 million. Canada also wanted renewed exemption from U.S. controls on lending and investing. The Board agreed to the exemption because the Treasury had agreed with the Canadians (Board Minutes, March 7, 1968, 9–10; memo, Robert C. Holland to FOMC, "The Two-Market System for Gold," Board Records, March 29, 1968, 15). After suspending sales to the London market, the Paris market gold price rose to $44 an ounce, a 26 percent discount of the dollar. The London market did not reopen until April.

They acquired dollars. For the U.S., the sale of gold meant a reduction in international reserves.

Six reserve banks proposed a 0.5 percentage point increase in the discount rate to 5 percent. Two banks proposed 5.5 percent and New York asked for 6 percent, an extraordinary 1.5 percentage point increase, the largest change since 1931. Chicago asked for 0.25, an increase to 4.75 percent. Clearly there were differences of opinion about the severity of the problem and the appropriate response.

Governor Maisel supported a 5 percent rate but insisted that "any solution to the gold problem should be compatible with what was best for the domestic economy" (Board Minutes, March 14, 1968, 15). Sherrill agreed about the domestic economy and, like Brimmer, Robertson, and Mitchell, preferred the 5 percent rate. This made a majority, but Chairman Martin was reluctant to impose a discount rate on directors who had voted for a different rate. He favored treating the reserve banks as members of a system and did not want to make the reserve bank directors less secure about their role in setting the discount rate. He proposed allowing the bank directors to reconsider. Chicago, St. Louis, and Dallas revised their requests, and the Board approved the 5 percent rate. New York would not revise its increase below 5.5 percent, and the Board was not willing to grant so large an increase. The Board's press release cited the international position of the dollar as the reason for the increase, despite New York's absence.[45]

The FOMC's telephone meeting also had difficulty agreeing on Coombs's proposal to increase the size of the swap lines by 50 percent with some main countries other than Britain. The Board's staff opposed the increase first because it signaled that foreign central banks would not want to hold additional dollars and second because it would increase short-term claims against the remaining gold stock. They preferred to force some change in international financial arrangements and thought that the United States would be in a better bargaining position if it held more gold and had fewer liabilities (Maisel diary, March 15, 1968, 26). Mitchell, Robertson, and Maisel supported the staff, but Martin and Daane supported the manager. FOMC approved the increase in swap lines.

On March 16 and 17, central bank governors of the United States, Belgium, West Germany, Italy, the Netherlands, Switzerland, and Britain met

45. In New York's absence the statement is not credible. Martin told President Johnson about the need for a discount rate increase before the vote. The president accepted the decision. Bremner (2004, 196), quoting Wilbur Mills, records that the president "was scared almost out of his body when he heard that people in Europe were having trouble exchanging dollars for foreign currency."

in Washington to decide on common strategy to stop the drain of gold through the London gold pool. The managing director of the IMF and the general manager of the Bank for International Settlements attended also. France did not participate (memo, Walt Rostow to the president, Department of State, March 12, 1968).

The first day's meeting was contentious. Martin asked Governor Carli to introduce his proposal for a two-tier market. The British and Dutch introduced their proposal to increase the gold price, devaluing the dollar against gold. Instead of devaluing, the United States mistakenly wanted to maintain the $35 price but restrict purchases and sales to central banks, the Carli proposal.[46] The Germans were uncertain, and the Italians, Belgians, and Swiss strongly opposed an increase in the gold price. Martin presided, allowed discussion to continue, then announced at the end of the day that the gold price would not be increased (Coombs, 1976, 168). That left Carli's proposal. The following day, Sunday, the United States agreed to borrow from the IMF to redeem the dollars that central banks had acquired by supplying gold to the pool and agreed to establish what it had previously feared—a two-tier gold market. "They decided no longer to supply gold to the London gold market or any other gold market. Moreover, as the existing stock of monetary gold is sufficient in view of the prospective establishment of the facility for special drawing rights, they no longer feel it is necessary to buy gold from the market. Finally, they agreed that henceforth they will not sell gold to monetary authorities to replace gold sold in private markets" (Krooss, 1969, v. 4, 3168).[47]

The Bank of England pointed out that closing the London market would move trading to other markets in Paris and Zurich. They proposed to keep the market open but restrict sales and purchases by central banks. The new rule set two restrictions. Gold in official monetary reserves at the time of the meeting could be used for transactions between monetary authorities

46. Switzerland agreed to this arrangement but said it was obligated under Swiss law to buy from and sell gold to Swiss citizens.

47. The two-tier gold market was discussed and discarded earlier. Arthur Okun explained that much of the contingency planning after 1965 was done by the Deming group, chaired by Treasury Undersecretary Frederick Deming, a former Federal Reserve Bank president. The other members were Dewey Daane of the Board of Governors, Okun while he was a member of the Council of Economic Advisers, Francis Bator of the National Security Council, and Anthony Solomon of the State Department. This group both preferred to pay out gold and doubted that other countries would agree to close the gold window. Okun claimed that in March "the outflow got up to hemorrhage proportions. It was at this point, I think, that the negotiability of the two-tier system first became clear. . . . They wanted to stop their losses of gold. They did not want to keep paying it into the gold pool" (Okun, Oral History, Interview II, tape I). Okun credits Guido Carli, governor of the Banca d'Italia, with the idea of the two-tier system.

**Table 5.3** Gold and Short-Term Claims, 1966–70 (in $ millions)

| | GOLD | | | SHORT-TERM CLAIMS | | |
|---|---|---|---|---|---|---|
| *Date* | *France* | *Germany* | *Japan* | *France* | *Germany* | *Japan* |
| Dec. 1966 | 5238 | 4292 | 329 | 1070 | 2538 | 2671 |
| Dec. 1970 | 3532 | 3980 | 532 | 2267 | 7520 | 5150 |

Source: Board of Governors (1976, 919–20, 958, 961).

at $35 an ounce. Gold not in official monetary reserves, including any new production, could be purchased or sold in the free market.[48] Participants recognized that if the market price fell below $35, some central banks might try to take advantage of the price spread.

The U.S. gold stock rose slightly in 1969–70. One reason was that Germany and Japan, the countries with large payments surpluses at the time, limited gold purchases. France had regularly demanded gold, but it experienced a payments deficit in 1968 and 1969, so it had to sell gold.

The German decision was formally stated in a March 1967 letter from President Karl Blessing of the Bundesbank to Chairman Martin supported by a letter from the chancellor of the West German government. Germany committed to refrain from purchasing gold from the U.S. Treasury (Solomon, 1982, 111). The decision came "following threats of a partial troop withdrawal" (Holtfrerich, 1999, 384). Japan did not make a public pledge or require direct pressure. It simply accumulated dollars and did not demand much gold.

Table 5.3 shows the change in short-term dollar assets and gold between 1966 and 1970 for France, Germany, and Japan. After it recovered from the 1968 strikes, disruptions, and wage increases, France accumulated dollar assets and did not replace the gold sold before the August 1969 devaluation of the franc. But it must have been clear to everyone that the agreement eroded the gold base of the fixed exchange rate system. De facto, the dollar was no longer convertible for most purposes.

The March 16–17 meeting took a long step toward ending the Bretton Woods system. It solved the short-term problem but left the long-term problem untouched. Vietnam spending had increased. The projected United States budget deficit reached a postwar record ($25 billion), and the

48. The commitment not to sell official gold (no longer to supply) was much stronger than the decision not to buy (no longer necessary because the existing stock is sufficient). The claim of sufficiency reflected the belief that the SDR would soon be approved as a source of international reserve growth. The Board's staff pointed out that IMF members had a right to obtain foreign currencies for gold and to repay the IMF in gold. The gold could be obtained from (or sold to) the market (memo, Holland to FOMC, Board Records, March 29, 1968, 9). Among large gold holders, France, Australia, and South Africa did not subscribe to the agreement. The last two were important gold producers.

dollar remained overvalued. The Johnson administration did not devalue the dollar against gold and offered no other adjustment toward long-term equilibrium. The Federal Reserve did not commit to a less inflationary policy. Until 1970–71 there was little pressure from Congress or others to develop a long-term policy.

The meeting solved the immediate problem by introducing another exchange control; this one went to the basis of the system. It could only work as long as countries feared the consequences of collapse and did not ask to exchange dollars for gold. Closing the gold market, passage of the surtax in June, the small budget surplus in fiscal 1969, a new administration in 1969, higher interest rates, and a capital inflow from the euro-dollar market postponed the long-term problem. Firm resistance at the Washington meeting to the British-Dutch proposal to devalue the dollar showed that United States officials had not yet concluded that they had to adjust. The most likely explanation is that they hoped that what they said was true; creation of SDRs and the surtax would solve their problem.

In the squabble over the discount rate with New York, the majority and minority set out their positions. The difference in the two positions was not in their analysis but in the goals each sought to achieve. New York recognized that a deflationary or disinflationary policy was the only way to keep the dollar price of gold fixed. A 6 percent discount rate would show "determination . . . to defend the dollar at all costs" (Maisel diary, March 18, 1968, 5). Maisel then wrote that the Board "should reject the concept that the defense of the dollar is worth 'all costs'" (ibid.) He was willing to "hold the growth rate of the economy to 4 percent and perhaps even to 3.5 percent, but anything beneath this is not logical . . . [F]or equilibrium to come about at existing exchange rates there would have to be a much faster rise in European prices and it does not seem likely that this can be brought about" (ibid., 6). The choice, he said, was additional controls or eventual devaluation of the dollar.

Martin did not share Maisel's view. He told the American Society of Newspaper Editors that the United States was in a crisis—"the worst financial crisis that we have had since 1931." But he added: "This is not a disaster story. The world would not come to an end if we did that [devalued]" (extemporaneous remarks, Martin speeches, April 19, 1968, 4, 5).[49] Press reaction to the speech called Martin an alarmist. Like many of his contemporaries, Martin believed that devaluation of the dollar

49. He noted that some economists preferred floating rates. That would be "the greatest setback, financially, that this country has faced, certainly in my lifetime, and I think it will take us a long time to recover from it" (Martin Speeches, April 19, 1968, 5). But his speech showed willingness to consider devaluation despite his reluctance.

or floating rates would end the postwar system and bring back trade restrictions.

When the London market reopened on April 1, gold sold for $38 an ounce. The price remained between $38 and $43 for the next year, then fell to $35 following sales by South Africa (Solomon, 1982, 124). The price remained close to $35 until new disruptions culminated in the formal end of U.S. gold sales in 1971. The two-tier agreement remained in effect until November 1973, when the market price was almost $100 and the official price had increased to $42.22 (ibid., 127).

Between November 1967, when Britain devalued, and March the federal funds rate increased nearly a percentage point, from 4.12 to 5.05. Growth of the monetary base remained at a 6 percent annual rate. In response to a question, Martin reported that the European central bankers held mixed views about the desirability of additional rate increases. They preferred a reduction in the budget deficit by fiscal contraction. Robert Solomon added that the Europeans would accept a rise in interest rates that shifted about $200 million in euro-dollars a month to the United States, reducing the capital outflow. A more aggressive policy would likely bring matching increases abroad.

Despite a decision at the April 2 meeting to make only a modest change toward firmer policy, short-term rates rose following the meeting. By mid-month, the Board agreed to increase the discount rate to 5.5 percent and the regulation Q ceiling rate to 6.25 percent. Much of the argument for the changes referred to the balance of payments. Before making the changes, the Board notified the Secretary of the Treasury and the Council of Economic Advisers. The Council informed the president. No one objected, but the White House staff asked the Board to delay the announcement until the following Monday, "pending an opportunity for the President to discuss the matter with the Chairman" (Board Minutes, April 18, 1968, 13). The Board agreed to delay the announcement (ibid., 14). This was the first time that the White House interceded to delay announcement of an action already voted. The Board Minutes do not report on the discussion with President Johnson, but the Board announced the rate increases after the meeting.

## MINTING PAPER GOLD[50]

For the years 1960–67 as a whole, the non-U.S. members of the G-10 (including Switzerland) acquired 150 million ounces of gold, an increase

50. Except as noted, this section follows Solomon (1982, chapter 8) and Meltzer (1991). Solomon was an active participant in most of the meetings. For details of the negotiations, see Solomon (1982).

of one-third over their holdings at the end of 1960 (IMF, 1990, 65). Every country except Britain and Canada added to its holdings. Britain sold 38 million ounces, the United States 164 million ounces. France acquired two-thirds of the G-10 increase, 100 million ounces. The following year, it sold 40 million ounces to delay devaluation.

The steady decline in the United States' gold stock pushed the liquidity issue to the forefront. From 1965 to 1968, the major countries discussed changes in the international monetary system to increase the stock of settlement balances (liquidity). The outcome was the special drawing right (SDR) widely described as "paper gold," a new reserve asset to be used for settlement between countries. The intention was to free the provision of international means of payment between central banks or monetary authorities from dependence on the supply of gold and U.S. dollars. Although most of the emphasis was on finding a solution to the "Triffin problem,"[51] France often tried to get attention to the adjustment problem. The United States usually assumed that its payments deficit would end.

The French argued, correctly, that there was no reason for the liquidity discussion as long as the United States and Britain had large payments deficits.[52] France opposed any planning for a new reserve asset as long as world dollar balances continued to increase. Its spokesmen wanted to end the special role of the dollar as a reserve currency, what President de Gaulle called its "exorbitant privilege," but they opposed putting control of a new money at the IMF. They preferred a new form of credit controlled by the G-10.

On important votes, the other European countries did not support France. This was particularly true of French proposals to increase world reserves by raising the gold price and reestablishing gold as a "neutral currency" (Solomon, 1982, 136). But the principal European countries agreed with France, for a time, that the new source of reserves should be a repayable form of credit, not an addition to international money as the U.S. proposed.[53]

51. Haberler (1965, 46) wrote, "Some of the ingenuity now so lavishly spent on how to guard against the possibility that international liquidity may become scarce could be more profitably applied to the more basic and neglected problem of how to improve the adjustment mechanism." Policy officials ignored all such comments.

52. The French position was that the special position of the dollar gave the United States the great advantage that it could settle its payments deficit by printing more of its own currency. The United States' position accepted the claim that it had a unique position, but recognized that it had committed to maintain convertibility of dollar claims into gold. After March 1968, this response was less prominent (Report of the President's Task Force on Foreign Economic Policy, Department of State, S/P Files, Lot 70D194, November 25, 1964, 23). The United States also paid interest on the foreign claims.

53. One early French proposal known as the Collective Reserve Unit (CRU) would have tied growth of international money to the stock of monetary gold, acting as a multiplier of the

The major issues that had to be resolved included whether the new units would be credit or money, who would get the new units, whether the new unit would be tied to gold, and who would decide on the size and frequency of additions to the stock—how many votes would be required and who would be able to vote. The United States and France generally differed on these issues. The U.S. task was to move ahead without attacking the French position in a way that would end the meetings.

By June 1967, the group had resolved several issues. However, France continued to insist that reserves supplied by the new mechanism had to be repaid. Differences about who would have power to veto additions to reserves also remained. One reason for the deadlock was that France and others believed that the United States intended to pay off its liabilities by creating new pieces of paper unrelated to gold or other assets. The French did not want a system that would permit the United States to pay its debts with a new paper asset.

France gained a concession when the Group of Ten agreed to name the new unit a special drawing right (SDR). Unlike other IMF drawings, however, the new unit was transferable and remained available for future transfers. France accepted the decision to make the new units permanent. This left only decisions about voting as a major issue. At the IMF annual meeting in Rio de Janeiro in September 1967, the members voted to approve the new asset as a supplement to existing reserve assets.[54] Finally at Stockholm on March 29 and 30, 1968, ministers agreed on the SDR and once again reaffirmed their commitment to the $35 per ounce gold price. To obtain agreement by the Europeans (other than France), the United States accepted that the European Union, like the United States, could veto any future increases in IMF quotas.

The IMF could issue SDRs only if an 85 percent majority approved. Under the 1944 Bretton Woods enabling legislation, Congress had to approve any increase. When approved, IMF members could create an asset to serve as a substitute for gold in settlement between central banks and governments but not as payment for quota increases at the IMF. France reiterated the need for adjustment and did not sign the agreement until autumn 1969. Congress quickly approved the amendments to the IMF agreement, and President Johnson signed the agreement on June 19, 1968. The agree-

existing gold stock. The United States wanted increases in reserves to remain independent of the gold stock. The CRU proposal called for action by the Group of Ten. The United States favored action under the IMF, where it could veto proposals.

54. France tried to the end to get agreement on an increase in the gold price. It proposed making the U.S. use profits from depreciation to redeem part of its outstanding liabilities.

ment received enough support to enter into effect on July 28, 1969. The first issue of SDRs came on January 1, 1970.

Robert Solomon, who did a great deal to achieve agreement on the SDR and the broader issue of providing liquidity, summed up the experience. At the time he thought that the decisions in March to close the gold market and to adopt the SDR "may turn out to have marked a turning point in world monetary history" (FOMC Minutes, April 2, 1968, 13). In his book, he revised this conclusion. "Even if establishment of a reserve-creating mechanism was a necessary condition for international payments balance . . . earlier attention should have been given to introducing greater flexibility of exchange rates" (Solomon, 1982, 167). Much earlier, Haberler and Willett (1971) criticized the decision to devote much time to the liquidity problem and not to the adjustment problem.

The case for SDRs was far less than compelling. As the French never tired of pointing out, the system had excess liquidity. The United States argued that this would not always be true, that ending the U.S. payments deficit would, sooner or later, lead to a liquidity shortage.

This argument suffered from two weaknesses. First, U.S. representatives had no plan for achieving balance and spent little effort on that problem. Second, the argument was false or, at best, incomplete. The United States could add to reserves by buying other stable currencies, just as those countries bought dollars. The Council of Economic Advisers (1964, 145) recognized that this argument was correct.

Principal world monetary officials had made enormous effort to solve the lesser of two problems while ignoring the more serious problem. French efforts to shift the emphasis met with hostility. To the last, at Stockholm, the French Finance Minister, Michel Debré, reminded his colleagues that they had neglected the adjustment problem. Perhaps because of the history of French policy, the others rejected his plea. Within three years, the Bretton Woods system broke down, exchange rates changed, the gold price increased, and the international monetary system later acquired an adjustment mechanism. SDRs remained in the system.

It seems unlikely that the SDR would have become a dominant medium of exchange or store of international reserves if the fixed exchange rate system had survived. Developing countries treated SDR allocations as a wealth transfer; most quickly exchanged them for hard currencies. Furthermore, the SDR did not dominate alternatives. Gold is an established store of value with a long history. SDRs had to compete with currencies that had superior properties—the dollar and later the mark and the yen. Balances held in each of these assets paid interest. At first SDR balances did not earn interest and could not pay interest since there was no source of revenue or earnings.

Revaluing gold would have solved the liquidity problem, as the French insisted. French proposals did not limit future changes in the gold price, so they were open to the charge that expectations of future devaluation would lead to a run on the dollar. Much earlier, Keynes (1924) had proposed a commodity standard in which gold served as a medium of exchange. He tied the gold price to the price of a commodity basket. In 1922, Irving Fisher persuaded a congressional committee to hold hearings on a similar proposal for a compensated dollar (Meltzer, 2003, 182–83).

When governments agreed to the SDR in 1968, the U.S. price level was approximately 2.5 times its 1929 level. If the gold price had increased in the same proportion, the 1968 gold price would have been $52, making the U.S. gold reserve $17.6 billion, $1.6 billion more than its total liabilities to central banks and governments. The Bretton Woods system could have continued. Of course, it could not have continued indefinitely or even very long without some restriction on U.S. monetary policy, a restriction that U.S. authorities were unlikely to accept. That was true of any solution that tried to maintain fixed exchange rates.[55]

## NEW PROBLEMS

The major decisions taken in March brought temporary calm to financial markets.[56] Britain still held blocked foreign balances that it could not repay and had a large short-term debt that it wanted to extend over a longer period. Riots in France and an 11 percent wage increase weakened the franc in exchange markets. Inflows into Germany threatened inflation or revaluation of the mark.

55. Eichengreen (2004, 18) discusses other ways in which governments could have sustained the Bretton Woods system longer.

56. The gold embargo restored calm but did not convince many market participants that the solution would last. Hayes received letters from some of the skeptics. His response to George Clark of First National City Bank expressed concern about giving most attention to the payments problem. Hayes was more concerned about that problem than most of the FOMC. Nevertheless, he wrote:

> The economic and social results of such drastic action would be very bad—and whatever short-term gain might seem to result for the balance of payments would be far overshadowed by the long-term damage inflicted on the economy. . . . I do not believe that our balance-of-payments problem can be solved in the context of a seriously weakened U.S. economy. (letter, Hayes to Clark, Correspondence, Federal Reserve Bank of New York, June 3, 1968)

Although his judgment about a draconian policy seems correct, he neglects many alternatives that would have lowered the inflation rate.

The first mention of renewed British problems came at the May 21 Board meeting. Governor Robertson reported on negotiations between the Treasury and the British government to refinance Britain's external debt, much of it outstanding since World War II. Coombs described the pound as "in extreme danger" (FOMC Minutes, May 28, 1968, 17). In the six months following devaluation, Britain had borrowed $2.6 billion. Coombs expected renewed drawings on the swap line and a possible request to increase the line, and he was pessimistic about Britain's ability to repay within the standard time frame. He suggested that the Federal Reserve consider turning down the British request. "In his judgment the British situation had come very close to being hopeless" (ibid., 15). The FOMC rejected his proposal. Chairman Martin reported that Britain agreed to repay all its swap credit, if it drew $1.4 billion from the IMF.

Britain had borrowed in aggregate between $5 and $6 billion, according to estimates, much of it to defend the exchange rate before the November 1967 devaluation. In addition, overseas holdings of blocked British pounds reached $7 billion, of which governments and central banks owned $4 billion (ibid., 27–28). Coombs said that it might take thirty years or longer to pay off the debt.

Solomon was less pessimistic than Coombs. He did not believe that the $2.40 exchange rate was untenable, and he urged the FOMC to consider the risk to the financial system if Britain floated its currency. "The Committee would have to be prepared to bear the responsibility for the chaos into which the international monetary system would be thrown. A run on the dollar by foreign central banks would undoubtedly follow" (ibid., 19). That clinched the argument.

Martin and Hayes supported Solomon. The FOMC voted to let the British continue drawing up to an additional $800 million on the swap line and to extend additional credit by purchasing up to $400 million of British pounds with an exchange rate guarantee. The British could use these longer-term funds and IMF borrowing to repay the swap line. Martin recognized that the debt could become illiquid. Like Solomon, he thought that risk was smaller than the risk that the British would float the pound.

Solomon's analysis proved correct. Britain's problems following devaluation proved temporary. The trade balance turned favorable within a few months. By 1969, Britain had a payments surplus of $1 billion. It began to repay the debts incurred in 1967–68. Also, the central banks of Europe, Japan, Canada, and the United States now supported an arrangement under which the British agreed to maintain the dollar value of the balances held as official reserves. The foreign central banks provided long-term dollar loans to permit holders of balances in London to diversify their assets. The

United States' share, $600 million of the $2 billion total, was made by the Treasury as swaps through the Exchange Stabilization Fund (ESF).[57] Since the ESF lacked the resources, the Federal Reserve agreed to warehouse the funds for the Treasury. This support of a longer-term loan raised both legal and policy issues. The Board's counsel ruled that legality was not an issue. The Board would enter into swaps as it had done since 1962.

Governor Brimmer opposed on policy grounds because the agreement allowed the Treasury to borrow at long term from the Federal Reserve. Others expressed concern but not opposition. The result was an agreement that allowed the Treasury to warehouse for up to a year. The Federal Reserve could then demand payment, but the agreement did not say that the Treasury had to pay. Treasury would have to go to Congress to ask for funds, a step that warehousing avoided (Maisel diary, July 2, 1968, 11). President Johnson approved the agreement with the Federal Reserve.[58]

That ended the British problem for the present. France's problem began with widespread strikes and demonstrations in May 1968. France was not alone; several countries experienced student demonstrations that year. France's demonstrations spread to the economy when the strike became general. The Bank of France and the financial markets closed.

Coombs described a general flight from currency, not just in France but elsewhere as well. The demand for gold increased, and the higher price "panicked a lot of small central banks into buying gold from the United States" (FOMC Minutes, May 28, 1968, 4). France continued to lose gold and foreign exchange, $1.8 billion in May and June, more than 25 percent of its balance at the beginning of the year. The franc began to trade at a discount as rumors and fears of devaluation spread. France had not participated in the expansion of the swap network. It drew its entire $100 million from the Federal Reserve in early June, and it began to negotiate for an increase to $700 million. Despite its often hostile or contrary attitude, the European countries and the United States agreed to extend more credit.

57. The swaps of dollars for pounds were three-month renewable loans that could be drawn upon for three years and, after a two-year grace period, would be repayable in the next five years. This gave the loans a maturity of up to ten years. The Bank of England gave an exchange value guarantee for about two-thirds of the outstanding balances (Board Minutes, July 2, 1968, 4–5; Maisel diary, July 2, 1968, 4–6).

58. The Treasury would receive pounds sterling on swaps for dollars with the Bank for International Settlements (BIS). When the Treasury's Exchange Stabilization Fund (ESF) needed additional dollars, it would sell pounds to the Federal Reserve and simultaneously buy pounds forward from the Federal Reserve. When the forward sale became due, the Federal Reserve could put the contract to the Treasury (ESF). The Treasury could put the contract to the BIS, which could put it to the British. The Board recognized that it was at risk.

France also sold gold, including $400 million to the United States in June. Between May and December, U.S. gold reserves rose $400 million.

The European Commission staff estimated that the settlements in France would raise wages 23 percent in 1968 and 1969 and prices 10 percent. It projected that higher costs and prices would induce a $1 billion payments imbalance. Devaluation seemed likely (Fowler to the president, Department of State, June 6, 1968).

The United States' concern was that weakness in the French financial system would make the international payments problems much worse. If a run from the franc triggered a large devaluation, the British could be forced to float. "There would be repercussions on the dollar and, perhaps, general monetary chaos—with everyone trying to get out of currencies and into gold. . . . The U.S. might have to cut the gold convertibility link to the dollar and float itself. And that would destroy the present system and probably badly cripple world trade" (ibid., 2).

Aside from loans, the expressed need was for a revaluation of the mark and realignment of the European currencies. The next months illustrate the problem of adjusting exchange rates under the Bretton Woods system even when the dollar was not directly involved. West Germany had reduced interest rates in 1967 during a mild recession. Rates remained low in early 1968. As imports fell during the recession, Germany's current account surplus rose, but the capital account deficit during the recession reduced upward pressure on the mark. The market anticipated that higher future interest rates would bring a reduction in the capital account deficit or possibly a surplus. Fears of French devaluation after the general wage increase and higher French prices induced capital outflow from France to Germany.

In September, after the capital flow to Germany rose, the Bundesbank proposed a revaluation of the mark, but Karl Schiller, the Economics Minister, rejected the idea (Holtfrerich, 1999, 385). In Germany, as in the United States, the government, not the central bank, decided exchange rate policy. Speculation resumed in November. The Bundesbank purchased $2.8 billion, mainly from England and France, to maintain its exchange rates.[59] The United States pressed for parity adjustments, a modest (less than 10 percent) devaluation of the franc and a 10 percent revaluation of the mark. President de Gaulle announced that France would not devalue. Germany put a special duty on exports and a special tax allowance on imports, each 4 percent, but the change was insufficient to stop the capital

59. The Bank of France lost $1.1 billion of reserves, and the Bank of England lost $800 million. The gold price remained about $40. Coombs claimed that the crisis originated in an effort by France and Britain to get Germany to revalue by 10 percent.

flow. The German chancellor, Kurt Kiesinger, pledged publicly that his government would not revalue the mark. Germany closed its exchange market on November 20 and 21.

A meeting of the Group of Ten, described as acrimonious, achieved very little. Much of the meeting pressed Germany to appreciate more and France to depreciate less than a threatened 15 percent devaluation. The Germans remained adamant; the French agreed, finally, to a maximum devaluation of 11.11 percent, but did not commit to do it. Although the meeting did not accomplish much, it showed a growing recognition of a need for parity changes and the difficulty of getting them. Germany put a 100 percent reserve requirement on short-term bank liabilities to foreigners, France reduced its budget deficit and increased exchange controls, and the central banks agreed to lend France $2 billion (Solomon, 1982, 160–61).[60] The U.S. share was $500 million, $300 million from the Federal Reserve.[61] The FOMC increased the French swap line to $1 billion and extended the term to one year as with other large countries. France increased some tax rates, reduced public spending, tightened price controls, restricted imports, subsidized exports, and imposed exchange controls. Germany and the United States agreed to sell marks forward at a 3 percent premium and to split the earnings with the Bundesbank. Following these actions, inflows into Germany reversed (FOMC Minutes, November 26, 1968, 15–16).

Coombs proposed that any further assistance to France be done by the Treasury. The Treasury would act as principal, but the Federal Reserve

60. France's technocrats wanted a 15 percent change in the mark-franc exchange rate, but neither government would accept a change. The British said that if France devalued by 15 percent, it would float the pound. French officials accepted the German tax changes on imports and exports as almost a 4 percent appreciation, so they offered an 11.11 percent devaluation, subject to de Gaulle's approval. He did not approve (Maisel diary, November 25, 1968, 3).

61. The German response to criticism at the meeting suggests why adjustment became infeasible under Bretton Woods. After making the obvious point that revaluation and devaluation had symmetric effects on exchange rates, Economics Minister Karl Schiller complained that German revaluation "would appear to be a punishment for a sound German policy" (telegram, embassy in West Germany to the White House, Department of State, 214, November 21, 1968). Secretary Fowler replied that no one wished to punish Germany. Germany had a persistent surplus since 1961. He claimed that it was a structural, not a cyclical, surplus. (At other times, Germany argued that it needed a current account surplus because it paid the offset for U.S. military costs.) During a break in the meeting, the Dutch representative proposed that Fowler talk to the Italian representatives. If Germany revalued by 10 percent and Italy by 5 percent, he offered a 5 percent revaluation of the guilder. The Italian representatives said revaluation by Italy was politically impossible (ibid.) The following day Schiller talked about the need to realign "all important parities" but indicated his belief that such a change "was not politically possible and is dangerous." He denied that the German surplus was structural, blaming U.S. corporate purchases of German industry for the surplus. Pierre-Paul Schweitzer of the IMF "said he was frightened at the Schiller proposal" (ibid., 216, November 21, 1968).

would assist because "under existing arrangements the Treasury could ask the System at any time to warehouse some of its holdings of guaranteed sterling if the Stabilization Fund's resources were inadequate to meet outstanding commitments" (ibid., 22–23). Although members expressed some concern about the possible long-term nature of this commitment, they took no action to change it.

Maisel (diary, June 9, 1968, 7–8) expressed his view about why the two-tier gold market did not set off a run on gold by central banks. He explained that the Europeans were "extremely reluctant" to permit exchange rate adjustments. Also, "the Europeans no longer felt in a position to threaten the United States with gold withdrawals. They were very much concerned over the potential cost to them if the international monetary system broke down" (ibid., 8). Once again, he portrayed the Europeans as concerned with the benefits to them, not the public good of an international system. Political costs had a major role.

After the failed November meeting, Stephen Axilrod at last said the "positive lesson . . . is a need for a more flexible means of correcting payments imbalances" (FOMC Minutes, November 26, 1968, 52). He was not optimistic about reaching agreement. "In the case of Germany, for example, the major obstacle to revaluation appears to be the political fallout from a drop in farm prices that would result from an appreciation of the mark" (ibid., 53).

A quiet period on exchange markets continued until March 1969. France did not recover the reserves it lost after May 1968, suggesting that the quiet period was a lull, aided by severe exchange controls, not an end to the French problem, an overvalued real exchange rate.

Several new events revived talk of franc devaluation. President de Gaulle retired on April 28 after losing a referendum on regional policy. West Germany's strong recovery from recession produced an enlarged current account surplus. The central bank responded by raising interest rates to slow inflation. A suggestion by the German Finance Minister that Germany might revalue as part of a multilateral realignment stimulated "the heaviest flow in international financial history," $4 billion inflow (DM 17 billion) to Germany in ten days (Solomon, 1982, 162). Throughout, the Bundesbank Council urged revaluation. By late spring the Economics Minister, Schiller, joined them, but the government, after intense debate, refused to go along. Instead, it voted to accelerate debt repayment and take other fiscal measures.[62]

62. In late June, Arthur Okun sent President Johnson a message warning that "the monetary system which lies as the basis of international commerce and trade has been impaired"

On August 8, France devalued by 11.1 percent. Solomon (1982, 163) was skeptical about the need for devaluation at that time. He suggested that the French government "felt it imperative to put an end to the expectation that they would devalue" (ibid., 113). Others saw the devaluation as an effort by France to undervalue the franc to stimulate its economy as in 1927 and on other occasions. Following devaluation, France removed exchange controls.

In the September German election the Social Democrats favored revaluation and the Christian Democrats opposed. The Bundesbank again closed the foreign exchange market three days before the election. The new Social Democrat government reopened the market and permitted the mark to float. Soon after the new government revalued the mark by 9.3 percent to DM 3.66 per dollar and removed the special taxes on exports and subsidies to imports introduced the previous November (Holtfrerich, 1999, 389). Following revaluation, capital flow reversed to such an extent that Germany drew on its IMF quota for the first time.

The German revaluation reduced Germany's current account surplus in 1969 and 1970 and induced a record capital account deficit in 1969. The revaluation came during the period of rising interest rates in the United States that increased the U.S. capital inflow. For 1968 and 1969, the United States had a surplus on the official settlements account. That helped to put the balance of payments problem aside for the rest of the Johnson administration. Its last act was to extend its controls on capital flows, and increase the ceiling permitted for direct investment. Once again, the Cabinet Committee pointed to tourism, trade, and overseas military spending as problems, but it made no new proposals (letter, Fowler to the president, Johnson Library, FO4–1, December 11, 1968).

## A NEW ADMINISTRATION

At the end of 1968, the United States had $33.8 billion of dollar claims against a $10.9 billion gold stock. Between 1964 and 1968, the trade and current account surpluses had changed from $6.8 and $5.8 billion to $0.6 and −$0.5 billion. This was the first current account deficit since 1959.

Anyone looking at this development was likely to conclude that the present arrangement could not be sustained. As a candidate, President Nixon opposed the restrictions on capital flows, but he did not propose any solution to the payments problem. The new Undersecretary of the Treasury,

(memo, Okun to the president, Confidential Files, FI9, Box 53, Johnson Library, June 21, 1968). The problem was the persistent U.S. payments deficit and the belief that it would continue. Okun pointed out that a new British devaluation or other currency change would harm the dollar.

Paul Volcker, recognized that without restrictions on capital and possibly tourism and trade, there were two solutions: either a multilateral agreement or unilateral action to permit exchange rates to adjust. The other possible solution—deflation—was so universally rejected that it was never mentioned. Exchange controls, pressures on some foreign governments, and a temporary surge of euro-dollar borrowing to finance domestic banks propped up the international monetary system in 1969.

The newly elected Nixon administration appointed a task force, chaired by Professor Gottfried Haberler, to recommend an international economic policy. Haberler made the case for wider bands, increased exchange rate flexibility and an end to capital controls. In a separate memo, Milton Friedman made the case for floating the dollar at the very start of the new administration. He warned that "later events may force the administration to take the same measures that it could at first take voluntarily, but if so, the measures will then involve great political and social cost" (Friedman, 1968a, 1).[63]

Arthur Burns summarized the task force report for the new president. The payments position "is very precarious." He favored the elimination of exchange controls calling them wasteful, inefficient, and a tax on growth, and he warned that pressures against the dollar could become a problem. He proposed "confidential negotiations with the key industrial countries . . . with the main American objective being to secure quickly a significant realignment of parities of some currencies" (Department of State, Summary of the Report of the Task Force on U.S. Balance of Payments Policies, January 18, 1969, 1). He proposed wider bands and small "automatic adjustments," a crawling peg, and separately a one-time realignment. He opposed a floating rate and revaluation of gold, and he warned that "if a 'gold rush' develops, the United States should suspend gold convertibility" (ibid.).

Separately, the new Treasury Undersecretary for Monetary Affairs, Paul Volcker, chaired a group similar to the Deming group in the Johnson ad-

63. Official views had started to change. Britain's 1967 devaluation and discussion of French devaluation and German revaluation in November 1968 brought adjustment to the fore and removed parity changes from among the unmentionables. In both countries, proponents of exchange rate adjustment, including central bankers, moved the discussion from academia to official institutions. Solomon (1982, 168) mentions the desirability of a depoliticized process for exchange rate adjustment. The United States government was slow to support discussion of greater flexibility (ibid., 171). The Economic Report of the President, however, mentioned "greater flexibility of exchange rates" within the Bretton Woods system (Council of Economic Advisers, 1971, 145). Later, the report recognized "the political consequences inherent in exchange rate decisions have made countries hesitant to undertake said adjustments" (ibid., 152).

ministration. It did not recommend a floating rate, in fact gave it little attention. It confined discussion of exchange rate policy to fixed rates or limited flexibility.[64] The memo did not take a position for or against limited flexibility. It suggested, however, that more flexible exchange rates would remove a restraint against inflation and "might worsen our current account deficit" if other currencies depreciated against the dollar (Department of State, Long-Term Aspects of U.S. International Monetary and Exchange Policies, Volcker group, January 30, 1969). Elsewhere in the memo, the group recommended prompt issuance of $3 to $4 billion a year of SDRs for five years.

With limited support and some strong opposition to floating, President Nixon retained the existing arrangements at the start of his administration.[65] The principal new thrust was the effort to get SDRs issued. The timing was helpful because the United States had raised interest rates as part of domestic policy. As a by-product it had an official settlements surplus at the time, and the French had made that a precondition for agreement. The principal issue in dispute within the administration was removal of exchange controls and the interest equalization tax when it expired in June. With these changes, Treasury estimated that the goods and services account would have to increase by $13 billion to achieve permanent balance.

All parties in the new government supported removal of controls in principle, but, prompted by his staff, National Security Adviser Henry Kissinger urged delay and deliberation. By late January, concern about foreign reaction to removing controls and the estimated increase of $2.1 billion of foreign direct investment, if the administration eliminated controls, caused further delay. Discussion with European officials aroused concern that an ambitious decontrol program could harm the administration's efforts to issue SDRs. This had priority, and the priority was not questioned. Major decontrol that would widen the reported payments deficit by as

64. I worked for Paul Volcker briefly in the Kennedy administration. At the time, he was committed to a fixed rate system. Although he may have moderated his views in 1969, they had not changed. As noted below, he was pragmatic; he recognized that the current arrangement could not be sustained.

65. Before President Nixon traveled to Europe to discuss international monetary arrangements, he received memos from Paul McCracken at the CEA and Arthur Burns, his counselor. McCracken opposed any increase in the gold price except as part of a total package "that makes it worth our while." Burns agreed about gold, then added, "Let us not develop any romantic ideas about a fluctuating exchange rate: there is too much history that tells us that a fluctuating exchange rate, besides causing a serious shrinkage of trade, is also apt to give rise to international political turmoil" (Nixon papers, Box 442, February–March 1969, Trip to Europe). President Nixon did not have much interest in international economics. Volcker and Gyohten (1992, 61) described him as unwilling to see finance as a binding constraint on his foreign or defense policies.

much as $2 billion strengthened some European concerns that the United States wanted to use SDRs to avoid "discipline." In any case, the need for SDRs would be reduced by a large payments surplus.

By March, the Volcker group was ready to propose a long-term strategy. This was a major step away from the short-term crisis management of the Johnson administration. With modest changes in response to events, the Nixon administration followed both of the proposals in turn.

The strategy called for "either (a) negotiating substantial but evolutionary changes in present monetary arrangements, or (b) suspending the present type of gold convertibility and following this with an attempt to negotiate a new system" ("Summary of a Possible U.S. Approach to Improving International Monetary Arrangements," Department of State 119, March 17, 1969). The paper proposed a two-year period to terminate at the end of 1970 during which active negotiations, with high-level support, would try to achieve several objectives: (1) issue $15 to $20 billion of special drawing rights over five years; (2) increase IMF quotas in 1970 but not at the expense of the SDR allocation; (3) seek appreciation of the mark and other currencies of countries in surplus; (4) begin intensive consultations about moving parities, wider exchange rate bands, or a combination of the two; and (5) make other adjustments including relaxation of capital controls. The memo ruled out a change in the gold price.

If negotiations failed to achieve adjustment, the United States would act unilaterally to end gold convertibility. Then in "calm and unhurried negotiations," the United States would try to reconstitute a system with greater exchange rate flexibility and other features of the earlier negotiations (ibid.) Volcker suggested about two years of efforts to change the system by multilateral agreement before taking a unilateral approach.[66] He was not optimistic about what negotiations would achieve, but he was less enthusiastic about ending the gold peg. His recommendations were based on what he thought would happen (Volcker and Gyohten, 1992, 67–69).

On April 4, President Nixon retreated from his campaign promise to remove capital controls and accepted the recommendations of the balance of payments task force. The new guidelines raised the ceiling for foreign direct investment by $400 million to $3.35 billion (Department of State, memo, Treasury Secretary Kennedy to President Nixon, April 1, 1969).

66. Solomon (1982, 169) noted that the Deming group circulated to "senior colleagues of a number of countries" proposals for discussion of wider bands and crawling pegs for exchange rates. The main reason given for failure to get agreement was European concern that the United States would practice "benign neglect" of the effects of its policies abroad (ibid., 170).

The Federal Reserve relaxed lending restrictions as part of the program (Board Minutes, March 27, 1969, 16–17).[67]

Martin was unable to attend an October 22 meeting on the revision of capital restrictions for 1970. He sent a letter outlining his views on the balance of payments. The improvement in the official settlements balance was temporary, he said, the result of a $410 billion euro-dollar inflow that had ended. As the official settlements deficit increased, foreign monetary authorities would acquire dollars leading to a "large draw down of U.S. reserves (gold, our IMF position, SDRs)" (letter, Martin to Kennedy, Board Records, October 21, 1969, 2). Then he added a critical point: "foreigners' response would be influenced by whether they regard the large deficits as temporary or permanent" (ibid., 2–3). Martin added that dismantling capital controls, when faced with a large deficit, would disturb foreign observers and lead them to "conclude that the U.S. deficit is here to stay" (ibid., 3).

In October, probably influenced by the Volcker proposals, the Federal Reserve staff proposed a study of the consequences of increasing exchange rate flexibility. The proposal listed wider bands for exchange rates, adjustable parities (e.g., crawling pegs), and wider gold-price margins, but it excluded floating rates. Later, the staff discussed some of the issues with foreign counterparts. The principal concern was the absence of "discipline." A few participants favored increased flexibility, but several opposed wider bands as unnecessary or harmful to international stability. Members of the European Economic Community expressed particular concern that exchange rate flexibility would disrupt internal agricultural trade because the pricing formulas would change with the exchange rate (Greater Exchange Rate Flexibility: Report on Bilateral Technical Discussions, Board Records, October 1969).[68] This hardly seems a strong reason for rejecting major reform of general benefit.

67. Chairman Martin continued to participate in meetings of the Cabinet Committee on the Balance of Payments. Secretary of State Rogers was a member also, but the National Security Adviser (Kissinger) was not. President Nixon saw foreign economic policy in its political aspect and had many of the discussions moved to the National Security Council, where Kissinger was present (Department of State, memo, C. Fred Bergsten to Henry Kissinger, April 14, 1969).

68. There were other proposals for change. William Dale, the Treasury representative at the IMF, proposed an end to gold convertibility, "sooner, rather than later" ("Limited Gold Convertibility in a Cooperative Framework," Volcker papers, Department of the Treasury, March 10, 1969). He proposed unilateral action to replace what he called "pseudo convertibility" with a rule for limited convertibility. The U.S. would sell gold at $35 an ounce to countries as long as the ratio of gold to imports in the buying country's official holdings were no higher than in the United States after the sale. Countries would converge to a common ratio. Dale did not specify how the rule would change if the world price exceeded $35 an ounce.

These conversations and others suggested that multilateral agreement on systemic changes would prove difficult. Appeals to the "discipline of fixed exchange rates" seem particularly odd, since neither the United States nor Britain was willing to restrict demand enough to maintain the exchange rate. True, neither country completely ignored its balance of payments deficit when it became a problem, but both were reluctant, or unwilling, to exert the necessary discipline. Nor would the surplus countries approve of policies that restricted demand in the deficit countries to a degree that significantly reduced their own exports. And the surplus countries would not adjust. The architects of the Bretton Woods system thought they had designed a fixed exchange rate system freed of the problems of the 1920s gold standard. In principle, exchange rates could adjust to clear permanent imbalances; in practice they did not, at least not for the principal surplus countries or for the principal reserve currency country.

Some small relief came in 1969. Early in April, the Federal Reserve raised the discount rate to 6 percent and increased reserve requirement ratios for demand deposits by 0.5 percentage points. Ten banks had requested an increase in the discount rate. Chairman Martin spoke about "the credibility gap" faced by the Board and the administration; "neither was willing to take the hard action required if inflation was to be stopped" (Maisel diary, April 3, 1969, 53).[69] Later in the year, after an election, West Germany floated its exchange rate to reach a new fixed rate 9.3 percent above the old rate. No major country followed. Some adjustment had been achieved, but it was insufficient.

On June 23, Secretary Kennedy sent the president a long options paper explaining what choices he could make about international economic policy. The paper, prepared by the Volcker group, reiterated the choices presented earlier. There were three options.

First, the United States should obtain multilateral agreement on increased exchange rate flexibility and adjustment. Part of this program included early activation of special drawing rights (SDRs). The U.S. proposal called for $4 to $4.5 billion a year for five years. The Europeans proposed $2 billion a year. The memo favored the multilateral approach but warned that "multilateral agreement may fail to move rapidly enough to achieve

69. All Board members agreed on the discount rate change. Maisel opposed the change in reserve requirements because he believed it would reduce growth of the aggregates, tightening policy. He issued a strong dissenting statement but was persuaded to shorten and soften it (Maisel diary, April 3, 1969, 53–56). Interestingly, differences of opinion still existed about whether increases in reserve requirement ratios would tighten policy. "Maisel described Martin, Robertson, Daane and probably Brimmer [as] believing that Board should push as hard as possible to stop inflation" (ibid., 53).

the objective and relieve the present strain" (Summary of Basic Options, Paul Volcker inter-agency group, Nixon papers, June 23, 1969).

Second was suspension of gold convertibility in part, on a negotiated basis, or wholly. The principal disadvantage came from the unilateral approach. Cooperation might end over trade and investment with the establishment of a dollar bloc and a European gold bloc. But this approach would force surplus countries to revalue.

Third was an increase in the gold price. This would require congressional approval and would be contentious. Also, a large change would be inflationary, and any change would be disadvantageous to countries like Canada and Japan that had held dollars and had not asked for gold. Gowa (1983, 137) found that only Arthur Burns, counselor to the president at the time, favored devaluation against gold. The dollar, he said, was overvalued, and the Bretton Woods system would remain at risk until adjustment occurred. By devaluing early, the president could blame the action on the Johnson administration's policies. Burns's opponents wanted to demonetize gold and substitute SDRs. They feared that devaluation would strengthen the role of gold (ibid., 138).

Two notable features of the memo and discussion are the absence of any discussion of more restrictive policies and the acceptance of the remaining capital controls that the president, as a candidate, promised to eliminate. However, the memo repeatedly recognized the importance of reducing inflation and ending the Vietnam War while avoiding deflation and unemployment.[70] Of course, it did not say how this could be done.

The Volcker group cited three major problems. First, it questioned whether existing arrangements would continue to finance large United States deficits. Second, confidence in the United States had declined. "The uneasy feeling abroad that United States deficits are in danger of becoming uncontrolled erodes our bargaining position" (Paul Volcker inter-agency group, Nixon papers, June 23, 1969, 8). Third, after reviewing the principal sources of the deficit, it concluded that the long-term outlook was unfavorable. Further, devaluation against gold does not necessarily change exchange rates.[71] Others can follow. The conclusion was "Until appropriate

70. The memo noted the diminished role of gold. The cumulative payments deficit of $24 billion from 1958 to 1968 had been financed only 40 percent ($10 billion) by gold sales (summary of basic options, Paul Volcker inter-agency group, Nixon papers, Annex I, June 23, 1969, 6). A few months later, Robert Solomon wrote to Arthur Burns urging no change in the gold price. The principal reason was that it would hamper the movement toward a multilateral system based on SDRs (memo, Solomon to Burns, Volcker papers, Department of the Treasury, March 16, 1970).

71. There was some basis for this concern. When the issue came up, some governments threatened to follow any devaluation of the dollar. Among other possible repercussions, the

changes can be made in commercial policy, world trading rules, and/or monetary arrangements, our balance of payments position will continue to require the protection of capital controls" (ibid., 18).

The memo turned near its end to negotiations over creation of SDRs. It again compared the U.S. position to the European, then added, "Failure to achieve agreement on a large amount would be one of the important factors pointing toward a shift to the second [unilateral] option of suspension" (ibid., 42). The group expressed a willingness to negotiate but not to take the $2 to $2.5 billion that the Europeans proposed. The SDR agreement reached in late July allocated $3.5 billion the first year and $3 billion in each of the second and third years. Also, countries agreed to increase IMF quotas by 30 percent.

In a separate memo, Paul McCracken supported the "evolutionary approach" through multilateral negotiations. He disagreed with the Volcker group on two points. He did not believe that greater flexibility of exchange rates would "unsettle the foreign exchange markets," and he placed less emphasis on getting a larger allocation of SDRs. The "additional liquidity can only make a modest contribution to the adjustment process" (McCracken to the president, Nixon papers, June 25, 1969, 1–2). Excessive exchange rate rigidity, he said, was the main reason for current problems. McCracken suggested also that he was less certain about the contribution of capital controls and preferred a phased reduction.[72]

Discussion of greater exchange rate flexibility began in March. In December 1969, Robert Solomon forwarded to the FOMC a staff report on progress and problems. In all of the discussions, participants assumed that the dollar would remain pegged to gold at $35 an ounce and that other currencies would peg to the dollar. The report recognized that the dollar could remain overvalued for long periods (Greater Exchange Rate Flexibility: Report on Bilateral Technical Discussions, Board Records, December 30, 1969, 1–2). Foreign participants were more concerned about the lack of monetary discipline that would result from wider bands or more frequent adjustment.

memo reported that the Japanese said their government would fall. Also, countries would ask for compensation for their losses to be paid from profits on the devaluation of the dollar. The report never considered Irving Fisher's proposal for a compensated dollar that would tie the gold price to an international commodity basket.

72. Henry Kissinger's memo on the Volcker group proposal supported the main conclusion but added a skeptical note: "It will be extremely difficult to reach a negotiated multilateral agreement on a sufficient scale within a relevant time period unless the alternatives are clearly perceived as worse by the key Europeans" (Department of State, Kissinger to the president, June 25, 1969). Kissinger then asked how long they should pursue the multilateral approach. His answer was that commitment to that approach could last longer if we removed constraints on our behavior (capital controls, tied foreign aid, etc.).

One of the Europeans' main continuing concerns about wider exchange rate bands again came from their agriculture policy. Any change in exchange rates would be reflected in agricultural prices causing political and economic repercussions within the European Community.[73] The community was trying to find ways to narrow exchange rate bands for its group. "Most of the reactions [to wider margins] . . . is that margin widening is unnecessary and a belief that the results would be positively harmful" (ibid., 5). Some countries considered a 5 percent margin tantamount to a system of floating rates. Participants raised fewer objections to 2 percent bands, but "there was no evidence of any enthusiastic support for margin-widening" (ibid., 7).

Criticisms and objections to wider bands carried over to other proposals such as crawling pegs. Participants expressed more interest in a one-sided arrangement, in which surplus countries would appreciate but deficit countries would not depreciate. The intent was to preserve discipline and avoid competitive devaluation.[74]

Although the discussions were preliminary and at the technical level, they gave very little support to those who favored multilateral negotiations. A discussion with the French Minister of Economy, Valéry Giscard d'Estaing, drew a more positive response. At an informal discussion, the minister accepted the idea of limited exchange rate flexibility for the dollar against the European currencies after inflation had been lowered and the gold price increased (telegram, American Embassy in Paris to Secretary of State, Nixon papers, August 4, 1969, 3).

Events changed attitudes. When the Group of Ten deputies discussed increased flexibility, Solomon reported that "there is more support for, and less opposition to, limited flexibility" than in earlier discussions (FOMC Minutes, May 5, 1970, 12). A crawling peg, or more frequent adjustments, attracted most support. Wider bands did not appeal to the Europeans.

### *Euro-dollars*

The inflow of euro-dollars became a principal concern in 1969. The problem was that the System had increased interest rates but had not changed regulation Q ceilings. To offset the loss of time deposits, banks borrowed in the euro-dollar market. Complaints from European countries rose be-

73. Under the Common Agricultural Policy, agricultural prices were the same in member countries and expressed in a common unit. A revaluing country would have to reduce agricultural prices and a devaluing country would have to raise them. The revaluing country would then increase subsidies to producers.

74. Gowa (1983, 144–47) argues that Volcker did not actively pursue exchange rate revaluation by surplus countries during this period.

cause the flow of euro-dollars toward the United States increased pressure for higher interest rates in their countries. The Federal Reserve, for its part, did not raise regulation Q ceiling rates because it feared again that the market would interpret the increase in the volume of CDs as evidence of monetary ease and, therefore, lack of commitment by the Federal Reserve to its announced anti-inflation policy.[75] Some members of FOMC subscribed to this view.

By mid-February, two positions began to develop at the Board and FOMC. Brimmer wanted controls on euro-dollar borrowing by domestic banks. His reasoning was that euro-dollars were not subject to bank reserve requirements. Hence, banks could make "unwarranted reductions in reserve requirements" (Hackley, Board Minutes, February 19, 1969, 11) Most governors agreed, but Governor Robertson objected that the Board did not understand enough about these operations to regulate them. This did not prevent action. The vote directed the staff to prepare and publish amendments to regulations affecting reserve requirements.

At most FOMC meetings the System reported complaints from the Europeans about the effect of higher euro-dollar rates on rates in their markets.[76] The Board staff proposed a marginal reserve requirement on euro-dollar borrowings by placing a reserve requirement ratio on deposits above some initial ceiling, but it wanted to avoid subjecting these deposits to regulation Q ceilings. Governor Mitchell was not convinced. He thought that acting without more knowledge of the effect was a mistake (Board Minutes, May 28, 1969, 13). Only Governor Brimmer urged prompt action. A month later, the staff returned with more information. They proposed a 10 percent reserve requirement ratio on deposits above a base period value, and they now argued that the current capital inflow, followed by an outflow at a later date, would affect the stability of the dollar exchange rate.

By June banks borrowed about $1 billion a week on the euro-dollar market. Interest rates reached as high as 13 percent for overnight loans. Pressed by some European governments, the Board issued new regulations for comment and on August 13, 1969, imposed the restrictions effective October 16. Banks that borrowed from foreign branches, or purchased

75. This reasoning is repeated by the staff and members of FOMC. It suggests that euro-dollar borrowings are a less than perfect substitute for bank CDs. A more plausible explanation is that corporations deposited surplus funds in the euro-dollar market instead of the domestic CD market to earn the higher return, and banks borrowed in the euro-dollar market instead of the CD market.

76. A typical example is Robert Solomon's report (FOMC Minutes, April 29, 1969, 38): "The WP-3 discussion was concerned not with the posture of U.S. monetary policy but with whether the United States should not do something to temper the effects of its tight money policy in the Euro-dollar market."

assets from those branches, and foreign branches that made loans to customers in the United States, became subject to 10 percent requirement for all transactions above a 3 percent base of deposits. To restrict a later return flow to the euro-dollar market, the Board lowered a bank's base by the full amount by which liabilities to foreign branches fell below the 3 percent base. The intent was to restrict growth of the euro-dollar market and moderate flows. Governors Mitchell and Daane dissented, claiming, in Mitchell's words, that "specific evidence that overall monetary restraint has been significantly diluted is lacking" (Board Minutes, June 25, 1969, 18). Both agreed that the regulation was complex and difficult to enforce. With hindsight they might have added that the new regulations encouraged banks to seek alternative sources of funds, such as commercial paper. This probably contributed to the rapid growth of bank related commercial paper and the Penn Central crisis the following year.[77]

The new regulations did not end criticism. As domestic rates in the United States declined in the 1969–70 recession, the flow reversed. Now Europeans complained about the sizeable reflow of dollars. At the January 1970 meeting of OECD's Working Party 3, critics recognized the cause of their problem. "Regulation Q once again came in for considerable criticism. Some delegates went so far as to say that there would not be a Euro-dollar market if it were not for regulation Q" (FOMC Minutes, February 10, 1970, 17). These criticisms continued. The flows were sizeable; between December 1968 and November 1969, "liquid liabilities to commercial banks abroad" rose $10.2 billion, 71 percent of the December value. A year later, these liabilities were back to $18.6 billion, a decline of more than $6 billion.

## *The Franc and the Mark*

Coombs warned the May 27 FOMC meeting that "the present international situation was the most dangerous of any that had yet been encountered" (FOMC Minutes, May 27, 1969, 7). Germany's failure to revalue put pressure to devalue on Britain, France, Belgium, Denmark, and possibly some others. A string of devaluations would "have ominous implications for the U.S. foreign trade position which was already bad enough" (ibid.).

77. Maisel (diary, June 26, 1969, 77–78) claims that the decisive change was Chairman Martin's decision to support the new requirements. He had met with some European central bankers who wanted action. Also, with the federal funds rate above 9 percent, banks had raised their prime rates to 8.5 percent, setting off complaints from members of Congress. "Martin supported it because he was mad at the banks [for] using it to such an extent" (ibid., 78). Mitchell disliked the regulation Q ceiling and "felt that this was a logical way around [it]" (ibid., 78). At the same meeting, Martin opposed an increase in the discount rate to 6.5 or 7 percent, despite the 8.5 percent prime rate.

Coombs also expressed concern about the euro-dollar market. He feared that foreigners would take "drastic restrictive action on the credit side in order to protect their reserve positions" (ibid., 8). Also, there would be some "spectacular bankruptcies."

The only action the FOMC took was to increase the amount of warehousing for the Treasury. The reasoning was that France would have to sell gold to repay the large volume of recent borrowing on its swap lines. The Treasury was reluctant to buy the gold at the time, so it wanted the alternative of warehousing with the Federal Reserve. The FOMC agreed to the increased warehousing (ibid., June 24, 1969, 15–17).

France continued to borrow and lose reserves until it devalued by 4.25 percent on August 10 from 4.94 to 5.15 francs per dollar. France did not give any advance notice to the IMF or its European Community partners, as required by IMF rules, or to the United States, so the devaluation surprised the Federal Reserve and other observers. No countries (other than those that pegged to the franc) followed, but Belgium increased its swap line.[78] At its next meeting the committee unanimously approved increases in the swap lines for Austria, Denmark, and Norway, bringing the total to $10.98 billion.

A special meeting of the FOMC on August 12 showed greatest concern about avoiding effects on employment. Robert Solomon "in effect said that the balance of payments should not be used to influence domestic policy" (Maisel diary, August 13, 1969, 100). Euro-dollar borrowing had started to decline, but the general belief at FOMC was that the interest differences remained large enough to avoid a major decline in the official settlements deficit. By late October, euro-dollar rates had fallen to 9 percent (from 11), partly as a result of the forthcoming recession in the United States and partly as a result of an unwinding of positions in the German mark following revaluation.

Following Germany's revaluation by 9.3 percent to DM 3.66 per dollar, British payments went into surplus. The British chose to repay the European central banks and made only a token payment to the Federal Reserve. This irritated FOMC members. The United States was the largest creditor, with 71 percent of British debt (FOMC Minutes, November 25, 1969, 8). The Treasury did not support the Federal Reserve's position about prompt

78. The Belgian increase aroused some FOMC members. Phillip Coldwell complained that the FOMC responded to each crisis but did not consider the size of the contingent liability or its long-term implication. The FOMC asked the staff for a study of the basic purposes, ultimate size, maturity, and other aspects of the swap network (FOMC Minutes, September 9, 1969, 3). It must have been clear that the swaps had gone far beyond the original "experiment."

British repayment. The Federal Reserve's claims on the swap line now had sixteen months maturity, well above the earlier twelve-month maximum.

Hayes and Coombs expressed their irritation at the lack of Treasury support and at the Bank of England's delay in repaying the United States. Some FOMC members expressed concern about the future of the swap lines, but no one proposed changes. The problem ended when Martin negotiated a better payment schedule by getting the Bank of England to reduce its payment to the Treasury and increase repayment of the swap line (FOMC Minutes, December 16, 1969, 10). Early in 1970, the Bank of England repaid the Federal Reserve and cleared its arrears.

## BEGINNING OF THE END

"All in all, the official decisions, the academic debate, the performance of the markets, and the resentment about the restraints on policy sent a message that the Bretton Woods system was in deep trouble, and to a growing number, not worth saving" (Volcker and Gyohten, 1992, 47). The problems became more pressing as the long expansion of the 1960s ended. By September 1969, the monthly federal funds rate peaked at 9.19 percent and started to fall. In January the ten-year Treasury rate and in February the CPI inflation rate reached temporary peaks.

The System and foreign governments were concerned about the prospect of a capital outflow to the euro-dollar market as domestic interest rates fell. To encourage banks to bid for time deposits, the Board, after discussions with the FDIC, the Home Loan Bank Board, and the Comptroller, raised ceiling rates on all types of savings deposits and negotiable CDs from 0.5 to 1.25 percentage points. The maximum rate for a one-year CD reached 7.5 percent. Opposition to the change came from two sources. Hayes and some others wanted to avoid the impression that FOMC had eased credit (despite the higher rates). He proposed regulation of commercial paper by applying a marginal reserve requirement ratio comparable to the ratio applied to euro-dollars earlier. Home Loan Bank officials' main concern was the competitive position and profitability of thrift associations. They negotiated agreements on higher ceiling rates for their members (FOMC Minutes, January 15, 1970; Maisel diary, January 20, 1970, 9–15).

An additional concern was to avoid a repeat of the 1966 experience, when the interest rate structure permitted commercial banks to drain sufficient deposits from other lenders to cause a major decline in lending for housing and state and local governments. Housing starts in 1970 remained at about the 1969 level. In 1966, housing starts had fallen 21 percent.

The System was less successful in managing the capital outflow of $9.3 billion, much of it reflow to the euro-dollar market. The official settlements account went into surplus at $2.7 billion in 1969. On the liquidity definition that included changes in liquid liabilities to non-official holdings, the deficit was −$7 billion, a record.

On January 1, 1970, countries received the first allocation of SDRs. The U.S. share was $867 million in 1970 followed by $717 and $710 million in 1972 and 1973. The Treasury issued $200 million of the initial allocation to the Federal Reserve, increasing bank reserves and base money. The total allocation was $3.1 billion. In the same year, foreign exchange reserves of all countries increased $14 billion, and total reserves reached $91 billion, a 50 percent increase for the decade and a 22 percent increase for 1970 (IMF, 1971, 19). Countries did not agree to issue SDRs again until 1979. The SDR became an unimportant sidelight of international finance.[79]

Despite the recession, the reserve banks kept the discount rate at 6 percent. The federal funds rate declined over the course of the year from 9 percent in January to 4.9 percent in December; growth of the monetary base rose from the recession low (3.8 percent) in January to 6.4 percent in December. By either measure, monetary policy eased, although the real value of annual monetary base growth was only about 1 percent. Stock prices continued to fall through June until they were 30 percent below the December 1968 peak.

Euro-dollars continued as a major problem for foreign central banks. For West Germany, following revaluation, the more serious problem was a successful effort by the trade unions to increase their income. In 1970, gross hourly wages rose 13.9 percent and unit labor costs 11.6 percent (Holtfrerich, 1999, 310). Faced with rising labor costs and renewed capital inflow, Germany raised its discount rate to 7.15 percent and introduced a reserve requirement against new foreign deposits at German banks. The major inflow problem was still in the future.

On May 31, Canada decided to float its dollar. The Canadian dollar rose modestly, from U.S.$0.932 in May to U.S.$0.984 in September. This was the first large country to (again) abandon the fixed exchange rate system. In September, Canada reduced its discount rate. The decision had no effect on Federal Reserve policy.

Throughout 1970, principal attention was on domestic concerns. An occasional comment at FOMC suggested that policy should be as tight as possible, given domestic concerns. Usually, Hayes or his representa-

79. At the turn of the year, the administration issued new credit restraint guidelines, slightly more relaxed than 1969. The Board was reluctant to relax its lending guidelines. It accepted the administration's proposal when Chairman Burns assured the members that the revisions were "quantitatively insignificant" (Board Minutes, January 5, 1970). The new guidelines removed the exemption for Japan.

tive made this case. It did not have much effect on Burns or decisions.[80] Burns's main concern was the rising unemployment rate and, of course, the Penn Central bankruptcy and its aftermath. In September, Pierre-Paul Schweitzer, managing director of the IMF, caused a stir by urging the United States to finance its deficit using reserve assets, not euro-dollars. This irritated U.S. policymakers but did not affect policy.

Solomon (1982, 177) reported that by spring 1970 domestic interest rates had fallen below euro-dollar rates, causing banks to repay euro-dollar holdings in excess of their reserve free bases. The payments deficit reached $3 billion in the fourth quarter and nearly $10 billion for the year. German reserves rose by about $6 billion as German companies borrowed euro-dollars to circumvent the relatively high interest rates at home. Belgium, the Netherlands, and Switzerland also experienced large inflows. Unlike Germany, these countries had not agreed formally to refrain from demanding gold, so they requested exchange guarantees on their swap lines (ibid., 177).

The FOMC and the Board returned frequently to consider possible actions the System could take to absorb euro-dollars or get U.S. banks to increase their holdings. At a Board meeting in November, Burns asked Robert Solomon for a staff recommendation. Solomon suggested reducing reserve requirements on demand deposits to release reserves equal to the amount of a bank's euro-dollar borrowing (Board Minutes, November 24, 1970, 7). Neither this nor other proposals became policy.

Europeans complained about the easy monetary policy and urged the United States to rely more on restrictive fiscal policy. And Coombs reported that attitudes in Europe had started to turn. "Rather strong resistance was developing to the SDR operation and strong impetus was being given to the European Monetary Union—not simply as a long-range plan but also as a contingency plan in the event of a breakdown in the international payments system" (FOMC Minutes, February 9, 1971, 8). This change probably reflected the growing belief that the United States would not act to stop the outflow. Earlier, "an intensive discussion of limited exchange rate flexibility . . . [showed] more support for, and less opposition to, limited flexibility than was indicated in the earlier discussion in the Fund" (FOMC Minutes, May 5, 1970, 12).

The U.S. gold stock reached a local peak of $11.9 billion in February 1970, $1.2 billion above March 1968, when the two-tier system began. In

80. As the recession ended, Burns told the FOMC: "The Committee members recognized the risk on the international side of moving to lower rates but most thought it was necessary to take that risk" (FOMC Minutes, November 17, 1970, 101).

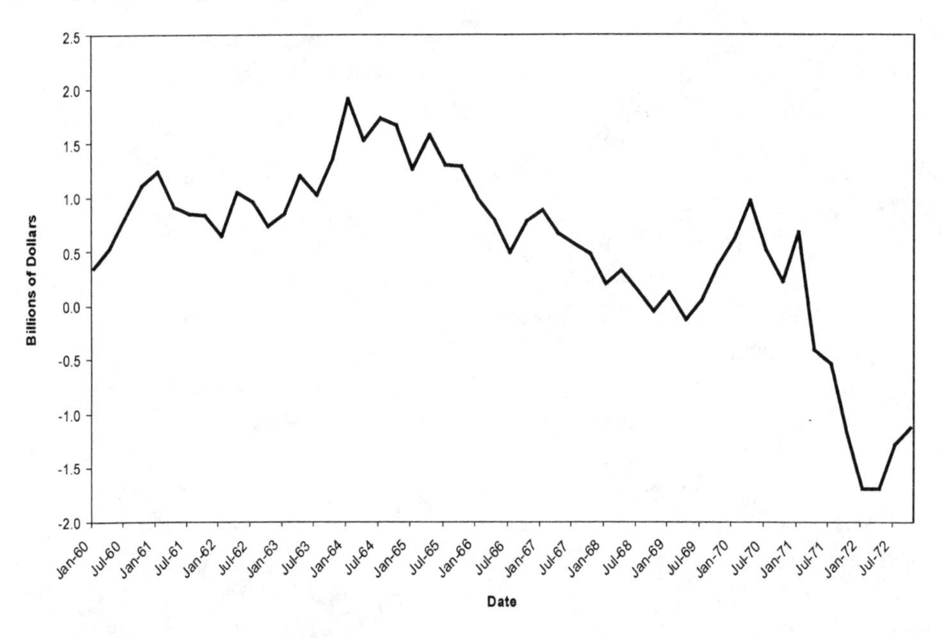


Chart 5.5. U.S. current account balance, 1960–72.

August, it began the final decline leading to the end of the $35 gold price. By May 1971, the stock was below the March 1968 level. Part of the decline reflected requests from countries that had to pay part of their increased IMF quota in gold.

Until 1970 or 1971, changes in the U.S. current account balance mainly reflect changes in relative unit labor costs. After 1970, the situation changed dramatically. The current account deficit and relative unit labor costs are positively related (Meltzer, 1991, 70–71). Chart 5.5 shows the current account balance. The balance fell from 1964 to 1969, rose during the recession, then plunged. The United States now had a current deficit in addition to its net capital, military, and foreign aid spending abroad. To an observer at the time, the prospects for an end to the dollar outflow seemed remote or unlikely.

There was no sense of panic within official institutions. Robert Solomon again told the FOMC in January that "he felt there was no reason for the balance of payments to be a variable influencing the decisions in the domestic sphere" (Maisel diary, January 13, 1971, 1). It was important "to do something about the [euro-dollar] problem . . . to show its [our] good faith" (ibid., 2). The main reason for restricting the euro-dollar outflow was to convince the Europeans that we would cooperate. That was important for two reasons, avoiding a crisis and issuing more SDRs. "If a crisis occurred they would be more willing to cooperate" (ibid.) Despite rapidly growing international reserves, Solomon's concern was to issue more SDRs. The Europeans had agreed to the first allocation because of the official settlement surplus; if euro-dollars outflow increased the official settlement deficit, "everyone could well argue that there shouldn't be any new creation until the official settlement deficit of the United States had been stopped" (ibid.).[81] This had been the French position all along.

At a March 12 meeting of the Board and the Council of Economic Advisers, Maisel asked Herbert Stein about the Council's view of the balance of payments. The response surprised him: "we would be better off suspending payments and letting the dollar or other currencies float in the exchange market. . . . [Secretary] Connally felt even more strongly that this was true" (Maisel diary, March 12, 1971, 28).

This was not the official Council view. A lengthy memo from Chairman Paul McCracken to Peter Peterson, head of a new Council on International Economic Policy, proposed increased flexibility of exchange rates but did not mention floating the dollar. McCracken noted that part of the difference between the U.S. and the Europeans reflected the relative importance of the United States in world trade but the small relative size of trade as a share of U.S. GDP. He concluded that the United States had an obligation to achieve balance in its economy but, if payments problems remained, the surplus countries would have to adjust. And he suggested that this was likely to occur because a decline in the U.S. trade deficit would create or increase deficits elsewhere, leading to exchange rate adjustment by the deficit countries and renewing our problem (memo, McCracken to Peterson, Nixon papers, Box 98 Council on International Economic Policy, April 5, 1971).

Some explicitly opposed both floating rates and neglect of the payments imbalance. Coombs regularly expressed concern about a gathering "speculative crisis. . . . Corporation treasurers and other traders were now beginning to hedge against the risk of parity changes over the weekend—the first time that type of speculation had been seen in nearly two years" (FOMC Minutes, April 6, 1971, 3). European central banks reduced their discount rates, but the market interpreted the reduction as a response to international flows; the flows increased. Then Coombs warned: "In recent

81. The main action was a Treasury decision to have the Export-Import Bank issue debt to the euro-dollar banks. This would absorb euro-dollars. To increase banks' incentives to buy the new securities, they became eligible for inclusion in a bank's reserve base used to calculate reserve requirements on euro-dollars. To supplement the Treasury's action, the Board began offering repurchase agreements to absorb euro-dollars, as much as $1.5 billion in the first month (Maisel diary, January 13, 1971, 8).

years the market has been listening to a great deal of official discussion of the virtues of exchange rate flexibility. . . . [W]idespread uncertainty had developed in financial markets both here and abroad as to whether the dollar and other major currencies would in fact be forcefully defended if they came under pressure" (ibid., 4).[82]

The predicted crisis came the next month. The capital outflow reached $4 billion in the first week of May following an announcement by the German Research Institutes that floating the mark was necessary to stop inflation. The Bundesbank stopped purchasing dollars followed by the central banks of Switzerland, Netherlands, Belgium, and Austria. The Treasury issued a statement saying that there was no reason for changing exchange rates. The mark appreciated against the dollar by about 4 percent, from 3.63 in April to 3.51 in June. Appreciation continued.

Volcker did not share the Treasury position. He saw the crisis as an opportunity and urged that the United States should "permit [the] foreign exchange crisis to develop without action or strong intervention by the U.S." (paper prepared in the Department of the Treasury, Department of State, May 8, 1971, Department of the Treasury). After the crisis developed, the United States would threaten to suspend gold convertibility, impose trade restrictions, and reduce overseas military support in Europe and Japan.[83] Volcker proposed five major changes: (1) a significant revaluation by major European countries and Japan; (2) an agreement to shift more of the military costs of defense to Europe and Japan; (3) a relaxation of trade restrictions by Europe and Japan; (4) sharing of foreign aid; and (5) greater exchange rate flexibility, phasing out of gold, and avoidance of exchange controls.

A memo to Volcker from the U.S. executive director of the IMF reinforced his view that the currency revaluations were a possible opportunity for reform. The memo proposed to get agreement on a $6 to $8 billion change in the United States payment position to be achieved by realignment of exchange rates. The U.S. would agree to give up its reserve currency position in exchange for exchange rate realignment and greater

82. Coombs reported that he had started forward operations in marks to stabilize the dollar. This surprised Burns and the others, since they had not been asked or told. Coombs had cleared the operation only with the Treasury. The outflow of dollars to Europe and Japan reached $2.4 billion in February and over $4 billion in March.

83. On June 3, Congressman Henry Reuss introduced a resolution calling for an end to gold convertibility and a floating dollar unless a new international monetary conference convened to resolve outstanding issues. In the Senate the following day, Senator William Proxmire, chairman of Senate Banking, said that the Treasury would soon accept floating, though the administration denied it (*Congressional Record*, June 4, 1971, 18148–49).

contribution by the Europeans to expenditures for world security (Volcker, 1970).

From Volcker's perspective, the two years he committed to negotiations were up. It was time to move unilaterally and force the changes that other countries were reluctant to make. Secretary Connally and the president had not yet reached that conclusion, but soon thereafter the secretary persuaded the president to take a modified version of Volcker's proposal as part of the New Economic Policy.

Directors of the New York reserve bank voted to increase the discount rate by 0.5 percentage points to 5.25 percent. Their aim was to slow the dollar outflow by reducing the interest spread between New York and Europe. With inflation at 4 percent or more, the 5.25 percent rate seems a modest move. The action received little support at the Board. It decided to do nothing and informed New York that the Board rejected the higher discount rate. This lack of response reinforced the growing belief that the United States followed the policy of "benign neglect" publicly advocated by Gottfried Haberler and others.

Germany found that it faced a standard problem; it had to sacrifice one of three policies—unrestricted capital movements, independent policy to control domestic inflation, and fixed exchange rates. It tried first to get agreement on a joint float of the European currencies but found no support. Instead of additional controls of capital flows, as France and others proposed, it continued to float. The mark appreciated by 3 or 4 percent and the Swiss franc by 7 percent (Maisel diary, May 11, 1971, 39). Japan announced that it planned no parity change.

The United States was prepared for larger exchange rate changes. Volcker had commissioned a study of the overvaluation of the dollar. It suggested that the overvaluation was 10 to 15 percent (Volcker and Gyohten, 1992, 72). While he did not urge a floating rate for the dollar, he advised Secretary Connally and others that he "was pessimistic on prospects for negotiating a large enough change in parities to deal with the situation" unless the system underwent major reform (ibid., 73).[84]

In a meeting with President Nixon, Volcker and Burns disagreed. Volcker warned that the German decision to float the mark would subject the dollar to speculative pressure and would encourage speculators to sell U.S. assets. Protecting the dollar would require large-scale borrowing. The short-run effects of dollar devaluation might be negative, but exports

84. Volcker wanted to float at least temporarily: "Burns was against me. I wanted to get to a more sustainable rate, maybe with a much wider band" (Volcker, 2001).

would increase and the U.S. could remove capital controls. He added that any defense of the dollar had to include reduction in the inflation rate.

Burns wanted the president to speak out against the German decision to float. His argument was political. "If the Germans move, they're going to blame us, and our political opponents at home are going to blame us." He urged the president to call an international conference for the coming weekend (White House tapes, conversation 490-24, May 4, 1971).

The immediate problem ended with West Germany and the Netherlands floating and revaluations by Switzerland and Austria. Burns wrote to the president and Secretary Connally warning that the crisis was not over and that the United States might have to suspend gold sales. He proposed some tactics. The best course, he said, was to "make it appear that other governments had forced the action on us" (letter, Burns to the president, Burns papers, BN1, May 19, 1971). He urged the president to pay out as much as $2 million in gold before closing the gold window and blame the countries demanding gold. That would improve our bargaining position in the negotiations that followed.

Although the German decision to abandon the fixed rate system signaled growing dissatisfaction with U.S. policies, Paul McCracken minimized its importance. He told the president that the "four countries who changed their exchange rates account for roughly 11 percent of the developed world's GNP" (McCracken to the president, Nixon papers, Box 42, May 17, 1971, 1). He proposed an unchanged policy and suggested that the president "communicate to Arthur Burns that you support fully the expansive monetary policies of the Federal Reserve this year" (ibid., 2). This was bad advice. The exchange rate system had lost support. A few weeks later, McCracken rethought his position and urged the president to promptly support implementation of the IMF's flexibility study calling for wider bands and a moving peg (ibid., June 2, 1971, 2).

Secretary Connally reacted strongly to McCracken's changed position. His sharp response suggests that he had not yet shifted to the decision he urged on the president only six weeks later. His response to McCracken was that he favored increased exchange rate flexibility "without—and this is the key—undermining confidence in the dollar and the general stability of the monetary system. Should we fail, forces of economic nationalism and isolation in one country after the other—including the United States—could become unmanageable."

The Quadriad meeting on June 5 shows the lack of importance attached to international policy. The summary of the meeting made no mention of international economic policy and offered no suggestions for a less expansive domestic policy. Burns again urged a price-wage policy and followed it up with a memo proposing a six-month price-wage freeze beginning in January (memo, Burns to president, Nixon papers, June 22, 1971).[85]

At the end of May, Secretary Connally made a speech to an international banking conference in Munich. He forcefully restated the United States' position: others must share more fully the burdens of maintaining the open trading system and paying for common defense. He ended by forswearing devaluation, a change in the gold price or continued inflation.[86] Connally elaborated on his policy views after a Quadriad meeting with the president late in June. There would be no change in policy, at least not yet.

Volcker had a different idea. With John Petty and William Dale, he developed an operational plan for a unilateral suspension of gold payments, devaluation of the dollar, restoration of convertibility, and reform of international arrangements. He proposed to float the dollar until it reached a new equilibrium without gold convertibility. Connally insisted that Volcker add an import surcharge; although Volcker opposed the surcharge, he did include it. This memo became one part of what the administration called a New Economic Policy after August 15. The rest of the program included a domestic anti-inflation policy "to persuade foreign governments that were not to bear alone the full burden of correcting the dollar's overvaluation" (Gowa, 1983, 148). The proposals included wage and price control and a cut in government spending.

The Federal Reserve divided over the benefits of devaluation. Coombs, Daane, and probably Burns wanted the Germans, Dutch, and others to go back to the old parity and fix their rates. Burns preferred exchange controls to devaluation, and he opposed Volcker's proposal to float. Solomon, Maisel, and most of the other Board members accepted the revaluations and wanted Japan to revalue as well. The staff estimated that by 1973, the revaluations that had occurred, and a 10 percent appreciation of the yen,

85. Coombs told the FOMC that "the reaction of the other European governments to the floating of the mark had been uniformly hostile" (FOMC Minutes, June 8, 1971, 5). Later that month the governments agreed not to place any deposits in the euro-dollar market. The French resisted because the "United States was not offering to do anything" though it was responsible for current problems (ibid., June 29, 1971, 8).

86. The following anecdote describes Connally's approach. Volcker asked him whether he wanted to dismiss devaluation so strongly. "We might have to end up devaluing before too long. . . . 'That's my unalterable position today. I don't know what it will be this summer'" (Volcker and Gyohten, 1992, 75). Volcker did not consider changing the gold price. This "would have been considered an enormous psychological defeat for the United States, as well as financially unsettling" (Mehrling, 2007, 174).

would reduce the payments deficit by $750 million (Maisel diary, June 8, 1971, 49–50).[87]

On July 27, Connally presented his recommendation to the president calling for a wage and price freeze, closing the gold window, a tax on imports, and tax reduction. Nixon wrote in his memoirs: "Even I was not prepared for the actions he proposed" (quoted in Matusow, 1998, 113). The president accepted the full program but decided to wait for Congress to return on September 7 before closing the gold window and possibly postpone the price and wage freeze until January 1972, as Burns had proposed.

Events took control. Belgium and the Netherlands asked that their swap lines be paid and closed. This was a major step away from the 1968 agreement to avoid a gold drain. The trade balance worsened. The OECD and BIS members other than France "agreed that a wider band would be better and they had also agreed that occasional floats for brief periods to change rates would be all right" (Maisel diary, July 15, 1971, 69).[88] The discussion suggested that adjustment had more support and opened the possibility of agreement at the September IMF meeting.[89]

McCracken did not know about the president's decision, but he recognized that some change had to be made. On August 9, he described the deteriorating trade position, growing overseas investment by domestic corporations, and increased reliance on foreign plants to service the domestic market. After rejecting proposals to insist either upon fewer restrictions against U.S. exports in Europe and Japan or deflation, McCracken joined those who favored either a "border tax" on imports and a credit for exports, devaluation against other currencies, or a floating dollar (McCracken to the president, Nixon papers, Box 42, August 9, 1971).

The Joint Economic Committee made a major contribution to ending gold convertibility. Before leaving for summer recess, the committee, led by Congressman Henry Reuss, issued a report that: (1) declared that the dollar was overvalued; (2) declared that the IMF should recommend exchange rate changes for countries in fundamental disequilibrium; (3) cited the United States as a country in fundamental disequilibrium; and (4) urged

87. Maisel described the Treasury as opposed to devaluation but that he did not agree with the official position. He explained the Treasury's position by saying that "you might be worse off after the move" (Maisel diary, June 8, 1971, 50). Volcker, as noted, held a different view.

88. Burns wrote a letter to the president at about this time saying that the Japanese ambassador told him that Japan would agree to revalue as part of a multilateral adjustment but not unilaterally (Burns to the president, Burns papers, August 5, 1971).

89. Maisel (diary, July 15, 1971, 69) notes that Burns and Connally did not get along and did not meet regularly. They had little direct communication.

**Table 5.4** U.S. Liabilities to Foreign Official Institutions, 1970–71 (in $ billions)

| Date | 1/70 | 7/70 | 1/71 | 7/71 | 8/71 |
|---|---|---|---|---|---|
| Total | 16.0 | 20.6 | 24.2 | 36.2 | 43.9 |
| Western Europe | 6.9 | 10.1 | 14.3 | 23.0 | 26.0 |
| Asia | 4.6 | 4.2 | 4.6 | 7.6 | 11.8 |

Source: Board of Governors (1980, 349).

the U.S. governor of the IMF (Connally) to ensure that the IMF take on this responsibility (James, 1996, 217–18).

If markets needed to be convinced that the dollar would be devalued, the Joint Economic Committee report provided that evidence. Flows from the dollar to foreign currencies rose during the week of August 9. On August 11, OMB director George Shultz met with the president. The president explained Connally's program. Shultz was against price and wage controls, but the president had decided. The president said that only the three of them would know what he planned to do ( Shultz, 2003). Shultz, a skilled negotiator, advised the president that he would need to impose the temporary 10 percent tax on imports that Connally recommended to supplement closing the gold window. That would force negotiations on exchange rates and other issues.

Table 5.4 suggests the size of the flows into foreign central bank reserves in 1970–71. West Germany held the largest share of West European reserves, and Japan held the largest share of Asian reserves. The market expected devaluation of the dollar to come principally through revaluation of the mark and the yen.

The remaining issue was how to make the announcement. The president again considered doing it in steps, but Connally urged a one-time announcement. If they just closed the gold window, it would look as if they were forced to do it and had to take time to decide what else to do. The president liked the idea of a bold program; it reminded him of his decision to go to China. They would go to Camp David to work out the details. "Connally suggested that at Camp David all should be encouraged to participate in the discussion, without their letting on that the decisions had already been made" (recording of conversation among President Nixon, Secretary Connally, and Budget Director Shultz, Nixon Executive Office Building Tapes, conversation 273-20, August 12, 1971, 5:30–7 p.m.).

The capital outflow forced action in August that would have been delayed until after September 7. "We were on the brink of a market panic that willy-nilly would force us off gold. If we were going to take the initiative of suspending the convertibility of dollars for gold and present it as the first step of a considered and constructive reform package, the decision would not wait" (Volcker and Gyohten, 1992, 76).[90] Volcker notified Connally, who talked to the president. The decision to go to Camp David that afternoon came quickly.

## CONCLUSION: WHY FIXED EXCHANGE RATES ENDED

The Bretton Woods system of fixed but adjustable exchange rates broke down because no major country or group of countries was willing to subvert domestic policy to improve international policy.[91] Exchange rate stability was a public good; no country was willing to pay much to supply it. The United States chose to maintain high employment even if its policy required rising inflation, as it did after 1965. When problems arose, it used capital controls to hide the problem temporarily. The Johnson administration developed many clever stopgaps, but it would not adopt a long-term solution. And it mistakenly kept the target unemployment rate at 4 percent. They would not accept that meeting their domestic concerns was incompatible with their international standard or that the 4 percent unemployment rate was too low for stable inflation.

Policymakers recited a standard mantra that recognized three problems: liquidity, adjustment, and confidence. Despite the rising stock of dollar reserves abroad, they gave greatest effort to creating more liquidity, and almost none to reaching agreement on an adjustment mechanism that could have sustained the fixed exchange rate system. The United States predicated its policy on the belief that other countries would match any devaluation of the dollar. This seems highly plausible for some countries, but

90. Some versions of these events, including Haldeman's diary, cite a British demand for $3 billion in gold as the triggering event. Solomon (1982, 185) corrects the amount, which was actually $750 million; also, the request was for an exchange rate guarantee, not for gold (Volcker and Gyohten, 1992, 77). Volcker explained that the British request came after the decision to go to Camp David had been made. He called Charles Coombs to permit him to make one last plea for retaining the $35 gold price. Coombs took a call from the New York bank saying that the British had asked for $3 billion in gold. This message was garbled. "The momentum toward the decision was by that time, in my judgment, unstoppable" (ibid., 77). When I asked George Shultz about the amount, he said, "The size of the demand was not the point because there would obviously be a run" (Shultz, 2003).

91. The papers in Bordo and Eichengreen (1993) suggest *inter alia* the following reasons: (1) change in relative productivity growth (225–26); (2) higher saving rates abroad (261); (3) the permanence of systemic shocks (266); (4) increasingly efficient capital markets (509); (5) a desire by some Europeans to discipline the United States by preventing it from devaluing to pay off its liabilities; and (6) subordination of international to domestic policy (617) The last of these (Feldstein, 1993) seems to me the most fundamental in that the other problems would have been more easily resolved if countries had been willing to accept temporary changes in the level of employment caused by exchange rate adjustment or devaluation of the dollar. More generally Obstfeld and Rogoff (1995) show that most fixed exchange rate systems lack durability.

implausible for the principal surplus countries, especially Germany. So they solved a problem that was unimportant by agreeing on special drawing rights or SDRs and ignored the more critical adjustment problem.

The United States had the greatest responsibility because the system had become a dollar standard and most of the main problems came from an excess supply of dollars. This was particularly true after 1968 when gold sales effectively ended. But the surplus countries, West Germany, Japan, and for a time France and Italy, were also unwilling to take actions that would preserve the system. These countries would not willingly revalue their currencies enough to reduce their trade surpluses, or reduce restrictions on agricultural and other imports from the United States, or inflate. Although greater exchange rate flexibility became more acceptable by 1971, countries were far from agreement on the particular form it would take.

Time ran out before agreement could be reached and before there was reason to believe that a new agreement was possible. Working against agreement was the loss of confidence in the ability (or willingness) of the United States to redeem its liabilities. An odd result was that after forcing an end to the fixed rate system, countries and their citizens accumulated vastly more dollars after the dollar became legally inconvertible. The reason again was full employment policy.

Loss of confidence reflected more than the growing stock of dollar liabilities and the reduced U.S. gold stock. Under fixed exchange rates, unless countries follow the rules or respect the public benefit, exchange rate stability is lost. A common lesson of Bretton Woods, the interwar gold standard, the Tripartite Agreement, and other efforts at cooperative solutions to fix exchange rates or bands is that enforcement of the rules is weak at best. Countries act in their perceived self-interest; typically they overweight short-term costs and underweight any long-term benefits.

In the early 1960s, when the United States' gold stock was large relative to its external liabilities, it was not difficult to believe that the U.S.'s problems were temporary. The strong expansion increased productivity growth and kept inflation low until 1965. President Kennedy's concern strengthened this belief. By the late 1960s, it became increasingly clear that the trade balance had declined, the flow of dollars had increased, the Johnson administration would not slow the economy to reduce inflation, and the Federal Reserve had abnegated much of its independence by accepting policy coordination. The new administration after 1969 was unlikely to shift policy from domestic to international concerns. And the Federal Reserve would not even raise its discount rates during a period of exchange market turmoil. Many in the administration and some at the Federal Reserve preferred to end the fixed exchange rate system. As markets learned about willingness to end the exchange rate system, confidence that it would survive withered.

One contentious issue about the breakdown is the role of money growth. Bordo (1993) and Darby, Lothian, et al. (1983) concluded that excessive money growth in the United States was the principal source of domestic inflation and its transmission by capital flows to the rest of the world. Bordo (1993, table 1.31) shows that the loss of gold did not deter the Federal Reserve from expanding domestic credit (see also appendix to chapter 4). Cooper (1993, 106) challenged that conclusion, claiming that the difference between growth of money and output in 1970 was no greater than in several previous recessions.

I believe Cooper misses the point for several reasons. First, productivity growth declined in the late 1960s, but money growth did not. The persistent excess increased. And it was the persistent excess, not the temporary change, that the Europeans and Japanese had to absorb persistently. Second, the system was much weaker and the U.S. gold stock much smaller in 1970–71 than in the earlier years that Cooper cited—1954, 1958, and 1967. And the U.S. current account surplus had become a sizeable deficit. It was reasonable to believe through 1964 that the increased trade balance and real exchange rate appreciation would end the problem. By 1970–71, this belief had withered. The steady decline in the current account surplus after 1964 and the rise in U.S. unit labor costs suggested that the current account deficit would continue.[92] Third, and most important, by 1970–71 the rest of the world had ample reason to believe that exchange rate stability ranked far below higher employment as an administration objective, so inflationary policies would continue. Fourth, the U.S. budget deficit increased on average. Federal Reserve policy would not raise interest rates enough to slow monetary expansion. A prudent observer would expect capital outflow to continue.

There were few voices in the Nixon administration that would fight for the fixed exchange rate system. Only Burns openly opposed a suspension of gold payments. At the Federal Reserve Arthur Burns, Alfred Hayes, and Charles Coombs wanted to maintain convertibility and defend the exchange rate, but they offered no effective means of doing so while expanding the economy. The latter was, of course, critical for President Nixon because reelection was his main objective.

The design of the Bretton Woods system had fundamental flaws. It re-

92. Eichengreen (1996, 129) also cites the importance of the persistent or permanent current account deficit in the system's breakdown.

flected the prewar experience, especially the British problem of reconciling employment and exchange rate stability in the 1920s. Countries could borrow from the International Monetary Fund to adjust to a temporary problem; they could devalue if they faced a fundamental disequilibrium. The agreement gave insufficient attention to distinguishing temporary from permanent or fundamental disequilibrium. Also, the designers wanted to make adjustment symmetric for deficit and surplus countries, but they neglected the political pressures against revaluation in surplus countries. Surplus countries viewed revaluation as a penalty for success instead of as a reward for better policies. With the passage of time, the system became more rigid. Britain delayed devaluation several years before 1967. France delayed devaluation in 1968. Japan never revalued; it supported the yen by buying dollars for a few weeks even after August 15, 1971.

By 1970–71, it must have been clear to outside observers that the United States did not intend to follow policies consistent with a fixed exchange rate system. Abroad, the German and Japanese current account surpluses seemed persistent. Sooner or later, these currencies were likely to appreciate. The United States trade account declined steadily after 1965. By 1971, the account was in deficit. The run from the dollar began. Germany added $3.1 billion to its reserves in the first six months of 1970. German money growth rose from 6.4 percent in 1970 to 12 percent in 1971. German consumer prices rose 1.8 percent in 1969 but 5.3 percent in 1971. Despite rigid exchange controls, Japan could not escape U.S. monetary expansion. Japan's reserves nearly tripled in the first nine months of 1971, rising $8.6 billion. The Japanese ($M_1$) money stock rose 25 percent in 1971.

The U.S. capital outflow dwarfed previous (but not later) experience. For the full year 1971, the deficit on capital account was almost $30 billion, after $12 billion in 1970. Of this amount $40 billion became dollar reserves of other countries. Japan and Germany accumulated $11 billion each, and Britain acquired $10 billion.

The 1960s witnessed renewed efforts to solve international monetary or economic problems by coordinating policy actions. At a fundamental level, the problem was to find a way to maintain a public good. In practice, this usually meant that surplus and deficit countries were supposed to agree on different mixes of monetary and fiscal policy actions. Discussions produced few concrete steps. Foreign countries accepted the expansions implied by the flows of U.S. dollars, but they did not systematically reduce government spending or raise taxes to slow their expansions and lower domestic interest rates. And, as discussed earlier, the United States focused mainly on domestic objectives. The dialogue about coordination, once started, was hard to stop. It continued into the 1970s and 1980s. Countries that faced a balance of payments deficit usually favored coordinated action. Countries in surplus usually opposed.

By 1971, Germany accepted that appreciation of the mark was the best way to prevent domestic inflation. The German government tried to get agreement from other European countries for a joint float against the dollar, but France and Italy opposed. They disliked inflation but were unwilling to accept the cost of adjustment. Once again coordination failed. Germany especially had less aversion to exchange rate adjustment than to continued inflation.

One of the lessons of 1965–71, known as the policy trilemma, is that independent monetary policy, fixed exchange rates, and capital mobility are incompatible. As long as low unemployment was the principal policy objective on both sides of the Atlantic, the choices for the Europeans were inflation, greater exchange rate flexibility, or rigid capital controls. The experience of 1965–71 taught many about the choices they had to make; President Nixon's decisions at Camp David forced them to take the first steps to greater exchange rate flexibility.

SIX

# Under Controls: Camp David and Beyond

The frequently heard argument that "needed" fiscal and monetary stimulation will be possible if there is an "adequate incomes policy" is proof enough of the most pernicious aspect of controls. It suggests why controls or any reasonably formal incomes policy are likely to lead to more inflation and not to less.
—Shultz, 1975, 4

On August 15, 1971, President Nixon announced the New Economic Policy to the nation and the world. Consumer price inflation was at a 3.6 percent average rate for the eight months of 1971 before controls began. In the eight months after controls ended in April 1974, the average inflation rate was 12.2 percent. Inflation rose, as Schultze suggested it would. Of course, the reason inflation rose may be unrelated to the control program.[1] Part of the increase resulted from the oil price increase. This raised the price level. Since the increase occurred over time, the rate of price change increased also. But that increase was temporary, unlike the price level change. Once oil prices reached a new level, the rate of price change declined.

This chapter tells a story of failure: failure of ideas that in one form or another had dominated policy analysis and professional economic opinion since the 1940s, failure also in the narrow sense that policy did not reduce inflation or restore price stability, and failure of the Federal Reserve and the government to maintain the internal and external value of money. No single reason explains these failures. The two principal reasons were: (1) the simple Keynesian model, augmented by price and wage controls to

1. Using service prices that are less influenced by oil prices, for the same two periods, the data show 4.5 and 12.5 percent (Kosters, 1975, table 9, 40–41).

reduce inflation with lower social cost, was flawed, based on faulty reasoning; and (2) Federal Reserve independence proved inadequate. Political concerns dominated economic policy both in the decision to impose price and wage controls and in the unwillingness to raise interest rates high enough to stop inflation.[2]

Arthur Burns and the Federal Reserve were central to both failures. Burns had earlier opposed Keynesian reasoning, but in office he accepted large parts. The president's decision to adopt price and wage controls was a victory for Burns's mistaken view that direct intervention in price and wage decisions was necessary to control inflation. And he sacrificed Federal Reserve independence and credibility for political reasons to a degree not seen since Marriner Eccles in the 1930s or perhaps never before.

Dependence on a simple Keynesian framework such as the model of Ackley's (1961) textbook was not the only analytic mistake. Freezing prices and wages did not reduce aggregate demand. The individual's nominal budget remained unchanged. Individual prices could be constrained, but spending was not. Controls could prevent some price level increases, but at best spending and inflation—the rate of price change—would be reduced temporarily. Chart 6.1 shows the brief temporary success in 1972. Measured rates of price change fell slightly after controls, but inflation surged once controls became voluntary or ended in 1973. Although the measured rate of price change rose and fell during the 1970s, it did not return to the range just prior to controls. Of course, the large surges in measured rates of inflation in 1973 and 1979 include the one-time effects of dollar devaluation and oil price increases as well as inflation properly measured.[3]

Also, the Federal Reserve and administration economists repeated an old error—they failed to distinguish real and nominal values. In part for that reason, the Federal Reserve remained reluctant to raise interest rates high enough to end inflation. This behavior reinforced the widespread belief, based mainly on its response to unemployment, that the Federal Reserve would not persist in a policy to end or substantially reduce inflation. The belief grew that any reduction in inflation would be temporary.

There is no evidence showing that inflation was lower after controls than before. Four-quarter forecasts for the GNP deflator rose from 3.1 percent before to 5.6 percent after controls. Twelve-month growth of average

2. Even President Nixon described the decision to control prices and wages as political. "The August 15, 1971 decision to impose them was *politically* necessary and immensely popular in the short run. But in the long run I believe it was wrong" (Nixon, 1978, 521; emphasis added).

3. The administration and Congress raised social security benefits in 1971 and restored the investment tax credit to increase spending.

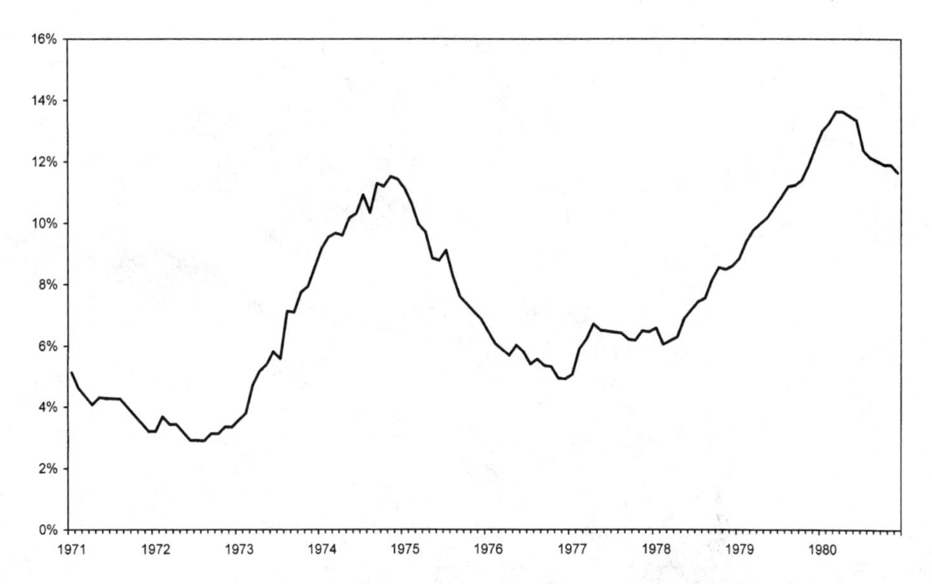


Chart 6.1. CPI inflation, 1971–80, measured year-over-year.

hourly earnings is much less affected by special factors like the 1973–74 oil shock. This measure declined only from 6.8 to 6.4 percent. Chart 6.2 shows the earnings data. Earnings decelerated slightly during the early months of controls but rose in 1972 to the highest rates of increase up to that time.

Those responsible for administering price and wage controls made, at most, modest claims for their success in lowering inflation. The budget director at the time, George Shultz, claimed a small, transient effect (Shultz and Dam, 1998, 71–72, 80–81). But Shultz also recognized that controls encouraged an easier monetary policy. He noted that West Germany had lower inflation and avoided controls (ibid., 80). And Arnold Weber, administrator of the Cost of Living Council and a member of the Pay Board set up to control wages, concluded that "wage controls . . . will not slay the inflationary dragon" (Weber and Mitchell, 1978, 406), although he credited wage controls for stabilizing wage increases. Elsewhere, his study claimed that the "Pay Board's program was aimed largely at the union sector" (ibid., 311). Only 30 percent of private non-farm employment was unionized at the time, so the Pay Board did not expect to control aggregate wage growth.[4] Paul McCracken denied any long-term affect. "Did our wage

4. Econometric studies produced mostly negative results. See McGuire (1976), Oi (1976), and Gordon (1973). For example Gordon (ibid., 778) concluded that "controls will have no long-run effect on inflation" but consumed real resources and caused shortages.

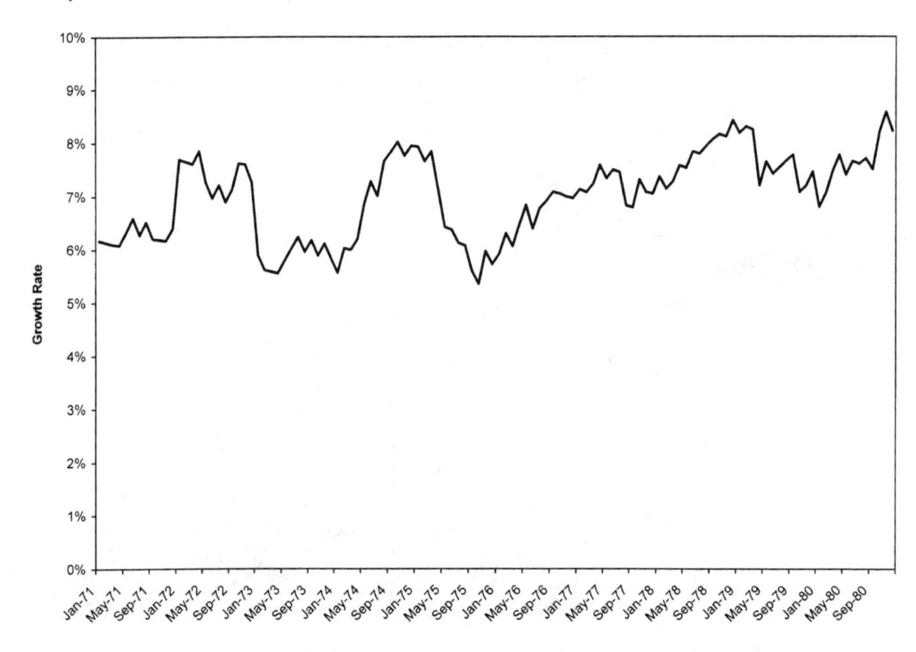


Chart 6.2. Average annualized hourly earnings growth, twelve-month moving average, 1971–80.

and price effort leave us with a better performance in terms of inflation? I would say 'no, it did not'" (Hargrove and Morley, 1984, 348).[5]

Though controls failed as economic policy, they succeeded as political policy, at least until the election.[6] The administration claimed that controls would prevent inflation from rising during a period in which "fiscal and monetary policy [would] exert a more expansive thrust than was prudent

5. The main proponent within government, Arthur Burns, claimed more than political expediency. He cited effects on public psychology. "Properly executed, such a policy could change the psychological climate, help to rein in the wage-price spiral, squeeze some of the inflation premium out of interest rates, and improve the state of confidence sufficiently to lead consumers and business firms to spend more freely out of the income, savings, and credit available to them" (Burns, 1978, 131). Burns did not reconcile spending "more freely" with lower inflation.

6. The program was mainly a political act. "In political terms, . . . he knew it would stun his critics and befog the issue that could best be used against him. Nixon hated to do it, but he loved doing it" (Safire, 1975, 527). McCracken described the program as mainly a political decision pressed by John Connally. "It was very clear that the President's popularity rating was low, in part because there was this almost tidal wave of demand for wage and price control. . . . I could see how a good political leader, not being excessively concerned with economic matters, would think that was the right way to go" (Hargrove and Morley, 1984, 350). Matusow (1998, 112) cites Haldeman's notes for July 23 to show that President Nixon told Connally the time had come to act on a wage-price freeze.

earlier where the inflation objective was more vulnerable" (Council of Economic Advisers, 1972, 101–2). The other parts of the program included: (1) an embargo on gold sales, (2) a 10 percent surtax on imports, (3) reinstatement of the investment tax credit, (4) reductions in government spending, (5) elimination of excise taxes on purchases of domestically produced cars, and (6) acceleration of planned income tax reductions. The investment tax credit and the temporary elimination of excise taxes on cars stimulated investment and consumption. The 10 percent surcharge on imports shifted purchases from imports to domestic production and gave an advantage when bargaining for exchange rate changes. Price and wage controls were intended to prevent a surge in prices from the devaluation of the dollar and increased spending.

The stimulus program worked. Industrial production had started to increase before the new program, but the rate of increase rose to a 10 percent annual rate by the election. Housing starts increased, and real GNP growth surged to 7 percent in the first three quarters of 1972. President Nixon's favorite benchmark, the unemployment rate, fell to 5.5 percent just before the election. And, most important for the president, he won the 1972 election.

## AT CAMP DAVID

On August 13, 1971, the president took fifteen principal advisers to the presidential retreat at Camp David. He had made all the main decisions in meetings with Treasury Secretary John Connally, Peter Peterson, and George Shultz on August 2 and 12.[7] The plan called for no action until September, when Congress returned, but the start of a run on the dollar forced earlier action.

> There were signs of improvement ahead, but patience had worn thin, and we ran out of time. Demands for action poured down on the White House from all sides. Media criticism of our policies became intense. . . . Most of

7. Connally, Peterson, and Shultz were at Camp David along with Arthur Burns, Paul McCracken, and Herbert Stein from the CEA, Paul Volcker from Treasury, and H. R. Haldeman, John Ehrlichman, and William Safire from the president's staff. Safire was there to write the president's speech. Arnold Weber, Caspar Weinberger, Kenneth Dam, Michael Bradfield, and Larry Higby from the Office of Management and Budget, Treasury, and the White House staff participated also. Although the meeting made a major change in foreign economic policy, the president did not invite Secretary of State William Rogers or National Security Adviser Henry Kissinger. Neither knew about the program in advance, although the president made an effort to inform Rogers on August 14. Burns's involvement shows his involvement as a presidential adviser, despite Federal Reserve independence. It is similar to Eccles's role in the Roosevelt administration.

> the critics and many of the economists hammered away on one theme: the need to have some program of mandatory government control of prices and wages. (Nixon, 1978, 517)

The group met from 3:15 to 7. The president cautioned them against leaks and told them not to make telephone calls. They were told not to tell anyone, even family, where they were. Paul Volcker briefed the group on gold losses that day. Then he told the group that action was needed on both international and domestic policy (Haldeman, 1994, 341). The president let Connally outline the proposed actions.[8]

Some of the economists opposed the import surcharge without much effect. The main dispute was over the decision to close the gold window. Arthur Burns urged the president to adopt the rest of the program but leave the gold price unchanged. He proposed that the president negotiate a cooperative agreement to depreciate the dollar but received no support. "He warned that I would take the blame if the dollar were devalued. '*Pravda* would write that this was a sign of the collapse of capitalism' . . . [H]e worried that the negative results would be unpredictable; the stock market would go down; the risk to world trade would be greater. . . . As events unfolded, this decision turned out to be the best thing that came out of the whole economic program I announced on August 15, 1971" (Nixon, 1978, 510–20).[9]

The meeting was to decide how to implement the new policy, not whether to do it. Burns's argument did not change the proposal. For the rest of the meeting, small groups worked out some details of how the program would be implemented and how it would be announced; William Safire and President Nixon prepared the president's speech to the public with some assistance from Herbert Stein.

President Nixon's main concern was to lower the unemployment rate

8. Nixon (1978, 519) described "strong, skeptical, support among those present for the freeze and other domestic actions." Shultz (2003) opposed wage and price controls when he learned about the program in early August. "President Nixon said, 'I want to do it.' He had decided, so the argument was over." McCracken had also opposed controls publicly just before the Camp David meeting.

9. James (1996, 212–15) notes that the participants did not discuss floating rates as a practical solution to the payments problem. As late as May 1971, James reports that Pierre-Paul Schweitzer, the IMF managing director, told Secretary Connally to devalue the dollar to a new parity. Connally opposed and urged Schweitzer to get Japan to revalue. Connally's attitude at this time is suggested by his widely quoted statement to foreign governments: "The dollar is our currency, but it's your problem." James (1996, 218) attributes the change in Connally's position to the issuance on August 6 of a statement by the Joint Economic Committee calling for devaluation of the dollar. Earlier President Nixon had agreed to suspend convertibility on Connally's recommendation based on Volcker's proposal.

before the election.[10] As Stein noted, the public and the president identified full employment with a 4 percent unemployment rate (Stein, 1988, 158). Before controls and devaluation, the administration had to fight off criticism that only obstinacy and slavish devotion to free markets prevented use of some type of wage-price policy. Before August 1971, the administration took some actions to respond to the critics, especially in the construction industry, where large local wage increases became troublesome.

Administration economists answered the critics but did not satisfy them. One reason is that they did not make their best case. Inflation, the sustained rate of increase in a broad-based price level, cannot be controlled by changing price levels of individual goods. Aggregate demand or spending is not affected. If prices are controlled, the reported price index may not rise that month, but with unchanged monetary policy, the public has as much spending power as before. They can continue to spend; they have no reason to save all or any gain from buying at controlled prices.

A common argument used by administration economists and others was that controls could lower inflation by reducing expected inflation. This argument would be strengthened if reduced government spending and money growth accompanied controls. Reduced stimulus to spending would support smaller growth of spending and eventually lower inflation; controls might possibly speed the adjustment. Not much is known about possible effects of controls on anticipations. But controls cannot lower inflation without a reduction in aggregate demand.

International issues received most attention in the first day's discussion. The president rejected use of the 1917 Trading with the Enemy Act to impose an import surcharge.[11] Congress was about to consider a surcharge, and the president wanted to move first. Connally argued that a temporary surcharge would help to get the exchange rate adjustment the United States wanted.

Arthur Burns disagreed about the decision to close the gold window and

10. President Nixon began the discussion saying, "[N]o one is bound by past positions." William Safire, his speechwriter commented: "Least of all . . . himself. . . . [E]very economic speech . . . there was a boilerplate paragraph on the horrors of wage and price controls" (Safire, 1975, 519–20).

11. "I don't want to corrupt my national security power" (Safire, 1975, 512). The current account deficit for 1971 was $1.4 billion, 0.1 percent of GDP. The merchandise trade deficit reached $2.3 billion, 0.2 percent of GDP. Compared to what came later, the size of the problem was tiny. Many in Congress favored devaluation of the dollar. Before major international meetings, Senator Jacob Javits and Congressman Henry Reuss would introduce legislation calling for devaluation. Guenther (2001) reports that Volcker would go to Javits's office to plead for support for administration policy, to no avail.

float the currency.[12] He urged delay. The action was unilateral and sacrificed the goodwill of other central banks and governments. In addition, he argued that the rest of the new program would strengthen the dollar.

Connally and others rejected these arguments. They did not want to appear to be forced to close the gold window. A run on gold had started. It was best, they said, to announce the whole program and present it as actions taken at their own initiative. Paul Volcker, who had previously favored fixed exchange rates, pointed out that they had little choice. The stock of gold was less than one-third of dollar liabilities to foreigners, and foreigners were demanding gold. Although Burns was not convinced, the president was.[13]

Burns did not give up.[14] When the group met the following day, only a memo prepared by Charles Coombs supported the fixed rate. President Nixon announced that he decided to stop selling gold. The main discussion was about how to present it to the public without appearing to be defensive. The president proposed to claim that the dollar was "under assault by international speculators." Closing the gold window protected the dollar (Ehrlichman notes, August 14, 1971).

The president then told George Shultz to assign people to work out the details of the programs. Connally and Volcker did tax policy and, with Burns, monetary affairs; McCracken and Stein worked on the details of the wage-price freeze; Shultz and his OMB staff worked on budget cuts (Safire, 1975, 517). Each group had prepared earlier, so they completed their assignments promptly.

Participants spent much of their time on Saturday going over the details of various programs or discussing what the president would say on Sunday night. One issue was control of interest and dividends. Both Connally and Burns urged the president not to include interest and dividends under the proposed ninety-day freeze of prices and wages. The law did not authorize control of interest rates and dividends, but a separate law authorized credit controls.

12. Connally warned the president never to use the word "devalue." Devaluation required an act of Congress, but suspending gold convertibility did not (White House tapes, conversation 547-9, July 27, 1971).

13. The Quadriad met with the president to discuss Burns's objections. "After that meeting I was told by Volcker to do my draft of the speech assuming we would close the gold window" (Safire, 1975, 518). The discussion about timing the announcement of the gold decision until after the other announcements was a reprise of a discussion between Connally, Shultz, and the president the day before. President Nixon decided to make the announcements all at one time (White House tapes, conversation 273-20, August 12, 1971).

14. His insistence is surprising. According to John Ehrlichman, Burns told the president in December 1970 that at some point he "might have to sever the link between the dollar and gold" (quoted in Wells, 1994, 66–67).

After the president announced the new program, labor union leaders and leading congressional Democrats protested exclusion of interest and dividends from the program.[15] Burns did not want to put interest rates under the freeze because that would transfer authority for monetary policy to the new Cost of Living Council, in effect to John Connally, the council's head. The Federal Reserve would be back in the position it had been in from 1942 to 1951, before the Accord.

To satisfy the critics, the administration decided on an informal program. In October, President Nixon asked Burns to chair the Committee on Interest and Dividends. Burns discussed the appointment with the Board of Governors on October 5. They agreed that Burns should serve. "The only questions raised were those of the powers of the committee related to those of the Board" (Maisel diary, October 20, 1971, 1). A main concern was that the committee would be heavily influenced by politics, since three members were cabinet officers. They expressed particular concern in this regard about Preston Martin of the Home Loan Bank Board, later vice-chairman of the Board of Governors. The Board concluded that the committee not have mandatory power to fix interest rates, and that it should avoid giving directions about open market operations and confine its attention to consumer credit and mortgage rates.

Thus, Burns became chairman of the Committee on Interest and Dividends.[16] Market-determined rates remained unregulated; the committee's responsibility applied only to dividends and so-called administered rates such as the prime rate or bank rates on consumer loans. Chairing the committee created a potential conflict of interest. If monetary policy actions raised market rates, banks expected prime rates (and others) to rise. The unions and Congressman Patman would oppose any increase in administered rates as a cost to consumers and business, so Burns might be reluctant to raise open market rates. This conflict is one explanation of expansive policy in 1972.[17]

15. At Secretary Connally's briefing for reporters on Sunday evening, he answered a question about interest rates by saying, "[W]e did not do it because we didn't know how effectively to do it" (Connally press conference, Nixon papers, Shultz Box 8, August 15, 1971, 8). In fact, the law that Congress had passed did not authorize control of interest and dividends, as he knew.

16. The other members were the Secretaries of Treasury, Commerce, and Housing and Urban Development, and the chairs of the Federal Home Loan Bank Board and the Federal Deposit Insurance Corporation. The Federal Reserve staff served as committee staff. As usual, Burns dominated the meetings so much that the others rarely attended.

17. Dewey Daane, a member of the Board of Governors at the time, objected to Burns taking the chairmanship of the Committee on Interest and Dividends. "I always thought it

The group did not decide what came after the ninety-day wage and price freeze. It left that decision to a committee headed by Herbert Stein. Stein had experience with decontrol after World War II and Korea, and he wanted to end controls "promptly and in an orderly way" (Stein, 1988, 181). He shared the view that the president repeated several times at Camp David and emphasized in his speech: controls should not become permanent. When the press asked Secretary Connally about the inconsistency between earlier statements opposing price and wage controls as unworkable, he denied that the administration had adopted controls. Nixon "put on a wage price freeze for a limited period of time, 90 days, with the idea that this would be voluntarily adhered to by the American people" (Connally press conference, Nixon papers, Shultz Box 8, August 15, 1971, 9).[18]

The proposed fiscal program provided a small reduction in the deficit. The proposal reduced tax rates by $6.2 billion, about half from the new investment tax credit. The planned 10 percent surtax returned $2 billion, and proposed budget cuts reduced spending by $6.6 billion. The largest proposed reductions were made in general revenue sharing and by deferring a federal pay increase. These actions required congressional approval. Most spending reductions were not realized. This did not surprise President Nixon. Burns warned him in conversation that congressional Democrats would want to increase, not decrease, spending. The president responded: "That's always their way—to increase government spending. Our way is to increase the private sector" (White House tapes, conversation 7-152, August 15, 1971).

In the next Economic Report of the President, the Council of Economic Advisers warned about the danger of relying on controls to stop inflation. The CEA and others in the administration and the Federal Reserve ignored the warning.

> If monetary and fiscal policy keep the growth of demand moderate, the price and wage controls can bring about more quickly and surely the lower rate of inflation that competitive forces would cause in such circumstances. But if demand is allowed to grow excessively, the price and wage control system

very, very inappropriate for him to wear that hat and be trying to hold down interest and interest payments, when to do the Fed's job properly, you had to be pushing interest rates up" (Hargrove and Morley, 1984, 377). Burns accepted the chairmanship so that Connally wouldn't get it (Brimmer, 2002, 20).

18. Stein later wrote, "As I look back to that weekend twenty years ago . . . I am amazed to recall how unconcerned and ignorant we were about what would happen next. . . . We did not foresee that the public would love the ninety-day freeze so much that we could not retreat from it very quickly" (Stein, 1994, 5).

will lose its value. Correspondingly, if the presence of the price and wage control system becomes an excuse for laxity in monetary and fiscal policy, the system's effect on controlling inflation will be negative. (Council of Economic Advisers, 1972, 96)

There was little basis for the more optimistic possibility.

## AFTER CAMP DAVID

The president drafted his own speech with revisions by his speechwriter, William Safire. On Sunday evening, he delivered the speech on television. The public accepted the new program enthusiastically. On Monday, the Dow Jones average rose 32.9 points, representing the largest one-day increase in dollar value to that time. The principal criticism came from economists,[19] but labor union leaders grumbled also. George Meany, president of the AFL-CIO, wanted free collective bargaining, but he could do nothing, so he went along with the freeze at least initially (Shultz, 2003).[20]

The president's address emphasized the role of speculators as the cause of dollar instability. He did not avoid the word "devaluation" but, reverting to populism, he reassured the public that the change in international policy affected only those who "want to buy a foreign car or take a trip abroad. . . . [For t]he overwhelming majority of Americans who buy American products in America, your dollar will be worth just as much tomorrow as it is today" ("The Challenge of Peace," Nixon papers, August 15, 1971).

Connally went further. He denied devaluation. "I don't know that it's going to devalue at all. I think it is going to stabilize it. . . . With respect to some currencies it may go down, and with respect to others it may go up. I think it is going to change, but to say it is going to be devalued, I am not prepared to say that" (Connally press conference, Nixon papers, Shultz Box 8, August 15, 1971, 5). This was misleading. Connally also doubted that the gold price would change. He maintained this position in subsequent negotiations until he was forced to accept an increase. Since the United States did not buy or sell gold, the posted price had no economic significance.

19. Karl Brunner and I organized one group of about a dozen economists. We predicted that controls would not reduce inflation and published an op-ed in the Wall Street Journal. The public's response differed. A public opinion poll asked, "'Is the president doing a good job?' Taken right after wage and price controls started, the poll showed that the percentage who thought the president was doing a good job had virtually doubled and held there" (Paul McCracken in Hargrove and Morley, 1984, 334).

20. Shultz (2003) explained that the Business Council (representing major U.S. corporations) had a rare vote on price and wage controls. The vote for controls was overwhelming. Only two voted against.

### *International Negotiations*

The government made a major change in policy without thought about its long-term consequences.[21] No one at Camp David had a clear idea about what would happen when they closed the gold window and imposed a surtax on imports. At his August 2 meeting with the president, Connally said: "We may never go back to it [convertibility]. I suspect we never will" (White House tapes, conversations 268-6 to 269-1, August 2, 1971). But beyond this conjecture, he had no more than a loose plan to use the surtax as a bargaining chip to obtain trade concessions for exports, especially agricultural exports. And he expected to negotiate a new set of exchange rates without announcing a change in the gold price. The latter required congressional approval, which he and President Nixon wanted to avoid.

The Federal Reserve's Board of Governors met on Sunday evening, August 15, to hear Chairman Burns's report of the Camp David meeting, to watch the president's speech, and to discuss the international policy change. Burns explained that Undersecretary Volcker and Governor Daane would leave that evening for London, where they would explain the president's program to officials of principal European countries and get some preliminary views of the scope for currency realignment. Governor Daane added that he and Volcker would then travel to other European capitals to hold bilateral meetings.

Burns "said he agreed with Treasury officials who felt the dollar was overvalued, but he was not persuaded that the overvaluation was great" (Board Minutes, August 15, 1971, 4). Maisel mentioned devaluation of 10 percent. Unless that devaluation could be achieved and agreement reached on greater flexibility of exchange rates, the United States should not enter a new agreement. But Burns, Brimmer, and Robertson urged Daane to push for prompt agreement. And Robertson proposed to end the Voluntary Foreign Credit Restraint Program (ibid., 5).

Monday, August 16, was a holiday in Europe. Foreign exchange markets were closed, and they remained closed for the rest of the week. In Japan, markets remained open. The Bank of Japan purchased dollars to keep the existing exchange rate and to prevent large losses to Japanese banks that the government had urged to hold dollars (Toyoo Gyohten, in Volcker and Gyohten, 1992, 93). Also, "the Japanese were too naïve in believing President Johnson and President Nixon when they repeatedly pledged that

21. Looking back long after the events, Paul Volcker was critical of the program. "The inflationary pressures that helped bring down the system did not abate for long; they got much worse as the controls came off and plagued the country for a decade or more" (Volcker and Gyohten, 1992, 80).

the United States would not devalue the dollar. . . . So we thought that the real U.S. objective was not to devalue the dollar but to free it from gold and try to stabilize its value as quickly as possible. Supporting the dollar at the parity of 360 yen, we believed, would meet the interests of the United States and be taken as an act of cooperation" (ibid.). In two weeks Japan increased its reserves by 50 percent, from $8 to $12 billion. $M_1$ balances rose 25 percent (ibid., 94). Critics blamed the subsequent inflation in 1973–74 on this decision.

Representatives of France, Germany, Japan, and Italy joined the British at the London meeting. Volcker opened the meeting by explaining the president's program and asking for initial reactions of the foreign participants.[22] He insisted that he had not come to open negotiations and explained that one of the reasons for the international measures was to head off rising protectionist pressures. A main reason for using executive authority to impose the surtax was that legislation would be easy to adopt but hard to repeal. The United States wanted a long-term solution, he said, and it would not be satisfied with short-term measures. "The U.S., at this stage, had no program that it was going to spring on anyone. . . . [W]e would not be satisfied without a reform that would repair the erosion that had taken place in the U.S. position over the years" (memorandum of conversation 170, United States Department of State, August 16, 1971). However, the president had decided that the price of gold would not change.

The European reaction focused on the surcharge. Several complained that they could not negotiate new exchange rates until the U.S. removed the surcharge. They also expressed concern about problems of keeping exchange markets closed versus reopening them. They asked Volcker what objective the United States had in mind. "Mr. Volcker said the U.S. should have a period of surplus" (ibid.). He also mentioned removal or reduction of barriers to U.S. exports, especially agricultural exports, and greater contribution to the common defense and security. Later, he quantified the objective as a $13 billion change in the U.S. trade position—from a $4 billion deficit to a $9 billion sustained surplus. This shocked the Europeans. "Few of our trading partners really wanted to see any significant deteriora-

22. One of the Japanese participants, Masaru Hayami, later became governor of the Bank of Japan. He described the European reaction as claiming that they could not reopen their exchange markets until the United States announced a new parity (Hayami, 2002, 2). They soon gave up that position. By the end of August all major countries had floated except France. France imposed exchange controls and adopted two-tier exchange rates. Volcker described the European response. "They were stunned and didn't know how to react. . . . [T]heir idea of an appropriate exchange rate change was very small—certainly well under 10 percent—and then simply put the old system back together again. That didn't make any sense, from our perspective" (Mehrling, 2007, 175).

tion in their own trade positions" (ibid., 81). Although most recognized the benefits of a stable system, they were not disposed to provide or maintain a public good if it required them to bear a major cost.

Volcker and Daane went on to Paris, where they met the next day with the French finance minister, Valéry Giscard d'Estaing. The minister was most interested in the extent of U.S. intervention in the foreign exchange market. Volcker said that except in unusual circumstances, the United States would not intervene. "Basically, the U.S. had not changed the parity of the dollar. Others would make that decision; we could not. We did not assume that there would be no changes in parities. We simply didn't know in which direction the dollar would move" (ibid.). Giscard questioned whether the United States expected to return to a fixed exchange rate system. Volcker gave a qualified yes; the system had to change in the direction of wider bands and fewer crises.

A few days later, Germany proposed a joint float of European currencies, but France opposed and, like Belgium, adopted a two-tier system bolstered by exchange controls. The Europeans made a formal complaint against the surcharge on exports. European irritation was out of proportion to its effect on them. The main effect was on Japan and Latin America (Solomon, 1982, 189; Nixon papers, Shultz Box 7, August 25, 1971).[23]

At a series of meetings, the developed countries gradually recognized the issues to be resolved and the positions that had to be negotiated. Early in these discussions, the Europeans rejected as too large both the proposed $13 billion swing in the United States' trade balance and the argument that the United States should have a trade surplus to cover some of its development assistance and defense spending.[24] But they accepted that a realignment of exchange rates was necessary. All but the United States agreed that realignment would require adjustment by the United States. Also, "there was nearly unanimous agreement among them that the surcharge was an obstacle to the achievement of an adequate realignment of exchange rates and should be removed as soon as possible" (FOMC Minutes, September 25, 1971, 3).

At most of the meetings, the foreigners expressed concern about in-

23. The Academic Consultants to the Treasury endorsed the basic program but preferred to eliminate the surcharge at an early date. Some favored floating; others preferred a large devaluation against principal foreign currencies and increased flexibility. None supported a return to the Bretton Woods arrangements or gold convertibility.

24. Volcker reported on a meeting at the OECD. He explained that the U.S. balance-of-payments surplus had to increase to $9 billion from −$4 billion, a $13 billion swing. The representatives offered to provide $3 billion, $2 billion of it from Germany. The French, Dutch, and Belgians explained why they would not help. The Japanese remained silent (Volcker and Gyohten, 1992, 83).

creased protection, dual exchange rates, capital controls, and a return to the "miseries of the 1930s" (ibid., 5). Secretary Connally continued to insist on the $13 billion swing, a U.S. trade surplus, no dollar devaluation, maintenance of the surtax, and agreements on trade barriers and sharing of defense costs.[25]

Currency markets were thin for most currencies, and trading was limited to commercial transactions. Trading costs had increased, and there were "virtually no capital flows" (ibid., 15). Forward markets existed only in British pounds and German marks. Governor Brimmer pointed out that capital controls were a main reason for the absence of capital transfers.[26]

Connally was in charge of negotiations for the United States. He started with three objectives: exchange rate adjustment, reduced barriers to trade (especially to U.S. exports), and increased foreign contributions to the common defense and the cold war. "Somewhere along the way between August 15 and the Smithsonian meeting of December 17–18, the defense sharing objective was dropped and the request for reduced trade barriers abroad was watered down to a few trivial demands" (Solomon, 1982, 191).[27] He was in no hurry to reach agreement. The surtax and appreciation of foreign currencies against the dollar helped U.S. exports and reduced imports. By early October, the yen had appreciated about 8 percent, the mark 9.5 percent, the Dutch guilder 7 percent, the British pound 3 percent, and the French financial franc about 2 percent.

Connally tried to get agreement without devaluing the dollar against gold. On this too, he had to retreat. Foreigners, particularly France, insisted on some dollar devaluation as part of any agreement. Solomon (ibid., 191) described Connally as "every inch the politician. . . . [H]is keen intelligence enabled him to grasp the substance of the economic problems he was

25. In late September, Congressman Henry Reuss introduced legislation to float the dollar. The administration rejected it.

26. The Board's staff estimated that to achieve balance the United States would have to increase net exports by $8 to $10 billion above 1970 (Maisel diary, August 25, 1971, 85). Chairman Burns said that "the experiment with floating exchange rates . . . was unlikely to prove successful. . . . Such [academic] arguments seemed highly reasonable until one realized that they involved the tacit assumption that there were no governments and no political pressures in the world. . . . [R]estraints were apt to multiply" (FOMC Minutes, September 21, 1971, 16–17). Burns favored negotiations leading to the prompt reestablishment of fixed exchange rates, and he favored retaining the surcharge to speed agreement (ibid., 18). Volcker had commissioned a study that found that the dollar had to be devalued by 10 to 15 percent to restore equilibrium (Volcker and Gyohten, 1982, 72).

27. Connally initially asked for a 24 percent revaluation of the yen and 18 percent for the mark. He settled for much less, 16.88 for the yen and 13.6 percent for the mark. Gyohten suggests that Japanese negotiators had authorization to go to 20 percent. He describes Connally as a "superb negotiator, a magnificent deal maker" who never humiliated the Japanese (Volcker and Gyohten, 1992, 97).

forced to deal with, [but] he brought to the job no broad vision of how to improve the economic welfare of his own country or the world."

Connally was not eager to reach agreement quickly. He may have recognized that the long period of an overvalued dollar and the presence of capital controls had distorted both trade and capital flows. No one could estimate accurately how much the dollar had to depreciate to achieve equilibrium. Bilateral rates were also a problem. Delay let markets make some of the adjustment and encouraged Europeans to reach an agreement that would eliminate the surcharge. By insisting on his demands, he delayed agreement.

Connally's aggressive demands irritated not only foreigners but members of the administration. Burns wanted a more conciliatory approach and a prompt return to fixed exchange rates. Henry Kissinger, the assistant for national security, opposed Connally's confrontational approach, and his emphasis on burden sharing invaded the political domain that Kissinger considered his own.

The result was that Connally's approach created opposition both at home and abroad. The change in market exchange rates for the dollar also changed bilateral rates between trading partners, particularly France and Germany. German officials expressed concern about the appreciation of the mark relative to the French franc. Perhaps for that reason French officials supported Connally's position that favored delay in reaching agreement (ibid., 195). But they insisted on an increase in the gold price. French officials said that the franc price of gold was "an important political issue in France, given the widespread and long-standing custom of the French population to hold gold as a hedge against inflation and political uncertainty" (U.S. Department of State, letter from Arthur Burns to the president, 183, October 14, 1971). A revaluation of the franc against the dollar with an unchanged dollar price of gold would lower the franc price of gold and penalize gold holders. This was unacceptable to French politicians.

In a meeting with George Shultz on October 25, the president expressed concern about the slow pace of negotiations and urged Shultz to "take a more aggressive role in bringing the international monetary crisis to resolution" (ibid., Editorial Note 187, October 25, 1971). The president continued to oppose any change in the gold price. At a meeting of the Quadriad on October 28 to discuss Connally's trip to Asia, the president authorized Shultz to work with Kissinger on negotiations during Connally's absence. Connally had set out a negotiating position that included a significant realignment of parities, no return to convertibility for at least two years, and a substantial reduction in the role of gold. He thought currency realignment less important politically than trade concessions.

**Table 6.1** Exchange Rate Realignment (percentage)

| | WITH A CHANGE IN THE GOLD PRICE | WITHOUT A CHANGE IN THE GOLD PRICE |
|---|---|---|
| Japan | 15–16 | 10–11 |
| Germany | 10–12 | 6–7 |
| France, Italy and Britain | 5–6 | — |

Source: Memo 209, Peter Peterson to the president, U.S. Department of State, November 27, 1971.

The United States changed its position on the gold price soon afterward. Three factors played a role. First, Congressman Henry Reuss and Senator William Proxmire introduced legislation permitting the president to devalue against gold as part of an international agreement that adjusted exchange rates. They assured the administration that Congress would approve a change in the gold price promptly. That reduced the president's concern about politically motivated resistance.

Second, delay increased uncertainty. At first, the administration attributed the uncertainty to concerns about the next phase of price and wage controls. After the new program became known, uncertainty continued. The stock market had boomed after August 15, but in October and November stock prices fell sharply. The president's friends on Wall Street blamed Connally's policy and warned that continued uncertainty would delay recovery. In late November, the president told Connally to break the impasse (Matusow, 1998, 174–75).[28]

Third, the Europeans agreed to a larger dollar devaluation if the United States accepted an increase in the gold price. Table 6.1 shows the substantial differences proposed at the time. Peter Peterson, an assistant, drove home the point by estimating that each percentage point of realignment increased net exports by $800 million. The president could translate the four to five percentage points of difference in exchange rates into $3 to $4 billion of net exports and a corresponding increase in employment. That effectively ended his resistance to a change in the gold price and moved toward a solution.[29]

The most important next step came at a meeting in the Azores between Presidents Nixon and Pompidou (France) on December 13 and 14. The presidents agreed to a $3 (8.6 percent) increase in the gold price to $38

28. "Nixon had grown tired of the whole business and was anxious to move on" (Matusow, 1998, 177). Soon afterward he reached agreement with President Pompidou of France to put the issue aside.

29. Opponents of an increase in the gold price agreed that it would (1) reward those who held gold against developing countries that did not, and hurt Japan, which held its reserves in dollars; (2) encourage a shift from dollars to gold in anticipation of additional changes in the gold price; and (3) partly reverse the effort to reduce the role of gold in the international system (Solomon, 1982, 197–98). Only the first proved correct.

**Table 6.2** Smithsonian Exchange Rate Changes

| | REVALUATION AGAINST THE DOLLAR | TRADE-WEIGHTED REVALUATION |
|---|---|---|
| Japan | 16.9 | 11.25 |
| Germany | 13.6 | 4.75 |
| Switzerland | 13.9 | 6.0 |
| Netherlands | 11.6 | 3.25 |
| Belgium | 11.6 | 3.75 |
| Britain | 8.6 | 1.75 |
| France | 8.6 | 0.25 |
| Italy | 7.5 | 1.75 |
| Sweden | 7.5 | N.A. |

[a]Calculations by the Federal Reserve staff (Solomon, 1982, 210).

an ounce. They also agreed that other countries would revalue their currencies and widened the former one percentage point band on parities. To satisfy President Nixon, they made a vague statement about trade negotiations. President Pompidou did not insist on convertibility of the dollar.[30]

At the end of the same week, the Group of Ten ministers met at the Smithsonian Institution in Washington with Connally presiding. The members agreed on realignment of exchange rates and a simultaneous end to the 10 percent surcharge. The United States agreed to the 8.6 percent devaluation of the dollar against gold, but it deferred submitting the new gold price to Congress until after an agreement on removing trade restrictions. After much discussion about effective changes and bilateral rates, countries agreed to the changes shown in Table 6.2. Canada, the largest U.S. trading partner, announced it would continue to float. France had argued throughout that it would not revalue the franc. It accepted devaluation of the dollar against gold and the implied change in the dollar price of francs.

Solomon (1982, 309–10) reported that Federal Reserve staff calculations suggested that the trade weighted dollar devaluation was about 7 percent against all currencies and 10 percent against the Group of Ten. It estimated that dollar devaluation would increase net exports by $8 billion above 1972 levels, $5 billion less than Volcker had proposed.

30. Agreement with France was easier than usual. A memo by Paul McCracken explained that the French had approached him in late November to express concern about the effects of floating rates on German-French relations and suggest that without renewed leadership from the United States "it might be difficult for European unity to survive" (memo, McCracken to Kissinger, Nixon papers, McCracken Box 43, November 24, 1971, 2). Between October 1969 and November 1971, the mark appreciated about 20 percent against the French franc (McCracken to the president, ibid., December 1, 1971).

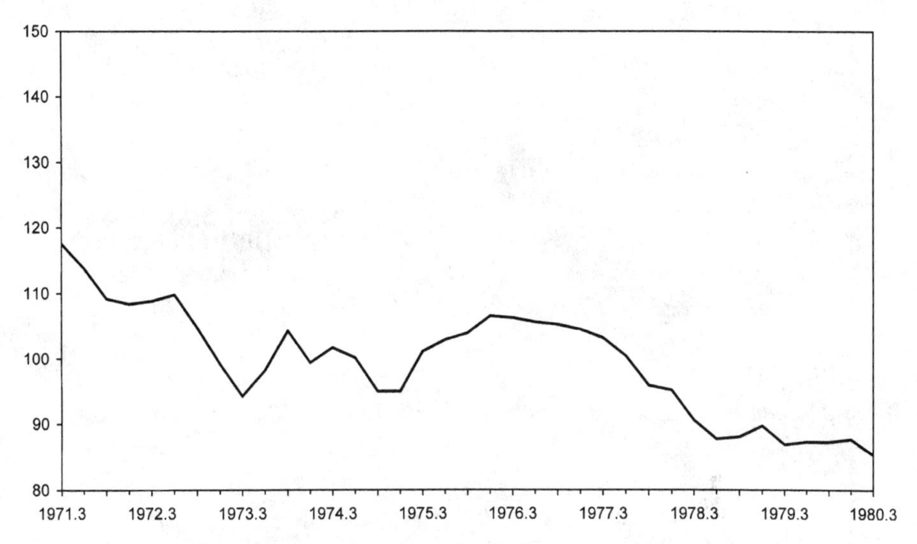


Chart 6.3. Trade-weighted real exchange rate, monthly, 1971:7–1980:12.

The net swing in the United States' current account balance was sharply negative in 1972, falling from −$1433 to −$5795 millions. Principal currencies appreciated against the dollar in 1973 and the balance reversed, rising to $7140 million, a swing of $8.5 billion from 1971 and $12.9 billion from 1972.

President Nixon, always looking to make startling changes, called the Smithsonian agreement "the most significant monetary agreement in the history of the world." It was far from that. There was still no accepted procedure for adjusting misaligned exchange rates. The dollar remained inconvertible. The group did not discuss monetary and fiscal policies of participating countries, so there was no assurance that the United States would treat maintenance of its new gold parity as a restriction on its domestic policies.

The dollar's weighted average exchange rate fell almost immediately, declining nearly 4 percent between December and February (Board of Governors, 1981, 441, table 64). Base money growth remained at 6 to 7 percent. Within a few months, the annual increase in the consumer price index rose above 7 percent, the highest rate of increase since the Korean War. The new exchange rates came under pressure. United States policy emphasized domestic concerns after devaluation just as it had before. Since the dollar remained inconvertible, it now faced one less constraint.

Chart 6.3 shows the trade weighted real exchange rate. After an initial devaluation, the real exchange rate remained unchanged for a few quarters after the Smithsonian agreement. Then it plunged downward and continued to decline, with occasional brief interruptions, until 1978. Charts for the dollar-mark and dollar-yen exchange rates show similar patterns.[31]

### *After the Smithsonian*[32]

The Smithsonian agreement had two fundamental weaknesses. First the dollar was not convertible and there was no restriction on U.S. monetary policy. Annual growth of the monetary base remained in a 7 to 8 percent range until the end of 1972. It then rose to 9 percent or more. The federal funds rate declined from 5.6 percent in August 1971 to a low of 3.3 percent in February 1972.[33] Price controls hid the inflation, so it appeared to decline until a few months before the 1972 election. Second, the Europeans did not like the agreement. They feared a loss of exports and were concerned about bilateral rates within Europe. They soon narrowed the width of bands around their bilateral exchange rates to one-half the Smithsonian bands (±2.25 percent).

One of the main concerns prior to 1971 was that countries would not choose to hold inconvertible dollars. The monetary system would break down. In fact, holdings of foreign exchange reserves, mainly dollar securities, by foreign central banks and governments rose much faster after August 1971 than before. Table 6.3 suggests the size of the holdings. They continued to increase for three principal reasons. First, many countries preferred to subsidize exports instead of permitting their nominal exchange rate to adjust. To keep their prices from rising to adjust real exchange rates, governments used exchange controls to limit capital inflows. Second, prices of most internationally traded commodities were posted in dollars; the dollar remained the currency used in most transactions. Third, the Federal Reserve directed its policies to domestic not international objectives. Money growth rose and fell to achieve domestic objectives.

Adjustment to the new system took time. The period from December

31. Makin (1974, 14) quoted the *Economist*'s comment at the time of the Smithsonian agreement. "The most important point about the new pattern of world exchange rates is that it will not last for long."

32. Connally's methods irritated not just Arthur Burns but also the Europeans and the Japanese. At a meeting with the president, George Shultz complained that Connally functioned as deputy president for both domestic and international affairs in addition to serving as chairman of the Cost of Living Council, and that he was "Secretary of the Treasury with vast responsibilities that he is not carrying out. . . . Connally has no staff and no time to do it" (Haldeman 1994, January 19, 1972, 399). The president later told Haldeman that Connally had decided to resign. He left in April, and Shultz became Treasury secretary.

33. Paul Volcker commented on Arthur Burns: "Despite his enthusiastic support of fixed exchange rates, he seemed to me to have a kind of blind spot when it came to supporting them with concrete policies" (Volcker and Gyohten, 1992, 104). Volcker added that President Nixon's only interest was to avoid crises.

**Table 6.3** Foreign Exchange Reserves outside the United States (in billions of SDRs)

| YEAR | FOREIGN EXCHANGE RESERVES |
|---|---|
| 1962 | 45.4 |
| 1972 | 146.0 |
| 1980 | 337.3 |

Source: Economic Report of the President, various years.

1971 to March 1973 was marked by frequent exchange rate problems, currency adjustments, and renewed crises. Gyohten described it: "As it became increasingly apparent that the divergence of economic fundamentals among major economies was not disappearing, the effort to restore a regime of fixed parities . . . was in fact doomed to failure" (Volcker and Gyohten, 1992, 128). That realization occurred slowly. Several failed efforts and experience with floating convinced governments and central bankers that the system could work without fixed parities everywhere. European governments could have regionally fixed rates while permitting their currencies to float jointly against the dollar, the yen, and other currencies. That reconciled France's desire for a fixed exchange rate on most of its trade with Germany's desire for a joint float against the dollar. It also reconciled the United States policy of "benign neglect" of the exchange rate with European intervention to avoid adjustment, reducing this source of frequent conflict.

The first European approach became known as "the snake in the tunnel." The tunnel was the band around the Smithsonian parities. When the dollar reached the band, central banks intervened, usually to buy dollars at the lower band. The snake referred to the narrower band within which initially six European governments fixed bilateral exchange rates. In May 1972, Britain, Denmark, and Ireland joined the snake.[34]

Britain's membership did not last. It had joined the European Common Market, requiring adjustment of its trade. The initial effect was a deficit. This occurred with rising inflation. By late June Britain abandoned the snake and its Smithsonian rate, permitting its exchange rate to float.[35] Denmark withdrew from the snake, and the Italian lira came under pressure.

34. The snake reduced the flexibility of dollar exchange rates. Depreciation of one or two currencies against all others required intervention to preserve the snake's bilateral rates. The outer band mattered only if the dollar depreciated against all currencies in the snake.

35. Secretary Shultz told President Nixon that the Smithsonian agreement could break down. He proposed what he called "limited initiatives." The aim was to show that the United States would support the Smithsonian rates, a step that Connally had refused to take. Shultz limited intervention to no more than $2 billion. The Germans especially complained to Shultz, Kissinger, and others about Connally's policy (memo 234, Shultz to the president,

Next, pressure shifted to the dollar, in part because the trade deficit increased substantially in the initial response to devaluation. Treasury reactivated the swap line and intervened to maintain the exchange rate. The dollar remained in a narrow range against the European currencies and depreciated slowly against the yen until February 1973.

The July 1972 decision to reactivate swap lines permitted the Federal Reserve "to draw foreign currencies whenever it believed that sales of these currencies would have a useful effect in helping to reestablish orderly conditions in the foreign exchange markets" (FOMC Minutes, July 18, 1972, 3). Burns believed that the chief benefit came from showing leadership toward more stable international arrangements and defense of the Smithsonian rates. Charles Coombs pointed out, however, that stable rates meant that the Federal Reserve would support the dollar-yen exchange rate. He did not think that exchange rate was appropriate (ibid., 5). Also, Burns said, "primary responsibility . . . lay with the foreign central bank" (ibid.). Federal Reserve purchases would be smaller than foreign purchases.[36] Many of the FOMC members praised Burns's initiative. None objected to reopening the swap lines.

With the presidential election over, the United States ended the second phase of price controls by moving to a more voluntary system. Soon after, Italy established a two-tier foreign exchange system. Lire flowed to Switzerland, so Switzerland floated its exchange rate. Dollars flowed to Germany, anticipating revaluation of the mark. Germany tightened exchange controls. The Bundesbank bought $5.9 billion in early February to support the exchange rate. Japan bought $1.1 billion, then closed its foreign exchange market. Germany soon followed (Solomon, 1982, 229–30).

Paul Volcker proposed a 10 percent devaluation of the dollar against gold and other currencies, provided Japan would revalue by 10 percent and the Europeans would stand still. To satisfy George Shultz, the new Treasury secretary, the United States would lift exchange controls includ-

---

Foreign Relations of the United States, V. III, undated probably July 18). Commitment to the snake remained weak.

The impetus for intervention came from Burns in response to repeated European complaints that the U.S. did nothing to maintain the Smithsonian parities. In March, the French had threatened to use exchange controls (FOMC Minutes, March 21, 1972, 13). Italy left in December 1972, France in January 1974. Germany learned not to repeat the inflexibility of Bretton Woods rates for the center country. It revalued four times between March 1973 and October 1978. The Dutch guilder and the Norwegian krone also revalued once. Other currencies devalued several times (Schwartz, 1987b, 31).

36. Burns mentioned that an alternative to using swaps was borrowing from the IMF. "A Fund drawing would be accompanied by a great deal of publicity, it would raise questions of surveillance, and it would accomplish nothing that could not be accomplished with System drawings on swap lines" (FOMC Minutes, July 18, 1972, 13).

ing the interest equalization tax.[37] Japan agreed to a revaluation of at least 7 percent, and by February 10 everyone had agreed on the additional 10 percent devaluation of the dollar. U.S. capital controls remained in place until January 1974. Volcker recognized at the time that nothing had been said about monetary policy. "The Fed was not ready, and no one except me seemed at all eager to press the point" (Volcker and Gyohten, 1992, 107).

The new agreement was less inclusive than the Smithsonian. Switzerland, Britain, and Italy joined Canada by floating. Further, the agreement did not last a month. Exchange markets reopened on February 14. By February 23, the gold price reached $89, more than twice the official price of $42.22, and the dollar weakened. On March 1, the Bundesbank bought $3.6 billion, then closed the exchange market. Once again the mark floated.

During the first quarter of 1973, foreign central banks, mainly in the G-10, bought $10 billion. The purchases were more than 17 percent of G-10 foreign exchange balances at the end of 1972. Combined with strong beliefs that the United States did little to sustain the agreed parities, the inflow was sufficient to convince even the French to end the Bretton Woods system of fixed exchange rates with the dollar (Meltzer, 1991, 79).

On March 16, 1973, a new system took shape. The continental European countries agreed to a joint float against the dollar, and the Japanese yen also floated. Countries agreed to intervene in exchange markets at their discretion.[38]

Participants at the March 16 meeting may have believed that floating was a temporary expedient, a step along the path to an improved par value system. Agreement had not been reached despite several years of meetings and proposals.[39] The oil embargo, the rise in the oil price and its effect on

37. Others in the administration and the Federal Reserve agreed with Shultz. Volcker (Volcker and Gyohten, 1992, 107) says "the effectiveness of the controls was becoming more limited, and they had become an important irritant for international business." The Federal Reserve had relaxed some of its voluntary controls in November 1971. Also, Commerce Secretary Maurice Stans proposed to weaken and end controls on foreign investment (letter Burns to Maurice Stans, Burns papers, Box B_B14, January 26, 1972). Burns agreed with the proposal but urged delay in implementing it.

38. Arthur Burns participated in the March 16 meeting. Volcker described him as fearing "floating with a passion" (Volcker and Gyohten, 1992, 113). At lunch, he attempted to reverse the decision. "With some exasperation, I said to him, 'Arthur, if you want a par value system, you better go home right away and tighten money.' With a great sigh, he replied, 'I would even do that'" (ibid.). But he didn't. Annual growth of the monetary base remained above 9 percent.

39. Before going to the March 16 meeting, Burns called a special meeting of the FOMC to discuss intervention in the foreign exchange market. Two opinions emerged. The first thought a European joint float would solve the problem and eliminate any need for intervention. John Balles (San Francisco) and Robert Mayo (Chicago) were spokesmen for this view.

payments and imbalances, and the difficulty in reaching agreement on a new arrangement convinced the skeptics to accept floating as a permanent solution for major currencies. The Europeans continued by fits and starts to adopt fixed exchange rates and eventually a common currency within their region.[40]

During the summer of 1973, Coombs argued repeatedly for intervention, often with Burns's support. At first his aim was to prevent depreciation but he became more ambitious. "Towards the end of July, I [Coombs] requested and secured Chairman Burns's approval to switch . . . from purely defensive tactics to a more aggressive approach, designed to push the dollar rate up toward more realistic levels. After some delay, the Treasury also concurred. . . . Early in August, however, the situation turned completely the other way and the dollar was suddenly favored" (FOMC Minutes, August 21, 1973, 11–12).

The weighted average value of the dollar fluctuated between monthly averages of 109.98 in January 1973 and 92.71 in July. See Chart 6.3 above. It then rose to 107.08 in January 1974. Fluctuations against the mark were much larger but in the same direction, down from January to July then up to the end of the year. Coombs did not mention that the U.S. inflation rate rose between 1972 and 1974 at a faster rate than inflation in Germany and several other countries. And neither he nor others who favored intervention expressed an opinion about the "correct" value that they wanted to maintain.

After an informal agreement in January 1974 to permit floating rates, the finance ministers of the main developed countries agreed in November 1975 to an amendment of the International Monetary Fund agreement that permitted a country to float its currency. Effective January 1, 1976, countries could have either fixed or floating exchange rates. Although the initial experience with floating rates raised many criticisms of the size and

---

Alfred Hayes and Charles Coombs argued that a joint float would be followed by exchange controls. They argued that the main problem was lack of confidence. Intervention was necessary to restore confidence. As on several previous occasions (1928, 1936) the proponents of intervention and cooperation did not mention that real exchange rates had to adjust to restore equilibrium.

At the March 16 meeting in Basel, the United States made clear that the dollar would float and that it would intervene only if necessary to keep the market orderly. Coombs was in despair. The international system, he said, "has broken down so completely that it is difficult to describe even in general terms what is left of the system and how it may be expected to function in the future" (FOMC Minutes, March 19–20, 61). Obviously not all central bankers believe markets can achieve equilibrium.

40. The United States and the Europeans continued to disagree about the role of gold (Volcker papers, National Archives, RG 56–79–15, Box 1, March 6, 1974). Eventually, gold was phased out of the system.

frequency of changes, major currencies continued to float. More than four years after President Nixon's decision to suspend convertibility, new and more flexible arrangements were in place. Gradually, countries relaxed capital controls finding them unnecessary with a floating rate.

## THE DOMESTIC CONTROLS PROGRAM

The New Economic Policy, announced on August 15, established a second arrangement for affecting prices and later interest rates. Monetary policy actions continued as before, but the new policy constrained most, but not all, prices and wages. Agricultural prices were a main exception. Interest rates responded to monetary actions, but the Committee on Interest and Dividends responded to congressional concerns by monitoring rates charged on mortgages and consumer credit. Its greatest influence was on dividends; it limited corporations to either a 4 percent increase or 25 percent of annual earnings.

Burns testified against legislation that mandated control of interest rates. Competition, he said, was much more effective in financial markets than in product and especially labor markets.[41] He now claimed that was why he favored mandatory controls on prices and wages but not on interest rates (Burns, 1978, 135–36). He promised Congress to monitor carefully the rates paid by consumers and farmers to assure that they promptly followed reductions in open market rates. His statement recognizes political concerns to protect particular groups.

Congress did not make interest rate controls mandatory perhaps because market rates had fallen at the time Burns testified (November 1, 1971). Burns continued with the dual role of chairman of the Board of Governors and chairman of the Committee on Interest and Dividends. He turned down an appointment to the Cost of Living Council, but he served as an adviser. He believed that full recovery without inflation required increased profits and lower wage growth, so he wanted wage growth held to 3.5 to 4.5 percent (Wells, 1994, 81). This ran counter to the concerns of union leaders, especially their concern that wages would be restricted and profits allowed to rise (ibid.).

Although union officers didn't like it, the ninety-day freeze proved popular with the public. The president and several of his advisers disliked the program's popularity. They preferred to weaken controls after ninety

41. "Large segments of the labor market are fenced off from effective competition by trade unions or governmental regulation" (Burns, 1978, 136). The Board favored voluntary control of interest rates on loans to consumers with "no attempt to limit those interest rates set in the open market" (memo, Holland to Burns, Burns papers, Box B_B14, October 5, 1971).

days, but they found it expedient to plan an effective and popular next step (Stein, 1988, 181).

*Phase 2*

Herbert Stein, chairman of a small planning group, considered a wide range of options including total decontrol. "My main interest was in getting out of controls promptly and in an orderly way" (ibid., 181).[42] But the freeze remained popular, so Stein offered the president two options—(1) stay close to the freeze or (2) permit wages to increase 5.5 percent and prices 2 to 3 percent (ibid., 182). The president chose the second and announced the new program on evening television on October 7.[43] He emphasized, not his concern, but his commitment to the program. After presenting his program to create new jobs, he turned to controls. "We began this battle against inflation for the purpose of winning it, and we are going to stay in it till we do win it" (Shouse, 2002, 45).

The revised program had a seven-member Price Commission and a fifteen-member Pay Board, the latter designed to placate George Meany, president of the AFL-CIO. The Pay Board had five members each from labor, business, and the public. When Stein told the press that the Cost of Living Council would act as overseer for both boards, Meany objected. The administration retreated, and the two boards remained independent. The president appointed C. Jackson Grayson to head the Price Commission and Judge George Boldt to head the Pay Board.[44]

The Pay Board adopted a standard that limited wage increases to 5.5 percent but permitted an additional 0.7 percent for increased benefits. But in one of its first actions, it approved a 17.5 percent increase for coal miners. The Price Commission showed its independence by refusing to allow coal companies to increase prices by the same percentage.

Table 6.4 shows changes in average hourly earnings, productivity, and consumer prices during the period around phase 2. Real growth of hourly earnings rose 3 percent on average, the same as in 1970–71. Hourly earn-

42. Separately, the president asked Arthur Burns for a proposal. Burns gave it to the president in person on September 24. He did not favor decontrol until 1973, after the election, again showing the political basis of the program (Burns papers, Box B_N1, September 23, 1971).

43. Within the administration, President Nixon explained that if he did not maintain controls, "the Democrats would win the presidency and they would impose permanent controls" (Stein, 1988, 182). For 1972, the administration predicted 6.25 percent increase in real GNP and 3.25 percent inflation. This was close to consensus.

44. Meany was not the only critic. Ralph Nader testified in Congress that the program did not control profits, agricultural prices, and new housing and that it was easier to control wages than prices (Shouse, 2002, 46–48). The president invited seven people to serve as chairman of the Pay Board. All declined (Weber and Mitchell, 1978, 24).

**Table 6.4** Quarterly Increases in Hourly Earnings Productivity and Consumer Prices 1971–72 (annual rates)

| DATA | HOURLY EARNINGS | CONSUMER PRICES | OUTPUT PER HOUR |
|---|---|---|---|
| 1970–71[a] | 7.4 | 4.4 | 3.5 |
| 1971:3 | 6.3 | 4.0 | 2.5 |
| 1971:4 | 5.2 | 2.3 | 4.7 |
| 1972:1 | 8.0 | 3.4 | 5.2 |
| 1972:2 | 5.6 | 3.1 | 5.1 |
| 1972:3 | 5.0 | 3.6 | 6.6 |
| 1972:4 | 7.6 | 3.6 | 3.6 |
| six-quarter average | 6.3 | 3.3 | 4.6 |

[a]Second quarter to second quarter.
Source: Weber and Mitchell (1978, 284).

ings increased more than the 5.5 percent standard, but real earnings remained below productivity growth. Reported consumer price inflation slowed from the 1970–71 rates. The administration could claim that inflation had slowed, and contrary to their fears, labor unions could not claim that wage increases had slowed more than prices. Corporate profitability benefited from the greater increase in productivity growth than in real wages that typically occurs in an expanding economy.[45]

Increased profitability pleased Burns. He claimed that labor unions caused inflation. With slow growth, profits and investment declined. His strong beliefs about the political importance of wage-price controls before the election coexisted with his dislike of labor unions and the need to control wages. Wells (1994, 81) described his efforts to strengthen wage control and moderate price controls.[46] But he also expressed concern about rising meat prices in a letter to the president in June 1972. The same letter expressed disappointment about slow productivity growth. His discussion of individual price increases suggests the extent to which he confused inflation and relative price changes. This problem became acute when oil prices rose in 1973 (letter Burns to the president, Burns papers, Box B_N1, June 24, 1972).

In January 1973, motivated by reelection, the recovering economy, rising stock prices, the unemployment rate at 5 percent, and its preference for decontrol, the administration relaxed phase 2 standards. From January 11

45. Phase 2 restricted profit growth by limiting margins to the best two of three fiscal years before August 15, 1971. Phase 3, beginning in January 1973, relaxed the limit slightly (Kosters, 1975, 16).

46. Burns's criticisms of the functioning of the controls program bought a rebuke from the White House (Wells, 1994, 83). Matusow (1998, chapter 7) traces the ups and downs of the programs and the reasons that the labor unions left the Pay Board in March 1972. Only Frank Fitzsimmons of the Teamsters agreed to remain on a reconstituted board.

to June 13, 1973, phase 3 controls depended mainly on self-administration and, for large firms, reporting of agreements. The Pay Board and the Price Commission ended; their remaining duties devolved to the Cost of Living Council.

Phase 3 was mainly the work of George Shultz, Donald Rumsfeld, and Herbert Stein. Before the president announced the program, they talked with the heads of principal labor unions, corporations, members of Congress, and others. They learned that dissatisfaction with phase 2 had increased and reported that the program should rely more on voluntary compliance. The principal complaint from both business and labor was the "difficulty of obtaining prompt, reasonable decisions" (memo, Shultz to the president, Nixon papers, January 8, 1973, Tab A).

Phase 3 came after the election. The administration intended to make the transition out of controls. Unfortunately, the change to phase 3 was "premised on a view of the price outlook that was far more optimistic than the inflation trend that actually emerged" (Kosters, 1975, 23).

The problems came from bad luck and bad policies. The very expansive monetary and fiscal policies of 1972 began to affect prices in 1973. Bad weather in the Soviet Union increased demand for food crops and produced a rapid increase in food prices. The first evidence came in December 1972 (ibid., 24), but the administration had to decide whether the increase was temporary or persistent and what to do in either case.

At first, it ignored the problem. At a Quadriad meeting on December 11, Stein exulted about rising output and falling inflation. With the election won, discussion turned to inflation. Burns wanted to set a target of 1.5 to 2 percent for calendar 1973, but Stein objected "that so low a goal would seem incredible" (memo, Stein to the president, Shultz papers, Box 3, December 11, 1972). President Nixon sided with Stein. Soon afterward, Burns sent a copy of a speech that made inflation "the most critical problem that we now face.[47] And the problem is of such gravity that a broad governmental effort is required to cope with the threat of a new inflationary spiral" (letter, Burns to the president, Burns papers, Box B_N1, December 28, 1972). The letter promised cautious assistance from monetary policy but added that "monetary policy cannot do the job alone, since any such attempt would threaten another credit crunch." A month later, he told the

47. In a letter to Burns commenting on his speech, the president wrote that he agreed that inflation was "the most critical problem we now face" and that "the *only* responsible course is to fight inflation hard, and this is precisely what I intend to do" (letter, Nixon to Burns, Burns papers, Box B_N1, January 5, 1973). The president set an objective of 2.5 percent inflation by year-end. His administration's forecast called for 6 percent growth and 3 percent inflation.

president that his staff analysis expressed concern that inflation would increase. He shared their concern (letter, Burns to the president, Shultz papers, Box 4, January 29, 1973).

On June 13, the president ended phase 3 by freezing prices for sixty-nine days. This decision again rejected the advice of his principal advisers, especially Shultz and Stein.[48] Stein outlined the economic and political dimensions. The economy had been in a very different place in August 1971. There would be more shortages now. Productivity growth had slowed. Prospects for wage increases were better than in 1971. There would be less conviction that controls would be temporary. This would affect compliance and investment.

Stein's principal political concern was that Congress would approve a comprehensive, temporary freeze, a popular remedy. That would hurt the president's ability to lead and "the Republicans could be hurt in the 1974 elections" (memo, Stein to the president, Shultz papers, Box 5, April 9, 1973). Although Stein opposed the freeze, he must have known that his reference to the 1974 election would push the president toward the price freeze.

Burns favored the freeze. On June 1, he wrote the president a letter with detailed recommendations for policy changes (Burns papers, B_N1, June 1, 1973). The letter warned of the public's unhappiness and unease. Like President Carter's famous 1979 speech warning of public anxiety, Burns, too, blamed inflation for "a crisis of confidence" (ibid., 3).

His first proposal was "reimpose mandatory controls for Tier I [large] firms" (ibid., 4).[49] Then he proposed rolling back prices for firms that violated profit guidelines, suspending all agricultural price supports, sales of materials from government stockpiles to lower raw material prices, prohibiting foreign orders for food exports, and other measures affecting wages and imports. To reduce spending, Burns proposed compulsory savings for corporations and individuals. To meet public concerns about energy, he proposed a tax based on horsepower.

In the last paragraph of his letter, Burns added "that the Federal Reserve has been trying hard to bring monetary policy to bear on the problem of

48. Shultz became Secretary of the Treasury when Connally left in 1972, and Stein replaced McCracken as chairman of the Council of Economic Advisers at the end of 1971. Shultz resigned and left the administration soon after the freeze.

49. In April Burns had proposed "an immediate 45 days freeze over a broad range of prices." Following the freeze, he wanted reforms "to reduce substantially the existing abuses of economic power by the labor unions and corporate giants." He suggested other structural reforms as well (memo, Burns to John Ehrlichman, Burns papers, Box B_B89, April 13, 1973).

**Table 6.5** Outlays and Deficits, 1970–73 (in $ billions)

| YEAR | BUDGET OUTLAYS | DEFICIT |
|---|---|---|
| 1970 | 168.0 | 8.7 |
| 1971 | 177.3 | 26.0 |
| 1972 | 193.8 | 26.4 |
| 1973 | 200.1 | 15.4 |

Source: Office of Management and Budget (1990, 16).

inflation, that our efforts in this direction will continue, but that we will also try to avoid a credit crunch of the 1969 type" (ibid., 7).

This differed from Herbert Stein's opinion. Stein (1988, 183) wrote:

> It was also part of the exercise that the revival of demand should be restrained. The Nixon team prided themselves on being alert to the error which other governments had fallen into and assured themselves and others that the controls would not seduce them into excessive expansionism.
>
> But they did fall into the trap. . . . The President, on the advice of his economists, decided that government expenditures should be rapidly increased during the first half of calendar 1972 . . . after which they would be restrained.

Federal budget outlays increased almost 20 percent, from $168 billion in 1970 to $200 billion in 1973. Table 6.5 shows annual data for these years. The administration increased spending with assistance from Congress, but it did not control monetary policy. For that it required help from the Federal Reserve and particularly from Arthur Burns.[50]

## FEDERAL RESERVE ACTIONS, 1971–73

The years 1971–73 are among the worst in Federal Reserve history. The Federal Reserve did not "fall into the trap" of excessive expansion under price controls. It entered by choice. Some members voted for expansion to reduce unemployment. Arthur Burns shared this objective, but he also remained committed to the reelection of President Nixon. He may have adapted monetary policy to achieve a political end. If so, he required help from other members of FOMC, and he was able to get it. There were few objections at the time from Congress or FOMC members.

50. Phase 4 followed the brief freeze. It lasted from August 12, 1973, to April 30, 1974. The administration decontrolled wages and prices during this period. Only 44 percent of CPI prices were subject to control at the start of phase 4. This fell to 12 percent at the end (Kosters, 1975, 26–27). Controls on oil and energy prices remained until the Reagan administration. I have not found an explanation of what this phase could accomplish beyond a cosmetic showing of administration concern.

**Table 6.6** Unit Labor Cost in Manufacturing (1977 = 100)

| YEAR AND QUARTER | UNIT LABOR COST | YEAR AND QUARTER | UNIT LABOR COST |
|---|---|---|---|
| 1970–1 | 72.3 | 1972–1 | 72.5 |
| 1970–2 | 72.5 | 1972–2 | 72.8 |
| 1970–3 | 72.7 | 1972–3 | 73.0 |
| 1970–4 | 72.8 | 1972–4 | 73.0 |
| 1971–1 | 73.2 | 1973–1 | 74.3 |
| 1971–2 | 73.3 | 1973–2 | 75.3 |
| 1971–3 | 73.3 | 1973–3 | 75.7 |
| 1971–4 | 72.4 | 1973–4 | 77.4 |

Source: Department of Commerce, 1989, November, 99.

At the last FOMC meeting before the New Economic Policy (NEP), the Board's staff raised its estimate of GNP for 1971 by $3 billion, all in real output. They projected real growth at 3.8 percent in the second half of the year and 5.3 percent in the first half of 1972. And they expected money growth to slow in the fourth quarter, as it in fact did (Maisel diary, July 29, 1971, 72). Reported real GNP growth remained at 1 percent in the second half of 1971 but rose to 8.5 percent in the first half of 1972.

The Board welcomed the NEP. Many of them believed that cost-push by unions and businesses caused most of the inflation. The freeze would end that and make possible a return to high employment with lower inflation. Markets interpreted the new policy as anti-inflationary. Short- and long-term interest rates fell after the announcement.

Following the start of controls, the staff projected less reported inflation for the second half. It reduced projected inflation from 4.9 to 3.4 percent. The reported rate was 5 percent, very close to the forecast before controls. However, unit labor costs rose very little in the second half of 1971, but they rose more rapidly after controls than before. Table 6.6 shows unit labor costs during these years. In 1973, they rose rapidly.

Maisel (diary, August 25, 1971, 85) described the August FOMC meeting as probably the longest ever. It lasted eight hours. Three topics added greatly to the discussion: the report of the Committee on the Directive, whether or how to implement new procedures, and whether to purchase federal agency issues to assist the housing market.

The Committee on the Directive proposed that the manager should achieve a reserve target subject to a proviso clause that limited interest rate changes. The committee was unanimous, and the Board's staff supported the proposal. All agreed that the change was a marginal adjustment that would improve control of the monetary aggregates. They did not discuss even keel, changes in Treasury deposits, or other technical issues. The manager argued that a reserve target should not be the main issue. The desk could improve control of reserves and the aggregates by permitting wider fluctuations in the federal funds rate.

The FOMC took no action on the proposal. It agreed to have additional studies of the effect of a reserve target on interest rates and to return to thc discussion after more had been learned. Nevertheless, it directed the manager to moderate growth of the monetary aggregates consistent with a floor of 5 percent for the federal funds rate. Several members expressed concern about staff projections showing a considerable slowdown in money growth during the fourth quarter.

A few presidents, Hayes, Kimbrel, and Clay, wanted monetary policy to "reinforce the President's move toward less inflation" by slowing growth of money (Maisel diary, August 25, 1971, 90). "Almost everyone else on the Committee agreed that the incomes policy . . . was to reduce the need for monetary restraint but that monetary policy ought not to increase restraint" (ibid.). Words like "ease," "restraint," and "neutral policy" continued in use without clear definition or relation to some measurable quantity.[51]

The Federal Reserve came into the NEP period with high money growth. Monetary base and $M_1$ money growth rose at 7.4 and 7.6 percent average annual rates in the first eight months. By August, twelve-month growth rates of the base and money were 8 and 7.2 percent respectively. Most members of the FOMC said they favored slower growth of the aggregates. Nevertheless, they allowed the federal funds rate to fall gradually from 5.57 percent in August to 4.91 percent in November. Free reserves rose.

At the October 19 FOMC meeting the staff forecast $M_1$ growth at 2.5 percent for the fourth quarter and 4.5 percent for the first quarter of 1972. They urged a reduction in the federal funds rate to 5 percent or less (Maisel diary, October 21, 1971, 2). Burns spoke first and urged no change. His concern was that if interest rates declined in 1971, they would have to rise in 1972. Rising rates in 1972 "could result in serious difficulties. That possibility worried him a great deal" (FOMC Minutes, October 19, 1971, 49–50). Burns did not explain the source of his discomfort, and no one pressed for an explanation. They probably understood that Congress and

51. Under growing pressures from Congress, Burns persuaded the FOMC to purchase agency issues. A large minority opposed, as they had for the five years since Congress authorized the purchases. But Burns had soon to testify about housing. "It would be useful politically if the System were operating in agencies" (Maisel diary, August 25, 1971, 91). The staff report suggested, it would have little effect on housing. Purchases began in September. The Board announced the first purchases and indicated that total purchases of five agencies issues came to $61 million and had about a two-year maturity (memo, Holland to FOMC, Board Records, September 24, 1971). This is one of several examples of failure to distinguish between mortgage credit and the real resources required to build houses.

the administration would criticize rising interest rates in an election year. The members divided almost equally but later compromised on a statement calling for "moderate growth in monetary and credit aggregates" (Annual Report, 1971, 189).

A week later, Paul McCracken wrote to President Nixon warning about recent slow growth in money. His memo suggested that real growth should reach 7 to 8 percent in 1972 to reduce the unemployment rate. Lower unemployment required 8 to 10 percent nominal GNP growth and 7 to 8 percent money growth (memo, McCracken to the president, Nixon papers, WHCF, Box 43, October 27, 1971).[52]

### *Nixon and Burns*

Following the FOMC meeting, Burns met with the president for more than two hours. Paul McCracken, George Shultz, John Connally, and others were present. When the discussion turned to monetary policy, Burns repeated the views he expressed at the FOMC meeting. If he pushed interest rates down now to increase money growth, they would have the "unsavory task of just watching them go up next year. . . . What I would like to do is prevent as much as I can an increase in interest rates next year" (White House tapes, tape 1327, October 28, 1971).

The president later responded by recalling his experience in 1960, when Burns warned in February about tight Federal Reserve policy. In the cabinet meeting, President Eisenhower sided with those who wanted a cautious policy because they feared inflation. President Nixon then explained his priority: "I don't want the same mistake again . . . I don't want to have a runaway inflation . . . [but many elections] have been lost on the issue of unemployment. None has been lost on the issue of inflation. . . . Unemployment is always a bigger issue than inflation" (ibid., tape 1328).

On November 9, the Board discussed a 0.25 percentage point reduction in the discount rate to 4.75 percent and a reduction in stock market margin requirements from 65 to 55 percentage points. The latter reflected con-

52. Burns's relations with the president continued to fluctuate over a wide range. The president told Burns at one point that he wanted his input on Federal Reserve appointments, so that Burns would have support for his proposals. William Sherrill resigned to accept the presidency of a bank in November and left in December, but Burns and others knew early in the fall that he would leave. Burns found a candidate and recommended him to the president as a person who would be "of inestimable assistance to me in the effective discharge of the Board's functions and responsibilities" (Burns to the president, Burns papers, Box B_N1, October 8, 1971). By the time the position became open, the president was irritated and anxious about slow monetary growth. He did not take Burns's candidate but instead appointed John E. Sheehan on December 23, 1971. Sheehan remained less than 3.5 years. He was a businessman influenced by John Connally.

cerns about falling stock prices. At the time of the meeting, the principal stock price indexes had fallen below their August 15 level.

Market rates had fallen relative to the federal funds rate and the discount rate. Board members expressed concern about differences in forecast for 1972. The staff and most economists were relatively optimistic; businessmen had become relatively pessimistic.

The Board approved the reduction in the discount rate but delayed the reduction in margin requirements. A main reason for delay was that several members argued against actions to influence stock prices or those perceived as such. By December 3, uncertainty about the international system had declined. Stock prices rose, and the Board reduced the margin requirement.[53]

Nixon and Burns met frequently both before and after the October-November meetings. In the months before the Camp David meeting, the president was strongly against controls that Burns thought necessary. The president wanted faster money growth, but Burns warned him several times that if interest rates were pushed down in 1971, they would likely rise in 1972.[54]

The relationship was not easy. On March 19, 1971, the two met alone. Burns complained about leaks to the press criticizing the Federal Reserve and him. The president again expressed his unhappiness about Burns's calls for wage-price policy. But Burns cited his loyalty to Nixon and service to the country.

> I am a dedicated man to serve the health and strength of our national economy. And I have done everything in my power, as I see it, to help you as President, your reputation and standing in American life and history. (White House tapes, conversation 470-18, tape 371, March 19, 1971)

Nixon mentioned the importance of lower inflation.

In April and May, the president was most concerned about the dollar outflow and the Germans' decision to stop buying dollars. At a May 4 meeting with the president, McCracken, Volcker, Connally, and Burns asked the

53. As usual, Governor Robertson objected that margin requirement legislation directed the use to control of stock market credit, not prices. There was no evidence of credit expansion for carrying shares. He voted for the change, however. No one else expressed concern about the regulatory change.

54. As early as February 19, 1971, Nixon explained his reasons for opposing price controls and urged lower interest rates (White House tapes, conversation 454-4, tape 271, February 19, 1971). Two weeks later, Burns urged the president not to give so much attention to the money supply. On June 7 and 8, the president again urged lower interest rates and stressed the importance of housing for reducing unemployment (ibid., conversations 59-4 and 60-1, June 7 and 8, 1971).

president to publicly urge Germany not to float its currency. The president gave a political reason: "They're going to blame us, and our political opponents at home are going to blame us" (ibid., conversation 490-24, tape 556, May 4, 1971). Connally wanted the float. He spoke of devaluation. "Even a twenty percent devaluation may not help us through 1972. You might have another crisis next year" (ibid.).

By mid-June, public opinion surveys showed the public concerned as much about inflation as about unemployment. In May and June, consumer prices rose 6 to 7 percent at annual rates. President Nixon asked: "What do we do to make people think that we care? We need to convince people that we're trying." Burns's response was a wage-price freeze from early in 1972 to July or August of that year. Then the president added: "You know I care more about unemployment than inflation. You know that . . . . " Then, probably reflecting briefing by his advisers, he added: "But I think that perhaps the best way of getting a hold on the unemployment problem is to subdue the inflationary expectations" (ibid., conversation 519-11, tape 750, June 14, 1971).

Two weeks later, the president was starting to consider some policy changes. Burns opposed any increase in spending and tax reduction. Then he brought up the wage-price freeze, saying he would not do it, but he would jawbone price and wage increases. "I have to do something with regard to foreign imports. I think Congress is going to pass a quota bill and if I was sitting there I'd vote for it . . .

"Connally: I would too" (ibid., conversation 531-16, tapes 808–9, June 28, 1971).

Nixon and Connally then criticized Burns for not supporting administration policy. Burns defended himself and predicted that events would drive the administration to adopt an incomes policy. He repeated that he supported the president. "No one has tried harder to help you" (ibid.).

On October 28, the president discussed the negotiations with the Europeans about the dollar. They mentioned floating rates, but the IMF opposed. Connally's main concern was Japanese trade barriers. Discussion then turned to domestic policy.

Burns said that if the Federal Reserve pushed interest rates down, he would have the "unsavory task of just watching them go up next year. . . . [W]hat I would like to do is prevent as much as I can an increase in interest rates next year." The conversation ended with the president reminding Burns about 1960 and the loss of the election to Kennedy over rising unemployment. "By February, we're past the point of no return . . . let's make sure we make our decisions" (ibid., conversation 606-2, tapes 1327–28, October 28, 1971).

The president then addressed Burns. "Maybe we're talking about an entirely different subject than was the case when McChesney Martin was running the Board." Burns replied: "I think we are" (ibid.).

### *Nixon and Burns in 1972*

The president wrote to Burns on November 4 about an article in the *New York Times* about slow money growth. Then he added:

> I have been flooded with calls . . . from people in Wall Street for whose judgments I have the greatest respect with regard to the Fed's policy of holding the money supply down for too long a period. . . .
>
> I do want you to know that there is nothing I feel stronger on than this money supply problem and that the crescendo of complaints that I have been receiving, not only from the New York financial community but from other places . . . expressing the same concern convinces me that you owe it to yourself, as well as to our goal of getting the economy to move smartly up in the months ahead, to re-evaluate your decision with regard to holding the money supply down and to take some action to move it up" (Burns papers, Box B_N1, November 4, 1971).

At its November meeting, the FOMC voted unanimously for "somewhat greater growth in monetary and credit aggregates over the months ahead" (Annual Report, 1971, 194). The staff remained optimistic about growth and employment, but Mitchell, Maisel, and Burns were skeptical. The forecast ended with a 5.3 percent unemployment rate in fourth quarter 1972 "which he [Burns] felt was still too high and unsatisfactory" (Maisel diary, November 17, 1971, 7). (Like others, Burns believed that 4 percent was full employment.) He added that slow money growth convinced some that Federal Reserve policy was too tight. "He thought for this reason that we ought to start getting some expansion" (ibid.). Morris (Boston), Mitchell, Maisel, Kimbrel (Atlanta), and Robertson joined Burns in advocating more expansive policy. Hayes (New York), Mayo (Chicago), Clay (Kansas City), and Daane wanted either no change or less aggressive policy action. Following the meeting, the federal funds rate fell.

Burns had no problem finding support in the FOMC for more expansive policy. There was not unanimity, but he had sufficient support for increased money growth to get agreement.

The president was not satisfied. At a meeting with the president, Burns complained about public pressure (White House tapes, tape 1480, November 24, 1971). He was sure he knew the source. He gave the president the commitment he wanted.

Burns: There is a campaign on to write me letters to urge more expansion. I will make good on my promises.
Nixon: I have no doubt about it. I just want to be sure I'm not misreading you.
Burns: Burns does not forget.
Nixon: I'll keep them off your back.[55]

At the November 14 FOMC meeting, reports and staff continued to express optimism, but the unemployment rate did not change. The staff expected slow money growth to end; their forecast called for 7 and 8 percent growth for $M_1$ and $M_2$ in first quarter 1972.

Maisel described the debate on current policy as "one of the most protracted that there had been" and "the greatest split there had ever been between the presidents and the Board" (diary, December 15, 1971, 10–11). Burns told the members that "the System was getting a good deal of criticism on the fear that the monetary policy appeared to be inconsistent with the New Economic Policy. If one used the aggregates as a measure of monetary policy, he said that people in the administration, perhaps the President too [*sic*], had raised questions with him as to whether the System had been trying to offset the New Economic Policy which obviously required that demand rise" (ibid., 10). He urged them to state that their goal for $M_1$ growth was 6 to 7 percent.

The division was about as before. Presidents Hayes, Kimbrel, and Clay wanted a more restrictive policy. Mayo and Morris were somewhat more expansive. Among Board members, Mitchell, Daane, and Burns "wanted a very aggressive move. . . . Robertson and I [Maisel] went along and Brimmer dragged his heels only slightly" (ibid., 11).

The instructions to the manager were very explicit. The Committee voted several times, once to set upper and lower bounds on the federal funds rate, 3.75 to 4.62. Then the committee voted on the desired money growth rate, 5 percent for December and January, and it instructed the manager to reduce the funds rate if money growth fell below the target. Each vote was split, but the final vote was unanimous.[56] The funds rate

55. The president continued to express concern, and Burns tried to reassure him. In a letter, he described his policy by quoting his recent public statement. "The System will provide adequate reserves to finance a vigorous, but sustainable expansion" (letter, Burns to President, Burns papers, Box B_N1, November 24, 1971, 2).

56. Maisel (diary, December 10, 1971, 8) reports on a reduction in the discount rate to 4.5 percent effective December 13 at three reserve banks. By December 24, the 4.5 percent rate became uniform.

dropped to a 3.5 percent average for January; money growth remained low in December but rose to a 10 percent annual rate in January.

Burns met with the president and George Shultz on December 22. The president again brought up money growth. Burns explained that he had had trouble with the reserve bank presidents. "I had difficulty at the last meeting. I kept them there until four o'clock to get what I want" (White House tapes, conversation 640-3, tape 1588, December 22, 1971).

Nixon: "You're independent (laughter), independent (laughter). Get it up! I don't want any more angry letters from people. . . . The whole point is, get it up!" (ibid.).

After Burns left, the president remarked to George Shultz: "He made his commitment. You heard it again" (ibid.). Shultz pointed out that the FOMC had voted to increase the money growth rate and the reported growth rate rose the previous week, but it could have been random fluctuation.[57]

The president believed that Burns had committed to an expansive monetary policy that would achieve strong growth and lower the unemployment rate. Burns, on his side, worked to get higher money growth. Instead of concentrating only on interest rates, the account manager sent the FOMC members his recommendation that the FOMC suspend until the next meeting the lower bound on interest rates charged on repurchase agreements so that he could supply more reserves (Holland to FOMC presidents, Board Records, December 22, 1971). The FOMC voted nine to one to suspend the floor on the rate. Governor Robertson objected that the manager should use open market operations, not repurchase agreements. In 1972, the FOMC changed to require bidding for repurchase agreements, so the rate became market determined.

The FOMC meetings in 1972 became the subject of charges and claims about Burns's efforts to expand money growth to help President Nixon's campaign for reelection. Sanford Rose (1974, 186, 188) made two shocking charges: (1) "A majority of the FOMC recognized the need for a turn to a more restrictive monetary policy in 1972, but Burns held out for continued stimulus, arguing that the Fed should do nothing that could snag the ongoing recovery or cause interest rates to rise any more rapidly than they already were rising"; (2) Burns left an FOMC meeting for an hour.

57. The president was not the only one receiving angry letters about money. Milton Friedman wrote to Burns: "What in God's name is happening" (letter, Friedman to Burns, Burns papers, Box B_K12, December 13, 1971). Friedman compared money growth to experience in 1959 and found "a far sharper slowdown . . . than in 1959" (ibid.). On his computation $M_1$ growth averaged 0.4 percent for the past four months, down from 10.8 percent from January to August.

When he returned, he told the committee, "I have just talked to the White House." The implication was that the FOMC adopted an easier policy out of concern for possible retaliation by "the White House" against Federal Reserve independence.

The minutes that later became available show that the first, more general, charge is false. Although some members dissented at times, a majority never opposed the policy. The second, more specific, charge is not only implausible, everyone at the meeting has denied it.[58] Wooley (1984, 161) interviewed almost all FOMC members. They said "such a blatant tactic would have been strongly repudiated." My interviews confirm this result, as did Abrams (2006) and Governor John Sheehan. No one to whom I spoke that was present at the meeting recalled the incident. All denied it occurred. Sheehan (2002, 14) pointed out that the Board was dominated by Democrats. "I never in monetary policy observed anyone voting because he was a liberal Democrat or a conservative Republican. . . . Every time that Burns went up to Capital Hill, Proxmire would beat up on him, that you're not expanding the money supply enough."

Wooley (1995, 8) returned to the issue after the Nixon, Burns, Haldeman, and Ehrlichman papers became available. His new conclusion was that "Rose was much closer to the truth than Fed officials wanted to admit or than many scholars believed." This conclusion is also contentious. Others who have studied the period concluded that Burns, and many others, accepted that there was ample slack in the economy. The unemployment rate remained at 5.6 percent as late as October 1972. The standard presumption was that full employment would not be reached until the unemployment rate was about 4 percent (Matusow, 1998, 187–90; Wells, 1994, 99–101). Wells quotes Walter Heller and Herbert Stein as favoring expansive policy because of the distance from full employment. Wooley (1984, 168) lists several prominent economists who usually advised the Democrats. Until August 1972, none favored more restrictive policies. And he quotes leading Democratic members of Congress as favoring "fairly rapid money growth"

58. Issues about Burns's role continue. Joseph Burns, a son, responded to criticism of his father in a letter to the *Wall Street Journal*. "In hindsight, there is little question that monetary policy in 1972 was expansionary, but the evidence strongly contradicts the assertion that Arthur Burns manipulated it to support Nixon's re-election campaign" (Burns, 2004, A15). The first part of the quoted statement is true; regrettably the second part is at best ambiguous. The issue arose at the Board meeting in 1978 after a *New York Times* article claimed that Burns aided President Nixon's reelection. The Times asked for early release of the 1972 transcript. Burns opposed but said that he would agree to release it to the president if asked by the president. He then denied that the record contained any matters of personal concern. "There's nothing in that record that would concern me for one moment. . . . [T]he Chairman's record in 1972 was an honorable record" (Burns papers, tape 6, August 16, 1977, 22).

(ibid., 175). As late as July, the Joint Economic Committee warned the Federal Reserve not to tighten its policy (ibid., 176).

Both positions have support. Ample evidence cited above supports the claim that President Nixon urged Burns to follow a very expansive policy and that Burns agreed to do it. Evidence also suggests strongly that many economists and politicians believed that the economy was far from full employment, and they wanted to reduce unemployment using highly expansive policies. Much of the previous literature neglects the fact that typically the FOMC voted unanimously. There were rarely more than three dissenting votes. At several meetings, including the critical meetings in January and February 1972, Hayes (New York) made a strong case for less expansive policy. He never drew more than two additional votes. Burns's policy drew support from such independent-minded Board members as George Mitchell, Sherman Maisel, and Andrew Brimmer, all appointed by Presidents Kennedy and Johnson. And Governor J. L. Robertson (one of the most independent members, initially appointed by President Truman) did not dissent until September, long after the economy had strengthened.

Burns was able to get a majority vote of the FOMC because he could appeal to beliefs that considerable resources were idle, that inflation would be held back by price controls, and that their principal mandate was to contribute to full employment. This was compatible with service to the president's reelection campaign. There is no doubt that he urged an easier policy in January 1972 after his discussions with President Nixon. He cited the unemployment rate and compared Treasury bill rates in previous periods of unemployment to conclude that bill rates were high (FOMC Minutes, January 11, 1972, 64). Most members agreed. Even Hayes favored 6 to 8 percent growth in $M_1$ for the next two months (ibid., 69).

Based on the FOMC's usual measures of policy thrust, monetary policy tightened in 1972. The federal funds rate reached a monthly average low in February, 3.29 percent; by June it was 4.46, and by October and November it was just above 5 percent. Reported inflation (under controls) for the most recent twelve months rose only from 3.3 percent in January to 3.45 percent in November, so the real federal funds rate ranged from zero to one percent. The Society of Professional Forecasters put the year-ahead increase in the deflator between 3.4 and 3.7 percent, about the same as before price controls. Free reserves fell from $152 million in January to −$300 million in October–November. Twelve-month average growth of base money, however, rose from 7 percent in January to 8.4 percent in November. The November rate of increase was the highest annual rate since 1946. It was soon exceeded. Twelve-month growth of $M_1$ rose from 6.5 percent in January to 7.8 percent in November.

The FOMC divided again. It did not readily accept Burns's choice of directive. Many wanted less expansive reserve growth than he did, and some objected to the shift from money market indicators to reserve growth. After a break, during which Burns and some staff redrafted the proposed directive, the committee reached agreement on projected reserve growth of 20 to 25 percent from December to January with a floor of 3 percent to the federal funds rate. Monetary base growth from December to January rose from 2 percent to 11.5 percent at annualized rates, then fell back to 7.4 percent in February. As is often the case, the aggregates and the money market measures have different implications about the direction of policy. This time, however, the FOMC gave more attention to the monetary aggregates. At its January 11 meeting, the FOMC voted nine to three to "promote the degree of ease in bank reserve and money market conditions *essential to greater growth in monetary aggregates over the months ahead*" (FOMC Minutes, January 11, 1972, 95; emphasis added). Hayes, Brimmer, and Kimbrel (Atlanta) dissented. Hayes's and Brimmer's dissents made clear that they opposed reference to a reserve target not to the money growth decision. Only Kimbrel objected to "pushing short-term rates down to unsustainably low levels" (ibid., 96).

Responding to administration pressures to "get it up," Burns advanced the date for the January meeting by a week. Time was critical. Most studies suggested a lag of six to nine months from the start of monetary ease to the response of output, and President Nixon had said that February was the cutoff point. To stimulate the economy and reduce unemployment no later than the third quarter, monetary growth had to move up substantially from one percent $M_1$ growth in fourth quarter 1971. $M_2$ had increased nearly 8 percent, and interest rates had declined, but the president watched $M_1$, and Burns wanted it to increase.

The staff had accurately forecast slow $M_1$ growth at the end of 1971. They now forecast a reversal, 10 percent $M_1$ growth in the first quarter with unchanged money market conditions and a 5.4 percent unemployment rate in the fourth quarter. Both forecasts proved accurate, although money market conditions eased in the winter.

In late January, the president met with the Quadriad. Burns described his efforts and spoke about opposition from Hayes especially but Brimmer also.[59] The president sent him a letter, marked "eyes only," commending Burns's efforts to increase money growth and promising to appoint a new

59. The president supported Burns's criticisms of Hayes. In language reminiscent of Morgenthau's in the 1930s, he concluded that the bankers were "timid," reluctant to lend and wanted higher, not lower, interest rates, and that Hayes would represent their viewpoint in opposition to Burns (letter, Nixon to Burns, Burns papers, Box B_N1, January 28, 1972).

member, to replace Maisel, who "will follow your leadership" (letter, Nixon to Burns, Burns papers, Box B_N1, January 28, 1972, 1). The president then expressed his "absolute confidence" in Burns's pledge and Burns's "absolute assurance that the money supply will move adequately to fuel an expanding economy in 1972" (ibid.).[60]

Then came the threat. "What could happen out of all of this is that a major attack on the independence of the Fed will eventually develop. I do not want this to happen—particularly I do not want it to happen when the Chairman of the Fed is a man in whom I have such enormous confidence and for whose economic advice I have such great respect" (ibid., 3).

Despite his annoyance, and possible anger, Burns replied a few days later. "I have read and reread your recent letter. I share your basic thought, and I am confident that monetary policy will promote rather than impede economic expansion this year" (Burns to the president, Burns papers, Box B_N1, February 3, 1972, 1). The rest of the letter criticized the president's budget message because there was not enough stimulus.[61]

President Nixon's interest in policy actions continued for a few months. In mid-February, he described the economy as "in fairly good shape" but he wanted "to do *everything* to help the expansion" (Ehrlichman notes, February 14, 1972; emphasis in the original). Although money growth had increased, the president continued to be annoyed by Burns. He accused him of "putting himself on all sides," telling Congress that the deficit was too high and telling the president to increase fiscal stimulus (ibid.).[62] When Burns joined the meeting, he assured the president that there was no reason for complaint. The money "supply was growing and interest rates had fallen" (ibid.). The president asked about Burns's problems with Alfred Hayes. Burns reassured him.[63]

With real growth reported in the minutes at 9.5, 5.5, and 8.5 percent in the first three quarters and revised real growth at 9.1, 8, and 4.2 percent,

60. Burns wrote at the end: "Absolute assurance! What nonsense! No answer to be made to this letter. It's outrageous" (letter, Nixon to Burns, Burns papers, Box B_N1, January 28, 1972, 5).

61. By mid-year $M_1$ and $M_2$ had increased 8 and 11 percent respectively. In testimony to the Joint Economic Committee, Stein lauded monetary policy.

62. The president decided to have no more Quadriad meetings "for AB [Arthur Burns] to lecture others" (Ehrlichman notes, February 14, 1972). President Nixon's relation with Burns went up and down throughout Burns's tenure. Burns often lectured the president on policy and politics, sometimes at length.

63. Sheehan (2002, 23) reports that Hayes had little influence. "Burns despised him." At a meeting later that day, the president told Ehrlichman that he wanted weekly reports from each cabinet member showing the spending they authorized to stimulate the economy.

the unemployment rate declined slowly from 6 percent in December 1971 to 5.5 percent in September 1972. President Nixon asked about money growth less often.

In September, Burns told the president that $M_1$ growth averaged 8 percent so far that year and he "promised" that it would remain expansive until November. Interest rates had remained "level, below August 1971" values (Ehrlichman notes, September 7, 1972).

Once the election was over, the president had little interest in monetary policy. He had won decisively. The benefits of expansion helped; the costs were in the future. He shifted attention to the budget, impounding spending on many programs. Also in January 1973, the administration began phase 3 of the controls program despite the 5 percent increase in the GNP deflator for third and fourth quarters 1972.[64] Large increases in prices, especially food prices, began in the winter of 1973 and made phase 3 unpopular. But monetary stimulus in 1972 and annual base money growth of 9 percent in the first half of 1973 added to the problem.[65] By March-April, the president considered alternatives, including a new freeze of prices and wages. Shultz warned that there was no longer much excess capacity, so it would not work as well as phase 1. In April, he told the president that "Burns did the job before the election, and we're paying some price now" (Ehrlichman notes, April 5, 1973). Burns, for his part, believed that firms and unions expected inflation to continue, so money growth had to remain high (Wells, 1994, 99). Incomes policy had to change these anticipations.

For the year 1973, the GNP deflator rose 8.3 percent, fourth quarter to fourth quarter. Consumer prices accelerated throughout the year; the twelve-month moving average rose from 3.4 percent in December 1972 to 8.4 percent in December 1973. Growth of annual average hourly earnings declined from 8.1 percent in December 1972 to 6.3 percent in December 1973; real wages fell and dissatisfaction rose.

The presidential tape recordings and letters and the Ehrlichman notes

64. Herbert Stein sent a memo to the president on January 8, 1973, to tell him that wholesale prices of farm products increased in December by the largest percentage in 25 years. For the year 1973, producer prices of farm products rose 41 percent. Stein suggested some specific measures—sell agricultural stocks—to slow the rate of increase (memo, Stein to the president, Nixon papers, January 8, 1973).

65. At a breakfast in the White House, Chairman Wilbur Mills of the House Ways and Means Committee chided Burns because the "Fed did everything to help in the election" (Ehrlichman notes, January 9, 1973). Democrats did not criticize the expansive policy before the election. Wells (1994, 101) quotes Walter Heller and Senator William Proxmire as arguing that the economy was far from full employment in 1972, so there was no risk of inflation.

leave little doubt that President Nixon urged Burns to accelerate money to aid his election and that Burns agreed. There are two alternative explanations, however, that cast Burns in a more favorable light.

One alternative attributes the very expansive 1972 policy to the conflict of interest that Burns faced as chairman of both the Board of Governors and the Committee on Interest and Dividends (CID). The argument is that Burns wanted to avoid congressional action to put controls on interest rates. By letting money grow rapidly, the Federal Reserve kept market rates from rising and avoided interest rate controls.

This explanation has two problems. First, the 1972 FOMC and Board minutes contain few references to the CID. If it was a serious conflict, Burns would have used it to support monetary expansion. Most members of FOMC would likely have supported expansion if required to prevent surrender of monetary policy to a control board. Second, during the period that most concerned the president—fourth quarter 1971 and first quarter 1972—the federal funds rate remained below its August 1971 average. In fact, it did not regain that average until December, after the election. The banks' prime rate showed the same pattern. There is no sign of a surge in the prime rate that the Federal Reserve or the CID had to counter. Open market rates are more responsive to market pressures. Ten-year constant maturity Treasury bonds do not show a sustained increase until August or September, and these yields did not pass their August 15, 1971, level until May 1973.

The second alternative was suggested earlier. Congress and most FOMC members wanted to reduce the unemployment rate. Many believed that the prevailing rate was far above the 4 percent level that they wanted to reach. Burns shared this belief and it fit well with his desire to help the president gain reelection.

### *The Directive*

Previous efforts to control money growth were ineffectual and produced general dissatisfaction. Burns again asked the Committee on the Directive to suggest changes. The committee's third report again recommended a system of targets and indicators (Brunner and Meltzer, 1967). The FOMC would use the staff forecasts and their judgment to set paths for final objectives, inflation and output growth, then relate those paths to an intermediate objective or indicator variable such as money growth. To reach money growth, the FOMC could use as an operating target reserves or money market conditions, but the Committee on the Directive favored a measure of reserves called reserves against private deposits. This measure excluded reserves against volatile government and interbank deposits.

The committee—Governor Maisel and Presidents Morris (Boston) and Swan (San Francisco)—wanted to (1) extend the time period over which the FOMC sets its objectives, (2) permit corrections as new information arrived, (3) issue more explicit operating instructions, (4) improve control of the monetary aggregates, and (5) allow money market variables such as the federal funds rate to fluctuate more widely (Third Report of the Committee on the Directive, Federal Reserve Bank of New York, Archives, Box T10282, FOMC 70–78, January 17, 1972). The proposed directive would instruct the manager to target reserves subject to a ±100 basis point deviation around the expected change in the federal funds rate.

The committee put the burden on the staff to estimate money demand and supply functions to relate interest rates and money in a way that was compatible with the output and inflation objectives.[66] The report recognized that the operating target (or "handle" as the FOMC called it in its discussion) could be reserves or an interest rate. It chose a reserve measure because it concluded that demand for money was more variable and less predictable than supply. Anticipating the New York response, the report said that the market would learn quickly that every change in the federal funds rate was not a policy change, and it would adapt to the new regime. No one suggested announcing the change to speed the adjustment, or to explain it to people whose decisions required judgments about policy actions and their consequences.

The New York trading desk responded to the proposal by making its own proposal after explaining its opposition to reserve targeting. Its response put the benefit to market participants ahead of responsibility to control inflation. The main complaint was that the federal funds rate (and money market conditions) would fluctuate over a much wider range and that many of the changes would be capricious, the result of random changes in reserves. The desk argued correctly that it was "the fallibility of projections that is the problem" ("Reserve Targets," Alan Holmes to the FOMC, Board Records, January 19, 1972, 6). Holmes pointed to sizeable changes in float and argued that it helped the market if the desk offset these changes by changing reserves to keep the funds rate unchanged. "Frequent and violent fluctuations in the funds rate . . . would no longer provide much of a clue as to nonborrowed reserve levels" (ibid., 7).

The FOMC discussed the report at a special meeting on February 14. Maisel's opening remarks emphasized four points.

66. The New York bank's copy of the report has penciled comments: impossible, very difficult, or too much to expect next to these staff assignments. Despite the choice of controlling reserves and money, the report did not suggest improving control by changing from lagged to contemporary reserve requirements. The System repeated this error in 1979–82.

> First, the FOMC did not have a clear enough picture of the relationship between changes in operating variables . . . and changes in the intermediate monetary variables. Second, there was insufficient understanding of the relationship between changes in the intermediate variables and changes in the economy . . . Third, there tended to be insufficient discussion of developments with respect to the demand for money. . . . Finally, the time period on which the Committee focused in its policy deliberations was often too short. When the Committee set its targets for intermediate variables for only a month or two ahead, it was dealing with a period in which current operations could not have much effect; and it was not taking into account the longer-run implications of its decisions. (FOMC Minutes, February 14, 1972, 5).

This was a very damning statement about an organization that was nearly sixty years old. The claim, especially the last one, was that their procedures were inadequate to achieve their objectives. And to leave no doubt about his intention, Maisel soon added: "It was the Open Market Committee's practice to try to achieve its objectives for the intermediate monetary variables by calling for gradual changes in the Federal funds rate from meeting to meeting. But that particular control mechanism was a poor one" (ibid.).

The two other members of the directive committee agreed. The only suggestion by Frank Morris called for a narrower band on the funds rate than the ±100 basis points in the committee's report. Neither president softened the criticism of FOMC procedures and accomplishments. The staff agreed that policy could be conducted more effectively using a reserve target.

The manager, Alan Holmes, described the desk as "less than wildly enthusiastic about shifting to a reserve target" (ibid., 10). He expressed concerns about how it would work in practice and was skeptical about the quality of forecasts of the real economy, projections of the monetary aggregates and reserves. He gave as an example the January 1972 experience. The desk thought it had exceeded the projected growth rate set by the FOMC, but it found that it was well below the projection when it used the new seasonal adjustment factors. "The revision of the 1971 monthly growth rates for total and nonborrowed reserves, which ranged up to 10 percentage points for individual months, had quite disturbing implications for the implementation of reserve targets" (ibid., 12). One part of the manager's problem was to distinguish persistent and permanent changes. The directive committee gave insufficient attention to this issue. The manager smoothed transitory changes such as float by keeping a constant interest rate and absorbing or providing reserves. A reserve target removed this solution but did not provide another. Hence interest rates in the short term would change over a wider range. But the manager's procedure did not distinguish permanent or persistent changes in demand.

These, and other issues about operations in practice, returned again in 1979–82, when the System adopted a nonborrowed reserve target. A particularly important issue required an FOMC decision about how much variability in the federal funds rate they would accept to damp fluctuations in their reserve measure. Although not discussed explicitly, the underlying issue required some decision about how to separate temporary and persistent changes and how much of each to offset. That problem remains.

A related measurement issue received more attention but was not resolved satisfactorily. Some members thought the permitted inter-meeting change in the federal funds rate should be narrower than the Committee on the Directive proposed, but none of these suggestions commented on what this would do to monetary control.

A second major unresolved issue was the time span over which the FOMC kept monetary aggregates on the desired path. Maisel stressed the need for looking and acting over a longer period than the time between meetings. The FOMC could make adjustments at each meeting, but the path would remain unchanged until new information suggested the need for change. This would shift the FOMC's attention to the longer-term effects of its actions. The manager and several of the members found it difficult to accept this proposal.

New York did not accept it. Hayes argued that Maisel had not provided evidence that the committee proposal would improve control. He then denied that money growth mattered. "It had been nowhere demonstrated that total or nonborrowed reserves had any strong or direct effects on the ultimate goals for the economy" (ibid., 21). He ended with a forceful statement of the New York view—the FOMC should set some broad objectives, propose some intermediate targets for the aggregates and interest rates, and leave discretion to the manager about how to trade off in the markets. "Given the vagaries of projections, and the after-the-fact revisions, it seemed to him a misguided effort for the members of the Committee to attempt to provide detailed guidance four or five weeks in advance for the specific reserve operations that might best serve the underlying objectives" (ibid., 22–23).

Others raised points that had to be resolved. Partee recognized that lagged reserve accounting and lagged effects of prior changes in interest rates would hinder the manager's efforts to hit a reserve target. As noted in chapter 4, lagged reserve accounting made precise control infeasible. Accurate seasonal adjustment would also prove difficult (ibid., 16–17). Brimmer asked about even keel operations and management of the Treasury account (ibid., 30–31). Both he and Daane opposed the change. Daane called the proposal "utopian" (ibid., 34). Bruce MacLaury (Minneapolis) also opposed the change, but in a perceptive statement he recognized that some thought "the members were not psychologically prepared to call for changes in interest rates of the size required to achieve the desired growth rates in the monetary aggregates, but they would permit such changes to occur if they could be described simply as a by-product of the Committee's pursuit of a reserve target" (ibid., 39).[67]

Most members took a stand. At least ten favored some steps—modest in some cases—in the direction urged by the Maisel committee. Five opposed, including Brimmer, Daane, and Hayes. They chose to stay with the existing procedures, perhaps allowing wider fluctuations in interest rates but retaining an interest rate target. Burns's summary called for a range for the growth of reserves, a band less than the 200 basis points favored by the directive committee for fluctuations in the federal funds rate, orderly adjustment of the federal funds rate within the band, and judgment by the manager to decide whether the reserve and funds rate targets would achieve the intermediate objectives for growth of $M_1$, $M_2$, and bank credit.

Burns described his summary as an intermediate step (ibid., 48). It did not shift the focus from the money market to longer-term objectives, as the Maisel committee had urged, and it did not propose a procedure for concentrating on the longer-term, persistent pressures for inflation or recession. Another opportunity was wasted. This was unfortunate since Maisel, the principal spokesman for changes, soon afterward completed his term and left the System.[68]

Discussion of monetary control brought renewed interest in how it would work and what to expect. A staff memo reported the results of a computer simulation to study the effect of variability in money growth.

67. This argument also returned in 1979 when the System again decided to gain more control of money growth. Supporting the report, Frank Morris used 1968 as an example of a money market directive leading the FOMC to resist a rise in interest rates, thereby supplying "more reserves than any member would have thought desirable at the time" (FOMC Minutes, February 14, 1972, 44). His concern was that without a reserve target, the same result would occur in 1972.

68. The following is Governor Brimmer's description of the presidents at about this time. "All of them (with the exception of St. Louis) remain highly eclectic and pragmatic. . . . and show no signs of being led astray by simple prescriptions" (memo, William Gibson to Herbert Stein, Nixon papers, White House Central Files, Herbert Stein Correspondence, January 3, 1972, 2). This was not a group inclined to accept rule-like procedures.

Using a 6 percent annual $M_1$ growth rate achieved at a steady rate and at 10 percent for two quarters and 2 percent for two quarters, the study found that "economic behavior is essentially the same whether money grows at a constant rate or whether money fluctuates around that rate for one or two quarters" (memo, James Pierce to Axilrod, Burns papers, Box B_B114, February 2, 1972, 1). Deviation from path lasting three or four quarters had more sizeable effects.

Chairman Burns asked the staff to "comment on the deficiencies of adopting a fixed rule guiding monetary growth" (memo, Partee to Burns, Burns papers, Box B_B114, Feb. 3, 1972). The response brought out three issues that divided the System and its critics over a fixed money growth rule and discretionary action. First, proponents of a fixed rule wanted the Federal Reserve to focus on medium- to long-term responses. The Federal Reserve countered that the demand for money could change permanently, so the rule would not produce the predicted stability. Second, the Federal Reserve put much greater weight on short-term changes and the need to adjust to them. The critics claimed that if the System did not act, the market would. Third, the System tried to smooth the economy counter-cyclically. The critics claimed that monetary policy was often procyclical, a source of instability.

Partee's memo discussed policy at or near turning points in economic activity. His conclusion was that policy was bad or procyclical at four, good or counter-cyclical at four, and fair at one. Three of the four "bad" cases were the recessions starting in 1948, 1953, and 1957. A few months later, William Poole revisited the issue. After examining trends and deviations from trend, he concluded that "a substantial and relatively prolonged drop in money growth preceded every postwar business cycle peak" (memo, Poole to Partee, Burns papers, Box B_B81, November 20, 1972, 3). Policy was procyclical.

The staff later evaluated experience using a reserve target (memo, Axilrod, Pierce, and Wendel to FOMC, Board Records, June 8, 1973). It concluded that the evidence was "mixed" (ibid., 2). Reserve targets have been "helpful," even allowing for constraints to respond to money market conditions, Treasury finance, and the like. Problems arose with monetary control however, when the multiplier relating reserves to money shifted. The degree "to which RPDs [reserves against private deposits] are helpful is enhanced if the RPD target range is narrow" (ibid., 2). This required larger changes in the federal funds rate.

The 1972 experience was a forerunner of the 1979–82 experience. Regrettably, the FOMC did not learn from the earlier experience how to improve monetary control. They did not introduce procedural changes such as contemporary reserve accounting or develop techniques for estimating the multiplier such as those later developed in Rasche and Johannes (1987).[69]

## *Policy Failures*

Under pressure from President Nixon to increase the money growth rate in early 1972, Burns considered reducing reserve requirement ratios in early January. The Board took no action at the time. Soon after it considered a structural change in reserve requirement ratios to recognize that growth of suburbs made the distinction between country and reserve city banks less useful and often inequitable. And the perennial issue of System membership remained and even increased as inflation raised the cost of holding non-interest-bearing reserves.

Legal issues had often blocked change. The Banking Committees of Congress opposed changes that favored city banks over country banks. The staff in Reserve Bank Operations found a way around Congress; they proposed to amend regulation D by redefining a reserve city to include "all those cities or localities that contain a bank with net demand deposits of over $200 million" (Board Minutes, February 29, 1972, 8). This would avoid a request for congressional action but not the scrutiny of its members. Country banks would have lower reserve requirements than reserve city banks as before. Once a bank reached $200 million in deposits, it would become a reserve city bank; its reserve requirements would increase without Board action.

Discussion showed how the role of reserve requirements had changed. Initially they recognized geographical differences and the practice, developed under the National Banking Act, for country banks to hold reserves at city correspondents—hence the name reserve city banks. One initial purpose of the Federal Reserve System was to pool and centralize reserves. Increased speed of transportation and communication facilitated pooling at Federal Reserve Banks. The main reasons for differential reserve requirements became political pressure, membership, and a payment for authorization to issue deposits. The Board favored country banks to encourage membership and respond to pressures from Congress.

The proposed reduction in reserve requirement ratios would release reserves. With a fixed interest rate, the System would sell bills and ab-

69. Charles Goodhart (1984) later formulated Goodhart's law to explain why control of a target was unsuccessful. The point was that once the central bank used an empirical relation to develop a target, the relationship changed. Market participants would change their behavior. This would not be true if the goal, say price stability, was clear. Countries using inflation targets have not faced the problem described by Goodhart.

**Table 6.7** Reserve Requirement Ratios, November 1972: Size of Net Demand Deposits ($ millions) (row 1) and Ratios (percent) (row 2)

| 0.2–2 | 2–10 | 10–100 | 100–400 | Over 400 |
|---|---|---|---|---|
| 8 | 10 | 12 | 13 | 17½ |

Source: Board of Governors (1981, 39).

sorb the reserves. With a total or nonborrowed reserve target, the manager would withdraw the newly released reserves also. Nevertheless, the Board wanted to counter the release. It decided to recognize the faster speed of check collection by amending regulation J to require payment of checks on the day they were presented instead of delaying for a day. This reduced "reserve availability credit" and float. Since float was an interest-free loan to the banks that received credit for reserves due, the move reduced bank reserves.[70] Reducing float reduced the monetary base and permitted the Board to show that the change in reserve requirement ratios had not eased monetary policy.[71] After further study by the staff, the Board announced both changes on March 27 as proposals for comment.

The change hurt non-member banks. They did not get a reduction in reserve requirements, but they lost the interest-free loan. Many were members of the Independent Bankers Association. The association demanded a public hearing. When the Board denied the hearing, it offered "informal consultation," but the association threatened to sue, claiming loss of wealth by its members without due process. The Board, citing statutes, replied that it was within its regulatory authority. Efforts to get an injunction failed, but the Board delayed the regulations until the court decided.

On November 9, 1972, the new system became effective. Table 6.7 shows the new requirements when fully implemented effective November 16. The Board modified its original proposal by creating more size categories, and it offered to lend to non-member banks, either directly or through commercial banks. The new ratios replaced the prevailing ratios of 17 percent on the first $5 million of deposits and 17.5 percent thereafter for reserve city banks. For country banks, the ratios had been 12.5 percent to $5 million and 13 percent thereafter. Minimum and maximum ratios

70. The System counted deposits (and money) as measured by bank balance sheets, not customer balance sheets. Reserves were assessed on collected items. By reducing the time span, banks lost a day of interest-free loan.

71. It is unclear why Board members considered "easing" a problem. At the time, most favored an easier policy. The press release announcing the two changes recognized that "open market operations would be adapted as needed . . . to neutralize the effects on monetary policy" ("Reserve Requirements," Board Minutes, March 27, 1972, 3). One possible reason is that some members of Congress would object to reducing government revenue.

remained 10 and 22 percent for demand deposits at reserve city banks and 7 and 14 percent for country banks.

On July 19, 1973, the Board raised reserve requirement ratios on demand deposits by 0.5 percentage points for all deposits over $2 million. Small banks continued to pay 8 percent up to $2 million.

The Board had put 10 percent reserve requirements on euro-dollar deposits in 1969. The next year, it raised the ratio to 20 percent. In 1972, the Board lowered the requirement ratio to 10 percent.

Under procedures agreed upon on February 14, the FOMC set a target growth rate of reserves against private deposits. Burns proposed 6 to 10 percent at the February 15 meeting. Second, he proposed the federal funds range of 2.75 to 3.75 percent as a constraint. Third, he set the quarterly average growth of $M_1$ at 7 to 8 percent and 12 percent for $M_2$. Fourth, if the targets were not being met or were incompatible, the manager would notify the chairman, who would decide whether to call a special meeting.

Burns and Hayes disagreed at every meeting. Hayes did not like reserve targets, and he wanted the federal funds rate to rise faster than it had. At times, Daane, Brimmer or MacLaury (Minnesota) joined him. But Hayes did not dissent after February. The only dissent was Coldwell (Dallas) in July; he expressed concern about reserve and money growth in the light of fiscal expansion and international concerns. As discussed earlier, this followed the British decision to float the pound, the pressure on the United States to abandon the Smithsonian agreement, and the special meeting of FOMC to decide on reactivation of the swap lines to reduce market pressure on the exchange rate.

Burns repeatedly reminded Hayes that their objective was reserve growth, not the funds rate. By midsummer, several members praised the experiment as a success. Gene Leonard (St. Louis) referred to the praise the System received in the press (FOMC Minutes, July 18, 1972, 29). And Robertson mentioned "the success that had been achieved . . . over the past six months," although he attributed much of the achievement to chance (ibid., 58). But Hayes, looking ahead, saw three "unfavorable elements . . . excessive fiscal stimulus, the price situation, and the situation in international financial markets" (ibid., 48). Burns replied that "it would be most unfortunate to drop an experiment which thus far had been working quite well" (ibid., 49).[72] His evidence was the recovery, not the problem of future

72. To control spending growth, President Nixon "impounded" spending approved by Congress. Other presidents had impounded but never to the same extent. These actions angered many in Congress, who saw the action as an increase in executive power over spending and a reduction in their favorite projects. In 1974, Congress passed the Impound-

inflation. He pointed to new housing starts, on their way to a record year and to real GNP growth.

In September, with the economy growing strongly, Brimmer and Hayes wanted to slow money growth. They did not dissent, but Robertson and MacLaury (Minneapolis) did. With the unemployment rate above 5.5 percent, Mitchell wanted an accommodative (expansive) policy, but Burns wanted slower growth of the monetary aggregates than in past months. The directive noted that new regulations D and J affecting reserves were scheduled to take effect, so they decided to "give more than customary attention to money market conditions, while continuing to avoid marked changes in conditions" (Annual Report, 1972, 171). The federal funds rate remained near 5 percent.

September's renewed emphasis on money market conditions did not end the reserve targeting experiment. The next month Burns tried to institute two changes, one sensible and one not. He told the FOMC that they should set targets for money six months ahead, subject to revision at each meeting. This change was long overdue; it would have forced more consideration of the consequences of their actions and given less attention to transitory changes. The second told the Committee that its "main responsibilities were to set targets and to issue specific operating instructions to the Desk. . . . [H]e did not believe it was desirable for the Committee to engage in lengthy discussions of projection procedures or of the relative merits of the projections made at the Board and the New York Bank" (FOMC Minutes, October 17, 1972, 33–34). If adopted, this would have reduced attention to differences in the medium-term consequences of their actions.

The members rejected both proposals. Brimmer criticized the absence of prior notice to the members. He said "that the projections were needed to provide information on expected outcomes" (ibid., 47). Burns replied that "the key question concerned actual outcomes" (ibid.). The Committee did not agree to set a six-month target, but Burns got agreement that 7 percent growth of reserves and $M_2$ and 6 percent growth of $M_1$ would be reasonable for the fourth and first quarters. Actual $M_1$ and $M_2$ growth averaged 6 and 9.5 percent mainly because both growth rates slowed markedly in February and March 1973. Fourth-quarter money growth was far above the target.

In November, Hayes warned that the economy was moving up strongly.

---

ment Control Act of 1974. Among other changes, the act limited the president's use of impoundment. However, the Nixon administration also proposed revenue sharing with the states under which the states received transfers and had no incentive to restrict demand for transfers.

He urged caution but not immediate action. In November and December, the FOMC set its six-month targets for $M_1$ growth at 6 or 5 to 6 percent.[73]

Revised regulations D and J became effective on November 9. The uncertainty surrounding the effect of these changes may have contributed to a surge in member bank borrowing. Between October and December, monthly average borrowing almost doubled, from $550 million to $1.05 billion. It continued to increase, so the entire change was not just a transitory response to regulation. By March 1973, borrowing reached $1.8 billion with free reserves at −$1.5 billion. The federal funds rate rose from 5 to 7 percent in the same period, an unusually large move at the time. The GNP deflator increased at a 5.2 percent annual rate in the fourth quarter.

Economic expansion brought substantial increases in real wages and incomes generally. President Nixon won reelection in a landslide; he carried all states but Massachusetts and the District of Columbia with 60 percent of the vote nationally. This was the peak of his economic and political success. The president celebrated his victory by refusing to spend large sums that Congress appropriated and by sending Congress a 1974 budget with a $14 billion reduction in spending. Real spending would decline. And with the election finished, the wage and price panels ended, replaced by voluntary compliance monitored by the Cost of Living Council.

Burns led the Committee on Interest and Dividends to a solution of their regulatory problem. As often with price controls, political concerns became important. The Committee voted to split the prime rate. On loans up to $350,000 to farmers and small business, lenders had to keep the interest rate below market rates. Although continually monitored, large borrowers paid close attention to the market rate.

As the administration began to loosen price and wage controls, the inflationary outbreak surprised them. By March 1973, annualized consumer price increases reached 4.6 percent led by a 75 percent annual rate of increase in meat prices. The GNP deflator rose 6 percent (annual rate) in the first quarter. The surge in inflation during the winter came from the expansive 1972 policy actions, the loosening of controls, and the shock to food prices from small grain harvests in the United States, the Soviet Union, and elsewhere. The Soviets replaced part of their poor harvest by buying in the United States.

73. At the November meeting, Burns mentioned that the Committee on Interest and Dividends had taken "informal action" on the prime rate and that it "might take further actions" on administered rates (FOMC Minutes, November 20–21, 1972, 98). The Committee delayed the increase in the prime rate to 6 percent until December 27. With market rates much higher, Burns did not say what economic effect he expected. Perhaps the move was entirely political to satisfy congressional populists.

President Nixon wanted action. Criticism of the administration from members of Congress and the public demanded action. Weakened by the Watergate scandals and mindful of the popular response to price controls in 1971, the president rejected his advisers' warnings that price control would not be effective at that time. Inflation was rising, not falling as in 1971. Even John Connally, called back to advise, opposed a new freeze (Matusow, 1998, 230). Not Burns. He urged the president to tighten controls to show the public that the president shared their concerns (Wells, 1994, 115). On June 13, 1973, the president, in a bid for political support, announced phase 4, a sixty-day freeze of prices but not wages. Again, he exempted agricultural prices though they were a main source of price level changes. For a man who professed to abhor price controls, the president seemed eager to use them if they served his purpose.

The freeze did not stop the rise in prices. Controls on wholesale and retail food prices, with agricultural prices uncontrolled, quickly caused shortages. Public reaction was negative. After thirty-five days, the president ended the freeze early.[74] The combination of this one-time price level effect, an increase in oil prices later in the year, and the inflation generated by growing aggregate demand brought measured rates of consumer price increases to 8.4 percent by December 1973 and above 10 percent in 1974. Expected inflation in the Survey of Professional Forecasters rose steadily in 1973 and 1974. Long-term interest rates began to rise.

The rise in short-term interest rates in the first eight months of 1973 is extraordinary, but so was the rise in reported inflation. The GNP deflator rose from an annualized 5.2 percent rate of increase in fourth quarter 1972 to 8.4 percent in third quarter 1973. The twelve-month moving average rate of increase in consumer prices doubled from December to August, rising from 3.6 to 7.2 percent. Data suggest that the public treated most of the price increase as a one-time rise. Ten-year constant maturity Treasury yields rose one percentage point, but Treasury bill rates rose from 5 to 8 percent. Adjusted for inflation, bill yields remained about unchanged and ten-year rates fell. The real federal funds rate rose.[75]

74. Matusow (1998, 222–32) provides a succinct account of prices and the second freeze. Oil prices remained controlled until 1981. Different regulation of retail and producer prices created shortages and long lines at gas stations.

75. The eight-month period is troubling for those who use the unemployment rate to predict the inflation rate. The unemployment rate declined only 0.4 percentage points to 4.8 percent between December and August. Measured inflation rose 3 percentage points. Growth of the monetary base increased one percentage point to 9.3 percent. Growth rates of $M_1$ and $M_2$ fell. Since much of the record increase in reported inflation was a one-time change in the price level from the grain harvest and other one-time changes, it had limited effect on employment and long-term interest rates.

The FOMC saw its task as control of reserve and money growth. It acted aggressively by its previous standards but, as the data show, it was not aggressive enough. Although member bank borrowing rose to $2 billion, the largest borrowing since 1921, the discount rate rose to only 7.5 percent, three percentage points less than the federal funds rate in August 1973. The banks' prime rate for large borrowers soon thereafter reached 10 percent. Throughout this period, banks could borrow at the discount window and relend in the federal funds market. The reserve banks tried to prevent this operation with some success, but borrowing did not decline until September.

Judged by the traditional measures—member bank borrowing, free reserves, and the federal funds rate—1973 is one of the most aggressive periods of restraint in Federal Reserve history to that time. The FOMC repeatedly raised the federal funds rate to keep growth of reserves against private deposits within the range it selected based on staff estimates of money growth. Yet the period has to be judged as a policy failure. The inflation rate continued to rise.

Several factors contributed to the failure. First was the operating procedure. The staff estimated the growth of reserves and the level or range of the federal funds rate consistent with desired growth of money. Inaccuracy was a problem throughout. Several times, the FOMC had to meet between meetings to increase the band on the federal funds rate. Although the FOMC remained committed to controlling reserve and money growth, subject to a money market constraint, the constraint frequently restricted policy action until it was raised. The result was that the manager maintained the federal funds rate and exceeded the reserve target.

For example, at its May 15 meeting, the FOMC set the desired growth rate of reserves against private deposits (RPDs) at "9 to 11 percent while continuing to avoid marked changes in money market conditions" (Annual Report, 1973, 169). RPDs rose at a faster than expected rate, despite an increase in the federal funds rate. The FOMC met twice between meetings to raise the permitted level of the funds rate. Instead of remaining unchanged, the federal funds rate rose from 7.75 to 8.5 percent. It was not enough. At the June 18–19 meeting, the FOMC changed planned RPD growth to 8 to 11.5 percent and permitted the federal funds rate "to vary somewhat more . . . than had been contemplated at other recent meetings" (ibid., 175). But the constraint continued to bind; RPDs rose at more than an 11.5 percent rate, and the FOMC voted to let the funds rate rise more than it had planned. No one dissented until the July 17 meeting, when Darryl Francis (St. Louis) agreed with the committee's objectives but said "the objectives would not be achieved because of the constraint on money market conditions" (ibid., 186). He was soon proved correct. On August 3, there was another inter-meeting increase in the funds rate. Francis dissented again, for the same reason, at the next meeting, August 21, 1973.

Second, throughout the Great Inflation the Board's staff interpreted errors in forecasting money growth as evidence of shifts in the demand for money, not as random shifts in supply or errors in their models of money supply growth. This permitted them to excuse their errors as unpredictable, random events even when they were repeated month after month as in 1973. The FOMC learned nothing. A related problem occurred in the period from 1979 to 1982, when the FOMC again tried to set a target for unborrowed reserve growth.

Chairman Burns asked the staff to explain why the errors in June and July 1973 were shifts in the demand for money. Its explanation is not reassuring. It started by describing the demand for money as a function of a short-term interest rate and nominal GNP. In the first quarter, GNP and interest rates rose; the model predicted a 6 percent increase in $M_1$ demand. Demand rose much less, so the staff concluded that the demand for money shifted down. "We take the shortfall of actual $M_1$ growth from that predicted from the model as evidence of a downward shift in the money demand function" (memo, Lyle Gramley to Burns, Burns papers, Box B_B80, July 31, 1973). This accepts the demand function as a true representation. The memo acknowledged that Federal Reserve policy could have raised the money growth rate "if the Fed had set out single-mindedly to keep $M_1$ growing at (say) 6 percent. . . . But it would have had to drive down interest rates substantially below actual levels to accomplish this" (ibid.). The writer, Gramley, did not recognize that this is a very different argument from his claim that the demand for money shifted. It attributed the shortfall (and subsequent excess growth) to the constraint on short-term interest rates that altered the growth of RPDs and the supply of money. The same error—explaining all excess or shortfall in money growth as the result of shifts in demand—reappears repeatedly.

A related but distinct error was Charles Partee's argument that easing wage and price controls in January 1973 "might necessitate a somewhat faster rate of monetary growth to finance the desired growth in real output under conditions of greater cost-push inflation than would have prevailed with tighter controls" (FOMC Minutes, January 11, 1973, 70). Here the unwillingness to risk a recession or even slower real growth dominates any concern about higher inflation.[76]

76. At the February 13 meeting, FOMC members learned that the agreement that month to devalue the dollar against gold from $38 to $42.22 an ounce would cause an 11 percent

Third, forecasts underestimated both growth and inflation. In February, the staff forecast that the GNP deflator would increase 4.25 percent in 1973 and that nominal GNP would rise 8.5 percent (FOMC Minutes, February 13, 1973, 144, 163). The actual price and GNP increases, fourth quarter to fourth quarter, were 8.3 and 11.9 percent. Partee did not offer a numerical estimate but forecast that "real GNP would grow at satisfactory but not ebullient rate for the remainder of the year" (ibid., 183–84).[77] The Council of Economic Advisors believed that fears of inflation were exaggerated. "There is still good room for expansion of non-farm output as evidenced by figures on capacity utilization and unemployment rates of adult male workers. We expect a marked change in the food price situation after mid-year" (memo, Stein to the president, Shultz papers, Box 5, March 2, 1973).[78] A few weeks later Stein wrote: "The money value of GNP rose extraordinarily in the first quarter—at an annual rate of about 13 percent. This is almost 30 percent larger than we forecast at the beginning of the year. Most of the increase is in prices, but the increase of real output also surpassed our forecast a little" (memo, Stein to the president, Shultz papers, Box 5, April 17, 1973). He recommended suspension of the investment tax credit and money growth held to 5 to 6 percent.[79]

---

loss on its outstanding swap lines. The administration sent Congress a bill to devalue the dollar to $42.22 per ounce of gold. The bill also gave the president authority to raise tariffs. Burns supported the proposal as necessary (FOMC Minutes, February 13, 1973, 4). Also, the Voluntary Foreign Credit Restraint Program ended.

77. The staff expressed considerable uncertainty about the effectiveness of so-called phase 3 controls. Burns sent the president a copy of the staff analysis. He urged the president to speak publicly about the "enforcement of desired conduct on wages and prices" (Burns to the president, Nixon papers, Box 33, January 29, 1973). He also urged the president to "appeal to the public to reduce its buying" and suggested a "meatless day each week" to bring down meat prices (ibid., 3). His concern was that rising food prices would increase wage demands. Despite higher inflation, average hourly earnings rose less in 1973 than in 1972. For December of each year, the rate of change for that year was 8.1 and 6.3 percent. The reported 1973 inflation rate includes the start of higher oil prices that could not be predicted early in the year.

78. These changes occurred at a time that the dollar was devalued by 10 percent (mid-February). Burns considered the devaluation necessary, but he did not like it. He continued to oppose a floating exchange rate (Wells, 1994, 107). In March the dollar floated. That ended the Smithsonian agreement and the effort to fix the dollar exchange rate. Volcker wrote that "despite his enthusiastic support of fixed exchange rates, he [Burns] seemed . . . to have a kind of blind spot when it came to supporting them with concrete policies" (Volcker and Gyohten, 1992, 104). The Council used a 4 percent unemployment rate as the natural rate, so it overestimated excess capacity (Orphanides, 2002). Pierce (1998, 7) pointed out that the Board's model used to estimate inflation and output did not allow for any effect of money growth until later in the decade.

79. The GNP data showed 8 percent inflation and 6 percent real growth. Consumer expenditure rose at 16 percent annual rate in these early data.

**Table 6.8** Forecast and Actual Inflation, 1973–74 (GNP deflator in percent)

| Date | 73:2 | 73:3 | 73:4 | 74:1 | 74:2 |
|---|---|---|---|---|---|
| Government | 5.5 | 4.0 | 3.6 | 4.3 | 3.5 |
| Average 3 Private Forecasts | 4.1 | 3.6 | 3.6 | 3.8 | 3.2 |
| Reported Inflation | 7.5 | 8.8 | 7.4 | 9.6 | 12.3 |

Source: Stein to the President, Nixon Papers, box 96, May 1, 1973; reported inflation from St. Louis FRED program.

Taking account of the first quarter results, the Council and private forecasters revised their forecasts. Table 6.8 shows that the forecasts by both government and private forecasters were as much as nine percentage points lower than reported inflation. As noted, part of the difference reflects one-time increases in oil and food prices.

Late in March, Partee summarized the staff position. It expected real growth to fall to 4 percent by year-end, and it anticipated that inflation would rise despite slower increases in food prices. He cautioned against a tough anti-inflation policy on the grounds that the FOMC would not persist in lowering inflation. "As unemployment rose, there would be strong social and political pressure for expansive actions, so that the policy would very likely have to be reversed before it succeeded in tempering either the rate of inflation or the underlying sources of inflation" (FOMC Minutes, March 19–20, 1973, 6). He favored 5.5 percent $M_1$ growth.[80]

Robert Black (Richmond) asked a critical question: Should they raise the accepted level of the unemployment rate to 5 from 4 percent? Partee avoided the issue by responding that inflation would continue, according to the model, even at 5 percent unemployment rate (ibid., 28).[81]

In testimony to Congress, Burns gave a different explanation. He explained that "fundamentally, it is the expansion of the money supply over the long run that will be the basic cause of inflation" (quoted in Wells, 1994, 111). Money growth ($M_1$) reached 8.2 percent in first quarter 1973, but Burns did not urge a much more restrictive policy. He told the BIS members that "there is an acute political problem regarding interest rates. Congress and the unions have become quite concerned about interest rates. Congress could unwisely legislate statutory limits on interest rates or

80. The FOMC voted at the March 19–20 meeting to authorize negotiations to increase swap lines with other central banks by up to $6 billion in the aggregate. The swap lines totaled $11.7 billion before the increase.

81. The model used a Phillips curve relating unemployment and inflation. Partee acknowledged that the model had not worked well until they adjusted for "special factors" (FOMC Minutes, March 19–20, 1973, 30). The government did not change its goal for unemployment to 5.1 percent until 1976.

fail to act promptly to approve an extension of the Economic Stabilization Act" [wage and price controls] (ibid.).

At the FOMC meeting, Burns expressed concern about a possible recession by the end of the year. He warned the members that "the Federal Reserve had a history of going to extremes" (FOMC Minutes, March 19–20, 1973, 108). It was now trying to do something it had not done ever before—slow inflation without bringing on recession. He accepted the higher inflation rate and urged the FOMC to accept a pause in restraint. Seven members agreed, but five disagreed. Robertson, Brimmer, and Hayes suggested changes in the ranges that would make Burns's proposal acceptable. The compromise called for the federal funds rate to remain between 6.75 and 7.5 percent, M1 growth at 4 to 7 percent near term, and RPD growth of 12 to 16 percent. This proposal passed unanimously. During the period between meetings, deposits grew more slowly than expected, so the manager let the federal funds rate decline to 7 percent.

Burns's concern about recession was misplaced. Industrial production declined in March, but the decline did not continue. Inflation, not recession, became the problem. Although the federal funds rate was at the highest level ever reached, after adjusting for current or anticipated inflation, the real funds rate was about 3 percent.

The unemployment rate remained in a narrow range around 4.9 percent during the first six months of 1973. Guided by the Phillips curve, the staff described the rise in inflation as "an aberration" resulting from the end of phase 2 controls and dollar devaluation (FOMC Minutes, April 17, 1973, 4–5). They did not anticipate continued inflation at the first quarter rate. The model predicted 4 to 4.5 percent for the next two to three years, based on a 4.5 to 5 percent unemployment rate. In response to a question, Partee agreed that the "tradeoff between unemployment and the rate of advance in prices had become less favorable recently" (ibid., 9). The model forecast could be reconciled with the data only by assuming that the Phillips curve had shifted. He blamed the shift mainly on phase 3.[82]

Brimmer and Balles (San Francisco) said that the 1973 surge in the inflation rate was a lagged response to the monetary and fiscal stimulus in 1972. But $M_1$ and $M_2$ growth slowed in the first quarter and were below the FOMC's objective, so Daane opposed any increase in the federal funds

82. In a statement reminiscent of the 1920s, Robert Black (Richmond) thought that prices were "beyond the control of the Federal Reserve." Partee agreed (FOMC Minutes, April 17, 1973, 10). Statements of this kind remain ambiguous. Was inflation independent of monetary policy, or did it mean that the System would not attempt adequate restriction? Or did Black refer to one-time price level changes?

rate.[83] Hayes agreed with Brimmer and Balles that the System should tighten by lowering the money growth rate, raising the discount rate and the funds rate, and removing remaining regulation Q ceilings. To prevent higher inflation, "firmer wage and price controls were needed . . . [but] controls were not of much use in the absence of appropriate fundamental policies and in the present situation monetary policy was one of the fundamentals" (ibid., 72).

Balles urged the FOMC to consider ways to improve control of money. He suggested controlling nonborrowed reserves and the monetary base (ibid., 75). The FOMC made no changes. After much discussion, it agreed to seek moderate growth in the monetary aggregates. In April, the funds rate remained unchanged, but $M_1$ and $M_2$ growth rose more than the FOMC's desired path of 5 to 5.5 percent.

As market interest rates rose, the prime rate and rates on consumer credit began to increase. Banks raised the prime rate to 6 percent (from 5.25) in December 1972. Early in February, four New York banks raised the rate to 6.25 percent. As head of the Committee on Interest and Dividends (CID), Burns spoke to the bankers and persuaded them to rescind their announcement. Congress had renewal of authority to control prices and wages under consideration, and neither Burns nor the bankers wanted Congress to include interest rates in the bill. By the end of February, however, the 6.25 percent prime rate had become general. CID issued guidelines that permitted banks to increase their lending rates as money markets rates rose, but they were supposed to adjust for the zero rate of interest paid on demand deposits.

Pressed by Congress, especially Congressman Wright Patman, Burns and the CID urged the banks to limit their rate increases. But markets imposed higher marginal costs as open market rates rose. By September 1973, the federal funds rate averaged 10.8 percent, an increase of 5.5 percentage points since December 1972. The prime rate reached 10 percent, an increase of 4 percentage points in the same period.[84] These data suggest a possible modest effect of CID efforts, since the lending rate rose less than the borrowing rate. We do not know how other terms and conditions of

83. The FOMC voted to release the 1967 Minutes after deleting some passages in the discussions of foreign currency.

84. Interest rates on three-month certificates of deposits rose from 5.67 to 10.71 percent in about the same period. In April, Burns asked the president to let him resign from the CID. The conflict of interest that some had foreseen was now apparent to all. The Federal Reserve's standing was hurt by the conflict. The president asked him to stay on, and he remained.

the loans changed, whether banks restricted prime rate loans, or whether borrowers shifted to other markets.

Burns recognized that any success he had in reducing lending rates increased spending and borrowing. He felt powerless to let rates rise, reluctant to hold them down. In April, a Senate bill called for lower interest rates, a rollback of rate increases. The bill failed by only four votes in the Senate (Wells, 1994, 113). The close vote was more than enough to frighten Federal Reserve officials, who were rarely comfortable about relations with Congress. Burns responded by ruling that banks had to split their lending rates. On April 16, the CID established voluntary guidelines for bank interest rates. Farmers and small business with less than $1 million in assets received a lower rate than other borrowers. Two days later, banks raised the prime rate to 6.75 percent.

In the next few months, as inflation rose, the System allowed market interest rates to rise to levels never experienced in the previous sixty years of Federal Reserve history. Although the Board was often hesitant to raise the discount rate, by July it had reached 7 percent, the highest level in Federal Reserve history to that time.[85]

From May through August–September, the System worked to control money growth and inflation. President Nixon worked to control spending growth. The administration called this "the old time religion"—a program to control inflation by traditional means. Nominal budget outlays in 1973 rose 3.2 percent, a real reduction of at least 5 percent. The budget deficit fell from $20 to $15 to $8 billion between 1972 and 1974, and annual $M_1$ growth declined from 8.8 percent in December 1972 to 5.3 percent a year later. It continued to fall. By the end of 1973, industrial production started to fall.

Supplementing fiscal and monetary restraint was the president's effort to end phase 3 by freezing prices, discussed above. The attempt failed. Phase 4 of the controls program replaced it. This was a reworking of phase 2. That also had little effect; the explanation at the time was that the economy was closer to full employment. In fact, the rate of increase in hourly earnings, which Burns considered central to inflation control, rose during the period of controls and phase 4.

At the May FOMC meeting, Partee put the issue squarely. After forecasting that the rate of expansion would slow, he told the committee:

85. One of many examples of hesitation and reluctance to raise the discount rate came in June 1973. On June 25 and 26, the Board disapproved requests for a 7 percent discount rate ostensibly because the request came too soon after the June 8 increase to 6.5 percent. Three days later, June 29, it approved the 7 percent rate. Consumer prices rose 8.2 percent at annual rate that month.

> Inflationary pressures are likely to remain substantial. . . . I do not have much hope that these underlying inflationary forces can be dampened appreciably without profoundly adverse consequences for the economy later on. (FOMC Minutes, May 15–16, 1973, 22)[86]

The Council of Economic Advisers finally recognized that it had to give up the idea that full employment meant a constant 4 percent unemployment rate (Hargrove and Morley, 1984, 399). Part of "the old time religion" was a willingness to accept larger increases in the unemployment rate as a cost of reducing inflation. Some members of the FOMC did not accept that reasoning. At the May meeting, Eastburn (Philadelphia), Black (Richmond), Coldwell (Dallas), Winn (Cleveland), and Daane expressed concern about too much restraint.[87] The GNP deflator rose at an 8.6 percent annual rate that quarter, about the same rate as the CPI.[88]

Instead of protecting the value of money, the May meeting concerned itself with trivia. It considered a proposal to increase the cost to banks of issuing large CDs by increasing the marginal cost of these deposits. The proposal increased reserve requirement ratios for time deposits to 8 percent. This combined the standard 5 percent and a marginal increase of 3 percent for increases in large-denomination CDs and commercial paper above the average amount outstanding for the week ending May 16. The new requirement became effective on June 7. The Board approved the requirement on May 16. At the same meeting, it reduced the reserve requirement for euro-dollars from 20 to 8 percent, the same as large time deposits. In September, the Board increased the marginal reserve requirement ratio to 8 percent, making the effective requirement on new time deposits 11 percent.

The Board also suspended regulation Q ceiling rates on time deposits of

86. Governor Daane reported that the BIS members, especially the Europeans, were eager to control euro-dollar markets. The United States had made euro-dollar holdings subject to reserve requirements. In 1973, they increased the requirements, raising the cost of euro-dollars. See below. Coombs complained that the United States did not intervene to prevent the dollar from falling. All other countries intervened. Coombs never accepted that coordination and intervention could not prevent the readjustment of real exchange rates. Although he recognized that the Watergate scandal reduced the demand to hold dollars, he believed that intervention could offset it.

87. Burns briefed the members about the "political crisis" (Watergate) affecting the country. He warned that it was likely to reduce "confidence." Stein claimed that the president remained active in policy discussions and had taken the lead in pushing for a second freeze and phase 4 (Hargrove and Morley, 1984, 400).

88. Despite concerns about disintermediation and housing, new housing starts remained at a robust annual rate above 2.2 million in the second quarter. The likely source of error was failure to distinguish real and nominal interest rates.

$100,000 or more with initial maturity of ninety days or more. This was the first liberalization of CD rates since ceiling rates were suspended for maturities of less than ninety days in June 1970.

MacLaury (Minneapolis), Francis (St. Louis), and Black (Richmond) pointed out that corporate borrowers would not be deterred by the small increased cost intended by the proposal. They would borrow in other markets. These critics did not favor controlling credit, because they did not think it could work.

The Board, however, was unwilling to take a decisive action, so it resorted to weak or cosmetic actions. On April 4, it sent the first of several letters asking banks to voluntarily restrict loan commitments. The Comptroller and the chairman of the FDIC sent similar letters to their members. On May 21 and 29, the Board sent letters to member banks urging them to voluntarily restrict growth of loans and certificates of deposits in an effort to control inflation. There is no indication that the Board thought about what would happen to the funds that did not go into time deposits or that the bank did not lend. The episode recalls the mistaken attempt to control credit expansion by exhortation in 1929. Despite the warnings they heard, the FOMC did not take decisive action.

The June 1973 FOMC meeting brought out the division between those who favored a more restrictive policy and members more concerned about a possible recession if policy tightened. The FOMC voted for slower growth of the monetary aggregates. It reduced its objective for money growth in the second half from about 5 to 4.5 percent and reduced its near-term objective to a range of 4 to 8 percent. The top of the range for the federal funds rate rose to 9.25 percent.

Several private forecasts expected a recession in late 1973 or early 1974. Lyle Gramley said the staff expected slower growth but not a recession. By the end of the year, the staff expected growth to fall to 3.5 percent.[89] Brimmer asked Partee why they did not expect a recession. Partee replied that they projected an investment boom, an improvement in net exports, and moderate money growth.[90]

Frank Morris (Boston) explained why he thought the System had to

89. Actual growth of GNP fell to 1 percent annual rate in the second quarter and −0.4 in the third. The fourth quarter reached 3.6 percent, as the staff predicted. They did not foresee the weakness in the second and third quarters. The GNP deflator rose 8.6, 8.4, and 10 percent (annual rates) in the second to the fourth quarter.

90. The dollar had depreciated 17 percent from its Bretton Woods value against a weighted average of sixteen foreign currencies. The staff forecast that nominal GNP would rise 7 percent if money rose 5.25 percent. The implicit rise in velocity was close to trend growth at the time (FOMC Minutes, June 18–19, 1973, 21).

reduce money growth modestly. He thought the basic problem was fiscal. A 6 percent unemployment rate would weaken the consensus between the administration and Congress to reduce growth of government spending. Burns agreed. He thought that "to achieve price stability it was necessary to avoid recessions" (FOMC Minutes, June 18–19, 1973, 34).[91]

The FOMC voted in June and July to tighten further, and between meetings it adjusted upward the tolerable level of the funds rate. Despite sharp differences of opinion, recorded votes were unanimous

The FOMC was not oblivious to the increase in current and anticipated inflation. The staff saw "clear and present danger of further overheating." They blamed strong economic growth and "monetary aggregates growing at unacceptably high rates" (FOMC Minutes, July 17, 1973, 43). Burns drew the right conclusion: "The basic reason [for rapid monetary growth] was that the System had been supplying reserves to commercial banks at a very fast rate. The rapid growth of the monetary aggregates was a most disturbing development; if it persisted there would be considerable justice to a charge that the System had fostered the inflation now underway" (ibid., 57–58). He wanted growth of M1 and M2 to slow to 3.75 and 4.75 percent for the second half, with 3.5 to 5.5 percent growth of reserves, but he thought this would require near-term 11 to 13 percent growth of reserves.

The FOMC remained divided. Most members wanted to avoid a recession and to reduce inflation, but they differed on the best way to achieve both objectives and on the weights they gave to each. Citing international as well as domestic concerns, Hayes and Daane wanted to tighten more than most others. Burns supported their position. He was now committed to an anti-inflation policy, and he was able to get majority support.

The economy operated at about 96 percent of capacity in the second quarter. Those who opposed a tighter policy thought the economy would slow. They feared a recession and either explicitly or implicitly preferred higher inflation to recession. Since they did not distinguish between real and nominal interest rates, they expressed concern about the consequences of a federal funds rate above 10 percent. Stephen Axilrod warned them that the funds rate could rise to 15 or 20 percent. Peter Sternlight agreed.

Bucher, MacLaury (Minneapolis), Black (Richmond), Holland, and Sheehan, all relatively new appointees, favored less restraint. Sheehan expressed their position best: "Experience suggested that the Government

91. At the time, the staff's model implied that a 1 percent increase in the unemployment rate would reduce the inflation rate by 0.7 percent within six quarters (FOMC Minutes, June 18–19, 1973, 42). Later experience showed that this estimate was too pessimistic.

could not permit the kind of recession that might serve to bring inflation under control without giving rise to political pressures that would result in a massive Federal Government deficit" (ibid., 95).

To a degree, the System was in the same position as in the pre-Accord period. In the 1940s, it knowingly risked inflation because it did not have political support before the Douglas hearings and the Korean War. Now, it risked higher inflation because Congress, the administration, and most likely the public would respond to a recession by demanding expansive policy actions. Inflation would increase.

The FOMC voted for Burns's six-month target growth rates for the aggregates but eased his near-term target for RPDs and federal funds. Francis (St. Louis) dissented. He agreed with the six-month money targets, but "the desired growth rates would not be achieved as a consequence of the constraint on the federal funds rate to 9 to 10.5 percent" (ibid., 104).

At the August meeting, Burns repeated Francis's message. Failure to control money growth, he said, "fundamentally resulted from a failure to control RPDs" (FOMC Minutes, August 21, 1973, 53). But the federal funds rate did not change, and Francis dissented for the same reason as in July.

To the extent that the FOMC had a long-term strategy, it was to avoid recession. Lyle Gramley, a member of the staff and later a member of the Board, expressed the strategy succinctly:

> The urgent task is to assure that aggregate demand slows somewhat further, and then remains at a moderate pace long enough for the inflationary process of recent years to unwind. But it is equally urgent to accomplish this without precipitating a recession. If economic activity weakens too much next year, the pressures to reopen the monetary spigot would almost certainly become too powerful to resist. (FOMC Minutes, September 18, 1973, 73)

Alas, the staff and the members did not know how to reduce inflation while avoiding recession. They were not alone. The FOMC proposal was very similar to the 1969–70 policy of slowing inflation while letting the unemployment rate rise to 4.5 percent, but no higher. It had not worked. A repeat effort suggests that Gramley (and others) continued to believe that they could manage inflation by keeping the unemployment rate slightly above its erroneously estimated equilibrium value.

On the international side, the trade-weighted dollar depreciated sharply in the spring and summer, falling 30 percent against the mark between January and July. Pressure to intervene rose. Coombs proposed a $5.95 billion increase in swap lines to bring the aggregate to $17.68 billion, an increase of 51 percent. The FOMC approved the increase and gave a subcommittee (Burns, Hayes, and Mitchell) authority to act on its behalf.

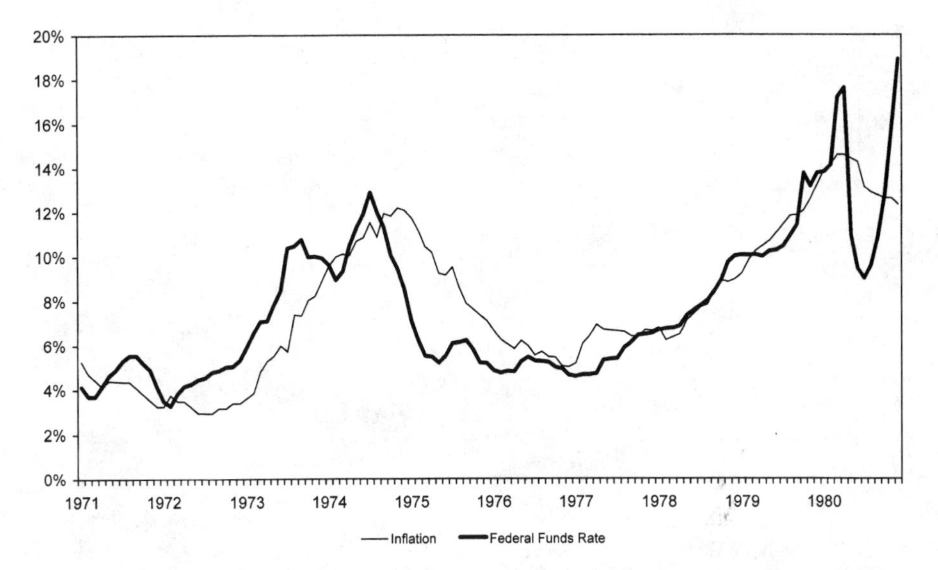


Chart 6.4. Federal funds rate and inflation, 1971–81. Inflation measured as year-over-year CPI.

On July 9, the FOMC held a telephone conference. The dollar had fallen an additional 10 percent against the mark and the franc and by lesser amounts against other currencies. The subcommittee had approved intervention and sharing risks with the Europeans. Only Francis (St. Louis) opposed the interventions. He said that the United States had embargoed grain exports when others wanted to buy grain and failed to make progress in reducing inflation. Hayes, Burns, and Daane supported intervention, claiming that the problem was lack of confidence and concern that the United States did not care about the exchange rate. Following the intervention, the dollar rose.

The federal funds rate reached a local peak in September 1973 at 10.78 percent for the month. Ten-year Treasury bonds peaked at almost 9 percent in August, and twelve-month monetary base growth reached a local peak in July. By year-end 1973 the twelve-month increase in consumer prices reached 8.4 percent, more than 5 percentage points above the December 1972 average. President Nixon decided to follow a less inflationary strategy (Matusow, 1998, 283). Burns received the signal. By March 1974, the federal funds rate started to rise to a new local peak in July at 12.9 percent, almost 4 percentage points above its February value.

Chart 6.4 compares these and later changes in the federal funds rate to the reported rate of increase in consumer prices. Through most of the early 1970s, the funds rate followed the inflation rate and generally is above

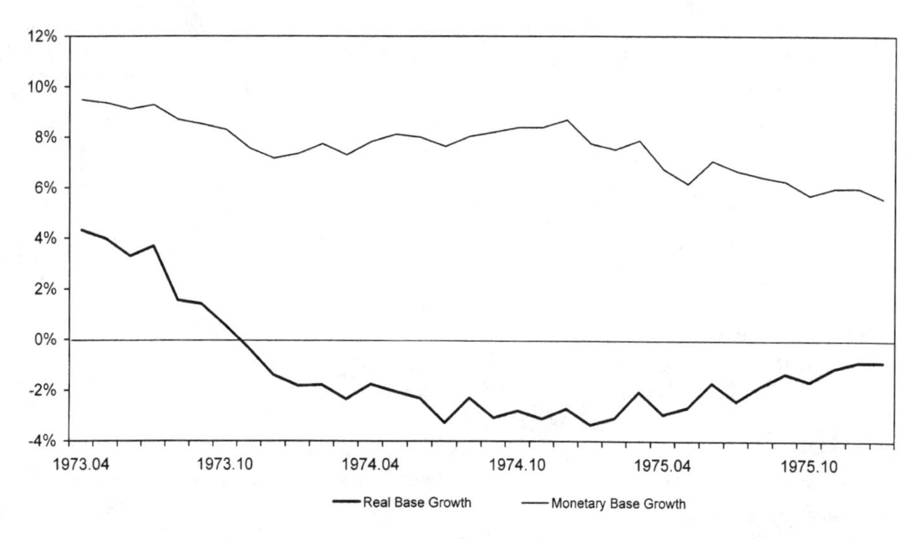


Chart 6.5. Monetary base growth versus real base growth, April 1973–January 1976. Growth measured year-over-year.

the reported inflation rate. By the middle of the decade this was no longer true. The rise in the inflation adjusted (or real) funds rate suggests monetary policy tightened in 1973. Data for growth of the real monetary base gives the same interpretation. Although the funds rate declined beginning in August 1974, growth of the real value of the monetary base, shown in Chart 6.5, did not change direction until early 1975 coincident with the recession trough.

*Discount rates.* Despite many requests for changes, the Board did not approve any discount rate changes in 1972. The discount rate remained at 4.5 percent. Between January and March all the requests asked for lower rates, usually a reduction of 0.25 but sometimes 0.5. Only Philadelphia, St. Louis, and Kansas City made these requests. The Board turned down the requests, in part because borrowing remained low, in part because the Board expected interest rates to rise.

Beginning in September, all the requests asked for increases of 0.25 or 0.5. The reserve banks cited rapid money growth and concerns about inflation. The Board often divided, but there was only one dissent, by Governor Brimmer, on September 1. The Board's expressed reasons for denying the requests included several references to the Committee on Interest and Dividends. Burns urged his colleagues not to increase an "administered rate" (the discount rate) when his committee urged banks to keep their administered rates unchanged. Several members expressed reluctance to use the discount rate to lead market rates.

Burns's argument against discount rate increases is a clear case of the conflict of interest that several feared in 1971, but the conflict lasted only a few months. By December, the elections were over, and opinions had changed. Market rates had increased. The main issue was timing. Burns proposed that the Board wait until mid-January, after the Treasury financing. On January 15, 1973, the Board raised rates by 0.5 to 5 percent. The requests cited concern about the rate of economic expansion.

The Board also approved discount rate increases in February (0.5), March-April (0.25), May (0.25), June (0.5), July (0.5), August (0.5). After the August 14 increase, the discount rate was 7.5 percent, an increase of 2.5 percentage points in little more than half a year. These most unusual actions followed market rates and reported inflation. By August, the federal funds rate was 10.5 percent, consumer prices had increased 7.2 percent in a year, and the ten-year Treasury bond yielded more than 7 percent. The relatively low discount rate acted as a subsidy to member bank borrowing. Borrowing doubled from $1.05 billion in December 1972 to a peak of $2.2 in August 1973. Increased borrowing contributed to base growth. Twelve-month base growth reached 9.3 percent in June, a rate of increase last experienced at the end of World War II. In July, the Board increased regulation Q ceiling rates by amounts from 0.25 to 0.75, depending on the maturity.

Effective April 19, 1973, the Board revised regulation A on discounting by member banks. It approved longer-term borrowing to meet seasonal needs. Banks without access to national money markets, mainly small banks, could borrow for periods up to ninety days and could renew the loan for the season. The amendment also reaffirmed the System's commitment to lend in emergency or unusual circumstances.

*Margin requirements.* From December 1971 to April 1972, the Standard & Poor's index of stock prices rose 17 percent. At a meeting early in April, the staff expressed concern about the speculative character of the increase. It urged the Board to consider an increase in margin requirements. The staff memo noted that since the reduction of margin requirements from 65 to 55 percent in December 1971, credit extended by brokers had increased 35 percent and the number of margin accounts had increased by 60,000. The Board took no action.

The S&P index fell in May, but stock market credit rose. The Board divided over whether there was a problem. Burns thought that stock market credit had not grown out of line with other credit, but Governor Sheehan was "shocked" by the increase and wanted to increase margin requirements (Board Minutes, June 7, 1972, 4). Both Sheehan and Robertson wanted to raise margin requirements to 70 percent (from 55). Mitchell and

Daane favored 65 percent. Burns favored the smaller increase but deferred action to consult the SEC and the Price Commission.[92]

Part of the System's problem arose from money illusion. Neither the staff nor the members distinguished real and nominal changes. The S&P index passed its 1968 peak in nominal value in March 1972. Consumer prices increased almost 20 percent in the interval, so the real value of stock prices remained well below values at the start of the inflation. The non-indexation of tax rates and depreciation explains much of the loss in real value (Feldstein, 1982).

Between June and November, margin credit increased about 3.5 percent, the S&P index by 6.5 percent. A majority of the Board—Mitchell, Daane, Bucher, and Brimmer—opposed a change in margin requirements at that time. Brimmer especially noted that there was no evidence of a significant increase in stock market credit. "In his opinion, changes in margin requirements should not be geared to the behavior of stock prices—but the actual use of stock market credit to purchase or carry securities" (Board Minutes, November 11, 1972, 11). He might have added that the 1934 Securities and Exchange Act said the same.

Burns wanted an increase. He spoke to SEC Chairman William Casey, who warned that some brokerage firms had financial problems and that an increase in margin requirements might harm them by reducing trading volume. Nevertheless, Burns said he favored "a preventive approach" and wanted to show that the System was acting against inflation. Robertson agreed. Acting now could reduce expectations of inflation. Neither explained how that would work or why they did not act more directly. Credit to purchase shares could be obtained in many ways.

With Brimmer dissenting, the Board approved an increase in margin requirements from 55 to 65 percent effective November 24. Stock prices reached a peak in December 1972 and continued to fall until December 1974. At that point, the S&P index was back to its March 1963 nominal value. The decline owed much more to inflation, the oil price shock, uncertainty about the functioning of government resulting from the Watergate scandals, and the resignation of the president in August 1974.

*Regulation Q.* As market rates rose, the Board relaxed or ended ceilings for large CDs; it did not change the rates on small (below $100,000) CDs

92. "Registered margin credit at broker-dealers and banks" reached a local peak in December 1972; the outstanding balance in May or June 1972 was between 45 and 50 percent higher than a year earlier (Board of Governors, 1981, table 23, 184). The Board's only action at about this time was a technical adjustment to the rule permitting substitution of securities in margin account collateral.

until July 5, 1972. On July 5, the Board approved increases of 0.5 to 0.75 on passbook saving accounts and consumer CDs. Also, it removed the ceiling rate for four-year CDs with a $1000 minimum denomination. At the time, deregulated six-month large negotiable CDs paid 9 to 10 percent.

The new certificates proved attractive. Three weeks later, the Board restricted issuance of four-year certificates to 5 percent of a bank's total deposits. Certificates above the limit could receive no more than 6.5 percent interest. Effective November 1, the Board removed the 5 percent limit but placed an interest rate ceiling of 7.25 percent. The other banking agencies adopted the same restriction.

*Membership.* The System tried several times in its history to require membership. This was a major issue for Eccles in the 1930s. It resurfaced in 1972. As interest rates rose, the cost of holding reserves that earned no interest became burdensome for many banks.

Burns wrote a letter to Herbert Stein decrying recent loss of membership. Between 1960 and 1972, 675 banks had left the System through withdrawal or merger. The System acquired 102 state-chartered banks in this period but 1,483 newly chartered banks elected to remain non-members. Burns recognized the principal reason for loss of members was the increased opportunity cost of holding reserves (letter, Burns to Stein, Nixon papers, WHCF, Box 33, November 15, 1972).

Burns did not request compulsory membership. He offered to permit non-members to borrow at the discount window if they held the System's required reserves. He recognized that the Federal Reserve's obligation as lender of last resort extended beyond its membership to the financial system.

The weak part of his argument was that requiring non-member banks to hold the same reserve requirement ratios "would facilitate the effective implementation of monetary policy" (ibid., 2).[93] Shifts of deposits between member banks with different reserve requirements, between demand and time deposits, or between member and non-member banks had small, mainly transitory, effects on the magnitude of the money stock produced by changes in reserves or base money. The longer-term effect of the relative growth of non-member banks was to reduce the average reserve requirement ratio for the entire monetary system. This change occurred with sufficient regularity that it should not have posed a control problem.

93. A letter from a former senior staff member, David Lindsey, in the mid-1980s showed that the staff recognized that the argument was incorrect, especially when the FOMC controlled the funds rate.

**OTHER ISSUES**

During the years 1971–73, the Treasury, at last, began to auction securities with more than a year until maturity, reducing the importance of even keel. Innovation in banking continued. The Board had to decide what to do about close substitutes for demand deposits such as negotiable orders of withdrawal (NOW accounts) that circumvented interest rate regulations. Financial markets increasingly accepted the challenge of regulation to find ways to legally avoid restrictions. Slowly the Board learned that lawyers and bureaucrats make regulations but markets decide how to circumvent them.

### *Personnel Changes*

Three Board members and four presidents changed in 1971–73, and Peter Sternlight replaced Alan Holmes as manager of the open market account in 1973. Table 6.9 shows the changes in Board members and presidents. Board members especially changed more frequently than in the past. Their real income declined with inflation.

Burns wanted replacements to the Board who would support his positions. His often close relationship with President Nixon gave him more influence on appointments to the Board than Martin had, but his fluctuating relationship with the president limited his influence at times. By May 1973, the majority of the Board owed their positions either to President Nixon or to Burns. This was particularly true of Robert Holland, who had served on Burns's staff. He was the first of several staff members promoted to the Board. None of the new members stayed very long.

Burns used his office, personal standing, and approval power to influence the choice of reserve bank presidents. In the first instance, the reserve bank directors chose the president, but the Board had to approve the choice. Although there is no way to measure his influence, he seems to have been more involved in the choices than either Martin or some of his own successors. One way of increasing his influence was to have the directors submit several names to the Board instead of a single candidate.

### *Delegation of Authority*

Legislation during the 1960s increased the Board's responsibilities. In addition to new regulations affecting consumers, the Board had to decide a greatly increased number of mergers, acquisitions, and holding company actions. The approval or rejection process slowed. By late 1971, half the applications took more than the ninety days of review that the Board had set as a standard for the staff (Board Minutes, January 4, 1972, 3).

A staff memo proposed that the Board delegate to the reserve banks

**Table 6.9** Personnel Changes 1971–73

| BOARD MEMBERS: | NEW | LEAVING | |
|---|---|---|---|
| January 1972 | John E. Sheehan | William Sherrill | Left in 1975 |
| June 1972 | Jeffrey M. Bucher | Sherman Maisel | Left in 1976 |
| May 1973 | Robert Holland | J. L. Robertson | Left in 1976 |
| PRESIDENTS: | | | |
| July 1971 | Bruce MacLaury | Hugh Galusha | Minneapolis |
| September 1971 | Willis Winn | W. Braddock Hickman | Cleveland |
| September 1972 | John Balles | Eliot Swan | San Francisco |
| August 1973 | Robert Black | Aubrey Heflin | Richmond |

authority to approve acquisition of mergers, membership, and acquisition of new banks by holding companies. Its letter to the reserve banks set out some uniform standards to apply. The Board's staff continued to review decisions and supporting documents (letter, Board to Reserve banks, Board Minutes, January 17, 1972). In 1973, the Board broadened the authority of the reserve banks over holding companies.

### *Securities Auctions and Even Keel*

Changing to a monetary or aggregate target required the System to reconsider even keel policy. The commitment assured "reasonable stability in narrowly defined money market conditions such as the Federal funds rate and net free or borrowed reserves"[94] (memo, Staff to FOMC, Board Records, July 17, 1970, 2). Its origin was the 1951 Accord that separated the responsibilities of the Treasury and the Federal Reserve for debt management.

An earlier study by Stephen Axilrod found that in the past even keel sometimes "enlarged [the] rate of increase in the monetary aggregates" (ibid., 4). After the shift to monetary targets, the desk and the FOMC "sought to achieve target growth rates in the aggregates only on an average basis over periods of several months" (ibid., 7). The desk did not get estimates of the monetary aggregates for a week, so the manager "tended to maintain day-to-day money market conditions within fairly narrow ranges for a number of days at a time, shifting to new target ranges only at relatively discrete intervals after firm data on the aggregates showed persistent deviations from their target paths" (ibid., 9). Hence, the desk

94. Usually even keel did not apply to bill auctions, but the FOMC made exceptions during large cash offerings. The time span for even keel varied with the offering and the market environment (memo, Staff to FOMC, Board Records, July 17, 1970, n. 2). The Board's staff and the FOMC never considered how much the Treasury paid for even keel. The market knew that the FOMC waited until after a Treasury sale to raise interest rates. There should be information in the asymmetry between periods of rising and falling rates.

could continue even keel actions much as before. This helped the dealers to avoid losses during the period between securities sales and their distribution to portfolios. The memo recognized, however, that if the Treasury auctioned bonds and notes, the System could apply even-keel in a less rigid way.

The memo recognized that neither the market nor the staff could estimate accurately future values of market interest rates, reserves, and money growth. It proposed to retain the old procedure for even keel. The major change was the adjustment of interest rates once it became clear that the reserve and monetary targets would not be met (ibid., 13).

Beginning in 1970, the Treasury began auctioning notes and later bonds. Previous attempts in 1935 and 1963 failed, so the Treasury introduced auctions slowly, starting with shorter-term coupon securities and keeping procedures close to the familiar Treasury bill auction.[95] As the variance of Treasury yields increased, it became much harder for the Treasury to price the bonds or notes (Garbade, 2004, 35).

The first auction in November 1970 successfully sold eighteen-month notes. After several similar note offerings in 1971, the Treasury auctioned two-, three-, and four-year notes in 1972 and twenty- and twenty-five-year bonds in 1973. By the middle of 1973, the auction had become the established method for selling notes and bonds. At first the Treasury announced the coupon and let the market set the price. In September 1974, it allowed the market to bid on the basis of yield. After the auction, the Treasury set the coupon to meet the yield. To facilitate bidding, in 1975 the Treasury permitted "when issued" trading. Bidders would know the approximate yield at the time they placed their bids.

Auctions reduced the use of even keel procedures but did not, at first, eliminate them. The January 1973 auction of twenty-year bonds prevented "the desk from exercising as much restraint on the growth of reserves as otherwise would have been desirable" (memo, Fred Struble to Axilrod, Burns papers, B_B81, August 2, 1973). Gradually, even keel disappeared as a major constraint on Federal Reserve actions to control inflation.

### *Revision of FOMC Procedures*

After Sherman Maisel left, Andrew Brimmer took up his efforts to focus more on long-term objectives. Brimmer wrote that "our present proce-

95. Friedman (1960, 64–65) criticized the Treasury's use of fixed-price offerings as inefficient. Later, he showed that in fact the Treasury at times offered substantial premiums because it misjudged market yields. He proposed a single price sale so that small investors could get the same price as large investors. The inefficiency arose because the Treasury did not know the market-clearing price, so it often paid a premium.

dures do not integrate adequately our short-run policy decisions with a strategy that adapts monetary policy to the longer-run needs of the national economy. . . . [W]hen the principal focus of the Committee's attention is on the probable effects of its policy decisions on financial variables in the immediate weeks ahead—as is often the case—a grave danger exists that the long-run course of monetary policy will turn out to be almost an incidental by-product of short-run decisions" (memo, Brimmer to Holland, Board Records, April 14, 1972, 1).

Brimmer's memo recognized that the FOMC had to develop strategies capable of reducing inflation. Concentration on control of short-term monetary changes did not assure that longer-term goals would be met. In fact, Brimmer claimed that the opposite had occurred; concentration on short-term changes had come at the cost of reduced attention to long-term goals. He proposed that the FOMC hold three "outlook meetings" a year.

Congressman Henry Reuss also wanted changes. In a January 14, 1972, letter, he urged the System to adopt seven guidelines for monetary policy. His aim was to improve control of inflation and unemployment or growth. His proposal, like Brimmer's, would have shifted attention to longer-term objectives.

Burns's reply emphasized the importance of discretionary changes, avoidance of a rule for money growth, and the need to take account of resource utilization, lags in response, fiscal policy, and other factors that Reuss mentioned. Reuss suggested setting three-month monetary targets. Burns replied: monetary targets "should be evaluated over a period of at least six months" (letter, Burns to Reuss, Board Minutes, February 7, 1972, 2).

Reuss also stated that the Federal Reserve had to assist the housing industry by purchasing issues of the housing agencies and by buying long-term securities at times of monetary stringency. He neglected to say that credit and money are fungible. Burns's reply noted that the FOMC had purchased agency issues since September 1971 with little effect on the housing industry. He did not point out that the supply of housing depended on real resources. Burns also was skeptical of the System's ability to change the shape of the yield curve. This was an improvement, perhaps reflecting experience in the 1960s, when the System tried to lower long-term rates while raising short-term rates.

Burns ended his response by again citing the importance of "confidence." Confidence affected not just spending but also the demand for liquidity. This, he said, contributed importantly to the length of the lag in monetary policy (ibid., 4). Burns seemed to think of confidence as an autonomous influence.

In June 1973, the staff reviewed experience with RPD control. It concluded the results were "mixed and difficult to interpret" (memo, Axilrod to FOMC, Board Records, June 8, 1973, 2). Control would be improved if the RPD target range was narrow and the federal funds constraint was wider. The memo showed that the RPD targets were almost never hit. The procedure had a much better record of controlling longer-term money growth than short-term ranges (ibid., 14, 28).

Surprisingly, the account manager was more positive than the staff about the experiment. He disagreed, however, about the desirability of widening the bands on the federal funds rate. Unless the bands became very wide, "one could not expect the portfolio adjustments of banks and their customers to proceed so rapidly as to offset unforeseen shifts in the demand for money within a four to five week interval" (memo, Alan Holmes to FOMC, Board Records, June 3, 1973, 2). As before, the manager put the interests of the banks ahead of inflation control.

An October memo from Arthur Broida to Governor Sheehan explained the way the procedures worked in practice. Its summary explained that "the Committee has not felt rigidly bound to the terms of some precisely defined experiment. Rather, it has felt free both to modify the general framework of the experiment on the basis of experience, and to adapt the approach to the special circumstances that arise from time to time" (memo, Arthur Broida to Governor Sheehan, Board Records, October 26, 1973, 6).

A System committee reported on the effects of lagged reserve accounting on monetary control. The members agreed on the direction of effect but differed on the magnitude. The Committee concluded that lagged reserve accounting:

> (a) significantly reduces the ability to hit a total reserve or RPD target . . . ;
>
> (b) is a less significant limitation on the System's ability to control reserves and monetary aggregates over the longer run;
>
> (c) adds to the tendency for day-to-day money market variability; and
>
> (d) increases somewhat the range over which the Federal funds rate needs to fluctuate if monetary aggregates are to be controlled by use of a reserve handle.(First Report of the Staff Committee on Lagged Reserve Accounting, Board Records, August 10, 1973, 2)

The Committee estimated that, short-term, a two-week lagged reserve system caused the federal funds rate to vary from ten to twenty-five basis points more than contemporaneous reserve accounting (ibid., 10). The report emphasized the Committee's uncertainty about the estimate, but it recommended returning to contemporary reserve accounting. The principal objection cited in the report was bank relations. Some banks preferred the lagged arrangement because they had better control of required reserves and could hold smaller balances on average. The banks' interest prevailed.

The FOMC reinstituted control of reserves in 1979. Despite the 1973, report it retained lagged reserve requirements and did not restore contemporaneous reserve accounting until after returning to control of money market conditions, when it no longer mattered for monetary control.

The memos make clear that senior staff understood the problems with System efforts to increase control of monetary aggregates. The System would neither permit wider variation in the federal funds rate nor adopt procedures that made reserve control easier.

### *NOW Accounts*

The combination of inflation and regulation created opportunities and heightened incentives to circumvent regulation. The Board responded by trying to limit the exceptions. By the end of the decade, there were numerous exceptions. Soon after, interest rate regulation ended.

In July 1970, a Worcester, Massachusetts, savings bank asked the state regulator to permit its customers to issue negotiable orders of withdrawal (NOW). The orders drew on the customer's savings account and were payable through a commercial bank.[96]

The banking commissioner denied the request. After almost two years, the Massachusetts courts ruled in favor of the savings bank. Beginning in June 1972, savings banks opened NOW accounts. Deposits in NOW accounts rose rapidly but remained less than one percent of total savings deposits after eight months. New Hampshire savings banks followed soon after.

The new accounts posed competitive problems for commercial banks. Savings banks were not members of the Federal Reserve System, so they had lower reserve requirements and could hold reserves in interest-bearing Treasury bills. Also, they could pay higher interest rates on savings accounts than commercial bankers. And regulation Q prohibited interest payments on demand deposits. Technically, NOW accounts were not demand deposits, but they were available on demand. The NOW orders transferred the balances as if by check.

Congress approved legislation in September 1973 that permitted the ex-

96. The origin and development of these accounts here follows the report to President Frank Morris of the Boston bank by his staff, dated March 29, 1973 (Board Records, March 29, 1973).

ception. The Board limited NOW accounts to individuals in Massachusetts and New Hampshire, two states with many savings banks, and it limited interest payments to 5 percent a year. To restrict use, the Board limited the number of NOW orders on an account to 150 a year, and it restricted advertising of NOW accounts to Massachusetts and New Hampshire. Of course, several of these restrictions proved difficult to monitor and enforce. Nothing prevented a person from having more than one account.

President Nixon appointed a Commission on Financial Structure and Regulation, called the "Hunt Commission" after its chairman, Reed Hunt. The commission recommended equality of reserve requirements achieved by requiring all institutions that issued demand deposits to join the Federal Reserve System. The Board did not ask for universal membership but it favored uniform reserve requirements for all banks (including savings banks) that offered demand deposits or NOW accounts (letter, Tynan Smith to William E. Simon, Burns papers, Box B_B24, April 5, 1973).[97]

The Hunt Commission also proposed eliminating interest rate ceilings on time and savings deposits. The Board favored delay and "a controlled phase-out" at the Board's discretion (ibid., 2). Nothing happened. The "right time" for removing ceiling rates had not come.

### *Release of Policy Decisions*

Chairman Burns appointed a subcommittee of four members to recommend how much and what kinds of information the System should release to the public. The subcommittee could not agree. Brimmer and Morris (Boston) favored the most liberal policy. They argued for the release of information on targets for growth of the monetary aggregates after a ninety-day delay and claimed that this would reduce uncertainty. They also favored release of the federal funds constraint. They hoped that release of information would increase the quality and relevance of criticism by outsiders.

Daane opposed release of any quantitative information such as target growth rates or interest rate constraints. He argued that the quantitative data served as guides to the manager. They developed out of a general discussion, which the manager heard. The policy decision included the nuances and qualifications that members offered in their statements. Releasing the data without the qualifications would be misleading. And

97. Tynan Smith was secretary of the Board of Governors; William E. Simon was deputy secretary of the Treasury and later secretary. I served as adviser to the homebuilders and their representative on the Hunt Commission.

the quantitative data on RPD growth and the federal funds target were, at times, inconsistent. The inconsistencies could be reconciled within the members' discussion, but this would not be available.

A fourth member, Robert Mayo (Chicago), proposed to publish only the longer-term targets for $M_1$ and $M_2$ and the bank credit proxy (total deposits). This information would help the market and other observers to understand the thrust of policy action.

A month after the report, Burns responded. He opposed publication of the six-month targets for the monetary aggregates at the end of each three months because it would permit outsiders to know what to expect in the next three months. Despite qualifications stating that these targets could change monthly, the information would affect interest rates. "The risk of misinterpretation . . . is great" (Board Minutes, November 15, 1973, 2). He was less concerned about publishing short-run targets, but he remained cautious. No one proposed that explanations accompany the data to reduce misinterpretation. There were few changes at the time, but the issue returned.

### *Watergate*

During the 1972 election campaign, agents connected to the Republican Party and President Nixon's campaign were arrested when they broke into Democratic Party offices at the Watergate. The police found Federal Reserve notes in the possession of the criminals arrested at the crime scene. Senator Proxmire and other Democrats conjectured that the Federal Reserve might be involved. The money was in $100 bills and totaled $6,300. Banks had to record large transactions, so there was a record somewhere showing who withdrew the currency. In a letter to Burns, Proxmire asked for information about the issuance of the notes, the name of the person receiving the notes, and how they were paid for.

Burns replied that the Board had no information. He promised to cooperate as fully as he could.

A week later, Congressman Patman asked for the information. Governor Robertson replied. He did not disclose any information or admit to having any. But he refused to answer questions because the U.S. Attorney had advised them that early release of information "would impede the investigation and, in the event of prosecution, could jeopardize the defendants' right to a fair trial" (letter, Robertson to Patman, Board Minutes, June 28 1973).

Although the exchanges became more rancorous, the Board did not release the information.

## CONCLUSION

Experience from 1971 to 1973 points up the advantages of keeping the central bank independent of government and able to choose its actions to maintain the internal or external value of money. More than any other president, President Nixon tried to use monetary policy to create conditions favorable to his reelection. In Arthur Burns, he had a chairman who shared his views and was willing to accommodate his president.

As chairman, Burns had a powerful role, but he required the votes of at least a majority of the FOMC. He could secure these votes because several members always voted with the chairman. But politics and authority alone do not explain what happened. Burns encountered little opposition, and he cited only two opponents—Governor Andrew Brimmer and New York bank president Alfred Hayes. Brimmer's memo in April 1972, cited above, explains one of the principal reasons for policy failure. They never developed and implemented a long-term or even six-month program.

Ideas had an important role. Several members favored Burns's expansive policies because there were idle resources. Their main concern was to achieve full employment; preventing inflation or maintaining the internal value of money was of lesser interest. The external value of money was neither an important goal nor a Federal Reserve responsibility. Proponents of ease drew support, or took comfort, from prevailing Keynesian doctrine that taught that it was possible to trade off a bit more inflation to reduce unemployment and that the tradeoff could be improved by controlling prices and wages. They favored government-administered guidelines and guideposts, and they welcomed the president's decision to adopt price and wage controls. Surprisingly, Arthur Burns, who had earlier pointed out the flaws in this reasoning, became the main proponent of controls or guidelines in this period. He pressed the president to adopt guidelines.

Pierce (1978, 365) quoted Burns's testimony in 1973 that in 1972 "monetary and fiscal policy moved in the right direction . . . [but] in retrospect it appears that restraint should have been greater." That was as much error as he would admit while he remained chairman. But those who criticized him after inflation rose included many who had urged more expansive policies in 1972 using much the same reasoning as those who supported the expansive policies. Prominent members of Congress took this position.

The mixture of politics, analytic error, and unwillingness to defend central bank independence was not restricted to the Federal Reserve and the administration. Many economists and members of Congress shared these views. The errors were costly. The surge in inflation took the annual measured rate of consumer price inflation from about 4 percent when price and wage controls began to more than 10 percent in 1974, when the administration gave up these efforts (except for oil). Wage increases, less subject to the one-time effects of food and energy prices, rose from about 6 to 8.5 percent annual rate.

Other errors contributed. The Federal Reserve did not distinguish between one-time price changes and long-term rates of change. The one-time changes in food and oil prices would pass through, leaving the maintained rate of inflation unchanged if policy remained non-inflationary. Reported inflation rates would decline after a year at most. By failing to distinguish between temporary and permanent changes, the Federal Reserve misdirected its policy and increased unemployment. The underlying problem was failure to decide, or even discuss, whether its objective was price level stability or zero or low inflation (rate of price change). The former required action to roll back or roll up one-time price level changes. The latter did not.

Sherman Maisel made notable efforts to give more attention to longer-term consequences and to improve operating procedures. He had very limited success. The FOMC formally adopted reserve targets, but it constrained its actions within a narrow band of short-term interest rates. The account manager gave most attention to the interest rate constraint. The staff recognized the problem and informed the FOMC, but policy action did not change. After Maisel's term ended, Andrew Brimmer raised some of the same issues with even less effect.

The Great Inflation continued and increased in these years for two main reasons. First, political concerns weakened whatever independence the Federal Reserve had just at the time when an independent central bank was most needed. The Federal Reserve accepted the political goal of achieving low unemployment even if it risked increased inflation, as it did. Second, analytic errors and inappropriate operating procedures supported these choices. Both problems continued for the rest of the decade.

Members recognized political concerns. Burns told Congress that "it is the expansion of the money supply over the long run that will be the basic cause of inflation" (quoted in Wells, 1994, 111). But he told the members of the Bank for International Settlements that Congress and labor unions disliked "high" interest rates, and Congress was likely to legislate ceilings. And he told the FOMC that "to achieve price stability it was necessary to avoid recessions" (FOMC Minutes, June 18–19, 1973, 34).

Governor Brimmer told the FOMC that its concentration on short-term changes neglected longer-term goals. Reading the minutes, one notices a striking difference between the major effort given to deciding on small differences in the federal funds rates or the money growth target and the much greater difference between the target and actual money growth. Discussions at the meeting presume that the manager would control money growth carefully though everyone knew that this was not so.

Behind most of these errors lay a political concern. As Burns, Frank Morris, and Charles Partee reminded the members, they could try to reduce inflation only as long as unemployment remained low. Once unemployment rose, they would be urged to expand and the government would take fiscal actions. Burns recognized that no country had succeeded in reducing inflation without increasing the unemployment rate. That made the Federal Reserve cautious and quick to abandon anti-inflation policy.

From 1971 to 1973 the country experienced the consequences of one of the major errors in economic policy—the attempt to control the price level by controlling most, but not all, relative prices. The proponents of the policy, Arthur Burns and John Connally, did not understand that unless monetary policy became less expansive, spending would continue to rise, raising prices. President Nixon had chosen controls to reduce employment enough to win the 1972 election. He pressured Burns frequently to increase money growth. Burns did so with the support of a majority of the FOMC urged on by prominent members of Congress. At a time when central bank independence was most needed to safeguard the value of money, the Federal Reserve failed the test.

By the time that Burns recognized that inflation was a major problem, it had become well entrenched. Too many promises had been broken, so credibility was impaired. The cost of a major reduction in inflation had increased. And President Nixon in his last days in office wanted easier monetary policy (Matusow, 1998, 298).

Poor forecasts added to the problem. Chart 6.6 compares the private Society of Professional Forecasters forecast to reported inflation. The forecast is consistently lower than actual inflation. Federal Reserve staff projections were usually close to the survey. Largest errors include periods with oil price increases, but large errors are not limited to these periods. Emphasis on short-term changes and neglect of longer-term consequences contributed to the poor performance both in this period and its continuation. Orphanides (2001, 2002) developed these points.

Herbert Stein (1988, 206), who participated in many of the policy decisions, put greater emphasis on political pressures. "Everything turned out to be more difficult than it seemed in advance. That was notably true of the effort to check inflation. No one knew how much the anti-inflation fight

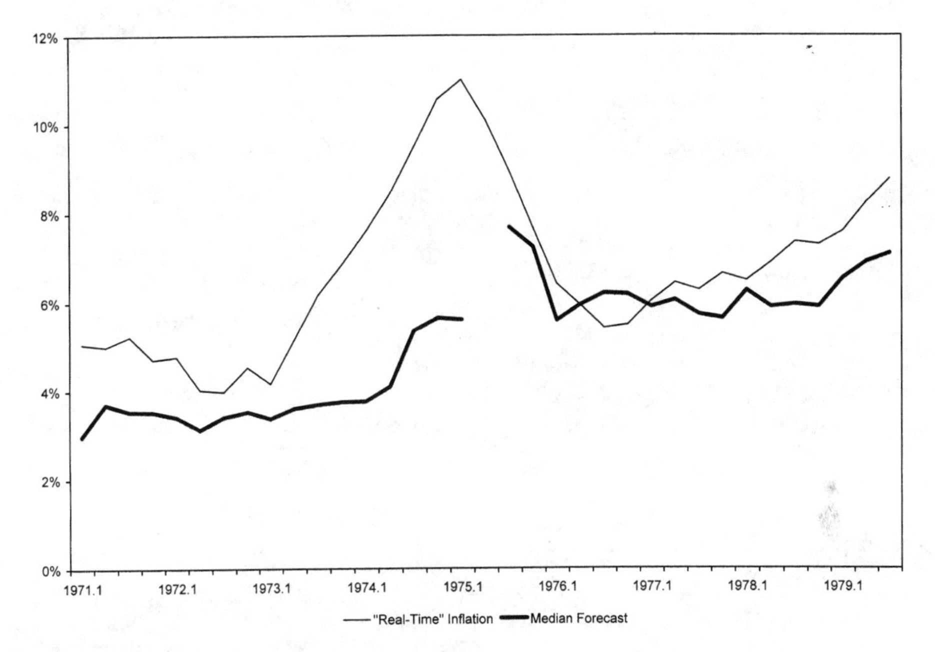


Chart 6.6. Median forecast from Survey of Professional Forecasters versus "real-time" inflation, 1971:1–1979:3. Inflation measured as four-quarter change in implicit GNP deflator.

would cost. When they got some inkling of the cost, they—the President and his advisers—were unwilling to pay it and also thought the public was unwilling to pay it."

## APPENDIX TO CHAPTER 6

The results of the vector autoregressions shown in Chart 6.A1 differ in several ways from the results for other periods. Among the off-diagonal responses, the response of discounts to the base is much stronger than in the 1950s or other periods. (Compare Chart 2.A1 in the Appendix to Chapter 2.) This likely reflects, in part, policy action during 1979–80, when the FOMC set targets for nonborrowed reserves and forced the banks to borrow to meet required reserves, and during other periods of reserve targeting in the 1970s. A less important change is the disappearance of a response of the gold stock to the monetary base, government securities, or discounts. Under floating rates, the gold stock rarely changed. The Federal Reserve rarely sold gold from 1968 until the floating in August 1971. Growth of the base was driven by open market operations in government securities. Discounts leave no significant effect on the base, but discounts reduced government securities.

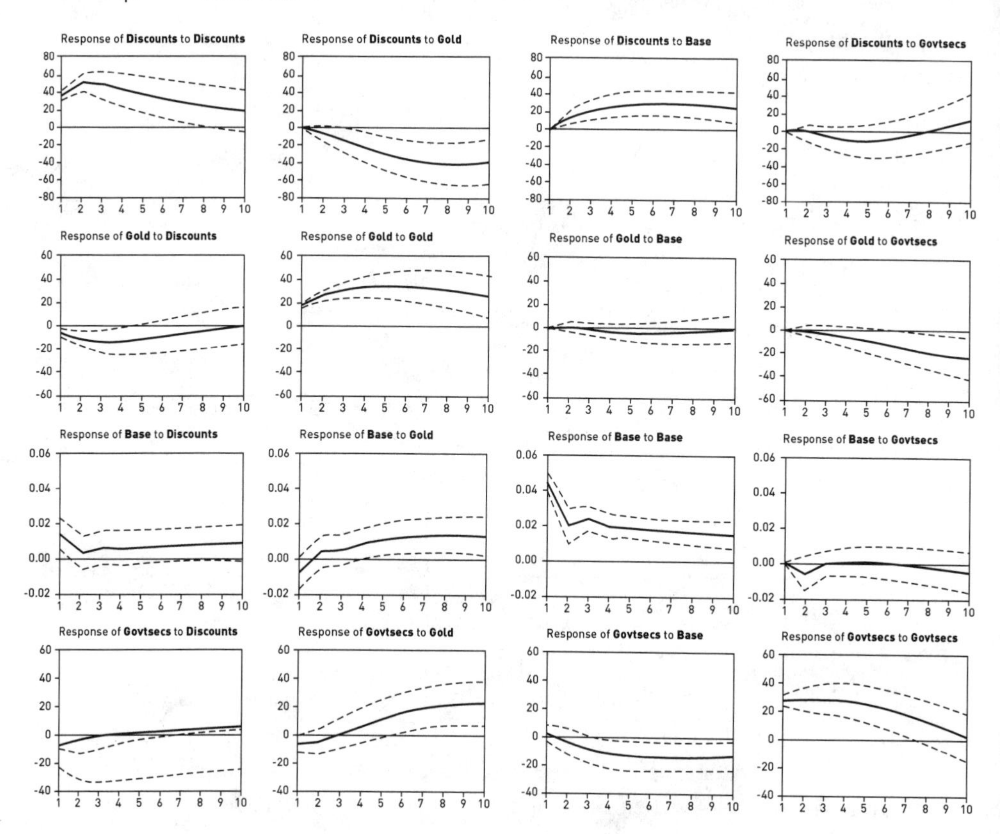


Chart 6.A1. Response to one S.D. innovations ±2 S.E.

The estimation proceeded as before. There are four variables representing the monetary base and its three principal sources—discounts, gold stock, monetary base, and government securities. (For more discussion on the procedure, see the Appendix to Chapter 2.) Data are monthly from October 1971 to December 1980. Estimates are again based on 2 lags, 11 seasonal dummies, and a constant.

SEVEN

# Why Monetary Policy Failed Again in the 1970s

"The history of money demonstrates the difficulties which men have to distinguish the permanent from the temporary." . . . [M]aking this distinction is a constant imperative.
—William McC. Martin, Jr., quoting Karl Bopp, in Eastburn, 1970, 35

Econometric models play an important role at the Federal Reserve Board. . . . That said, the economic environment is a forbidding one for models: appropriate specification and identification of models is elusive; data are faulty and subject to revision; the economy is in a constant state of flux; and events not contemplated at the time of model design frequently buffet the economy.
—Reifschreider, et al., 1996, 47

The years 1973 to 1979 were the least successful period for postwar Federal Reserve policy. Consumer price inflation rose from an annual rate of 3.6 percent in January 1973 to 10.7 percent in July 1979. Part of the increase represents the temporary effect of oil price increases. Although Federal Reserve officials may have distinguished "the permanent from the temporary," they did not act on that information.[1]

The policy failure had both political and economic causes. Arthur Burns, who served as chairman of the Board of Governors until spring 1978, lacked both the courage and the conviction to restore low inflation or price stability. He believed that inflation was endemic in a modern economy, and though he started at times to reduce inflation, he did not persist when unemployment rose above 6 or 7 percent. Like his predecessor, Martin, he

1. Conventional estimates put the one-time oil price increase at one-third of the inflation rate. That leaves 7 percent as the maintained inflation rate in 1979.

spoke often and forcefully about the dangers of inflation, but his actions generally were much less forceful. His successor, William Miller, was a business executive. He had little professional experience and knew little about monetary policy. Both chairmen gave too much heed to perceived political constraints and too little to the costs of inflation.

Political pressures were only one of the reasons for rising inflation. The FOMC made several errors and had some bad luck. The oil price increase was non-monetary and did not require a monetary response. Error or misinterpretation caused them to treat the decline in output as a recession instead of a permanent loss of wealth and output, in effect a response to a tax paid to foreign oil producers that transferred wealth. Also, the main effect of the oil price increase was on the price level; the increase in reported rates of price change was temporary. The job of the central bank was to prevent the relative price change from spreading to non-energy prices. Once oil prices stopped rising, inflation would converge to or near its previous rate of change if monetary policy did not ease. Ignoring the difference between the temporary and persistent rate of price change or responding to the loss of output contributed to inflation. Countries that did not make this error, notably Germany and Switzerland, had much lower inflation rates (Issing, 2005, 334).[2] The different inflationary responses suggest that policy responses to the decline in output following the increase in the relative price of oil was an important determinant of the size of subsequent inflation. What of the oil price increase itself? A study by Barsky and Killian (2004) concluded that in the United States the dominant inflation impulse came from monetary policy. The oil price increase raised consumer prices relative to the deflator because of the greater weight given to this price in the CPI. But the effect on measured inflation was temporary; the rate of increase rose then fell back.

Policymakers were slow to recognize that productivity growth had slowed. Reduced real growth called for slower money growth to avoid raising the inflation rate. Productivity growth is highly variable, so it seems right to assign some of this error to bad luck, especially since decades of research have not explained the productivity slowdown satisfactorily.[3]

The Board's staff and the FOMC used a Phillips curve relating inflation negatively to the output gap (the difference between actual and potential—full employment—output) to predict inflation. Orphanides (2001) showed that the output gap as reported at the time was subject to large persistent

2. A staff study by Pierce and Enzler (1974) analyzed the oil price increase as a permanent change in the price level. Like much of the best staff work, this did not affect the FOMC.

3. A recent study (Nordhaus, 2004) using industrial data finds the slowdown concentrated in energy-intensive sectors.

errors caused mainly by errors in estimating potential output. The gap reported at the time was generally much larger than the gap in the data as revised later. Staff estimates, therefore, implied lower inflation than actually occurred. This persistent error misled policymakers at the FOMC and in the administration and encouraged excessive expansion.

Later research showed that the output gap has not been measured precisely and perhaps cannot be. Using a large number of different models, Staiger, Stock, and Watson (1997) reported that they could not distinguish several different measures of the natural rate. The clear implication is that the Phillips curve model is not a reliable way of predicting inflation in the short run. Unfortunately, there is no systematic alternative that makes reliable predictions. This raises a fundamental question: Why does the Federal Reserve give so much attention to unreliable short-term changes in output and unemployment that include transitory elements? This concentration on short-term changes and the heavy weight given to unemployment changes caused much of the inflation problem of the 1970s.[4] Chairman Martin's statement at the start of the chapter recognizes part of that problem.

Serious as were the errors in Phillips curve forecasts of inflation, other errors contributed to the poor performance. These included excessive concern for short-term changes and failure to distinguish between persistent and temporary or transitory disturbances when implementing policies.[5] This was particularly true in responding to the price level effects of rising food and oil prices in 1973–74. Stein explained these responses as responses to public and political pressures to "do something."[6] Also, mistaken policies defended or imposed by politically potent groups or their

4. Feldstein (1997) computed the gain from ending inflation allowing for the cost in unemployment during the transition. He found the gain to be positive. Abel (1997) strengthened Feldstein's result using a general equilibrium model.

5. Burns (1974, 1–2) testified that "[w]e have come to recognize that public policies that create excess demand, and therefore drive up wage rates and prices, will not result in any lasting reduction in unemployment." Unfortunately, he did not always act as if his statement was true. I am grateful to David Lindsey for supplying the quote.

6. As Stein put it,

> The decisions at the top are very much constrained by what the public wants, or by an administration's perception of what the public wants, which I think is often quite wrong but is very important in their decision making. (Stein in Hargrove and Morley, 1984, 407)

And

> The Director of the Cost of Living Council and the new Federal Energy Administrator were unwilling to raise the [oil] price, mainly for fear of the political reaction. (Stein in Hargrove and Morley, 1984, 403)

representatives often made rational policy unattainable. Matusow (1998, Chapter 9) gives several examples following the first oil shock. Consumer gasoline prices remained frozen, but wholesale oil prices could increase. And import quotas restricted supply. Despite long gasoline lines and other inconveniences, oil price controls remained until 1981.

None of these explanations accounts for the persistence of inflation and its increase during the 1970s. There is no doubt that the Federal Reserve made errors; the problem is to explain why it continued to make the same or similar errors.[7]

When Gerald Ford replaced President Richard Nixon, he declared inflation to be the main policy problem. One of his early efforts, known as the WIN program (Whip Inflation Now), was more a public relations effort than a policy initiative. The program began just as output started to fall. As unemployment rose, the administration shifted its emphasis. It asked for tax reduction, and the FOMC lowered the federal funds rate. That ended the anti-inflation effort and the WIN program. But it reinforced the strengthening view that anti-inflation programs would not last long enough to end inflation.

For the Federal Reserve, this meant reduced credibility. Burns, like Martin before him, made many strong statements about the evils of inflation. His actions increased inflation on average. The low credibility encouraged Congress to act. It passed resolutions and later the Humphrey-Hawkins Act, which required the Federal Reserve to announce monetary targets to aim for lower inflation.[8] It did not achieve the projections. Even worse, it built its positive errors into its projections.

President Ford's experience with the WIN program was not a unique event. It was one of three parts of the main problem. The Federal Reserve, Congress, and successive administrations put less weight on rising inflation than on rising unemployment. Rising unemployment called for more stimulus, an end to the anti-inflation program. After gaining this experience, the public doubted that the Federal Reserve would persist, so they

7. In 1973 Karl Brunner and I organized the Shadow Open Market Committee, with assistance from James Meigs and William Wolman of Argus Research, to point out policy errors and propose alternatives. Membership at the time included Robert Rasche, Anna J. Schwartz, James Meigs, William Wolman, and Homer Jones. The group met every six months to comment on policies and errors.

8. Arthur Burns testimony to Congress in 1974 is one of many examples. "A return to price stability will require a national commitment to fight inflation this year and in the years to come. Monetary policy must play a key role in this endeavor, and we, in the Federal Reserve recognize that fact. We are determined to reduce over time the rate of monetary and credit expansion to a pace consistent with price stability" (quoted in Broaddus and Goodfriend, 1984, 3). The quote shows that Burns understood that he had to control monetary emissions if he was to lower inflation.

chose brief spells of unemployment to wage reduction. Wages became more sticky, reinforcing loose talk about stagflation and contributing to the mistaken belief that guidelines or controls were needed. Second, the Federal Reserve overemphasized short-term, often random changes and neglected the longer-term consequences of its actions. Controlling inflation required patience and persistence that it did not have at the time. Also, it lacked both a longer-term objective and a means of reaching it. Third, control procedures were harmful. The FOMC persistently misinterpreted interest rate declines as evidence of ease and increases as tightness. This error gave its actions a procyclical bias. And it failed to establish adequate procedures for controlling money growth.[9]

Some members of FOMC understood the need for regaining credibility by sustaining anti-inflation policy. No reader of the minutes or transcripts can fail to see that there was not much agreement on the need for commitment of this kind. By 1978, there were three distinct groups. One proposed sustained anti-inflation policy. The second was unwilling to risk recession even as the reported inflation rate rose to 8 or 9 percent. Burns was usually part of this group. A third group remained in the middle of the two. The result was considerable talk but no sustained action.

Starting in 1973, the principal currencies floated, not always freely. But it is the first period in modern history with no major currency fixed to a commodity. Gold lost its position in the international system. Learning to operate without a reserve currency tied to a commodity or with a fixed exchange rate proved difficult for central banks. Oil shocks, recycling of oil revenues, and later the Latin American debt crisis and the anti-inflation policies in several countries increased exchange rate variability. Many observers decried the instability of floating rates, and many sought evidence of excess burden. Western European countries especially established arrangements for a joint float, often without restricting policies in the individual countries. It took years before governments accepted the discipline that fixed exchange rates required. Table 7.1 shows price and wage changes during 1973–79 in leading industrial countries.

Average annual inflation rates ranged from less than 5 percent in Germany to 15 percent in Italy. Since all of the countries experienced the same

9. In 1973, the Congressional Joint Economic Committee proposed some changes in monetary policy. At the time, the CPI rose 11 percent for the month and the unemployment rate was 4.9 percent. The proposed changes called on the FOMC to not permit interest rates to rise above present levels. "If possible interest rates should be reduced" (JEC Report, 1973, Box 35602, New York Federal Reserve Bank, March 26, 12). The report also urged a standby credit allocation system to assist home buyers, local governments, and small businesses. Also, the report called on the System to buy mortgages and state and local securities. There was more, but the general direction is clear. Inflation control was of lesser interest.

**Table 7.1** Price and Wage Changes, Major Countries, 1973–79

| COUNTRY | CUMULATIVE PERCENT CONSUMER PRICE CHANGE | CUMULATIVE PERCENT HOURLY WAGE CHANGE |
|---|---|---|
| United States | 49 | 54 |
| Canada | 53 | 52 |
| Japan | 57 | 92 |
| France | 61 | 90 |
| Germany | 27 | 95 |
| Italy | 90 | 77 |
| United Kingdom | 87 | 94 |

Source: Economic Report of the President (1983, 286–87).

oil shock, that shock cannot explain the very different behavior of inflation in these countries.

Arthur Burns remained chairman of the Board of Governors until replaced by G. William Miller in April 1978. Miller had little experience with monetary policy. He had served as a director of the Boston Federal Reserve bank. His appointment owed much to his work in the presidential campaign and his friendship with Vice President Walter Mondale. He left the Federal Reserve to become Secretary of the Treasury in August 1979. Table 7.2 shows the personnel changes during 1973–79.

Two notable appointments, Henry C. Wallich and Paul A. Volcker, joined the FOMC during this period. Wallich was a Yale professor at the time of his appointment with years of practical and academic experience. He had worked as an international economist at the New York Federal Reserve bank and served as a member of the Council of Economic Advisers in the Eisenhower administration. In 1958, he joined the Treasury as head of tax analysis. In March 1974, he joined the Board of Governors, replacing Dewey Daane. He strongly opposed inflation but did not always favor control of money growth.

Paul A. Volcker became president of the New York bank in August 1975. He had a long experience in the System, beginning in 1949 at the New York bank and later in the bank's research division under the direction of Robert Roosa. Roosa brought Volcker to the Treasury in 1962. He worked in both Democratic and Republican administrations, rising to Undersecretary of Monetary Affairs in the Nixon administration. Volcker was always an anti-inflationist.

Turnover of Board members increased during the period. Some complained that Board salaries did not adjust for inflation, so their real incomes fell. One seat, occupied by Governors Robertson, Holland, Lilly, Miller, and Volcker, changed four times during the six-year period. For the first time, two of the new governors, Holland and Partee, came from

**Table 7.2** Personnel Changes, 1973–79

THE BOARD

| *Date* | *New Appointment* | *Replacing* |
|---|---|---|
| 6/11/73 | Robert Holland | J. L. Robertson |
| 3/8/74 | Henry Wallich | J. Dewey Daane |
| 10/29/74 | Philip E. Coldwell | Andrew F. Brimmer |
| 7/14/75 | Philip C. Jackson | John E. Sheehan |
| 1/5/76 | J. Charles Partee | Jeffrey M. Bucher |
| 2/13/76 | Stephen S. Gardner | George W. Mitchell |
| 6/1/76 | David M. Lilly | Robert C. Holland |
| 3/8/78 | G. William Miller | David M. Lilly |
| 9/18/78 | Nancy H. Teeters | Arthur F. Burns |
| 6/20/79 | Emmett J. Rice | Stephen S. Gardner |
| 7/27/79 | Frederick H. Schultz | Philip C. Jackson |
| 8/6/79 | Paul A. Volcker | G. William Miller |

RESERVE BANKS

| *Date* | *New Appointment* | *Replacing* | *Bank* |
|---|---|---|---|
| 1/1/75 | Ernest T. Baughman | Philip E. Coldwell | Dallas |
| 8/1/75 | Paul A. Volcker | Alfred Hayes | New York |
| 3/1/76 | Roger Guffey | George H. Clay | Kansas City |
| 3/22/76 | Lawrence K. Roos | Darryl R. Francis | St. Louis |
| 4/16/77 | Mark H. Willes | Bruce K. MacLaury | Minneapolis |

the senior staff, and one governor, Coldwell, was a reserve bank president at the time of his appointment. Many of the appointees were professional economists or experienced in financial markets.

Miller claimed that the president accepted his suggestions for appointments to the Board while he was chairman. He recommended Nancy Teeters, the first female member, Emmett Rice, the second black, and, just before leaving, Frederick Schultz, a Florida banker. Schultz became vice chairman of the Board.

Congress made several changes in financial regulation that broadened the Federal Reserve's regulatory and supervisory activities and enlarged its staff by about 50 percent. Bank holding companies expanded by acquiring non-banking subsidiaries. The Board in 1970 assumed responsibility for one-bank holding companies. Truth-in-lending legislation and consumer credit protection became main activities. The Freedom of Information Act and other programs required increased transparency and information. To house the expanded staff, the Board supervised construction of the new Martin building, which opened in 1974.

Of the changes Congress authorized in this decade some altered the banking and financial systems permanently. By the end of 1979, nearly 2,500 bank holding companies held 70.6 percent of banking assets

(O'Brien, 1989, 51). Growth of non-bank financial institutions and inflation eroded regulation Q and restrictions that separated banking and other financial firms. By the end of the 1970s, the burden of several costly regulations became apparent. Deregulation began.

### THE ECONOMY IN 1973–79

Rising inflation was the main economic event of the period. Chart 7.1 shows the percentage change in the deflator for private consumption during the 1970s. The two peaks roughly coincide with increases in oil prices, but it is less clear that oil price increase caused most of the price increase properly measured. Unlike the consumer price index, the deflator is much less affected directly by oil prices, and its peak rates of inflation remained well below the rates recorded by the consumer price index. The consumer price index, however, was widely used to adjust wages and other contracts and it was widely quoted at the time.

It is true, nevertheless, that the peaks in oil price increases shown in Chart 7.2 correspond to the peaks in general measures of the price change. Part of the increase resulted from the world increase in aggregate demand in 1973 stimulated by expansive policies in several countries.

Real growth in the United States made a large contribution to robust world growth in 1972. Chart 7.3 shows this surge and the recession that followed. It was the deepest recession of the postwar years to that time. Inflation continued at a high level during the recession, so there was much talk about "stagflation," inflation at a time of high persistent unemployment. By this time producers and consumers had learned that anti-inflation policies did not persist once unemployment rose, so they were hesitant to change their beliefs about long-term inflation. Measures of anticipated inflation remained at about a 5 percent annual rate, and ten-year Treasury bond yields remained about 7 percent.

Chart 7.3 also shows the real interest rate computed from the ten-year Treasury bond and the anticipated rate of inflation from the Society of Professional Forecasters. The rate moves in a very narrow range. In contrast, growth of the monetary base, especially the real value of the monetary base, fluctuated over a wide range. Real base growth rose during the boom in 1972, fell in advance of the recession in 1973–74, and rose during most of the expansion during the middle of the decade. Chart 7.4 shows these data.

Chart 7.5 shows the surge in the base growth compared to output growth in 1973–74, its subsequent collapse in 1974–75 and the new surge at the end of the 1970s. Inflation rose, pushed by excessive monetary stimulus and lax monetary and fiscal policies. By contrast, inflation remained low in 1963–64, when the base and real GDP rose at about the same rate.

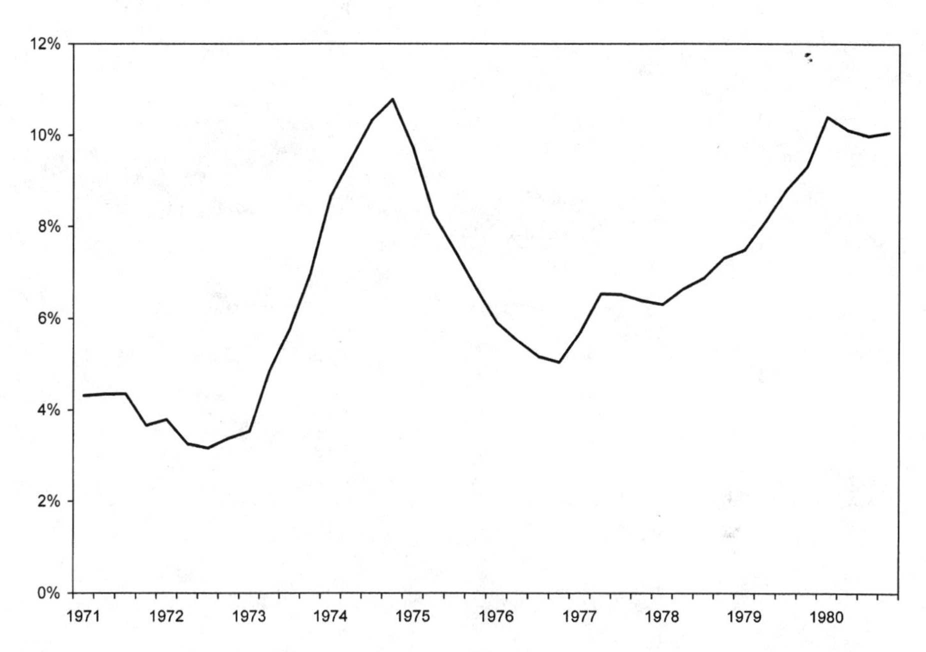


Chart 7.1. PCE inflation, 1971–80. Measured year-over-year.

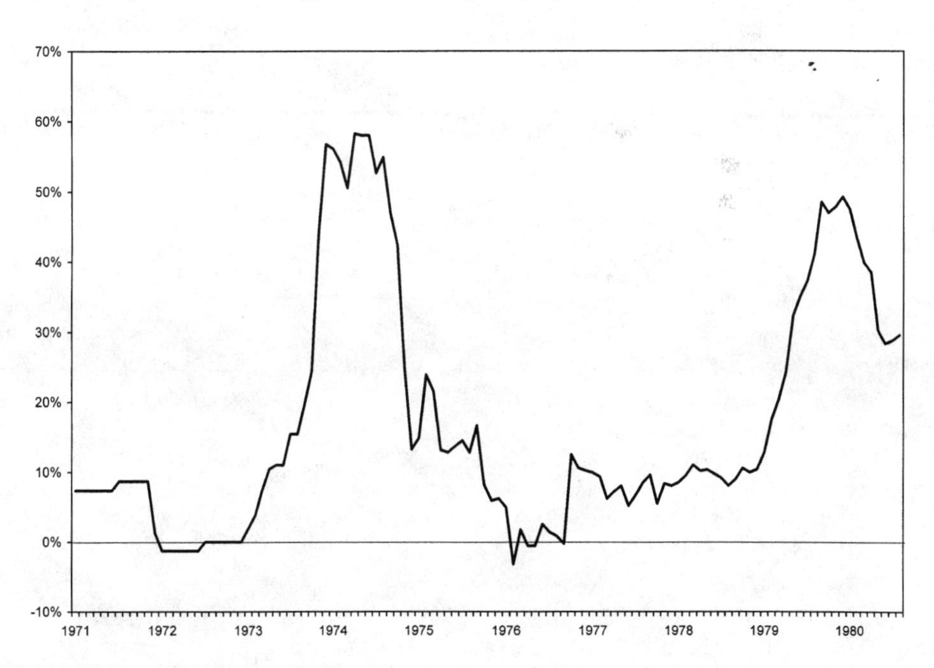


Chart 7.2. Price change of domestic crude oil, 1971–80. Measured year-over-year.

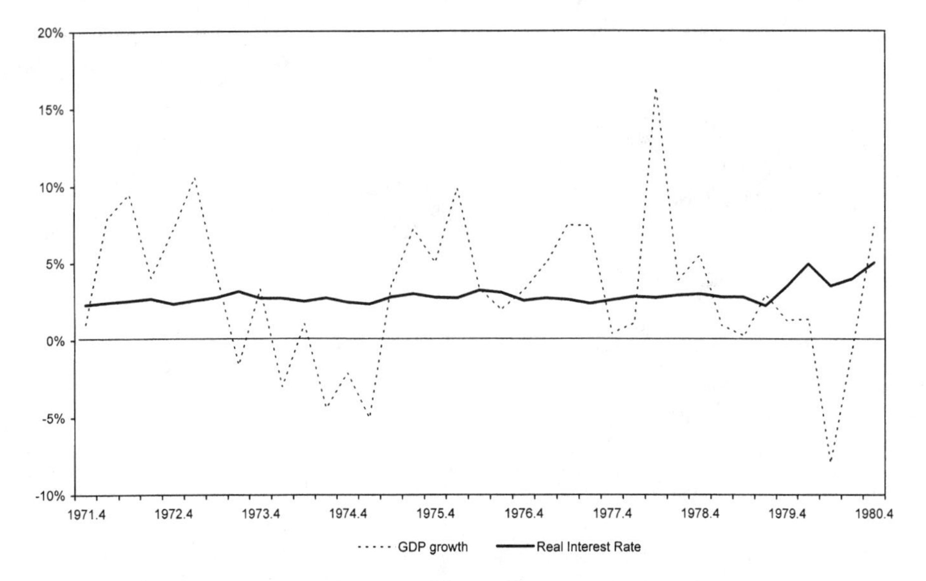


Chart 7.3. Real GDP growth versus ex ante real interest rate, 1971:4–1980:4.

Chart 7.4. Monetary base growth versus real base growth, October 1971–December 1980. Growth measured year-over-year.

Productivity growth declined during the 1970s as shown in Chart 7.6. The relatively high nominal base growth maintained through the decade and falling productivity growth contributed to average inflation over the decade. As in Nordhaus (2004), slower productivity growth was in part the result of the oil shocks during the decade. Variable inflation contributed

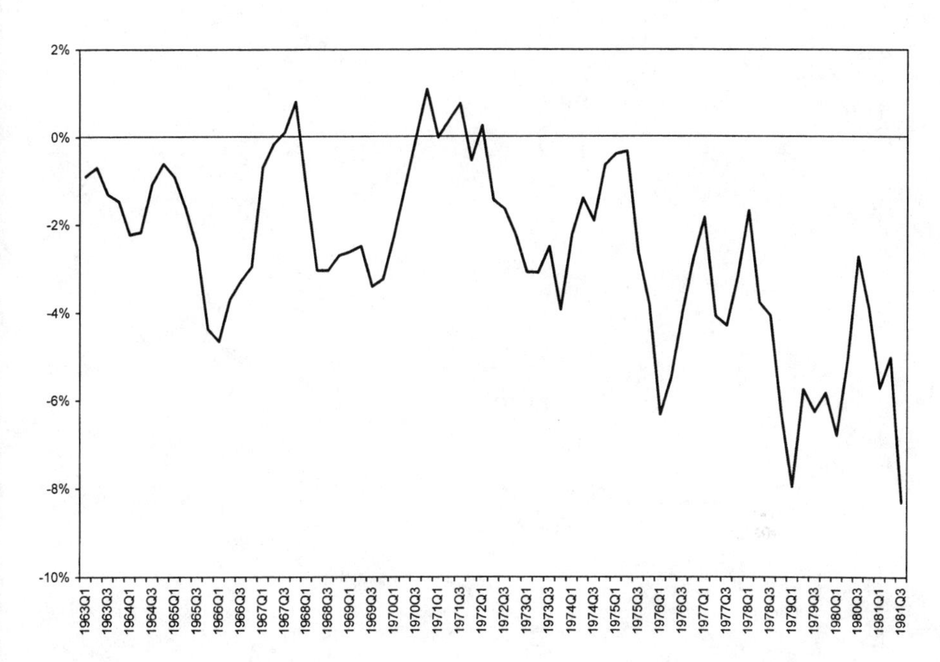


Chart 7.5. Year-over-year monetary base growth minus year-over-year real GDP growth, 1963:1–1981:3.

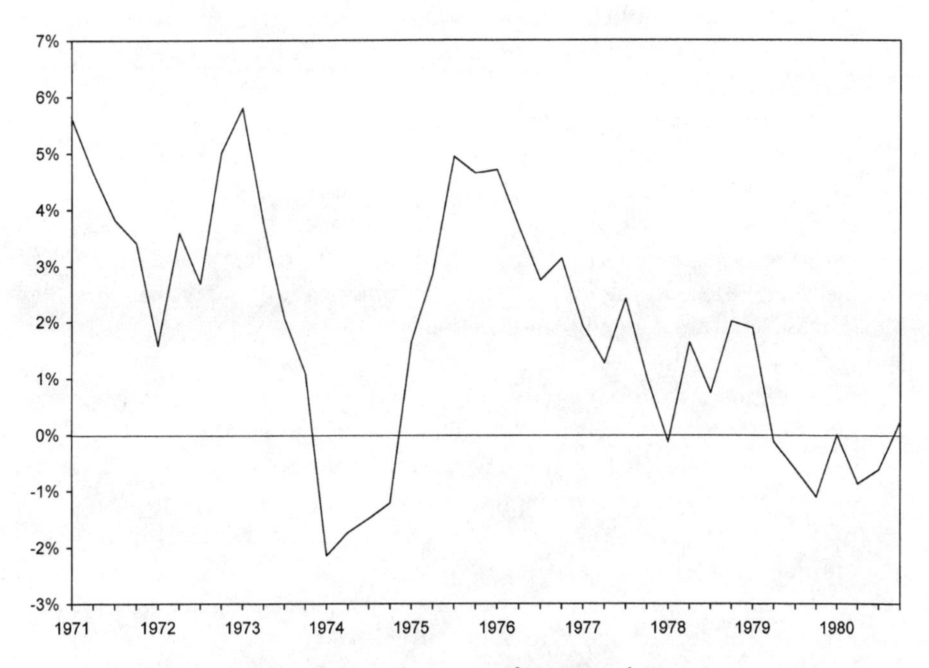


Chart 7.6. Output per hour, business sector, 1971–80. Measured year-over-year.

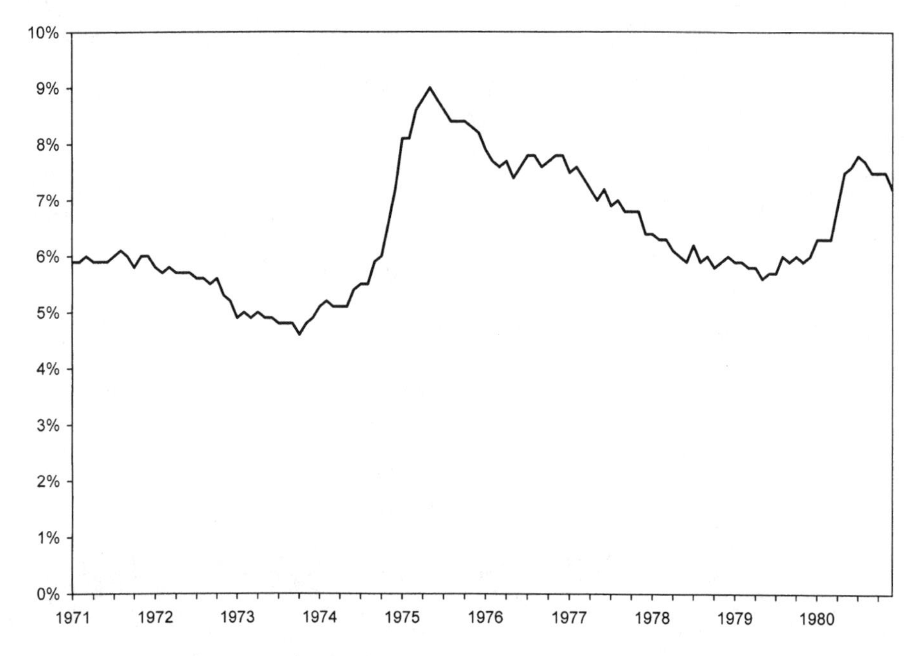


Chart 7.7. Civilian unemployment rate, January 1971–December 1980.

also by making it difficult for producers to make long-range plans and by focusing their attention on short-term gains. Federal Reserve actions reinforced these tendencies.

The civilian unemployment rate in Chart 7.7 follows the same general path (with opposite dips) as productivity growth. The unemployment rate fell as productivity and real growth rose, and it rose during recessions, when growth of productivity and real output fell. Chart 7.7 shows the peak in the postwar unemployment rate at 9 percent. In 1982, the unemployment rate reached a higher peak, 10.8 percent, near the end of the recession that ended the high inflation period.

Much economic theory of the cost of inflation discusses the cost of a fully indexed inflation. All prices adjust fully to the anticipated inflation rate. The 1970s inflation was far from that theoretical construct. Congress did not index personal income tax rates until the 1980s. Interest rates on time and demand deposits remained controlled. The government controlled energy prices. The controlled rates and prices did not adjust to inflation.

One consequence was that it was privately profitable to use talent and personnel to develop alternatives that avoided regulation. These innovations introduced variability into monetary aggregates and eventually their

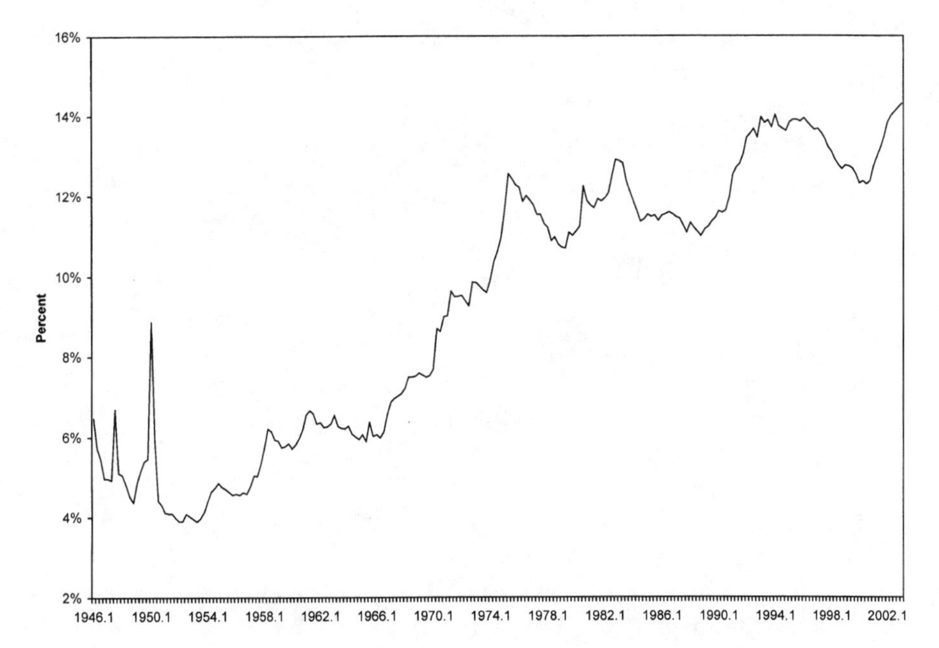


Chart 7.8. Transfer payments as a percentage of personal income, 1946:1–2003:1.

redefinition. A second consequence was that savings and loan institutions faced long periods in which the yield on their portfolios remained far below the interest rates permitted to be paid on their liabilities even though these rates remained below open market rates. The savings and loans suffered loss of income and deposits. Inflation and their decisions about risk taking eventually destroyed many of them at substantial cost to taxpayers.

Finally, Chart 7.8 points out a major change in the use of resources. Beginning with the start of President Johnson's Great Society spending in 1965–66, transfer payments as a percentage of personal income doubled in less than a decade. The change in administration in 1969–70 slowed the growth rate for a short time. The rate of increase rose following the slowdown until the proportion reached more than 12 percent of personal income. This surge reflects the introduction and growth of many so-called poverty programs but also transfer programs for health care. These programs shifted resource use from production to consumption and probably contributed to slower productivity growth as resources were drawn to the new federal programs. The small changes in the last half of the 1970s reflect mainly changes in income. A new, smaller surge in transfer payments occurred at the end of the 1980s.

The data summarized here, particularly data on the Great Inflation, encouraged an extensive literature on the causes of the inflation by both political scientists and economists. Before turning to the details of the period, we examine some of these explanations.[10]

Tufte (1978) offered a political interpretation. Based on work such as Kramer (1971) and many later studies, he showed that election outcomes depend positively on unemployment, real disposable income, and similar variables and negatively on inflation. Quoting Nordhaus (1975, 185), Tufte argued that "politically determined policy choice will have lower unemployment and higher inflation than is optimal." Barro and Gordon (1983) reached a similar conclusion in a different model by assuming that the desired unemployment rate is below the so-called natural rate.

One problem with these models is that they explain policy outcomes for a period restricted to the Great Inflation. They explain neither the period before nor the one after the Great Inflation. To explain observed changes in the inflation rate, the models require improbably large changes in the so-called natural rate of unemployment. They suggest why it can be politically costly to reduce an inflation that has started, but they do not adequately explain either why inflation ended or, once ended, why it did not return. Second, the political models explain what politicians prefer, but they avoid an explanation of why an ostensibly independent Federal Reserve cooperated.[11]

Economists' explanations fall into three groups. The first cites theoretical errors; policymakers used the wrong model to choose actions or interpret data. A second is misinformation; policymakers believed that their actions would reduce or prevent inflation, but the data misled them. Third, officials neglected or dismissed money growth as important for inflation. This is a special case of the first explanation that merits separate consideration. I discuss each in turn.

### *Theoretical Errors*

There is little reason to doubt, and abundant evidence to support, the conclusion that in the late 1960s the Council of Economic Advisers under Gardner Ackley and the Board's staff under Daniel Brill relied heavily on a simple Keynesian model with a non-vertical, long-run Phillips curve.

10. The summary is based on Meltzer (2005).

11. Many economists invoke the inflation tax as a cause of inflation. The inflation tax—the cost to money holders from a fall in the real value of their balances—transferred wealth to the government, so the government gained from inflation. It gained also as taxpayers moved to higher tax brackets. I have found no evidence that suggests that this encouraged inflation or that policymakers chose this tax. Concern about unemployment was far more important for monetary expansion and Federal Reserve actions.

Romer and Romer (2002b) develop this reasoning.[12] Combining this model with a belief that in James Tobin's familiar phrase—it takes many Harberger triangles to fill an Okun gap—we get a rationalization or defense of inflationary policies.[13]

Another explanation of this kind points to the misinterpretation of interest rates or neglect of the distinction between real and nominal interest rates. This was a long-standing Federal Reserve problem (Meltzer, 2003). According to Taylor (1999), Clarida, Gali, and Gertler (2000), and others, until 1981, the Federal Reserve did not increase the market interest rate enough in response to inflation to offset the negative effect of inflation on (ex post) real interest rates and on expected future interest rates. Orphanides (2003a, 2003b) shows that, at the margin, the Federal Reserve's response to its (flawed) inflation forecasts would have been sufficient to compensate for inflation. It remains true, however, that ex post real short-term interest rates remained negative during much of the 1970s.[14]

If we accept Taylor's interpretation and conclude that the Federal Reserve did not raise nominal interest rates enough, we are left with two questions. First, didn't the market recognize the error and raise (the more relevant) long-term interest rates and other asset prices? Second, then as now, the Federal Open Market Committee looked at many different series. They knew that inflation continued and rose at times to new levels. How could they fail to see (or learn) that their actions were inadequate to slow or stop inflation? The data in Chart 7.1 above, or similar data for the period, were available at every meeting.

There is little doubt that the simple Keynesian model as used at the time, such as is found in Ackley (1961), with a non-vertical long-run Phil-

12. In Hargrove and Morley (1984) Council chairmen state their interpretations. Okun (1970) explained that he regarded Friedman's (1968b) explanation of the vertical long-run Phillips curve as of little practical relevance.

13. The argument is flawed. Tobin compares the one-time loss from unemployment (Okun gap) to the loss from non-indexed inflation (Harberger triangle). Losses from inflation continue as long as inflation continues. Fischer (1981) shows many ways in which inflation is costly that are not captured in the Harberger or Bailey triangle. See also Feldstein (1982) for effects on capital.

14. Recent papers compare two explanations of negative real short-term rates. Collard and Dellas (2004) attributes the result to chance, principally unfavorable shocks (oil); Velde (2004) cites policy errors. These are not alternatives. Both could be and probably were relevant. One problem is that the bad luck mainly affected the price level, not the maintained inflation rate. A market that recognized temporary and permanent changes would have different responses of short- and long-term interest rates to such changes, hence different responses of economic activity. Between the end of December 1972 and December 1973, three-month Treasury bill rates rose from 5.13 to 7.50 percent; ten-year constant maturity Treasury bonds rose only from 6.40 to 6.87 percent. This is one illustration of the difference between the two definitions of inflation. The Federal Reserve did not recognize the distinction at the time.

lips curve, misled policymakers in the 1960s by overstating the role of fiscal policy, especially temporary changes, understating the role of money growth, failing to distinguish between anticipated and unanticipated inflation and between the effects of temporary and permanent tax rate changes, and neglecting the role of inflationary anticipations on interest rates, wages, and prices. However, in the 1970s the Nixon administration economists did not share many of these beliefs. They accepted that the long-run Phillips curve was vertical, and they emphasized the importance of money growth for inflation. Nevertheless, under their guidance, inflation increased before the oil price shock of 1973 and continued through their term in office. Despite their beliefs about money and inflation, they urged faster money growth in 1970–72 and at other times.

At most, reliance on the simple Keynesian model is part of an explanation of the start of the inflation. There has to be more to the story because it is the Federal Reserve, not the Council of Economic Advisers, that makes monetary policy. William McChesney Martin, Jr., was chairman of the Board of Governors at the start of the inflation and until 1970. Martin did not rely on explicit economic models, Keynesian or other.[15] He said many times that he did not find economic models useful and he gave most attention to market data and market participants, not economists. This reinforced the short-term focus of Federal Reserve actions and the neglect of longer-term consequences. Arthur Burns was an empirical economist who disdained deductive models. Martin and Burns made many speeches opposing inflation and pointing out its costs.

Gordon (1977, 276) concluded that his model based on a Phillips curve failed "to explain the increased variance of inflation during 1971–76 as compared to the pre-1971 period." The model did better at explaining the cumulative change. Gordon concluded that the short-run Phillips curve became steeper after 1971, but he offered no explanation of the change. The change in the estimated coefficients of his equations from estimates for earlier periods suggests that the underlying structure had changed. The likely reason was that the public had learned to expect inflation and

15. Of course, anyone who makes repeated decisions and does not act haphazardly can be described as having a framework in mind. This is far different from saying that Martin had an economic model relating interest rates or free reserves to output and prices. As he often said, he thought of policy as a river that had to be controlled enough to irrigate the fields without flooding them. After reading Martin's statements in Board and open market meetings, in White House conferences, and in the question-and-answer sessions in Congress (as opposed to statements that his staff wrote for him) I cannot find an economic model. In 1963–64 as a temporary member of the House Banking Committee staff, I interviewed Chairman Martin and asked him to explain how he thought monetary policy worked. He explained about rivers irrigating fields.

increased expected inflation in response to higher actual inflation.[16] A common finding at the time was that the tradeoff between inflation and unemployment became steeper (a more inflationary cost of reducing unemployment) as time passed.

Subsequent work showed that the short-run Phillips curve did not give reliable forecasts of inflation. That should have been clear from the large errors in forecasts of inflation during the 1970s. (See below and Orphanides (2003a).) As the charts above suggest, inflation and unemployment tended to increase together in the 1970s and, subsequently, to decline together. A summary of some recent research concludes, "The short-run Phillips curve should be viewed as a limited tool for forecasting purposes" (Lansing, 2002, 3).

### *Misinformation*

In a series of papers, Orphanides showed that the information available to policymakers from 1977 to 1992 differed, at times substantially, from the data published subsequently for output and inflation. One paper (Orphanides, 2001, Figure 2) shows that the output gap, as measured at the time, was generally larger than the output gap based on data recorded in the revised national accounts. The difference was often sufficient to mislead policymakers adjusting policy in response to the output gap and inflation. In Orphanides (2003a) he showed that the principal sources of error were two misperceptions: (1) through much of the 1970s, policymakers assumed that full employment meant an unemployment rate of about 4 percent; they were slow to recognize that the so-called natural rate of unemployment had increased; (2) productivity growth slowed in the late 1960s or early 1970s (see Chart 7.6 above), but policymakers continued to expect a return to the higher productivity growth of earlier postwar years.

Orphanides's explanation has considerable verisimilitude, as he shows. I would add that policymakers erred in treating the output loss following the 1973 and 1979 oil shocks wholly as evidence of recession, instead of partly a one-time transfer to the oil producers that permanently reduced the level of output. This contributed to the mismeasurement of the output gap and the desire to raise output by monetary expansion. This is an example of the pervasive problem created by failing to distinguish between one-time changes and maintained rates of change. The problem remains currently in discussions of inflation targeting. At the time, West Germany,

16. Sargent (1999) developed an explanation that depends on the belief that there was a permanent (or long-run) tradeoff between inflation and unemployment. Sargent (2002, 80–85) supplemented that explanation by pointing to several additional errors.

Switzerland, and Japan did not make that error and experienced less inflation despite greater dependence on imported oil. This shows that alternatives were known.

The more general point based on Orphanides's work is that the Federal Reserve underestimated inflation throughout the Great Inflation. The persistence of the error raises a question: Why did the FOMC members not recognize the error after a few years and adjust their procedures and policy actions?

### *The Role of Money Growth*

A noticeable change occurred in the 1960s. By 1960–61, policy had driven the CPI inflation rate from an annual rate of 3.5 percent in 1958 to 1 percent or less in 1959–61. Under the influence of Winfield W. Riefler, Chairman Martin at times testified about keeping the average rate of monetary growth close to the average rate of output growth.

After Riefler retired at the end of 1958, this model of inflation disappeared from the Board and its staff. Malcolm Bryan of the Richmond reserve bank and D. C. Johns and Darryl Francis of the St. Louis bank brought this analysis to the Federal Open Market Committee in the 1960s and 1970s without much impact on decisions. Governor Sherman Maisel, at the Board from 1965 to 1972, is an exception. He often urged a policy of controlling money growth. He was not, however, willing to control inflation if it required more than a modest increase in the unemployment rate.

Friedman and Schwartz (1963) emphasized the importance of money growth for inflation. Their work was well known but largely ignored by most members of FOMC. Economists in the Nixon administration understood the importance of money growth for inflation but yielded to political pressures.

Chart 7.5 above suggests that, in addition to its error in measuring growth of potential real output, neglect of money growth—here growth of the monetary base—contributed to the policy error. Growth of the base in excess of output growth leads the inflation rate throughout the period. Excess growth of the base would have been a useful statistic for future inflation. The Federal Reserve Board staff gave it little weight.

Economists in the Nixon administration did not neglect money growth. They watched reported money growth closely and overemphasized the effect of short-term changes. Their larger error was that most often they wanted to increase money growth to reduce the unemployment rate, and they encouraged President Nixon to talk to Arthur Burns about money growth frequently, as shown in chapter 6.

By 1974 and perhaps earlier, most FOMC members recognized that sustained inflation occurred only if supported by money growth. The House Committee on Banking and Currency took testimony from several Federal Reserve presidents, and it sent a staff member, Robert Weintraub, to question each president and Board member about the reason they believed the country experienced high inflation and high nominal interest rates.

Answers about the cause of inflation varied in detail, but the role of money growth was common. President Francis (St. Louis) said that inflation and high interest rates "stem from the same source—an excessive trend rate of expansion of the Nation's money stock since the early 1960s" (House Committee on Banking and Currency, 1974, 166). He blamed the Federal Reserve's actions for the result. Others rationalized the FOMC's actions citing energy and commodity price changes or unemployment as reasons for the FOMC's actions. All accepted the long-term influence of money growth as a dominant factor, but several cited short-run concerns. For example, President Mayo (Chicago) said, "No one will deny that inflation is directly concerned with the relationship between the quantity of goods and the quantity of money" (ibid., 195). But he soon retreated to a claim that other "factors outside the influence of the Federal Reserve played a very important role in the unprecedented inflation of 1973 and 1974" (ibid.). His statement is correct only if the definition of inflation includes one-time price level changes in addition to persistent changes. Failure to distinguish between maintained inflation and price level increases contributed to the Federal Reserve's inept policy. The cost of rolling back the price level increases added greatly to the perceived cost of an anti-inflation policy. Controlling the sustained (monetary) inflation and permitting the price level changes to pass through would have left the price level higher but not the inflation rate.

President Balles (San Francisco) testified that excessive money growth was the principal cause of inflation. He claimed that pressures to support housing construction, concerns about unemployment, and "excessive deficit financing" were background causes (ibid., 98). President Eastburn (Philadelphia) testified that "whatever immediate events may cause prices to rise . . . a higher price level can not be maintained without sufficient money" (ibid., 121).

There is little reason to doubt that FOMC members recognized their role in creating inflation, although many offered explanations defending their actions or sought to justify them. Arthur Burns was less forthright, perhaps trying to shift responsibility away from the Federal Reserve. Even he accepted that "monetary policy must not permit sufficient growth in money and credit supplies to accommodate all of the price increases that are directly and indirectly attributable to special factors. . . . A monetary policy that accommodates all of these price increases could result in an endless cost-price spiral and a serious worsening of an already grave inflationary problem. The appropriate course for monetary policy is the middle ground" (ibid., 243). Burns said some price increases should pass through, but not all. He then cited the annual 6 percent growth of money as appropriate for the present but too high for the longer-term. Reducing the growth rate "must be achieved gradually to avoid upsetting effects on the real economy" (ibid., 254). This recognized both inflation and the cost of containing inflation as major concerns. Action did not follow recognition.

The 1974 hearings bring out forcefully the political constraints that Congress tried to impose on the Federal Reserve. Congressman Reuss urged credit allocation to priority uses. Burns opposed, urging market allocation, but Andrew Brimmer wrote a letter favoring a system of credit allocation (ibid., 274–76). Other congressmen wanted more assistance to housing and other politically popular uses. Still others used the hearing to complain about the $1.2 billion the Federal Reserve lent to prevent failure of Franklin National Bank. Chairman Patman included several criticisms, including one that contrasted the Federal Reserve's support of Franklin with the Bundesbank's refusal to support the Herstatt bank (ibid., 298).[17]

The hearings and Weintraub's interviews showed general agreement about the long-term role of money but little agreement about the desirability of monetary control. One central problem that the hearings did not develop was the role of interest rate targets.[18]

*A remaining puzzle.* The references earlier in this chapter to Orphanides, Sargent, Taylor, and Romer and Romer offer explanations of the Great Inflation compatible with the more general statement that policymakers ignored economic theories that were available, repeating a similar error made in the 1930s. Indeed the monetarist critique at the time emphasized neglect of long-standing propositions, as Franco Modigliani (1977) later acknowledged.

17. Elsewhere in the hearings, Burns recognized the problem caused by below-market ceiling rates under regulation Q. He did not propose removal and questioned whether it was appropriate to raise the ceiling because it would increase costs for thrift institutions (House Committee on Banking and Currency, 1974, 285).

18. Neglect of money growth and reliance on interest rate changes to interpret policy resulted in procyclical changes in money growth. When output fell and borrowing declined, market interest rates declined also. The Federal Reserve interpreted the decline as evidence that policy had eased, so it permitted money growth to decline. Rising output and borrowing raised interest rates. The Federal Reserve interpreted higher nominal interest rates as evidence of restrictive policy, so it permitted money growth to increase, adding to inflationary pressures.

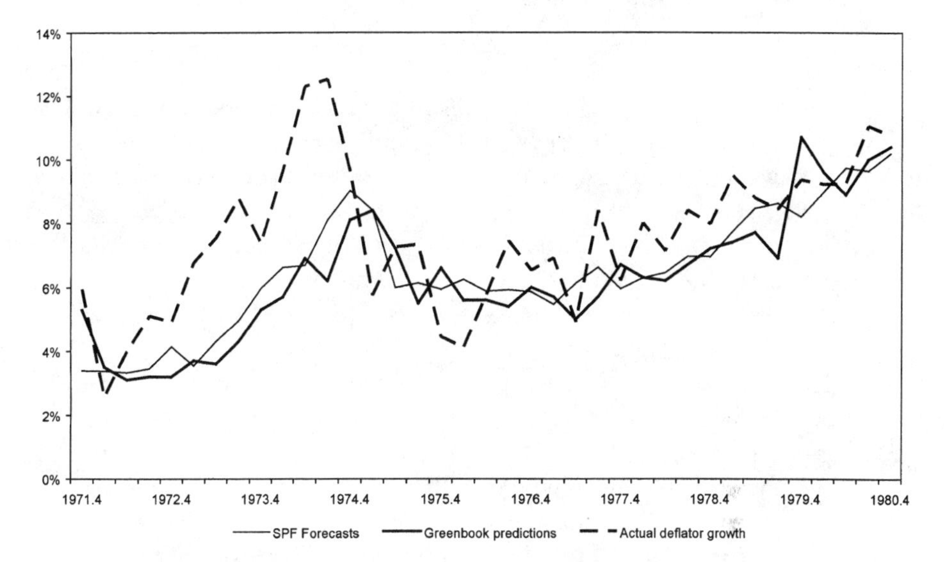


Chart 7.9. SPF versus green book forecasts of GNP/GDP implicit price deflator annualized quarterly growth, compared with actual deflator growth, 1971:4–1980:4.

The remaining large puzzle is to explain why this happened. Why did the Federal Reserve dismiss for years the long-run vertical Phillips curve, procyclicality of monetary policy, and the effect of inflation on nominal interest rates, wages, and anticipations more generally? Why did they ignore the finding of some of their own staff that concluded that the long-run Phillips curve was vertical? Critics pointed out these errors at the time. Propositions that attribute the Great Inflation to analytical errors of one kind or another ought to be supplemented by an explanation of why the error persisted for fifteen years before policy changed. As is well-known, policymakers began anti-inflation policies as early as 1966 and several times after—1969, 1973, 1978–79, and 1980. They were aware of the Great Inflation but, until 1979–82, they did not persist in policies to end it.

My main objection to explanations based on persistent policy errors is that they are incomplete. Federal Reserve officials could observe inflation rates. They knew that their policies had not ended inflation. Most often inflation was above their forecast. Chart 7.9 shows that the forecast errors were too large and persistent to be ignored. Yet the System did not change course. Burns was a distinguished economist, influenced more by data and induction than by deductive theories. Yet he failed to stop the inflation and, at times, saw it rise to rates never before experienced in U.S. peacetime history. Most of the FOMC members were not ideologues or slavish adherents to a particular theory. Several regarded themselves as practical men, meaning not attached to any particular theory and willing to discard analyses that did not work.

One additional caveat is that the Federal Reserve is not a monolith. Members of the Federal Open Market Committee (FOMC) have independent views. Particularly in the 1960s, they were mostly non-economists. They had considerable difficulty agreeing on how to implement actions, as Maisel (diary, 1973) documents fully. The staff, or part of it, had a model, but insiders who have written about the 1960s and 1970s often emphasize inconsistency in the choices made by the FOMC (Lombra and Moran, 1980; Pierce, 1980, and Maisel, various years).

The international character of the Great Inflation is sometimes advanced as support for explanations based on errors in economic theory. The claim is that many countries made the same errors, particularly denial of the natural rate hypothesis, claiming that unemployment in the long run was independent of inflation. All experienced inflation. Once policymakers everywhere accepted the natural rate hypothesis, time inconsistency theory, understanding of the need for credibility, and rational expectations, inflation declined.

Appealing as this argument is to economists, it fails to separate the start of inflation and its continuance. The start of inflation occurred under the Bretton Woods system of fixed exchange rates. Surplus countries experienced inflation because they would not appreciate their currencies to stop the inflation, and those that did appreciate made at most modest increases until 1971. They were fully aware of the problem; they did not want a solution that reduced their exports or slowed the growth of output and employment. They opposed dollar depreciation. Once the fixed exchange rate system ended, Japan, West Germany, Switzerland, and Austria reduced their inflation rates. Others permitted inflation to continue or increase.

The United Kingdom was the principal deficit country besides the United States. It comes closest to support the policy errors (or preferences) explanation. Policymakers in both U.K. parties accepted and used a simple Keynesian model. The long delay of sterling devaluation from 1964 to 1967 and the policy measures chosen are evidence of the reluctance to slow growth (Nelson, 2003b).

The Great Inflation resulted from policy choices that placed much more weight on maintaining high or full employment than on preventing or reducing inflation. For much of the period, this choice reflected both political pressures and popular opinion as expressed in polls. Many accepted James Tobin's view that inflation would increase before the economy reached full employment, or they claimed that eliminating inflation required an unacceptable increase in unemployment. Inflation did not fall permanently until public opinion polls showed the public willing to bear the cost. Then it became acceptable politically to shift more weight to inflation control and less to unemployment when choosing monetary policy actions.

## THE 1973–74 RECESSION

Neither the administration nor its critics and outside observers anticipated the 14 percent surge in food prices followed by a surge in oil prices in 1973.[19] None predicted the steep decline in output that followed.

The 1973–74 increase in consumer prices was the largest since 1947, following the end of wartime price controls. This time removal of price controls, devaluation of the dollar after 1971, poor harvests abroad, and increases in oil prices added to the underlying rate of measured inflation resulting from the excessive monetary and fiscal expansion of 1972. Although some of the Board's staff recognized the distinction (Pierce and Enzler, 1974), the administration and the Federal Reserve did not distinguish between these sources of rising prices. Monetary contraction—slower monetary growth—could reduce the maintained rate of inflation driven by growth of aggregate demand by reducing growth of aggregate demand. Using monetary policy to counter the price level increase resulting from one-time reductions in the supply of food or fuel lowered the equilibrium price level by reducing aggregate demand. Reductions in both supply and demand induced reductions in output and employment. A proper policy response to the oil price increase would have recognized that it was a tax on oil users paid to foreign producers. To reduce the loss of welfare, the administration could have reduced domestic tax rates.[20] Or it could do nothing about the price level shock and allow it to pass through the economy. It was not a monetary problem, as some FOMC members recognized.[21]

19. Wells (1994, 111) quotes Burns as offering a political explanation of rapid money growth but not attributing the increase to the election. "Fundamentally, it is the expansion of the money supply over the long run that will be the basic cause of inflation." To slow its growth, the Federal Reserve had to raise interest rates but, Burns said: "In the United States, there is an acute political problem regarding interest rates. Congress and the unions have become quite concerned about interest rates. Congress could unwisely legislate statutory limits on interest rates, or fail to act promptly to approve extension of the Economic Stabilization Act [controls]." This shows a willingness to sacrifice independence.

20. The source of this error was failure to distinguish between the maintained or persistent inflation rate and other increases in the reported price level. An anti-inflation policy can have different goals. It can keep the maintained rate of inflation at zero and permit price level shocks to drive the price level to fluctuate around an expected zero long-run rate of inflation. Or it can aim for price level stability by offsetting increases and decreases in the price level. The second option probably requires larger changes in output and employment.

21. Members of the staff correctly analyzed the oil shock and other one-time changes as affecting the price level, temporarily raising the rate of price change. See Pierce and Enzler

Secretary George Shultz and Council members Paul McCracken and Herbert Stein recognized in 1971 that a price and wage control program carried the risk that monetary and fiscal policy would be overly expansive (Hargrove and Morley, 1984, 356). Nevertheless, that was what they urged.

In addition to policy errors, administration economists relied on faulty data. They believed that the economy had idle capacity that later data revisions removed. They believed that with idle capacity and a 6 percent unemployment rate at the start of 1972, their stimulus program would create jobs not inflation. Stein later recognized their error. "We all thought, 'we're a long way from full employment . . . and the inflation rate is low'" (Hargrove and Morley, 1984, 396).

Once the election was over and members recognized the consequences of their actions, the administration reversed course. The president proposed reductions in government spending, and he tried to impound $12 billion in spending that Congress had authorized. He determined to hold fiscal 1974 spending to $269 billion.[22] Money growth declined also. From a peak twelve-month rate of increase of 9.3 percent in July 1973 annual base growth fell to less than 6 percent in late 1975 after controls relaxed or ended. Chart 7.4 above shows that annual growth of the real base turned negative in the fall of 1973. It remained negative for almost two years. Chart 7.10 compares real base growth to the real interest rate. Real base growth reached its trough in January 1975, two months before the National Bureau recorded a trough to the recession. As in several earlier recessions, real ten-year interest rates (using predicted inflation) remained in a narrow range. These rates declined modestly before the recession, remained in a narrow range during the recession, again declined modestly before the trough, and rose during the early months of recovery. Chart 7.10 shows these data.

The Council of Economic Advisers forecast for 1973 that inflation would fall to 2.5 percent and that real growth would approach full employment, still considered a 4 percent unemployment rate. Instead, the four-quarter average increase in the GNP deflator reached more than 8.25 percent and rose 10 percent (annual rate) in the fourth quarter. Real GNP rose 3.5 percent, but in the last three quarters, the average rate fell to 1.4 percent. The unemployment rate remained about 5 percent. Despite the commitment

(1974). I am grateful to David Lindsey for this reference. There is little evidence that the FOMC accepted this analysis or discussed its implication for their response.

22. He achieved his spending limit, but Congress resisted his unprecedented use of impoundment. They removed this power. Earlier in October 1972, Congress increased social security payments by 20 percent just before the election and for the first time indexed social security benefits so they would increase with prices automatically.

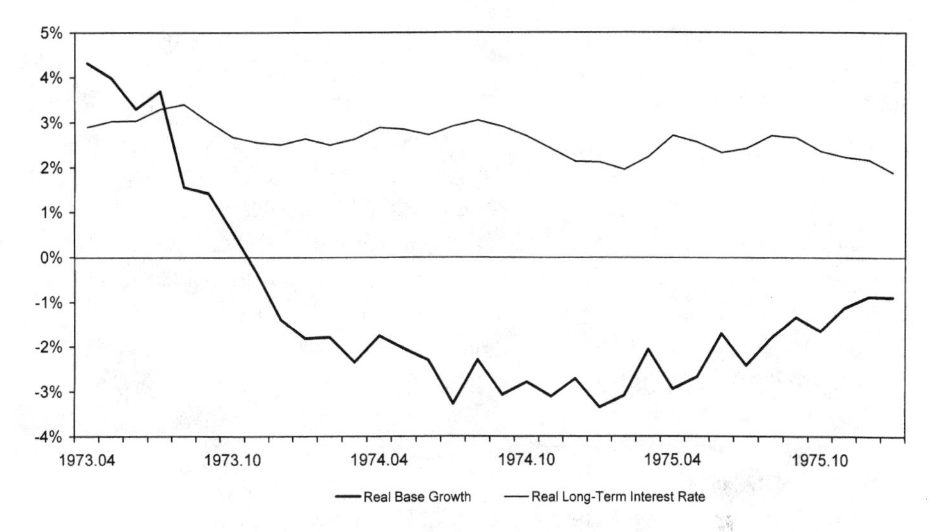


Chart 7.10. Real base growth versus real long-term interest rate, April 1973–January 1976. Real base growth measured year-over-year; long-term interest rate measured as yield on ten-year Treasury bonds.

to reduce inflation, the Society of Professional Forecasters raised the expected four-quarter inflation rate from 3.7 percent to 5.4 percent between fourth quarter 1972 and 1973. A year later, it reached 7.7 percent. Hourly wage growth increased from 6.3 to 8.1 percent, and ten-year interest rates rose 0.5 percentage points to 7.4 percent.

Food price increases that began with large grain purchases by the Soviet Union ended with the new harvest. Oil price increases began at about the same time. At first oil prices more than doubled to $5 a barrel. By year-end 1973, the oil price reached $11.65 a barrel. Instead of allowing domestic gas and oil prices to reflect market prices, the administration maintained price controls. These controls began in August 1971, so they froze prices when heating oil was relatively cheap seasonally and gasoline relatively expensive. Subsequent supply problems reflected this policy. Heating oil became scarce in the winter, when its price usually rose.[23]

The National Bureau dates the peak of the expansion in November 1973 and the trough of the recession sixteen months later in March 1975. The recession was the longest since the Great Depression and the deepest since 1937–38. Real output fell 4.9 percent, more than in any postwar recession

23. On October 23, 1973, most members of OPEC, led by Saudi Arabia, imposed a boycott on exports to the United States and the Netherlands, demanding a change in their policy of supporting Israel and to punish the United States for supplying weapons to Israel in the 1973 war. The boycott had little effect on supply. Oil shipments shifted. The United States received its oil from non-Arab producers. The boycott soon ended.

to date (including 1981–82). The unemployment rate reached 9 percent in May 1975 after the recession ended.

Prior to the recession, the FOMC could not agree on appropriate policy or how to conduct it. Policy called for controlling growth of monetary aggregates by controlling growth of RPDs (reserves against private deposits) to reduce inflation; the members never discussed how much unemployment they would accept to reduce inflation. In practice, differences persisted.[24]

At its August 20 meeting, the FOMC recognized that part of the recent surge in wholesale prices reflected the early end of the June 13 price freeze on July 18. Interest rates had increased during the summer as money growth slowed. In July, the Board removed interest rate ceilings on consumer time deposits of $1000 or more and four years maturity. It raised ceiling rates on shorter maturities. At the end of July, the System decided to rescue a Treasury offering by purchasing $350 million of a $500 million issue. The Treasury purchased almost half of the twenty-year bond issue for its trust accounts.

To offset growth in RPDs that was more rapid than expected, the FOMC raised the maximum federal funds rate from 10.25 to 11 percent. As in its later experience from 1979 to 1982, the spread between the federal funds and discount rates induced a surge of borrowing to more than $2 billion in August.[25]

The staff forecast called for much slower growth, 1.2 percent average real growth for the four quarters of 1974. "The dilemma that the Committee faces . . . is in deciding how to weigh the very real prospect that growth in the economy will be slowing to minimal levels against the very real risk that there may be enough remaining strength to keep unacceptable pressure on critical resources and hence on our structure of costs and

24. The Board also increased marginal reserve requirements from 5 to 8 percent on certificates of deposit and commercial paper on May 16. The new requirements became effective June 7 but applied to the increase after May 16. At the same time, the Board removed the ceiling rate on all ninety-day single-maturity time deposits of $100,000 or more. On May 21, the Board sent a letter to large banks asking that "the rate of credit extension be appropriately disciplined" (Annual Report, 1973, 88–89). The federal funds rate rose, but annual monetary base growth also rose. The Board increased reserve requirements by 0.5 percentage points on June 29. It exempted the first $2 million of a bank's deposits to pacify members of Congress who wanted to protect small banks and to reduce the loss of members. With bank credit continuing to grow rapidly, on September 7, the Board increased the marginal reserve requirement from 8 to 11 percent. Three months later, the Board restored the 8 percent marginal requirement.

25. The System intervened in the foreign exchange market in July to stop dollar depreciation. The August rise in market rates reversed the decline. The System repaid the $273 million swap in August with an $8.5 million profit. Coombs was elated and urged more frequent, more visible, and larger interventions.

prices" (FOMC Minutes, August 21, 1973, 21). In response to a question, Charles Partee, a senior staff member, said he expected a recession in late 1974 (ibid., 30). The staff report urged the FOMC to choose between higher employment and lower inflation. The member's responses show their thinking. President Hayes (New York) wanted to slow inflation before it became embedded in wages. "He did not see much evidence that high interest rates were in themselves bringing demand pressures under control thus far." And he described the increase in nominal rates as "severe restraint" (ibid., 14–15). However, he failed to mention that real rates of interest had changed very little and were modestly lower (Chart 7.10 above). Governor Brimmer thought a recession was likely to come sooner than most expected. "The issue before the Committee would be not whether but how soon monetary policy should be eased" (ibid., 32–33). Burns, Hayes, and Francis disagreed. As usual before the recession started, they gave priority to inflation control. Burns said that "reduction in the rate of inflation would require an environment of tighter budgets and a relatively restrictive monetary policy" (ibid., 39).

Governor Bucher believed "the Fed had overreacted in the past and had created undesirable shocks in the economy" (ibid., 61). President Coldwell (Dallas) wanted to lower growth of RPDs and ignore $M_1$, but Governor Holland thought the Committee should focus on interest rates. And Governor Daane wanted to remain restrictive, but he didn't believe the System could achieve a precise target.

President Balles brought expectations into the discussion. He quoted a newspaper article saying that "the Federal government doesn't want to see the economy suffer either a recession or more inflation. If there is a choice, however, federal officials lean heavily toward more inflation" (ibid., 67). He thought that some measures of money had to slow. Part of the problem was the narrow range kept on the federal funds rate. Governor Brimmer responded that "policymakers faced with a choice between more or less inflation and more or less unemployment were inclined to accept a little more inflation" (ibid., 73).

Divided on several dimensions, the FOMC was unlikely to agree on decisive action. They made no effort to discuss the reasons for disagreement; they agreed to make no change. Chairman Burns summarized the comments as favoring $M_1$ growth of 1 to 4 percent, RPD growth of 11 to 15 percent, and the funds rate between 10 and 11 percent. The Committee changed RPD growth to 11 to 13 percent. It voted ten to one, with one absence. Darryl Francis dissented because of the narrow range for the federal funds rate. He did not believe the desk would hit the money target. Burns had recognized that "failure to bring the monetary aggregates under control in recent months fundamentally resulted from a failure to control RPDs" (ibid., 53). Yet he did not set a wider range for the funds rate or support Francis's effort to do so.

Soon after the meeting, data showed that RPD growth remained above the target. The desk responded by raising the federal funds rate by 0.25 to 10.75 percent, and the Board on September 7 increased reserve requirements against large-denomination CDs.[26]

Industrial production followed a very variable path during the fall, then fell 19 percent in December. Stock prices generally declined. The average annual increase in the CPI rose above 8 percent in November. The federal funds rate reached a peak in September and declined gradually, suggesting less restraint. As usual, policy moved procyclically. Monetary base growth declined from 9 percent in July to 7 percent in December, suggesting increased restraint.

The Federal Reserve faced stagflation, defined as falling output and rising inflation. On the staff's analysis, this was a puzzling outcome. Inflation was supposed to decline along the Phillips curve as output fell relative to potential. After the September 18 FOMC meeting, market rates dropped precipitately, and money growth fell below the target. At a special meeting on October 2, the FOMC voted six to five to permit a modest further decline in the funds rate. The minority wanted a larger move. A week later, at another special meeting, after Chairman Burns returned from Africa, the FOMC met (by telephone) again. The asymmetry in Burns's policy is evident. Although he had hesitated to respond to rising inflation, he warned the members that the FOMC "would be failing to meet its responsibilities to the economy and to the nation" (FOMC Minutes, October 10, 1973, 5). He favored providing "reserves aggressively" (ibid., 3). The funds rate would fall from 10.5 to 10. The Committee deleted the word "aggressively" and voted unanimously to make the policy change.[27]

26. On September 14, the Shadow Open Market Committee (SOMC) held its first meeting. Its initial statement said "economic policies could have been better in the past and can be better now." It proposed gradual reduction in money growth to a non-inflationary range, and it criticized the Federal Reserve for failing to adopt a long-term plan to lower inflation at lowest cost. Karl Brunner and I, with help from William Wolman and A. James Meigs of the Argus Research Corporation, organized the meeting. The SOMC continued to meet semiannually into the twenty-first century. Karl Brunner died in 1989, and I left in 1999. The SOMC hoped that its semiannual meetings would suggest that the FOMC give less attention to short-term changes.

27. Burns's policy reversal is informative about his concerns. He wanted to lower inflation without increasing the unemployment rate. Usually he dismissed short-term changes in money growth as non-informative, mainly random fluctuations. At this meeting, he seized on the brief decline in money growth to urge an aggressive expansion. He told the FOMC: "He had strongly advocated the highly restrictive monetary policy that had in fact been pursued in

Policy eased again on October 16. The federal funds rate remained near 10 percent from October to December. The professional forecast of inflation rose to 5.4 percent, an increase of 1.75 percentage points in a year. The oil embargo was in effect, and oil prices had increased when the FOMC met for the November meeting. Burns said he was "less confident about the direction of monetary policy" (ibid., November 20, 1973, 83). He thought that current economic problems were not primarily monetary. "Monetary policy might be able to play a marginally constructive role . . . but it could not offer a solution to the problems that the nation was on the threshold of experiencing" (ibid., 84–85).

Morris (Boston) disagreed. He thought a recession was likely, and he wanted more stimulus to offset the energy problem. "In addition to an easier open market policy, he would urge that some more overt easing action be taken" (ibid., 87). Burns resisted, and he prevailed, so Morris dissented. Reported money growth rose above the short-run targets. The FOMC voted on November 30 to let the excess growth remain and to keep money market conditions unchanged. Thus, they augmented the effect of the oil price increase on the price level by raising the inflation rate.

The initial staff estimate of the effect of the rise in oil prices was optimistic (memo, Effects of Oil Supply Cutbacks, Burns papers B_B3, December 1, 1973).[28] It did not consider the substantial costs created by price controls and waiting lines. Matusow (1998, chapter 9) describes the many mistakes made to prevent energy prices from rising.[29] President Nixon's concerns about the Watergate investigation and his desire to retain popular support probably contributed to the decision. Controls on energy prices remained until ended by President Reagan in 1981.

The rise in oil prices raised import costs. The value of imports rose

recent months. It now appeared that the objective—to moderate the growth of the monetary aggregates—had been achieved. . . . [T]he narrowly defined money supply had shown virtually no growth over the third quarter. . . . If the System were to allow the period of very low or negative growth in the money stock to continue much longer, . . . it would be failing to meet its responsibilities to the economy and to the nation" (FOMC Minutes, October 10, 1973, 4–5). "Mr. Daane remarked that he had not seen the kinds of significant changes in the economic situation that would warrant a sharp change in monetary policy" (ibid., 7–8).

28. Barsky and Killian (2004) cast doubt on the importance assigned to the oil shock in inflation and output in the 1970s. They show that the timing is a problem. They accept that a fixed-weight consumer price index would increase with the oil price, but they find little support in the deflator. "There is no convincing empirical evidence that oil price shocks are associated with higher inflation rates in the GDP deflator" (ibid., 124). There is an effect on the price level.

29. Matusow (1998, 267) gives a vivid description of the rage some drivers developed when they had difficulty buying gasoline. The Council of Economic Advisers favored decontrol, but political concerns prevented it. "Our failure to deregulate was one of the great mistakes" (Stein in Hargrove and Morley, 1984, 403).

almost $15 billion, 25 percent, in 1973. Exports increased more than $20 billion. The United States had its largest current account surplus in nominal dollars since 1947 and the first net inflow of private capital since 1968. The strong surge in exports helped to sustain output growth in the fourth quarter. The staff expected continued strong export growth in 1974 and forecast that nominal GNP would rise 8 percent in 1974 if money growth remained at 5 percent. The staff did not expect a recession at its November meeting even though the National Bureau later dated the start of the recession in that month. As often happened before and after, the forecast was wide of the mark, and it missed the start of a steep decline.

Not so for the basic analysis of the oil shock. Ralph Bryant of the Board's international staff understood what had happened. He told the Committee that "this will be a very special kind of recession, and it is not at all clear whether orthodox anti-recession policies will be appropriate" (FOMC Minutes, December 17–18, 1973, 41). Bryant saw the analytic problem as estimating the primary effects of reduced supply and the induced effects of uncertainty on demand. In addition, countries would have to finance large changes in their international payments.

The staff forecast was less accurate. It assumed that policy remained unchanged, but the budget deficit would rise as the economy slowed. Output growth would be about zero for the year. The outlook for employment and growth had been poor before the oil shock. It would be poorer, and inflation would rise.

Burns gave his view. He did not accept the staff forecast, but he recognized with them that the oil shock differed from an ordinary recession and called for different actions. He gave three reasons. "The continuance of sharp inflation clearly required caution and some restraint in carrying out a policy of monetary easing. The need for caution and restraint was also indicated by the energy shortage; . . . it was doubtful whether it [monetary policy] could overcome the short-run limitation on the nation's capacity to produce. Finally, . . . the sharp divergence was likely to occur in the fortunes of individual communities. . . . [A]t a time of energy shortage, monetary policy—instead of aiming to bring recession to an end—should merely aim to keep the recession becoming deeper than the restricted capacity to produce in itself required" (ibid., 70–73). This was a correct appraisal. He favored a slight easing.

### *Release of Information*

Renewed dissatisfaction with its operating procedures and growing external criticism of its results induced a new study and a lengthy discussion after the November FOMC meeting. Burns described the criticism: "it was issuing virtually meaningless directions to the Desk, that it was engaged in an exercise in obfuscation, and that it was following muddleheaded procedures" (FOMC Minutes, November 20, 1973, 78). The problem, as Burns described it, arose from misunderstanding. "The Committee did adopt specific targets, but . . . it could not reveal them for a time because of possible market effects" (ibid., 78–79). He proposed to provide the information after the fact, when the market could not profit from trading on the information.

Members were divided on this issue, as on most others. All favored giving more information but differed on what they should give and when. There were short-run targets, long-run targets, and revisions to targets. Some wanted to release information after three months, others after six months. Neither Burns or other members mentioned the benefits from giving correct information to the market.

Those expressing caution made two main arguments. Additional information would give the critics more information. They would see the difference between projections or plans and outcomes.[30] Also, giving more information would allow market participants to predict what the Federal Reserve planned to do and profit from it.

Surprisingly, no one suggested that the FOMC should improve its procedures and its control of inflation or that their problem arose in part from the lack of effective control. No one urged an end to quarterly control or concentration on longer-term outcomes. Some argued that the targets were not policy decisions, so they did not have to reveal them; Governor Holland described this as "sophistry" (ibid., 73).

At a more fundamental level was the Committee's understanding of the role of information. The discussion emphasized political and public relations problems and neglected efficiency. Several of those who wanted to release full information, with a lag, wanted to silence criticism. They did not argue that announcing targets would induce the market to help achieve the System's goals. The FOMC was in transition on this issue, as on many others. The old tradition allowed central banks to be secretive. But this tradition arose under the gold standard and public support for a balanced budget (except in wartime.) These restrictions were generally

30. Robert Mayo (Chicago) gave a succinct statement of this concern. "The record of misses would be interpreted too narrowly and used in new attacks by hostile critics in the Congress. That record could be described by those critics as providing evidence that monetary policy and the Federal Reserve as an institution were inept; that the Federal Reserve staff was incompetent; and that the Federal Open Market Committee should be modified or abolished" (FOMC Minutes, November 20, 1973, 80). Mayo did not mention the benefit of more accurate information to the market and thus to the System. No one suggested that random elements made short-run control difficult.

believed to be adequate to limit the damage a central bank could do. After abandoning the gold standard rule and accepting some responsibility for employment, growth, and inflation, the central bank inevitably became subject to democratic political pressures. Having lost its rule, and subject to the unpredictable actions of central bankers, the public wanted more information to protect itself. The central bank did not yet recognize that by releasing information and acting to achieve its targets, the market would help to achieve its targets and avoid mistakes or misinterpretations costly to both sides. Only in 1994 did the Federal Reserve start to announce its short-term objective.

Discussion at the November 1973 meeting did not reach a conclusion. FOMC members did not have common beliefs about how monetary policy affected the economy, which variables made good targets, or how the desk should operate to meet the targets. Without some common framework, differences were hard to reconcile. The members did not attempt to do so.

Burns stopped the discussion but returned to it in December. At the time, the FOMC published the RPD target in the Record of Policy Action and in the report of the meeting. Burns proposed to include short-term targets for $M_1$, $M_2$, and the funds rate also. Some wanted to add long-run targets; others wanted to release long-run targets but not short-run. Coldwell thought money targets got too much attention; he wanted to suppress them. Daane wanted to eliminate RPDs from the record and to limit statements to qualitative references. Like several others, he was embarrassed by the size of the errors they made.

Governor Mitchell did not accept that releasing more quantitative information would help the public understand what they did. Then he described the problem. "The basic problem—that such records would not articulate the Committee's theory about the manner in which monetary policy worked—was a consequence of the fact that the Committee as a whole did not have such a theory, although individual members might" (FOMC Minutes, December 18, 1973, 15–16).

No one responded to Mitchell. The Committee voted nine to two (Hayes not voting) to publish quantitative information on all of the short-run targets. Daane and Mayo dissented. None of the long-term targets would be published.[31]

The FOMC reopened discussion of publishing long-term targets the

31. The staff issued its "First Report on Lagged Accounting" on August 13, 1973. It would return to the topic several times in the next decade. The conclusion of all the reports was similar. "If reserve aggregates are used the contribution of lagged reserve accounting is, if anything, negative" (First Report, Federal Reserve Bank of New York, Box 110282, August 13, 1973, 1). The staff did not agree on the magnitude or whether there was a long-run

following April. A study prepared by Gary Gillum of the Philadelphia bank said that the choice of long-run targets constituted a policy decision and, therefore, they had to be published by law. The memo also answered the criticism that publication of six-month targets after three months could disrupt markets by giving speculators information about future actions. Gillum argued correctly that better information would improve market efficiency (memo, "The Place of Long-Run Targets in the Policy Record," Board Records, April 9, 1974).

Beset by problems arising from the Watergate break-in, President Nixon was more concerned than ever with the political. He reappointed Burns for a second four-year term as chairman but gave little attention to monetary policy. Burns, for his part, devoted much time and attention to preventing Congress from passing Congressman Patman's bill calling for a regular audit of the Federal Reserve by the General Accounting Office (now known as the Government Accountability Office). The audit called for examination of administrative and financial transactions, including open market purchases and sales.

Burns's efforts to defend independence from audit contrasts with his willingness to respond to congressional and administration pressures to inflate. The Federal Reserve called on banks, current and former reserve bank directors, and other allies to lobby members of Congress. Burns was willing to have an audit of administrative operations. The Senate did not act, and the issue was put aside, not without much resentment from the proponents about the intense lobbying (Wells, 1994, 130).

In 1975, Congressman Patman tried again to restrict Federal Reserve independence by reviving his proposal to require the Federal Reserve's budget to become subject to congressional appropriations. In practice, the Federal Reserve banks received the earnings on the government debt in their portfolios. The Board assessed the reserve banks semiannually to pay its expenses. The rest of the banks' income returned to the Treasury. The proposed legislation would have ended that system.

The legislation also set a ceiling on Board and bank spending, required Senate confirmation of bank presidents, and required the president to include representation of labor and consumer interests when choosing members of the Board. In his testimony against the legislation, Burns explained that independence was critical for successful monetary policy but could not be absolute. "The System is duty-bound to implement the will of Congress expressed in legislation" (Burns's testimony on S.2285,

effect. But they did agree that it significantly reduced their ability to manage a total reserve or RPD target between meetings and that it increased short-run interest rate variability.

Box 35607, Federal Reserve Bank of New York, October 20, 1975, 4). The legislation did not pass.

Henry Reuss replaced Wright Patman as chairman of House Banking after the 1974 election. He introduced a bill requiring the Federal Reserve to maintain at least 6 percent money growth. This was the start of legislation that became the Humphrey-Hawkins legislation requiring the Federal Reserve to announce targets for monetary aggregates twice a year. Reuss's bill also called for credit allocation. Burns was highly critical. It lost in committee on a twenty-to-nineteen vote.

### *Policy Actions*

In August 1973, the price of a barrel of crude oil increased from $3.56 to $4.31. The price rose again in January 1974, this time to $10.11. As soon as oil price increases began, the Boston bank requested a lower discount rate. Between October 1 and year-end, Boston requested a 0.25 reduction to 7.25 percent five times. The Board rejected each of the requests without dissent. Its reasoning is unclear. At the time the federal funds rate remained between 9.5 and 10 percent.

Burns's analysis recognized that a supply shock called for a different response than a reduction in demand. He did not recognize, or at least mention, that the price change was a change in relative prices, not an increase in the maintained rate of inflation; implicit in his analysis, however, was recognition that the main effect was on the level of output.

Table 7.3 shows what happened after the oil shock and the policy decision. The federal funds rate declined moderately, as Burns proposed, but growth of the monetary base declined, tightening policy and adding the effects of monetary restriction.

The Standard & Poor's (S&P) index shows the public reaction to the oil shock, the 15 percent decline in industrial production, the rise in prices and expected inflation, and monetary contraction. The stock price index declined 40 percent, wiping out nominal gains since 1963. It did not again reach the January 1973 nominal value until 1980. The Society of Professional Forecasters raised its four-quarter inflation forecast by 3.6 percentage points, much less than the increase in the deflator or growth in money wages. Real wages fell as part of the permanent adjustment to the supply shock.

Most of the FOMC members praised Burns's analysis.[32] With Hayes dissenting, they voted for a short-run funds rate of 8.75 to 10 percent and

32. The administration also analyzed the oil price increase as a supply shock. Secretary Shultz told the international energy conference in February 1974 that the problem was not monetary or financial and could not be offset by financial actions. He urged continued or

**Table 7.3** Responses to Policy and the Oil Shock

| VARIABLE | AT TURN | | NEXT TURN | |
|---|---|---|---|---|
| Federal funds (%) | 10.78 | 9/73 | 8.97 | 2/74 |
| Base growth (%)* | 9.3 | 7/73 | 7.2 | 3/74 |
| S&P index | 118.4 | 1/73 | 68.1 | 9/74 |
| Industrial prod. index | 71.9 | 11/73 | 61.3 | 3/75 |
| SPF inflation (%)** | 4.1 | 73/III | 7.7 | 74/III |
| Hourly earnings (%)* | 5.8 | 5/73 | 8.2 | 9/74 |
| CPI (%)* | 5.6 | 7/73 | 11.5 | 12/74 |
| GNP deflator (%)** | 8.6 | 73/II | 14.3 | 74/III |

*Twelve-month moving average.
**quarterly values at annual rates

$M_1$ growth of 3 to 6 percent. They committed to "foster financial conditions conducive to resisting inflationary pressures, cushioning the effects on production and employment growing out of the oil shortage, and maintaining equilibrium in the country's balance of payments" (FOMC Minutes, December 17–18, 1973, 105). This was an error. The oil price rise transferred wealth to the oil producers. It forced a reduction in real wages and profits that the Federal Reserve could not prevent.

The difference between statements and actions is great at this time. The funds rate followed the Committee decision, but the economy did not. Several members made excellent statements about what should be done. Bruce MacLaury (Minneapolis) "anticipated major sectoral [*sic*] dislocations, great uncertainty, and a sharp reduction in consumer demands. While he expected more inflation than the staff did, much of the increase would be a one-time adjustment to higher cost energy. . . . [H]e thought that monetary policy should not do very much about a one-time price adjustment and that it probably could not do very much about cost-push inflation" (FOMC Minutes, December 17–18, 1973, 79–80). John Balles (San Francisco) also recognized that the price increase "stemmed from supply shortages, of which oil was the most spectacular instance. . . . [T]he System had no choice but to validate price increases that stemmed from supply shortages, because a failure to do so would probably result in unacceptable declines in production, income, and employment" (ibid., 84). President Coldwell (Dallas), who described the boom in his region, wanted faster money growth.

That did not happen. Money growth slowed over the next six months. The immediate response was faster growth in RPDs and money in part because the desk purchased securities sold by foreign central banks.

increased aid to the poorest countries and the development of arrangements to recycle the increased revenues of the oil-exporting countries.

**Table 7.4** Measures of Ease and Restraint

| MONTH | FEDERAL FUNDS (%) | BASE GROWTH (%) |
|---|---|---|
| January | 9.65 | 7.69 |
| February | 8.97 | 7.20 |
| March | 9.35 | 7.71 |
| April | 10.51 | 8.09 |
| May | 11.31 | 7.97 |
| June | 11.93 | 7.64 |

On January 11, the FOMC voted not to adhere to its money target but to maintain money market conditions. By March 1974, it began to raise the federal funds rate to slow money growth. Despite declining output, the federal funds rate rose from an average of 8.97 in February to 12.92 in July. Twelve-month average money base growth remained between 7.2 and 8.1 percent. Table 7.4 compares the monthly average federal funds rate to the twelve-month moving average of the monetary base growth in the first half of 1974. The two measures again gave different indications of policy. Reported inflation continued to rise.

The FOMC minutes for the first half of 1974 show the committee struggling with the one-time effects of the oil shock, concern for recession, and a desire to slow inflation. A typical statement by Arthur Burns during the winter recognized that "the economy was suffering from a shortage of oil and other materials rather than a shortage of money" (FOMC Minutes, January 22, 1974, 109). Then he urged an increase in money growth or made some other statement about ease.[33] In Table 7.4, movements of the federal funds rate give a correct picture of desired policy action. On a few occasions in February and March, the FOMC had to decide whether to raise the funds rate to slow money growth. Burns recommended holding the funds rate, citing the fragility of financial markets.

Hayes and Francis dissented at the January meeting because they opposed a tilt toward ease. In February, the FOMC raised the short-term $M_1$ target from 3–6 percent to 6.5–9.5 percent. Four members dissented. Bucher, Morris, and Sheehan wanted a wider range for $M_1$ growth and a lower federal funds rate. Francis wanted slower money growth. Actual money growth exceeded the target. This was one of the occasions when

33. Stein described the administration's position as seeking a $5 to $10 billion reduction in spending. The recession prevented efforts to reduce the budget deficit. "We could never have any dispute with the Federal Reserve about how restrictive monetary policy was going to be because they never described their future policy in terms that enabled us to criticize it" (Hargrove and Morley, 1984, 403). The Council favored decontrol of oil prices, but Congress voted controls. "Failure to deregulate [was] one of the great mistakes" (ibid., 403).

the FOMC accepted the chairman's proposal to let money growth exceed the target range.[34] But just before the February FOMC meeting, the Board unanimously disapproved a 0.25 reduction in the discount rate to 7.25 percent. The principal reason was that the slowdown arose from the supply side. The discount rate remained far below the funds rate, so borrowing banks received a considerable subsidy.

Rhetoric of the period included many unconditional statements about controlling inflation. At times, Burns warned the FOMC about moving to a Latin American inflation. Practice differed, as in February. Concerns about unemployment continued to dominate concerns about inflation and to receive first priority. Challenged to explain the very expansive policy in 1972, Burns asked: "What would you have wanted the Federal Reserve to do in a year like 1972, when the year started out with an unemployment rate of 6 percent and didn't go below 5.5 percent until November?" (quoted in Pierce, 1979b, 492).[35]

With rising inflation, criticism of monetary policy increased. In September 1973, Senator Proxmire sent Burns a letter criticizing monetary policy for erratic growth of money and too high an average rate. Burns wrote a twenty-eight-page reply, the main points of which included his views on the economy and economic policy. The economy "is inherently unstable" (Burns papers, Box B_B81, Money Supply, November 6, 1973, 6). A market economy, left alone, generates "imbalances" and fluctuations. "Flexible fiscal and monetary policies, therefore, are often needed to cope with undesirable economic developments" (ibid., 7).[36] To be effective, policy actions had to be discretionary. One of the reasons he gave was that "when the economy is experiencing severe cost-push inflation, a monetary growth rate that is relatively high by a historical yardstick may have to be tolerated for a time" (ibid., 11). The reason he gave was that high money growth avoided some "adverse effects on production and employment"

34. On March 18, the Arab oil embargo ended. The staff expected little effect.

35. Otmar Issing (2005, 329–30), chief economist at the Bundesbank, compared Germany's less inflationary experience. He gives credit to the use of targets for money growth beginning December 1974. Monetary control contributed directly to control of inflation. Also, it informed price and wage setters that their excessive demands would lead to excess supply and unemployment. VonHagen (1999, 414–19) described the start of this policy. It continued through the 1970s and beyond. Between 1972 and 1979, consumer prices in West Germany rose 27 percent, half the rate in the United States (55 percent) (Council of Economic Advisers, 1983, 286).

36. This is a Keynesian perspective. The monetarist view was opposite. If government policy, especially monetary policy, is stabilizing and predictable, market forces restore or maintain economic stability. The Federal Reserve temporarily adopted the monetarist view in the 1980s.

(ibid., 12).[37] He did not mention that the Federal Reserve could not restore the loss of income or wealth.

Consistency was not Burns's strength. In March, Burns told the FOMC that "he was much impressed by the size of the Federal deficit in the five fiscal years 1970 through 1974 . . . While the Federal Reserve always would accommodate the Treasury up to a point, the charge could be made—and was being made—that the System had accommodated the Treasury to an excessive degree. Although he was not a monetarist, he found a basic and inescapable truth in the monetarist position that inflation could not have persisted over a long period of time without a highly accommodative monetary policy" (FOMC Minutes, March 9, 1974, 111–12).

Burns's conclusion that the problem was failure to control money growth soon had an effect.[38] In April, the System began to raise interest rates. To bring money growth within its target range, the FOMC agreed to an intermeeting increase in the funds rate to 10.25 percent. The Board approved a 0.5 increase in the discount rate to 8 percent on April 25. The FOMC set its target rate for money growth at 3 to 7 percent with the funds rate between 9.75 and 10.75.[39] Soon afterward, the members approved Burns's proposal to raise the funds rate to 11 percent. Governor Bucher dissented. The Nixon administration had now changed its policy and would oppose a tax cut.[40]

Preliminary data for first quarter 1974 showed a 6.3 percent annual rate

37. Burns ended the letter by discussing monetary policy in 1972–73. He accepted that "in retrospect, it may well be that monetary policy should have been a little less expansive in 1972. But a markedly more restrictive policy would have led to a still sharper rise in interest rates and risked a premature ending of the business expansion without limiting to any significant degree this year's upsurge of the price level" (Burns papers, Box B_B81, November 6, 1973, 25). Burns, like Eccles in the 1930s, blamed the lack of Federal Reserve control of nonmember banks for poor control of money. He also asked for better control of government spending. Although Burns discussed variability of velocity as a problem, he did not mention any of the proposals to permit NOW accounts nationally or pay interest on demand deposits. These were under discussion within the System at the time ("Selected Options for Implementing Interest Payments on Deposits," Federal Reserve Bank of New York, Box 240, 10, January 18, 1974).

38. Burns explained that central banks had to control inflation "because weak governments could not cope with the problem" (FOMC Minutes, March 9, 1974, 139).

39. The FOMC approved the manager's proposal to submit non-competitive bids at Treasury bill auctions. Previously, the desk had submitted competitive bids at the auction to replace bills in the open market account and on behalf of the Treasury and foreign central banks. Growth in foreign and System holdings since 1970 increased the System's bid from about 30 to more than 50 percent of the offering. The manager's main concern was that the desk would not get all the bills it wanted at its competitive bid. The non-competitive bid guaranteed their share at the average auctions price. The FOMC agreed (memo, Alan Holmes to FOMC, Board Records, March 15 and April 8, 1974).

40. At the April meeting, Burns told the FOMC that the administration's position at the beginning of the year was that a recession must be prevented and that whatever needed to be done would be done (FOMC Minutes, April 16, 1974, 85).

of decline in real GNP and an 11.5 percent rise in the GNP deflator. Using this measure of inflation, the real federal funds rate was zero or negative. To slow the growth of RPDs, the FOMC made an inter-meeting increase of 0.25 in the funds rate. By late May, the rate was 11.75 percent.

The FOMC did not permit banking problems to interfere with its efforts to slow money growth. Early in May, the Franklin National Bank (New York) told the Comptroller of the Currency and the Federal Reserve that the bank had extensive losses in the foreign exchange market. The Federal Reserve lent $1.723 billion through the discount window to prevent the bank from failing, and the New York reserve bank took over management of the bank's exchange portfolio. The loans served only to delay the failure until October, when the regulators merged Franklin with another bank. The Federal Deposit Insurance Corporation assumed Franklin's debt to the Federal Reserve. The Board cited fear of financial collapse as the reason for sustaining the bank. This showed a misunderstanding of its role as lender of last resort, and it encouraged risky behavior. The proper Bagehotian response would have allowed Franklin National to fail while lending to support the financial system. Failure did not require the bank to close. It required that stockholders and management bear the loss. In fact, the bank's branches remained as part of the European American Bank.

Negotiations leading to the Federal Reserve loan in May were complicated by concerns that an Italian businessman, Michele Sindona, had a major interest. Hayes and his staff wanted Sindona to provide $40 million of additional equity. Sindona agreed to $30 million at the time and $20 million to be paid later.

Before Franklin failed in October, the New York bank encouraged the Treasury's Exchange Stabilization Fund to take over Franklin's foreign exchange portfolio. The Treasury did not agree. The Franklin case went to court where a judge agreed to declare Franklin insolvent. The European American Bank (EAB) acquired most of Franklin's productive assets in May 1976, in part to cancel a debt and the rest for cash (Franklin National Bank, Box 741A, Federal Reserve Bank of New York, October 25, 1974). European American also assumed deposit liabilities.[41]

Contrast the German resolution. In June, the Bundesbank learned the Herstatt Bank was in a position similar to Franklin National. The bank failed. There was a scramble for liquidity, and interest rates rose. The

41. The loan to Franklin paid an interest rate of 7.52 percent, below the 8.5 percent earned on the System portfolio. At liquidation, the FDIC paid the Federal Reserve the nearly one percentage point of additional interest. The FDIC collected the principal and interest on assets that EAB did not acquire. One result of the Franklin and Herstatt failures was creation of an international Committee on Banking Regulations in Basel (Borio and Toniolo, 2006, 21).

Bundesbank and other European central banks prevented any additional failures but allowed Herstatt to fail and liquidate.

In the winter of 1974, President Nixon reappointed Burns as chairman. That provided continuity during the uncertainty arising from the Watergate scandal. But in May, George Shultz left the government because he opposed President Nixon's second effort to freeze prices (Shultz, 2003, 15). Shultz had served as coordinator of economic policy for the administration. His departure set off a struggle to assume his role between William Simon, the new Treasury secretary, and Roy Ash, the budget director. Neither received Shultz's authority or his central position, and neither could acquire his leadership role.

Early in 1975, dissatisfaction with economic outcomes raised new challenges. Many real estate investment trusts, financed by leading banks, borrowed short-term and lent long-term to finance real estate. As real estate prices fell, the real estate trusts faced insolvency. Feedlot operators who fed cattle suffered losses as meat prices fell. The operators had borrowed heavily. The high nominal interest rates added to their burden. Other distressed borrowers included airlines hurt by fuel prices and electric utilities caught between higher fuel prices and many state regulators reluctant to raise prices (Wells, 1994, 141–42).

At the June FOMC meeting, the committee voted eleven to one (President Clay dissenting) to hold the funds rate between 11.25 and 12.25 percent. By early July, the funds rate was between 13 and 13.5 percent, the highest ever reported to that time. The desk tried unsuccessfully to lower the rate, while remaining within the money targets. The desk explained that banks wanted to hold reserves because of the Franklin National and Herstatt failures. The FOMC decided to let the rate remain where it was. On June 10, Burns changed his mind. He wanted a lower funds rate, between 12 and 13 percent. Governors Bucher and Sheehan wanted more decisive action to lower the rate. President Winn (Cleveland) opposed any action to lower the rate. "Our experience indicates a bias for quantities to exceed upper limit of range of tolerance. Would like to see a few periods in which achievements were in lower end of range" (telegram, Winn to Burns, Board Records, July 10, 1974).

The recession was in its eighth month in July. At a 12.92 average for July 1974, the nominal funds rate was three percentage points above the rate at the National Bureau peak. The unemployment rate shows one likely reason; it rose only from 4.8 percent to 5.5 percent during this period. That was about to change. The unemployment rate reached 6 percent by October and 7.2 percent by December.

That ended the anti-inflation policy. The federal funds rate began to fall.

By December it was down to 8.5 percent. And it continued to fall for the next six months despite high and, until December 1974, rising consumer price inflation.[42]

In July the FOMC voted to reduce $M_1$ growth to the range 2 to 6 percent during July and August, but after reporting 1.7 percent for July, the FOMC raised the proposed $M_1$ growth rate to 5.5 to 7.5 percent. Real base growth fell through 1974 and 1975. Real long-term interest rates also fell, but falling real base contributed to a large decline in real GNP (see Chart 7.10 above).

President Nixon resigned, and President Gerald Ford took office on August 9, 1974. Financial market rates rose with the heightened political uncertainty beginning in mid-July. In the month to August 9, Treasury bill rates rose 1.3 percentage points to 8.75. Long bond rates also rose by smaller amounts. Both rates began to fall after a month. The dollar strengthened, however.

Burns sent a twelve-page memo to President Ford outlining an anti-inflation program. He told the president that "the nation is in the grip of a dangerous inflation" (Burns to the president, "Agenda for an Immediate Economic Program," Burns papers, Box B_B24, August 12, 1974, 1).[43] Monetary policy had borne too much of the burden. He urged the president to meet with the congressional leaders and agree on at least $5 billion in spending reduction. (Outlays for 1975 reached $332 billion.)

Much of Burns's program called for interference in price and wage setting. He urged President Ford to pledge a balanced budget for 1976, avoid price and wage controls, reconstitute the Cost of Living Council and the Construction Industry Stabilization Committee, and pursue a tough antitrust policy. He favored "temporary restraint on export of grains" (ibid., 5) in the event of rising food prices. And he proposed an enlarged public service employment program to absorb some of the unemployment caused by the anti-inflation policy.

Burns returned from a meeting with the president and legislative lead-

42. Concern about leaks from the meeting arose periodically throughout System history. To limit or prevent leaks, beginning in August Chairman Burns limited attendance to Board members, presidents, the managers, and a few essential staff members during the part of the meeting devoted to monetary policy and the directive. Customary attendees would remain at other parts of the meeting (Board Records, August 1, 1974).

43. Burns's advice was not uniformly accepted within the administration. Old and mistaken ideas do not disappear. David Packard, undersecretary of defense, sent a memo giving his views of the causes of inflation. He recognized that "tight monetary policy is about the only real pressure on inflation." But it had become counterproductive because it increased costs, delayed investment, and caused "serious, even dangerous distortions." He agreed with Burns that the administration should reestablish the Cost of Living Council (David Packard to the president, White House Central File, Box 31, Ford Library, August 20, 1974).

ers on August 20. He told the FOMC that the president had said he would like a new Cost of Living Council and that he would avoid price and wage controls. The president hoped to keep total outlays under $300 billion in fiscal 1975. And he announced a "summit meeting" on inflation to solicit advice and focus attention on the problem.[44]

The president announced his ten-point program on October 8, 1974. It called for a one-year 5 percent tax surcharge on high-income taxpayers and corporations, an increase in the investment tax credit, increased unemployment benefits, public service jobs in areas with high unemployment, a budget ceiling of $300 billion for the 1975 fiscal year, and a voluntary program to control inflation—the WIN program (Whip Inflation Now). WIN initially captured the popular imagination, but the program did not have congressional support. The 1974 congressional election was only weeks away, so most Congress members would not support either a tax increase or reductions in spending, not even the $4.4 billion by which the president proposed to reduce the increase in the last Nixon budget (Greene, 1995, 72).

The rest of the WIN program was entirely public relations.[45] It could do nothing to stop inflation; the opposition in Congress pointed to the neglect of a deepening recession. This doomed the tax increase and any other part of the program that required legislation. By the time the president announced the program, industrial production had fallen in three of the last four months. A 35 percent (annual rate) decline in November followed by a 50 percent decline in December doomed WIN.

44. Burns's relations with President Ford and his administration were excellent. He described President Nixon as trying "to interfere with the Federal Reserve both in ways that were fair and . . . unfair. Mr. Ford on the other hand was truly angelic. I met with President Ford frequently, alone in the privacy of his office. He never inquired about what the Federal Reserve was doing. He never even remotely intimated what the Federal Reserve should be doing" (Burns, 1988, 136). Burns added that he was informally a member of the president's economic team. "It was a one way street" (ibid., 138). He discussed administration policies but did not mention Federal Reserve plans. Alan Greenspan, who replaced Herbert Stein as chairman of the Council confirms Burns's role (Hargrove and Morley, 1984, 429).

45. The president's aide, Robert Hartmann, compared WIN to President Roosevelt's Blue Eagle program, part of the NRA intended to show public support for higher prices and wages in 1933. Memos at the time compared it to the Army-Navy E (for efficiency) in World War II. Companies that pledged not to raise prices for one year would receive an IF flag (inflation fighter) similar to the E flags during World War II. Advocates suggested that "the American people would serve as policemen to make sure the program works" (memo to the president, Inflation Fighter Program, Robert T. Hartmann papers, Ford Library, August 30, 1974, 2). The name of the sender was cut out of the memo. A WIN song was written and recorded. The program began as independent suggestions from a Pennsylvania's businessman, William J. Meyer, and a financial journalist, Sylvia Porter. Sylvia Porter became chair of a large voluntary citizen's campaign.

That was the end of the WIN program. Annualized consumer price inflation reached a local peak of 11.5 percent that month. The following month the Ford administration replaced the 5 percent tax increase with a proposed 12 percent tax reduction in the form of rebates of 1974 tax payments. It also proposed to increase the price of imported oil. Congress passed a much larger tax cut and increased spending.

The economy and the Congress doomed Ford's hope of reducing the budget deficit. Although he vetoed many spending bills, the budget deficit rose to $5.5 billion in 1975 and $70 billion in 1976, a new record. That left inflation control entirely to the Federal Reserve, displeasing Burns.[46] Despite his many speeches about the dangers of inflation, policy gave pride of place to reducing unemployment.

During the fall, evidence increased that the recession would become deeper and last longer. Burns's initial reaction was to lower the funds rate gradually. He typically said, "[A]ny drastic change . . . would be a great mistake, although some further easing would be appropriate" (FOMC Minutes, December 17, 1974, 85).

Henry Wallich proposed a temporary policy of increased money growth. To avoid another surge of inflation, the committee would later slow money growth. Burns opposed. In a clear statement of the time inconsistency problem, Burns said, "The members might plan now to slow growth later on, but when the time arrived, they would find it a difficult step to take" (ibid., 104).

In mid-November, the Board reduced reserve requirement ratios for demand and time deposits. The new demand deposit ratios applied only to banks with $400 million or more. Their ratio became 17.5 percent instead of 18. Adjustments to time deposit ratios lowered the ratio to 3 percent for most categories (Annual Report, 1974, 95–96).

Table 7.5 shows the decisions and approximate outcomes reported in the FOMC minutes from September to December 1974. By the November meeting, the committee had an estimate of −3 percent for third-quarter growth and a projected faster decline in the fourth due in part to a coal strike. Inflation in wholesale and consumer prices showed no evidence of decline until 1975.

The table shows, as usual, that the manager always met the funds rate

46. The CEA chairman, Alan Greenspan, explained that inflation and other instabilities increased the risk premium and reduced investment. "[T]he only way to [reduce risk and inflation] in the long term was to bring down the rate of increase in money supply, which in turn required that Federal financing be brought down" (Hargrove and Morley, 1984, 418). Greenspan explained that the Federal Reserve controlled a short-term rate. Increases in the deficit, therefore, resulted in faster money growth and more inflation.

**Table 7.5** Policy Actions, Autumn 1974

| MEETING DATE | $M_1$ | | FUNDS RATE | | DISSENT |
|---|---|---|---|---|---|
| | *Planned (%)* | *Reported (%)* | *Planned (%)* | *Reported (%)* | |
| September 10 | 3–6 | 2(Q3) | 10.5–12 | 11.3 | Hayes |
| October 3 | | | 10.25–12 | 11 | Hayes, Winn |
| October 14–15 | 4.75–7.25 | 5 | 9–10.5 | 9.75 | Clay |
| October 31 | | | 9.5 | 10 | |
| November 18–19 | 6.5–9.5 | 7 | 8.5–10 | 8.75 | |
| December 16–17 | 5–7 | 2–2.5 | 7.5–9 | 7.5 | Mitchell, Wallich |

target but met the money target only occasionally. In September and October, the dissenters wanted slower money growth or higher interest rates to lower inflation. In December, Wallich and Mitchell's concern was the deepening recession.

William Fellner, a member of the Council of Economic Advisers, sent a weekly memo to the president to inform him about monetary policy. Most of the memos supported the reduced growth of monetary aggregates as the way to reduce inflation. By November, reported $M_1$ growth had fallen to 3.7 percent annual rate for the most recent twenty-six weeks. Fellner said, "The numbers . . . are compatible with a reasonable degree of anti-inflationary pressure" (memo, Fellner to the president, Burns papers, WHCF Box 1, November 8, 1974). When Burns praised President Ford for not interfering in monetary policy, he did not note that William Fellner and Alan Greenspan generally approved of what he did. Greenspan was the new chairman of the Council of Economic Advisers, replacing Herbert Stein.

Support changed in the winter of 1975. Money growth ($M_1$) fell to −0.6 percent from December to February. Fellner recognized that the Federal Reserve had "vigorously to expand money in periods of falling interest rates and economic decline" (ibid., February 14, 1976). Fellner cautioned against treating the decline in short-term rates as evidence of ease. Greenspan repeated this point in a memo prepared for a meeting between the president and Burns in early March. Soon afterward money growth rose. In July, Greenspan warned the president about upward pressure on interest rates (ibid., July 7, 1975).

Beginning in 1975, borrowing declined and the federal funds rate came down rapidly. Once the oil price surge ended, reported consumer price inflation slowed. The decline in reported inflation induced an increase in growth of the real monetary base (Chart 7.4 above).

Judged by the decline in the federal funds rate, the Federal Reserve eased policy decisively in 1975. The change coincided with the rapid in-

**Table 7.6** Key Variables, December 1974–76 (%)

| YEAR | BASE GROWTH | FEDERAL FUNDS | CPI INFLATION | UNEMPLOYMENT RATE |
|---|---|---|---|---|
| 1974 | 8.8 | 8.5 | 11.5 | 7.2 |
| 1975 | 5.8 | 5.2 | 6.8 | 8.2 |
| 1976 | 6.7 | 4.6 | 4.7 | 7.8 |

crease in the unemployment rate in the winter of 1975. Table 7.6 outlines changes in some principal variables in three Decembers. Using CPI inflation shown in the table, the real federal funds rate was negative throughout. Real base growth turned positive early in 1976. Unemployment was not affected, most likely because the public expected easier policy and higher inflation.

The manager summed up experience in a difficult year. "The use of aggregate targeting has probably contributed to the clarity of monetary policy discussions, but policymaking itself has not proved easier. Evidence of structural change in the financial system has reduced the policymaker's confidence in the stability of the linkage between operational instructions and desired long-run economic goals" (Holmes, 1975, 207). Among the major changes he mentioned were the end of ceiling rates for large CDs that made banks more confident about sources of funds, and thus more willing to lend, and belief that inflation would continue. Banks included adjustment clauses in loan contracts and adopted a floating prime rate. The manager did not oppose the use of monetary targets, but he asked for greater flexibility in the choice of particular monetary targets.

At the FOMC meeting, the New York bank began with relatively pessimistic news and forecasts. The Council and the Federal Reserve staff predicted that the recession would continue for the first six months of 1975. In fourth quarter 1974 output declined at a 9.1 percent annual rate. Later revisions changed the decline to 1.6 percent, an extreme example of the cost of reliance on current data.[47]

The president's advisers recommended a $91.5 billion tax cut, three-fourths to individuals in the form of a one-time rebate. They also proposed an increase in the investment tax credit from 4 to 12 percent for utilities and 7 to 12 percent for all other corporations. The advisers proposed to decontrol oil prices and impose a windfall profits tax on oil companies. There

47. Data are from Runkle (1998, 5). *Business Conditions Digest* for October 1988 reports the decline as 3.5 percent. Runkle shows that in the sample he used, 1961 to 1996, initial estimates are biased estimates of the final data. For real GNP the difference was as large as the 7.5 percentage point underestimate in 1974 or a 6.2 percentage point overestimate. This raises an issue to which I will return in chapter 10: Why base policy actions on noisy short-term data? See also Orphanides (2001) and Meltzer (1987).

would be no new spending programs, but the Treasury and the Federal Reserve would prepare legislation for an agency like the Depression-era Reconstruction Finance Corporation to take over failing financial institutions. Congress approved only tax reduction and added additional spending for low-income individuals.

The Federal Reserve began the year by reducing the federal funds rate target to 6.5–7.25 percent, intending to maintain money growth at 3.5–6.5 percent. On January 20, the Board reduced reserve requirement ratios by 0.5 percentage points for demand deposits of $400 million or less and by 1 percentage point above $400 million effective February 13. The new range ran from 7.5 percent to 16.5 percent based on size of deposits. Also during the first quarter, the Board rejected several requests to reduce discount rates, but it approved 0.5 percentage point reductions on January 3, February 4, and March 7. The discount rate declined from 7.75 to 6.25 percent.

By March, the monthly average funds rate was down to 5.5 percent, a 50 percent decline from the previous September. This was hardly the slow, deliberate ease that Burns claimed he wanted. Growth of the monetary base declined from 7.5 percent for the fourth-quarter average to 6 percent for the first quarter, a tightening of policy. First-quarter $M_1$ growth, reported at the time, was 3.9 percent. Once again, the federal funds rate and nominal base growth gave different signals. However, CPI inflation declined, so growth of the real base rose. In the second quarter, the recession ended.[48]

Keynesian economists had learned about the importance of money growth. In congressional testimony and public statements, they urged much more expansive monetary policy, 10 percent money growth or higher, and predicted dire consequences if the Federal Reserve did not accept their advice.[49] Burns resisted. The FOMC $M_1$ target was 5 to 7.5 percent. He dismissed the Keynesian critics: "Most economists who move from platform to platform these days . . . pay very little attention to the business cycle. They have never studied it thoroughly, or, if they have, they have forgotten what they once knew" (quoted in Wells, 1994, 158). Burns

48. In the weekly memo to the president on monetary policy dated February 14, 1975, Alan Greenspan and William Fellner noted that the System's easier policy, including lower reserve requirement ratios, had not raised money growth rates. The memo recognized that the decline in interest rates reflected weak credit demand. "Movements in the monetary aggregates will also tend to *reflect* the business cycle instead of countering it unless the Fed moves vigorously to expand money in periods of falling interest rates and economic decline" (Fellner and Greenspan to the president, Ford Library, WHCF FI Box 1, February 14, 1975; emphasis in the original). Burns's efforts to reduce inflation brought strong criticism of Federal Reserve policy from the labor unions and some members of Congress. But he also received support from others in Congress (Wells, 1994, 137).

49. Wells (1994, 158–59) cites James Tobin and a "committee of prominent Keynesians" as the authors of these claims.

claimed that in the first year of recovery, velocity growth rose above trend. He relied on velocity growth to end the recession. He was right. Recovery began in April 1975.

In March, President Ford met with Arthur Burns to express his concern about money growth and to get Burns's assessment of the recession and recovery. The president stressed the importance of having recovery in 1975 without a new surge of inflation in 1976 (briefing paper, Greenspan to the president, Ford Library, WHCF FG, Box 156, March 10, 1975).[50] Soon after $M_1$ growth rose.

The Board's staff recognized by May that the decline in output had slowed or stopped. They did not recognize that recovery began until August. By that time, growth was at a 7 percent annual rate after rising 4 percent in the second quarter.

## CONGRESSIONAL INTERVENTION

Reports of deep recession, sustained inflation, historically high interest rates, and a 9 percent unemployment rate brought heightened attention to Federal Reserve policy. Although the Constitution gives Congress power over money creation, few members found the details interesting enough to learn about the processes. Usually they relied on a few interested members to inform them when an issue arose. Periods like the deep recessions of 1920–21 or 1929–33 brought more attention. In the 1970s, many people shared Poole's conclusion that "the 1972 boom was purchased at the cost of the 1974–75 recession" (Poole, 1979, 482).

These criticisms and the economic problems in 1974–75 renewed public and congressional interest. Burns's active lobbying against Congressman Patman's efforts to bring more direct control succeeded. Despite strong resistance, however, Congress passed a resolution in March 1975 over Burns's strong objections.

Members of Congress expressed annoyance at Burns's refusal to tell them the planned rate of money growth.[51] One response was a bill requir-

50. As Council chairman, Alan Greenspan held meetings of the treasury secretary, budget director, and Federal Reserve chairman with a small group of business and academic economists. At the February 1975 meeting, I urged Chairman Burns to recognize that monetary base growth was procyclical. He made clear that his concern was to lower interest rates and did not want a large decline required to get an increase in base growth. The March 7, 1975, statement by the Shadow Open Market Committee made the points public. At the White House meeting, Chairman Burns asked me to tell him what would happen if he adopted my proposal that he make up the shortfall of 8.5 billion in $M_1$ and return to a 5.5 percent growth rate. Burns's letter of April 12, 1975, said that would be unwise. In fact, he increased $M_1$ about as much as I suggested by the end of March (Burns papers, Box K24, Ford Library, April 12, 1975).

51. Burns's desire for secrecy and his idea of independence were probably central. However, in an interview, James Pierce, an associate director of research at the time, explained

ing the System to make $M_1$ grow 6 percent or more in 1975 and to allocate credit toward national priorities. Burns argued that $M_1$ was not a good indicator, that velocity changed erratically so that the System could not rely on a specific target.[52] He properly opposed credit allocation as impossible, a new type of real bills notion. The System could not know what the final use of credit would be.

As finally approved, Congressional Resolution 133 required the Federal Reserve to reduce long-term interest rates and to report quarterly to the House and Senate Banking Committees on its planned rate of money growth.[53] This requirement became part of the Federal Reserve Reform Act of 1977. Most commentary on these targets points to the way in which the Federal Reserve evaded congressional intent by announcing four targets for one-year growth—$M_1$, $M_2$, $M_3$, and the Bank Credit Proxy (total deposits)—revising the announcement each quarter, and shifting the base. The last, known as base drift, was probably the most serious. When money growth exceeded the target, the new target started from the overshoot (or undershoot). Thus, maintained money growth bore little relation to the target until the Volcker years after 1980–81.

After some experimentation, the FOMC set its target as the four-quarter rate of change beginning in the most recent quarter. Most, but not all, the errors were excess growth. Table 7.7, adapted from Broaddus and Goodfriend (1984, 7), shows the ranges and the errors for 1975 to 1984.

On average the error was 1.3 percentage points compared to an average 5.6 midpoint, or 23 percent. Most of the errors are positive; actual growth exceeded the target midpoint. Some of the errors arose because of changes in the composition of $M_1$; NOW accounts are an example.

Nevertheless, Resolution 133 was a step toward increased transparency. For the first time in the Federal Reserve's history, after more than sixty years, Congress tried to supervise its agent more effectively, and the

that the Board's forecasts did not relate money and output. Lyle Gramley prepared the green book forecasts of the real economy. They were independent of money growth. "Here was the central bank making forecasts without knowing what its monetary policy was. I'd make myself very unpopular going into that meeting saying what's your monetary policy assumption? . . . They wouldn't listen because they were old-fashioned business economists" (Pierce, 1998, 9).

52. In a comment on this section, Jerry Jordan described the outcome of a meeting held at the FOMC about this time. Four recommendations for a target came to a vote. Money growth received seven votes. Three money market measures (federal funds, free reserves, nonborrowed reserves) each received four votes. Burns ruled that a majority opposed money growth, so he eliminated it and revoted on the other three.

53. The legislation owed much to the efforts of the late Robert Weintraub, a staff member of the Banking Committee. Weintraub persuaded Senator Proxmire of the need for monetary targets.

**Table 7.7** Targets and Actual $M_1$ Growth Rates, 1975–84 (%)

| YEAR, FOURTH QUARTER TO FOURTH QUARTER | TARGET | MIDPOINT | ACTUAL | ERROR |
|---|---|---|---|---|
| 1975–76 | 4.5–7.5 | 6.0 | 5.8 | −0.2 |
| 1976–77 | 4.5–6.5 | 5.5 | 7.9 | 2.4 |
| 1977–78 | 4.0–6.5 | 5.25 | 7.2 | 2.0 |
| 1978–79 | 4.5–7.5 | 6.0 | 6.8 | 0.8 |
| 1979–80 | 4.0–6.5 | 5.25 | 6.9 | 1.7 |
| 1980–81 | 3.5–6.0 | 4.75 | 2.4 | −2.4 |
| 1981–82 | 2.5–5.5 | 4.0 | 5.0 | 1.0 |
| 1982–83 | 4.0–8.0 | 6.0 | 4.3 | 1.7 |
| 1983–84 | 4.0–8.0 | 6.0 | 5.2 | −0.8 |

public had a noisy indicator of intended future System policy. Additional steps eventually produced meaningful increases in transparency at all major central banks. Since the Federal Reserve had not replaced the gold standard rule with an alternative rule, greater transparency was needed to improve private forecasts of inflation or disinflation. The Federal Reserve was able to evade this step, but the issue was now open and would return.

In testimony on May 1, Burns announced a target of 5 to 7.5 percent for $M_1$ for the year ending March 1976. The announcement of explicit targets was a first. Unfortunately, the Federal Reserve chose to undermine Resolution 133 instead of using it to reduce inflation and maintain price stability.

Internally, members expressed concern about the unreliable control of monetary aggregates. In July 1973 the FOMC reactivated the Subcommittee on the Directive. The subcommittee's first report, on March 10, 1975, recommended use of nonborrowed reserves (total reserves minus member bank borrowing) in place of RPDs. The claim was that the manager's control of the instrument would improve. The report recognized that none of the reserve aggregates permitted precise short-run monetary control. It proposed setting a nonborrowed reserve target for the interval between FOMC meetings (memo, Subcommittee on the Directive to FOMC, Board Records, March 10, 1975). This was the apparent basis for choosing nonborrowed reserves as the target when the System adopted reserve targeting in October 1979.

Dewey Daane gave another prominent view of thinking within the FOMC. Daane served as a governor from 1963 to March 1974. A year later, he gave a speech expressing his personal views and responding to many of the Federal Reserve's critics. His emphasis on fiscal policy errors is familiar from many members' statements.

Daane said that the "recession-depression was an *inevitable concomitant* of the inflation that preceded it, and that is far from being eliminated. . . . [M]y best judgment of the present recession is that it traces primarily from the earlier inadequacies of stabilization policies, particularly fiscal policy although I would not altogether absolve monetary policy, of which I was a part, in contributing to an inflation that could not go on uncorrected" (Daane "The Other Side of the Looking Glass," Burns papers, Box K7, Ford Library, April 9, 1975, 6; emphasis added). Daane did not explain how inflation induced recession as an inevitable concomitant. Much of the rest of his speech sharply criticized "the simplistic view that $M_1$ growth rates are the sole determinant of economic activity" (ibid., 8). Simplistic is right!

The FOMC continued to use the federal funds rate as its principal target. A careful study at one of the reserve banks summarized its actions during September 1974 to September 1, 1979. "This period is unique in that the Fed controlled the funds rate so closely that market participants could identify most changes in the funds rate target on the day they were first implemented by the Fed, and these changes were reported by market participants in the financial press the following day" (Cook and Hahn, 1987).

## REGULATION 1974–75

In 1975, Congress considered and eventually approved legislation requiring greater openness and access to government decisions. As originally proposed, the bill would have required that meetings of FOMC and the Board be open to the press and the public. This constituted a very large change from the tradition of secrecy.[54]

Burns wrote a strong letter to Abraham Ribicoff, chairman of the Senate Committee on Government Operations, requesting exemption from the act. He argued that FOMC and Board meetings discussed problem banks and "sensitive materials relating to businesses, financial institutions, and foreign central banks and governments" (Burns papers, WHCF, Box BE1, Ford Library, June 17, 1975, 1). As a conciliatory gesture, Burns accepted that open meetings remained feasible for discussion of various consumer regulations such as Truth in Lending, Equal Credit Opportunity, and the like.

54. Kenneth Guenther (2001) was an assistant at the Board doing political liaison in this period. His first assignment was to organize the Federal Advisory Council to work against "government in the sunshine legislation," later called the Freedom of Information Act. Legislation of this kind had become law in Florida. Florida's senators pushed for similar legislation for the federal government. The Federal Reserve had help from the Federal Communication Commission because it, too, wanted an exemption. Congressional discussion shows the typical confusion between decision making and its consequences.

Burns's efforts succeeded. FOMC and most Board meetings remained closed to the public, though reports of the meetings became available sooner than in its past, and some meetings were open to the public.

As usual, the Board discussed and approved many regulatory changes. Attempts to circumvent regulation Q ceilings raised new issues every year. Defining the powers permitted to bank holding companies raised issues repeatedly. Also, 1974 provided an opportunity to end the Voluntary Foreign Credit Restraint Program on January 29, 1974. Truth in Lending legislation required many interpretations of banking actions.

Legislation in 1974 ended the forty-year ban on private ownership of gold. The Board sent a letter to the reserve banks urging them to send letters to district banks warning them that gold was not a reserve, it was a speculative commodity, and urging them to adopt precautions against price fluctuations if they made loans or sold gold to their customers.

Growing regulatory responsibility under consumer protection legislation and the Bank Holding Company Act encouraged the Board to divest some of its responsibilities. On several occasions in 1974, the Board directed responsibility for holding company acquisitions, bank mergers, and one-bank holding companies to the reserve banks. It restricted reserve bank decisions to actions similar to those on which the Board had ruled previously.

The Board made a policy decision to encourage longer-term time deposits by lowering reserve requirement ratios on certain types of deposits. For example, on October 16, 1975, it reduced from 3 to 1 percent the reserve requirement ratio for time deposits with four years initial maturity. The Board also reduced reserve requirement ratios on euro-dollar deposits to equality with domestic certificates of deposit. This action recognized that adoption of floating exchange rates reduced the need for restrictions on capital movements.

## POLICY ACTIONS IN RECOVERY

The recovery that began in second quarter 1975 was moderately robust, 6.1 percent average real growth in the next four quarters. Growth then slowed to 1.7 percent in second and third quarter 1976. Consumer price inflation fell from 9.8 percent in March 1975 to 4.8 percent at the 1976 election. Money wage growth declined from 8 percent in March 1975 to 5.7 percent in October, then rose to 7 percent at the election. Real wage growth turned positive. Unemployment reached 9 percent in May 1975, then declined to 7.8 percent at the election. Inflation declined as output rose and the unemployment rate fell. The Society of Professional Forecasters' forecast for four-quarter inflation remained in a narrow range, 5.9 to

6.2 percent throughout. Ten-year Treasury yields rose from 8 to 8.5 percent at the start of the recovery, then declined to 7.4 percent in November 1976. This measure of real yields remained positive.

The temporary tax cut increased disposable income at the start of the recovery, stimulating spending. The Federal Reserve followed a relatively cautious path, holding the federal funds rate between 4.8 (February 1976) and 6.2 percent (September 1975). At the election, the funds rate was 5 percent, slightly lower than at the end of the recession. Burns and a majority of the FOMC seemed determined to avoid another surge of inflation during the recovery. Twelve-month average growth of the monetary base fell from 7.9 to 6.8 percent during the recovery to November 1976. Although Burns professed admiration for President Ford, monetary policy did not turn highly expansive in 1976 despite slow real growth after first quarter 1976 and a 7.8 percent unemployment rate. The Federal Reserve had learned from its experience after 1972 not to repeat the 1972 stimulus despite an unemployment rate that was two percentage points higher in 1976.

William Simon became treasury secretary in May 1974, when George Shultz left. Simon opposed most stimulus programs and emphasized tax reduction and tax reform to increase productivity and encourage investment (MacAvoy, 2003). The Democratic majority in Congress did not share his views. They added spending and increased tax reduction, enlarging the budget deficit. Simon encouraged the president to veto a large number of spending programs, but despite the economic recovery, the budget deficit reached $60 and $76 billion in 1975 and 1976.

Congressional Democrats and many economists urged counter-cyclical fiscal actions. Simon generally opposed. Instead of viewing government spending as a means of stabilizing the economy, he argued that spending became permanent, increased deficits, and crowded out private spending. Simon renewed the claim that the economy would do a better job of restoring full employment with low inflation if left on its own. He favored fiscal policies that "were business cycle neutral" to increase long-term growth (ibid., 214). He told the Congress: "[F]ree competitive markets are the most effective way to increase output" (ibid., 215). Congress had not heard such comments from a treasury secretary since Secretary Humphrey in the Eisenhower administration, twenty years before. Like Humphrey, Simon did not convince a majority that short-term stimulus was both undesirable and possibly counterproductive.[55]

55. A milder version of the difference in approach was the discussion of the 1977 budget in Lynn and Schultze (1976). Lynn was the budget director in the Ford administration; Schultze had been budget director in the Johnson administration and became chairman of the Council of Economic Advisers in the Carter administration. In the question period,

**Table 7.8** Policy Changes, Inflation, and Unemployment, 1975–76 (%)

| MONTH | FEDERAL FUNDS | MONETARY BASE GROWTH | CPI INFLATION | UNEMPLOYMENT RATE |
|---|---|---|---|---|
| May 1975 | 5.22 | 6.3 | 9.1 | 9.0 |
| Sept. 1975 | 6.24 | 6.2 | 7.6 | 8.4 |
| Feb. 1976 | 4.77 | 6.1 | 6.1 | 7.7 |
| June 1976 | 5.48 | 6.3 | 5.8 | 7.6 |
| Dec. 1976 | 4.61 | 6.7 | 4.7 | 7.8 |

The Federal Reserve was more determined than in the previous ten years to reduce inflation while reducing unemployment rates. Between the end of the recession and the 1976 election the FOMC changed course five times, judged by the federal funds rate. Table 7.8 shows these changes, the twelve-month moving average of monetary base growth, consumer price inflation, and the monthly unemployment rate.

The inflation rate fell to the level prevailing in March 1973 under price and wage controls. The FOMC showed itself capable of substantially reducing inflation while the unemployment rate slowly fell, contrary to the Phillips curve. Growth of the monetary base fluctuated around 6 percent. As the table suggests, base growth began to rise late in 1976.

Burns responded more to the inflation rate than in the past, but he was aided by rising economic growth and falling unemployment.[56] Although several of the Keynesian economists had left the FOMC since 1972, and he influenced the choice of replacements, his policy met opposition.[57] President Eastburn (Philadelphia) dissented at the April 1975 meeting.[58] Governors Bucher and Coldwell dissented to an interest rate increase intended to slow money growth at the June meeting. Money growth contin-

Robert Weintraub pointed out the large difference between forecasts and outcomes in 1975 (ibid., 35).

56. Alan Greenspan did not accept the Phillips curve as a useful tool. "Unemployment was never seen as a necessary condition for bringing down the rate of inflation. . . . [S]ince the unemployment rate and inflation rate both went up together, we always argued it was possible to bring them down together. Over the longer run there's no question that that's right. The question is whether we could succeed in doing it over the shorter run" (Hargrove and Morley, 1984, 445). Greenspan retained this view later when he served as chairman of the Board of Governors.

57. At the time, the Shadow Open Market Committee (SOMC) blamed the Federal Reserve's operating procedures for the slow rate of money growth (reported 1.5 percent from June 1974 to February 1975). The March 1975 SOMC statement explained the decline in money growth ($M_1$) as a counter-cyclical mistake arising from the failure to recognize that the decline in market interest rates resulted from the weak economy, not from expansive Federal Reserve policy.

58. More than previous chairmen, Burns influenced the choice of reserve bank presidents. The law gave the Board final choice of the candidates that the Banks selected. Burns took a more active role in the selection process than Martin had.

ued to increase, so Burns had a telephone meeting to vote on an additional increase in the upper limit of the funds rate to 6.25 percent. This time Governors Bucher, Holland, and Mitchell dissented. This is another of the very few times when three governors dissented together. Alan Greenspan's weekly memo to the president noted the rapid growth but did not express concern. Money growth soon slowed. The action showed that at this time Burns watched money growth rates but did not attempt control.[59] The Federal Reserve lost much of its remaining credibility as SPF inflation forecasts rose.

Governor Holland dissented to an increase in the funds rate at the July meeting. $M_1$ growth slowed.[60] The FOMC kept the federal funds rate unchanged, but it raised the top of the range to 7 percent. The FOMC rejected a reduction in the funds rate because the reduction "might have to be reversed shortly—a sequence that could seriously compound uncertainties in financial markets" (Annual Report, 1975, 222).[61] The Federal Reserve has usually been averse to reversing its actions in a short period. Five changes up and down in the federal funds rate in 1975–76 were unusual.

Misled by data suggesting modest economic growth that was later raised and rising inflation, the FOMC promptly voted for a modest increase in the funds rate at the September 16, 1975, meeting. By October 2, the committee recognized that money growth had slowed. It voted to reduce the funds rate from 6.36 percent toward 6 percent or lower. At the October meeting, it voted to further reduce the funds rate to 5.75 or possibly 5.5 percent.[62]

59. $M_1$ and $M_2$ grew 11 and 13 percent in the second quarter. The announced intention called for 5 to 7.5 and 8.5 to 10.5 for the year to June 1976. The FOMC changed the target base to second quarter at its July meeting. It set the near-term growth rates to 3 to 5.5 and 8 to 10.5 percent. Also, the Board reduced discount rates by 1.5 percentage points in three stages—January 6, February 5, and March 10. On March 10, the discount rate was 6.25 percent. These changes followed the market.

60. European countries were in recession. They urged the United States to reduce its interest rate to help their recoveries. Burns and the administration resisted (Wells, 1994, 173).

61. A principal uncertainty was the possible default by New York City on its debt. The Ford administration refused assistance at first because New York did not offer a credible plan to achieve budget balance. At first Burns agreed with the president, but a New York default would damage the New York banks as debt holders. Also, the dollar declined, alarming the Europeans. After the state and city acted, the Ford administration agreed to lend several billion dollars, repayable by 1978. Congress approved (Wells, 1994, 175–77). Burns's reasoning again confuses the Federal Reserve's responsibility for sustaining the market, not the banks.

62. Twelve-month monetary base growth had declined from 8.8 percent in December 1974 to 5.7 percent in October 1975. At its September meeting, the SOMC urged the FOMC to maintain a 5.5 percent rate of money growth. This was within the 5 to 8 percent short-term range and the 5 to 7.5 percent medium-term range set by the FOMC. The minutes report a staff estimate of 11 percent nominal growth in the third quarter. Actual growth was 16.2 percent.

Opinions about appropriate policy differed as 1975 ended. A change in regulations permitted businesses to hold interest-bearing savings accounts up to $150,000 at member banks. This reduced measured $M_1$ growth. But monthly reported average hourly earnings rose rapidly (10.5) percent in November, even as CPI inflation rates continued to fall.

The FOMC's November decision called for a reduction in the federal funds rate and an increase in money growth. Paul Volcker and Philip Jackson dissented because they were uncertain about current conditions and, Volcker added, uncertain about the outlook for New York City. David Eastburn dissented for the opposite reason. He wanted a more expansive policy. "Too much emphasis on money market conditions had misled the Committee in the past" (Annual Report, 1975, 244). He wanted less emphasis on money market conditions.

Money growth rates declined after year-end 1975. The manager reduced the funds rate. Uncertainty about the reason for slow money growth, problems of seasonal adjustment in December–January, and evidence of continued economic growth limited the Committee's response to money growth. On December 24, the Board announced a small reduction in reserve requirement ratios, from 3 to 2.5 percent, on time deposits with 180 days to 4 years initial maturity. The new requirement became effective on January 8. The staff estimated that the reduction released $380 million in reserves, but as usual, the release was temporary; at unchanged interest rates borrowing declined. On January 5 the Board cited the release of reserves as a reason for delaying requests from Kansas City and San Francisco to reduce the discount rate. Eleven banks requested a reduction to 5.5 percent. The Board approved on January 16, 1976, citing a desire to bring the discount rate closer to open market rates. At the time, the federal funds rate was below 5 percent. Governor Coldwell dissented; he preferred a reduction of 0.25 because he thought the 0.5 reduction would signal a move toward greater ease.

Monthly average federal funds rates in 1976 remained in a narrow range between a low of 4.77 percent in February and a temporary high of 5.48 percent in June. In November, the month of the election, the funds rate was 4.95 percent.

At each meeting the FOMC set a one-year rate of growth in $M_1$ and $M_2$, a rate of $M_1$ and $M_2$ growth for the current period, and a federal funds rate target. The manager always hit the funds rate target, but frequently missed the money target. The modest rise in the federal funds rate in May and June may be a mild response to relatively rapid money growth in April and May. I find no evidence, however, that the one-year targets for money growth had any influence on the funds rate target. Perhaps most surpris-

**Table 7.9** Planned and Actual $M_1$ Growth, January–November 1976 (percent at annual rate)

| MONTH | PLANNED | ACTUAL | ANNUAL | PERIOD |
|---|---|---|---|---|
| January | 4–9 | 1.5 | 4.5–7.5 | 4Q to 4Q |
| February | 5–9 | 6.5 | 4.5–7.5 | 4Q to 4Q |
| March | 4–8 | 6.5 | 4.5–7.5 | 4Q to 4Q |
| April | 4.5–8.5 | 15.0 | 4.5–7.0 | 1Q to 1Q |
| May | 4–7.5 | 6.0 | 4.5–7.0 | 1Q to 1Q |
| June | 3.5–7.5 | 0 | 4.5–7.0 | 1Q to 1Q |
| July | 4–8 | 6.8 | 4.5–7.0 | 2Q to 2Q |
| August | 4–8 | 6.0 | 4.5–7.0 | 2Q to 2Q |
| September | 4–8 | 0 | 4.5–7.0 | 2Q to 2Q |
| October | 5–9 | 14.5 | 4.5–6.5 | 3Q to 3Q |
| November | 3–7 | 0 | 4.5–6.5 | 3Q to 3Q |

ing is the absence of any effect of the unsuccessful attempt at monetary control in 1976 on the procedure adopted in 1979. The main difference in the two periods was the tight control of the funds rate in the earlier period. Control of money growth did not improve.

Table 7.9 shows the planned and actual rates of $M_1$ growth up to the 1976 election. The FOMC always choose an $M_2$ range, but I have omitted these from the table. Also, the FOMC chose annual targets for $M_3$ and the bank credit proxy (total deposits).

The FOMC planned a four percentage point money growth range most of the year. Money growth was outside that range in six of the eleven months. Burns and the Committee recognized that control was unsatisfactory, as discussed below, but the Committee did not change its operating procedure or permit the federal funds rate to fluctuate over a wider range. The real federal funds rate was negative.

In February, Burns announced the proposed money growth rate for 1976 as 4.5 to 7.5 percent, a reduction of 0.5 in the lower bound. Since the FOMC also moved the base from the third to the lower fourth quarter 1975 value, it signaled an interest in continuing to lower inflation. Burns's testimony reinforced this message.[63]

At the April meeting, some members urged the FOMC to lower the upper bound on one-year money growth by as much as one percentage point to show its intention to reduce inflation. The committee reduced only the

63. As reported at the time, annual average $M_1$ growth in 1975 was 4.4 percent, but much of this growth reflected rapid growth in the second quarter. In early March, the Shadow Open Market Committee expressed concern that the rapid deceleration of money would reduce growth of output and lead to more expansive policies and higher inflation. The SOMC favored a gradual policy, an end to shifting the base for projections (base drift) each quarter, and specific reforms to improve monetary control.

upper bound and only by 0.5. The discussion showed more interest in reducing inflation than was typical of FOMC discussions. But it occurred while the economy recovered and the unemployment and inflation rates both declined.

There were only two dissents in 1976. A strong report of first-quarter expansion (7.5 percent) and reported rapid money growth encouraged the FOMC to increase the federal funds rate at the May meeting. Governor Coldwell dissented because he regarded the increase as excessive and likely to require a reversal. He thought the strong money growth was transitory.[64] Paul Volcker dissented at the July meeting from a decision to widen the band on the funds rate from 5.25–5.75 to 4.75–5.75. He thought increased money growth in July was transitory. The funds rate averages in July, August, and September were 5.21, 5.29, and 5.25 percent.

In July, members recognized that delaying action to change policy would bring them close to the presidential election. MacLaury (Minneapolis) and Guffey (Kansas City) proposed to slightly increase the money growth rate in July; the Committee voted to do so. This time, however, neither Burns nor the FOMC proposed to repeat the 1972 expansion. Occasional comments suggest the election was a consideration, but the minutes have few explicit statements. The FOMC did reduce the federal funds rate in October and after the election in November and December, but the belief at the time was that economic growth had slowed. Burns told the July meeting that "over the next few years we should get our monetary growth ranges down to a level where they are consistent with general price stability" (Burns papers, FOMC, July 19–20, 1976, tape 7, 8).[65] Unfortunately, actions did not correspond. The projected ranges showed good intentions that were not realized.

The staff estimated that growth in third quarter 1976 reached 4.5 percent and that the deflator rose 5.2 percent. Revised subsequently, real growth was 1.7 percent and inflation increased to 5.9 percent. These data are one of many examples of the often wide divergence between early re-

64. Coldwell dissented also from the decision on March 15–16 to eliminate publication (after five years) of the memoranda of discussion. (These are the records I refer to as minutes.) The FOMC agreed to put more information into the annual records of policy actions published in the Board's Annual Reports. The chairs of the Senate and House Banking Committees criticized the decision and asked the FOMC to reconsider. In July, the FOMC voted eleven to one to reaffirm its decision. Governor Coldwell dissented again.

65. Following Burns's statement, members discussed the market's response to short-term changes. Balles (San Francisco) and Burns described the market's response as irrational. Burns added that the FOMC and the desk also respond irrationally to new data (Burns papers, FOMC, July 19–20, 1976, tape 7, 16). No one suggested basing policy on longer-term changes, but Balles proposed smoothing data using moving averages.

ports and later revisions, especially for real growth. The divergence again raises the question: Why did the FOMC respond to the preliminary data? As Orphanides (2001, 2003a, 2003b) has shown, use of preliminary data was a main source of error in choosing policy actions.[66]

The staff projected an increase in real growth in the quarters ahead. None of the members disagreed with the projections, although some expressed uncertainty about the timing of the increase and the effects of an automobile manufacturing strike then under way (Annual Report, 1976, 259). The projection differed from the claim by the Democrats' candidate for president, James Carter, who suggested that a slowdown was under way and proposed more fiscal stimulus. Some FOMC members favored small fiscal stimulus, but the Committee preferred tax reduction to spending increases.

After rejecting proposals for reductions in the discount rate in September and October, the Board approved a 0.25 point reduction to 5.25 on November 19. Eleven banks asked for the reduction. St. Louis joined the following week. The action followed the market in recognizing slower real growth in the fourth quarter, the decline in market rates, and the belief that growth would slow in 1977. In December the Board turned down several requests for additional discount rate reductions. But it slightly reduced reserve requirement ratios for demand deposits by 0.5 points to 7 and 9.5 percent for deposits of 0 to $2 million and $2 to $10 million and by 0.25 points for all other demand deposits. The staff estimated that the action released $550 million in reserves, but with unchanged interest rates, the manager absorbed the additional reserves. The move intended to reduce the loss of members by reducing membership costs.

Soon after these moves, the staff recognized that the 1976 slowing of industrial production and economic growth was temporary. By year-end, the staff described the very large increase in industrial production (19.8 percent annual rate) in November as larger than could be explained by the end of the auto workers' strike.[67]

66. The FOMC voted in August to continue open market operations in agency securities. It claimed these operations were "useful in achieving the Committee's reserve objectives" (Annual Report, 1976, 252). The more likely reason was pressure from Congress to intervene in the agency market, especially housing market securities.

67. Purchase of federal agency issues became controversial. Burns recognized that congressional pressure to aid the housing industry was a main reason for purchases. Coldwell opposed strongly. Volcker recognized the political pressures but urged restraint, especially for FNMA purchases. Burns concluded that it was not worth a fight with Congress (Burns papers, FOMC, August 17, 1976, tape 6, 8). The issue returned in November, when several objected to the purchase of transit bonds for Washington, D.C. Some in Congress asked why FOMC could help Washington but not New York, pointing up the problem arising from credit allocation.

## THE 1976 ELECTION

James Earl Carter narrowly defeated Gerald Ford in the 1976 election by 1.7 million votes out of 86 million. With inflation (deflator) at 7.1 percent and a new administration, the anti-inflation program ended. Four years later the deflator reached 12 percent, partly a result of a second large oil price increase.

During the campaign, and after, Carter's principal advisers tried to hark back to the successful experience of the Kennedy administration's program to "get America moving" after the very restrictive policies of the late Eisenhower administration (Biven, 2002, 27). Although candidate Carter did not offer an explicit program, he emphasized the long and deep recession in 1974–75 and the slow recovery. He promised full employment by 1979 and expressed much less concern about inflation (ibid., 29, 34, 36). He explained that he had never been asked about inflation during the campaign, only about employment (Carter, 1982, 65).[68]

Comparisons to the 1960s neglected an important difference. The Kennedy program came after a successful anti-inflation program had convinced all but the most skeptical that the United States would not inflate. Also, it came at a time of faster productivity growth. These factors reduced both actual and expected inflation. Few, if any, in 1961 believed that peacetime inflation rates would reach 8 to 10 percent. Few in 1977 doubted that these inflation rates could return.

Several Carter administration economists, like the Kennedy administration economists, believed that they could use wage and price guideposts to limit inflation. In a magazine interview, Carter told the editors what he understood from his advisors. "My economic advisors and I agree that until you get the unemployment rate down below five percent, there's no real danger of escalating inflationary pressures" (quoted in Biven, 2002, 36). He wanted "more humane and economically sound solutions to cooling inflation" without increasing unemployment (ibid.). In a speech to the AFL-CIO, he accused the Ford administration of using "the evil of unemployment to fight the evil of inflation—and—having the highest combination of unemployment and inflation in the twentieth century" (ibid., 37). Four years later, Ronald Reagan used the same argument against Carter.

Labor unions objected to strong interference in wage setting, so the administration adopted a modest guidepost program. As inflation rose, guideposts became more explicit but no more effective. Stuart Eizenstat,

68. President Carter attributed part of his difficulty in getting his programs through Congress to his position as an outsider. As a "southerner, born-again Christian, a Baptist, and a newcomer," his election owed little to traditional Democratic groups in Washington (Carter, 1982, 11).

**Table 7.10** Consumer Price Inflation Forecasts and Realizations, 1977–79 (%)

| YEAR | FORECAST | REALIZATION |
|---|---|---|
| 1977 | 5.3 | 6.8 |
| 1978 | 6.0 | 9.0 |
| 1979 | 7.5 | 13.0 |

Source: Bivens (2002, 56).

the Domestic Policy Adviser, described the guidepost policy as enough "to make all constituencies mad without accomplishing the result" (Eizenstat, 1982, 79).[69]

Two problems arose. First, the administration's economists were unwilling to accept a temporary increase in unemployment to gain a permanent reduction in inflation, and the public in 1976–77 was not greatly concerned about inflation. By 1979, concern had increased. Second, administration economists underestimated the rate of inflation. Forecasts of inflation, based on the Phillips curve relating inflation to the unemployment rate, were inaccurate. Table 7.10 shows the forecasts and realizations of inflation in 1977–79. All three forecasts underestimated the inflation rate, in part because of one-time increases in food and oil prices, in part because of mistaken beliefs about the natural rate, but also because monetary base growth from 1977 to 1979 averaged 8 percent or more.

Part of the forecast error resulted from the unanticipated oil price shock. Chart 7.11 shows the two sharp increases in consumer price inflation following the two large oil price increases in the 1970s. The oil price increases in 1973 and 1979 came at a time of rising inflation. In contrast, Chart 7.12 shows the much smaller increases in nominal wage growth in 1973–74 and 1978–79. Together, the two series imply a substantial decline in real wages in both periods. Despite repeated claims by Arthur Burns and others about the role of labor unions, labor unions did not recover their losses. The oil price increases were a tax paid to foreigners that had to be borne by wages and profits. The different response of wages to demand stimulus and supply shocks suggests the importance of separating these persistent and transitory effects in discussing and responding to price increases.

At a more fundamental level, Carter's choice of advisers included mainly people who believed that the economy had to be closely managed. This fit well with Carter's predilections. In contrast to Greenspan, Simon, and President Ford, they did not believe that they could rely on a robust private sector to restore full employment at low inflation if government adopted

69. President Carter's adviser from his years as governor of Georgia warned him that wage-price guidelines were ineffective unless supplemented with general macroeconomic policy. Carter replied: "I understand from this what will not work. What will?" (quoted in Biven, 2002, 54).

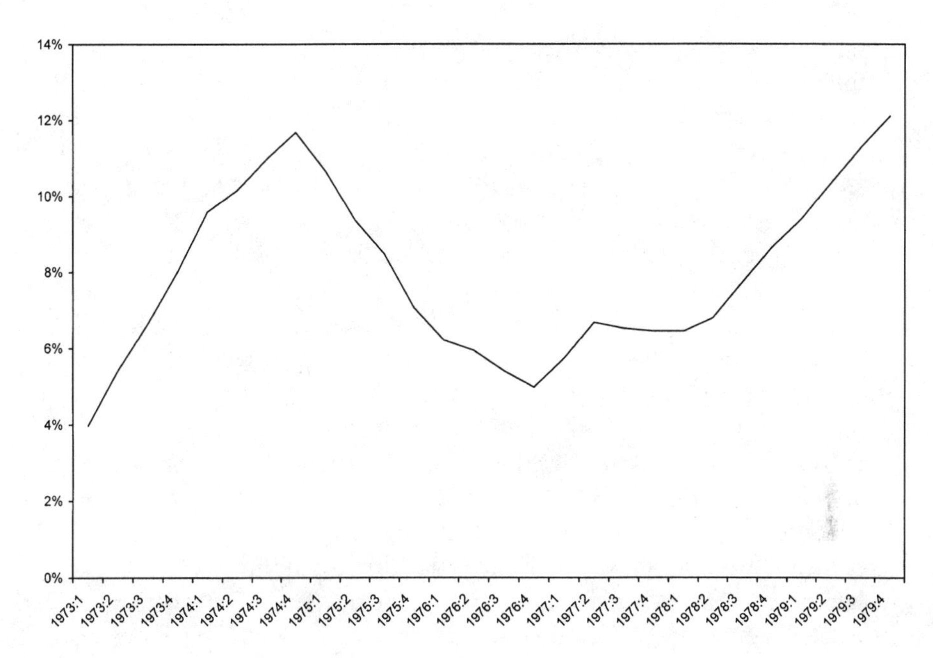


Chart 7.11. Annualized quarterly CPI, twelve-month moving average, 1973–79.

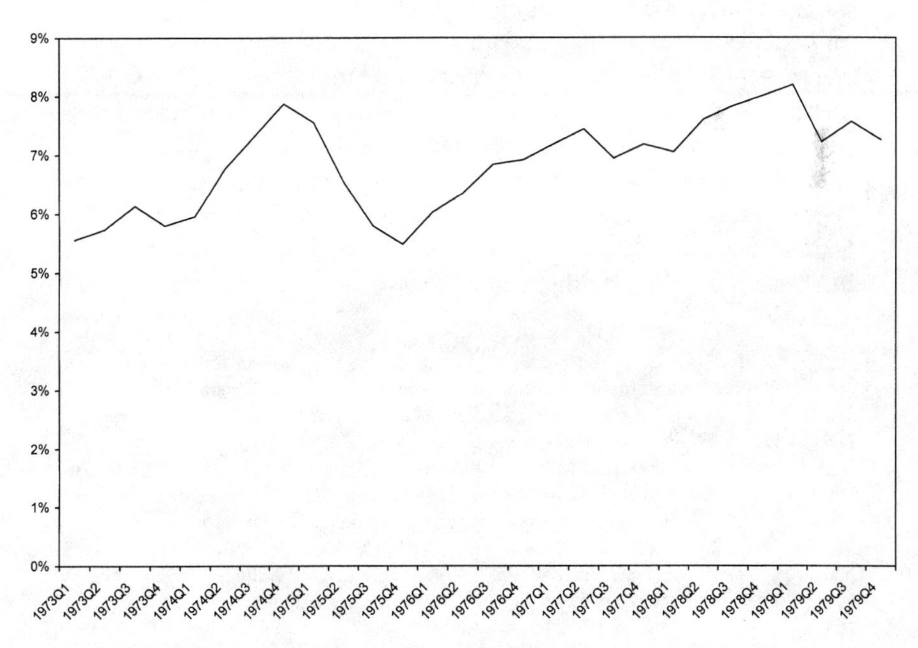


Chart 7.12. Annualized growth in quarterly nominal wages, 1973–79, twelve-month moving average.

non-inflationary policies. They were Keynesians with a strong belief that their task was to manage the details because without their intervention, the private sector would be unstable. A briefing paper for President-elect Carter told him: "There have been few spontaneous recoveries in the years since World War II" (quoted in Biven, 2002, 125). Advisers explained that several econometric models showed declining growth in 1977. They were wrong. The 1977 recovery is evidence against the Keynesian view.

To expand output and increase employment, the Carter administration proposed to reduce corporate taxes, increase depreciation allowances for small businesses, give a $50 rebate to households on 1976 income taxes, increase revenue sharing for state and local governments, and create additional public service jobs at a total cost of $15 billion. Ray Marshall, secretary of labor, proposed public employment programs. This did not appeal to Schultze, but it did to Carter. President Carter was torn between his alleged fiscal conservatism and the political pressures from the liberal side of his party (Hargrove and Morley, 1984, 463).[70] By spring, congressional opposition, recovery, economic expansion, and the unpopularity of the $50 rebate changed the program (Hargrove and Morley, 1984, 480; Carter, 1982, 12). In April President Carter dropped the rebate and the business tax cut. Congress adopted an employment tax credit in place of public service jobs, increased the standard income tax deduction for individuals and gave assistance to state and local governments. The stimulus package transferred $6 billion in 1977 and $17 billion in 1978. The original proposal had $15 billion in each of 1977 and 1978 (Biven, 2002, 82).

Arthur Burns openly opposed the administration's program. Burns believed that budget deficits and labor unions were major causes of inflation.[71] He wanted a lower budget deficit and stronger guidelines for wage increases. This open conflict with the administration was not forgotten

70. Charles Schultze served as budget director during the Johnson administration. He is a highly regarded economist, active in the Democratic Party. Several of Carter's advisers described him as a fiscal conservative. In fact, budget deficits for the four years 1977–80 reached $226.8 billion. Total federal outlays rose 44 percent in nominal terms and 13 percent in real terms between 1977 and 1980. Outlays increased by one percentage point relative to GNP. This growth is not conservative compared to experience up to that time, but it is modest compared to budget and deficit increases during the Reagan administration.

71. The Shadow Open Market Committee in March warned that the new administration had shifted priorities. The committee said that this change would bring higher inflation. In September, it warned that money growth had returned to the high levels of 1968, 1972, and 1973. Government spending growth increased also. After the fact, Stuart Eizenstat said that their biggest mistake was underestimating inflation at the start of the administration and failure to act against it (Eizenstat, 1982, 79). Eizenstat was chief Domestic Policy Adviser to the president. Later, he favored price and wage controls as a short-term response to the 1979 oil price increase.

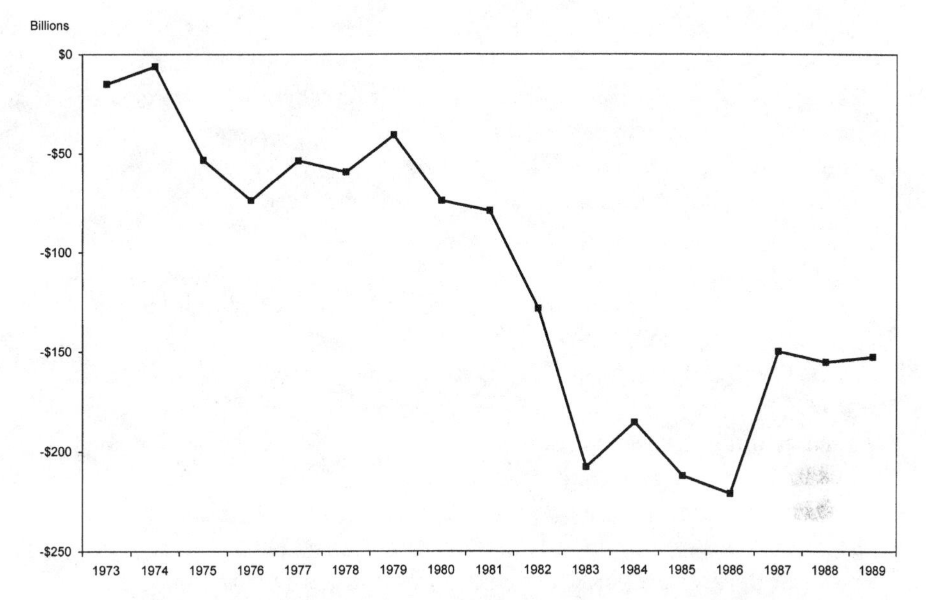


Chart 7.13. Federal budget deficit, 1973–89.

when his second four-year term as chairman of the Board of Governors expired in February 1978.

Expressed concern about the budget deficit had little influence on the size of the actual deficit compared to President Ford's budgets. Chart 7.13 shows that deficits in 1977 and 1978 are about the same as in 1975. The 1979 deficit fell to about $40 billion, in part because of stronger growth. Compared to the deficits that came in the Reagan presidency, these deficits though historically large, seem modest.[72]

Burns's opposition to the administration program did not go as far as tightening monetary policy enough to bring down inflation.[73] Although

72. Critics of budget deficits often claim that deficits increase real interest rates. This claim is hard to accept as a major influence for the United States given the United States' experience since 1980. Large deficits of the Reagan years, surpluses in the late years of Clinton's presidency, and renewed deficits in the Bush presidency from 2001 leave little visible effect on real interest rates. One possible reason is Ricardian equivalence. A more likely reason is that many countries manage their exchange rates by buying the debt issued by the U.S. to finance its budget deficits.

73. Burns believed that monetary velocity would rise rapidly during the early months of a cyclical recovery. In an exchange with Congressman Henry Reuss on February 3, 1977, about the Carter fiscal program, he denied the need to increase the money growth rate. Unlike Martin in 1968, he did not blindly accept coordinated action.

Dr. Burns. I cannot overemphasize the point that no matter how you define the money supply . . . for periods of intermediate duration, such as a year or a little longer, the

the federal funds rate rose during the rest of his term as chairman, the rise was gradual and often less than the increase in inflation. As noted earlier, monetary base growth remained historically high. Between December 1976 and February 1978, the twelve-month average base growth rose from 6.7 to 8.7 percent. Despite Burns's frequent strong statements about the evils of inflation, his policies continued to finance inflation and fostered inflationary expectations. When Burns took office in February 1970, the Society of Professional Forecasters predicted 3 percent inflation for the next four quarters; when he left in March 1978, the forecast had doubled to 5.9 percent.

Just before the election, FOMC members and staff forecast sluggish growth in the world economy. They were uncertain about what to do and did not think that the private sector could produce a revival unaided. Burns said that classical liberal financial policy "may no longer work in [an] environment in which inflation coexists with recession or sluggish economic expansion" (Burns papers, FOMC, October 19, 1976, tape 4, 7–8). Not everyone shared the pessimism, but it was widespread.[74] The sluggish economy with continued inflation would be called "stagflation," a term that, perhaps inadvertently, covered up the role of anticipations of future inflation. Burns explained stagflation as a result of an unanticipated, large, worldwide recession in 1973–75. This increased uncertainty and pessimism everywhere (ibid., tape 4, 8). He thought "a cut in taxes accompanied by a cut in expenditures, . . . concentrated in large part in a

dynamic factor is not so much the rate of growth of the money supply as the rapidity of its turnover.

The Chairman [Reuss]. That is precisely why I put to you at the start of the discussion the assumption that velocity would increase at approximately the same rate, around 3 percent that it has in the post-World War II period. . . .

Dr. Burns. But I can not accept your assumption, and I do not accept it. I am assuming that the increase in velocity will be appreciably larger than that. (Hearing before the House Committee on Banking, Federal Reserve Bank of New York, Archives Box 110282)

The testimony is one example of Burns's allegedly uncooperative attitude. In the event, velocity increased about as he forecast. In November 1976, an international group of sixteen economists called for coordinated expansion by the United States, West Germany, and Japan. Paul McCracken and Arthur Okun represented the United States. Despite inflation the concern was mainly unemployment.

74. At about the same time, U.K. Prime Minister Callaghan moved toward more liberal policies. "We used to think that you could just spend your way out of recession. . . . I'll tell you in all candor that that opinion no longer exists. And that insofar as it ever did exist, it worked by injecting inflation into the economy and each time that happened the average level of unemployment has risen" (quoted by Burns, Burns papers, FOMC, December 21, 1976, tape 5, 1). Burns's opinion was that Keynesian views still dominated in the United States and had misled Carter.

reduction of business taxes . . . would help to restore confidence," (ibid., tape 6, 5). He was less confident about the benefit of monetary ease.

The FOMC had learned about the cost of policy coordination. Several expressed the point more or less explicitly. The general view was that they must avoid inflation. Volcker expressed concern about the pessimism in statements by members of FOMC. He blamed the election campaign (not the candidates) and suggested the election result would reduce uncertainty and pessimism. He did not favor fiscal expansion and criticized Eastburn and Gramley for endorsing a political program to reduce tax rates (ibid., 5, 5).

In November, Burns proposed reducing the upper bound and midpoint of the federal funds target while also reducing the lower limit on $M_1$ growth. The Committee did not accept his recommendation for $M_1$ growth. Instead of Burns's proposed 3 to 7 percent, the FOMC chose 5 to 9 percent unanimously, the same range as in October. The difference showed a shifting concern toward moderate stimulus and Burns's expressed concern to continue reducing the inflation rate. President Baughman (Dallas) urged restraint. He thought the Carter administration would ask for fiscal stimulus, followed by price-wage restraint. Kimbrel (Atlanta) reported that businessmen had started to increase list prices in anticipation of price controls.

Several members urged the Board to agree to proposed reductions in the discount rate. The Board soon afterward accepted the recommendations. Volcker stated the FOMC's position in December. "Some stimulus could be productive, but [he] preferred to see it in a mild fiscal package" (ibid., tape 8). As usual, most of the discussion was about a difference of 0.12 or at most 0.25 in the funds rate. Wallich was the most vocal about the risk of inflation.

Burns looked back at policy in 1976. He claimed that the FOMC had performed "admirably," citing the continued expansion and decline in interest rates (ibid., tape 4, 1–2).[75] He agreed with a subcommittee report that suggested that control of monetary aggregates required a longer term program. Again, Burns did not propose or undertake steps to improve control of money growth.[76]

A subcommittee chaired by Governor Partee reported on the results of using a nonborrowed reserve target in 1976. The central issue was whether the System could improve operations by using a nonborrowed reserve tar-

75. In fact, the monthly average federal funds rate began the year at 4.87 percent, rose to 5.4 in June, then declined to 4.65 in December.

76. The FOMC voted to extend the authorization for direct purchases of securities from the Treasury.

get with less emphasis on the federal funds rate. The subcommittee concluded that a nonborrowed reserve (NBR) target was more likely to be hit than a reserves against private deposits (RPD) target used earlier, but that control of short-term money growth would not improve. To hit the money stock target, NBR was no better than the federal funds rate target (ibid, December 21, 1976, tape 3, 1–9).

The subcommittee opined that adopting an NBR target gained little if the FOMC continued to seek control of money for a two-month period. It proposed to abandon the NBR target.

President Balles (San Francisco) drew a more appropriate conclusion. The committee should seek balance between short-run interest rate stability and keeping monetary aggregates within a twelve-month growth range chosen once a quarter. He wanted to let interest rates fluctuate more than in the past to improve control of money growth and inflation (ibid., tape 3, 16–18).

The subcommittee report and subsequent discussion again failed to get the FOMC to look ahead far enough to control money growth and inflation. Even after it gave up tight control of the funds rate in 1979–82, it did not act on the information learned from the Partee committee study or on Balles's conclusion. The focus remained on the short-term. Another missed opportunity!

President Carter's first budget director was a Georgia banker, Bert Lance. Lance was a fiscal conservative who opposed the proposed 1977 stimulus package. An alleged scandal about his banking practices before he joined the administration forced him to resign in summer 1977.[77] He was exonerated later. President Carter (1982, 12) believed that Lance knew less about economics than other advisers but was better able to deliver information because of their long relationship.

Other members of the economic advisory group were Treasury Secretary Michael Blumenthal, a businessman; Stuart Eizenstat, a Georgia lawyer who served as Chief Domestic Policy Adviser; and Council chairman Charles Schultze. These four became part of the Economic Policy Group (EPG). Carter added others to the group, so it became unwieldy and ineffective. He blamed Blumenthal for its ineffectiveness. This contributed to his decision in 1979 to replace Blumenthal as treasury secretary with

77. At the Shadow Committee meeting in March 1977, Beryl Sprinkel and I expressed concern about the end of the disinflation policy. Sprinkel, a bank officer, knew Lance and arranged a meeting with him in May 1977. The argument that got Lance's attention was that a stimulus policy in 1977 would likely require an anti-inflation policy that would increase unemployment in 1979–80, when President Carter would run for reelection. Lance asked us to stay in touch and come back, but he left soon after.

G. William Miller (Carter, 1982, 19–22). One part of his concern was the inability to get a uniform recommendation. He often had to decide between alternatives. For this, too, Carter blamed Blumenthal's lack of leadership. He thought the EPG was ineffective under Blumenthal, but it improved when Miller became treasury secretary (Carter, 1982, 19–22). Miller liked the change to Treasury and did an effective job of managing the financial transaction that released the hostages held by Iran.

Before the inauguration, the economists responsible for international economic policy expressed concern about the effect of the stimulus package and a larger fiscal deficit on net national saving and the exchange rate. Shortly after the inauguration, the new president sent Vice-President Walter Mondale and some economists to talk to the principal countries with payments surpluses—West Germany and Japan—about coordinating policies. The main idea was that if all three expanded spending, relative positions would remain about the same and the dollar would not devalue.

All three countries had excessive unemployment. The response by Japan was cautious but generally positive (Biven, 2002, 103). The response in Germany was negative. Chancellor Helmut Schmidt pointed out that although exchange rates might remain stable, worldwide inflation would be the "inevitable result" (ibid., 99; Volcker and Gyohten, 1992, 145–48).[78] Nevertheless, Germany's efforts to reduce its budget deficit stopped in 1977–78, and the Bundesbank allowed money growth to exceed its preannounced targets. But the German official position remained opposed to greater policy coordination with the United States. It attributed the "high current account deficits in the United States . . . not to any low level of demand, but to massive public sector debt as well as to the consequent low level of savings in the country" (Kitterer, 1999, 199).

President Carter's personal style influenced policymaking also. He thought it was his responsibility to be fully informed about details of all policy positions, so that he did not require the assistance of an aide (Carter, 1982, 17). He recognized also that he sent too many recommendations to Congress at one time (ibid., 23). And he felt very much the outsider in Washington and believed that leaders of Congress had not campaigned for him. As a "southerner, born-again Christian, a Baptist, and newcomer," he believed he had no obligation to major lobbying groups and former Democratic leaders (ibid., 6–7). He described his economic aims as a balanced budget, lower inflation, and deregulation of trucking, airlines, communi-

78. Schmidt asked for the estimated effect of the stimulus package on inflation in the United States. "When [Fred] Bergsten replied it was expected to raise the inflation rate by only 0.3 percent Schmidt is reported to have been 'incredulous'" (Biven, 2002, 99).

cation, banking, finance, and oil and gas prices (ibid., 45). These aims did not please many congressional Democrats (ibid., 66). And he blamed his failures also on the oil price shock.

## FEDERAL RESERVE ACTIONS, 1977–78

The election removed a government that gave much attention to reducing inflation and brought in a government that gave priority to reducing unemployment. See Table 7.10 and Charts 7.1 and 7.7 above.

Actual and expected inflation rose. The unemployment rate remained unchanged. The 1979 oil price increase was a one-time increase that overstates the underlying inflation rate. The Federal Reserve responded by increasing the federal funds rate. By December 1978, federal funds adjusted for expected inflation exerted disinflationary pressure.

At the start of the period, several reserve banks requested discount rate reductions. The Board rejected six requests in December 1976 and three in January 1977. It pointed to evidence of a strengthening economy.

Early in December 1978, President Carter announced that he chose a businessman, G. William Miller, to replace Arthur Burns as chairman of the Federal Reserve. Burns, who had done much to sustain and increase the Great Inflation, was replaced in part because he was considered too much an anti-inflationist. Schultze also complained that Burns was more than willing to comment on administration policy at Quadriad meetings with the president but unwilling to tell the president what the Federal Reserve would do (Schultze, 2005). Schultze wanted more policy coordination; Burns guarded Federal Reserve, and his own, independence as a principle he insisted upon despite often yielding to administration pressure. This created an unsatisfactory outcome. He did not control inflation and did not gain the trust and confidence of the Carter team. Most of all, Carter did not get along well with Burns, as he later said.

Table 7.11 shows planned and actual federal funds and short-term money growth targets during the rest of Burns's term as chairman. The minutes give $M_1$ growth and the funds rate as ranges, usually one-half percentage point for the funds rate and four to six percentage points for $M_1$ growth.

As before, the manager always came close to the federal funds target, although usually modestly below. The manager and the FOMC did not respond forcefully to the much wider discrepancies between actual and planned money growth. Particularly in April, July, and October, money growth was highly inflationary. Reactions remained mild.[79]

79. The New York bank staff compared the use of the federal funds rate and nonborrowed reserves as operating targets. The main conclusions were that (1) either could be used to

**Table 7.11** Planned and Actual Actions (%)

| MEETING DATE | PLANNED $M_1$ | ACTUAL $M_1$ | PLANNED FUNDS RATE | ACTUAL FUNDS RATE |
|---|---|---|---|---|
| *1977* | | | | |
| January 17–18 | 5 | 4.5 | 4.625 | 4.61 |
| February 15 | 5 | 1 | 4.625 | 4.68 |
| March 15 | 6.5 | 6 | 4.75 | 4.69 |
| April 19 | 8 | 20 | 4.875 | 4.73 |
| May 17 | 2 | 1.1 | 5.50 | 5.35 |
| June 21 | 4.5 | n.a. | 5.50 | 5.39 |
| July 19 | 5.5 | 18 | 5.50 | 5.42 |
| August 16 | 2.5 | 5.5 | 6.00 | 5.90 |
| September 20 | 4.5 | 7.75 | 6.25 | 6.14 |
| October 17–18 | 5.5 | 12 | 6.50 | 6.47 |
| November 15 | 4 | −1 | 6.50 | 6.51 |
| December 19–20 | 5.5 | 7.6 | 6.50 | 6.56 |
| *1978* | | | | |
| January 17 | 5 | 7.25 | 6.75 | 6.70 |
| February 28 | 3.5 | −1.0 | 6.75 | 6.78 |

Source: Annual Reports 1977, 1978.

In 1977, the Board also approved two increases in the discount rate; one on August 29 raised the rate to 5.75 percent; the other on October 25 set a 6 percent rate.[80] On January 6, 1978, the Board approved a 6.5 percent discount rate. The rise in interest rates shown in Table 7.11 suggests, and the Board's announcement stated, that the adjustments recognized market actions that had occurred previously. Beginning in May, the Board rejected discount rate increases ten times before the August increase and three additional requests before the October increase.

The reserve banks were ahead of the Board in seeking to slow inflation. As the Board noted: "In proposing those increases the directors of the Federal Reserve Banks in question stressed the outlook for rising prices and the

control monetary aggregates, (2) neither target was better than the other, (3) the federal funds rate target permitted greater money market stability, and (4) market interest rates would be more variable, if nonborrowed reserves became the principal target. The memo questioned whether money market stability was advantageous (Richard Davis to Paul Volcker, Federal Reserve Bank of New York, Archives Box 110282, August 15, 1977). The memo does not say how the comparison was made, but it does not suggest that the variability of interest rates under a nonborrowed reserve target and interest rate targeting achieved the same monetary growth. A reserve target required an increase in interest rate volatility compared to past practice. The memo shows also that Volcker had considered some of the issues that arose in 1979–82 years before he changed procedures. The memo does not discuss the effects on the maintained rate of money growth or how to lower inflation.

80. Governor Wallich dissented from the August increase because of "hesitation in some key indicators of economic activity and the associated uncertainty about the duration of the economic expansion" (Annual Report, 1977, 150).

desirability of providing a signal of the System's determination to continue pursuing an anti-inflationary monetary policy" (Annual Report, 1977, 142). The Board expressed concern that an increase in the discount rate would be "misconstrued as an indication of a major shift in monetary policy" (ibid.). The underlying reason was that despite an average increase of consumer prices of more than 6.5 percent (annual rate) per month between May and August, the unemployment rate remained between 6.9 and 7.2 percent. Despite his anti-inflationary rhetoric, Burns again failed to respond effectively to inflation. In the meetings, he often proposed less expansive policies, but he did not fight for them. The FOMC responded weakly to monthly money growth rates as high as 18 percent annual rate. Burns was not alone. Dissents from FOMC decisions remained rare in this period. John Balles (San Francisco) expressed concern in January about rapid growth of $M_2$, but did not follow through. Phillip Coldwell dissented in June because he wanted a 0.25 percentage point reduction in the lower bound on the funds rate. Coldwell dissented again in July, joined by Jackson and Roos (St. Louis). Each favored a less expansive policy. But Governors Lilly and Wallich dissented in September because they believed monetary policy was too restrictive. At the time, growth of $M_1$ for the year ending in third quarter 1977 "had exceeded by a considerable margin the upper limit of the range set at its meeting in early November 1976" (ibid., 292). However, at the same meeting Frank Morris (Boston) and Larry Roos (St. Louis) dissented for the opposite reason. They regarded as inadequate the policy response to the money growth rates reported at recent meetings. Morris and Wallich also dissented in October, one again favoring faster money growth, the other slower. Roos dissented again in December, and Lilly, Morris, and Partee dissented in early January from a decision to raise the upper limit on the funds rate by 0.25 to 7 percent principally to strengthen the dollar.

At the May 1977 meeting, the FOMC began to increase the federal funds rate. The average rose to 5.4 in May from 4.7 percent in April. At the time, both the twelve-month-average consumer price increase and average rate of monetary base growth were 6.5 percent. Expected inflation increased to 6.5 percent. $M_1$ growth from May to July averaged about 4 percent using the revised definition of $M_1$ that included NOW accounts and other transaction balances.

Burns urged a reduction in the $M_1$ target to 0 to 4 percent with federal funds at a 5.5 percent midpoint. Volcker and Wallich proposed −1 to 4 percent, but Burns did not want a negative number. Six members wanted the lower bound on the funds rate at 5 percent; four wanted the upper bound at 6 percent. By unanimous decision the FOMC accepted 5.25 to 5.75, Burns's midpoint and also his range for $M_1$ growth.

The narrow range and unanimous vote understate the division within the Committee. Willes (Minneapolis) said that businessmen needed continued evidence of he System's willingness to combat inflation. He wanted "a significant step toward moderation in the rates of growth in the aggregates" (Burns papers, FOMC, May 17, 1977, tape 3, 16). Partee responded, opposing the degree of monetary "tightness" that Willes called for. "We also have the objective of maintaining reasonable growth . . . [W]e're talking about a growth rate of around six percent or perhaps a shade below which we need unless we're to accept this unemployment rate as a permanent thing" (ibid., tape 3, 11–20).

Partee noted that the Committee had tightened in the spring of 1975 and again in 1976 but reversed policy soon after. He believed they did no harm. Earlier, Partee mentioned a congressional response, a topic that rarely became explicit. "What would be a Congressional response to a higher unemployment rate?" Burns cut off the discussion (ibid., tape 2, 11–12). Others mentioned the effects on wages, prices, and interest rates from an increase in expected inflation, a sign that FOMC members started to give attention to anticipations of inflation in the private sector. Guffey mentioned speculation in farm real estate, a major problem for the farm sector after 1979.

The modest move to a higher federal funds rate at first had no effect on longer-term rates. By October the ten-year rate began to rise, in anticipation of rising inflation. By year-end, it increased forty basis points, from 7.4 to 7.8 percent. It continued to rise in 1978 to 8.7 percent in July 1978. By that time twelve-month CPI inflation was 7.5 percent and rising.

The FOMC never discussed and never decided how much unemployment they would accept to reduce the inflation rate. They had different objectives and rarely expressed a clear view.[81] Their votes and discussion are the main clues to their beliefs. For example, Burns talked often about the objective of price stability or reduced inflation, but he recognized and perhaps overemphasized the political constraints. In January 1977, he urged the members to "consider the degree to which, if any, our monetary policy should contribute to unwinding the inflation from which our economy has been suffering since the mid-1960s. . . . [N]o other branch of government . . . has anything approaching an articulate policy for bringing down the rate of

81. One of the rare exceptions was a brief discussion in February 1977. Morris (Boston) said that "there is a need for the Committee to make policy in a longer term time frame than we've been accustomed to in the past. I thought I would ask if the staff has a concept of what the optimum growth path ought to be for the economy over the next few years" (Burns papers, FOMC, February 15, 1977, tape 1, 10). A brief discussion followed, but action did not change.

inflation" (ibid., January 17–18, tape 7, 1). Then he expressed concern about the unemployment rate, the new administration, the new Congress, and the possible interpretation of an anti-inflation action as an effort to frustrate the efforts to expand employment. That covered all the possibilities. He proposed leaving the annual target for $M_1$ growth unchanged at 4.5 to 6.5 to limit that criticism, but he proposed lowering the bottom of the $M_2$ and $M_3$ ranges by 0.5 percentage points. Morris (Boston) argued that the proposal lacked substance, suggesting it was mainly cosmetic.

Burns replied to the criticisms by defending the small change in $M_2$ and $M_3$ growth. "It will take us ten years [to return to price stability]. Ten years if we're lucky" (ibid, tape 8, 2).[82] Governor Coldwell pointed out that they did not achieve the annual targets. "I don't hear many Committee members, perhaps excluding President Balles, who keep reminding us that our short-run ought to be somewhat consistent with our long-run targets" (ibid., tape 8, 4–5).

With the obvious divisions, the short-term focus, and the absence of a common, coherent framework and an agreed objective, the System was ill-equipped to end inflation. Political concerns and weak independence heightened the problem.

In March, the FOMC missed another opportunity to consider the longer-term effect of its actions. Governor Wallich said the FOMC would improve its policy "the earlier we face up to the prospect of rising interest rates" (ibid., March 15, 1977, tape 4, 4). Burns opposed. "We ought to be very cautious about any anticipatory movement that we make. And we're capable of responding and responding very promptly without anticipating these very short-term adjustments" (ibid., tape 4, 7). Of course, this neglects changes in maintained anticipations.[83]

Political concerns affected Burns's decision about the choice of annual targets for money growth. He told the FOMC that before President Carter announced his energy policy he proposed to reduce $M_1$ growth by 0.5 percentage points. Uncertainty changed his proposal to "a much

82. Although the staff used a model, Burns had little confidence in econometric models. "I have managed to get to my present age without paying much attention to what these equations have to say. . . . I see no reason for learning these things at the present time" (Burns papers, FOMC, June 21, 1977, tape 1, 24–25). His successors, Volcker and Greenspan were also disinclined to accept model forecasts.

83. Burns publicly opposed President Carter's fiscal program. In March, he told the FOMC, "I don't think it is going to make any difference one way or another as far as the real economy goes." He explained that higher interest rates and inflation would offset any positive real effect (Burns papers, FOMC, March 15, 1977, tape 1, 17). He also opposed Carter's energy program, describing it as overly complicated, likely to increase uncertainty and reduce growth (ibid., April 19, 1977, tape 3, 23–24).

milder recommendation." He eliminated the proposed reduction (ibid., April 19, 1977, tape 5, 4). Then, remembering his repeated concern about inflation, he warned: "There is never a good time to lower the monetary growth ranges, yet unless we work at it . . . I don't see much future for our economy" (ibid.).

For the first time, Wallich recognized that the measured rate of price change included one-time price changes resulting from "external shocks." He wanted the committee to decide whether to accommodate the shock or ignore it. His analysis showed the lack of clarity about inflation and price level changes. Accommodating the shock—not responding—"would just build the price increase into the economy permanently as a continuing rate of inflation" (ibid., tape 6, 2). The oil shock was a price level change that would increase the rate of price change temporarily as it passed through. Actions to offset the price level effect was a long step toward taking the price level as the goal instead of the sustained, expected rate of inflation.

President Black urged a reduction in the proposed money growth rates. The present is about "as good a time as we are likely to get" (ibid., tape 6, 4–5). But he voted for Burns's proposal. Only Partee dissented from the very mild move because of uncertainty, withdrawal of President Carter's proposed $50 rebate, and the continued high unemployment rate.

At the time, the unemployment rate was about 6 percent. The full employment rate was no longer 4 percent. Mayo thought it was 5.5 percent. The staff used 4.86 percent, a precision that amused the members. As with most decisions, the Committee did not attempt agreement on full employment or reconciliation of diverse opinions.

Wallich concluded from his observations that high unemployment did not reduce inflation. This denied the relevance of the Phillips curve relating the two, a main hypothesis in the staff model. "Our projections say that doesn't have that effect and I think we could begin trying something else" (ibid., September 20, 1977, tape 3, 18). He proposed an incomes policy, similar to the policy the administration used without obvious benefit.

Sometimes the committee chose a money market directive. At others, it chose an aggregates directive. The difference was in the degree of control or the width of the range for the federal funds rate. Although this decision brought out frequent differences of opinion, the data do not show any major differences in outcomes.

The Committee required four votes to reach agreement in September. Burns proposed $M_1$ growth of 2 to 7 or 3 to 7, $M_2$ at 4 to 8, and a 6.125 mean funds rate. Roos wanted $M_1$ at 0 to 5, didn't care about $M_2$, but his mean funds rate was 6.5 percent. Wallich proposed $M_1$ at 2 to 9 percent, $M_2$ 5.5 to 9.5 and the funds rate at 6.125. Eastburn had $M_1$ at 0 to 7, $M_2$ at 0 to 9, and the funds rate at 6.25. Very similar values for the funds rate covered a wide range for proposed money growth. No one suggested reconciling these numbers or discarding some combinations as unlikely.[84]

The first vote on Burns's proposal was seven to five in favor. He wanted more support. He raised the maximum growth rates and the funds rate. Votes changed but the division remained seven to five. When he changed the proposal to a money market directive, the vote became eight to four. Burns accepted the seven-to-five vote on his proposal and criticized the members' inflexibility.

Some of the presidents wanted the Board to reduce reserve requirement ratios, principally to retain members. As the opportunity cost of reserves rose, member banks converted to non-member banks. Between 1970 and 1977, 133 state member banks gave up membership, more than 10 percent of the total. The number of non-member banks increased by 1,116. In 1977, 69 banks converted from member to non-member status, followed by 98 in 1978 (Board of Governors, 1981, 490, 495).

At Burns's last FOMC meeting, February 28, 1978, the staff reported that the consumer price index rose at a monthly rate of 0.8 percent in January, almost twice the monthly average for the previous six months. "Considerable concern was expressed that the rate of inflation might accelerate significantly as the year progressed. . . . Such price behavior . . . would pose difficult questions concerning the appropriate role of monetary policy" (Annual Report, 1978, 132). Yet the committee kept the projected rate of $M_1$ growth unchanged at 4 to 6.5 percent for the year after rebasing to accept the excess growth in 1977. After some discussion, the Committee accepted the proposed rate unanimously.

The February meeting showed a marked change in members' comments. The majority recognized the need to reduce inflation and lower money growth. Even Burns was explicit about the need to control money growth. They recognized also that Federal Reserve credibility was low. Several favored rebuilding credibility before attempting to lower money growth, but they did not offer a plausible set of actions. They recognized that achieving the announced yearly money growth rate was important. Instead of reducing projected money growth, the FOMC voted to maintain the growth rate unchanged.[85]

84. At the August meeting, Volcker expressed "a sense of futility" in picking money growth rates given errors ranging up to 15 percent and differences in the alternatives of only 0.5 (Burns papers, FOMC, August 16, 1977, tape 4, 22).

85. Wallich complained, "We think we want to avoid triggering the funds rates because if it goes down it hurts the dollar and if it goes up it hurts housing . . . But we don't really gain anything, we just postpone" (Burns papers, tape 5, 9, February 1978). Burns disagreed.

Why did the Federal Reserve renew inflationary monetary policy? Unlike some of their predecessors, Committee members recognized that rapid money growth caused inflation. That was why they selected money growth targets, even if they did not meet them. Doubtless there are many reasons in a nineteen-person committee. Three stand out.

First was the relative weighting given to the employment and inflation objectives. With Congress and the administration controlled by Democrats many of whom gave more weight to unemployment than to inflation, the FOMC acted as if they could control inflation only when the unemployment rate was relatively low. Opinion polls showed that reducing the unemployment rate was most important to the public at the time. Congressional opinion probably reflected the polling data.

Members of the administration shared these views. They wanted to get the economy to grow faster and lower the unemployment rate. They urged Burns to coordinate his actions with their goals. One of several occasions came at a breakfast in June 1977. Schultze reported to Carter that Burns was "sensitive" about administration criticisms of the interest rate increases in April and May. He urged Burns to keep monetary growth compatible with their planned economic growth. Burns explained that he was willing to be flexible, but Schultze concluded that he would not "prevent substantial interest rate increases" (memo, Schultze to the president, Schultze papers, Carter Library, Box A96018, June 10, 1977).[86]

Preparing for a Quadriad meeting in November 1977, Schultze wrote to the president about the state of the economy and topics to discuss with Burns. A main point was that monetary velocity had slowed from about 6 percent early in the recovery to a 2 percent rate in 1977. The Federal Reserve had announced that $M_1$ growth would be between 4.5 and 6 percent for the year ending third quarter 1978.

> If velocity continues to rise at a slow pace, a relatively high growth rate of money will be needed to accommodate satisfactory growth in output. . . . To meet our growth targets, nominal GNP will have to grow about 11 percent from 1977 to 1978 (5 percent real growth and 6 percent inflation). If velocity grows by 2 percent, *$M_1$ growth of 9 percent would be needed.* If the Fed tries to hold growth of $M_1$ within its target range, and velocity increases are small, *interest rates will rise very sharply* and the recovery will be damaged" (memo,

86. Schultze wanted policy coordination. His idea of coordination differed from Ackley's in the Johnson administration. For Schultze, coordination meant "really talking together frankly" (Hargrove and Morley, 1984, 483). He believed Burns would not be frank or open whereas Volcker, who pursued a more independent policy than Burns, was willing to discuss his plans.

Schultze to the president, Schultze papers, Carter Library, November 9, 1977, 3–4; emphasis in original)[87]

Schultze made no mention of the failure of the Federal Reserve to meet its many targets.

Schultze also advised the president that the Council had lowered its forecast of 1978 growth because of reduced growth in mid-1977. He urged the president to ask Burns how the Federal Reserve would respond to the administration's tax reform bill. "A tax cut can keep the pace of expansion from lagging *if money and credit are permitted to increase fast enough to keep the higher growth rate of the economy from pushing up interest rates* (ibid., 1–2; emphasis in original). Agreeing to coordination was unlikely to appeal to Burns, though he would probably do it when the time came.

The substance of the memo suggests the weights that the Carter policymakers gave to real growth and inflation. With a reported unemployment rate of 6.8 percent at the time, reducing unemployment was the main goal. Schultze told the president: "A weaker economy next year because of inadequate growth of money and credit *will affect prices very little, and real output and employment a lot* (ibid., 4; emphasis in original). The unemployment rate declined to 6 percent by the following November; the annual rate of increase in consumer prices rose from 6.4 to 8.5 percent. A new surge of inflation was under way. The increase in inflation began before the oil price increase.

In a memo to Treasury Secretary Blumenthal, written at the same time, Schultze was more explicit about his concerns. Unless policy gave greater stimulus, he expected "a stagnation of overall unemployment in the 6.5 percent area; no improvement and more likely a worsening of unemployment for blacks and other minorities; a continuation of inflation in the 6 to 6.5 percent neighborhood" (memo, Anti-inflation Component of a 1978 Economic Program, Schultze papers, Carter Library, November 9, 1977, 1). He described the economic and political consequences as "severe," and he urged "a meaningful anti-inflation program" (ibid., 2).

Schultze proposed a voluntary program that combined tax reduction and wage-price guidelines. If an employer certified that wages and benefits increased by no more than 6 percent, employees' taxes would be reduced up to 1.5 percentage points up to $20,000. For each 1 percent that employers reduced their weighted average rate of price increase, the government would reduce corporate tax rates by 1 percentage point up to a maximum of

87. Real GNP rose at an average 4.8 percent in the year ending third quarter 1978. The GNP deflator rose at an 8.9 percent average. $M_1$ growth was less than 5 percent. The monetary base rose about 9 percent.

2 percentage points. "The objective behind the approach is to break the momentum of the current price-wage spiral in 1978 and lay the groundwork for moderate union settlements and price increases in 1979" (ibid., 3–4).

Again, as with President Nixon's price and wage controls, the proposal blamed unions and business, not government policies for inflation. And again, the underlying belief was that the way to reduce inflation was to change union and management actions without adopting restrictive policy. Surprisingly, Schultze described the proposal as "the only hope for moderating inflation" (ibid., 6). In a later memo, he considered variations on this proposal and alternatives, including guidelines and reduced aggregate demand by monetary and fiscal actions. He rejected the latter as too costly.[88]

Second, many members of FOMC, including Burns, either were reluctant to reduce money growth enough to lower inflation because of concern for recession or did not believe that money growth was a main cause of inflation. When Burns wrote to President Carter offering a twenty-point anti-inflation program, he did not mention monetary policy. He emphasized reductions in federal spending, tax policy to encourage investment, deregulation of transport, vigorous enforcement of anti-trust laws, public hearings on price and wage increases, and reduction of the minimum wage for teenagers (memo, Burns to the president, Schultze papers, Carter Library, Box A96-01B, March 31, 1977).

Most of Burns's proposals had one-time effects on the price level that would appear as a temporary reduction in the inflation rate. Burns never distinguished between permanent and temporary reductions in aggregate spending. He blamed unions and budget deficits for inflation and only occasionally mentioned money growth.

Third, this was not his only analytic error. He did not develop adequate procedures for controlling money growth. Even when there were large errors, as when the FOMC planned for 8 percent money growth in April 1977 and experienced 20 percent growth, it did not improve procedures. The staff "explained" most of the errors by saying that the demand for

88. Burns told the House Banking Committee in July that inflation could not proceed without "monetary nourishment;" but he explained that the Federal Reserve could not act quickly. "The shock of abrupt adjustment after so many years . . . would be excessively risky" (Burns statement, Carter papers, Jimmy Carter Library, July 29, 1977). This view contrasts with the administration's approach as soon became apparent. In Schultze's absence, Lyle Gramley, a member of the Council and a former Federal Reserve senior staff member, told the president that prolonged growth of the money stock at current rates would have adverse effects eventually but he opposed an increase in interest rates at that time (memo, Gramley to the president, Carter Library, August 11, 1977). Eizenstat urged the president to call Burns to oppose any interest rate increase.

money shifted. They did not admit that better control procedures might have warned them that the funds rate had to fluctuate over a wider range. They did not want to admit that answer because they believed that frequent changes in interest rates would disturb the money market and thereby damage the financial system in ways that they never explained. The Federal Reserve again chose protection of the money market instead of protection of the public.[89]

In January 1978, with the dollar falling and inflation rising, Schultze sent a memo to President Carter proposing a new set of guidelines for wage and price increases as part of an overall program of fiscal restraint, improvements in productivity, and reduction in excise taxes. There is no mention of monetary policy. He did not mention his earlier proposal to lower tax rates as an incentive to lower wage and price increases.

President Carter accepted the program with considerable skepticism. He wrote on the cover page: "Charlie. The program seems (inevitably I guess) very general in nature and mostly wishful thinking. However, I'll do all I can to make it successful" (memo, Schultze to the president, Schultze papers, Carter Library, Box A96–01B, January 7, 1978).

In 1977, the United States ran the largest current account deficit up to that time. Much of the increase represented the arithmetical effect of higher oil prices. The cost of oil imports rose from $8 billion in 1973 to $47 billion in 1977. The large current account deficit and increased inflation induced a fall in the dollar. In the first year of the new administration, the trade-weighted dollar fell from 105 to 97, more than 7.5 percent. Depreciation against the mark reached 13 percent, and 29 percent against the yen.

The administration program called for coordinated fiscal expansion by the United States, West Germany, and Japan. The metaphor was that these countries would be the locomotive of the world economy, raising growth everywhere without much change in currency values. Trading partners, particularly Germany, complained about dollar depreciation, but they were reluctant to join in coordinated expansion. They could either purchase the dollars to finance the current account deficit, permit additional exchange appreciation, or try to sterilize the inflow. Germany, especially, would not sterilize the dollar inflow, so it missed its monetary target (by 100 percent in fourth quarter 1977) (Biven, 2002, 116). In December 1977 and January

89. As often happens in government, some staff tried to find personal motives for Burns's differences with the administration. A staff member wrote to the president that interest rate increases were "bringing the economy down." Burns thus appears as the "inflation fighter" making the president look bad and responsible for the decline in the stock market (memo, De Jongh Franklin to the president, Carter Library, November 2, 1977). The memo suggests the bad feeling between Burns and the White House staff.

1978, the United States, under foreign pressure, intervened. It increased its swap lines with Germany and raised the federal funds rate and the discount rate, and the president announced that the United States would intervene to prevent disorderly markets (ibid., 120).[90] At the February FOMC meeting, Henry Wallich argued that there was too much intervention, but Burns argued that it was necessary to prevent additional dollar depreciation (Burns papers, tape 2.1, February 1978). Later, he reversed his position, saying that intervention delayed more fundamental steps to restore the integrity of the dollar (ibid., 2.5).

In Burns's last three months at the Board consumer prices rose 7.1, 7.7, and 8.9 percent (at annual rates). Inflation control became a more lively issue. In advance of the February 22 Quadriad meeting, Schultze told the president that growth of monetary velocity had fluctuated over a wide range. The Federal Reserve should therefore widen the bands on money growth, but should avoid further interest rate increases. He blamed "institutional factors" such as the increased minimum wage and higher payroll taxes for the rise in inflation. And he added, "It would be most unfortunate to sacrifice real output objectives in the name of inflation control without giving your anti-inflation program a real test" (memo, Schultze to the president, Schultze papers, Carter Library, February 21, 1978, 3). The anti-inflation program refers to the voluntary guidelines recently adopted.[91]

Soon afterward, Schultze sent the president a tutorial on inflation, its causes, and the reasons it continued despite persistent unemployment. The main reason he gave was that in modern economies prices and wages are not very sensitive to modest and short-lived periods of economic slack. "Once an inflation has been underway for a while, workers and employers behave as if it will continue. . . . It therefore is very difficult to use the traditional tools of monetary and fiscal policy to bring inflation to a halt once it has begun in earnest" (memo, Schultze to the president, Schultze papers, Carter Library, March 14, 1978, 5). Schultze explained the persistence of inflation by citing downward inflexibility of prices and wages. Each new round of inflation started from a higher base. He did not relate the down-

90. The report on foreign exchange operations in February acknowledged that the desk exceeded its authority by purchasing more than $100 million in gross transactions per day. The FOMC set limits on gross and net transactions (Burns papers, tape 1, 13; February 1978).

91. The administration considered, but opposed, Senator Proxmire's bill to consolidate the bank regulatory agencies into a single banking agency. The bill passed the Senate but not the House. Eizenstat and Schultze gave some reasons for not taking up the proposed reform at that time. One reason was that they believed that Congress would increase "detailed regulation that substitutes for market competition—exactly the opposite direction from the thrust of your other regulatory reform initiatives" (memo, Eizenstat and Schultze to the president, Schultze papers, Carter Library, March 8, 1978, 4).

ward inflexibility to the belief that the Federal Reserve and the government would end efforts to reduce inflation when unemployment rose. But he mentioned more widespread expectations of continued inflation as one of the reasons for persistence. And he expressed concern about the long-term trend toward higher inflation. "As we move toward lower rates of unemployment, increasing labor market tightness will, at some point or other, lead to an acceleration in the rate of advance of wages" (ibid., 13).

Two days after Schultze's tutorial, Blumenthal and Schultze told the president that "the price outlook is deteriorating." They warned the president that consumer prices would rise 7 to 7.25 percent, about 1 percentage point more than their earlier forecast. (The twelve-month average rate reached 8.6 percent in December 1978.) "Absent other convincing anti-inflation programs, the classic resolution of the inflation problem is likely to take the form of tightening financial markets, even with the Federal Reserve lagging rather than leading the market" (Blumenthal and Schultze to the president, Schultze papers, Carter Library, March 15, 1978, 3). To prevent this outcome, Blumenthal and Schultze proposed: (1) reduced wage increases for federal employees, (2) asking state and local governments to reduce wage increases and lower sales and property taxes, (3) other similar actions to delay increases or reduce prices in regulated industries. They also proposed that the president meet with unions and businesses to urge moderation and especially smaller executive compensation increases.

## APPOINTMENT OF G. WILLIAM MILLER

President Carter's advisers opposed Burns's reappointment to a third term as chairman. In December 1977, Blumenthal and Schultze sent the president a memo describing the qualities that a chairman should possess. It was an anti-Burns memo, critical of Burns's weights on inflation and unemployment. Among other comments, they said, Burns was "more concerned with inflation than unemployment"; he was willing to "thwart administration goals to reduce unemployment"; and he "has stirred up opposition to many of your policies." "We should not expect a Fed chairman to follow an administration policy line, but he should work closely with us" (memo for the president on The Role of the Federal Reserve, Box 16, R. J. Lipshitz Files, Carter Library, December 10, 1977, 1–2).

Burns had openly opposed the administration's initial fiscal program. Also, he gave speeches about the dangers of inflation, though he did not run restrictive policy for long. Schultze criticized his lack of cooperation. At meetings, Burns commented on administration policies, but citing independence, resisted talking about Federal Reserve policy or accepting comments (Schultze, 2005).

Washington gossip at the time cited Burns for reluctance to act as a team member with Carter's officials, his less-than-satisfactory relations with Secretary Blumenthal, and his decision to raise interest rates in 1977. Gossip also cited his decisions to control money growth and emphasize disinflation despite his failure to implement these policies. Burns tried hard to get reappointed. He wanted to be reappointed by a Democrat, perhaps to remove the charge that he had used monetary policy to reelect President Nixon. When Hubert Humphrey, a friend of Vice-President Walter Mondale's, made a very critical speech about Burns's policy, he recognized that he would be replaced (Guenther, 2001, 10–11).[92]

Carter put Mondale in charge of the search. Mondale's search narrowed the choice to three industrialists and one economist. G. William Miller, CEO of Textron, had been active in Democratic Party politics. Miller had served as a director of the Boston Federal Reserve bank, a position that gave him exposure to and limited understanding of Federal Reserve activities. He had headed a successful business group that found employment for Vietnam veterans, and had taken a minor but active role in the 1976 campaign. Reginald Jones of General Electric was "conservative," but he was also "expansion minded about economic growth and cooperative." Irving Shapiro of Dupont, and Bruce MacLaury of the Brookings Institution were the other two (memo to the president on the Federal Reserve Chairmanship, the Federal Reserve Board, Box 16, Carter Library, December 23, 1977). The advisers liked all of the candidates, including those who said they lacked enough knowledge of monetary matters. The critical attributes were acceptability to the business and financial community and willingness to "work cooperatively with the Administration while preserving the independence of the Fed" (ibid., 1).

They chose Miller, perhaps because "Miller shares your basic goals and views. He would be an independent Chairman, but he would also be cooperative and easy to work with" (ibid., 4). Miller, however, was concerned about his lack of knowledge and background. The memo dismissed this statement. He "can learn the job quickly; he will have a good staff available; there are no arcane mysteries which would elude him" (ibid., 4).

Miller had spoken about inflation and unemployment months before he was considered for appointment. He believed that fiscal and monetary policies could reduce the unemployment rate "from 8 percent to 5.5 percent (or perhaps even 5 percent) within two years without triggering a renewed bout of inflation" (quoted in Romer and Romer, 2003, 29). At his Senate

92. Burns hired Milton Hudson from JP Morgan to lobby financial institutions to support Burns's reappointment (Guenther, 2001, 11).

confirmation hearing, Senator Proxmire expressed strong opposition. He thought Miller lacked knowledge needed for the job

At his confirmation hearing Miller denied that the standard Phillips curve gave the tradeoff between inflation and unemployment because it included workers who received unemployment compensation as unemployed. Miller thought they should be counted as employed. "A significant portion of the unemployed act in an economic sense as if they were employed" (ibid., 30). Hence, expanding to return them to work would not greatly change the inflation rate. This argument must have appealed to the expansionists like Eizenstat in the Carter administration. However, Miller did not give greater weight to unemployment than to inflation. When asked about his priority, his answer was "we can tackle both to achieve what we really need—full employment with price stability" ("Swearing in William Miller," Box 19, Carter Library, March 8, 1978, 4). This appealing answer was not entirely consistent with his earlier statements.

Burns stayed on at the Federal Reserve to ease the transition but left before the March meeting. Miller took the seat of David Lilly, who resigned as governor in February 1978 after serving twenty months. Miller served for only seventeen months before becoming treasury secretary.

Miller's conjecture about inflation proved incorrect. In Burns's last month, February 1978, the unemployment rate was 6.3 percent, and the twelve-month CPI inflation rate was 6.2 percent. The GNP deflator rose at a 5.9 percent annual rate in that quarter. When Miller left in August 1979, the unemployment rate was 6 percent, and CPI inflation reached 11 percent. This rate included the one-time effect of an oil price increase. The GNP deflator is less affected by oil price change; it reached 8.5 percent in third quarter 1979.

Burns had not reduced the inflation rate during his eight years as chairman, but under Miller inflation increased. The irony of the decision to replace Burns because he was regarded as uncooperative and independent was that a more independent Paul Volcker soon after replaced Miller. Poole (1979, 484) summed up Burns's leadership of the Federal Reserve: "The tragedy of Burns's leadership . . . is that he did not put in place the monetary policy he advocated so vigorously. . . . Arthur Burns's Federal Reserve policy permitted money growth zigzags to accumulate to produce one of the most inflationary policies over an eight year period of any eight year period since the establishment of the Federal Reserve System."[93]

93. After leaving the Federal Reserve, Burns chaired the Committee to Fight Inflation. The members were distinguished former policy officials of both parties. Their reports rec-

Carter administration policy added to the problem. Looking back, Stuart Eizenstat, the president's Chief Domestic Policy Adviser, acknowledged several mistakes. The biggest mistake was underestimating the economy's strength in 1976 and the underlying rate of inflation. Treasury Secretary Blumenthal was the first inside the administration to urge a policy shift, but he left before it could be accomplished (Eizenstat, 1982, 79–84).

Miller's lasting achievements as Federal Reserve chairman were legislative. To accomplish regulatory changes, Miller had to improve working relationships with Congress. In 1978, Congress passed the International Banking Act, placing foreign banks and branches in the United States under rules similar to those applied to domestic banks. Miller worked with Congress to get changes in the Humphrey-Hawkins Act that made it acceptable to the Federal Reserve. And he worked with Congressman Henry Reuss on the Depository Institutions Deregulation and Monetary Control Act (DIDMCA), which authorized reserve requirements for non-member banks and phased out interest rate controls including regulation Q. Miller had moved to the Treasury before DIDMCA passed, but he was a major influence on its development and passage. The act led to expansion and modernization of United States financial institutions.

## POLICY ACTIONS 1978–79

As mentioned, the administration decided at its inception that it did not favor use of monetary and fiscal policy to reduce inflation. The cost in higher unemployment and lost output seemed too great. Instead it proposed voluntary wage-price moderation as part of its April 1977 program.[94] Schultze later said, "We had an anti-inflation program, so-called, in April 1977 . . . none of which meant anything" (quoted in Biven, 2002, 134). By the time Miller took office, inflation had increased and the program was dead. The administration blamed increases on food prices. Real wages rose slowly, but productivity slowed even more, so unit labor costs rose more than 8 percent in the year ending first quarter 1977 (memo, Schultze to Carter, Carter Library, Box 194, May 11, 1977).

ognized the importance of monetary control. It excused Federal Reserve actions. "The ability of the Federal Reserve System to combat inflation has in the past been limited by lack of understanding and support in the Congress" (Committee to Fight Inflation, 1980, 3).

94. The program included extension for two years of the Council on Wage and Price Stability (COWPS), which had administered President Nixon's wage and price controls. Also, the program called for deregulation of communications, trucking, and other industries. This was one of the more successful economic initiatives taken during the Carter presidency. While governor of Georgia, Carter had listened to a Georgia economist who now advised him that jawboning and guidelines would not work, so he was not surprised that guidelines failed.

At his first FOMC meeting, March 21, 1978, Miller told the members:

> We have all these policy dilemmas we are speaking about. Relative growth rates are such that we are going to have these large current account deficits. Then our choices are going to narrow down to whether we'll take a lower growth rate in our economy because it doesn't look like we are getting the relative speedings in other economies. [A lower growth rate] is something that I think many of the economic advisers in the Administration are now willing to accept because the alternative is to see the dollar under pressure and our resources to change it are not great. And that in itself feeds inflation into our economy and creates a whole series of other [developments] that lead us down an unhappy trail. (FOMC Minutes, March 21, 1978, 9)

Governor Partee expressed "amazement" that the administration would favor a lower growth rate. President Eastburn (Philadelphia) suggested that a recession might be needed. Wallich insisted on the need to reduce inflation. No one pointed out that lower growth during a recession would produce mainly a temporary reduction in current account balances. The effect on the exchange rate was uncertain.

In April 1978, Blumenthal and Schultze sent a memo on inflation that began on an ominous note. "During the past several months, a growing concern has developed around the country about the outlook for inflation. Your April 11 announcement of steps to implement the anti-inflation program was an important step in dealing with the inflation problem. Realistically, however, the chances are no better than 50–50 that the anti-inflation program will lead to significant moderation of wage and price increases—even if it is followed up vigorously and continuously" (memo, Schultze and Blumenthal to the president, Schultze papers, Carter Library, April 13, 1978).[95] A memo to Vice President Mondale reported adverse polling data. The president's rating on managing the economy had fallen from 47 percent to 24 percent. "Moreover, other recent polls show a dramatic shift in public concern over inflation as opposed to unemployment" (quoted in Biven, 2002, 137). This proved to be a step on the path to monetary restraint.

The Carter administration was incapable of devising a successful strategy for reducing inflation. Labor unions, an important support group, op-

95. The new program followed the program outlined in the 1978 Economic Report. Voluntary steps to decelerate wages and prices sector by sector, reductions in government wage increases to set an example, etc. Robert Strauss, a persuasive Texas lawyer, became counselor on inflation to persuade business and labor. Large corporations offered cooperation. The AFL-CIO did not (Biven, 2002, 137–38). And the coal miners negotiated a three-year 38 percent increase in wages at this time.

posed both wage controls and guidelines and higher interest rates. Business groups would accept price guidelines only if unions accepted wage restrictions. That would have been a program, but inflation can be hidden but not ended by such means. The administration wanted tax reduction, not an increase, in 1978. And it opposed raising interest rates enough to slow inflation. Its efforts consisted of cosmetic actions and the hope that they might succeed. Unfortunately for them, public opinion now saw inflation as a major problem.[96] Schultze (2005) recognized the problem, hoped to enforce the guidelines with greater effort, but he recognized that other effective actions had been ruled out by concern to avoid increasing unemployment.

The choice of Miller added to the problem of controlling inflation. George Meany, president of the AFL-CIO, wrote the president quoting and endorsing Miller's approach enunciated in a 1974 interview.

> Working our way out of inflation requires an allocation of the available but limited resources to areas of priority, thus reestablishing a proper balance between supply and demand. Allocation solely by controlling the aggregates—the supply of money and net federal spending—will bring about levels of unemployment and general economic hardship that are likely to be unacceptable. Allocation by direct controls involves even more difficulties. (letter, George Meany to the president, Schultze papers, Carter Library, May 19, 1978)

Meany added that Miller saw the need for a new approach, mainly selective controls including credit controls. He agreed. President Carter later requested the Federal Reserve to impose such controls.

Miller had apparently changed his mind. In his first press interview he explained that the Federal Reserve must achieve "a gradual slowdown in the expansion of the money supply" (Rowe, 1978). Miller also supported the president's program to moderate price and wage changes. And he recognized that shifting from unemployment to inflation would not achieve both objectives. "Society can not reach the goals of full employment growth and price stability independently" (ibid., D10).[97]

96. An example is a fourteen-page memo to the president signed by Schultze and Blumenthal dated April 13, 1978. Near the end of the memo, a White House staff member wrote about the recommendations. "This is an anti-climax . . . they say don't do anything. This is absurd" (memo, Schultze and Blumenthal to the president, Schultze papers, Carter Library, April 13, 1978, 14).

97. On his last day at the Federal Reserve, Arthur Burns spoke about inflation and the dollar. He favored pay cuts for government employees, an energy conservation policy, and tax cuts to increase investment. He also favored "massive intervention" to strengthen the dollar, supported by sales of gold, SDRs, and $10 billion of bonds denominated in foreign currencies (Rowan, 1978, A2). Burns placed greater importance on avoiding currency depreciation

**Table 7.12** Federal Funds and Reported Inflation, Monthly 1978–79 (%)

| DATE | FUNDS RATE | CPI INFLATION |
|---|---|---|
| *1978* | | |
| April | 6.9 | 10.7 |
| May | 7.4 | 11.2 |
| June | 7.6 | 12.4 |
| July | 7.8 | 8.6 |
| August | 8.0 | 6.7 |
| September | 8.4 | 9.0 |
| October | 9.0 | 9.6 |
| November | 9.8 | 6.6 |
| December | 10.0 | 5.3 |
| *1979* | | |
| January | 10.1 | 10.6 |
| February | 10.1 | 14.0 |
| March | 10.1 | 11.5 |
| April | 10.0 | 13.7 |
| May | 10.2 | 14.7 |
| June | 10.3 | 13.9 |
| July | 10.5 | 12.7 |

The Federal Reserve began to raise the federal funds rate in May 1978.[98] The monthly average rate rose from 6.9 to about 10 percent that year. At the time, the FOMC set annual growth rates for the monetary aggregates and two-month average growth rates for $M_1$ and $M_2$. It specified a federal funds rate believed compatible with the money growth rates. If a discrepancy arose, the committee held a telephone meeting to assess the situation. During 1978, the planned two-month money growth rates changed very little. Actual $M_1$ growth reported in the minutes rose as high as 19 percent (April), 11 percent (August), and 14 percent (September) without any decisive effect on FOMC actions. Most of the time $M_1$ and $M_2$ desired growth rates were 4 to 8 or 9 percent and 5 to 9 or 6 to 10 percent respectively. Table 7.12 shows the monthly average federal funds and monthly CPI inflation rates during Miller's term as chairman. Average federal funds rates were, as before, very close to policy rates specified by the FOMC.[99]

than on curtailing domestic inflation. In November, the administration adopted several of his proposals.

98. The minutes obtained from Burns's papers end when he left the Federal Reserve in March 1978. For the rest of 1978, we relied on the Annual Report supplemented by the minutes for May to December 1978 that Debby Danker made a special effort to edit and release in 2007. We greatly appreciate her effort.

99. At the April meeting, the FOMC had an active discussion of a proposal by President Baughman (Dallas) that the FOMC announce a three-year target for money growth. Only Roos (St. Louis) supported him. The Subcommittee on the Directive opposed because they

In Table 7.12, the measure of the real interest rate, ex post, is positive in only three months, August, November, and December 1978. The inflation data include the one-time price level increase from the oil price shock. Usually the FOMC did not distinguish this transitory effect on inflation, and neither did the administration. Wage increases are another measure of inflation; in April 1978 wages rose 8.3 above the previous April. In 1977, wages increased 7 percent from 1976.

In fact, the Council of Economic Advisers and the Secretary of the Treasury took the highly unusual step in June 1978 of meeting with the Board of Governors out of concern about the increase in interest rates that occurred in the spring. At the time, the ex post real federal funds rate was −4.8 percent.[100]

Schultze explained to the president that "the Board is *very* concerned about inflation. Some members of the Board appear to be prepared to tighten monetary conditions still further; . . . [T]hey seem willing to run some risks with tight money because of their inflation worries—Chairman Miller is under considerable pressure from some of the more vocal and articulate inflation-fighters on the Board. He, himself, is very sensitive to the danger of overdoing monetary restraints" (memo, Schultze to the president, Schultze papers, Carter Library, June 27, 1978).[101]

In the rest of the memo, Schultze spelled out his forecast for the economy for the next eighteen months. He expected real growth of 3.75 to 4 percent with productivity growth only 1 percent. This was slower growth than in early 1978. Schultze estimated that the underlying rate of inflation, excluding food and mortgage costs, was between 6 and 6.5 percent. Unit labor costs would rise 7 percent in the next year. He explained that his forecast assumed that $M_1$ would rise more than the 4 to 6.5 percent annual target and that Congress would approve a $20 billion tax cut, effective January 1.[102]

said no one would believe that they would achieve the three-year growth rate. Baughman argued that the FOMC needed to meet long-term objectives, but he argued in vain. In 2007, the Federal Reserve adopted the proposal as part of a plan to become more transparent.

100. Schultze had become more concerned about inflation. Early in May, he told the president about his concern and the need to tighten the 1979 and 1980 budgets. The president wrote on his memo: "A new Convert" (memo, Schultze to the president, Carter Library, May 8, 1978, 2).

101. Lyle Gramley attended the June 19 meeting at the Board. "I had some notion before we went that this was not the appropriate thing to do. It would be quite unproductive. And it was. If anything it may well have been counterproductive" (Biven, 2002, 141). Schultze had warned the president about interest rate increases in April. He thought they were appropriate. His concern was that they would continue too long and increase too much.

102. In late May President Carter reduced the proposed tax cut by $5 billion (to $20 billion) and postponed its effective date to January as an anti-inflation measure. He also requested some small spending cuts.

Schultze's memo indicated concern about additional interest rate increases. He suggested that the president discuss this with Miller at the Quadriad meeting the following day. Charts accompanying the memo showed growth of $M_1$ well above the 6.5 percent maximum target. Eizenstat was not persuaded. He told the president that the president's policies can "help avoid inflationary actions." The private sector was responsible for lowering inflation (Carter papers, May 9, 1978).

A quick reading of the April 18 FOMC minutes would suggest a major division over inflation policy. Verbal disagreements were sharp. But almost all proposals for $M_1$ growth called either for 4 to 8 or 5 to 9 percent. Similarly, all but one proposal called for either a 6.5 to 7.5 or 6.75 to 7.25 funds rate. The vote called for 6.75 to 7.5 with a conference call if the rate reached 7.25 percent. Within three weeks, the April–May money growth rate reached 13 percent, and the Board staff raised nominal GNP growth to 17 percent in the second quarter.

Chairman Miller described monetary policy as "prudent and decisive" (FOMC Minutes, May 5, 1978, 4). He thought the projected second-quarter GNP growth might be transitory, so he favored leaving the fund rate at 7.25. Ignoring years of delay, he said action would suggest that the committee was "too quick on the trigger" (ibid.). He favored a 0.5 increase in the discount rate the following week. Only Black, Willes, and Wallich favored an increase in the funds rate but only Black and Willes voted against Chairman Miller's recommendation. Once again, some of the reserve banks were most willing to act.

Although the administration adjusted its anti-inflation actions several times, Schultze did not expect much effect. His forecasts in May 1978 showed inflation unchanged for the next four years at about 6.5 percent. The unemployment rate forecast suggested that unemployment would remain about 5.5 percent. In the critical political year 1980, forecast inflation and unemployment rates were 6.7 and 5.4 to 5.7 percent respectively (Schultze to the president, Carter papers, Box A8013, May 13, 1978, 5).[103] Soon after he wrote that worsening inflation required giving inflation control a higher priority. But he opposed fighting inflation with monetary and fiscal policies alone. "Our best hope of getting inflation under control lies in a joint effort by businesses, labor and government to achieve deceleration in the rate of price and wage increases" (draft letter to George Meany, ibid., May 31, 1978).

103. In an interview, Carter said that he believed the economy would be in good shape in October 1980, based on projections received from Schultze and William Miller in May. He expected inflation to decline by 5 or 6 percentage points and the unemployment rate to fall also (Carter, 1982, 59).

Much more than in the past, FOMC members accepted that inflation was mainly a monetary problem. As Orphanides (2001 and elsewhere) emphasized, the level of the so-called natural rate of unemployment used to forecast inflation was uncertain. At the May 1978 meeting, the staff characterized the natural rate as difficult to estimate (FOMC Minutes, May 16, 1978, 6). Their estimate was 5.5 to 6 percent, far higher then the 4 percent rate used for many years. The members did not agree. Wallich thought 5.5 percent too low; Partee thought it too high. The disagreement shows a major reason for low reliability of inflation forecasts based on a Phillips curve.

Coldwell, Balles, and several others agreed with Wallich and urged the committee to slow the economy (ibid., 13–15). Jackson spoke about "a loss of public confidence . . . [that] will damage the economy" (ibid., 33). But Eastburn and Partee remained "pessimistic" about inflation. Partee added that a 1979 recession was now likely (ibid., 18). Axilrod cited some staff work showing that $M_1$ was a good indicator of future GNP. The divisions within the FOMC remained for the rest of the year, preventing effective anti-inflation actions.

At the June meeting, Chairman Miller proposed a moderate program of disinflation. "If we use a steady and sure hand to restrain the growth of the aggregates and bring it down at a more measured pace, then I think we see conditions for bringing the rate of growth down to a more sustainable level that will counter inflation but avoid . . . recession" (ibid., June 20, 1978, 18). Regrettably, he did not institute procedures to carry out his program.

The FOMC voted for an increase in the funds rate to the 7.5–8 percent range at the June meeting to recognize growing public and administration concern about inflation. Mark Willes (Minneapolis) and Willis Winn (Cleveland) dissented. Winn made a correct forecast: "If the committee did not act now to assure a reduction in the rates of growth of the aggregates, an excessively restrictive policy would be required later on if the committee's longer-range objectives were to be achieved" (ibid., 191).

On June 30, the Board voted three to two to increase the discount rate from 7 to 7.25 percent. Miller voted against and, against the advice from other governors, allowed his vote in the minority to be published. That had never happened before and it may have heightened concern about his control of policy. Not much happened. Earlier, on May 10, Miller had voted for an increase to 7 percent.

Members continued to make strong statements and take weak actions. In July's discussion, Governor Partee commented on the continued growth of $M_1$ in excess of their target. He favored holding $M_1$ in the 4–6.25 range (FOMC Minutes, July 18, 1978, 26). Mark Willes commented on that: "I don't see how we are ever going to deal with the inflation problem unless we do something to bring the rate of growth of money down" (ibid., 27). And Paul Volcker added that because of "so much base drift recently," the FOMC targets were a "farce" (ibid., 28).

Despite these strong statements, action was modest. With reported inflation running about 9 percent annual rate for several months, the FOMC voted seven to three for a funds rate target of 7.75 to 8 percent and an unchanged 4 to 6.5 percent $M_1$ target. Willes complained that the real interest rate was negative and could not be considered restrictive (ibid., 40–41).

The July meeting heard that hourly earnings and producer and consumer prices had increased faster in 1978 than in 1977. Nevertheless, Governors Jackson and Partee dissented from the decision to set annual money growth rates for $M_1$ and $M_2$ at 4 to 6.5 and 6.5 to 9 percent, as at several previous meetings. Jackson preferred a 4 to 7.5 percent band for $M_1$, and Partee wanted the upper limit at 8 percent. The lower limit was below the projected increase in nominal GNP, so it might require slower growth of real GNP.

The FOMC increased the mean target for the federal funds rate by 0.125. Presidents Baughman, Willes, and Winn dissented. They wanted "more vigorous measures" (ibid., 206).

Willes dissented again for the same reason at the August meeting. This time Governor Partee also dissented to favor an easier policy, citing the "marked slowing in real economic growth that now appeared to be in progress" (ibid., 215).

Partee's dissent came despite recognition by "all members of the committee" of the "high recent rate of inflation in prices and wages" (ibid., 210). Also, the Committee learned that labor leaders planned "to hold out in forthcoming contract negotiations for sizeable wage settlements" (ibid.). The suggested reason was concern that the administration would adopt mandatory controls.[104]

104. The archives contain many memos to the president from Schultze, Ambassador Robert Strauss (appointed to administer and get agreement on the voluntary standards), and Barry Bosworth, director of the Council on Wage and Price Stability (COWPS). One set of memos on environmental and health regulations suggests that opposition came not only from business and labor unions but from other parts of the government, in this case the Council on Environmental Quality. It objected to complaints that regulation increased inflation (again treating price level changes as inflation), and it urged the president not to weaken his commitment to environmental and health regulation for economic and especially political reasons. President Carter wrote, "I agree" on the memo. This aroused Schultze, who argued that the memo neglected the principal cost, a reduction in productivity. He urged the president to continue programs to improve regulation, reduce its cost, and deregulate where appropriate (memo to the president, Inflation and Environmental and Health Regulations, Schultze papers, Carter Library, September 18, 1978; memo, Schultze to the president, ibid., September

At last, Wallich and Willes observed that "interest rates adjusted for expected rates of inflation were not high and might even be negative" (Annual Report, 1978, 222). This rare explicit recognition of the difference between nominal and real rates had at most a modest effect on the FOMC's decision. It raised the mean federal funds rate target by 0.125 to 8.5 percent despite a reported increase in August of 14 percent (annual rate) for $M_1$ growth. "It was observed that for an extended period of time $M_1$ had been growing at rates in excess of the longer-run range adopted by the committee and that a slowing of growth was necessary in pursuit of the committee's objective of resisting inflationary pressures while continuing modest economic expansion" (ibid., 222).[105]

By October, the FOMC knew that President Carter planned to offer a new anti-inflation policy, but they were uncertain about the details. Many FOMC members were pessimistic about inflation control. President Roos pointed out that "we seem never to have really defined what we think would be the [desirable] rate of growth" (FOMC Minutes, October 17, 1978, 23).

Inflation had become a political issue. The administration developed a policy package to reduce inflation without raising interest rates. On October 24, President Carter presented the program to the nation in a nationally televised address. The centerpiece of the program was a stronger set of guideposts, including specific rates of wage and price increase that he asked the private sector to follow. Reductions in government spending, reductions in federal employment, a government pay freeze, and deregulation were additional one-time changes.

The announcement did not draw strong public support. Details aside, it was more of the same approach that had not worked. The biggest change came not in the program but in the president's explanation of why the country should support the program. The president described inflation as "our most serious domestic problem" (Shouse, 2002, 184).

The new program failed to prevent additional increases in interest rates. Following the announcement, the dollar continued to fall. Within a week, the administration announced a new dollar policy, including a Federal Reserve decision for a one percentage point increase in the discount rate, an unusually large increase. But that action also failed to reduce inflation.

President Carter never had much confidence that voluntary guidelines

29, 1978). Shortly after, Labor Secretary Ray Marshall wrote that "the private sector portion of the program is the most critical to bringing down the inflation rate" (memo, Ray Marshall to the president, Carter Library, October 13, 1978, 1). The president wrote, "I agree."

105. Willes and Wallich wanted a 9 percent funds rate. This was one percentage point above twelve-month average CPI growth and above SPF estimates of expected inflation.

would reduce inflation. We cannot know what he thought about the failures at the time or later, but we do know that he thought the public considered inflation to be the most important domestic problem. The combination of heightened public concern and the failure of his programs may have opened his mind to a more painful but more effective solution when he chose Paul Volcker as chairman.[106]

The November increase in interest rates was part of a coordinated policy action to strengthen the dollar. After reaching a local peak at 107 in June 1976, the trade-weighted average value of the dollar declined gradually for a year. It then fell from 103.8 to 86 between September 1977 and October 1978. During the same period, it declined almost 10 percent against the mark. Responding to domestic and foreign concerns, the administration and the Federal Reserve took steps to strengthen the dollar by raising the discount rate and the federal funds rate.[107] The percentage point increase in the discount rate was the largest increase in forty-five years. International concerns got the Federal Reserve to respond to inflation in a way that domestic factors did not.

The November increase in the discount rate was the seventh increase that year. The discount rate rose from 6 percent to 9.5 percent. Expected inflation remained between 7 and 8 percent. Most of the increases followed the market. A 0.5 percentage point increase on August 18 was an exception; the increase was a policy move to strengthen the dollar and reduce inflation.

Several governors dissented in 1978. In January, Governors Partee and Lilly thought higher rates threatened the recovery, so the vote was four to two with one absentee. On April 24, Governors Wallich and Jackson dissented from a decision to disapprove a 0.25 increase. They favored the August and November increases to strengthen the dollar.

With prices rising more than 9 percent, Vice-Chairman Gardner and Governor Teeters dissented from the October 13 decision to increase the discount rate by 0.5 to 8.5 percent at eleven banks. They claimed monetary restraint was sufficient.

The FOMC and the Board staff at the time blamed the increase in inflation on individual price increases. For example, at the April meeting,

106. On June 27, Vice President Walter Mondale sent a memo recommending appointment of Nancy Teeters as the first female Board member. The memo reported that the screening committee had considered nearly 100 women. The president asked to interview Teeters. He appointed her on August 28, and she took the oath on September 18. She completed Arthur Burns's remaining term (to 1984).

107. The international section of this chapter discusses the November program to strengthen the dollar.

the record cites "reduced supplies of meats and increases in payroll taxes and in minimum wages" for the rise in inflation during the first quarter (Annual Report, 1978, 157). Or, "expectations of a high rate of inflation seemed to be growing and, as a result, actions of businessmen and consumers might tend to make their expectations self-fulfilling" (ibid., 162). Later in the same meeting, the record refers to money growth. "Since the fourth quarter of 1976 the rate of growth of $M_1$ had exceeded the 6.5 percent upper limit of the longer-run range in every quarter except the one just ended" (ibid., 163). Subsequently in May, "committee members were deeply concerned about the recent acceleration of inflation and about prospects for prices" (ibid., 175). They voted for a 0.5 increase in the funds rate "to moderate growth of the monetary aggregates" (ibid., 177). One member recognized the monetarist complaint. "If further significant actions were not taken in the present circumstances, current monetary policy might be found in retrospect to have been procyclical" (ibid., 177).

Mark Willes (Minneapolis) dissented, as he did at most meetings that year. "He favored more vigorous measures to reduce the rate of monetary growth" (ibid., 180). For this and other dissents and his remarks at the meeting, he was warned to be more flexible.[108]

Some members of FOMC questioned the role of the short-term (two-month) targets for money growth. Credibility had been shredded by failure to achieve the targets. The members agreed that the manager could not be expected regularly to achieve two-month growth rates in $M_1$ and $M_2$ within the specified ranges for various reasons—"including the lag between changes in the federal funds rate and changes in these growth rates and the brevity of the period to which the operational paragraphs of any single directive applied. . . . The purpose of the 2-month ranges was to provide the manager with an indicator for determining when changes in the funds rate were appropriate" (Annual Report, 1978, 189). The committee dropped the statement that "the committee 'expects' the 2-month growth rates to be within the indicated ranges" (ibid., 189). However, the members affirmed that they intended to hold money growth within the one-year targets. They failed to do so in many years and, as noted, did not adjust the following year's projected growth rates for the excess or deficiency in the previous year.[109]

108. "The first time I started speaking out in meetings, one of the very senior staff people on the Board . . . took me aside and said, 'you need to understand the way this works. You're going to be more effective if you say your piece, but then kind of go along. . . . 'And I just said, . . . 'I'm going to say what I think is right'" (Willes, 1992, 4).

109. Pierce (1978) and Weintraub (1978) found that short-run targets had no effect. The FOMC changed its directive at this (June) meeting. It now read: "If, giving approximately

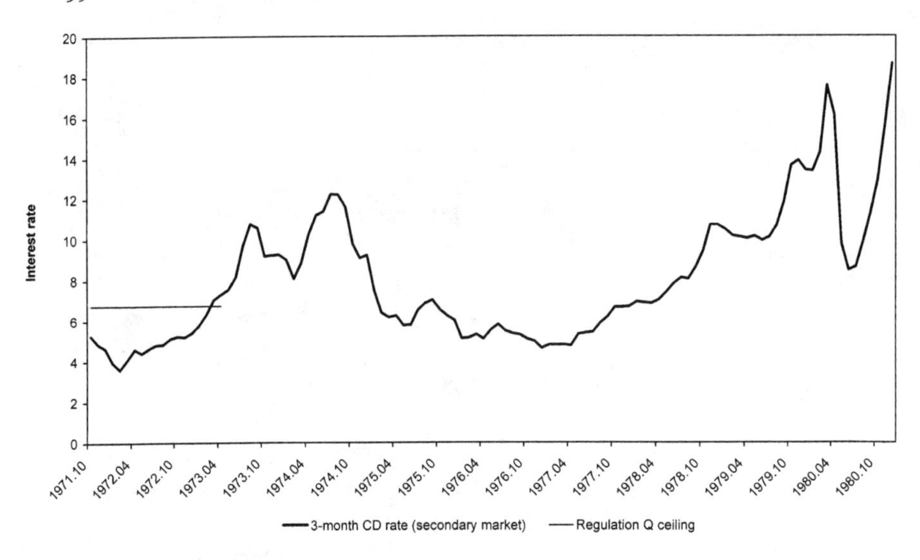


Chart 7.14. Three-month CD secondary market and regulation Q ceiling, 1971:10–1980:12.

New regulations permitted owners to transfer funds from saving to deposit accounts, the automatic transfer service (ATS). Growth of $M_1$ became more uncertain. The staff gave estimates of $M_1$ adjusted and unadjusted for ATS, but they had no record on which to base the estimates. Axilrod explained that both measures of $M_1$ conveyed useful information about short-run GDP changes. Partee pointed out that the Committee on the Directive found it difficult to relate near-term $M_1$ growth to longer-term (annual) $M_1$ growth rates (ibid., 26–29).[110]

Chart 7.14 shows that the CD (certificate of deposit) rate was above 10 percent when the ATS ruling occurred. Regulation Q ceilings for ninety days to one year held the rate to 5.75 percent. The maximum ceiling rate, 8 percent, required a deposit of seven years or more. Banks and financial institutions offered unregulated higher rates on so-called money market accounts and purchased CDs to pay the higher rates. A financial institution could buy an unregulated CD of $100,000 or more and sell small money market accounts that permitted the purchaser to share in the rate on the large CD less a fee to the institution. The accounts were not insured by the

equal weight to $M_1$ and $M_2$, their rates of growth appear to be significantly above or below the midpoints of the indicated ranges, the objective for the funds rate shall be raised or lowered in an orderly fashion within its range" (Annual Report, 1978, 191). Clearly, the FOMC recognized the source of its problem. Their failure was unwillingness to act forcefully.

110. At about this time, Congress amended Humphrey-Hawkins to require semiannual reports to Congress instead of quarterly.

federal government, but the default risk was small. Although it took about a decade for the change to occur, money market accounts and inflation drove out regulation Q ceiling rates. Congress did not outlaw the accounts because consumers found them attractive.

To take account of these changes, the Board's staff created a new measure of transaction balances originally called $M_1B$, that included as additions to $M_1$ savings deposits at commercial banks, NOW accounts at nonbank thrift institutions, and demand deposits at mutual savings banks. Shifts between demand deposits and the new additions would not affect the aggregate. This was the first formal recognition of a problem that would hinder efforts to control money growth.[111]

The attempt to coordinate policies internationally failed to maintain exchange rates. Within a few months, rising inflation in the United States and ineffective policies led to a sharp depreciation of the dollar. Misled by nominal interest rates, the administration worried about "tight money." A week after the October 17 meeting, the administration announced voluntary numerical standards for price and wage increases. The market responded unfavorably, believing the policy change weak and likely to be ineffective. The public had learned a main lesson about guideposts—they don't control inflation. On October 31, the FOMC delegated authority to Chairman Miller to act in concert with the administration to strengthen the dollar and reduce inflation "if he determined that the arrangements with the U.S. Treasury and with certain foreign monetary authorities were substantially as contemplated" in the FOMC's discussions (ibid., 238).

As noted earlier, the announcement on the morning of November 1 increased the discount rate by one percentage point to 9.5 percent, the largest increase since 1933, and imposed a supplemental reserve requirement of two percentage points on time deposits of $100,000 or more. Also, the swap lines with West Germany, Japan, and Switzerland increased by $7.6 billion (to $15 billion), and the United States agreed to "a program of forceful intervention in the exchange markets in coordination with foreign central banks to correct recent excessive movements in the exchange rate" (ibid., 239).[112] After these actions, the dollar reversed its October decline. Growth of the monetary aggregates declined in December. The manager's instructions at the December 19 meeting let the funds rate decline from

111. Nancy Teeters dissented from the modest increase in the funds rate out of concern for the effect of the many increases in interest rates since April (Annual Report, 1978, 238).

112. Treasury actions and background to the changes are below in the section on international monetary decisions. The dollar fell 1.6 percent against an average of G-10 countries between Friday and Monday, October 30 (before the monetary changes).

10 percent to the lower limit, 9.75 percent. Chairman Miller proposed to leave the rate unchanged, and the FOMC agreed unanimously.[113] But the Board tabled discount rate requests from Chicago and Dallas because money growth had fallen. The decision to table came on a three-to-two vote; Partee and Teeters voted to reject the requests.

At the December FOMC meeting members made three significant observations. Henry Wallich noted the bias in inflation estimates later analyzed by Orphanides (2001). According to Wallich, "we also seem to have a built-in bias toward a low inflation forecast" (FOMC Minutes, December 19, 1978, 11). He produced data showing the staff's persistent underestimate. Mark Willes commented on the reason the FOMC had lost credibility. The public "don't believe us when we say we are going to stick with it. They think at the least sign of trouble we are going to back off and I think that's too bad" (ibid., 14). And President Roos asked whether the Committee set its economic objectives or its monetary objectives first. "Have we actually, in our practices, ever discussed or agreed upon what our ultimate economic objectives would be and then attempted to make our monetary policy decisions consistent with the achievement of these objectives?" (ibid., 55).

No one followed up. Each of the points was a starting point for studying why their policies failed to produce the outcomes they hoped for. The comments remained on the record, but so did the failure to respond.

In December 1978, the oil-producing countries again raised prices. Oil prices (West Texas spot) increased from $14.85 a barrel in December 1978 to $32.50 a year later and to $39.50 by April 1980. Monthly rate of increase in consumer prices in the United States rose (at annual rates) from 5.3 percent in December 1978 to 10.6 percent in January 1979. That ended any remaining chance that labor unions would reduce their demands to the 7 percent guideline proposed in the president's October program. And it ended any prospect that Congress would approve selective tax reduction for groups that followed the administration's guidelines.

Schultze proposed more policy coordination. In preparation for the December 14 Quadriad meeting, he proposed that the president tell Chairman Miller that the 1980 budget (submitted in January 1979) would be tight. Too much monetary restraint would work with spending restraint to cause a recession. It would then be "politically difficult . . . to persist with stringent budgetary policies" (memo, Schultze to the president, Schul-

113. On November 19, 1978, Stephen S. Gardner, the Board's vice-chairman, died. He served less than three years and had been ill and absent from many of the meetings in 1978. His death reduced the number of Board members to five. Phillip Jackson resigned after 3.4 years of service on November 17.

tze papers, Carter Library, December 13, 1978). His preliminary forecast called for 2 percent growth in 1979, increasing modestly in 1980 if inflation declined.

Within a few weeks, Schultze and Blumenthal decided that policy was too expansive. "At the turn of the year in 1978–79, Blumenthal and I carried on a leaked campaign in the press to try to pressure Miller into tightening up. The leaked stories told that administration officials think the Fed ought to tighten up—normally it's the other way around . . . We got a very nasty note from the president at one time in effect saying lay off" (Hargrove and Morley, 1984, 485).[114]

Schultze saw the administration's problem in 1979 as the "very difficult task of cooling off a stubborn 12 year old inflation without (i) a recession; (ii) mandatory controls, or (iii) dismantling our assistance to those who really need it" (memo on the president's State of the Union speech, Schultze papers, Carter Library, January 17, 1979, 1). Then he explained why inflation persisted and why recessions and controls did not work. "No democratic nation can stick with such policies long enough to do the job. . . . Sharp recessions inevitably lead to renewed pressures for large-scale stimulus and there go the anti-inflation policies" (ibid., 1–2). There was no thought that presidential leadership could change these beliefs.

Schultze did not add the problems of forecasting accurately, a problem that plagued him during his term. Third quarter 1977 is an extreme example. The Council's first forecast called for a 3.9 percent increase in real GNP. The Council revised the number several times. In the final report, real growth reached 7 percent. This was not the only error of this magnitude. The Reagan Council's forecast for 1983 called for a modest recovery. Actual growth reached nearly 10 percent. These experiences, though worse than average, again raise the question: why did the Federal Reserve and the administration base policy heavily on short-term forecasts and neglect longer-term consequences?

### *Federal Reserve Action, January to August 1979*

Fischer (1984, 46) reproduced an index of public concern about inflation. After rising steadily from 1974, the index reached a peak in 1979, about 2.5 times its 1974 value. There is reason to question what the index mea-

114. Schultze attributed Carter's response to populism and the dislike of higher interest rates. Perhaps Carter's behavior can also be explained by a concern for Federal Reserve independence. The only previous effort by an administration to get the Federal Reserve to raise interest rates was in 1922, when Secretary Andrew Mellon urged the Federal Reserve to stop bond purchases by individual reserve banks. At that time, Mellon was ex officio, a member of the Federal Reserve Board.

sured, but there is no reason to doubt that the public wanted lower inflation in 1979.

At the first 1979 meeting, on February 6, the staff projected output growth of 2.1 and 1.4 percent in 1979 and 1980 and inflation of 8.1 and 7.4 percent with 6.25 percent growth in $M_1$.[115] Expected productivity growth was 1 percent (FOMC Minutes, February 6, 1979, 5).

Divisions within the FOMC were never greater than in early 1979. Paul Volcker, Mark Willes (Minneapolis), and Henry Wallich urged more restrictive policy to reduce inflation. Nancy Teeters, Charles Partee, and Frank Morris (Boston) were most concerned about a possible recession. Votes were narrowly divided, and most often the decision was to keep the federal funds rate unchanged. See Table 7.11 above. Twelve-month monetary base growth slowed to the 6 to 7 percent range from 8 to 9 percent earlier.

It was at this time that Secretary Blumenthal, joined by Charles Schultze, criticized the Federal Reserve and asked for higher interest rates until the president told them to stop interfering with the Federal Reserve. Blumenthal's action may have encouraged Chairman Miller to take the unprecedented step of announcing just before an FOMC meeting that there was no reason to raise the funds rate.

Discussions at the FOMC meetings bring out some of the reasons that differences continued. Mark Willes used a rational expectations argument to explain that "we can in fact have less inflation without more unemployment in 1980 if we have policies in 1979 that are . . . firmly held to so that people really believe we are going to follow through on them" (FOMC Minutes, February 6, 1979, 19). Henry Wallich reminded them of the persistent forecast errors. "The rate of inflation is always worse than we think it is" (ibid., 23). Wallich added that "real interest rates are barely positive and they're negative after taxes" (ibid.).

Nancy Teeters's statement is representative of those who emphasized the risk of recession. "I think the probabilities are on the side of a reces-

115. Procedures for setting longer-term money growth rates changed at this meeting. Instead of setting a growth rate each quarter for the next four quarters, the FOMC now set money growth for fourth to fourth quarter. In July, the FOMC gave Congress a preliminary estimate for 1980, and it could adjust the 1979 growth rate. Also, the staff proposed redefinition of the monetary aggregates to adjust for the changes in transaction accounts such as NOW accounts. The new $M_1$ included NOW balances, credit union share drafts, and demand deposits at thrift institutions. The additions increased $M_1$ by $4.8 billion, 1.36 percent. The staff removed $11.3 billion of demand deposits of foreign banks and official institutions, so the new $M_1$ was smaller than the old. The staff also developed $M_1+$ to include saving balances at commercial banks ($221.6 billion), and it redefined $M_2$ and $M_3$ (Federal Reserve Bulletin, January 1979, 17).

sion, but I don't see it occurring until the end of the year and the early part of next year" (ibid., 13). Paul Volcker also believed a recession was likely, but "the number one problem continues to be concern about the price level" (ibid., 10). Volcker also expressed concern about the dollar when the dollar was weak.

Henry Wallich complained about the changing base for the money targets. "We were essentially ratcheting [$M_1$] up by first going to the upper side of it and then by choosing a range that would make the upper side fall in the middle" (ibid., 29).

Chairman Miller often spoke first to give the FOMC what he called guidance. He did not think the monetary aggregates were reliable, especially when NOW accounts and automated transfers distorted the data. And he accepted the staff's standard explanation that the large and frequent errors in hitting the money targets resulted from shifts in the demand for money. The possibility that the interest rate target was inconsistent with the money target was rarely acknowledged.[116]

Miller was much more collegial than Burns or Martin. Although he was famous within the System for putting a "no smoking" sign on the Board table (which the others ignored), he consulted frequently between meetings and was much less inclined to act on his own initiative than Burns or Volcker.[117]

The staff's description of the economy's position in March 1979 called inflation prospects "dismal and the Administration's wage-price restraint program . . . in a great deal of difficulty" (ibid., March 20, 1979, Kichline appendix, 1).[118] Paul Volcker expressed most concern about inflation, although he repeated that "the odds are better than 50–50 that we're going to run into a recession" (by year-end) (ibid., 9). He wanted to increase the funds rate, but a six-to-four majority voted to leave it unchanged. Wallich, Kimbrel (Atlanta), and Coldwell joined him. Frank Morris (Boston) asked

116. One of the rare occasions was the March 20, 1979, meeting. David Eastburn (Philadelphia) asked, "How much validity is there to the idea that what is happening to money is supply induced and not demand induced?" (FOMC Minutes, March 20, 1979, 7). Stephen Axilrod at first replied that by setting an interest rate, the manager relinquished control of money. He soon realized that his answer evaded the question, so he added, "whether it's a demand or a supply phenomenon, it's very difficult to dissociate the two" (ibid., 8). He might have added "under their procedures." The staff continued to explain money growth errors as shifts in the demand for money.

117. He described his procedure. "My tendency is not to go off on these things [decisions] without first having a quick phone call so we can get everyone involved" (FOMC Minutes, conference call, July 19, 1978). This was Miller's last meeting before moving to the Treasury.

118. This view was widely held. The General Accounting Office tried to decide whether guidelines were effective. It concluded that "we could find no convincing evidence that the standards have had any effect on the rate of inflation" (quoted in Biven, 2002, 195–96).

for a counter-cyclical policy move. He recognized that a preemptive move was "unprecedented," so he proposed that the FOMC reduce the funds rate to 9.5 percent and "explain this unprecedented development of the Fed moving the funds rate down before we're actually in a recession" (ibid., 30). Morris added that the money supply [growth] had remained unchanged for six months.

Morris's proposal to act in anticipation of recession did not attract any followers. Fifteen years would pass before the FOMC in 1994 attempted to move counter-cyclically to prevent an increase in inflation.

Miller had to work to change a five-to-five vote to seven-to-three at the April 17 meeting.[119] Volcker, Coldwell, and Wallich wanted more restrictive policy than a short-term $M_1$ range of 3 to 7 or 3 to 8 percent and a 10 percent federal funds rate. Teeters wanted less restraint, and Kimbrel (Atlanta) wanted a "money market" directive, not an "aggregate" directive. At the time that meant that the manager did not change the funds rate until projected two-months growth of the aggregates reached the upper or lower bound. Usually, the chairman held a telephone conference before deciding whether to make an inter-meeting change. On the other side, Mayo, Balles, Black, Partee, and Miller voted for the directive with mixed reasons also.

Miller then announced the number for March housing starts, a number well below the staff estimate. On a new vote the FOMC voted seven to three for a 4 to 8 percent growth for $M_1$, 4 to 8.5 percent for $M_2$, and a 10 percent funds rate with bounds at 9.75 and 10.5. $M_1$ and $M_2$ received equal weight when making decisions.

The reasons given for differences varied. Volcker's main concern was the persistent underprediction of inflation. He believed the expected rate of inflation had increased, so a constant nominal interest rate implied a lower real rate, hence a more stimulative policy. Coldwell and Wallich agreed. Wallich wanted to raise the funds rate until the real rate became positive. Statements of this kind went unchallenged; none of the FOMC argued that interest rates were high, a significant improvement over the past.

The main reason for opposing more restrictive policy was fear of a recession. One of the more sophisticated arguments suggested that if a recession came, the System and the administration would be under pressure to take expansive actions, so inflation would rise in a year or two.

Months of slow money growth was one of the concerns at the April meeting. Ten days later, the FOMC held a telephone conference to respond to a 17.5 percent (annual rate) surge in $M_1$ growth during April. The FOMC agreed without objection to move the funds rate target to 10.25 percent.

119. If the vote remained tied, the existing directive remained in effect.

The staff forecast a 10.3 percent rate of increase in the business product deflator (annual rate) in the second quarter. Excluding food and energy price increases that were mainly one-time price level changes (temporary inflation), not persistent inflation, the rate of increase would be 8.25 percent. Using the persistent inflation rate, or second-quarter 1979 expected rate of inflation from the survey, real ten-year Treasury yields were only slightly positive. Despite low real yields, Governor Partee and President Morris forecast a recession.

Volcker objected. "If we're going to balance these risks of inflation and recession we have to run not too scared that the recession is going to be worse than we expect" (FOMC Minutes, May 22, 1979, 22). He proposed a wider range for monetary growth with a lower value for the acceptable minimum. Partee responded, "I come to exactly the opposite conclusion" (ibid.) He wanted to widen the range for the funds rate by allowing a decline from 10.25 percent. But he wanted to avoid weakness in the monetary aggregates, and he recognized that in the past, policy was procyclical at or near turning points. "To go to an interest rate target now at this turning point in the economy would be exactly the wrong prescription. . . . [W]e ought to have an aggregates target with modest growth. . . . not crunch the economy into . . . a very serious recession" (ibid., 23). His recommendation called for a 0.25 reduction in the funds rate (to 10 percent) and 1 to 5 percent $M_1$ growth for the next two months. At the opposite pole, Volcker wanted a 10.25 percent (unchanged) funds rate and the money ($M_1$) growth band from "a minus number up to 4.5 percent" (ibid., 28).[120]

Part of the FOMC had started to change. The rhetoric was more divided than the recommendations, as was often true. The main division was about objectives. Partee, Morris, Teeters, and their group believed that the Federal Reserve's main responsibility was to prevent recession or reduce the unemployment rate. Reducing inflation was a subsidiary responsibility to be achieved without causing much unemployment. This had been tried without success at the end of the Johnson administration and in the early Nixon administration.

Volcker, Wallich, and Coldwell, to different degrees, put greater weight on reducing inflation and preventing dollar depreciation. They interpreted the Employment Act of 1946 as a mandate to maintain the purchasing power of money. They were willing to tolerate temporarily higher unem-

120. The Senate Banking Committee considered repeal of the Credit Control Act of 1969. Schultze opposed repeal. Although he doubted that the administration would use the authority, he urged retention (letter, Charles Schultze to Senator William Proxmire, Schultze papers, Carter Library, May 22, 1979). Ten months later, the president invoked the act and requested the Federal Reserve to control credit.

ployment to reduce inflation. They would later add that low inflation reduced uncertainty, improved the quality of information in relative prices, and encouraged investment in long-term capital and productivity growth. Thus, low inflation encouraged economic growth and employment in the longer run.

Henry Wallich expressed the proposed change in strategy during a recession. "I think we are getting ourselves here in the spirit of [believing that] in a recession we've got to accelerate the aggregates. Now, that way, there will never be a reduction in inflation. In a recession interest rates should come down, but at constant rates of expansion of the aggregates; otherwise prices will go up indefinitely" (FOMC Minutes, July 11, 1979, 37).[121]

Under the Humphrey-Hawkins law, the Federal Reserve had to inform Congress in July about any revision to its monetary targets for the current year and its first estimate of the monetary targets for the following year. Miller and many others were very uncomfortable about making forecasts of money growth as much as eighteen months ahead. The several institutional changes affecting the money aggregates, particularly $M_1$, increased their discomfort. The introduction of automatic balance transfers (ATS) received most attention. A depositor could move balances between demand deposits and interest-bearing savings accounts automatically, so the data understated effective demand deposits. The FOMC had estimated earlier in the year that ATS accounts would lower $M_1$ growth by 3 percentage points in 1979. In the first six months, the actual reduction in $M_1$ growth was 1.5 percentage points. Thus, when reported money growth was 4.5 percent, the public had instantaneous access to an additional 1.5 percent, making effective money growth 6 percent. Forecasting the growth rate of ATS accounts and $M_1$ was more uncertain than earlier.[122]

Wallich started the discussion by stating a view that he described as widespread. "Wherever I go I sense there is less willingness this time

121. Mark Willes raised an issue about the staff's use of the Phillips curve in their model and forecasts. "Implicit in your inflation forecast . . . is a belief that there is a short-run tradeoff between inflation and unemployment. Can you tell me what data there are in the last decade that makes you think that such a tradeoff even exists?"

122. The 1987 Humphrey-Hawkins Act gave the administration a problem also. The act called for a 4 percent unemployment rate and 3 percent inflation by the end of 1983. In a memo to the president, Schultze and Budget Director James McIntyre reported that the goals were "unrealistic" and required assumptions that caused "serious problems for long-term budgetary control. . . . Because both inflation and unemployment are understated, the future year outlay totals are misleadingly low" (memo to the president, Schultze papers, Carter Library, May 19, 1979, 1). The memo told the president that they had to choose between realistic assumptions and assumptions consistent with Humphrey-Hawkins. They preferred realistic assumptions but would include a short section using the alternative assumptions.

around to accommodate the OPEC shock monetarily" (ibid., 16). Mark Willes added that "there is very little evidence that monetary policy can do anything to offset an oil price increase in terms of ameliorating its real effects on the economy. . . . [T]he one thing we can have a systematic impact on is the rate of inflation, and that should be our primary objective" (ibid., 20). But Frank Morris stated the contrary view. He thought that a deep recession had started. "I believe we could see the unemployment rate go as high as 9 percent next year rather than the 8 percent the staff has projected. In my view that would be counterproductive to the long-run anti-inflation fight. If we have that big a recession, the hope of keeping some constraint on fiscal policy is going to be diminished" (ibid., 17). Those who made this argument never considered that the Federal Reserve did not have to finance the deficit.

After much discussion, the FOMC voted for an $M_1$ growth range for 1979 of 1.5 to 4.5 percent, net of ATS deposits, and 3 to 6 percent for 1980. Wallich dissented on the 1979 vote, but the vote on 1980 was unanimous.

For the next two months, the FOMC voted unanimously for a funds rate kept at 10.25 percent, $M_1$ growth of 2.5 to 6.5 percent, and $M_2$ growth at 6.5 to 10.5 percent. The unanimous vote belied the different views. Referring to the funds rate, Morris said the manager should "move to 10 percent immediately . . . [T]he economy was clearly in a recession" (ibid., 43). Partee repeated the traditional argument that gave more weight to the prospect of recession than to actual inflation. He voted for 10.25 because of weakness in the dollar. He believed that West Germany, Britain, and others were deliberately appreciating their currency to reduce inflation. "I don't think we ought to get dragged along with them into a worldwide depression" (ibid., 46).[123]

At the Bonn summit in July 1978, President Carter had agreed to decontrol domestic oil prices as part of a multilateral agreement to expand economic activity and reduce inflation. Decontrol meant higher prices for gasoline and heating oil. It was rational economic policy but certain to be unpopular politically. The president delayed carrying out his commitment, but as the 1979 summit of developed country governments approached, he felt obliged to honor his explicit agreement.

On April 5, 1979, in a television address to the nation, President Carter announced that oil prices would rise steadily beginning on June 1 and con-

123. At the July meeting, Emmett Rice attended for the first time. He was sworn in on June 20, 1979, and resigned on December 31, 1986. He took the seat of Stephen Gardner, who died after less than three years on the Board. At this meeting, Chairman Miller complained about leaks to the press from FOMC meetings, an issue that arose many times in the past and would return.

tinuing for twenty-eight months until domestic oil prices reached world levels. To pacify congressional critics, he asked Congress to pass a 50 percent windfall profits tax to subsidize payments by low-income consumers for fuel and public transportation. Congress passed the tax about a year later. The Reagan administration completed decontrol early in its term. The Iranian revolution overthrew the shah, held American officials hostage, and raised oil prices beginning in December 1978.

President Carter returned from Camp David on July 15, 1979, and announced a new long-run energy program including subsidies for synthetic fuels production, mandatory conservation measures, and further decontrol of oil and natural gas prices but not gasoline (Solomon, 1982, 351). This speech is best remembered for his complaint that the public suffered from "malaise," although he did not use that word. Economically, its largest impact was the firing of Treasury Secretary Michael Blumenthal and his replacement with G. William Miller.[124] That left a vacancy at the Federal Reserve. Soon afterward, President Carter appointed Paul Volcker, a known anti-inflationist.[125]

The market's reaction to the president's speech started modestly but turned increasingly negative. At a telephone conference on July 17, Margaret Greene of the New York bank briefed the FOMC on the foreign exchange market. "The market responded to the Carter address with some disappointment—disappointment that some of the immediate questions about the economy have not been addressed and that the issues that were addressed were of a long-term nature" (FOMC Minutes, July 17, 1979, 1). The New York desk intervened to slow dollar depreciation. Since mid-June, the desk had sold $3.1 billion, mainly in marks. West Germany and Swit-

124. Blumenthal's relation with the White House staff, especially Eizenstat, and perhaps Carter had deteriorated. For Carter, inflation was a serious problem, and the advice he received seemed not to work.

125. Volcker made many speeches in the years before his appointment. In Senate testimony in 1976, he explained that inflation had many causes—oil price increases, devaluation—but included lax monetary policy. He did not accept the Phillips curve view that low inflation and low unemployment were alternatives. Sustained, disinflationary monetary and fiscal policies could achieve both. "We must choose a policy that in the somewhat longer run will be compatible with both" (statement, Federal Reserve Bank of New York, Box 35604, February 17, 1976, 9). Later that year, Volcker spoke to the American Economic and American Finance Associations. He recognized that all price increases (called inflation) were not monetary. Then he added, "Excessive monetary expansion is a sufficient condition for inflation, and in the longer run, it is equally clear that no important inflation can be sustained without money rising substantially faster than real income. . . . There is always some rate of monetary growth (perhaps zero) that will in principle achieve price stability" (Remarks, "The Contributions and Limitations of 'Monetary' Analyses," Federal Reserve Bank of New York, Box 35605, September 16, 1976, 18). No one earlier came to the Federal Reserve chairmanship with these views.

zerland bought $3.7 billion of bonds denominated in marks and francs (ibid., 2).

Miller seemed concerned that a renewed run against the dollar had started. He asked the members to consider whether intervention was called for and what its consequences would be for the domestic economy. Volcker proposed an increase in the discount rate and the funds rate as an alternative to exchange market intervention. "I am extremely skeptical that intervention will be adequate to handle a situation of this sort" (ibid., 5).

Several members commented that the president failed to address inflation, a major concern of the markets. Sentiment favoring a discount rate increase dominated. The Board met following the meeting. On July 19, effective July 20, the Board voted unanimously to increase the discount rate by 0.5 to 10 percent, an unprecedented level.

Two days later, July 19, Miller held another telephone conference. Stephen Axilrod reported that $M_1$ had increased well above its target for three of the past four months. He proposed raising the funds rate to 10.5 percent.

Margaret Greene reported that the dollar had again come under pressure. Intervention by the Federal Reserve and the Bundesbank had slowed the decline, but sentiment remained bearish. The System had used swap drawings on the Bundesbank to finance $1.5 billion of intervention. The FOMC decided to let the funds rate rise to 10.5 percent, as they had agreed earlier if money growth exceeded its upper target. International concerns influenced many, a marked contrast with 1971. The FOMC did not vote because the July 11 directive provided for the increase. Based on their comments at the meeting, Teeters and Eastburn (Philadelphia) would probably have dissented. Morris (Boston) had urged easier policy. The rapid increase in money changed his outlook; he now favored 10.5 or even 10.625 percent.

## INTERNATIONAL CRISES AND POLICIES

During the years from 1973 to 1979, the international system faced repeated problems and several crises. Many of the problems were new. Agreement by principal countries on how to respond came slowly. Principal countries floated their exchange rates but also intervened, heavily at times, to influence currency values. Individual currencies had floated before, notably the Canadian dollar in the 1950s, but the modern world had not experienced a time when there was no fixed anchor to currency values. To reduce risk in the past, asset owners could shift part of their wealth into a currency with a fixed exchange rate. No longer. Learning to function in a world of independent or interdependent individual countries policies took time.

The oil price increases in 1973 added another dimension. The effect of the oil price increase was similar to a tax on the use of oil paid to a foreign supplier or government. The tax reduced wealth and income in the importing countries and increased wealth and income of the oil-exporting countries. Several of the oil-importing countries, especially developing countries, ran large payments deficits.[126] The OPEC countries did not choose to lend to the developing countries, so banking institutions in the developed countries borrowed surplus dollars from OPEC and re-lent to the developing countries. For a time this process, called recycling, seemed satisfactory. By the early 1980s, both bank lenders and country borrowers learned that lending and borrowing was temporary assistance that did not eliminate the need for the developing countries to adjust spending to reflect their permanently reduced wealth and income.

Failure to distinguish between permanent and transitory changes in measured inflation reflected two persistent problems. One was policymakers' excessive concentration on near-term or current events and neglect of longer-term consequences of policy actions and other events. Second was the related but distinct problem of neglecting differences in persistent and temporary changes.[127]

Floating changed the role of gold in the international system. Historically, gold was used to settle international payments imbalances. With floating rates, exchange rate changes settled these differences. What role remained for gold? The United States and France had spent much time arguing about the role of gold during the 1970s. France wanted to return to a fixed exchange rate with settlements involving gold. The United States wanted to demonetize gold by floating and using SDRs when or if balances were settled by asset transfer.

Very often events settled the disputes and resolved differences. The oil price increases in 1973 put an effective end to discussions about fixed or floating rates (James, 1996, Chapter 9). Perhaps the main lesson from this experience was that, for fixed exchange rates to stabilize economies,

126. The effect of the oil price increase on the current account deficits of developing countries was a main concern at international meetings in the mid-1970s. In January 1975, the G-10 discussed a $25 billion fund to finance developing countries' balance of payments deficits, as a "last resort." The decline in spending and imports reduced these concerns following the oil shock but of course, raised new concerns about the depth and duration of the decline in spending and output (report of the meeting of G-10 ministers and central bank governors, January 16, 1975, Board Records). Throughout, the discussion did not distinguish between a recession and a permanent reduction in output. Recessions are temporary reductions in spending; the oil shock was a permanent wealth transfer to the oil-producing countries.

127. See Brunner, Cukierman, and Meltzer (1980) for a formal analysis.

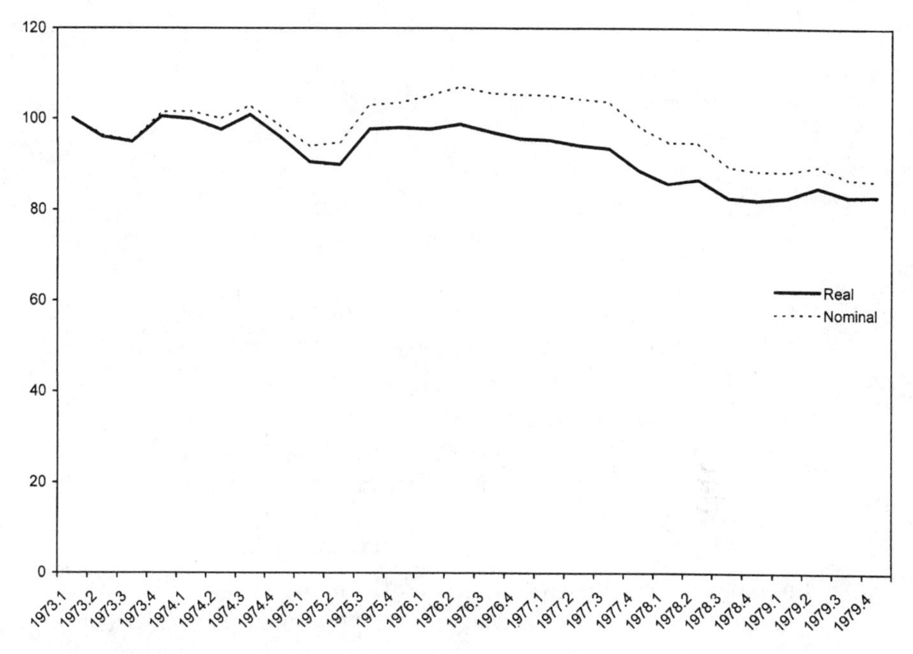


Chart 7.15. Trade-weighted exchange rates, 1973–79.

economic policies had to be compatible and external events relatively benign. This lesson was hard to learn; the Continental European countries tried several times to maintain a local fixed exchange rate system without enforcing common policies. Eventually, they adopted a common currency and a common monetary policy. And the market ended international policy discussions about recycling oil revenues by doing just that.

Chart 7.15 shows trade weighted nominal and real exchange rates for the United States for 1973 through 1979.[128] Slower inflation in the middle of the decade and higher inflation abroad slightly appreciated the nominal exchange rate in mid-decade. The real exchange rate depreciated steadily. By the end of 1979, the nominal trade weighted dollar was 14 percent below its early 1973 value; the real exchange rate depreciated more than 17 percent during the period.

Policy toward the dollar changed considerably. At times, policy called for "benign neglect." At other times, policymakers intervened actively to influence the exchange rate or its rate of change. Some United States trading partners, particularly the Europeans, intervened from their side. When

128. Real exchange rates use the Federal Reserve definition and weights and export and import prices.

the United States would not join them, they often claimed that the United States wanted to depreciate its currency to gain trade advantage.[129]

Chart 7.15 suggests the source of many conflicts—real and nominal exchange rates move together (Mussa, 1986). Inflation rates adjust slowly, so expansive or contractive policies in a large country have persistent real effects that affect other countries and that floating does not eliminate instantaneously. Another side of this finding is that payments imbalances adjust with a lag.

Despite French resistance,[130] IMF members adopted an amendment in 1976 that authorized countries to choose the exchange rate system they preferred. This included both fixed and floating rates, but it eliminated a rate fixed to gold (ibid., 272–73).

The United States Treasury, especially, wanted to reduce, then eliminate, the role of gold in the international monetary system. Arthur Burns was not convinced. But the Treasury persisted and reached agreement in July 1975.[131] The agreement also instructed the IMF to sell one-sixth of its gold holdings to finance aid to developing countries and to return an additional one-sixth to member countries. The agreement effectively ended squabbles over the role of gold for the next two years. It was not renewed in 1978. By that time, the issue had become less important. During the next two decades, several developed countries sold part of their gold holdings. However, diminution of the role of gold did not shift the monetary system toward SDRs, as the United States intended. Countries held reserves principally

129. Intervention can be sterilized or unsterilized. Unsterilized intervention changes the monetary base, so it is an open market operation using currency purchases or sales in place of securities. Sterilized intervention does not change the monetary base. The central bank offsets the change in international reserves by moving domestic assets in the opposite direction. In a market as large as the market for dollar securities, unsterilized intervention cannot have much effect on the exchange rate. The main portfolio change arises from possible differences in the risk of holding Treasury bills or foreign securities. A substantial volume of research identified an "information effect" of sterilized intervention. The central bank (or banks) signal that they regard the nominal exchange rate as over- or undervalued. The market responds by adjusting the exchange rate unless new information shows that the central bank was mistaken (Dominguez and Frankel, 1993; Sarno and Taylor, 2001). This seems an inefficient way to announce policy or give the market information that the central bank or government thinks relevant. The magnitude and duration of the response seems small but remains a subject of research.

130. Finance Minister Jean-Pierre Fourcade gave the official French attitude toward floating in 1974. "Floating rates, though 'an inevitable evil for the time being, will never constitute an acceptable response to the profound exigencies of a sound international payments system'" (quoted in Solomon, 1982, 268).

131. The breakdown of Bretton Woods with the closing of the gold window ended the two-tier system for pricing gold that began in March 1968. The United States did not eliminate exchange controls until 1974.

in dollars but also marks (later euros) and to a lesser extent yen and Swiss francs.

To carry out foreign exchange market intervention, the Federal Reserve increased its swap lines several times. Use of swap lines in transactions altered the monetary base of the foreign country unless it sterilized the Federal Reserve's action; for example, by selling marks for dollars, the Federal Reserve increased the market's holdings of marks. To prevent a domestic impact, the Bundesbank had to sterilize the sale by reducing domestic securities in its portfolio.

The Treasury was the dominant partner in United States foreign exchange operations after 1933. The Gold Reserve Act of 1934 established the Exchange Stabilization Fund (ESF) for this purpose and authorized the secretary, after consultation with the president, to intervene. The ESF did not have large resources, so it borrowed from the Federal Reserve by "warehousing" foreign exchange with the Federal Reserve as collateral. Since the Federal Reserve Act prohibited loans to the Treasury, warehousing evaded the restriction. Congress failed to interpret warehousing as a loan, so the practice continued.[132] The Treasury absorbed any losses if the collateral value declined.

The Federal Reserve's authority to engage in foreign exchange transactions was not explicitly recognized in the Federal Reserve Act. The legal staff interpreted the provision permitting the System to purchase and sell cable transfers and to hold foreign exchange in accounts abroad as sufficient to permit these transactions (Humpage, 1994, 3).[133]

Humpage (ibid., 16) produced a table of the Federal Reserve's realized and unrealized gains and losses from its dealings in foreign currencies between 1975 and 1992. Many of the gains resulted from holding foreign assets that appreciated relative to the dollar.[134]

Floating exchange rates permitted countries to control inflation. None managed to restore price stability in the 1970s, but significant differences emerged. Table 7.13 shows these differences on average for 1977–80 and in 1979 and 1980.

Differences in measured inflation rates reflect mainly sustained differences in monetary policy and the weight on oil prices in the country's

132. Members of the FOMC reopened the issue about legal authority in 1990 (Schwartz, 1997, 145).

133. For the legal reasoning see volume 2, book 1, chapter 3.

134. Humpage found relatively large gains from 1985 to 1987 and 1990, mainly from dollar depreciation. Overall, the cumulative gain for these years was $4.8 billion, or 0.66 percent of the Federal Reserve's payments to the Treasury. Humpage shows losses in eleven years and gains in seven.

**Table 7.13** Consumer Price Inflation (%)

| | 1977–80 | 1979 | 1980 |
|---|---|---|---|
| United States | 9.85 | 12.48 | 11.68 |
| Japan | 5.11 | 5.49 | 6.79 |
| Germany | 4.12 | 5.24 | 5.31 |
| Netherlands | 5.02 | 4.71 | 6.53 |
| Canada | 9.28 | 9.32 | 10.62 |
| France | 10.45 | 11.16 | 12.77 |
| Italy | 15.15 | 17.19 | 19.36 |
| United Kingdom | 12.37 | 15.90 | 14.08 |

Source: Darby et al. (1983, 515).

consumer price index.[135] Those who expected that a shift to floating rates would totally separate economies were disappointed. Capital movements continued, driven in part by the policy and inflation differences that underlie the table. The resulting volatility of exchange rates gave rise to considerable negative comment about floating rates, but little evidence of systematic effects of variability on trade flows. In time, policymakers remembered that whether exchange rates were fixed or floating, stability depended on the policies pursued. In the United States and many other countries, full employment was the main policy goal. The exchange rate reflected the actions taken to achieve the employment goal. Absorbing the increased price of oil also increased instability.

International agreements advised countries to cooperate.[136] One popular proposal called upon leading countries to limit floating by agreeing upon target zones for exchange rates. Such proposals attempted to move back toward fixed exchange rates with wider, perhaps much wider, bands within which exchange rates could change. They required an agreement to limit domestic policy actions and to change domestic policy when called for by a foreign government, but the proponents did not discuss the loss of control over domestic policy. Efforts by the Carter administration to get agreement for joint action in 1977–78 showed that countries gave different weights to employment and inflation. West Germany, in particular, was reluctant to risk higher inflation to reduce U.S. unemployment and finance

135. Mundell (2000, 335), using wholesale prices, claimed that the price increase in the United States from 1971 to 1982 was 157 percent. This exceeded the increases during any wartime period after independence.

136. The agreement legalizing floating exchange rates called on countries to achieve "orderly underlying conditions . . . for financial and economic stability." It "did not offer any real guidance as to how the requisite cooperation would be achieved" (Volcker and Gyohten, 1992, 143). Criticism of floating was widespread. Gottfried Haberler (1990, 157) quotes a criticism of floating rates by Pope John Paul II in 1988.

its overseas commitments for common defense and military assistance.[137] These problems continued to exist after exchange rates became free to float; international disagreement on how to manage the consequences remained.[138] Volcker summed up the problem: "Coordination becomes much more complicated when it moves into broad questions of trying to manage different economies at different rates of growth, or of influencing tax policy or energy policy. To a politician, that all implies some loss of sovereignty" (Volcker and Gyohten, 1992, 145).

The end of the Bretton Woods system did not eliminate differences among countries about how to share the cost of common defense or reconcile domestic demands to lower the unemployment rate or the inflation rate. Floating simply gave policymakers one more degree of freedom; they could permit the exchange rate to adjust, and they could choose to control domestic inflation. Foreign governments disliked these changes as much as or more than they disliked capital inflows. The United States, at first, chose to ignore the criticisms and the exchange rate. Later it intervened in the exchange market or proposed coordinated action to increase economic growth without changing exchange rates (Pauls, 1990).

## INTERNATIONAL POLICY ACTIONS

Early 1974 found the Federal Reserve and other central banks trying to adjust to the oil price increases without a clear idea about what to do. The Arab countries embargoed oil sales to the United States, but the embargo proved mainly that oil was fungible. It sold in an international market, so the actual effect was much less than the Arabs anticipated. The embargo failed and ended in March. Governor Daane reported on the January meeting at the Bank for International Settlements (BIS) in Basel. The United States proposed multilateral intervention to avoid competitive devaluations. BIS President Zilstra sensibly pointed out that "it was necessary to determine the appropriate exchange rates before intervening, in order to know what rate levels to aim for" (FOMC Minutes, January 21, 1974, 12). Needless to say, the central bankers had no way to answer that question. Burns looked on the bright side. Appreciation of the dollar would lower the inflation rate and restore "some semblance of price

137. James's (1996, 207) description of the breakdown of the Bretton Woods system remained applicable to the early years of floating. "The crisis of the Bretton Woods system can be seen as a particular and very dramatic instance of the clash of national economic regulation with the logic of internationalism. . . . [T]he description of the system followed very obviously and directly from the policies of the United States."

138. In a widely cited paper, Meese and Rogoff (1983) showed that exchange rates under floating approximately followed a random walk.

stability" (ibid., 20). But Coombs saw only disorderly markets driven by speculation.

In February, the United States called an energy conference in Washington. The discussion did not distinguish between a price level increase and continued inflation. Burns summarized his conversation with the finance ministers of leading countries by saying they were more concerned about maintaining aggregate demand than preventing inflation (ibid., February 20, 1974, 11).[139] The size of their problem measured by the gross increase in payments to the oil-producing countries was $60 billion in 1974, about 2 percent of the combined GNP of the OECD countries (Solomon, 1982, 307).

The United States removed exchange controls and freed capital exports and imports early in 1974. At first, the dollar appreciated. By February, the dollar was under pressure to depreciate. The Federal Reserve and the Treasury sold $155 million of foreign currency by mid-March to stem the decline (ibid., March 18, 1974, 47).[140] Failure of the Franklin National Bank in New York and the Herstatt Bank in Germany increased intervention during the summer. Countries continued to meet and discuss various reforms, but their policies remained independent.

Active intervention continued in 1975. The trade-weighted dollar moved over a relatively wide range. The monthly average reached lows in March and June, then recovered to the end of the year. In the year ending December, the dollar rose 6.5 percent against the mark. In part, dollar appreciation against the mark reflected the more rapid increase in West German hourly compensation and the greater domestic production of oil in the United States.

Several efforts to coordinate policy reflect dissatisfaction with floating rates. The Federal Reserve and others focused attention mainly on short-term events and ignored expectations of differences in inflation and growth. In January, the staff reported that several countries lowered interest rates to coordinate actions with the United States and Germany. In February Chairman Burns met with Presidents Karl Klassen of the Bundesbank and Fritz Leutwiler of the Swiss National Bank. They agreed on "more concerted intervention policies" based on daily conversations by operating officials. The three agreed to expand operations in periods of dollar weakness (FOMC Minutes, February 19, 1975, A-2).

139. Some of the ministers may have recognized that a relative price had changed and did not choose to force the price level down.

140. This was much less than Japan. Between the oil shock in October 1973 and January 1974, Japan spent almost $7 billion on intervention to slow yen depreciation (Gyohten in Volcker and Gyohten, 1992, 131).

**Table 7.14** Consumer Price Inflation, Selected Countries, 1973–77 (%)

| | 1973 | 1974 | 1975 | 1976 | 1977 |
|---|---|---|---|---|---|
| Japan | 11.7 | 24.5 | 11.8 | 9.3 | 8.1 |
| Germany | 6.9 | 7.0 | 6.0 | 4.5 | 3.7 |
| Italy | 10.8 | 19.1 | 17.0 | 16.8 | 17.0 |
| United Kingdom | 9.2 | 16.0 | 24.2 | 16.5 | 15.9 |
| United States | 6.2 | 11.0 | 9.1 | 5.8 | 6.5 |

Source: Solomon (1982, 300), based on OECD.

Very large differences in reported headline inflation rates and changes in reported inflation suggest that the mid-1970s was not a period in which exchange rates were likely to stabilize with or without intervention. Table 7.14 shows a sample of reported consumer price inflation rates during 1973–77. Reported inflation rates include both one-time responses to food and oil price increases and permanent or persistent underlying rates of inflation. There are few if any peacetime periods in which comparative inflation rates for industrial countries differed as much or changed as much from year to year. Given these data, exchange rate volatility should not have surprised central banks and governments. They did not agree, however, on the reasons for inflation.

Germany (and many others) criticized United States monetary policy as a main reason for exchange rate instability. They emphasized the excessive creation of dollars as a source of "monetary debauchery" for countries with current account surpluses and fixed exchange rates (Solomon, 1982, 301, quoting Otmar Emminger of the Bundesbank). This line of criticism usually did not mention that surplus countries could revalue. Maintaining or increasing employment and exports dominated their other goals. Others again pointed to the asymmetry of the international system based on the dollar.

Solomon (1982, 301–7) rejected Emminger's argument. Although he recognized that the capital inflow to Germany and Japan was historically high, he pointed out that German wages began to increase before the capital inflow. He blamed German inflation on food and oil price increases and rising foreign demand for German exports. And he quoted from BIS and OECD reports to show that the non-monetary explanation of inflation was widely held. Solomon recognized that comparisons of timing cannot be decisive, but he offered no other evidence. And he ignored the cumulative effect of expansive policies in the United States and abroad and the growing expectation in many countries that those policies would continue.[141]

141. Volcker had a more classical interpretation. He urged Burns to "tighten money" if he wanted to restore a par value system (Volcker and Gyohten, 1992, 113–14).

United States policy did not try to fix the exchange rate. Instructions called on the desk to "maintain orderly markets" but left the definition of "orderly" to the desk (FOMC Minutes, December 16, 1975, 44). The meeting of the G-7 at Rambouillet (France) in November "suggested that intervention might be more active than in the past. However, the language of the agreement was so loose that its meaning could be determined only in the course of experience" (ibid., 17).[142]

The considerable volume of U.S. foreign exchange intervention was entirely sterilized, so it had no monetary effect. The FOMC did not discuss effectiveness. Scott Pardee, responsible for operations at the New York bank, like his predecessor, believed intervention was effective but made no effort to gather evidence. Burns usually favored intervention. Despite his academic background and frequent public criticism of intervention as ineffective, he did not ask the staff to produce evidence of its effect.[143]

The facts about floating that most surprised policymakers were that volatility of exchange rates and large parity changes did not prevent recovery or noticeably reduce trade. Trade expanded and economies recovered from the oil shock, the surge in food prices, and economic mismanagement. As Volcker noted, the absence of crisis revised countries' concern about exchange rates (Volcker and Gyohten, 1992, 103).

The agreement between France and the United States to include floating as a legitimate option required a difficult series of negotiations. Pressed by Representative Reuss and his own inclinations, Treasury Secretary William Simon continued the negotiations through 1975. He was probably aided by the large imbalances that countries faced and the belief that the balance could not be settled without exchange rate adjustment. Also, the French position favoring fixed but adjustable rates had little support in

142. Rambouillet was the first G-7 summit of heads of state. These meetings began with George Shultz's "library group" consisting of the finance ministers of the United States, Britain, Germany, and France. Japan did not want to be excluded. It invited these four to meet at the Japanese embassy in Nairobi at the time of the IMF meeting in 1975. The French agreed to hold the next meeting at Rambouillet in 1976 and added Canada and Italy. The meetings began as an attempt to find acceptable common solutions to economic problems. Later it became a public relations effort for leaders of each of the principal countries.

143. Reports of international meetings at this time contain many endorsements of cooperative action. The international system organized special lending facilities to help developing countries finance balance of payments deficits resulting from the rise in oil prices and the decline in industrial countries' demand. However, individual country concerns were not lost. In his report on a July OECD meeting, Henry Wallich described the continued dependence of foreign governments on United States policy much as it had been under the Bretton Woods system. "Several [members of the BIS] also expressed satisfaction over the recent rise of the dollar in the exchange markets. The Germans and Swiss went so far as to indicate that they were hoping for a stimulus to their exports as a result" (Notes on Meeting of Bank for International Settlements, Board Records, July 29, 1975).

other countries. The agreement reached at Rambouillet became a new Article 4 of the IMF agreement in January 1976. The article stressed "stability" and called upon members to "promote stability by fostering underlying economic and financial conditions and a monetary system that does not produce erratic disruptions" (Solomon, 1982, 272).

Article 4 permitted countries to fix their exchange rate using SDRs or other base, but it forbade the use of a gold base. It also permitted floating. It is not clear that France recognized that it had accepted a permanent system of floating rates, but, in practice, most countries adopted some type of floating rate with intervention.

### *Gold*

Finance ministers and governments also had to agree on the role of gold. The difficulty with this decision arose not only from the problem of reconciling the French and United States positions but also from the lack of agreement among policy officials in the United States. In part because French citizens traditionally held part of their wealth in gold, France wanted rules that permitted purchases and sales at market prices, and they wanted the right to increase gold held as a reserve asset. United States policy favored the elimination of gold as a reserve asset, called demonetization, and replacement with SDRs. After July 1974, valuation of the SDR used a basket of principal national currencies excluding gold.

In June 1975, Burns sent a memo to the president making the case against gold transactions by central banks and governments at market prices. At the time, the official gold price was $42.22 per ounce; the market price ranged from $160 to $175 per ounce (memo, Burns to the president, Greenspan files, Burns papers, Gerald R. Ford Library, Box 10, June 3, 1975). The large difference in price created an incentive to distribute the profits on IMF country quotas and to revalue reserves of individual countries. France favored both. Burns opposed.

The gold deposited at the IMF belonged to the IMF (subject to restrictions), so the gain on the stock also belonged to the IMF. Members control IMF decisions, if they can agree. The United States could veto any action, so its agreement and congressional approval mattered. Some wanted to use the capital gain on gold to finance redistribution to developing countries. Others, especially France, wanted to return gold to member countries at the original price so that the gain would accrue to the member, not to the IMF.

Secretary Simon was willing to compromise with the French by allowing countries to revalue gold reserves at the market price, permit purchases and sales at market prices, and authorize countries to increase gold holdings above the level on May 1, 1975, if they wished. Burns opposed all three, especially removing the ceiling on a country's gold holdings. He quoted from the January 1975 statement by the IMF's Interim Committee stating the Fund's policy was to "ensure that the role of gold in the international monetary system would be gradually reduced" (ibid., 2). The aim was "to give the special drawing right the central place in the international monetary system" (Press Communiqué of the Interim Committee, Board Records, January 16, 1975, 1).

The first of Burns's two greatest concerns was that the proposal would increase the relative importance of gold as a monetary asset. "In fact, there are reasons for believing that the French . . . are seeking such an outcome" (memo, Burns to the president, Greenspan Files, Gerald R. Ford Library, Box 10, June 3, 1975, 3) The second was that a higher gold price and higher gold reserves would add up to $150 billion to the value of nominal reserves. "Liquidity creation of such extraordinary magnitude would seriously endanger, perhaps even frustrate, our efforts and those of other prudent nations to get inflation under reasonable control" (ibid., 4).[144]

Burns's memo did not carry the day. As usual in international dealings, the Treasury position prevailed. An August 1975 agreement by principal IMF members abolished the official price of gold and eliminated any requirement for using gold in transactions with the IMF. Also, the countries agreed that one-sixth of the Fund's gold holdings would be sold at auction to finance a transfer of wealth to developing countries, and an additional one-sixth would be returned to member countries in proportion to their quotas. Between 1976 and 1980, the Fund auctioned 25 million ounces and returned 25 million ounces to members (Schwartz, 1987b, 353). The new agreement expired in two years and was not renewed.

Congress repealed the 1934 prohibition on a citizen's private holdings of gold effective December 31, 1974. The law empowered the Treasury to offset any effect of private demand on the gold price by selling gold at auction. The Treasury auctioned gold in 1975, 1978, and 1979 (ibid., 353).

The agreements and actions during this period ended any remaining link between gold and money.[145] Countries were free to value gold at the price they chose and without regard to decisions by other countries. Gold no longer served as a numeraire for the monetary system. It was a com-

144. Burns assured the president that the United States would not be isolated on the issue. "I have a secret understanding in writing with the Bundesbank—concurred in by Mr. Schmidt—that Germany will not buy gold either from the market or from another government at a price above the official price of $42.22 per ounce" (memo, Burns to the president, Greenspan Files, Burns papers, Gerald R. Ford Library, Box 10, June 3, 1975, 6).

145. In 1975, the System ended reliance on gold certificates for interdistrict settlements. The new procedure used government securities to equalize approximately the average rate of gold holdings to note liabilities at each reserve bank.

modity with a historic past, a past that appealed to some. In the early 1980s, proponents of a link between the dollar and gold convinced the Reagan administration to establish a gold commission to examine the role of gold. It appointed Anna Schwartz as executive director. The Gold Commission report did not support a return to a gold-based currency.

I believe it is correct to say that we have not returned to a gold standard because we are familiar with its attributes, not because we are ignorant of its attributes. A gold standard puts great weight on the objectives of price stability and fixed exchange rates. Countries must be willing to accept the fluctuations in employment and output necessary to maintain long-term price stability. The public, the political system, and policymakers after World War II were more concerned with avoiding recessions. After 1980, when low inflation received increased weight in policymakers' objectives, a main argument for low inflation was that it encouraged long-term growth and employment. This argument gained support because the United States and much of the world had long expansions and relatively mild recessions in the twenty-five years after the 1979–82 disinflation.

### *Euro-dollars*

Partly as a consequence of regulation Q ceiling rates and partly to protect foreign governments and citizens from the threat of blocked accounts by U.S. government order, a market for interest-bearing deposits developed abroad. The market expanded rapidly first in Europe and then elsewhere. Most of the instruments traded in these markets were denominated in dollars, hence the name euro-dollar.

Growth of the market as an unregulated market was at first misunderstood. Some observers argued that the market permitted banks to avoid restrictive monetary policy. Some feared that the market would collapse, plunging the financial system into widespread default. Some, including members of the Board of Governors, wanted to subject euro-dollar deposits to high mandatory reserve requirement ratios.

In September 1979, the Board asked the members of the Federal Advisory Council whether major central banks should expand surveillance, regulation, and reserve and capital requirements for the euro-dollar market. FAC members showed better understanding than the governors. They issued a statement explaining that high legal reserve requirements do nothing to improve either the solvency or the survival prospects of individual institutions. Further, the FAC explained that the euro-market did not allow banks or other intermediaries to evade monetary policy actions. "So long as a central bank can regulate the monetary base and the size of its domestic commercial banking system, it has nominal GNP on its leash, and the dog will wag the nonbank-intermediary tail." There is no evidence that eurobank subsidiaries "or other financial intermediaries . . . permit any meaningful evasion of monetary restraint" (Board Minutes, Addendum, Federal Advisory Council, September 7, 1979, 4).

The Board did not attempt to close the euro-market by regulation. The market remains, but it is better understood as an efficient credit market.

### *Mexico*

The first of several financial crises in a Mexican election year came in 1976. Excessive fiscal and monetary expansion produced inflation and capital flight. Mexico delayed or limited exchange depreciation by drawing $360 million on its swap line with the Federal Reserve.

In the executive session to the November 16 FOMC meeting, Burns criticized the FOMC and the staff for asking too few questions and providing too little information about the Mexican financial position.[146] Mexico's position was "scandalous." They had no evidence that Mexico could service its debts. Nevertheless, he acceded to the Treasury by agreeing to share the cost of $150 million additional loan to Mexico. Burns explained participation as a way of preventing financial repercussions in the world financial system. A more plausible explanation was the desire to protect the liabilities of money market banks that had large loans to Mexico.

Mexico devalued the peso on August 31 and later repaid its loans by borrowing from the IMF. This was the first of four financial problems Mexico experienced at six-year (election) intervals. Volcker, who managed the 1982 crisis, forecast his approach at the 1976 meeting. He felt "very strongly" that "there is nothing we can walk away from, and we will be called upon from time to time for this kind of difficult operation" (FOMC minutes, executive session, November 16, 1976, 21–22). He compared the risk on the assistance to Mexico to the risk of a mismanaged situation and preferred to take the former.

### *Policy Actions 1976–78*

The years 1976–78 saw the return of higher inflation. The Federal Reserve let twelve-month growth of the monetary base rise from 5.7 to 9 percent

146. Burns overlooks the discussion in August 1976, when the FOMC voted to roll over the Mexican swap agreement. Coldwell objected, but Burns cited foreign policy concerns—politics—and Gardner added that the Federal Reserve would choose a different outcome but the Treasury was doing the negotiating (Burns papers, FOMC, August 17, 1976, tape 1, 4–6). Burns also failed to mention that he participated in the negotiation with Mexico. He described the negotiation at the time as requiring no action by the FOMC. "We [the Federal Reserve? the United States?] are no worse off and we may be significantly better off" (Burns papers, FOMC, September 2, 1976, tape 1, 8).

during these years. FOMC members recognized some of the main problems. Although the Committee discussed the control problem, very little changed.

Monetary control was not the only problem. At the start of the period, the staff forecast productivity growth at 3 percent per annum and suggested that it might be higher. In fact, it was much lower, adding to the inflationary pressure (Burns papers, FOMC, March 15–16, 1976, 35). At the April meeting, Wallich questioned the staff forecast for interest rates on the grounds that the staff did not take account of expectations. Gramley acknowledged that they did not (ibid., April 20, 1976, tape 2, 3). In January, Gramley warned that "forecasters should not give a great deal of weight to the statistics for a single month (FOMC Minutes, January 18, 1976, 46). The Committee ignored the advice.

The Committee disliked policy reversals. A New York staff study found seven or nine periods when it had to reverse a change in reserve availability or the funds rate during 1973–76. Holmes noted that most of the changes were small. Only two reversals had a market impact (ibid., 46).

Burns expressed concern and stressed the importance of avoiding reversals and financial market disturbances. Reluctance to risk policy reversals was another reason for responding slowly to conditions in the economy. President Mayo (Chicago) made a different proposal. Tight control of the funds rate caused exaggerated market reaction to small changes. He suggested wider fluctuations as a way of avoiding market overreaction to changes (ibid., 55). Coldwell agreed but no others took up the point. And no one proposed to reduce uncertainty by announcing the rate. But President Eastburn (Philadelphia) urged a narrow range for the money target and, as a consequence, more variability in the funds rate (ibid., 69).

The discussion at this meeting shows that several of the members understood a main reason they did not hit money growth targets came from the unwillingness to let the funds rate change. Unfortunately, there was never a consensus for change, particularly in 1976, when the inflation rate had fallen. Persistence then would have ended the inflation, probably at much lower social cost. At the April meeting, Henry Wallich urged a more restrictive policy to slow the expansion and further reduce inflation. Balles, Guffey, and Gardner offered similar or supporting statements. Volcker remarked he was "worried about the inflation thing" (Burns papers, April 20, 1976, tape 7, 10). The FOMC voted unanimously for a small reduction in the federal funds rate—from a midpoint of 5 to 4.875 percent.

Money growth continued to rise. At the May meeting, Burns described the growth rate as "unacceptable" (ibid., May 18, 1976, tape 6, 1). He proposed lowering the bottom of the $M_1$ range to 3.5 percent (up to 7.5) but received no support. Even though Volcker, Wallich, and MacLaury agreed about inflation, they treated Burns's proposals as too low. With Coldwell dissenting, the FOMC voted for a 4 to 7.5 percent range for $M_1$ growth.[147] The 0.5 percent difference suggests how much rhetoric differed from decisions.

In 1976, prospects for reducing inflation had improved. By the end of 1975, the trade-weighted dollar had appreciated to a point above its March 1973 value, but the dollar had depreciated relative to the mark and the yen.[148] This pattern continued through the next two years. Reported inflation and the unemployment rate both declined. By late 1976, consumer prices increased less than 5 percent a year. Disinflation was clearly visible in the data (see Chart 7.1 above).

The Federal Reserve and the Treasury took advantage of the appreciation to agree on a three-year repayment of the debt incurred to the Swiss National Bank, mainly in 1971. Of the $1.6 billion in borrowings at the time (including the BIS), $1.15 billion remained. This sum included $196 million to compensate for devaluation of the dollar (Annual Report, 1976, 280 n. 2). The United States and Switzerland agreed to repayment over a three-year period.[149]

With the change in administration in 1977, United States policy toward coordination changed completely. The new officials accepted an analysis by Professor Lawrence Klein, presented at an economic conference in 1976. Klein wanted increased fiscal stimulus to reduce unemployment. To avoid the capital outflow resulting from the increased spending, he proposed

147. At the May meeting, Partee accused Peter Sternlight of following an even keel policy during the Treasury financing. Sternlight concurred with Burns's description of a semi-even keel (Burns papers, FOMC, May 18, 1976, tape, 5, 2).

148. The staff reported that the dollar appreciated sharply against the British pound and the Italian lira, both countries with high and rising inflation (see Table 7.13 above). Early in June 1976 the Federal Reserve and the Treasury contributed $2 billion to a $5.3 billion pool of standby credits for the Bank of England.

149. Another example of policy attitudes at the time showed the aversion in many countries to tightening monetary policy or policy coordination. "It was suggested by a representative of [the OECD] secretariat that countries should coordinate their monetary policies with weaker countries taking the lead in tightening (raising interest rates) in order to avoid exchange market disturbances. This suggestion received little support. The representatives of Belgium and Sweden expressed concern about a tightening of German monetary policy. . . . The Swiss, Germans, and Americans generally indicated that they would follow appropriate monetary policies and coordination was unnecessary" (Report on Meeting of Working Party Three, Board Records, May 25, 1976, 7).

A problem arose in settling swap borrowings from Belgium. Devaluation of the dollar raised an issue about sharing the loss on the borrowing. The Treasury insisted on sharing the loss with Belgium; the Belgians insisted that the U.S. bear the loss. Holmes wanted to compromise by accepting most of the $14 million loss, but the Treasury was unwilling. The contract, however, favored the Belgians (Alan Holmes, notes, 1975, New York Federal Reserve, Box 007973 FOMC).

that West Germany and Japan, the principal surplus countries, should expand in coordinated step with the United States. The three countries would provide a "locomotive" that expanded world aggregate demand and raised incomes and output in other countries.[150] Reports done at the IMF and even the Bank for International Settlements supported this approach (Volcker and Gyohten, 1992, 147). It did not appeal to the strong-minded Helmut Schmidt, West Germany's chancellor. Schmidt saw the inflationary consequences and forcefully pointed them out to the Americans. Japan, as usual, hesitated but did not reject the proposal completely. However, increased expansion and higher inflation in the United States increased net imports. As Japan's current account surplus rose, criticism of Japan became shrill (Volcker and Gyohten, 1992, 154). At the London summit in May 1977, Japan agreed informally to achieve 6.7 percent growth. It reached only 5.4 percent, well above the average for G-7 countries but below the informal target. The Japanese government committed to 7 percent growth in 1978, but again fell short.

From September 1977 to October 1978, the West German mark, Swiss franc, and Japanese yen appreciated by about 11, 35, and 29 percent. Germany, Japan, and others strongly criticized United States policy, especially the failure to let energy prices rise to market levels and neglect of dollar depreciation.[151] Many foreigners charged that Treasury Secretary Michael Blumenthal "talked down" the dollar. They saw this as competitive devaluation.[152]

At a BIS meeting in January 1978, "Burns said developments in the exchange markets have been a source of considerable anxiety—even anguish—to all of us" (memo, Margaret Greene to FOMC, Board Records, January 9, 1978, 3). He expressed concern about the effect of dollar depreciation on foreign economies, and he told the members that the very recent increase in the discount rate was "governed entirely by international considerations" (ibid.). Most of the members praised Burns's efforts. Markets were more skeptical; the mark resumed appreciation.

150. Lawrence Klein, a prominent Keynesian economist, served as principal adviser to Governor Carter during the 1976 election campaign. He did not join the administration. A common complaint at the time was the variability of exchange rates. Taylor (2000, 14–15) showed the large increase in variability of nominal and real exchange rates compared to Bretton Woods. Real and nominal exchange rate variability were highly correlated.

151. A sixteen page memo summarizing a conference in May by representatives of the G-7 contains very little about United States' energy policy (macroeconomic assessment, Schultze papers, May 21, 1978).

152. Solomon (1982, 346) suggests that President Carter discussed dollar depreciation with King Khalid of Saudi Arabia. Shortly after his return from the Middle East, the Treasury announced an active effort to stabilize the exchange rate.

Wrangling and recriminations ended in an agreement at the Bonn summit in July 1978.[153] Germany and Japan announced that they would reduce tax rates to raise their GDP growth rates. They joined the locomotive. The United States agreed to control inflation and raise oil prices to international levels by late 1980. When he made the commitment, President Carter did not know how he would implement it. The main problem was political; so-called consumer groups opposed allowing the price to rise. "What Carter intended to promise at Bonn was not completely decided at the time he departed from Washington" (Biven, 2002, 160). A main problem was getting agreement with the Senate to tax oil, especially old oil to prevent oil companies from receiving windfall profits. Domestic advisers urged him to withdraw his promise. International advisers urged him to keep it.

He kept it. In April 1979, nine months after he made the commitment, President Carter announced a phased decontrol of oil prices over twenty-eight months beginning June 1. He asked Congress to tax windfall profits, but he did not make decontrol depend on the tax. A year later, in April 1980, he signed the tax bill.

The July decisions at the Bonn summit are often said to represent the high point of traditional Keynesian policy and policy coordination. Germany and Japan agreed to coordinate fiscal expansion and implemented the agreements. Decontrol of United States oil prices was a main achievement. Pressure from other countries facilitated the decision and advanced its timing.

The effects of fiscal expansion are difficult to separate from monetary changes at home and abroad and the second major oil shock at the end of 1978. In the United States, after a slow start in 1979, real GNP rose at a 3.7 percent rate in the third quarter, then fell (−0.8) in the fourth quarter following the start of the Volcker disinflation. In Germany, the Bonn agreement came just as the European Monetary System (EMS) required monetary policy to give greater attention to European exchange rates. Also, the Bundesbank shifted its announcement of the monetary growth rate from annual average to a four-quarter growth rate and reduced the announced growth rate. Bundesbank actions pressed other EMS countries to reduce inflation.[154]

153. President Carter would not commit to attend the Bonn G-7 summit until Germany agreed to raise its growth target and adopt a more stimulative fiscal policy. The contrast between the United States' emphasis on growth and Germany's concern about inflation tells much about the difference in priorities and in outcomes in this period.

154. Beginning in September, the FOMC began discussion of the terms for renewing its swaps with the Bundesbank. The Germans wanted to end the equal sharing of exchange rate losses. They offered, instead, to receive interest on the outstanding balance at the (lower) German interest rate.

Coordinated policy did not avoid exchange rate adjustment. Between May and October 1978, the dollar depreciated by 14 percent against the mark and 23 percent against the yen. From the start of the year to late October, the trade-weighted dollar lost nearly 25 percent of its value. The reported inflation rate approached 9 percent. Foreigners again accused the United States of talking down the dollar's value. Domestic critics reinforced these criticisms. This encouraged policy changes, especially after the G-10 dollar index fell nearly 4 percent in less than four weeks ending October 24.

The administration's approach reveals its thinking. On October 24, it announced policy changes intended to strengthen the exchange rate. The three principal changes were fiscal actions to slow aggregate demand, voluntary wage and price standards, and regulatory reform to increase efficiency and competition (Solomon, 1982, 349). President Carter said that monetary policy would be "responsible," but he gave no indication that the Federal Reserve would adjust its actions or give priority to lowering inflation.

Market reaction was swift and decisive. The day following the policy announcement the dollar fell about 1.7 percent against the mark and the yen. In the week ending October 20, the G-10 index fell another 4 percent. A new program began to take shape. This time, monetary and financial change had a major role. The Federal Reserve and the Treasury increased swap lines by $15 billion. The Treasury announced sales of $10 billion in foreign-denominated bonds with up to five years maturity, borrowed $3 billion from the IMF, and increased monthly gold sales.[155] The Federal Reserve raised the discount rate by one percentage point to 9.5 percent and put a supplementary reserve requirement of two percentage points on large time deposits. The dollar index rose 5.3 percent and this time it continued to rise. By November 20, the index was back to its level in early September.

Solomon (1982, 350) wrote that the November 1 program persuaded market participants, foreign governments, and others that "the U.S. monetary authorities were serious about defending the dollar."[156] To reinforce

155. Germany especially preferred sales of foreign-denominated bonds over swaps when the swaps were used to buy dollars. Swaps increased the German money stock but the sale of foreign bonds did not.

156. Toyoo Gyohten (Volcker and Gyohten, 1992, 159) called it a "big success," citing the depreciation of the yen from 176 to 200. An OECD meeting on November 30 was more critical. Foreign governments praised the change in the U.S. attitude toward dollar depreciation. The foreign members asked why it had taken the United States so long to act and expressed skepticism about whether exchange rate intervention would continue, particularly if the domestic economy slowed (memo, Edwin Truman to FOMC, Board Records, November 30, 1978, 1–2). At the November FOMC meeting, Scott Pardee (the manager) reported that the account sold $4.6 billion between the October and November meetings. $1.1 billion was for

**Table 7.15** Exchange Rate and Consumer Prices, Selected Dates, June 1976–October 1978

| DATE | FEDERAL RESERVE TRADE-WEIGHTED EXCHANGE RATE | CUMULATIVE CHANGE PERCENT | CPI | PERCENT |
|---|---|---|---|---|
| june 1976 | 107.05 | | 170.1 | |
| June 1977 | 104.35 | −2.5 | 181.8 | 6.8 |
| January 1978 | 96.73 | −9.6 | 187.2 | 10.0 |
| June 1978 | 94.74 | −11.5 | 195.3 | 14.8 |
| October 1978 | 86.64 | −19.1 | 200.9 | 18.1 |

Source: Exchange rate, Board of Governors (1981, 441).

this view, the authorities bought $6.7 billion in November and December by selling marks, Swiss francs, and yen. The Treasury issued $1.6 billion in mark-denominated bonds.

President Carter had been skeptical earlier about his advisers' recommendations to control inflation without reducing money growth and aggregate demand. The October–November experience demonstrated that outsiders would not regard an anti-inflation or exchange rate policy as credible if it relied mainly on wage-price guidelines. These policies had failed in too many countries, including the United States, too many times. We can not know what President Carter thought, but we know that in less than a year he appointed Paul Volcker to chair the Board of Governors after being told that Volcker intended to reduce money growth and raise interest rates.

The 1978 experience showed that a floating exchange rate could in principle permit the United States to pursue a strictly domestic policy with "benign neglect" of the exchange rate. Politically it had less chance despite the fact that almost all of the dollar depreciation during the period was a change in the nominal value that differed little from the price change during the same period. Table 7.15 compares the decline in the Federal Reserve's trade-weighted index from its local peak, June 1976, to October 1978 to the change in the consumer price index. The table suggests that domestic inflation played a major role in dollar depreciation; the real exchange rate changed little. The table also shows the sizeable nominal depreciation in 1978 that alarmed the Europeans.

Some of the concern may simply have reflected myopic failure to distinguish between real and nominal changes. All rates did not change together; in particular the mark appreciated approximately 28 percent in nominal terms during this period, so the Germans could (and did) complain about real appreciation, although Germany also experienced infla-

the Treasury. Most of the sales, $3.5 billion, came after the November 1 policy announcement. Pardee was exultant about the program's success.

tion. The 1976–78 experience showed that, while floating exchange rates increased freedom of action for limited policy changes, large dollar depreciation forced the administration to respond to the exchange rate for political reasons. Indexed, the November rescue package was larger in size than anything done during the Bretton Woods era to respond to international pressures.[157]

### *The Bank for International Settlements (BIS)*

One sign of increased concern about the international effects of central bank policies was the decision to become a member of the BIS. The United States played a major role in establishing the BIS in the 1930s, but it elected not to become a member or to purchase shares. It held observer status.

At the start, the New York Federal Reserve bank furnished the observer, but Congress stripped that power from the New York bank in 1935 and gave it to the Board. The Board discussed joining several times but did not act until the mid-1970s. In a letter to the general counsel of the BIS, the Board's staff inquired about liability of directors under Swiss corporate law and BIS regulations. And it questioned whether BIS statutes had to be amended to take account of the structure of the Federal Reserve. The Board was not a bank, as specified in the statute; the monetary authority was the System, not the Board; and the operating head was the chairman of the Board of Governors, not the president of a Reserve bank (letter, Theodore Allum to F. E. Klein, Gerald R. Ford Library, February 12, 1976).

When these and other technicalities were resolved, Chairman Burns became the U.S. representative. Henry Wallich became his alternate and usually attended the meetings.

## CONTROLLING MONEY AND FURNISHING INFORMATION

During 1976 to 1978 the monthly unemployment rate remained between 6 and 8 percent, and the twelve-month average rate of consumer price inflation ranged from 5 to 8.5 percent.[158] Many regarded this performance

157. The November 1 Federal Reserve action was a more decisive step, but it was not the only departure from "benign neglect" of exchange rates. For example at the January 17–18, 1977, meeting, the FOMC voted unanimously to lend up to $1.5 billion of foreign currencies to the Exchange Stabilization Fund for periods as long as twelve months. To get around the prohibition on direct loans to the Treasury, the action was again called "warehousing." Subject to review each year, the warehousing did not have a terminal date. Also, in December 1977, the FOMC responded to the relatively sharp dollar depreciation by authorizing the account manager to take account of "unsettled conditions in foreign exchange markets" in his operations (Annual Report, 1977, 321).

158. These are two months below 5 percent inflation at the end of 1976. Between December 1976 and December 1978, CPI inflation rose from 4.7 to 8.6 percent.

as poor. Among the critics, some wanted price and wage controls, some urged a return to the gold standard, and some called for control of money growth. The last group, called monetarists, presented an alternative analytic framework and criticized the Federal Reserve's procedures. Perhaps the most important technical criticisms were that the Federal Reserve misinterpreted its own policy actions by identifying changes in market interest rates with adjustments to the stance of monetary policy. It interpreted a decline in market interest rates as evidence of monetary ease even if growth of money and credit declined. And it interpreted an increase in interest rates as restrictive even if money growth rose. Also, the Federal Reserve routinely used market or nominal interest rates, instead of real rates, as its indicator of ease and restraint.

Gradually, poor or unsatisfactory outcomes and monetarist criticisms encouraged congressional action intended to give more attention to growth of the monetary aggregates. Unfortunately, the discussion almost always presented control of market interest rates and money growth as alternatives. There was no reason why the Federal Reserve could not eliminate its procyclical actions by adjusting the interest rate to reflect the maintained path of the monetary aggregates. In fact, the FOMC's introduction of proviso clauses specifying some measure of reserves or money growth were steps in that direction beginning in the early 1970s. The clause added a proviso that called for a change in the federal funds rate if money growth was deficient or excessive. One problem was that the account manager or the chairman was reluctant to raise interest rates when money growth or reserves exceeded the proviso clause out of concern about an increase in unemployment. This reflected beliefs about public and congressional attitudes, interpretations of the Employment Act, and the perceived relative social costs of unemployment and inflation.

FOMC members disliked congressional interest in its operations, procedures, and actions, but formally the Federal Reserve is the agent of Congress. Congress could change the Federal Reserve Act if it chose to do so. Heightened congressional interest aroused Federal Reserve concerns. Many of these concerns reflected the belief that the System was a guardian of the currency while members of Congress included (many) inflationary populists. Members did not say on the record that their failed policies and poor performance brought on increased congressional scrutiny and demands for increased oversight. And attempts to control inflation by raising real interest rates also brought the criticism that housing starts declined.

*Early Stirrings*

One pressure called on the Federal Reserve to release more information in a timely manner. Several issues about release of information had a long history in the tradition of central bank secrecy. Should the reserve banks share information about discount rate changes? How much information should directors be given when they voted on discount rates? What should the Board release to the public?[159] In 1971, a committee of presidents reconsidered these and other issues as part of the decision to make discount policy more flexible.

The committee proposed regular discussion of discount rate policy at FOMC meetings and at the regular meetings of the Conference of Presidents. The presidents requested notification from the Board when it approved a discount rate change at one of the banks. And they asked to receive notice of the Board's policy actions before they were released to the press and public. The committee also suggested changes in interbank exchange of information. It proposed that each reserve bank notify the Board and all other banks about the views of its board of directors on the discount rate and other policies.

On the difficult issue of information given to directors about Federal Reserve policy, the presidents proposed "some very general indication of the current monetary position of the FOMC, particularly on the occasion of a change in the direction of policy" (memo, Committee on Discounts and Credits to Conference of Presidents, Burns papers, BB25, February 5, 1971, 4). It called on the FOMC to issue guidelines. It permitted presidents to inform the board chair, in strict confidence, of Board decisions about discount rate changes at other banks "when it would appear such action is imminent" (ibid., 6). But other members would not be told except as to the "general nature of the situation in order that they may make a fully considered judgment" about discount policy action (ibid.).

The Board staff accepted most of the presidents' suggestions. It prepared a letter outlining what presidents could tell their boards about Federal Reserve actions (memo, Robert Holland to Burns, Burns papers, February 5, 1971).

Further stimulus to change in communications came after passage of legislation including the Freedom of Information and Government in the

159. The decision about whether the Board or the reserve banks announced discount rate changes was contentious in the 1920s. The Board asserted responsibility because changes became effective only if approved by the Board.

Sunshine Acts. Following the Freedom of Information Act, a student (Merrill) sued the Federal Reserve to release current information. The Merrill case (discussed below) forced the Federal Reserve to give more thought both to what the laws required and what legitimate reasons it had to withhold information about its actions to protect its ability to operate effectively.

### *Monetary Targets*

In spring 1975, Congress made a first attempt to instruct the System on ways to improve the conduct of policy. House Concurrent Resolution 133 proposed three major changes: (1) the Federal Reserve was to set a twelve-month target for money growth and announce it publicly; (2) it was instructed to maintain long-run growth of the monetary and credit aggregates commensurate with the economy's long-run potential to increase production; and (3) Congress increased its oversight by requiring the Board of Governors to report to Congress semiannually at open hearings before the banking committees.

Two correct implications of the resolution were that the Federal Reserve gave too much weight to current developments and too little to the longer-term consequences of its actions. And it neglected the role of money growth and the evidence that sustained inflation resulted from a sustained excess of money growth over real output growth. But the resolution recognized that, in an uncertain world, the Federal Reserve might wish to change its money target and report the reason for the change at the next semiannual hearing.

Two memos, one from the Philadelphia Reserve Bank and the other from the Board staff, took constructive positions on the proposed changes in procedures and response to the Congress. Philadelphia's memo described the resolution as "a useful affirmation on the part of Congress of the importance of long-term targets and the role of Congress as an overseer of the basic objectives and overall implementation of monetary-policy" (memos, David Eastburn to FOMC, Board Records, April 4, 1975, 1).[160] Although Philadelphia criticized specific details in the resolution, it urged the FOMC to "clarify its targets for the Congress and to assist in developing a framework for holding the Fed accountable in hitting its targets" (ibid., 6). The FOMC did not accept this suggestion, and it did not limit its reporting mainly to $M_1$ and $M_2$.[161]

160. Later in the memo, Philadelphia accepted a key criticism. "Congress expects the Committee to lengthen its horizon for monetary policy planning" (memo, Eastburn to FOMC, Board Records, April 4, 1975, 8).

161. Philadelphia warned that "introducing too many aggregates may appear as an evasive tactic . . . to avoid accountability" (memo, Eastburn to FOMC, Board Records, April 4,

The FOMC's Subcommittee on the Directive proposed introducing a new paragraph into the directive giving four-quarter ranges for growth of the monetary aggregates. In a separate paragraph, it would continue to state the federal funds rate target and the short-term money growth rates approved by the Committee. However, the subcommittee did not propose any means of achieving the longer-term money target, reconciling the short- and long-term targets, adjusting to target misses, or even reconciling the short-term targets for monetary aggregates and the federal funds rate. And, most importantly, it did not discuss whether the longer-term target to reduce inflation would cause a larger temporary increase in the unemployment rate than the FOMC was prepared to accept.

The St. Louis Federal Reserve bank strongly favored increased emphasis on monetary growth and longer-term policy, but it expressed concern about the compatibility of fiscal and monetary policies and market interest rates. In a letter to the Board and an article in its Review, St. Louis noted that the proposed $M_1$ growth rate would require the administration to finance a much larger share of its current deficit in the market. "Our desire is to make it clear that the achievement of the target growth in the monetary aggregates will not be easy, but clearly desirable. We feel strongly that outside pressures on the System will build for us to monetize more debt in an effort to hold down the inevitable rises in short rates and we want, in this rather hypothetical way, to illustrate the implications of such actions" (letter Jerry L. Jordan to Arthur Broida, Board Records, July 23, 1975).

Arthur Burns's testimony before the Senate Banking Committee tried to weaken Resolution 133 without much success.[162] The resolution passed. There is little evidence that it affected the FOMC's actual performance. It did increase oversight and information about monetary policy by introducing quarterly statements by the chairman at congressional hearings.

At about the same time, Congress approved the Government in the Sunshine Act. The Board tried to be exempt but did not fully succeed. Most policy meetings including FOMC meetings remained closed, but the FOMC voted to make reports of its meetings available to the public forty-five days after the meeting. Very slowly, it reduced the lag over subsequent decades. The release of information and summaries of policy discussion were additional steps from traditional central bank secrecy to greater transparency. The burgeoning academic literature following Kydland and Prescott (1977)

---

1975, 7). Contrast the Board staff's memo that proposed six measures of money growth (memo, staff to FOMC, Board Records, April 10, 1975, 5).

162. This sentence is based on conversation with the late Robert Weintraub, a senior staff member of the committee and a proponent and architect of Resolution 133.

greatly encouraged this development by making more explicit the advantages to society from pre-announced rule-like monetary policy procedures. That came later.

### *The Merrill Case*

In 1975–76, the Board had to explain to the federal courts why it kept its directives secret. In March 1975 a Georgetown University law student, David R. Merrill, filed a request under the Freedom of Information Act (FOIA) asking that the Board release the minutes (memoranda of discussion) of its January and February 1975 meetings.[163] Merrill claimed that FOIA required prompt release of the minutes, not the five-year delay that the Board had established. The Board turned down the request. Merrill sued, asking for release of the minutes and publication of the directive within a day of the meeting.

The Board's response to the court was a mishmash of poor or wrong arguments. We cannot know that the lawyers and economists who made these arguments believed them; possibly they were the best arguments they could muster to support the secrecy policy. And since the System maintained the policy for many years, it may have believed that at least some of the arguments were more right than wrong.[164]

Most of the information in the minutes about the economy was available. Release of minutes would show some members' interpretation of incoming data and their expressed concerns. New information would include differences of opinion and emphasis as well as the often very small differences about interest rates and money growth rates. Also, it would announce the target federal funds rate and associated growth rates of money and bank credit that the FOMC instructed the manager to achieve. Congressional hearings announced annual targets, so these were available. However, when the manager changed the market federal funds rate as specified by the FOMC, the market observed the change. Rare errors aside, anyone observing the market rate would know the target. Although it was not announced, it was not secret for more than a day.

According to Goodfriend's (1986) summary, the Board and its staff used

163. Discussion of the Merrill case is based mainly on Goodfriend (1986). At the time, Goodfriend was an economist and vice president of the Richmond Federal Reserve. His public discussion of the secrecy issue and the Board's arguments in the Merrill case produced a severe backlash from several of the Board's senior staff, but, to his credit, Goodfriend persisted and published the paper.

164. Of course, it is possible that the System maintained secrecy for reasons it was unwilling to state publicly. Cukierman and Meltzer (1986) and Cukierman (1992) argued in a rational expectation framework that the System used secrecy to surprise the public when it wanted to increase output or slow inflation.

six arguments to defend secrecy. It added a seventh after the district and circuit courts found for Merrill.[165] First, earlier disclosure interfered with orderly policy execution. Second, it permitted speculators to gain at the expense of others. Third, it would introduce additional disturbances in the markets; uncertainty would increase. Fourth, the cost of open market operations would increase. Fifth, orderly execution of market operations for other government agencies would become more costly or difficult. Sixth, it would impair the effectiveness of operations acting as agent for foreign banks and governments.

An internal staff memo gave the same arguments about speculative dangers and precipitate, disruptive responses. It claimed that uncertainty increased policy effectiveness because it made market participants cautious and prevented "precipitous" responses. And it ended with a warning. "If the FOMC is required to publish its Domestic Policy Directive at the beginning of the period to which it applies, its ability to discharge effectively its statutory responsibilities to carry out monetary policy in the national interest may be significantly impaired (memo, Board staff to FOMC, Board Records, April 10, 1978). A subsequent study by Donald Kohn of the Board's staff summarized the empirical evidence. It concluded that a 10 percent increase in interest rate volatility would increase the difference between bid and asked yields on Treasury bills by one basis point (0.01 percentage points) (memo, Kohn to Arthur Broida, Board Records, July 13, 1978).

When the Board appealed to the Supreme Court, it added that when acting on its account or as agent for the Treasury, transparency would cause commercial harm because the directive authorized buying and selling transactions and so did the instructions from the Treasury. Commercial harm was explicitly mentioned as a reason for secrecy under FOIA, so the Supreme Court in 1981 reversed the decision and found for Federal Reserve secrecy.

Burns's initial reaction to the district court's order favored releasing the directive information after a delay. The court order held unlawful the forty-five-day lag between a decision and its publication. It ordered prompt publication of the directive in the Federal Register. Also, it ordered prompt release of the "reasonably segregable positions" of the memorandum of discussion (minutes). Burns opened the February 17 meeting by recommending that, if the court order applied only to the domestic policy directive, the Committee could "comply with the spirit as well as the letter of the order and make public at the same time the short-run ranges of tolerance

165. I list the arguments in the text; Goodfriend (1986, 69–83) presented the Board's case more fully and offered a careful critique. He, too, found little merit in the Board's case.

adopted for the aggregates and for the Federal funds rate" (FOMC Minutes, February 17, 1976, 2). He favored asking Congress for authority to delay release of the directive for up to forty-five days, and proposed that a subcommittee, chaired by Governor Coldwell, reconsider the information included in the minutes. The members agreed.

Burns did not seek to release the targets for federal funds and money growth promptly. Instead, the Board's appeal asked the Circuit Court to reinstate the forty-five-day delay. Thomas O'Connell, the Board's counsel, opined that the district court had "simply pronounced what the law said" and would be upheld on appeal (FOMC Minutes, March 15–16, 1976, 5). O'Connell believed that annual money growth rates were "understandings, objectives, or goals" and did not have to be published on the same basis as the directive (ibid., 7). The Board's affidavit also asked to exempt confidential information received from foreign governments.

The "reasonably segregable positions" referred to "facts." The Board's appeal concerned mainly matters other than this material. Disagreement arose about what was "fact," but Burns's main concern was that released material would get to Congress. They would ask for supporting material, memos, and additional reports.[166]

Discussion of alternatives to releasing the directive promptly continued in 1976 and 1977. As O'Connell predicted, the Federal Reserve lost on its appeal at the Circuit Court. Much of the December 1977 meeting considered available options if the Merrill opinion prevailed at the Supreme Court and if Congress put the Federal Reserve under the Government in the Sunshine Act. Burns proposed asking Congress to legislate relief by excluding bank examination reports from coverage.

A subcommittee chaired by Governor Partee discussed changing the directive that the Committee wrote for the manager by giving the manager more discretion, replacing quantitative with qualitative information, and widening the ranges for the federal funds rate and money growth rate. The range for the funds rate would be one percentage point, but the subcommittee proposed an inside range of one-half percentage point for desk operations. This was a modest change. The transcript would omit the names and dissents of individual members. These would remain in the Annual Report, as before.

The subcommittee proposed to make few changes in the directive. In part, they did not want to avoid the finding of the court (ibid., tape 1, 17). The main proposal called for instructing the manager to adjust to chang-

166. Burns did not hold Congress members in high regard. "It's a talking committee and that would cause some mischief" (FOMC Minutes, Executive Session, March 29, 1976, 15).

ing financial conditions following early release of the FOMC record. This would "establish a degree of looseness between the specification of the manager's actions" and his performance. The purpose was to "provide an uncertainty in the markets mind" (ibid., tape 1, 18).

Concern about the release of information led to a discussion of procedures, one of the very few ever held. President Roos (St. Louis) called this a "revolutionary change in procedure" (Burns papers, FOMC, December 19, 1977, tape 2, 17). Henry Wallich proposed that the Committee should test its procedures to see if the range set for the federal funds rate was consistent with control of the monetary aggregates (ibid., tape 3, 1–2). Wallich doubted they would agree to widen the proposed range enough to make the two compatible. President Balles (San Francisco) spoke in favor of a target for the aggregates; Burns agreed that this was technically right but politically wrong. Congress would respond to increases in interest rates "just the way it had been doing" (ibid., tape 2, 16).

The discussion did not reach a consensus, in part because it concerned the FOMC's response if it lost the Merrill decision in the Supreme Court. It showed, however, that members were aware both of the reasons they did not succeed in controlling the aggregates and the importance of control of aggregates for inflation control. And Burns gave the reason; either he was not willing or did not feel able to assert Federal Reserve independence as a response to congressional complaints.[167]

After much further discussion, the Federal Reserve in 1994 began to publicly announce its federal funds target and other information at the end of each meeting. Some central banks began earlier. None of the alleged harmful consequences occurred. Some evidence suggests that markets are less volatile. For example, long-term interest rates changed very little in 2004–5, when the Federal Reserve increased the federal funds rate from 1 to more than 4 percent. A main reason was that its actions and talk convinced the market that the target funds rate would likely rise by 0.25 percentage points at each FOMC meeting. Long-term rates appear to have incorporated the anticipated path, so they did not react to each separate announcement.

### *New Procedures*

Aroused by the Merrill case, general congressional concern about excessive secrecy by the administration and the agencies, or specific concerns about

167. Unemployment was a political concern also. Later in the December meeting, Roos described the goals of monetary policy as maintaining economic growth and keeping unemployment at a reasonably low level. Burns responded that it was not the overall unemployment total but concentration among certain groups in the population. He then spoke about race and cultures (Burns papers, FOMC, December 19, 1977, tape 5, 19).

economic policy, the Federal Reserve renewed attention to the directive and release of information in 1976. Coldwell's subcommittee expressed concern about the ability to conduct monetary policy, if the court required prompt release of the memoranda of discussion (minutes). It proposed to use summaries of the discussion in place of actual statements and eliminate exchanges of views.

Burns moved to change procedures more radically. Both the Board and the FOMC had kept minutes of each meeting; for the FOMC the minutes started when the FOMC became an official entity under the 1935 Banking Act. Burns proposed to end the transcripts or minutes after the March 15, 1976, FOMC meeting and substantially increase the length of the policy record released after forty-five days and included in the Annual Report. The report would include views of individual members, but they would no longer be identified. They would continue to record dissents, and members would retain the right to give their reasons and identify themselves (FOMC Minutes, Executive Session, March 29, 1976, tape 1).[168]

Both banking committee chairmen objected strongly. Burns insisted that the minutes were used very little and that the only objections to the proposed change came from the two banking committee chairmen. Burns's major concern was that a future court might expand the information required to be released and thus become available to Congress.

The FOMC supported Burns and agreed in April to discontinue the memo of discussion (called Minutes here), expand the policy record, and release the record including the directive shortly after the next FOMC meeting instead of after forty-five days (FOMC Minutes, May 1976 tape 1). The vote in May to make this change was ten to one; Coldwell abstained because the decision reduced available information, and Holland did not participate. But Burns argued that the longer policy record increased the information available to historians.[169]

Under the new procedure, the FOMC secretariat would continue to

168. We relied on material from the Burns papers at the University of Michigan, hence the references to tapes for 1976 to February 1978. The Burns papers include transcripts for 1976 to February 1978 that did not become available until after there was a draft of this chapter. We appreciate the help we received from the Board staff in later providing the redacted transcripts.

169. Burns reopened discussion of the decision to eliminate the memo of discussion and took a new vote. The result did not change. Governor Wallich suggested that the policy record include names, but Burns objected and did not take a vote. The meeting also discussed a suit by Congressman Reuss claiming damages for losses he incurred because reserve bank presidents voted on FOMC policies but were not appointed by the president and confirmed by the Senate. Legal counsel said he expected the court would dismiss the suit because Reuss lacked standing. He was correct. During the discussion, Burns claimed Reuss should thank the FOMC for keeping inflation from rising more rapidly.

record and circulate the discussion transcript taken at the meeting as before. Members could correct the record. The intention was that the revised minutes would furnish the basis of the expanded record of policy action and then be discarded. They were not discarded, however. At a subsequent congressional hearing in 1993, the existence of the stored archives became known. Federal Reserve officials admitted the truth, although a congressional staff member, Robert Auerbach, claimed the opposite (Auerbach, 2006); Board staff cited the record, showing that no denials occurred. The FOMC resumed publication after 1993, with a five-year lag, and began editing the material for the years (working backward) from the 1980s to 1976 that had been stored but not published. Historians owe a debt to the House Banking Committee for opening the archives for these historically important years and restoring the prior procedure.

Discussion of the proposal at the May 1976 meeting kept sunshine legislation in the background though it was clearly the main force for change. Thomas O'Connell, the Board's counsel, expected that the sunshine legislation would not apply to the Federal Reserve. Burns urged members not to discuss applicability of the legislation to reduce the risk that Congress would remove the "ambiguity" in the legislation, on which the Board believed its exemption rested (Burns papers, May 18, 1976, tape 1, 4).

Practice changed less than the discussion suggests. The manager continued to give primary attention to control of the federal funds rate. This was explicit when the manager described his operations. "Incoming data on, and projections of the aggregates are compared with the [FOMC's] ranges each week to determine the Desk's posture with respect to reserve provision and the federal funds rate. The Manager's response to undesired behavior is constrained by a range of permissible variation in the weekly average federal funds rate" (Holmes, 1976, 413).

Burns proposed setting 4 percent bands for money growth rates and an inside (say) 2 percent band that he called a "zone of indifference." The manager could ignore money growth rates in the zone of indifference but was to respond outside the band. Burns hoped in this way to allow for the imprecision of the money growth estimates and their short-run variability (Burns papers, FOMC, February 17, 1976, 9–13).[170] The FOMC referred to the "range of indifference" at a few subsequent meetings. Within a few months, it disappeared from the discussion. FOMC members did not agree on the appropriate size of the range or how to use it.

170. The FOMC based the wide range chosen for the money growth rates on staff work reporting on thirty different seasonal adjustment techniques. They suggested a range of uncertainty about the "true" seasonally adjusted value.

Burns commented that the imprecision of the two-month ranges led him to question their usefulness. He proposed lengthening the period to up to six months. Others responded that his proposal put more weight on uncertain projections (ibid., 15–16). Burns's proposal suggested more attention to the medium-term and sustained changes. The members did not reach consensus or agree to change.

### *Operating Procedures*

As inflation rose, the FOMC recognized more fully than earlier that targeting the federal funds rate did not achieve its objectives. They experimented over the decade with different ways of reducing or controlling inflation by including in the directive targets for measures of reserves and money. Dissatisfaction with outcomes and problems in reconciling the interest rate and aggregate targets brought the topic back to their agenda several times.

The staff concluded that responding to monthly data was unwise. It reached a correct and long-delayed conclusion that to control inflation and improve outcomes the FOMC had to take a longer view and pay more attention to persistent evidence showing money growth rates above or below target (memo, staff to FOMC, Board Records, February 10, 1976). This was an opportunity to shift more emphasis to longer-term consequences. There is no evidence that the FOMC agreed.

A separate staff report also considered the effect of legislative changes and market innovations on the composition of financial balances. Some of the changes relaxed regulation to help thrift institutions adjust to inflation and regulation Q ceilings. The report concluded that the introduction of NOW accounts and other changes in saving accounts to make them more like transaction balances had reduced demand deposits. The staff proposed that the FOMC should give more weight to the broader aggregates without abandoning $M_1$ (memo, staff to FOMC, Board Records, February 10, 1976).

At a special meeting in March 1976, Governor Robert Holland, as chairman of the Subcommittee on the Directive, proposed replacing the target for RPDs (reserves against private deposits) with nonborrowed reserves (total reserves minus member bank borrowing). Since required reserves depended on lagged deposits, this proposal would renew the role of free reserves (excess reserves minus borrowing) for a short period. The federal funds rate would be a constraint; the manager would target nonborrowed reserves as long as the funds rate remained within the target range. The FOMC would resolve conflicts or inconsistencies by revising instructions.

Following his report, an exchange with Chairman Burns suggests that members of the FOMC did not agree on the operating target. Holland said it was the funds rate.

Burns objected. "That is not our operating target—we use the federal funds rate with a view to reaching certain monetary aggregates." Holland replied, "I think it is in practice our *only* operating target and that we need to have a structure that has a reserve measure in it, that is a workable one that the committee can work towards" (FOMC Minutes, special meeting, March 29, 1976, tape 2; emphasis added). Volcker agreed with Holland. "As long as the Federal Reserve used it [the funds rate] as its mechanism for implementing policy, the market would continue to interpret any move in the funds rate as an indication of a change in policy" (Burns papers, FOMC, March 15–16, 1976, 82).

Surprisingly, the FOMC did not explore the range on the target federal funds rate required to keep the monetary aggregates within their bounds most of the time. Nor did most members accept that to control monetary growth they would have to permit more frequent changes in the funds rate. Instead, Burns asked the staff to report on the forecast error in the aggregates under prevailing conditions. The reports showed large short-term errors, two-thirds of the time as much as 4 percentage points around the two-month money growth rate (ibid). Governor Wallich concluded the discussion again by pointing out that the System could improve control of the aggregates by permitting greater variability in the funds rate. The FOMC was not ready to accept this proposal.

Holland explained that the main reason for rejecting RPDs was that the manager could not control them effectively. Governor Partee pointed out that the data did not show that a nonborrowed reserves (NBR) target would be better. The staff agreed, but Axilrod said that NBR could be controlled better. Governor Holland said that politics, more than economics, was the reason "for not naming federal funds as the FOMC exclusive operating target" (ibid., tapes 3 and 4). Setting an interest rate "is a kind of lightning rod in terms of some of the public discussion" (ibid.). He might have added that the problem of choosing a nominal short rate was more acute during an inflation when nominal interest rates reached unprecedented levels. He favored allowing the funds rate to move within a one percentage point band adjusted up or down by 0.25 percentage points as growth of monetary aggregates changed. Contrary to the evidence presented earlier, this proposal put excessive weight on short-term, often random changes in the aggregates.

Governor Jackson and President Balles proposed the opposite alternative—controlling longer-term measures of money growth.[171] Governor Wallich suggested that this would have a better chance of success if the FOMC would permit the funds rate target to change more often. He thought that the funds rate should not be an objective of policy; it would become an instrument. He doubted that this could be done (ibid.).

The discussion did not reach a firm conclusion, but it showed that several FOMC members understood why their operating procedures did not control inflation. Burns and others were not willing to make the necessary changes, so policy continued much as before. Burns concluded that both monetary aggregates and interest rates mattered for monetary policy.

Vice Chairman Volcker pointed out that the FOMC did not know whether failure to control the aggregates resulted from the reserves multiplier or the funds rate constraint. He wanted better information (ibid., tape 5).

Burns ended the meeting by eliminating RPDs and telling Axilrod to prepare an article for the Bulletin. Axilrod replied that "the evidence would show that the committee chose to adhere to the FF [federal funds] rate constraint rather than the RPD target" (ibid.). This statement seemed to infuriate Burns. He replied sharply that "this was not a criticism of the Committee; it was evidence of the Committee's practical wisdom" (ibid.). He told Axilrod to write it objectively and to recognize that the FOMC acted wisely!

Neither Burns nor a majority of the committee accepted nonborrowed reserves as replacement for RPDs. They postponed a decision. Burns did not think much would change. The concerned public already believed that they did not give enough attention to reserve growth.[172]

171. President Balles's position was based on research at the San Francisco reserve bank. Balles asked his staff to determine whether the relation of $M_1$ to GNP had deteriorated. To his expressed surprise, the staff presented evidence that "all of the monetary aggregates tested gave roughly similar results in predicting both nominal and real GNP for the period 1960–74 as a whole. In this sense no other aggregate was significantly superior to $M_1$" (memo, James L. Pierce to Burns, Burns papers Box B-B81, April 3, 1974, 1). The memo concluded that the Board's staff obtained the same result using other techniques. Later, San Francisco repeated its study and concluded that emphasis should shift to $M_2$. The Board's staff repeated the test. The Board's equations show very little deterioration in either $M_1$ or $M_2$ variants (memo, staff to James Kichline, Burns papers, Box B_B114, June 3, 1977, 2).

172. Burns then asked whether monetarist economists would criticize the decision to drop RPDs. He accepted that they would. "We've gotten criticism from the monetarists no matter what we do. It's their destiny to criticize, it's their place in life" (FOMC Minutes, special meeting, March 29, 1976, tape 5). Also at the April 1976 meeting, Burns asked Holland to find an economic historian to write the Federal Reserve's history. Holland left the Board the next month to become president of the Committee for Economic Development without completing the assignment.

### *Reserve Management*

As part of the reconsideration of operating procedures, the System revisited lagged reserve accounting. Two main questions arose. First, would a return of contemporaneous reserve accounting improve control of the monetary aggregates? Second, would this change be costly to banks and discourage membership in the System?

The answers to both questions were yes, although arguments were made on the other side. Staff of the New York bank argued that elimination of lagged reserve accounting would increase interest rate variability. Market participants judged policy stance by the level of the funds rate, so their information would be less certain, and monetary control would suffer (memo, Paul Meek and Charles Lucas to FOMC, Board Records, February 17, 1976). Board staff reached the opposite conclusion. "For the purpose of controlling the monetary aggregates in the short run of a month or two via reserves, theoretical considerations and empirical evidence suggest that contemporaneous reserve accounting would be more effective than the existing reserve accounting system with a two-week lag. Linkages between reserves and the monetary aggregates in the short-run are loose in both cases, though less so without lagged reserve accounting" (memo, Reserve Requirement Policy Group to Board of Governors, Board Records, April 13, 1976, 1). The memo added that contemporaneous accounting would "probably reduce somewhat the amplitudes of movements in the funds rate over the longer run" (ibid., 1). Then it added that it had taken a survey of bank attitudes. Large banks with many branches strongly opposed a return to contemporaneous reserve requirements because it increased their costs of reserve management. They would likely hold more reserves.[173] It cost nothing to provide them.

The staff favored contemporaneous reserve requirements whenever they considered or reconsidered the issue. The Board always rejected their advice until 1984, when they returned to contemporary reserve accounting after it no longer mattered for control. The issue was important only during periods of monetary control using a reserve target. The record suggests

173. The Federal Reserve introduced the two-week lag in 1968. The main reasons were (1) to moderate the decline in the funds rate on Wednesday settlement days caused by banks selling their surplus reserves and (2) difficulties in hitting the free reserve target because of large revisions in required reserves and vault cash after settlement. Prior to the change, member banks could offset reserve deficiencies in one settlement period up to 2 percent of required reserves by carrying the deficiency over to the next period, but there was no carryover provision for surplus reserves.

that at the FOMC banks' opposition to their higher costs outweighed the social benefit of improved monetary control. This was clearly a misreading of Federal Reserve responsibilities.

The New York staff also ran an experiment on the use of a nonborrowed reserve target. Based on its findings, the Subcommittee on the Directive recommended against using a reserve objective in the directive because it "would not improve the Committee's ability to achieve short-run objectives for the monetary aggregates" (memo, Subcommittee on the Directive, Board Records, December 15, 1976, 5–6). The subcommittee recognized, however, that the main problem was failure to change the funds rate. Governor Wallich pointed out again that the System treated the funds rate target as a policy objective, not as an instrument for achieving control of monetary aggregates consistent with stable growth and low inflation. Further, Wallich said, these System actions encourage the market to put excessive weight on changes in the funds rate as policy indicators. Using the funds rate as an instrument, he said, would increase its volatility. Then he concluded, "I believe that good control of the aggregates, even at the cost of an unstable funds rate, would be superior to a well-controlled funds rate with the aggregates in danger of going out of control" (ibid., 2). President Balles agreed and added: "The pendulum has shifted too far towards interest rate stability at the cost of significant undershoots or overshoots from time to time in our twelve-month growth range for the monetary aggregates" (ibid.). He favored a nonborrowed reserves target.

Burns devoted much attention to the size of errors made in forecasts of reserve and money growth. Stephen Axilrod disagreed. A large part of the Board's problem came from its short-term focus. He claimed that if the objective was to have 6 percent $M_1$ growth six months ahead, "I could do it better by telling you what nonborrowed reserves to hit than what FF [federal funds] rates to hit" (FOMC Minutes, March 29, 1976, tape 3).

The staff of the Philadelphia Reserve bank also studied the reasons the FOMC found it difficult to control money growth reliably. It concluded that the main problems were weak linkage between the short-term and medium-term targets and large errors in the two-month projections for the aggregates. Underlying the short-term monetary control problem were "the constraints of modest week-to-week changes in the federal funds rate" (memo, "Perspectives on Controlling Monetary Aggregates Over Time," New York Reserve Bank, Box 110282, November 21, 1978, 4).[174]

174. The memo cites a study by Gary Gillum, then at the Philadelphia bank, that showed that $M_1$ projections for 1973 to 1977 appeared unbiased but had an average absolute error of 3 percentage points at annual rates.

These studies, and others done within the System, show that the principal technical reasons for poor monetary control were well understood both at the Board and several of the reserve banks. Richard Davis at the New York bank advised Paul Volcker that "nonborrowed reserves might prove a more effective means of hitting monetary targets by freeing the Committee from the burden of substantial direct responsibility for the short-run behavior of the money market" (memo, Richard Davis to Volcker, New York Reserve Bank, Box 110282, August 15, 1977, 2).

Lack of understanding cannot explain the System's failure, and I find it implausible to believe that lack of control was inadvertent. The FOMC was unwilling to take effective action and, as we shall see, subverted efforts by Congress to improve monetary control.

## *The "Missing Money"*

As noted earlier, Arthur Burns explained in testimony before the Banking Committee in 1975 that economic recovery and expansion would not require rapid money growth. He expected a rise in average growth of monetary velocity because the public's confidence would increase, so they would reduce average money balances. Base money growth fell from about 8 percent annual rate in much of 1974 to less than 6 percent in early 1976. It remained below 6.5 percent until late in 1976. By autumn 1976, the annual rate of consumer price increase was below 5 percent, less than half the 1974 rate of increase. This was Burns's most persistent effort to reduce inflation.

In January 1976, the staff began to inform the FOMC that money growth, particularly $M_1$, had fallen below the staff's expectations and forecast despite their efforts to reduce the funds rate. The staff's $M_1$ forecast was off by 6.25 percent at the end of 1975 (FOMC Minutes, January 18, 1976, 55). The staff made no connection to Burns's prediction about velocity (FOMC Minutes, March 15–16, 1976, 56–57). They attributed the decline to a shift in the demand for money.

A retrospective memo showed that reported quarterly average growth of $M_1$ and GNP were, respectively, 4.9 and 13.6 from first quarter 1975 to first quarter 1976, so velocity growth was 8.7 percent compared to a 3 percent postwar average. In 1976 and 1977, average velocity growth was 3.7 percent. If there was a puzzle, it was limited to one year[175] (memo, John Paulus to Board of Governors, Burns papers, Box B-B81, January 13, 1978, 2). Paulus gave three possible explanations. First, regulators had

175. Revisions later reduced average GNP growth to 10.6 percent for the four quarters of 1975 (Department of Commerce, October 1988, 99).

changed the rules to make savings accounts closer substitutes for demand deposits. Payments could be made by drawing against saving accounts. Second, higher nominal interest rates in 1973–74 increased incentives to economize on cash balances and adopt more efficient payment systems. Third, technical changes in payment systems brought many new techniques for more efficient payments. These changes were more important for businesses than for households. Staff estimates suggested that business experienced the largest part of the decline in average cash balances (ibid., 4–5).

At the time, the staff was most concerned by the persistent error in their estimates of the demand for money. Their estimates came from an equation, based on Goldfeld (1976), that had worked well in earlier periods but not in 1975. In retrospect, the Board's staff misstated and overstated the problem. First, the staff acted as if their demand equation was correctly specified so errors could only mean that the world had changed. Second, their framework implied that by setting the (or an) interest rate, the FOMC determined reserves and could ignore the supply side. At times, some recognized that the multiplier connecting reserves to money changed, but changes in growth of the money stock received little attention. The staff did not consider that some of the problem came from the imprecision of their estimates of the supply of money consistent with the FOMC's chosen federal funds rate. Or, when the staff recognized this problem, they could not convince the FOMC to change procedures. Also, the model gave little attention to anticipations.

Our interest is not in the details as perceived at the time. The incident shows the intense concentration on short-term changes, part of the reason for neglecting medium- and longer-term changes. Also, it shows the neglect of the money stock and its determinants and the conviction that staff equations correctly specified economic behavior.

Goldfeld (1976) studied the source of the error without changing the staff's conclusion. Laumas and Spencer (1980) changed the specification of the demand equation by replacing current income with permanent income. This removed part of the problem. Lucas (1988) and Hoffman and Rasche (1991) argued that there was no evidence of instability using specifications other than Goldfeld's. And Ball (2002, 18) concluded that the problem arose because the Board's equation did not properly specify the opportunity cost of holding money.

Chart 7.16 suggests the importance of specifying the appropriate opportunity cost. The chart compares the logarithm of base velocity to the reciprocal of the long-term interest rate on government bonds, quarterly,

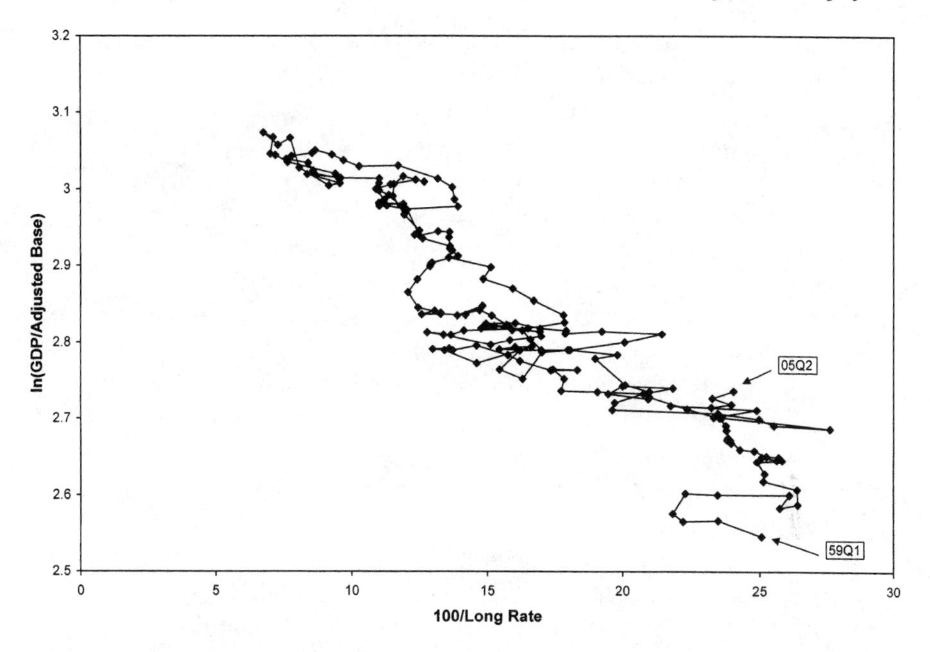


Chart 7.16. Base velocity and the long rate, 1959:1–2005:2.

for more than forty-five years. The scatter shows a relatively stable relation. Points for the middle 1970s, the period of "missing money," lie at the upper left and show no evidence of instability.

Striking evidence of the stability of the relation comes from comparison of the years of rising and falling interest rates and inflation. As long-term rates declined, velocity moved back along the path it followed when inflation rose.

The Board's staff, and most outsiders, usually disregard the effect of the long-term rate on the demand for money. This neglects the public's expectations of persistent inflation and other permanent changes except as they change the current short rate. It assumes that the short rate fully reflects expectations at longer maturities. In practice, the long rate and other relative prices affect the public's decisions to hold money instead of bonds or real capital. This is a more general problem than the "missing money" episode, and it leads at times to misinterpretation.

### *Humphrey-Hawkins Legislation*

Early in 1975, Congress citing its constitutional power to coin money and regulate its value adopted Resolution 133 instructing its agent, the Federal Reserve, to

(1) pursue policies in the first half of 1975 so as to encourage lower long term interest rates and expansion in the money and credit aggregates appropriate to facilitating prompt economic recovery; and

(2) maintain long run growth of the monetary and credit aggregates commensurate with the economy's long run potential to increase production, so as to promote effectively the goals of maximum employment, stable prices, and moderate long term interest rates." (memo, staff to FOMC, Board Records, April 10, 1975)

The resolution was unusual in several ways. First, Congress called on its agent to do a better job. Individual's complaints about the Federal Reserve were common; statements by the Congress were rare. Second, the resolution strengthened the role of price stability in the Federal Reserve's mandate. Interpretations of the 1946 Employment Act usually emphasized primacy of full employment. Third, Congress instructed the Federal Reserve to avoid excessive long-term growth of its monetary aggregates, partly endorsing monetarist criticism of the Federal Reserve.

Other sections of Resolution 133 required the Board to appear before the Banking Committee semiannually to present its objectives and plans for the next twelve months. The resolution began regular oversight hearings. Regrettably, few in Congress are informed enough to enter into a useful dialogue with the Board's chairman. The oversight hearings did not prevent the Federal Reserve from continuing to follow inflationary policies for several years. And the hearings did not get the Federal Reserve to give greater weight to the longer-term consequences of its actions.

Burns worked to weaken the resolution and succeeded in modifying it. Once the resolution passed, several members of FOMC and the Board's staff urged cooperation with Congress, reluctantly in some cases.

Continued dissatisfaction with economic performance, the high and variable rates of inflation and unemployment, the level of interest rates, and the heightened uncertainty of economic life brought additional legislation. The FOMC undermined the intent of Resolution 133 by failing to achieve the money growth rates it announced and by setting the new growth rate without compensating for over- or underperformance. Members of the FOMC discussed their record, and some proposed procedures for correcting "base drift." None was adopted.

Senator Hubert Humphrey and Congressman Augustus Hawkins introduced legislation that eventually became the Full Employment and Balanced Growth Act of 1978, known as the Humphrey-Hawkins Act. Humphrey began the process at a 1976 hearing on the thirtieth anniversary of the Employment Act of 1946. He commented, "It is my judgment that that law has, from time to time, been conveniently ignored" (Joint Economic Committee, 1976, March 18 and 19, 155). He left no doubt that he believed that Congress had to adopt new legislation to achieve "full employment with reasonable price stability" (ibid.).

The Speaker of the House, Carl Albert, accused the FOMC of holding a static position and ignoring evidence. "The Committee has steadfastly clung to the notion that tax cuts do not work, in spite of the success we have had with them, in the early 'twenties under Republicans, and in 1963, under President Kennedy. . . . We sorely need a fresh look at the concept of government control of the economy. We need to give up the preconceived notion that Washington knows best" (ibid., 144).

Arthur Burns and Alan Greenspan, then chairman of the Council of Economic Advisers, testified at the hearings also. Burns firmly rejected the idea that anyone could give an accurate numerical value for full employment. Any number was both unreliable and subject to change. The proper definition was that the number of people seeking jobs at prevailing wage rates is equal to the available jobs seeking workers. Then he proposed that the "[g]overnment has a responsibility of acting as an employer of last resort" (ibid., 148) at less than the minimum wage. He gave a number of reasons why, despite his usual conservative views, he believed this was necessary. The list included high tax rates that discouraged investment, environmental legislation, and archaic anti-trust laws. Burns did not consider that any lasting effect would be on real wages not employment.[176] Later, he changed his statement in response to an economist's proposal to have the government serve as "employer of last resort," adding "of course it should" (ibid., 206). And Burns endorsed nationalization of the railroads because they have been "overregulated" by government (ibid.).[177]

Burns criticized the use of numerical targets for unemployment, but he avoided criticism of the 3 percent unemployment goal (to be achieved in four years) in Senator Humphrey's bill. He criticized Humphrey's

176. Responding to academic critics, Burns was explicit about the distinction between real and nominal interest rates, noting that short-term rates were below the current inflation rate and that long-term rates, adjusted for inflation, were about 2 or 3 percent. Burns also responded to Professor Robert Eisner's argument that budget deficits were inflationary. Eisner said, "All you have to do is see to it that the deficit is financed exclusively by the selling of bonds" (Joint Economic Committee, 1976, 206). Burns's response restricted or gave up independence, similar to Martin's earlier. "If the Congress proceeds to appropriate money at such a rate, for us to fight the Congress would hardly be in conformity with the Congressional will" (ibid., 207). Burns added that, at times, the System resisted, but it had limited power to resist in practice.

177. Senator Humphrey's bill called for prevailing wages, including Davis-Bacon wages.

proposal to reduce Federal Reserve independence by putting control in the White House without directly confronting the senator. The 1976 bill had the president submit his recommendations for monetary policy. The Board would have to respond within fifteen days and explain any proposed deviation.

Alan Greenspan endorsed full employment as a goal but agreed with Burns that full employment should not be defined as a number and certainly not 3 percent of adults as the bill specified. He argued forcefully against making the government the employer of last resort or a guarantor of jobs.[178] Unlike Burns, Greenspan distinguished between productive employment and holding a job. If the job provided by government did not create value, it was like unemployment compensation. And an employer of last resort would discourage workers from looking for jobs or retraining (Senate Committee on Banking, Housing, and Urban Affairs, 1976a, 39, 51–55). Greenspan was no less forthright on the issue of planning. He did not oppose planning, but he opposed detailed numerical plans.

> The approach (in the legislation) . . . relies heavily on the ability of the economics profession to plan or outline fairly precisely the path that must be followed to achieve and then maintain full employment. I find the thrust of this argument troublesome. It presumes a detailed forecasting capability which is far beyond any realistic assessment of the present or immediately foreseeable capability of the economic profession.
>
> A modern industrial economic system based even partly on market phenomena is so complex that any model or statistical abstraction, no matter how complex, is still a gross oversimplification of the dynamics of the system. Models can never expect to achieve more than very rough approximations of the dynamics of the real world. (ibid., 33)

Greenspan added that in practice it would be difficult to separate political and planning aspects of forecasting and setting explicit numerical goals.[179]

The most inflationary provision in the proposed legislation was the requirement to avoid action against inflation until the unemployment rate remained at 3 percent. Several witnesses pointed out that this provision would be difficult to achieve in practice and would substantially increase

178. The reported unemployment rate at the time was about 7.5 percent, down from 9 percent a year earlier.

179. Governor Charles Partee made a similar statement when commenting on the section in the bill that required the Federal Reserve to commit to a twelve- to fifteen-month unalterable plan for monetary policy. Partee also voiced concern about the absence of a clear goal for inflation in the 1946 act and in Senator Humphrey's proposal.

inflation. Governor Partee noted that the tradeoff between inflation and unemployment had changed. He attributed the change to structural factors, immune from monetary and fiscal policy. Burns denied the tradeoff existed.[180]

Congress did not pass the 1976 Humphrey-Hawkins bill. Instead, in 1977 it amended the Federal Reserve Act to incorporate the provisions of Resolution 133.

The following year, Congressman Henry Reuss introduced legislation that added to the reporting requirements of Resolution 133, restricted Federal Reserve officials from encouraging banks and financial institutions to support or oppose legislation, and regulated potential conflicts of interest of reserve bank board members. The bill called for a Federal Reserve forecast of interest rates and monetary velocity for twelve months ahead and quarterly projections of the System's portfolio composition.

Burns testified against these new requirements and endorsed the practice under Resolution 133. The Board accepted the provisions broadening the categories of individuals being considered as directors of the reserve banks and providing for Senate confirmation of the chair and vice chair of the Board. But Burns objected strongly to prohibiting discussions of pending and proposed legislation with representatives of banks and financial institutions. And he opposed the provision putting reserve bank officers and directors under the conflict of interest provisions of the criminal code on grounds that they should not be treated distinctly ("Statement to Congress," *Federal Reserve Bulletin,* August 1977, 717–21).[181] The final bill reflected many of Burns's and the Board's objections.

Efforts by Congress to make the Federal Reserve more accountable and to reduce unemployment and inflation continued. By 1978, the Humphrey-Hawkins Act had become less inflationary. The target unemployment rate was now 4 percent; government was no longer the employer of last resort, avoiding inflation received greater attention, but reducing unemployment remained the principal objective. The House passed the bill without adding a numerical inflation target. The Senate bill set the target at 3 percent or less to be achieved by 1983. Both the House and Senate bills required the Federal Reserve to set targets for monetary policy that it believed were

180. In May, Chairman Burns testified in the hearings under Resolution 133. Senator William Proxmire pointed to a change in the Humphrey-Hawkins bill. The goal was a 3 percent adult unemployment rate. Burns rejected the proposal or any numerical proposal (Senate Committee on Banking, Housing, and Urban Affairs, 1976a).

181. The restriction on lobbying bankers was a response to the Banking Committee's access to minutes of the reserve bank directors meeting where much information about lobbying appeared (House of Representatives, 1977, 15).

consistent with the act.[182] Administration direction or guidance for monetary policy did not remain.

In spring 1978, William Miller replaced Arthur Burns. He testified in favor of the general objectives of the act. Like his predecessor, he opposed numerical targets. And he emphasized the importance of reducing unemployment and inflation (Senate Committee on Banking, Housing and Urban Affairs, 1976a, 210).

Governor Partee testified for the Board (ibid., 215). He praised the increased attention to inflation in the 1978 House and especially Senate bills, removal of the government as employer of last resort, and elimination of the 3 percent goal for the unemployment rate, but he objected to the numerical targets that remained.

The Board was particularly pleased that the legislation allowed greater flexibility to monetary policy. Objectives for monetary policy could change during the year as economic conditions changed. And Partee, in a break with the past, emphasized that "performance with respect to inflation has a critical bearing on the chances for actually achieving meaningful and sustainable full employment" (ibid., 214). He insisted that the improvements did not go far enough. Inflation control continued to take "a back seat" to unemployment.[183]

The 1978 legislation amended section 2A of the Federal Reserve Act by requiring the Board to report in writing to Congress by February 20 on its and the FOMC's objectives for the monetary and credit aggregates for the year ahead. In July, the Board had to report on its plans for the following year. This forced the Board to give more attention to medium-term objectives, a potentially important change. Also, the Board's report had to relate its plans to the administration's economic program for the year and to congressional goals.[184]

182. The goals specified in the act included more than unemployment and inflation rates. They included balanced growth, productivity growth, full parity income for farmers, and other objectives. Many of these objectives were outside the competence of the Federal Reserve. The 3 percent unemployment rate for adults twenty years and over remained in the bill (Senate Committee on Banking, Housing, and Urban Affairs, 1976a, 21).

183. One sign of change is the absence of discussion of guideposts and guidelines for wages and prices. Since the early Kennedy administration, officials and others argued that a market economy could not achieve full employment and low inflation without intervention in labor and product markets. This reasoning no longer appeared in official or congressional statements. Partee rejected it explicitly (Senate Committee on Banking . . . , 1978, 723). Partee insisted, however, that training programs would be needed to reach 4 percent unemployment rates.

184. News reports at the time suggest the intense struggle over the provisions of the act. Republicans in Congress wanted more emphasis on reducing inflation and government spending. Union lobbyists wanted more spending (*Washington Post*, October 13, 1978, A2).

By the time President Carter signed the legislation, a common belief was that the act would not achieve its stated goals. That proved to be correct. For its part, the Federal Reserve was no better at achieving announced monetary targets than before, and it continued to allow year-to-year base drift. In 2001, Congress repealed Humphrey-Hawkins, eliminated targets for money growth, but retained semiannual oversight hearings.[185]

The Subcommittee on the Directive proposed several changes in response to the new mandate. It recommended eliminating two FOMC meetings, in January and June, and moving the February and July meetings earlier in the month to allow time to prepare the statement for the oversight hearings. Also, the subcommittee proposed to state short-run targets for the aggregates as three-month moving averages centered on the month of the meeting to reduce the volatility of reported growth rates and to reduce the width of specified ranges.[186]

The act, like Resolution 133, explicitly absolved the Federal Reserve from responsibility for achieving its announced ranges. If it claimed that conditions had changed, it had to explain to Congress the reason for the change. In effect, this provision weakened the act. The System rarely achieved its targets for the monetary aggregates, and Congress eventually repealed the required announcement.

At the time, the Subcommittee on the Directive proposed changes to reduce "base drift"—building the next growth rate on the excess or shortfall in the previous year—and announcing calendar year growth rates twice a year instead of moving one quarter at a time. The committee saw the new legislation as offering an opportunity for dealing more directly with problems widely believed to inhere in the existing system (Federal Reserve Bank of New York, 1978, Box 110282, FOMC, 1970–78).

Other memos prepared at the time accepted many of the monetarists' criticisms. One recognized that lower money growth was a necessary condition for lower inflation and that targets for monetary aggregates were a

185. Passage of the act stimulated internal discussion of changes. Presidents Baughman (Dallas) and Roos (St. Louis) proposed steps to focus on longer-term consequences of policy actions. "The economic problems we are attempting to address now require attention to the longer consequences to a degree not heretofore experienced since the 1930s" (letter, Ernest Baughman to FOMC, Board Records, April 20, 1978). Both presidents proposed a three-year horizon. The letter concluded by recognizing the procyclical thrust of Federal Reserve policy actions. "We would be hard pressed to find a persuasive rationale that monetary policy in the past three years has been countercyclical" (ibid., 2).

Neither Burns nor many others were ready to make the needed changes in procedures to control inflation and make policy counter-cyclical.

186. Chairman Volcker dissented because the moving averages would "convey an exaggerated impression to the public of fine-tuned precision in the setting of ranges" (Federal Reserve Bank of New York, 1978, Box 110282, FOMC, 1970–78).

more useful measure than interest rates of the thrust of monetary policy. Another memo proposed use of a single aggregate target. Still another recognized that policy was often procyclical. "The need for serious adjustments is often deferred because of the procedure of shifting the base. The tendency for monetary growth to be procyclical is strengthened. The delayed adjustments are ultimately enlarged" (memo, "Perspectives on Controlling Monetary Aggregates over Time," Federal Reserve Bank of New York, Box 110282, November 21, 1978, 4).

Recognition did not influence decisions. Federal Reserve actions continued to be procyclical on average until 1994. Base drift continued, as did the announcement of multiple targets for monetary aggregates and inflationary monetary growth. Recognition of excessive attention to short-run changes was a large forward step. Unfortunately, it did not produce the required changes.

The importance of this memo should not be underestimated. It shows that internal memos reinforced external criticisms of policy and procedures. And it established that decisions to continue the procedures and policies had to be explained some other way than by claiming misunderstanding. Most likely is the primacy given to unemployment and the misinterpretation of interest rate changes. But underlying these errors was the influence of Congress and the general public. The FOMC continued to interpret a decline in interest rates as evidence of easier monetary policy even if money and credit growth slowed in recessions. Similarly, it interpreted higher interest rates as evidence of tighter policy despite more rapid growth of money and credit. This was the main reason for procyclical policy actions and the low or negative real interest rates found during the Great Inflation.[187]

## REGULATION

The 1970s were a period of active financial regulation. The Federal Reserve's responsibilities increased under the Truth in Lending Act, the Community Reinvestment Act, and the Equal Credit Opportunity Act (non-discriminatory). These changes required rulings and interpretations to keep up with new congressional legislation and practical problems.[188]

187. Tax policy became an active political issue in 1978 with the introduction of bills by Senator William Roth (Delaware) and Representative Jack Kemp (New York) that proposed large reductions in individual and corporate tax rates. Individual rates would be reduced from the prevailing 14 to 70 percent to 8 to 50 percent by 1980.

188. The Community Reinvestment Act of 1977 (CRA) responded to complaints that some banks did not lend adequate amounts to meet demands of low- and moderate-income

The 1970s were a time of dissatisfaction. Truth in Lending and the diversity of banking practices raised many issues, for example disclosure of discounts for cash or surcharges for the use of credit cards (Annual Report, 1977, 132). Administration of margin requirements continued to raise issues about matters such as substitution of securities in margin accounts and the extension of margin requirements to new instruments in a rapidly changing market. These seem remote from core Federal Reserve responsibilities. Inflation required changes in nominal values. For example, in 1998 the Board permitted banks to increase the limit on credit card loans to executive officers from $1,000 to $5,000. Congress proposed or passed legislation to restrict System practices, release additional information, change the regulatory structure, and regulate the growing number of foreign banks operating in the domestic market.

Potential default by New York City induced Congress to seek emergency loans from the Federal Reserve. The Federal Reserve Board attempted to draw a line between assistance to potential bankrupts and service as lender of last resort. It agreed to a temporary increase in bank discounts in the event of a major default, but it opposed loans to New York City. In the event of losses "that would seriously impair the capital of some banks," it argued that the Federal Deposit Insurance Corporation had statutory responsibility (*Federal Reserve Bulletin,* 1975, 635–36). In 1979, the System acted as fiscal agent for Treasury loan guarantees to Chrysler Corporation.

Support for housing in Congress induced the Federal Reserve to buy agency debt issues for its open market account. Between 1972 and 1976 System holdings of obligations of the Federal National Mortgage Association (FNMA) rose from $500 million to $2.9 billion. Between 40 and 60 percent of all agency issues held were FNMA obligations (memo, Stephen Axilrod and Alan Holmes to FOMC, Board Records, May 19, 1976, 9). FNMA was in part a private corporation; its shares were held by the public, but it retained some characteristics of a government agency, as Congress intended. The staff memo recommended continuing purchases, but it proposed to reduce the relative size of FNMA holdings. The memo showed concern for the effect on the interest rate paid by FNMA on its stock price, and on "the impression that the Federal Reserve is significantly reducing its activity in housing-related agency securities" (ibid., 1). Also, "there is a risk that Congress may come to believe that the System is not conforming

borrowers. Studies showed that the CRA reduced the spread between loans to such borrowers and other home buyers and that the loans were profitable (Laderman, 2004). Interest groups used the CRA to intervene in banks' proposals to expand, merge, etc.

to the intent of Congressional legislation . . . [S]uch action would be interpreted as a significant change in the System's attitude toward the residential mortgage market" (ibid., 7).

The System preferred not to own long-term securities, and it regarded agency securities as less marketable for resale, so its reluctance to hold FNMA obligations is not surprising. Political concerns overrode portfolio considerations in this case as in many others. Members of Congress and especially members of the Banking Committees would have objected strongly to refusal to purchase, or decisions to sell, housing securities. The System made no effort to show that buying agency securities had little effect on housing.

## REGULATION Q

There were more regulatory changes affecting regulation Q than any other part of Board supervision. Chart 7.14 above shows one reason; market rates rose far above regulated rates from 1972 to 1974, and after decontrol of rates on large CDs from 1978 on. By 1980, Congress was willing to remove all ceiling rates gradually.

The relative increase in market rates increased the profitability to banks of holding regulated deposits, so many actively sought ways of increasing services and return on such deposits to stem the outflow. Also, savings and loans typically lost time and savings deposits to banks. Since their portfolios consisted mainly of mortgages, they had fewer opportunities to increase portfolio returns. Their growing problems helped to convince Congress to reduce interest rate regulation.

Innovation was perhaps most important. As market rates rose above ceiling rates, mutual funds and others offered money market funds. These funds took advantage of the deregulation of ceiling rates on certificates of deposit of $100,000 or more that followed the Penn Central failure. Money market funds bought large certificates of deposit (CDs) and, for a small fee, offered participations to smaller depositors. The rapid growth of money market funds drained deposits subject to regulation Q from banks and especially non-bank thrifts. Banks bought many of the deposits from the market by paying market rates. By early 1980, money market mutual funds held nearly $50 billion compared to $335 billion in savings deposits.

By late April 1974, savings and loan associations had to borrow heavily from the Federal Home Loan Banks (FHLBs) to cover deposit outflow. The Reserve Board's staff estimated the increased borrowing at $50 million a day. At that rate, the FHLBs would exhaust their liquid assets by mid-May. The FHLBs could then borrow against a $4 billion line of credit with the Treasury. As a precaution, the Home Loan Bank Board asked the

Federal Reserve to offer standby emergency assistance (memo, Peter Keir to Board of Governors, April 30, 1974, Box 431.2, Federal Reserve Bank of New York). The Federal Reserve agreed to provide the emergency loans as lender of last resort. Loans from reserve banks to FHLBs would be for no more than thirty days and secured by collateral acceptable to the reserve bank. Borrowing could be renewed only if the FHLB system acted to eliminate the need for Federal Reserve assistance. Loans to individual member and non-member institutions were left to the decision of the FHLBs. The interest rate on loans to savings bank and thrifts would be two percentage points above the discount rate, a 10 percent rate at the time.[189]

These extensions of its emergency lending recognized the Federal Reserve as lender of last resort to the financial system. The earlier, very narrow interpretation of its role had given way gradually but had not been fully reflected in operating rules and procedures. The thrift problems forced decisions that extended the lender-of-last-resort function by recognizing finally the role of the central bank that Walter Bagehot insisted upon one hundred years earlier.

Small depositors attempted to acquire large CDs to earn open market rates. One method was to pool deposits. The Board proposed to prohibit pooling on January 29, 1975, inducing greater use of money market funds. Governor Coldwell dissented because he thought the prohibition was unenforceable. The Board withdrew the ruling two years later.

Later that year Governor Coldwell dissented again when the Board voted to support a one-year extension of its authority to control interest rates under regulation Q. Coldwell did not agree to a provision calling for an eventual end to ceiling rates. He said that small institutions would be harmed. Congress was not ready to remove controls. In December 1975, it approved a provision intended to protect thrift institutions from competition. The spread between interest rates paid by banks and thrifts could not thereafter narrow unless the Board notified Congress. Thrifts now came under interest rate regulation with the right to pay slightly higher rates than banks. Both rates were below open market rates, so withdrawals continued.

At about the same time, the Board permitted banks to open savings deposits for small businesses. Account balances had to remain below $150,000. Governors Bucher and Coldwell dissented because they opposed the limitation on accounts size (Annual Report, 1975, 133–34). Earlier in

189. The guidelines did not cover mutual savings banks since they were not members of the FHLBs and did not have a comparable organization. The New York and Boston Reserve banks prepared guidelines for their emergency borrowing. A few months later, the Board clarified its rules for lending to non-member commercial banks (memo, S-2276, Board of Governors, March 31, 1975. File 431.2, Federal Reserve Bank of New York).

the year, the Board revoked authority for banks to open NOW accounts for governmental units and authorized member banks to permit depositors to transfer or withdraw deposits by telephone. This repealed a restriction adopted in 1936 (ibid., 118–19).

NOW accounts began in Massachusetts and New Hampshire. They permitted banks to pay interest on liabilities with most of the properties of demand deposits. Congress extended the use of NOW accounts to the four remaining New England states, and the Board amended regulation Q in February 1976 to permit member banks to pay interest on these accounts. Several members of the Banking Committee wanted to extend NOW accounts nationally and to permit banks to pay interest on the public's demand deposits. The new Carter Treasury mistakenly opposed the proposed extension to New York, New Jersey, and Pennsylvania. Congress removed it from the bill extending regulation Q to June 1977 (letter, Blumenthal to Proxmire, Burns papers, Box B_892, February 23, 1977).

The Board in 1975 permitted banks to waive the penalty for early withdrawal of time deposits in IRA accounts if the depositor was older than 59.5 or disabled. An amendment on November 3, 1976, extended the waiver to Keogh retirement accounts. In 1977, the Board set a minimum maturity of three years for these retirement accounts and permitted banks to pay the highest rate allowed on long-term time deposits. The aim was to encourage retirement accounts and to assist banks and thrifts to gain deposits. Thrifts, as usual, could pay 0.25 percentage points above the interest rates permitted to banks. In December 1978, the Board further liberalized withdrawals from these accounts.

Several other actions modestly increased the attractiveness of time deposits or the incentive to evade the regulations. Banks and depositors tried to circumvent penalties for early withdrawal by making loans to depositors. The Board required that such loans be made at a rate of two percentage points above the rate paid on the deposit. In November 1977, it reduced the differential to one percentage point (Annual Report, 1977, 138).

The Federal Reserve Reform Act, approved November 16, 1977, extended regulation Q for an additional year to December 15, 1978. The Board soon thereafter permitted automatic transfers for individuals from savings accounts to checking accounts. This was particularly useful if a depositor overdrew a checking account, and it saved the customer the large fees banks usually charged for overdrafts. Both banks and depositors could choose to adopt or avoid automatic transfers. The new authority amended regulation Q by permitting depositors to receive interest on their savings account up to the date of withdrawal. The Board's announcement recognized that, in effect, the authorization was equivalent to allowing interest to be paid on part of a demand deposit account (Board Minutes, May 1, 1978).[190]

Pressured by the rise in market rates and loss of banks' competitive position, effective June 1, 1978, the Board, joined by the FDIC and Home Loan Bank Board, announced two new instruments intended to permit banks and other deposit takers to "compete for funds to assure an adequate flow of credit into housing and to meet other borrowing needs" (Board Minutes, May 11, 1978). Deposit takers could issue a six-month certificate with minimum denomination of $10,000 that paid interest at the average yield on a six-month Treasury bill set at the most recent weekly auction. Savings and loans were permitted to retain their 0.25 percentage point higher rates. Soon after, the Board ruled that banks could not compound interest on the six-month certificates (Annual Report, 1979, 90).

At the time that it made this change, the Board introduced a new 4-year certificate with an interest rate 1.25 percentage points (1 percentage point for S&Ls) below the auction yield on 4-year Treasury securities, and it reduced penalties for early withdrawal from time deposit accounts. The new instrument was not sufficiently attractive, so in December the regulators replaced the 4-year certificates with a 2.5-year certificate that paid 0.75 percentage points less than outstanding Treasury securities of the same term to maturity. The Board's statement was explicit about the problem. The action was taken "to help the small saver and to improve the ability of banks to compete for funds" (Annual Report, 1979, 93).

The same institutions could also issue an eight-year certificate of deposit, with minimum denomination of $1,000, that paid a maximum of 7.75 percent at banks and 8 percent at savings and loans and mutual savings banks. Later the Board eliminated the minimum denomination restrictions.

In 1978, banks in New Jersey, Pennsylvania, and Ohio began to issue bearer certificates of deposits with denomination of $100 or less. Some

190. This feature drew many negative responses, including from 370 savings and loans, the Federal Home Loan Bank Board, and 42 or 45 members of Congress. But 424 individuals wrote to favor the proposal when it was under consideration. To partly deflect the concerns, the Board permitted depositors to make automatic transfers from savings and loans to commercial bank checking accounts. At about this time, the Board considered allowing interest on demand deposits. Burns suggested permitting nationwide NOW accounts, interest on reserve balances, elimination of the reserve city classification, and a lower minimum for reserve requirement ratios (Board Minutes, February 14, 1977). The Board approved the changes. Governor Coldwell dissented because of the cost to banks and omission of pricing membership services (ibid., May 5, 1977).

banks highlighted the fact that they did not report the interest payment to the Internal Revenue Service (IRS) because the certificates were negotiable and they did not know who received the interest. Of course, the records showed who received the payment. Concern about tax evasion and about the effective breach of regulation Q ceilings concerned the Board. The IRS limited the practice by ordering banks to report the interest paid (memo, staff to Board of Governors, Board Records, March 15, 1978).

The following year, the Board changed the definition of deposits to include repurchase agreements of less than $100,000 with maturities of ninety-days or more. This closed a means of evading regulation Q ceilings. As deposits, the instruments would be subject to ceiling rates (ibid., 92).

The Board and other regulators never found a satisfactory way to maintain interest rate ceilings during a period of rising interest rates and a growing difference between regulated and open market rates. The gap between regulated rates and open market rates invited innovation to avoid regulation. This brief history shows the great resistance to removing ceilings. In part, the Board and Congress had multiple objectives: maintain the relative positions of banks and thrifts, increase (or avoid reducing) funding for home mortgages, and prevent or hinder innovation that avoided controls. As open market rates rose, deposits at money market mutual funds soared. Regulators kept busy trying to improve the competitive position of their members and, at the same time, prevent innovations that circumvented restrictions. Congress was unwilling to prohibit money market funds and other means of avoiding regulation but unwilling also to recognize the failure of regulation in an inflationary period. And consumers slowly learned that they were penalized if they held regulated bank liabilities.

Pressure to remove regulation Q ceilings rose. By the late 1970s, Senator William Proxmire, chairman of Senate Banking, proposed regular gradual increases in ceiling rates until they reached the level of market rates. Congress approved the gradual end to ceiling rates in 1980.

Regulation did not save the thrift associations or maintain housing finance in an inflationary period. It took years for some cautious and poorly informed savers to recognize the opportunity cost of keeping their balances in regulated deposits instead of moving them to money market funds. The former were insured by a federal agency; the latter were not, so this slowed the transfer. By the end of the 1970s, however, many learned. Although many members of Congress served as directors of thrift institutions in their district, it became increasingly difficult to defend a policy of taxing mainly small, ill-informed savers. And it became clear that regulation induced innovation to circumvent the rules, requiring new or different rules and, in turn, bringing new innovation.

*Reserves and Reserve Requirements*

As open market interest rates rose with inflation, the cost of reserve requirements rose. Many banks withdrew from the System. From January 1970 to January 1980, the proportion of commercial banks that were Federal Reserve members declined from 43 to 35 percent even as the number of commercial banks increased by about 12 percent. The System had been concerned about membership since its earliest days. Many now regarded the problem as acute.

One way to encourage membership was to reduce the cost of holding (non-interest-bearing) required reserves. In 1969, the Board subjected a member bank's euro-dollar borrowing to a 10 percent reserve requirement ratio. The next year, it increased the ratio to 20 percent. In May 1973, it lowered the ratio to 8 percent, and in April 1975 to 4 percent. On October 15, 1975, the Board reduced the ratio from 3 to 1 percent on time deposits with an original maturity of four years or more (Annual Report, 1975, 120, 134). In December, it reduced the ratio from 3 to 2.5 percent for time deposits with maturity of six months to four years (Board Minutes, October 15, 1975, 2).

To assist smaller member banks facing seasonal changes in loan demand, the Board modified regulation A to reduce restrictions on borrowing. For the first time, it permitted banks to arrange seasonal borrowing in advance, in effect providing a line of credit. The Board "expected that small banks in agricultural areas would be the principal beneficiaries" (Annual Report, 1976, 145–46).

Periodically during the 1970s, the System considered the costs and benefits of using a reserves operating target instead of the federal funds rate. The New York desk opposed the change, arguing that banks used the federal funds rate to judge the System's policy. A reserve target would increase variability of the funds rate and obscure the signal to the market. Heightened variability would make it more difficult for the desk to interpret changes in uncontrolled reserve factors (Paul Meek and Charles Lucas to FOMC, Board Records, February 17, 1976). A System subcommittee accepted this conclusion. It recommended against including a reserve objective in the short-run operating specifications. But it based this conclusion as much on the opposition of banks as on the control issue. In fact, it found that "contemporaneous reserve accounting would be more effective than the existing reserve accounting system with a two-week lag" (memo, Subcommittee on the Directive to FOMC, Board Records, April 13, 1976, 1). This decision failed to recognize the Federal Reserve's social responsibility and gave greater importance to the wishes of some of its members.

Governor Henry Wallich, a member of the subcommittee, noted correctly that "the problem with the funds rate is that . . . it tends to shift to the role of objective. . . . Inadequate control of the aggregates has at times been the result" (supplementary comment of Governor Wallich, Board Records, December 15, 1976, 1). He recognized that initially the funds rate would be less stable. After an initial period, however, other short-term rates would probably cease to move closely with the funds rate and would react only mildly to a jumpy funds rate (ibid., 2).[191]

This issue returned several times. A report from the subcommittee reviewed the issue again in 1977 and reached the same conclusion (memo, Reserve Requirement Policy Group to Board of Governors, Board Records, August 19, 1977). When the System in 1979 announced its intention to control nonborrowed reserves instead of the funds rate, it did not eliminate lagged reserve accounting. It did permit much larger changes in the funds rate, but banks could borrow reserves as needed to meet required reserves. The Board kept the discount rate well below the funds rate much of the time, so borrowing was subsidized and banks had an incentive to err on the side of deficient reserves. The Board and the FOMC again reviewed contemporaneous reserve requirements, but it did not adopt contemporaneous accounting until after it ended its experiment with reserve control.

In 1978, the Board reduced reserve requirement ratios by 0.5 percentage points for demand deposits at banks with deposits of $10 million or less and 0.25 for other banks. Vice Chairman Stephen Gardner objected that the addition to reserves was permanent. This repeated an old error. With the funds rate unchanged, the estimated $550 million reduction in required reserves had no monetary effect. The action was most likely taken to encourage banks to retain membership, although that was not mentioned. After the reduction, reserve requirement ratios ranged from 7 to 16.25 percent. The Board also eliminated reserve requirements for foreign deposits beginning October 5, 1978. This increased the appeal of eurodollar deposits at a time when depreciation of the dollar created resentment in Europe (Annual Report, 1978, 68–69).

The Board took a large step toward reform in June 1978 by voting to recommend that all depository institutions with transaction balances of $5 million or more be required to hold required reserves whether mem-

191. The subcommittee accepted Wallich's point, but it did not change its conclusion. "After a learning period under a reserve target, it seems probable that the banks and the public would become less sensitive to day to day fluctuations in the funds rate. On the other hand, the predictability of the relationship between reserves [and interest rates] might well deteriorate somewhat" (memo, Subcommittee on the Directive to FOMC, Board Records, December 15, 1976, 3).

bers of the System or not. It took this action "to provide for greater competitive equality among financial institutions and to correct the loss of Federal Reserve member banks by reducing the burden of membership" (letter, G. William Miller to Henry Reuss, Board Minutes, July 6, 1978, 1). The Board would charge members for the services the System provided and would pay some interest on reserve balances.

The House Banking Committee proposed to extend reserve requirements to all commercial banks but exempt thrift institutions. It also exempted the first $100 million of deposits. The Board disliked these provisions. It offered to exempt $25 million and claimed that with this provision only five thrift institutions would be required to hold reserves. Congress did not act for two years.[192]

### *Collateral and Settlement*

The diminished stock of gold and gold certificates and rising levels of reserves and deposits required a change in interbank settlement. In 1972, the Board adopted monthly reallocation to maintain a common ratio of gold certificates to Federal Reserve notes outstanding. Officials could approve interim adjustments, if they appeared desirable.

In 1975, the operations staff recommended that monthly gold transfers cease. Reserve banks other than New York would change once a year. New York would pay for withdrawals and receive deposits from the Treasury. Once a year, the Interdistrict Settlement Fund would reallocate securities in the System Open Market Account to balance accounts. Gold would remain as collateral for the note issue, but securities would be the principal collateral (memo, Maurice McWhirter and Alan Holmes to FOMC, Board Records, April 11, 1975). Step by step, gold lost its monetary role and main provisions of the 1913 Federal Reserve Act disappeared.

### *Supervisory Powers*

The Board issued many regulations about holding company powers, truth in lending, community reinvestment, and other topics. It enlarged the desk's authority to purchase bankers' acceptances. Many of these regulatory actions were of minor significance.

In a lengthy memo on May 7, 1975, the Board's staff joined the desk in discussion of the System's ability to change the shape of the yield curve. The issue arose under the usual pressure from Congress to assist the hous-

192. The System published a proposed schedule pricing its services in November 1978. The bankers on the Federal Advisory Council (FAC) responded and accepted the principle that the System should charge enough to cover its costs (Board Minutes, addendum for February 1–2, 1979).

ing industry by buying long-term securities to lower long-term rates. The basis of this belief is itself open to question; mortgages are a nominal valued asset, housing a real asset. And mortgage rates are nominal values. Any effect on mortgage rates does not assure an effect on housing (Meltzer, 1974).

The memo recognized that "the expectations theory now generally accepted as the best explanation of the term structure of interest rates and empirical tests of changes in the maturity distribution of securities held by the public suggest that even very large desk purchases of Treasury coupon issues exert only limited, short-lived effects on levels of long-term rates and their relation to short-term rates" (memo, Stephen Axilrod and Peter Keir to FOMC, Board Records, May 7, 1975, 1). The memo pointed out that during periods of high demand for long-term credit, the short-term effect may be useful. If they smooth rate changes, operations may reduce expected future rates and, thus, current interest rates. Also, the staff argued, even a small change in Treasury rates could widen the spread between Treasury and corporate bonds and induce a shift of buyers to corporates and an increase in corporate debt (ibid., 16).

An increase of this kind would be unlikely to persist. Once bondholders learned that the change in relative yields was temporary, it would be unlikely to reoccur. The expectations theory of the term structure is not a complete explanation of the yield curve, but observed departures are not likely to be exploitable except in rare cases.

In May and June 1978, the Board considered proposals to retain members. The main changes called for payment of interest on bank reserves at a rate 1.5 percentage points below the average yield on government securities with a limitation on total payments equal to 7 percent of the total net earnings of the Reserve banks. Since the System paid most of its earning to the Treasury, the cost would be borne by the Treasury. The Board also proposed to establish universal reserve requirements for all transaction accounts. That would remove one of the main advantages of non-member status. The first $5 million of deposits would be exempt from reserve requirements to assist small banks. Congress wanted much higher exemptions (letter, G. William Miller to Henry Reuss, Board Minutes, June 29, 1978).

Board members expressed concern that loss of members reduced effectiveness of monetary policy. These statements make clear that they did not understand that monetary policy influenced the economy by changing relative prices, the amount of money relative to the stocks of financial assets and real capital, and expectations of inflation. None of these factors depend on the number or proportion of member banks or the volume of required reserves.

A memo from Arthur Burns to Alan Greenspan as Council chairman gave the Board's reasoning. The memo asked the administration to oppose the sections of the Financial Reform Act of 1976 considered by the House Banking Committee that spring. The bill proposed to create a Federal Banking Commission to assume the bank regulatory and supervisory functions of the Board of Governors and the Comptroller of the Currency.

Burns wrote, "If the legislation passes in its present form, it could well frustrate the conduct of monetary policy and do serious injury to our nation's economy" (memo, Burns to Chairman of CEA, Burns papers, Box B_B23, March 8, 1976, 1). His explanation is an assertion that "there is a vital interaction between monetary policy and bank supervision. . . . The interaction is so strong that actions by this new Federal Banking Commission, either deliberately or inadvertently, could frustrate monetary policy and destroy the effectiveness of the Federal Reserve" (ibid.). He did not say that a banking agency would likely be subject to congressional pressure to allocate credit.

One example that he gave was that the Banking Commission could frustrate Federal Reserve efforts to increase or reduce money and credit by changing lending standards in the opposite direction. He argued also that supervision and regulation were critical for decisions made at the discount window.

Burns's arguments are unconvincing. A purchase of securities by the FOMC would, as before, change the stock of reserves, relative prices, and expectations. The Federal Reserve continued to make these arguments on the several occasions when interest in a banking agency rose. To date, Congress has not created a banking agency.[193]

### *Legislation*

To meet the requirements of the Government in the Sunshine Act, the Board approved a regulation that permitted observers to attend those parts of Board meetings that did not discuss information that the bill permitted to be kept from public scrutiny. The latter included material from foreign governments and central banks, banking problems, and monetary policy changes. The law required the Board to keep minutes or transcripts of the

193. Senator Proxmire was a leading proponent. The issue arose again in March 1978. Chairman Charles Schultze opposed the legislation partly because all of the banking agencies opposed. This would mean "substantial" political problems. "Very significant opposition would arise from some banking groups, most state banking supervisors, and Congressmen with connections to the banking industry" (memo, Stuart Eizenstat and Charles Schultze to the president, Schultze papers, March 8, 1978, 4). The memo also recognized the risk that Congress would impose many regulatory restrictions on the allocation of credit.

parts of the meeting that remained open to the public and to announce all meetings to the public in advance (Annual Report, March 7, 1977, 123).

### *Foreign Banks*

The International Banking Act of 1978 placed regulation of all foreign banks in the United States under the control of the Board. The legislation required branches of foreign banks to meet the same reserve requirements as domestic banks and gave them access to the discount window on the same terms. The act exempted banks operating in the United States prior to the legislation. Most major West German, Swiss, and Japanese banks were therefore exempt.

The System began to use matched sale-purchase transactions with foreign banks beginning in 1968. With the oil price increase in 1973 and after, several oil-exporting countries wanted assistance in managing their dollar deposits. The Federal Reserve adapted the repurchase agreement to acquire the deposit and simultaneously contract to return it at a fixed future date.

A main appeal of foreign accounts to the System was that they permitted the System to manage bank reserves "unobtrusively." The System took part in the transaction "whenever it needed to absorb reserves but did not wish to intervene overtly in the market." At that time, central bankers considered secrecy to be useful.

The staff recommended that the System authorize the transactions. A lengthy memo from Paul Volcker, then president of the New York bank, explored the positive and negative aspects before recommending continuation (memo, Volcker to FOMC, Board Records, June 14, 1977).

Effective February 23, 1979, the Board adopted a policy statement about the supervision of foreign bank holding companies' operations in the United States. The guiding principle was "national treatment" of each country's holding companies. The Board increased examiner surveillance of transfers between the parent and the subsidiary, including quarterly reports on transactions. This action recognized the growth of foreign-owned holding companies and their diversity. Recycling profits from the sale of drugs or other illegal transactions had increased.

## CONCLUSION: WHY INFLATION PERSISTED

Arthur Burns defended Federal Reserve independence repeatedly. Unfortunately, he held a narrow view of independence. He would not discuss proposed monetary policy actions at the Quadriad, and he resented efforts by President Nixon and his staff to influence his actions. Although he made many speeches about the dangers of inflation, he did not continue anti-inflation policy when unemployment and interest rates rose or when congressional pressure for more expansive policies increased.

The simple explanation of why inflation persisted and rose on average through the 1970s is that the Federal Reserve did not sustain actions that would end it. "That was basically political" (Axilrod, 1997, 20). It started several times. It was aware that its actions increased inflation. Periodically it brought the inflation rate down, notably in 1976 during the Ford presidency. It did not maintain independence. The election of President Carter on a promise of more job creation and more expansion ended disinflation. Although Burns criticized the new administration's fiscal plan, the Federal Reserve did not want to be accused of undermining the expansion.

There were many reasons for not insisting on independence and low or zero inflation. At the time, the public did not regard inflation as a major problem, and many in the Congress reflected that attitude. Except for the start of the Ford administration, reducing unemployment dominated reducing inflation in policymakers' minds. The Ford administration's program to "whip inflation now" gave way under popular and congressional pressure once recession started. Congress and successive administrations interpreted the Employment Act of 1946 as a commitment to full employment. Successive administrations and the Federal Reserve defined full employment as a 4 percent unemployment rate long after demographic changes falsified that definition. Low inflation was not mentioned explicitly in the act.[194]

In his 1979 Per Jacobsen lecture to the IMF in Belgrade, Burns recognized that he lacked political support for slowing money growth to end inflation. He was not willing to insist on independence to carry out the central bank's responsibility to maintain the value of money. His failure was not the first time the Federal Reserve had chosen not to rely on its statutory independence to change policies. In the late 1940s, it chafed under the policy of pegging interest rates, but it did not act until after Senator Paul Douglas showed support for independent monetary policy. The Federal Reserve under Martin engaged in policy coordination, thereby financing a rising budget deficit by issuing money.

The Federal Reserve also lacked a coherent framework. Arthur Burns was a distinguished empirical economist with little interest in economic models. His successor, William Miller, was a businessman with limited knowledge of monetary economics. Yet the record shows that some mem-

194. President Carter suggests that he wanted to reduce inflation but found little support in the Democratic-controlled Congress. He described the "stricken expressions" on the faces of the leadership when he talked about balancing the budget (Carter, 1982, 65–66).

bers of FOMC recognized the main errors and weaknesses in the Federal Reserve's framework repeatedly. The FOMC chose monetary targets. It recognized that maintaining a narrow constraint on nominal interest rates prevented the manager from achieving the monetary target. It did not change because it would not accept greater interest rate variability and higher rates. Members pointed out at times that when it missed its annual target, it started from the new level, thus building in the inflation implied by excess money growth.

Some members of FOMC recognized that judged by money growth, monetary actions were procyclical. The staff and the members interpreted falling or low short-term interest rates as evidence of more expansive policy.[195] Often it reflected a decline in borrowing during the recession. Money growth declined, adding to the recessionary impulse. And the FOMC interpreted higher nominal interest rates as evidence of anti-inflation action even if money growth increased. Almost always, the FOMC used nominal, not real, interest rates to gauge policy thrust.[196]

Although many members understood that reducing inflation required consistent long-term action, there is scant evidence of longer-term planning. Discussion at FOMC meetings was often between those who favored and opposed raising the federal funds rate an additional 0.12 or 0.25 percentage points. The staff did not consider expectations when making its forecast, as Lyle Gramley noted at one point; expectations entered the member's discussion mainly as evidence of public attitudes and concerns.

Staff forecasts of inflation relied on a Phillips curve. As Orphanides (2001, 2003a, 2003b) documented, inflation forecasts typically underestimated inflation. Further, the record of the 1970s showed that inflation and unemployment rose together, on average, propelled by expectations of inflation. These errors did not shift concern from quarterly near-term changes to longer-term implications of the FOMC's actions. Some recognized that FOMC actions had little effect on near-term changes and major effect on the maintained rate of inflation, but this occasional recognition did not lead to changes in procedures.

One important consequence was the failure to distinguish between permanent or persistent problems and transitory or short-term events. The oil price increases in 1973 and 1979 were the most notable examples. In part as a result of its short-term focus, the System did not distinguish the

195. The Board's staff recognized many of the errors but could not or at least did not convince a majority of the FOMC. Also, the St. Louis staff argued vigorously for disinflation and pointed out errors and failures of the FOMC majority.

196. "I don't think I ever used the words real funds rate in the blue book, but it was always in my head" (Axilrod, 1997, 21–22).

one-time price level change induced by the oil price increases from the persistent inflation induced by its policy. The former was real, the latter monetary. If the Federal Reserve had a coherent view of its objective, it might have recognized that preventing a one-time price level change by reducing aggregate spending worked to stabilize the price level. Controlling money growth worked to maintain inflation—the sustained rate of price change—and expectations of inflation.

Rising unemployment and inflation did not protect the Federal Reserve from congressional legislation. Congress found its performance less than satisfactory. It legislated objectives and required more reporting and oversight. The 1970s, like the 1930s, suggest that poor performance is a greater threat to Federal Reserve independence than effective action to maintain stability.

Despite its problems in the 1970s, the members of FOMC never discussed how their actions affected inflation and output or whether they could agree upon a framework for improving performance. They argued many times that lower average money growth was necessary to control and lower the inflation rate; they were unwilling to let interest rate variability increase. No one suggested bold, decisive actions to end inflation.[197]

197. A former senior staff member suggested reforms after he left the Board. One of his proposals called for disclosure—announcement of policy actions when they were made. He quoted a former Governor, David Lilly, as supporting prompt disclosure. Pierce attributed unwillingness to announce decisions to its "penchant for secrecy" (Pierce, 1979a, 249). Unwillingness to accept responsibility is a reason for the "penchant."

EIGHT

# Disinflation

The policies of the past have failed.
—Ronald Reagan in Council of Economic Advisers, 1982, 10

With the best staff in the world and all the computing power we could give them, there could never be any certainty about just the right level of the federal funds rate to keep the money supply on the right path and to regulate economic activity.
—Volcker and Gyohten, 1992, 166

In July 1979, President Carter spent two days at Camp David to reassess his presidency. Things had not gone well. Abroad a hostile government had replaced a friendly government in Iran. Militants soon thereafter seized the United States embassy in Teheran and held the staff hostage. Oil prices had increased, and some forecasters predicted that the price would rise to $100 a barrel, compared to $2 to $3 dollars in 1972. At home consumer prices rose 11 percent for the year and output had not increased for the first two quarters of the year. The unemployment rate was about 6 percent.

Forecasts brought little cheer. Predictions of recession were common; the Federal Reserve staff thought a recession was "imminent" (Volcker and Gyohten, 1992, 165). The Society of Professional Forecasters predicted that inflation would continue at the current 8 to 9 percent rate with nominal GNP rising about 8 percent. That implied zero real growth. The interest rate on ten-year government bonds at 9 percent suggested a real before-tax return near zero or negative. This was the highest reported nominal government bond yield in United States history to that time.

Some of the news conveyed by these data overstated the problem by failing to separate the one-time effect of a rise in oil prices from the persistent effect of excessive monetary growth. The GNP deflator, much less influenced by energy prices, rose 9 percent; hourly earnings increased 7.8 percent in the year ending in July, about the same as in the previous year. Even with these lower rates of inflation, the news was not good.

When President Nixon went to Camp David in 1971, he returned with announcements that the public thought would bring lower inflation and increased employment. President Carter's return created less enthusiasm. He blamed the public for their "malaise," although he did not use that word. Instead of announcing that problems required new policies, he asked his cabinet to resign. He soon announced changes. G. William Miller replaced Michael Blumenthal as Secretary of the Treasury. That left a vacancy at the Federal Reserve.

There were strong market pressures to fill the vacancy promptly. Disappointment and lack of confidence in U.S. policy started another run against the dollar. The gold price rose and the trade-weighted dollar fell to a new low. The president and his staff wanted to announce an appointment that would calm fears and reduce uncertainty about the administration's program. The problem was that the president's staff also wanted someone who would "cooperate" with them.[1] Paul Volcker had strong views strongly held. When he met President Carter for an interview, he was "mainly concerned that the president not be under any misunderstanding about my own concern about the importance of an independent central bank and the need for the tighter money—tighter than Bill Miller had wanted" (Volcker and Gyohten, 1992, 164).

Stuart Eizenstat (1982, 70), the Domestic Policy Adviser, described the circumstances at the time. "With inflation raging and the president's popularity plunging the president believed the economic situation was dire, and he wanted someone who would apply tough medicine."

To President Carter's credit, he appointed Volcker. Inflation was not just an economic problem. Polls showed that the public now listed inflation as a major problem, more serious than unemployment.[2] Several authors

1. Grieder (1987, 45) lists four names of people under consideration: Tom Clausen of Bank of America; Paul Volcker, president of the New York Federal Reserve Bank; David Rockefeller, CEO of Chase Manhattan; and Bruce MacLaury, president of the Brookings Institution. Grieder claimed that the president spoke to Clausen, who declined (ibid., 46). Biven (2002, 239) quotes Lyle Gramley, a former Federal Reserve staff member and, at the time, a member of the Council of Economic Advisers, as saying that Charles Schultze, chairman of CEA, expressed "reservations" about Volcker. Schultze denied that story. He was hospitalized at the time and did not take a position on the appointment (Schultze, 2005).

2. Charles Schultze confirmed the importance of public opinion as a reason for President Carter's concern (Schultze, 2005, 6). He blamed the oil price increase for the change. "It was the supply side shock inflation that turned the public mood very substantially" (ibid., 15). Robert Samuelson (2004, 21) quotes a survey taken in 1979. "For the public today inflation has

describe the president as uncertain about the consequences of his choice; Volcker had dissented against the FOMC consensus several times in the spring of that year, as Miller and Schultze knew. And his concerns about inflation were long-standing. Volcker had spoken about inflation and the need to reduce it many times. When he rejoined the Federal Reserve System as president of the New York bank, he told *Business Week* magazine that "we've got to deal with both inflation and recession at the same time" (Volcker papers, Federal Reserve Bank of New York, Box 35581, August 4, 1995). He criticized a policy of shifting primary concern from inflation to unemployment. He claimed that he was not a monetarist, but he accepted that proper monetary policy had to pay more attention to the long-term effects of its actions, particularly growth of the monetary aggregates.

Volcker discussed the role of money again after Congress passed Concurrent Resolution 133, stating that the Federal Reserve should maintain long-term growth of money commensurate with the economy's long-run potential to increase production. Volcker accepted the importance of monetary control. "To my mind, monetary aggregate targets are a useful—even a necessary—gauge of appropriate monetary policy action in bringing inflation under control. But they do not in themselves alter the real problems and hard choices imposed by the economic structure" ("The Role of Monetary Targets . . . ," galley pages, New York Federal Reserve Bank, Box 35606, December 30, 1977, 10).[3]

By January 1979, he compared the monetarist and cost-push positions and favored an eclectic approach that combined both. But he now described the monetary approach to inflation control as based on the proposition that "substantial and sustained changes in price performance are accompanied by or preceded by substantial and sustained changes in rates of money growth" (draft January 15, 1979, New York Federal Reserve Bank, Box 35581). He added that this relationship was "well established" for the long term but not generally in the short to medium run. No monetarist would have disagreed.

---

the kind of dominance that no other issue has had since World War II. The closest contenders are the Cold War fears of the early 1950s and perhaps the last years of the Vietnam War. But inflation exceeds those issues in the breadth of concerns it has aroused among Americans. . . . In a September 1979 survey, 67 percent of the public said that 'holding down inflation' was a bigger problem than 'finding jobs' (21 percent)."

3. Volcker made clear that he did not favor targeting reserve or money growth without restricting the range within which the federal funds rate could move. But he joined the monetarists in his criticism of the Federal Reserve staff's practice of explaining failure to meet reserve or money targets by claiming that demand for money shifted. "Portentously pointing to these 'shifts,' without further explanation seems to me something of a confession of ignorance" (Volcker papers, "The Role of Monetary Targets . . . ," galley pages, Federal Reserve Bank of New York, Box 35606, December 30, 1977).

As his thinking and observations developed during the 1970s, he moved toward a more monetarist position that he later called practical monetarism (Mehrling, 2007, 177). He recognized that ending inflation required control of money, and he recognized that this could be achieved either by targeting reserve growth or an interest rate. What mattered was how much the interest rate changed to achieve desired control. Commitment also mattered. Volcker understood that ending inflation would not be painless or quick. "I had begun thinking about how one could practically adopt some of these monetarist ideas . . . to make policy more coherent and predictable" (ibid.).

President Carter's summary of his first meeting expressed his own concern about inflation. "He [Volcker] made it plain, and it was mutual, that if he took the job he would want to do it in accordance with my previously expressed policy, that I wouldn't try to put pressure on him or interfere in his best judgment" (Biven, 2002, 239, based on an interview with President Carter). To his credit, President Carter honored his pledge not to pressure Volcker except for the brief period when he insisted on credit controls.

Several in the Carter administration believed that price and wage controls, guidelines, or incomes policy were an important element of an anti-inflation policy. These policies had been in place for several years, and in the summer of 1979, as inflation rose, the administration considered ways to strengthen them. Volcker believed that "if all the difficulties growing out of inflation were going to be dealt with at all, it would have to be through monetary policy. . . . [N]o other approach could be successful without a convincing demonstration that monetary restraint would be maintained" (Volcker and Gyohten, 1992, 164–65).

Volcker became chairman on August 6, 1979. Consumer prices rose at an 11 percent annual rate that month and average hourly earnings rose 7.8 percent. When he left the Board in August 1987, consumer prices had increased 4.2 percent in the most recent twelve months and average hourly earnings rose 2.2 percent. As far as most of the public was concerned, the inflation problem was over for the time.

President Carter gets credit for appointing him and President Reagan for supporting him through a deep recession. But Paul Volcker's major contribution stands out. Unlike 1966, 1969, 1973, and other times, he persisted in an anti-inflation policy long enough to bring the inflation rate down permanently. Despite the added burden of an oil price increase that raised the reported rate of price change, reported consumer price inflation fell from a peak annualized monthly rate of 17 percent in January 1980 to about 5 percent in September and October 1982, when policy operations changed. Interest rates on ten-year Treasury bonds reached 15.68 percent (October 2, 1981) and remained above 10 percent from July 1980 to November 1985. The unemployment rate remained at 7 percent or above for sixty-eight months from May 1980 to December 1985 and reached a postwar peak at 10.8 percent in November and December 1982.

Skepticism about the persistence of low inflation remained in October 1982. The interest rate on a ten-year Treasury bond remained near 11 percent and the Society of Professional Forecasters predicted inflation near 6 percent. Inflation forecasts did not fall to 2 to 3 percent until 1985–86, when the ten-year interest rate reached 7 to 8 percent. Apparently the public had learned to distinguish between permanent and temporary changes (Friedman, 1957; Brunner, Cukierman, and Meltzer, 1980). It became convinced that the long period of high inflation was over only after experiencing a sustained recovery with low or declining inflation rates.[4]

Paul Volcker had the background and experience to be a successful chairman. Early in his career he worked at the New York bank, later as its president, and he served as undersecretary for monetary affairs during the collapse of the Bretton Woods system and its aftermath. Foreign central bankers and New York bankers knew him and had confidence in him. He was knowledgeable and strong-willed, and he recognized the importance of reducing inflation. He was also determined and committed to the task. "You needed someone like Paul, a total technical command, political savvy in the best sense within the System and able to go and explain this to the country. . . . I think he was unique, and it wouldn't have been done this way without him. . . . Now in the end we might have done it one way or another, but they would never have had the nerve to raise interest rates so fast" (Axilrod, 1997, 9). "Paul was a very good chairman at the time . . . [H]e saw the time was right to kill inflation. . . . The President [Reagan] was willing to support him. The public was equally supportive and could get high interest rates from money market funds, so you weren't going to get flack for driving interest rates up with people stuck with low interest rates on their savings accounts. I thought that was crucial in keeping Congress from the battle" (ibid., 8–9).

Axilrod (2005, 241), who worked closely with Volcker, described him as "an eminently practical person, who very well understood how important it was for the health of the economy and the country to bring inflation down and restore the Fed's anti-inflation credibility. Moreover, he also had enough political astuteness to grasp that political and social conditions in the country at the time presented him with a window of opportunity for

4. This episode shows that the short-term interest rate does not express all the information in the term structure of interest rates or in asset prices and inflation anticipations. The Federal Reserve can manipulate the short-term rate. Changes in long-term rates, asset prices, and money growth suggest the degree to which market anticipations respond.

implementing a paradigm shift in policy that might well make the process of controlling inflation more convincing and quicker. In his choice of policy instrument, he was a practical monetarist for a three-year period."

No less important, Volcker believed the task of lowering inflation was important for the country and the world. By moving from New York to Washington to become chairman, he gave up $60,000 a year in income, one measure of his commitment to the task.

Volcker's method of operation was to work with a small staff. Joseph Coyne, in charge of the Office of Public Affairs at the time discussed Volcker's management style.

Q. He has a reputation of being a man who kept his own counsel, who didn't talk very much to the other Governors. Several complained that they really felt that they were out of the loop. . . . Is that fair?
A. Yes, that's fair.
Q. He worked mostly with the staff?
A. He worked mostly with the senior staff. (Coyne, 1998, 9–10)[5]

Volcker did not come to the Board with a complete plan, and he had not decided to change the FOMC's operating procedures. He had spoken about the role of money in inflation control on several previous occasions. The Board's staff, however, had experience with reserve control from earlier efforts in the 1970s. Volcker assigned to Stephen Axilrod and Peter Sternlight the development of a technical control system.

At about the same time, Congress made a major change in regulations affecting interest rates and money by passing the Depository Institutions Deregulation and Monetary Control Act (DIDMCA). The act gradually eliminated interest rate ceilings for banks and financial institutions and empowered the Federal Reserve to require non-member banks to hold reserves. In exchange, non-member banks obtained the privilege of discounting at Federal Reserve Banks. The Federal Reserve had sought a legislated change of this kind at least since 1937 (Meltzer, 2003, 486–87). The change was overdue, but the timing was poor since permitting new types of accounts and removing interest rate ceilings changed the public's preferred mix of monetary assets in a way that made forecasts of money growth difficult just at the time that the Federal Reserve chose to monitor money growth more closely.

5. From the Axilrod interview:

A. Many people on the staff thought they were excluded.
Q. Well, among the Governors also?
A. Yes, in a way they may have been excluded a bit from direct contact with him because he was more comfortable working with several people. (Axilrod, 1997, 10)

Appreciation of the dollar was a third major monetary event of the period. The Federal Reserve's trade-weighted index appreciated from 85 to 135, after adjusting for price changes, between 1980 and 1985. Appreciation worked to reduce measured inflation, but it deepened the recession by raising prices foreigners paid for U.S. exports.

The Federal Reserve and political administrations from 1966 on had postponed or interrupted efforts to reduce inflation. Financial markets and the public had become convinced that commitments to end inflation would vanish once unemployment began to increase.[6] Skepticism made the task more difficult; it was not enough to reduce the inflation rate temporarily. That had happened before, but it had not lasted. The public and financial markets wanted to see a permanent reduction in inflation, a reduction that persisted through the next expansion.

Past failures imposed two conditions: (1) anti-inflation policy had to continue after the unemployment rate increased; (2) inflation would not rise much during the expansion that followed the recession. Past experience made the task harder, but none of the principals anticipated how costly and painful disinflation would be. In practice, it was more costly than they anticipated but much less costly than predictions made by Keynesian economists at the time.

At his confirmation hearing, Volcker distinguished between real and nominal interest rates and explained that to reduce interest rates permanently, the Federal Reserve had to reduce inflation. He made the usual statements about the existence of non-member banks as a problem for monetary control and the changing nature of "money." But in response to a direct question, he described control of money growth as "indispensable . . . if we're going to have price stability. . . . If the growth of money is excessive over a period of time, we're going to have inflation" (Senate Committee on Banking, Housing, and Urban Affairs, 1979, 12). Volcker added later that he saw no reason to use credit controls.

## ANALYSIS AND BELIEFS

Several models or frameworks for analyzing the economy and monetary policy dominated systematic thinking at the time. The more popular Keynesian framework gave no special emphasis to money or money growth. Prices rose for many reasons, and inflation was the measured rate of price change. A leading Keynesian economist, James Tobin (1980a)

6. Pressures to ease rose in 1982. Congressmen Jack Kemp and James Wright (the majority leader) called for Volcker's resignation in 1982. Senator Edward Kennedy, Congressman Henry Reuss, Senator Robert Byrd, and thirty others introduced legislation requiring lower interest rates.

summarized Keynesian thinking about macroeconomics.[7] The economy had an inflationary bias; any effort to stabilize the rate of inflation required a sacrifice of real output. To reduce the bias and the loss of output from disinflation, government had to use incomes policy (ibid., 69). As a member of the Council of Economic Advisors in 1961–62, Tobin proposed and introduced wage-price guidelines in the United States. Despite the many failed attempts to use incomes policies at home and abroad, he and many others held to this view in 1980.

Tobin's analytic framework had five main features: (1) Prices are marked up over costs, particularly labor costs. (2) Changes in aggregate demand change prices, wages, output, and employment by changing the tightness of product and labor markets as measured by unemployment and operating capacity. (3) According to Okun's law, it takes a 3 percent change in GDP to change the unemployment rate by one percentage point. (4) At low unemployment rates, inflation increases and at high unemployment rates, inflation decreases, but the rate of decline is slower than the rate of increase. At the non-accelerating inflation rate of unemployment (NAIRU), inflation remains at the expected rate and the unemployment rate is constant. (5) Tobin saw little professional consensus on the relative effectiveness of fiscal and monetary policies and the proper indicator of monetary policy. He was pessimistic about the costs of the disinflation policy and highly critical of the Volcker policy (Tobin, 1987).

The Phillips curve was a core relation in this framework. It predicted that anti-inflation policy would increase the unemployment rate. Medium-term, this was not true; on average inflation and the unemployment rate rose in the 1970s and subsequently both declined in the 1980s. For medium- and longer-term policy, the positive relation was more important. Monetarists and rational expectationists explained the positive relation as a reflection of the dominating influence of expectations of inflation resulting from monetary expansion and policy errors. Volcker accepted this explanation. Subsequent studies showed that the forecasts had large errors principally because expected output or full employment output could not be measured accurately (Orphanides and van Orden, 2004; Stock and Watson, 1999).

Tobin (1983, 297) remained critical of the disinflation policies adopted in the United States and the United Kingdom at the end of the 1970s. "Like Okun, I would expect the process to be lengthy and costly, characterized by recession, stunted recoveries, and high and rising unemployment." He speculated that it would take ten years. As late as 1981, he urged incomes

7. Goodfriend (2005) has an excellent summary of Tobin's framework.

policies during a transition long enough to unwind the previous history of contracts, patterns, and expectations (ibid., 300).

A major difference between monetarists and Keynesians concerned the role of government. Keynesians saw the government's role as one of managing the economy to minimize social cost of change. Government had a leadership role in adjusting aggregate demand up or down to achieve optimal results. Monetarists emphasized long-term institutional prerequisites for stability. If institutions gave proper incentives to the private sector, the economy would adjust. Although there were differences about the relative importance of fiscal and monetary actions and about the economy's response to policy actions, the major difference was about the role of government. To monetarists, the economic system adjusted toward full use of resources if policies encouraged stability.

Monetarists agreed that reducing inflation would be socially costly. Failure of past attempts reinforced beliefs that disinflationary policies would stop once unemployment rose. Monetarists differed from Keynesians, however, by claiming that the Federal Reserve could reduce the social cost by increasing its credibility. Increased credibility affected price and wage adjustment by changing beliefs and anticipations of future inflation.

Monetarists accepted parts of the framework described by Tobin but emphasized the role of money growth for inflation and the long-run neutrality of money. Following Milton Friedman, they argued that inflation could not be reduced unless money growth declined relative to growth of real output, a proposition accepted by Volcker (Mehrling, 2007, 178). In the long run, the equilibrium levels of unemployment, output, and other non-monetary variables would be the same (after adjustment of tax rates) as before the disinflation. For the monetarists, price levels could change for many reasons, but sustained changes in the rate of price change resulted from excessive money growth—sustained growth of money in excess of output growth. They viewed the Federal Reserve's job as preventing sustained price level changes. They restricted the term "inflation" to sustained changes in the rate of price change.[8]

Monetarists blamed Federal Reserve policy for procyclical monetary actions and for increasing the amplitude of both recessions and inflation. They offered evidence that—measured by money growth—policy was expansive during periods of increasing aggregate demand and inflation and contractive in recessions. They traced much of this problem to the

8. Brunner, Cukierman, and Meltzer (1980) model permanent or persistent changes. Their model shows why unemployment and inflation can rise together, unlike the standard Phillips curve. And the model shows that a permanent disinflation can occur only if the public becomes convinced that policy will not bring back inflation.

misinterpretation of member bank borrowing and interest rate changes. The Federal Reserve interpreted the rise in nominal interest rates during periods of economic expansion as evidence of restrictive monetary policy despite rising money growth; it took the decline of interest rates in recessions as evidence of easier policy despite a decline in money growth. Also, Federal Reserve spokesmen interpreted an increase in borrowed reserves as contractive. Monetarists wanted the Federal Reserve to avoid procyclical actions by controlling money growth, including the effect of borrowing. They recognized that if the Federal Reserve changed interest rates to control money growth, interest rate control would be effective and counter-cyclical. But they did not emphasize the last point and insisted on the importance of controlling money directly. However, they did not give sufficient attention to deregulation in the 1980s that made monetary aggregates less reliable indicators of the thrust of policy action.

These monetarist criticisms of Federal Reserve actions emphasized the problem of using a short-term interest rate or money market conditions to describe monetary policy and to characterize the thrust of monetary policy as easier or tighter. A nominal interest rate must be judged against some benchmark such as sustained money growth relative to the growth of output or relative to the expected rate of inflation. Otherwise it contains little information about policy. Later, Taylor (1993) proposed an interest rate rule for judging the thrust of current policy actions that several central banks use. The Taylor rule advises the central bank to compare the nominal short-term rate to prevailing conditions, including current anticipations. Monetarists also insisted on the importance of policy persistence. The public had to be convinced that the Federal Reserve would persist in an anti-inflationary policy when unemployment rose, as they expected it would. If the public became convinced that low inflation would return, the social cost of reducing inflation would fall. Using this reasoning, Cagan (1978b) estimated a more rapid response to disinflationary policy than Tobin or Okun. The staff econometric model also predicted a more rapid response than Tobin.

Differences in the expected response of inflation to sustained disinflationary policy divided economists at the time. Nordhaus (1983, 254) described the Keynesian view of inflation. "Inflation is taken to be the sum of inertial, cyclical, and volatile or random forces. The inertial element is the inherited 'underlying' rate of inflation, particularly from wages, which changes slowly in response to experience and expectations."[9] Inertial infla-

9. Academic literature at the time was dominated by models with rational expectations. The then current vintage had little or no effect of policy actions on real variables. President Mark Willes (Minneapolis) mentioned this work at times, but he did not get a response.

tion was slow to adjust downward. Nordhaus described the principal cost of chronic inflation as the constraint imposed on economic activity. "The main reason policymakers have been unwilling to set higher targets for output and employment is simply their fear that higher targets would risk increasing inflation. . . . unemployment rates in the 2 to 3 percent range, and hence output 8 to 10 percent higher would surely have been much closer to the ideal output" (ibid., 265).[10]

By adopting the new procedures and undertaking a sustained effort to reduce inflation, the Federal Reserve staff accepted several main criticisms of the monetarists.[11] At Ohio State University on April 30, 1981, Stephen Axilrod and Peter Sternlight from the Federal Reserve debated Robert Rasche and Allan Meltzer from the Shadow Open Market Committee.[12] The topic was "Is the Federal Reserve's Monetary Control Policy Misdirected?" (Axilrod et al., 1982, 119–47). The debate brought out agreement on objectives and the means to reach them. The Federal Reserve accepted that it had to control money growth to control inflation, a position it had denied in the past.

Important differences remained about how to improve monetary control, particularly how to forecast the money multiplier more accurately and control quarterly or semiannual money growth more effectively. Federal Reserve staff repeated their claim that tighter control of money growth required unacceptable fluctuations in market interest rates. Axilrod and Sternlight mostly refused to recognize publicly that part, probably a large part, of the interest rate volatility resulted from restrictions they imposed such as lagged reserve requirements.[13] Axilrod, however, accepted that variability would be reduced and control improved if the Federal Reserve made institutional changes. He did not suggest why they failed to do so. And he accepted the monetarist proposition that medium- and long-term control of money growth was most important for control of inflation. This was progress at least at the verbal level.

10. Fischer (1983, 275) commented, "The neo-Keynesian synthesis of the late 1960s was that inflation was not a serious problem. . . . [D]isagreements within the profession on the relative importance of inflation and unemployment is a source of differing views on desirable policy."

11. Milton Friedman (1982) summarized the changing position of the Federal Reserve on the possibility of monetary control.

12. The Shadow Open Market Committee was a group of academic and business economists that met semiannually to critique monetary policy. Meltzer was co-chairman.

13. Although he did not say so in the debate, Axilrod made this argument each time the FOMC asked him to discuss lagged reserve requirements. The Board did not consider returning to contemporaneous reserve ratios until pressed to do so by members of Congress (Friedman, 1982, 111).

**Table 8.1** Changes in FOMC Membership, 1979–1981

| BOARD MEMBERS | | |
|---|---|---|
| LEAVING | APPOINTEE | DATE OF APPOINTMENT |
| Phillip Coldwell | Lyle Gramley | May 28, 1980 |
| Phillip Jackson | Frederick Schultz | July 27, 1979 |
| Stephen Gardner | Emmet Rice | June 20, 1979 |
| G. William Miller | Paul Volcker | August 6, 1979 |

| RESERVE BANKS | | | |
|---|---|---|---|
| LEAVING | APPOINTEE | DATE | BANK |
| Monroe Kimbrel | William Ford | May 28, 1980 | Atlanta |
| Robert Mayo | Silas Keehn | July 1, 1981 | Chicago |
| Willis Winn | Karen Horn | May 1, 1982 | Cleveland |
| Ernest Baughman | Robert Boykin | January 1, 1981 | Dallas |
| Mark Willes | E. Gerald Corrigan | August 1, 1980 | Minneapolis |
| Paul Volcker | Anthony Solomon | April 1, 1980 | New York |
| David Eastburn | Edward Boehne | February 1, 1981 | Philadelphia |

## PERSONNEL CHANGES

Both Board members and reserve bank presidents changed during the disinflation. Table 8.1 shows the changes. Lyle Gramley was a career Federal Reserve staff member who returned as a governor after serving on the Council of Economic Advisers. Frederick Schultz was a Florida banker; he served as vice chairman. Anthony Solomon had worked with Volcker in the Nixon administration, and Gerald Corrigan was a Volcker protégé.

## A NEW POLICY[14]

Both the Board and the FOMC were divided in 1979, as they had been for some time. One group wanted more restrictive policy action to reduce inflation. The other expressed concern about a possible recession. By early August, when Paul A. Volcker became chairman, many forecasters thought a recession was coming. Others thought it had started. The preliminary report of second-quarter GNP showed a 3.3 percent decline at annual rates, in part as a result of the oil price rise and the wealth transfer to the oil exporters. "By not tightening, the Committee compounded its earlier errors, allowing inflation to accelerate further only to postpone and raise the cost of restoring stability" (Orphanides, 2004, 171).

Volcker thought that a recession was likely, but before becoming chairman he had repeatedly said that inflation was a bigger concern. He dissented from the directives during the spring because he wanted more

14. An extended discussion of the policy change is Lindsey, Orphanides, and Rasche (2005).

restraint. At his confirmation hearing, he repeated his concern about inflation, emphasized the central role of money growth for inflation, and expressed concern about the persistence of inflationary expectations.

Preparing for a Quadriad meeting in late September, Charles Schultze expressed concern about the increase in interest rates during Volcker's chairmanship. He recognized "the dilemma facing economic policy generally and monetary policy in particular" (memo, Schultze to the president, September 25, 1979, 4–5). Growth of monetary aggregates had increased, but rising interest rates "have a delayed impact on the economy" (ibid., 5). Policy increased the risk of rising unemployment rates in 1980. Disinflation had not started but he urged the president to probe when Volcker could "begin easing a bit" (ibid.), although disinflation policy had not begun.

Volcker's concern was inflation. The FOMC used a federal funds rate target but also announced objectives for growth of $M_1$ and $M_2$. Its directives to the desk aimed to reduce money growth, and it had voted between meetings to raise the federal funds rate target to between 10.5 and 10.75 percent to keep $M_1$ and $M_2$ growth at annual rates between 2.5 and 6.5 and 6.5 and 10.5 percent respectively. At the August 14 FOMC meeting:

> [t]here was little disagreement with the proposition that for the near term modest measures should be taken to direct policy toward slowing growth of the monetary aggregates. Control of monetary growth was regarded as essential to restore expectations of a decline in the rate of inflation over a period of time. (Annual Report, 1979, 183)

FOMC members were aware both that their statements lacked credibility and that market participants paid attention to reported growth of the monetary aggregates, but the statement showed the beginning of a change in members' thinking.

In February 1979, the FOMC had agreed to hold growth of $M_1$, $M_2$, and $M_3$ to ranges of 1.5 to 4.5, 5 to 8, and 6 to 9 percent for the four quarters of 1979. The proposed slow growth of $M_1$ reflected an anticipated shift to NOW accounts.[15] At the August 14 meeting, the committee voted to raise the range for the federal funds rate by one-half point to 10.75 to 11.25 and to make the limits conditional on moderate growth of $M_1$ and $M_2$. President Robert Black (Richmond) and Governor Emmett Rice dissented. Black wanted slower money growth; Rice expressed concern about recession. He wanted policy to remain unchanged. Volcker, aware of the

15. NOW accounts were negotiable orders of withdrawal, similar in many respects to demand deposits, but they paid interest. New England banks began issuing NOW accounts. Legislation, discussed below, extended their use to the rest of the country.

political problem, favored a less inflationary policy, but he wanted to "keep our ammunition reserved as much as possible for more of a crisis situation when we have a rather clear public backing for whatever drastic action we take" (FOMC Minutes, August 14, 1979, 22–23). On August 30, the FOMC voted to raise the upper end of the funds rate band to 11.5 percent, citing high money growth as the reason. Rice again dissented.

If Congress had doubts about Volcker's intentions, they should have been dispelled by his testimony on September 5. He told the House Budget Committee about some of the costs of inflation. Unlike the Keynesians, he considered the costs higher than the costs of reducing inflation. One of the costs Volcker cited in his testimony was "the capricious effects on individuals" (Volcker, 1979, 738). A more specific cost cited was the reduction in after-tax returns to corporations. This return "averaged 3.8 percent during the 1970s . . . as compared to 6.6 percent in the 1960s. At the same time, the uncertainty about future prospects associated with high and varying levels of inflation tends to concentrate the new investment . . . in relatively short, quick payout projects" (ibid., 738–39). And he listed other costs including increased sensitivity, and more rapid response, of wages, exchange rates, prices, and interest rates.

He added that earlier in the postwar years, the response lag was longer, so real incomes increased more before inflation rose. Actions "all too likely to produce more inflation will in fact have only a small and short-lived expansionary effect. . . . [O]ur current economic difficulties are tightly interwoven. They will not be resolved *unless we deal convincingly with inflation*" (ibid., 740; emphasis added). This reasoning dismissed the Phillips curve tradeoff as irrelevant to current outcomes.

On August 13, the Board rejected a request from San Francisco to raise its discount rate by 0.25 percentage points to 10.25 percent. After discussion at the FOMC meeting the following day, the Board on August 16 approved a 0.5 increase in the discount rate to 10.5 percent to support its open market policy. However, the Board did not approve any further requests for increases that month.[16]

What proved to be a critical vote came on September 18. By a vote of four

16. The Shadow Open Market Committee (policy statement, September 17, 1979) remained skeptical. "The slow economic growth, high inflation, and high unemployment of the past decade cannot be blamed primarily on the oil cartel. Monetary policy caused consumer prices to rise at an average rate of 7 percent a year in the seventies. Mishandling of the 1974 oil price increase slowed the rate of investment and lowered the growth of productivity. Reliance on wage and price controls and on guidelines reduced the credibility of government without achieving any reduction in the average rate of inflation." The statement clearly distinguished between a real shock to supply and excess aggregate demand induced by monetary expansion. It urged the government to separate inflation and the real and price *level* effects of the oil price

to three, the Board approved an increase in the discount rate to 11 percent. Governors Partee, Teeters, and Rice dissented. They wanted to wait until they gained more information about the risk of recession. New York had asked for a 0.25 percentage point increase. Lindsey, Orphanides, and Rasche (2005, 196) show that the Federal Reserve made an announced tightening that morning. At the September 14 meeting, Cleveland, Richmond, Dallas, St. Louis, Minneapolis, and San Francisco asked for a 0.5 increase. The Board usually approved requests when made by so many banks, but it delayed its response on September 14 because only four members were at the meeting and they divided two to two. The opponents Rice and Teeters cited the "very high" interest rates at the time. They failed to distinguish between nominal and real rates.

When the Board reopened the issue on September 18, all members attended. Positions had not changed. Those favoring an increase cited strong money growth, high inflation and inflation expectations, and the spread between the discount rate and the market rate. Opponents emphasized the risk of recession and the high level of nominal rates.

Volcker was surprised and disappointed by the market's reaction to the discount rate increase and the vote. He thought the reaction would be positive. This was the second increase in the discount rate during his short tenure as chairman. But the market interpreted the vote very adversely. Instead of taking this as a decisive sign of the new chairman coming in and taking more decisive action, they said: "See the Federal Reserve is at the end of its rope. . . . Instead of being a constructive impact on market psychology, as I interpreted it, it worked the other way" (Volcker, 2001, 2).

The surprising response was a sharp increase in commodity prices and market commentary suggesting that the Federal Reserve would have difficulty further increasing interest rates.[17] This was a critical factor for Volcker; he recognized that small increases in interest rates would be difficult to get and might not be adequate. Also, despite its acceptance by the staff and academics, he did not believe that forecasts based on the Phillips

change. "The proper response to the oil price increase is a reduction in both government spending and taxes."

The Shadow Committee remained skeptical in February 1980, its first meeting after Volcker announced the new procedures. The committee urged the FOMC to control the monetary base. Research by Johannes and Rasche (1979) showed that the base multiplier could be predicted with greater accuracy than by Federal Reserve procedures. Rasche challenged Axilrod to explain why they did not adopt his procedure without getting a response (Axilrod et al., 1982, 122–23).

17. Between the second and third quarters, the Society of Professional Forecasters raised the predicted inflation rate by 0.6 percent to 9.67 percent.

curve were useful. What was plainly happening over a period of time, as the monetarists emphasized, was that both unemployment and inflation were rising, and further delay in dealing with inflation would ultimately make things worse, including the risk that any inflation would be large.

> In my own mind, I had about concluded that we could achieve several things by a change in our approach. Among the most important would be to discipline ourselves. . . . More focus on the money supply also would be a way of telling the public that we meant business. People don't need an advanced course in economics to understand that inflation has something to do with too much money. (Volcker and Gyohten, 1992, 167)

Characteristically, Volcker offered a public statement about the problem and his proposed action in an appearance on a popular television Sunday talk show. As the show opened, the moderator, reflecting past experience, asked:

> Moderator: At what point . . . do you expect your emphasis at the Federal Reserve will change from fighting inflation to fighting unemployment and recession?
>
> Mr. Volcker: Well, Mr. Herman, I don't think we can stop fighting inflation. That is the basic, continuing problem that we face in this economy, and I think that until we straighten out the inflation problem, we're going to have problems of economic instability. So it's not a choice either or, as I see it. I think we've got to keep our eye on that inflationary ball as we move along, particularly in the sense of keeping the money supply under control when moving to a reduced rate of growth in the money supply. (Volcker papers, Federal Reserve Bank of New York, transcript from *Face the Nation,* Box 97653, September 23, 1979, 1)

Later in the broadcast Volcker explained the difference between an oil price increase and maintained inflation. If the oil price stopped rising, "we can see the rate of inflation declining for that reason alone. What is important is that that explosion in oil prices doesn't get translated into the wage and price structure generally" (ibid., 12–13). Throughout the interview he emphasized that progress against inflation would be slow. In the past the "main deficiency in policy . . . has been not having enough concern over the inflationary danger" (ibid., 31).

Volcker left Stephen Axilrod and Peter Sternlight (the account manager) to prepare new operating procedures intended to improve control of money. On a trip to the International Monetary Fund meeting in Belgrade,

Yugoslavia, he briefed Secretary Miller and Council Chairman Schultze. They were not enthusiastic.[18] In Hamburg, Germany, he discussed his plan with Helmut Schmidt, the West German chancellor and Otmar Emminger, president of the Bundesbank. Both were old acquaintances from Volcker's days in the Treasury, and both urged him to go ahead. From their perspective, U.S. inflation and anticipations of continued and higher inflation weakened the dollar and appreciated the mark. This almost certainly brought pressure from German exporters, and they believed made it more difficult to prevent inflation in Germany.

Volcker left the Belgrade meeting early.[19] Gossip at the time said that he changed policy because he had been pressed hard to strengthen the dollar and slow inflation. In fact, he was well along toward that decision and had told the administration officials about his intention on their trip to Belgrade. "It was not true at all. I was just bored. I wanted to go home and get to work, so I went home and thought about it a little more" (Volcker, 2001, 3).

Charles Schultze believed that any restriction on monetary policy would increase unemployment, that the economy would be in recession in election year 1980, and that the policy would make it difficult for the president to win reelection. Doubtless he communicated these thoughts to President Carter and urged him to talk to Volcker. Soon afterward, Schultze changed his mind. On September 25, he sent a note to the president saying that "it is probably best that you don't call [Volcker]. . . . [M]y advice is not to twist Volcker's arm" (memo, Schultze to the president, Schultze papers, September 25, 1980). Reflecting his uncertainty about reserve targets, he urged the president to keep open the option of criticizing Federal Reserve actions later. "Even though I don't believe such a public protest would be wise, there is no use narrowing your options now" (ibid.). A handwritten note on the memo added: "Paul called. I made the points. His decision is possibly best, but he understands my problem" (ibid.).[20]

18. Secretary Miller said he did not think the change was substantive. He thought (correctly) they would have to raise interest rates even to 20 percent (Miller, 2002, 26). Volcker did not share that view. He did not anticipate interest rates at 20 percent. Lindsey, Orphanides, and Rasche (2005) quote several Board members supporting Volcker.

19. By coincidence, the IMF invited Arthur Burns to present the distinguished lecture named for Per Jacobsen, a former managing director. In his lecture, Burns explained that control of money was necessary to control inflation, but that monetary control was not possible in a modern country. He blamed unions, the welfare state, etc. The difference between Burns and Volcker is that Volcker left the Belgrade meeting early to do what Burns said could not be done—control money growth. The different responses of the two men suggests a difference in their character that contributed to success in one case and failure in the other. Robert Black (Richmond) gives more weight to foreign reactions at Belgrade (Black, 2005).

20. Recall that Blumenthal and Schultze used leaks to urge the Federal Reserve to tighten monetary policy at the end of 1978 (Hargrove and Morley, 1984, 485). Schultze did not object

President Carter did not act and did not threaten to oppose the policy if or when the Federal Reserve adopted it.[21] Volcker concluded: "My reading of the situation was that while the president would strongly prefer that we not move in the way we proposed, with all its uncertainties, he was not going to insist on that judgment in an unfamiliar field over the opinion of his newly appointed Federal Reserve chairman" (Volcker and Gyohten, 1992, 169). Public opinion polls contributed to the change. Concerns about inflation reached a peak in 1979. A growing number of people considered inflation at least as serious as unemployment (Fischer, 1984, 46). Politicians in Congress may have shared these concerns or reflected constituents' concerns. They more willingly accepted a more decisive disinflation policy.

Volcker returned to Washington on October 2 and called a special FOMC meeting for Saturday, October 6. On the preceding Thursday, he met with the Board. The discussion emphasized speculation in commodities, gold, and the exchange rate. The London gold price started a sustained increase from about $300 an ounce on August 21. On October 2, it reached a local peak of $426, a 42 percent increase in less than six weeks. The trade-weighted dollar had fallen sharply also, as shown in Chart 8.1. Note the decline following the split vote on the discount rate in mid-September and the appreciation following the Federal Reserve's policy change.

Volcker told the members that the staff had prepared some recommendations "designed to show *convincingly* the Federal Reserve's resolve to contain monetary and credit expansion . . . to help curb emerging speculative excesses, and thereby to dampen inflationary forces and lend support to the dollar in the foreign exchange markets" (Board Minutes, October 4, 1979, 1; emphasis added). The proposed actions included three possible actions: increasing reserve requirement ratios, increasing the discount rate, and shifting to a reserve target.

The Board took no action in advance of the FOMC meeting. It agreed on "the seriousness of the present situation and on the need for action

---

to Volcker's program to reduce inflation by raising interest rates. "I didn't want him to go to a monetarist set of targets. I wanted him to continue to target interest rates, in effect, just raise them a lot" (ibid., 486). Schultze later told Biven (2002, 242) that the genius of what Volcker did . . . was to adopt a system . . . in which he said we are not raising interest rates, we are just setting a non-inflationary path for the money supply, and the markets are raising the interest rates."

21. Schultze urged Volcker to give up the reserve target and raise interest rates in the conventional way. "Once you tell the world this is the money target and we are going to follow it no matter what happens to interest rates, you have to stick with it and you have no flexibility" (Schultze, quoted in Grieder, 1987, 119). Schultze worried that the Federal Reserve would not retreat in a recession.

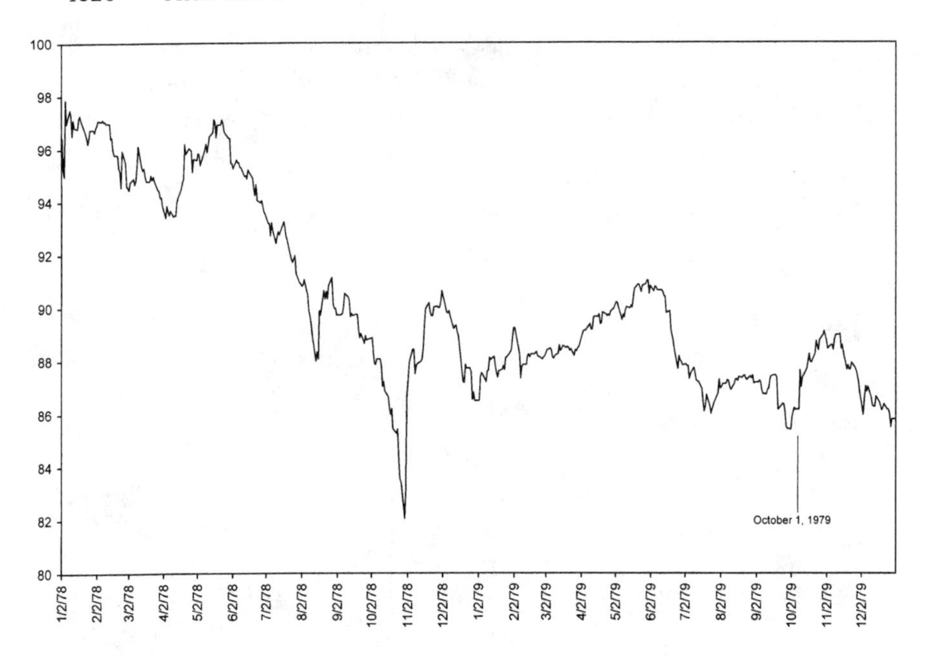


Chart 8.1. Daily exchange index (G-10) 1978–79.

along the lines outlined" (ibid., 3). It preferred the proposal for an increase in marginal reserve requirements on all increases in banks' managed liabilities, the most restrictive of the three proposals they were given. It was clear from the meeting that Volcker would not have opposition from Board members on Saturday.

The following day, the FOMC held a conference call. Volcker made two points at the start. They would make no decisions that day, and any decisions made the next day about operating procedures would be "an approach for between now and the end of the year" (FOMC Minutes, October 5, 1979, 1). He acknowledged that adopting new procedures could make it difficult to abandon them, but he insisted that they would if desirable.

The staff reported that both real GNP and money had grown faster than the FOMC expected. Much of the higher GNP growth was in inventories; the staff expected a reversal in the fourth quarter. Rapid money growth in the second and third quarters put $M_1$ growth above the annual target of 3 to 6 percent. $M_2$ growth was no better, 12 percent against a target range of 5 to 8 percent. The System's battered credibility had taken another hit. Volcker and others believed it would further damage their impaired credibility if they failed to slow money growth. Much of this discussion at the October 6 meeting was about how fast money should be permitted to grow from September to December 1979. Each member had a copy of an Axilrod-Sternlight memo showing that if $M_1$ grew at a 4.6 percent rate in the fourth quarter, growth for the year would be 5.3 percent.[22]

The memo indicated that the staff would estimate the monetary base and total reserves required to reach the FOMC's proposed money growth. They would subtract currency and average member bank borrowing from the monetary base to get an estimate of nonborrowed reserves. Use of average borrowing reflected inability to develop a reliable model of bank borrowing. The desk was supposed to provide the desired growth in nonborrowed reserves. The memo recognized that changes in the demand for money and the multiplier relating reserves to money or failure to control reserve growth could create problems, so the staff would reassess target values for each meeting. The memo and Volcker emphasized that judgment would have to be used to decide both when and how much to adjust. Volcker retained that discretion between meetings.

Volcker recognized that to control money growth, the System had to control total reserve or monetary base growth. Nonborrowed reserves (seasonally adjusted) were the operating target because, Volcker said, they could not directly control borrowing or currency demand. However, if total reserves rose too much, the desk would have to lower the nonborrowed reserve path to offset borrowing. He added that increased borrowing would initially raise the market rate and encourage a move back toward the path for total reserves and the monetary base (Volcker papers, Board of Governors, February 1980).

Volcker pointed to two problems the Axilrod-Sternlight memo neglected: lagged reserve requirements and weak control of discounting.[23] Banks had to hold required reserves against deposits held two weeks earlier. They could borrow to obtain additional reserves. Total reserves would increase, but not nonborrowed reserves. If the Federal Reserve increased the discount rate to reduce borrowing, the federal funds rate would rise.

22. The memo estimated that monetary base growth would average 8 percent in the fourth quarter. Actual growth was 8.6 percent.

23. "We are working with a two-week lagged reserve requirement. . . . [T]hat probably isn't the most desirable [arrangement] in the world if we are operating on this kind of system. . . . But we have it, and that's not something we can change overnight" (FOMC Minutes, October 6, 1979, 26). Banks, especially large banks with many branches, disliked contemporaneous reserve requirements because they were more costly to them. The Federal Reserve chose to support their preference, thereby placing their private benefit about the social benefit of improved reserve control. "With the volatility of the funds rate, more and more banks will be tempted to borrow. . . . How do we prevent that from happening?" (ibid., 32). In practice, the Federal Reserve subsidized borrowing in the next few years.

The FOMC did not then discuss the alternatives—control total reserves or the monetary base and restore contemporary reserve accounting.[24]

Monetarists criticized the procedures at the time, arguing that they made both interest rates and money growth more volatile. Growth of the money stock depends on reserve growth (or the monetary base). By holding to a fixed value (or growth) of nonborrowed reserves, banks had to borrow any deficiency to meet required reserves on deposits outstanding two weeks earlier, thereby increasing total reserves. Eliminating lagged reserve accounting would reduce borrowing and improve control of total reserves and money.

Further, keeping the discount rate as a penalty rate, slightly above the average federal funds rate, would reduce borrowing. Most often, the Federal Reserve subsidized borrowing in 1979–82 by allowing a wide spread, 4 or 5 percentage points, between the average federal funds rate and the discount rate. This encouraged borrowing and weakened control of money.

Some of these points arose at FOMC meetings. Volcker made both points on October 6 but made no effort to change the rules (FOMC Minutes, October 6, 1979, 26). Frank Morris (Boston) made the point about lagged reserve requirements at a telephone conference on October 22. "What happened confirms my feeling that it's going to be very difficult for us to execute control of reserves with a lagged reserves system. . . . It seems to me that reacting two weeks later and having our reserve levels determined by deposits two weeks earlier is continually just going to foul us up" (FOMC Minutes, October 22, 1979, 5). Others agreed, and Volcker said they were looking into it. But the Board did not change; possibly they regarded the problem as short-run and without much effect over a quarter of a year (Lindsey, 2005, 5). More relevant, they were unwilling to impose additional costs on the banks at a time when they perceived membership as a serious problem.[25]

24. Volcker did not propose to let the federal funds rate change without restriction on the size of the change. He told the FOMC: "In this process the federal funds rate is going to be constrained but constrained over a substantially wider range than has been our practice. . . . We operate on a day-to-day basis with almost no range at all. . . . In practice, the kind of range we have is one-eighth of a point roughly" (FOMC Minutes, October 6, 1979, 26). The Axilrod-Sternlight memo used similar language.

25. The System returned to contemporary reserve accounting in October 1982 just as they ended the policy of targeting a reserve aggregate. It no longer mattered. Lindsey speculates that pressure from Beryl Sprinkel, the first Undersecretary of Monetary Affairs in the Reagan administration contributed to the change (Lindsey, 2005, 5). Axilrod's first presentation to the Board analyzed lagged reserve accounting and came out against it, but Martin adopted it (see Chapter 3 ). Axilrod continued to recommend contemporary reserve accounting without effect.

At a special FOMC briefing on November 19, Axilrod and Sternlight explained how they controlled money growth. A straightforward way would have set a target for total reserve growth that would reduce inflation. If banks increased borrowing, the manager would supply fewer reserves by open market operations. To increase control, the Board would restore contemporary reserve accounting. A penalty discount rate would facilitate total reserve control. Changes in the multiplier relating reserves to the money stock would be offset by raising or lowering reserve (and base money) growth.

That was not the procedure adopted by the staff. Axilrod explained that the staff estimated the demand for money, believed to be consistent with the System's objectives, computed reserve growth to satisfy the demand for money, corrected for seasonal adjustment to get non–seasonally adjusted reserve growth as a four-week moving average, and assumed a value for member bank borrowing based on recent behavior to get unborrowed reserves.[26] This procedure introduced possible error at several places, and it gave too much attention to very short-run changes in the demand for money and too little to control of sustained money growth necessary for controlling inflation. Also, it required adjustments for float, currency, and shifts in the composition of deposits subject to different required reserve ratios. The manager added that the desk did not try to control the weekly data; it aimed at a four-week average (FOMC Minutes, appendix, November 19, 1979).

The Board's staff improved models of borrowing, but the FOMC did not use any until 1981. One reason was that the Federal Reserve treated borrowing as a privilege, not a right of membership. The meaning of privilege changed from time to time and introduced non-market considerations into banks' demand. Also, the System changed the rules to permit smaller banks to borrow more easily, especially for seasonal purposes. The difficulty in estimating the demand for borrowed reserves was well known

26. The staff was unable to estimate a reliable borrowing relation or a short-run demand for money. Axilrod noted that lagged reserve accounting made it "impossible" to hit the total reserve target. He argued, however, that it made little difference over three to six months (FOMC Minutes, appendix, November 19, 1979, 5–6). Control over longer periods would be less affected, but Axilrod's statement ignores the market's response to the short-run changes in reserve growth. Mark Willes (Minneapolis) commented on the procedure at the FOMC meeting the next day. "What we would end up with are reserves that are totally demand determined. . . . [W]e are trying to do just the opposite . . . to make reserves and, therefore, the aggregates supply determined. Yet the mechanisms we have set up would have just the opposite result" (FOMC Minutes, November 20, 1979, 20). Willes expressed skepticism as to whether the procedure could work except by chance. Important as his comment was, it did not elicit an answer and was ignored.

at the time. Axilrod and Sternlight avoided econometric estimates of borrowing. See Hamdani and Peristiani (1991, 59–61), who explained why the borrowing relation was non-linear and more variable at high levels of the spread between the federal funds and discount rates, a problem during much of 1979–82. Research at the Board cast doubt on these findings.

No less important, the System misunderstood the effect of borrowing. An implication of the Axilrod-Sternlight framework was that increased member bank borrowing was contractive because interest rates initially rose. This is very reminiscent of the Riefler-Burgess framework from the 1920s, or control of free reserves in the 1950s, when the System exercised control by forcing banks to borrow and, it claimed, to contract. The reasoning was now somewhat different, but the implication was the same: an unchanged value of total reserves was more expansive if member bank borrowing was smaller. The staff did not offer an adequate explanation. As in Riefler-Burgess, they presumed that as borrowing increased, total reserves unchanged, interest rates would rise.[27] One might think that having adopted a money stock target based on the monetary base or total reserves that members would have discarded this old error. That did not happen.

If the demand for money declined in recessions, the staff projection would call for a decline in reserve growth, deepening the recession. Similarly, in expansions, money growth would rise with the demand for money. This procyclical policy characteristic of nominal interest rate targeting, as practiced by the System, remained.

At the October 6 meeting, Volcker again emphasized the temporary nature of the procedural change and the importance of reducing inflation and of acting that day. "We can't walk away today without a program that is strong in fact and perceived as strong in terms of dealing with the situation" (FOMC Minutes, October 6, 1979, 5). He did not equate "strong" with a shift to reserve targets; he said repeatedly that he could continue with traditional procedures, although the Board had accepted the change earlier.[28] The main reasons for change were to give a psychological push to

27. "I would say that we aim at a given volume of reserves and that the composition of that volume of reserves makes a difference. If they're all nonborrowed, it's more expansionary than if a higher percentage of them is borrowed" (Henry Wallich, FOMC Minutes, January 8–9, 1980, 7). The account manager agreed, using the same fallacious argument about bank reluctance to borrow that Riefler (1930) had used. By March, average borrowing exceeded $2.5 billion.

28. "I am prepared, within the broad parameters, to go whichever way the consensus wants to go so long as the program is strong, and if we adopt the new approach so long as we are not locked into it indefinitely" (FOMC Minutes, October 6, 1979, 10).

"Mr. Eastburn . . . There is a credibility problem if we launch this and stop and go with it. So I really think we are committed to this if we go forward.

"Chairman Volcker: Well I don't want to accept that" (ibid., 15).

the idea that inflation would slow or end. Volcker put much emphasis on market psychology and its effect on anticipations.

He was disappointed. He expected an increase in short-term interest rates, but he was disappointed by the big rise in long-term rates. "They went up much more than I would have expected" (Volcker, 2001, 3) "You have this little illusion. You were taking a tough measure, and the market ought to respect it. You're the new Chairman of the Federal Reserve. It ought to have a salutary effect on expectations. Of course, it didn't" (ibid.).

The new program had three parts. First, the FOMC voted to adopt the new procedures and to bring $M_1$ growth to about 5 percent in the fourth quarter. The initial vote was twelve to five in favor, and eight to three among the voting members. Some of those who voted "no" wanted to raise the funds rate but not adopt the reserve target. All three then voted for the program so that it could be announced as approved unanimously. As part of the program, the FOMC permitted the federal funds rate to increase from about 11.5 percent to a range of 11.5 to 15.5, with an understanding that the FOMC would consult if the rate moved above 14.5 percent. Reflecting heightened concern, Nancy Teeters, who voted against a 0.5 percentage point increase in the discount rate in September, proposed that range. She favored a monetary target because it permitted the funds rate to fall.[29] Partee agreed.

Second, the Board met after the FOMC meeting. It approved a request from New York for a 12 percent discount rate, an increase of one percentage point. This was an unusual move intended to demonstrate that a strong program had started and to adjust the discount rate for the expected increase in market rates when the new program began. By the time the board voted on the New York request, Philadelphia, Cleveland, Richmond, Minneapolis, and San Francisco requested the 12 percent discount rate also. Within a few days, all reserve banks were at 12 percent.

Third, the Board raised marginal reserve requirement ratios by 8 percentage points for increases in managed liabilities at banks with $100 million of such liabilities.[30] This level eliminated all small banks, a move intended to disarm some congressional critics.

If the FOMC hoped for a positive response, the markets disabused them quickly. On Monday and Tuesday the Dow Jones average fell about 4.5 per-

29. Teeters (1995, 37) later wrote: "I was very concerned over the very aggressive move to fight inflation in October 1979 and the slowness in the willingness to back off as the recession deepened and dragged on into the middle of 1982."

30. Managed liabilities included: (1) time deposits in denominations of $100,000 or more with one year or less to maturity; (2) federal funds borrowings; (3) repurchase agreements on U.S. government and agency securities; and (4) euro-dollar borrowings from foreign banking offices (Board Minutes, October 6, 1979, 6).

cent. Gold prices fell at first but rose soon after. Reflecting the pervasive uncertainty and difficulty of interpreting what the announcement meant in practice, short-term rates fluctuated over a wide range. Long-term rates rose.

A week after the Federal Reserve's announcement, Charles Schultze sent a memo to the president describing his speech about inflation. He stressed voluntary wage price guidelines and fiscal restraint. He said very little about monetary policy (memo, Schultze to the president, Schultze papers, October 13, 1979).

In testimony to the Joint Economic Committee on October 17, Volcker repeated his main messages about the importance of ending inflation, the need for persistence, the central role of monetary control in an anti-inflation program, and the importance of public support. He did not hide his belief that inflation control would be costly and would require an adjustment of expectations.

The Federal Advisory Council (FAC) favored the new program unanimously but warned the Board that it must persist, despite the coming election and the "likelihood of a recession." If strong words and actions are not followed by results, "then holders of dollar-denominated financial assets in the U.S. and abroad will conclude that the recent changes are no more significant than the statements and policy changes of prior years which did not reduce inflation. Where rhetoric sufficed several years ago, tangible proof is now required" (Addendum to Board Minutes, November 1–2, 1979, 6). The FAC called on the Board to improve communications by announcing "its targets for the growth of the monetary base as well as for other aggregates" (ibid., 7).

### *Why the Change?*

A group that divided sharply in September over a 0.5 percentage point increase in the discount rate to 11 percent voted unanimously less than three weeks later for a 12 percent discount rate, a federal funds rate band up to 15.5 percent and other restrictive measures. They would soon approve still higher short-term interest rates. Also, the FOMC had discussed for years whether to control reserves or interest rates. They now voted unanimously to control reserves. And at least some recognized why their earlier efforts at reserve control failed.[31]

A sense of current or impending crisis often causes officials to adopt changes that they earlier rejected or even scorned. That brought floating

31. Robert Mayo commented on previous experience with reserve control. "I think the RPD [reserves against private deposits] experiment . . . failed we were too timid on the federal funds ranges that we associated with it, and it killed itself" (FOMC Minutes, October 6, 1979, 17).

exchange rates in 1971 or 1973. Now it brought "practical monetarism." Although the FOMC did not adopt the procedures that monetarists advocated, they now accepted the importance of controlling inflation by controlling money, permitting much wider fluctuations in market rates, and distinguishing between real and nominal interest rates.

Volcker was clear about the impending crisis. At the meetings on October 5 and 6, he referred repeatedly to the precipitate depreciation of the exchange rate and possible flight from the dollar and the rise in commodity prices. He didn't claim there was a crisis; he expressed concern that one would come if inflation continued (FOMC Minutes, October 6, 1979, 12).

Those who dissented at the September 18 meeting agreed that the commodity markets and exchange rate reacted negatively to their dissent. They too believed a crisis might occur. They supported a policy change that they would have opposed strongly three weeks earlier. Some, including Volcker, recognized that the FOMC was unlikely to vote for interest rates high enough to reduce inflation. By choosing a reserve target, it could blame the market for the level interest rates reached.[32]

It was also an opportunity to make a major change. The president did not object openly. Key legislators favored monetary control (ibid., 8, 9). European policymakers expressed alarm at the fall in the dollar and urged decisive action (ibid., 17). Perhaps most important of all, the domestic public expressed concern about inflation. Data from Gallup polls starting in 1970, when annual inflation reached 6 percent, show only 14 percent named inflation or "the high cost of living" as one of the country's most important problems. The percentage rose and fell with reported inflation. It did not remain persistently above 50 and as high as 70 percent until 1980–81.[33] Volcker persuaded his colleagues to seize the moment.

### *The Major Change*

The October 6 meeting did not dwell on the most important change. Perhaps without recognizing it, the System implicitly changed the weights on

32. Charles Schultze described the procedural change as "a political cover. They're not monetarists, but it allowed them to do what they could never have done. . . . They could never have done what had to be done if it looked as if they were the ones raising interest rates . . . But with fixed monetary targets they could just say, 'Who us?'" Volcker disliked suggestions that it was a public relations move to avoid blame for the rise in interest rates. "I never thought it was that. . . . It was a very common thing to say that we just did it to obfuscate" (Mehrling, 2007, 178; Hargrove and Morley, 1984, 486). Schultze also described the administration's guidepost policy. "We preached and promoted and jumped up and down, but with little effect" (ibid., 488).

33. I am indebted to Karlyn Bowman of the American Enterprise Institute for retrieving the polling data.

unemployment and inflation. It now regarded control of inflation as its principal current responsibility. That had happened before. The FOMC recognized that its previous efforts failed because it did not persist when the unemployment rate rose. The change in operating procedures intended to signal the change in the System's commitment to put greatest weight on inflation and expectations of inflation. Orphanides (2005, 1021) presents some evidence of this change. The change in objective was much more important and more durable than the change in procedures.

The FOMC may not have recognized the change, but Volcker certainly did. In response to a question from the press, he rejected the Phillips curve tradeoff as a useful tool. Even more than in his colloquy on *Face the Nation,* cited earlier, he emphasized the centrality of ending inflation.

> Question: How high an unemployment rate are you prepared to accept in order to break inflation?
>
> Chairman [Volcker]: That kind of puts me in a position of I accept or unaccept or whatever. You know my basic philosophy is over time we have no choice but to deal with the inflationary situation because over time inflation and the unemployment go together. . . . Isn't that the lesson of the 1970s? We sat around [for] years thinking we could play off a choice between one or the other . . . It had some reality when everybody thought prices were going to be stable . . . So in a very fundamental sense, I don't think we have the choice. . . . The growth situation and the employment situation will be better in an atmosphere of monetary stability than they have been in recent years. (Volcker papers, Federal Reserve Bank of New York, speech at the National Press Club, Box 97657, January 2, 1980, 6)

The Federal Reserve now claimed that a policy of maintaining low inflation would increase employment in the long-run. Instead of trading off higher inflation to get lower unemployment, policy would lower both. Twelve years after Friedman's (1968b) insistence on the effect of expectations, the Federal Reserve not only accepted that it could not permanently reduce unemployment by increasing inflation, but it now claimed that low inflation increased employment. Other leading central banks did the same. The way was open for inflation targets and other ways of recognizing that the principal, but not only, responsibility of a central bank was to maintain the value of money.

The changes in the Federal Reserve's perception of its responsibility eventually produced good results. In the following twenty-five years, the United States experienced two very long expansions followed by two relatively mild recessions. The variability of output growth declined. The

United Kingdom also had a very positive response to persistent low inflation. The new anti-inflation policy remained in place until 2004.[34]

The policy change appreciated the dollar against the European currencies. "The increase of U.S. interest rates and the exchange rate, as well as their volatility, gave rise to vociferous complaints. . . . [T]he principal objection was to the level that interest rates reached in 1981" (Solomon, 1982, 356). The European countries were forced to choose between higher interest rates and currency depreciation. The latter raised energy costs because oil was priced in dollars. Important, also, was the swing in the current account deficit as United States imports fell. By the second half of 1980, the United States' current account temporarily showed a surplus. Among the Europeans struggling with recessions, high nominal interest rates and declining imports were unpopular.

At the time and for many months, the market and the public remained skeptical about the response to the policy change. Short-term interest rates rose as expected, but the market expected higher short-term rates to persist, so long-term interest rates rose also. The three-month Treasury bill rate rose from 10.43 percent on October 5 to a local peak of 12.60 on October 26. It did not fall below 10.43 until May 1980. The ten-year constant-maturity Treasury bond, on the same October dates, rose from 9.53 percent to 10.89 percent. The long-term rate continued to rise, reaching 13.20 percent in February 1980, and did not temporarily fall below 9.53 until June 1980. Forecasts of expected inflation one quarter ahead reached a peak at 9.98 percent in second quarter 1980, but forecasts for four quarters ahead continued to increase until fourth quarter 1980. Using the inflation forecasts to compute real interest rates suggests that these rates remained modestly positive. But confidence in the Federal Reserve's ability or willingness to keep its commitment remained low.[35]

FOMC members recognized the skepticism. This time they intended to continue the anti-inflation policy until inflation remained lower permanently. President Carter did not criticize the policy publicly during his campaign, President Reagan emphasized policies for growth and low inflation. Principal members of Congress, too, provided support.

34. Lindsey, Orphanides, and Rasche (2005, 207) quote Volcker's comment on the *MacNeil/Lehrer Newshour* on October 10, 1979. "I am not saying that unemployment will not rise. I am saying that the greater threat over a period of time would come from failing to deal with inflation rather than efforts to deal with it."

35. Henry Wallich and Scott Pardee (manager of the international account) commented on European attitudes in November 1979. Wallich's statement emphasized the importance of lower inflation. Commitments were not enough. "I think inflation coming down will be the most convincing single thing" (FOMC Minutes, November 20, 1979, 3). Domestic market participants made the same point. It proved to be correct.

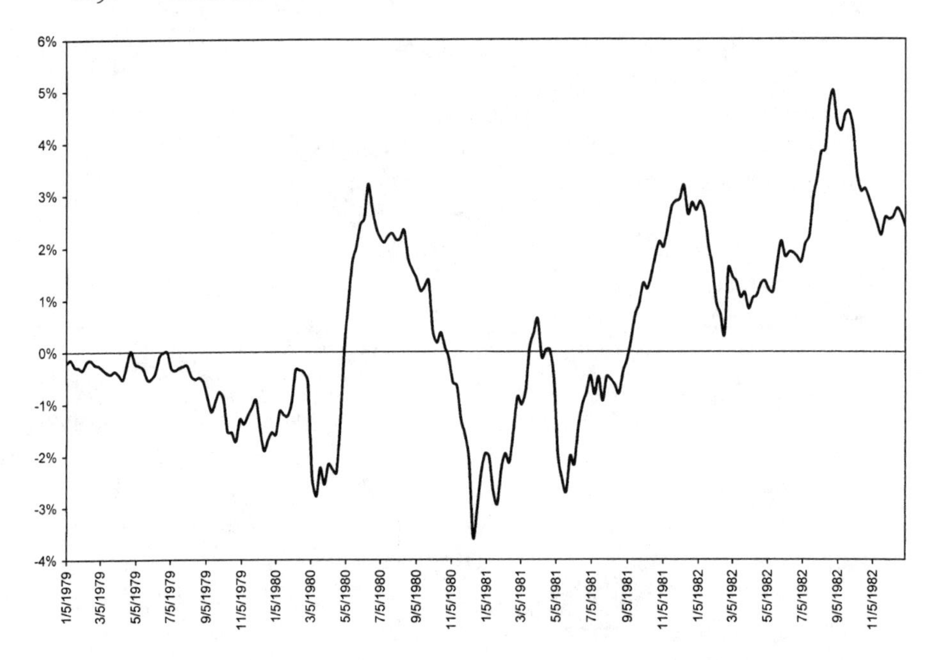


Chart 8.2. Spread, long-term ten-year bond and three-month Treasury bill, January 1979–December 1982.

The shift from interest rate to reserve targets, or the wider band on interest rate ranges, helped to implement and call attention to the change. Research suggests that the Federal Reserve's commitment to reserve targeting was less than many of them said (Cook, 1984).[36] A more transparent, coherent policy of controlling total reserves or the monetary base would have lowered the cost of reducing inflation. But persistence in a disinflation policy was the critical factor. As several members of the FOMC and the senior staff commented at the time, markets wanted to see what the FOMC would do when unemployment rose, when unemployment remained high, and when recovery came. Would inflation remain low in the next recovery? Would disinflation be permanent or, once again, a temporary break in a rising trend?

Policy actions and the anticipations they generated changed several times during the disinflation. Some of the public believed that Federal Reserve actions would lower inflation. Others had the opposite response;

36. Later, in an influential paper, Goodfriend (1991) analyzed interest smoothing in a model of Federal Reserve behavior. He showed that interest rate smoothing could generate an inflation process of the kind that occurred in the 1970s.

expected inflation rose at least for a time. Goodfriend (1993) called these episodes "inflation scares" and used the spread between long- and short-term interest rates to identify the scares. Chart 8.2 shows several periods when long-term rates increased relative to short. Periods such as spring of 1980, when the System abandoned its policy during the brief, sharp recession, or the fall of 1981 (with increased credibility in early 1982) or skepticism about the willingness to persist in disinflation during the summer of 1982 stand out in the chart.

Chart 8.2 suggests that the public distinguished between the one-time increase in price level (or a temporary rise in inflation) and changes in persistent inflation. The oil price increase in 1978–79 raised short-term rates relative to long-term rates. The spread started near zero in 1979 and drifted lower as short-term rates rose and long-term rates remained in a narrow range until the October policy announcement. The announcement raised short-term rates relative to long, suggesting that the market's initial response was perhaps uncertain as to its meaning and persistence.

The four-quarter anticipated inflation rate in the SPF survey rose slightly in fourth quarter 1979 to 8.2 percent, approximately equal to the increase in the deflator in fourth quarter 1979 but below the four-quarter average for 1980. Measured inflation rose after the announcement; the twelve-month rate of consumer price increase reached a peak of 13.70 percent in March 1980, but the deflator did not reach a peak (12.1 percent) until fourth quarter 1980.

### *Policy Actions, the First Phase*

Volcker spoke to the American Bankers Association convention on October 9, three days after the policy change. He outlined the changes, warned them to avoid loans that financed speculation in commodities, gold, or foreign exchange, and described the background to the new policy. He detected "a dramatic swelling of national concern about inflation," and he called attention to congressional support for monetary targets (Board Minutes, October 6, 1979, 5–6). The speech carefully distinguished monetary and other factors affecting prices, including energy and slow productivity growth, but he did not absolve policy of responsibility. "We can no longer blithely assume we can 'buy' prosperity with a little more inflation because the inflation itself is the greater threat to economic stability" (ibid., 9–10).

The initial implementation of the policy change was discouraging. $M_1$ growth for October reached a 14 percent annual rate, far above the 4.5 percent target for the fourth quarter. Axilrod estimated that bank borrowing reached $3.1 billion, twice the FOMC's estimate. He expected it to increase further. The federal funds rate rose to 17 to 18 percent, far above the FOMC's range and the highest rates ever recorded to that time. Trading was light (FOMC Minutes, October 22, 1979, 1).

In the first of many partly reinforcing actions, the FOMC telephone conference chose to keep to the nonborrowed reserve path and allow the federal funds rate to stay at 15 percent or above. That meant that borrowing would remain high. Willis Winn (Cleveland) and several others proposed an increase in the discount rate. Larry Roos (St. Louis) and Mark Willes (Minneapolis) proposed announcing the targets for total reserves and the monetary base, but Volcker rejected both proposals. A higher discount rate would "push market rates up further." He opposed giving the market more information. "We have more targets than we can meet already" (ibid., 9).

The result was a shift back to an interest rate target, keeping the ceiling at 15 percent and satisfying the demand for reserves by permitting banks to borrow from the discount window at less than the market rate. For the month of October, borrowing averaged $2 billion, twice the level of the previous January and $700 million more than in September.

Between October 26 and the next FOMC meeting on November 20, the Board rejected or deferred twenty requests for a 0.5 or 1 percentage point increase in the discount rate. The usual reasons were that the Board wanted to avoid higher interest rates and, in November, because money growth slowed from the torrid October pace. No one mentioned that persistent reductions in borrowing would assist in reaching the money growth targets. Instead, the Board backed away from its money targets. "Flexibility was necessary . . . rather than setting precise, fixed growth levels of the money supply by statute" (Board Minutes, November 9, 1979, 3).[37]

Volcker had difficulty getting people to understand the new procedure. The first question the public asked was "Are you going to stick with it?" He explained that interest rates could decline "when the economy declines particularly if the inflation rate is falling" (FOMC Minutes, November 20, 1979, 24). Years of experience had led the public to interpret any decline

37. Adding to the uncertainties, in November the Iranians occupied the U.S. embassy in Teheran and held the Americans captive. This also affected uncertainty about future oil prices. At the January FOMC meeting, Volcker explained to the presidents how he interpreted their requests for discount rate changes under the new operating procedures. "If you're sending the Board a message about the discount rate, you're sending us a message on where you think market rates should be . . . [t]his is why we didn't act in October and November. . . . It was our judgment that at least in the short run, it wasn't going to close the gap but was just going to put the market rates up further" (FOMC Minutes, January 8–9, 1980, 80). As Volcker noted, his argument depended on traditional Federal Reserve beliefs about banks' reluctance to borrow as in Riefler (1930).

in interest rates as easing and any increase as tightening. Communication that the policy had changed was difficult and made more so because the FOMC was itself less than certain about what it was willing to do and how long it would continue to subordinate control of interest rates to control of reserves and money growth.

Even a relatively hawkish member like Governor Coldwell showed ambivalence very early in the program by using interest rates to evaluate policy thrust. "I'd like to keep the Committee's focus on the inflation side for the moment. I do think the chances of [recession] are high next year; and we will have to face the problem of to what extent we allow the rates to go down next year" (FOMC Minutes, November 20, 1979, 19).

After listening to the November discussion and the large amount of time spent debating small differences, President Roos (St. Louis) said: "I think we have to set longer term targets and be prepared to do what is necessary to achieve those longer-term targets. One thing that I think would be devastating . . . [would be to] worry about whether we ought to reduce the upper limit of the fed funds rate from 15.5 to 14.5 percent" (ibid., 27).

$M_1$ growth ran ahead of the target range in October but slowed in November. By November, year-to-year growth of industrial production had fallen to zero. Money growth ran below target; borrowing declined, so the manager added to the path for nonborrowed reserves. When the FOMC met in early January 1980, many expressed satisfaction with the outcome.

What should they do next? Some wanted to announce money targets for the next three years. Willes (Minneapolis) and Roos (St. Louis) made the case for credible announcements to give the market as much information as possible and reduce expectations of inflation. The majority, led by Nancy Teeters, argued that the System had too little information and would have to change its path. They wanted no announcement beyond the one-year growth rates required by Humphrey-Hawkins.

Monetary innovation added to the difficulty of choosing a path and announcing it to the public. The staff prepared new definitions of money to take account of NOW accounts, automatic tellers, money market funds, and other new instruments. $M_1A$ and $M_1B$ replaced $M_1$; they differed mainly by the amount of NOW accounts. These were expected to increase, if Congress voted to permit the change. That made it difficult to specify growth rates. Following new legislation, the staff expected a large one-time change. The composition of other monetary aggregates also changed.[38]

38. $M_1A$ and $M_1B$ differed by adding into $M_1B$ NOW accounts, automated teller balances, credit union share balances, and demand deposits at mutual savings banks. $M_2$ added savings and small time deposits, overnight repurchase agreements, euro-dollars, and money market mutual fund shares.

However, only $M_1A$ and $M_1B$ were available weekly, so they received most attention from the Board's staff, the manager, and the marketplace.

A December memo from Charles Schultze expressed surprise that the economy avoided a recession. He noted that slow productivity growth had raised costs and prices but kept unemployment low. He expected recession in 1980 with mild recovery late in the year. Oil prices received most attention; he forecast an increase to $29 a barrel, but interest rate increases would cause a decline in housing starts and automobile sales. The forecast decline in GNP was 1.3 percent for the year followed by a small, 1 percent, increase in 1981. His forecast of the GNP deflator was 9 percent in 1980 and 9.3 percent in 1981; the forecast unemployment rate rose in both years to 7.8 and 8.7 percent respectively (memo, Schultze to the Economic Policy Group, Schultze Papers, December 13, 1979).

The Board's staff also forecast a recession in 1980, but it predicted a larger decline of 2.25 percent, followed by slow growth of 1.25 percent in 1981. The projected increase in oil prices was 60 percent in 1980. The inflation forecast called for 8 percent inflation in 1980 and slow decline thereafter. The actual inflation rate (deflator) was 9.9 percent, and real growth was near zero. Data for 1980, however, reflected President Carter's use of credit controls and the public's reaction.

Chairman Volcker expressed concern about inflationary expectations at the January meeting. "All the financial data are within our immediate objectives [but] I don't think we've made as much expectational progress . . . as conceivably might have been hoped" (FOMC Minutes, January 8–9, 1980, 32). The ten-year constant maturity bond yield continued to increase slowly. Between October 5 and January 4, it had increased one percentage point to 10.5 percent. Quarterly data on expected inflation from the Society of Professional Forecasters had increased also. In first quarter 1980, the expected increase in the deflator was almost 10 percent.[39]

Chart 8.3 compares actual and expected inflation from the Livingston survey. Forecasts show no evidence of heightened credibility. Forecasts for 1981 made in 1980 eventually exceeded actual inflation. Forecasters remained skeptical that the new program would succeed. Interest rate reduction in the spring of 1980 probably reduced credibility. Many observers saw it as a repeat of the response to a rising unemployment rate that ended previous attempts to reduce inflation.

What should the FOMC do? The more hawkish members, Coldwell

39. Volcker anticipated increases in the CPI for the next three months including some large increases (FOMC Minutes, January 8–9, 1980, 32). Monthly CPI inflation rates rose from 12.6 percent in December 1979 to 17.1 percent in January and March 1980. March 1980 was the peak monthly and twelve-month rate of reported CPI inflation.

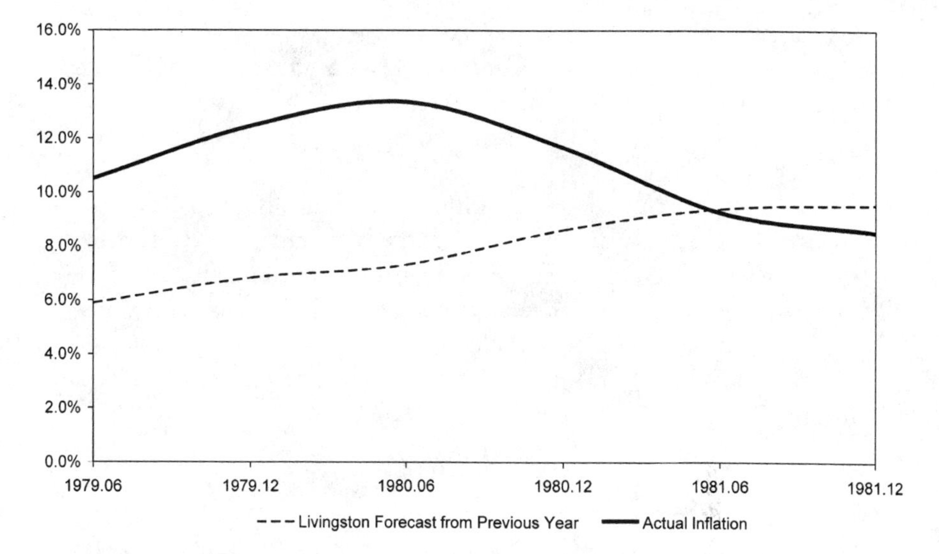


Chart 8.3. Mean inflation forecast from Livingston survey from twelve months prior to actual inflation, June 1979–December 1981.

and Wallich, wanted to reduce the $M_1$ growth rate to 4 percent. Partee and Teeters opposed any additional increase in interest rates as the economy headed into recession. The compromise called for 4.5 percent money growth with the federal funds rate range unchanged at 11.5 to 15.5 percent. Although the Committee was divided, the vote was unanimous.

The new procedure and the high variability of money growth forced some desirable changes in operations. The staff set monetary targets for a quarter ahead that, it believed, were consistent with its annual target. The FOMC gave attention to the credibility of its announcements of annual targets. Several expressed concern that "few people in the financial markets . . . believe that we're going to stick with the policy we announced October 6th" (ibid., 66).[40]

The FOMC could not decide on the relative weight to place on interest rates and money growth. Lawrence Roos (St. Louis) wanted to ignore rate fluctuations to concentrate exclusively on money growth. Most others dis-

40. President Morris (Boston) accepted part of the monetarist claim that traditional policy was procyclical. "Traditionally, following our earlier policies, we have supplied very little monetary growth in the early part of a recession. We have encouraged a sharper decline in the economy thereby. We lagged in reducing interest rates and then when the unemployment rate got really high, we turned around and produced very rapid rates of growth in the money supply. That led to very big swings in the economy, which I think are counterproductive in the long run to controlling inflation" (FOMC Minutes, January 8–9, 1980, 72).

agreed. The staff argued that interest rates and availability of credit affected decisions, so they could not be ignored. Henry Wallich wanted to avoid negative real rates in recession, and Robert Black (Richmond) expressed concern about effects on the exchange rate and foreigners' interpretations of policy.

The FOMC did not reconcile the different positions. Although it did not discuss how much fluctuation in interest rates it would tolerate, it made public the inter-meeting interest rate band in the delayed publication of the directive. This neglect, or deliberate omission, made the policy less transparent than it could have been. Although FOMC members worried about credibility, they would not agree with Mark Willes's frequent statements that, in effect, warned that to be more effective the System had to decide upon and announce a coherent strategy.

### *Goals and Control Procedures*

The Federal Reserve did not announce or choose a long-term goal for inflation. Nor did it specify whether its goal was to end the sustained rate of inflation resulting from excessive aggregate demand or, in addition, to prevent the price level increase resulting from the oil shock. In fact, they did not distinguish the two in their discussions.[41]

Monetarists argued that the proper goal was to end excessive aggregate demand by immediately slowing the rate of increase in the monetary base to a steady 6 percent rate (Shadow Open Market Committee, 1979 and 1980). The oil supply shock would pass through the economy; the price level would remain higher but the result would be a one-time increase spread over time. By trying to prevent the one-time price level increase, the Federal Reserve would use monetary policy to offset a real shock. This would require additional loss of output.[42]

The FOMC discussed lagged reserve accounting at its February 1980

41. To respond to frequent complaints about the opacity of their control procedures, the Board's staff prepared a memo describing procedures more fully. The memo emphasized the judgments that the staff had to make when deciding on the reserve path. Their procedure involved estimating the currency drain, the spillover into non-member bank deposits and into CDs that were not part of $M_1$ or $M_2$. One of the weakest links was the estimate of borrowed reserves. The staff assumed that borrowed reserves would remain "close to the level prevailing around the time of the FOMC meeting, though varying a little above and below that level" (memo, "The New Federal Reserve Technical Procedures for Controlling Money," Federal Reserve Bank of New York, Box 97657, January 30, 1980).

42. Economic theory does not conclude that price level stability—rolling prices up or back following one-time shocks—is preferred to constant expected inflation. The latter leaves the price level to vary as a random walk but maintains zero expected inflation for long-term planning.

meeting. No one disputed that lagged accounting made control of money under nonborrowed reserves target more difficult. The Board's staff report repeated and strengthened its earlier conclusions: it favored contemporary reserve accounting. However, most of the presidents believed that member banks generally favored lagged reserve accounting. The account manager, however, "came out feeling that there is not all that much advantage to it" (FOMC Minutes, February 4–5, 1980, 4).

The members divided on the issue. Those who spoke in favor usually added that they would not act immediately. Congress had under consideration legislation that would increase System membership. They did not want a ruling that agitated the banks. The FOMC took no vote and made no change.

In February 1980, Volcker testified again at Joint Economic Committee hearings. He reinforced and reiterated his main themes—inflation control had to have priority. This time he emphasized that forecasts were not very reliable. A major failing in the past came from "relying too heavily on uncertain economic and financial forecasts" (Volcker papers, Board of Governors, February 1, 1980, 2). He attributed many of the failures to "transitory and misleading movements in the latest statistics" (ibid.).[43] But neither he nor his successors followed a strategy that minimized short-run influences on their actions.

### *The 1980 Recession*

The National Bureau of Economic Research set January 1980 as the start of a mild six-month recession. Real GNP declined 2.5 percent, and the unemployment rate rose to a peak rate of 7.8 percent. Using a common unofficial measure of recession, two consecutive quarters of negative growth, the 1980 experience does not qualify as a recession.

Both the administration and the Board staff expected a recession at the February meeting. The staff was pessimistic about the depth of the recession, but they expected a larger decline in reported inflation, from 11.4 percent in 1980 to 8.6 percent in 1981.

The changed attitude on the FOMC became apparent. Despite the prospect of recession, the FOMC majority favored slower money growth. Governors Teeters and Partee favored an easier policy, but went along with the consensus. Many spoke about the uncertainty caused by redefinition of

43. Later, he described forecasts as equally likely to be right or wrong. He emphasized control of monetary aggregates, lags in response, and determination to continue anti-inflation policy (Volcker papers, Board of Governors, Summer 1980).

the aggregates, the oil shock, hostages in Iran, an election year tax cut, and differing outlooks for economic activity and inflation. But their own credibility and public commitment to slow money growth and inflation was a strong force favoring slower money growth.[44]

Several favored a wider band on growth of the aggregates to recognize their uncertainty and increase the prospect of meeting their targets. Mark Willes (Minneapolis) made the opposite case. "If the time pattern of the economy is very unpredictable, then there's no way we can respond to change it in a predictable way and, therefore, we ought not to be responding. We ought to respond less rather than more, the greater the uncertainty about the outlook" (ibid., 51). He favored picking a long-run non-inflationary path for money and keeping to it. His comment drew no response. Most of the others argued as usual over small differences in the annual growth rates for the various aggregates. The Committee, with two dissents, voted for a quarterly target of 5 percent for $M_1B$ and 6 percent for $M_2$. Governors Wallich and Coldwell dissented because they wanted a more restrictive policy for the next quarter. They agreed with the annual targets of 4 to 6.5 and 6 to 9 percent for $M_1B$ and $M_2$ growth.

The Board's Humphrey-Hawkins procedures required the System to announce its macroeconomic projections for the current and following year. The projections gave a range for inflation and real growth. The unusual feature was a relatively deep projected recession in 1980, as much as −5 percent for the year with a slow recovery in 1981. The FOMC expected the unemployment rate to rise to 8.5 percent by year-end 1980 with little change in 1981. The actual rate was 7.2 percent in December. Projections of inflation proved more accurate and no less pessimistic. For 1980 and 1981, the projected ranges reached 9 to 10 and 7.75 to 9.5 percent. Actual changes in the deflator were 9.5 and 8.6, in the middle of the projections.

Money grew more rapidly than anticipated in February. On February 22, the FOMC held a telephone conference to authorize an increase in the upper limit of the federal funds rate to 16.5 percent. A group that only narrowly approved an 11 percent discount rate in September for fear of recession voted unanimously for an upper limit of 16.5 percent for the federal funds rate after the recession started.

44. The February meeting came before President Carter asked for credit controls. Governor Frederick Schultz commented: "In the area of consumer credit, more and more banks are cutting back on the availability of consumer credit and are increasing the price and other factors. . . . Sears and Penneys and others have recently made those kinds of announcements" (FOMC Minutes, February 4–5, 1980, 43).

The monetary aggregates continued to increase above their short-term targets, and the federal funds rate approached the ceiling as the manager worked to reduce reserve growth. At a March 7 telephone conference, Volcker asked the FOMC to ratify an increase in the ceiling rate to 17.5 percent that he had made and to approve an 18 percent ceiling. The main issue was whether the lower bound should remain at 11.5 percent. Those most concerned about unwillingness to respond to recession wanted to avoid raising the lower bound. The FOMC cancelled its approval of the 17.5 percent ceiling and unanimously agreed to the wider band, 11.5 to 18 percent until their scheduled meeting on March 18. The funds rate was now four percentage points higher than ever before.

The discount rate remained at 12 percent, the rate set the previous October. With the federal funds rate at 17 percent, borrowing soared from $1.2 billion on average for January to $2.8 billion in March. The Board finally agreed to a one percentage point increase effective March 15 for nine reserve banks. By March 19, a uniform 13 percent discount rate was in effect. The action was late and insufficient. Heavy borrowing continued because the subsidy of about four percentage points made it desirable for banks to obtain reserves from the discount window.

For the week ending February 29, the ten-year note yielded an average rate of 13.2 percent. During February and March, the rate remained between 12 and 13 percent. Treasury bill rates reached a local peak of 15.37 percent on March 7. Banks could profitably borrow from reserve banks to hold Treasury bills.

To put these interest rates in perspective, compare them to peaks in Macauley's yields on American railroad bonds, 6.37 and 6.52 percent in 1865 and 1869 for longer-term yields. For shorter-term yields, at the earlier peak in 1873, a year of panic, stock exchange call loans averaged 14.2 percent. Of course, these are nominal yields. In 1981 consumer prices rose at 16 and 17 percent annual rates in February and March, and the Federal Reserve minutes report rising anticipations of inflation and skepticism about the effectiveness of the System's policy. Market participants are an impatient lot. After five months of rising inflation rates, they were not reticent about making their concerns known.

Chart 8.2 above compares long- and short-term nominal interest rates during the years of rising inflation. The negative spread in early 1980 has similar order of magnitude to the spread during the 1970s recession. On this measure, Federal Reserve policy is about as restrictive as in 1973–74 but not more so. Long-term rates rose with short-term rates but less than short-term rates. Nevertheless, the rise in long-term rates and the

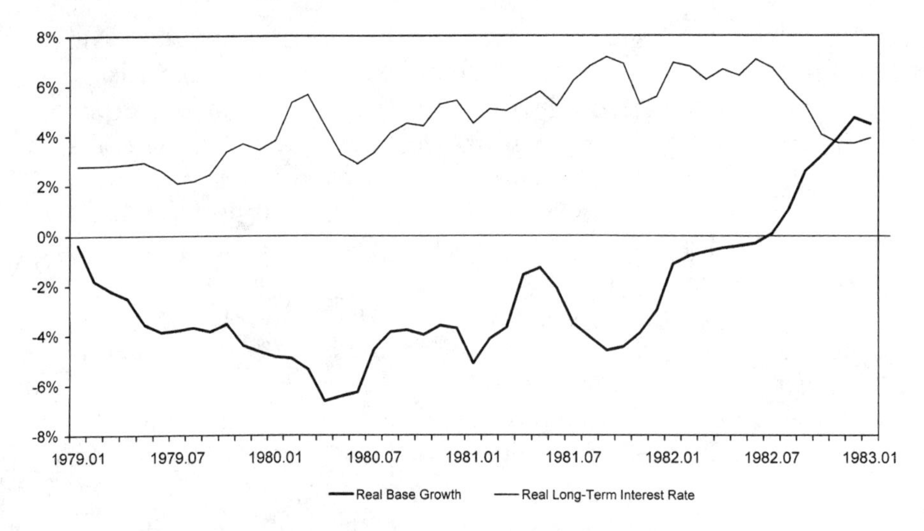


Chart 8.4. Real base growth versus real long-term interest rate, January 1979–January 1983. Real base growth measured year-over-year; long-term interest rate measured as yield on ten-year Treasury bonds.

size of the increase disappointed Volcker and his colleagues (Volcker and Gyohten, 1992, 170).[45]

Chart 8.4 compares annual growth of the real value of the monetary base to the inflation-adjusted (real) long-term interest rate. The two series move toward restriction in 1979 and early 1980 under the common influence of a rising expected inflation rate. Comparison with the 1970s recession (or the 1950s and 1960s) shows more accurately the severity of the restrictive policy. Real monetary base declined at a 6 percent rate. Real long-term rates hardly changed in the 1970s; in 1980, this measure of the real rate rose sharply to about 6 percent or more.

Chart 8.5 brings out more fully the effect of inflation. While the Federal Reserve struggled with little success to control the monetary aggregates, rising inflation sharply lowered their real growth. Judged by growth of the nominal base, the new monetary policy accomplished little. Annual growth of the nominal base rose from 7.7 percent in October to 8.2 percent in March. Real base growth, however, turned negative early in 1979 and

45. Lindsey, Orphanides, and Rasche (2005, 209–10) quote Volcker and other FOMC members as satisfied with the progress and the "success" of the new procedures in January 1980. This is probably a reference to slower money growth. They also report the support of Senators William Proxmire and Jake Garn of the Banking Committee for the aggressive policy. Proxmire expressed hope that the FOMC would continue the policy in a presidential election year.

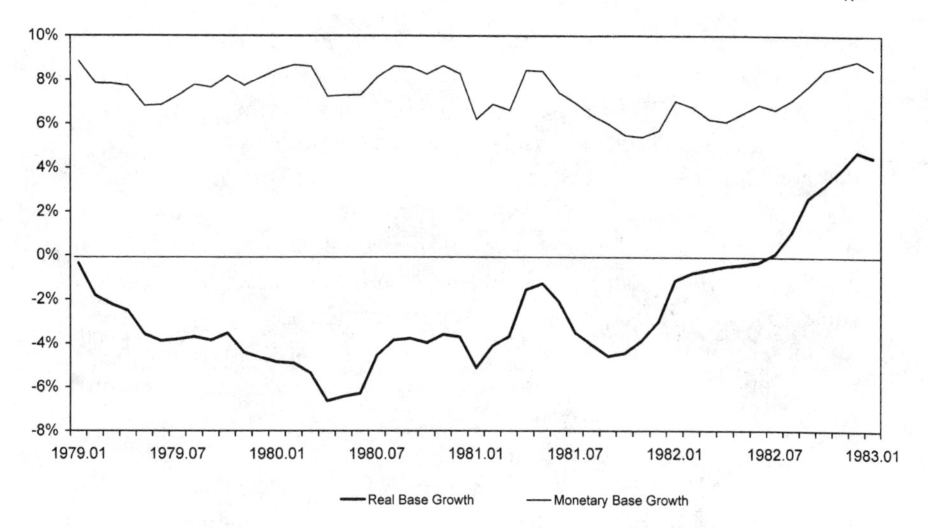


Chart 8.5. Monetary base growth versus real base growth, January 1979–January 1983. Growth measured year-over-year.

continued to decline until March–April 1980. Thereafter, the real value of the monetary base continued to fall, but the rate of decline slowed. The chart shows the persistence of policy. Real base growth remained negative for 3.5 years. It did not become positive until mid-1982, just before economic recovery at a time when nominal base growth rose and the real rate (Chart 8.4) declined.

The unemployment rate started to rise in the new year, but the rise was modest, reaching 6.3 percent in March. Unlike previous recessions, the rise in the unemployment rate did not create substantial pressure on the president and his administration. High nominal interest rates did. Principal members of Congress remained committed to an anti-inflation policy, but some criticized alleged monetary orthodoxy and blamed it for the level of interest rates. They hoped to slow spending at lower interest rates. They urged the president to use the powers granted in the 1969 Credit Control Act to ask the Federal Reserve to control consumer credit.

Responding to the criticism, on March 14, 1980, the Board split the discount rate by authorizing a three percentage point surcharge for banks with more than $500 million in deposits. With the funds rate at 17 percent or higher, the subsidy to borrowing remained. The Board renewed the basic discount rate at 13 percent to help smaller banks. Some members wanted a higher basic rate, but the majority opposed. The main reasons were concerns about congressional pressure, agricultural credit, and the slowing economy. The surcharge remained in effect until May 6, when eight banks voted to remove it. Henry Wallich opposed the decision. He believed that the market would interpret the decision to eliminate the surcharge and reduce the federal funds rate as an end to the anti-inflation policy.[46]

The idea of using credit controls spread. Thomas Timlen, acting president of the New York bank, reported on a meeting with business executives. They urged the System to control credit directly—not just any credit, or all credit, but consumer credit. They wanted limits on the "ability of consumers to borrow" (FOMC Minutes, March 7, 1980, 5).

Volcker opposed credit controls. He spoke publicly about his opposition. "I am not in favor of taking any direct measure to control consumer credit, or indeed, any other type of credit" (Volcker papers, Federal Reserve Bank of New York, address to the National Press Club, January 2, 1980, Box 97657, 3). He offered several reasons why controls would be hard to administer and ineffective. He asked: how could the Federal Reserve restrict people from using their credit cards?

A year before, on March 13, 1979, Charles Schultze prepared a memo on credit controls. He recognized the problems of administering controls, the disproportionate effect on lower-middle income groups, and the loss of employment in automobile production if controls increased down payments or shortened maximum duration of loans. He was not positive, but he did not recommend against controls (memo, Schultze to the Economic Policy Group, March 13, 1979, 7–8).

At a congressional hearing in December, Congressman John Cavanaugh asked Volcker about reserve growth, pointing out that the reason the System had difficulty controlling money growth came from the failure to control reserve growth. Volcker replied that the System controlled nonborrowed reserves. Cavanaugh asked whether borrowing also supported money growth. Volcker replied that borrowed reserves were different than nonborrowed, using the flawed Riefler-Burgess reasoning. "Banks are reluctant to borrow, and the mere fact of borrowing will exert some restraint" (Clark, *Wall Street Journal,* December 9, 1980, 1). Then, he added, "Relatively little borrowing doesn't exert much restraint. Relatively large borrowing exerts a lot of restraint. We now have—are back in the position of having a relatively large amount of borrowing, and there is a lot of restraint

46. On April 14 the Board voted down a request from the Cleveland bank to increase the discount rate by two percentage points. On June 12, the Board reduced the discount rate to 10 percent, and it renewed the surcharge at two percentage points. The Board again began to raise the discount rate on September 15. Governor Teeters opposed. By year-end, the discount rate was back to 13 percent with a three percentage point surcharge.

on the market." As Clark noted, the large volume of borrowing resulted from the wide gap between the discount rate and the federal funds rate.

The FOMC spent the winter raising the federal funds rate to contain money growth. Growth in February was far above target. Members expressed as much concern about the effect on market psychology and their credibility as on inflation, although the two were clearly related. Despite the recession, the dominant thrust at the March 18 meeting was to slow money growth; the FOMC agreed to let the federal funds rate vary between 13 and 20 percent.

Paul Volcker summed up the position that many of his colleagues took. "The worst thing we can do is to indicate some backing off at this point when we have an announced anti-inflation program.[47] We have political support and understanding for what we have been doing. People don't expect it to be too easy. . . . I would not give all that much weight to the degree of support we're going to get if this is dragged out indefinitely and we have to go through this process once again" (FOMC Minutes, March 18, 1980, 36).[48]

Since the staff tried to control growth of nonborrowed reserves, banks borrowed at the discount window to acquire reserves. The manager's report recognized the problem. "The level of borrowing remains one of the more difficult elements to cope with in our reserve targeting approach" (Report of Open Market Operations, FOMC Minutes, appendix, March 18, 1980, 2). Nevertheless, the Board continued to subsidize borrowing by holding the discount rate far below the federal funds rate. Volcker gave one plausible reason—concern that an increase in the discount rate here would encourage foreign central banks to raise their interest rates (FOMC Minutes, March 18, 1980, 7).

*Credit controls.* Prodded by the congressional Democrats, labor unions, and others, on March 14 the president addressed the public on television. He announced additional reductions of $13 billion in spending to reduce the prospective budget deficit, and he told the Federal Reserve to impose credit controls on borrowing. Most of his economic advisers opposed, but

47. Governor Partee summed up the opposing position. "I would hate to have somebody ask me what I was doing during the crash and have to remark that I was defending our credibility" (FOMC Minutes, March 18, 1980, 34). Partee was the most outspoken advocate of low interest rates during the recession.

48. When Senator Byrd (West Virginia), the majority leader, criticized Federal Reserve policy, the chairman of the Banking Committee, Senator Proxmire, defended the Federal Reserve and pointed out that small depositors were big losers because interest rates were below the inflation rate. "There is no way you can do it without more unemployment, without some business failures you would not otherwise have, without serious farm losses" (quoted in Grieder, 1987, 150). The next day Byrd became more supportive.

the decision was made for political reasons to provide an alternative to high interest rates (Biven, 2002, 247).[49]

The Federal Reserve opposed but did not resist. It drafted the new regulations. Schreft (1990, 33) claims that the Federal Reserve planned for the controls in February, before the president acted. Paul Volcker participated fully in the detailed budget discussions and in the credit controls decision;[50] the members were not surprised.

The economy had slowed before controls. Consumer credit grew little in February. The Federal Reserve intended its new regulations to have a modest effect. The Board asked creditors to comply voluntarily with its credit control program. Also, it raised the marginal reserve requirement on managed liabilities from 8 to 10 percent and required creditors to maintain a non-interest-earning deposit equal to 15 percent of the growth of certain assets obtained after March 14. This regulation also applied to money market mutual funds. In a reversion to earlier practices, the System warned banks and financial institutions not to lend for "speculative and nonproductive purposes" and to limit credit growth to 6 to 9 percent for the year. Also, it kept the surcharge of three percentage points on the discount rate charged large banks that borrowed frequently[51] (Annual Report, 1980, 76). The surcharge applied to 270 banks out of 5,459 (Schreft, 1990, 38).

The Board's vote was five to one to adopt controls. Most of the members disliked the proposal, but only Henry Wallich voted no. Coldwell had left the Board, and his successor, Lyle Gramley, had not been confirmed. Grieder (1987, 184) reports Wallich's statement reflected strong views about independence. "It's not an easy thing to vote against a president's wishes. . . . But what are we appointed for? . . . In the end it may be helpful

49. In 1969, Congress authorized the president to direct the Federal Reserve to impose credit controls. In principle, it could reject the request. Chairman Martin testified in favor, and President Nixon signed the bill into law.

50. Charles Schultze explained why Volcker imposed controls. "He was there at the table. . . . [I]f you play in the game, you have to abide by the decision" (Schultze, 2005, 11–12). Volcker (2001, 5–6) described Carter's attempts to cut spending over objections from his political advisers and his decision "to get the message to the consumer." But the president exempted automobiles and housing because they were in a slump. "All we had left was . . . unsecured installment lending and credit cards, which weren't all that big at that time" (ibid., 6). The Federal Reserve was unlikely to dismiss a direct presidential request. Volcker participated in the meetings with the president to decide on $13 billion in spending reductions and credit controls. Once more the Federal Reserve chairman functioned as part of the administration on a political issue. Schreft (1990) gives the legislative history and much detail about administrative and Federal Reserve positions. Volcker even accompanied members of the administration when they testified in Congress about budget cuts (Mehrling, 2007, 180).

51. On March 31, the Board rejected requests by Cleveland for a 16 percent discount rate and by St. Louis for a 15 percent discount rate. On April 14, it rejected a 15 percent rate at Cleveland.

to remind the president that it's not only his present concerns that matter." His substantive objection was that the Board relied on market prices to guide its policy. Credit restraint was a backward step. "It was likely to lead to efforts to circumvent it . . . and to considerable administrative burden" (Board Minutes, March 14, 1980, 11).[52]

Neither the Federal Reserve nor the president's advisers expected the strong public reaction. Although credit card use remained unrestricted, people cut up their credit cards and mailed them to the government or the Federal Reserve. "It wasn't just consumers who were sending the credit cards. I'm told business firms were going around canceling loans. They had been borrowing too much" (Schultze, 2005, 12). Between February or March and July 1980, the unemployment rate rose from 6.3 to 7.5 percent. Real GNP growth fell from 4.1 percent in the first quarter to −9.1 percent in the second. Industrial production declined at 25 to 30 percent annual rates in the spring. This was the sharpest decline in any postwar quarter.[53] The effort to reduce spending without raising interest rates had a much stronger response than traditional monetary actions.

No sooner had credit controls come into effect than the Federal Reserve agreed to a $1.1 billion loan to the Hunt brothers, who lost heavily speculating in the silver market. On March 26, a large brokerage, Bache Halsey, told Volcker that it had lent $200 million to the Hunts to buy silver. It was close to bankruptcy. The reason was that the silver market had collapsed. The price reached $52 an ounce in January; by late March it was down to $10. Twelve domestic banks, four branches of foreign banks, and five brokerages had lent more than $800 million. The Hunts had large losses and could not repay the loans all at once.

Subsequently, market participants learned that the Hunts had purchased futures to bet on a higher price. The contracts came due on March 31; settlement required an additional $665 million. If the Hunts defaulted as expected, the silver market and probably others would decline. Volcker and the Board wanted to avoid that outcome, but they were reluctant to open

52. He referred to experience earlier. Banks circumvented or avoided credit limits by shifting their loans to overseas branches not subject to controls. In April, the Board adopted a temporary seasonal program to assist member and non-member banks making loans to small businesses and farmers. Small housing contractors were an example of an affected group.

53. Frederick Schultz, vice-chairman of the Board of Governors, administered credit controls. Controls worked poorly. "Every time we put out a regulation to try to take care of one problem, we would find that we had created two or three others in the process" (Schultz, 2005, 346). "It shouldn't have done anything, logically. We didn't want it to be very much. . . . I never saw anything like it in my life! . . . [T]o the very day, to the very week, there was a sharp reaction" (Mehrling, 2007, 181).

the discount window to banks with good collateral. Thirteen banks, mainly those that had lent to the Hunts, agreed to extend long-term loans totaling $1.1 billion to avoid a panic.

The problem of controlling excessive money growth reversed soon after credit controls began; growth fell below the target. In place of conflict over how high to place the upper band on the federal funds rate, the FOMC argued over how low to place the lower band. Following the March meeting, the federal funds rate reached a weekly average of 19.38 percent. By the April meeting it was at 17 percent. A week later, the rate was 13.5 percent.

The staff report for the April 22 meeting lowered the forecast for output and reported on the very rapid decline then underway. Auto sales and housing starts had been weak in the winter. Housing starts plunged from an annual rate of 1.5 million in December to 900 thousand in April. Inflation remained high. Consumer and producer prices rose at 18 or 19 percent annual rate in the first quarter. Nothing like this had happened in the peacetime United States and rarely even in wartime. The staff forecast CPI inflation at 17 percent for the year. The actual rate was 11.7 percent. Volcker typically praised the forecasters but expressed deep skepticism about their accuracy. He did not add that his unwillingness to change procedures added to the difficulty of forecasting money growth, reserves, and other variables.

In the midst of the uncertainty created by monetary targeting and credit controls, on March 31, 1980, Congress passed the Monetary Control Act, giving the Federal Reserve additional powers that it had long sought but also deregulating financial institutions to promote competition (Timberlake, 1993, chapter 24). Effective September 1, 1980, all depository institutions maintaining transaction balances or nonpersonal time deposits became subject to reserve requirements. The law specifically included non-member banks, thrift institutions, credit unions, and money market funds. Non-member banks and thrift institutions could hold their reserves at Federal Home Loan Banks, the Central Liquidity Facility of the National Credit Union Administration, or with banks or other institutions that held reserves at Federal Reserve Banks (Annual Report, 1980, 66–67). In exchange, the Federal Reserve permitted these institutions to borrow at the discount window and Congress broadened their lending powers to permit them to compete with banks.[54] Congress also passed legislation gradu-

54. Kenneth Guenther served from 1975 to 1979 on the Federal Reserve staff. His duties included liaison with members of Congress, and he was active in the negotiations leading to the Monetary Control Act. Although the act passed while Volcker was chairman, much of the work was done by Chairman Miller, working with Congressman Henry Reuss. The act also required the Federal Reserve to price its services, such as check clearing, at market prices.

ally phasing out regulation Q interest rate ceilings and permitting interest payments on consumer transaction accounts. And it raised the maximum deposit insurance coverage to $100,000.

Historically high interest rates in the United States relative to foreign rates strengthened the dollar. As interest rates declined after March the dollar depreciated. The Federal Reserve, the Treasury, and foreign central banks intervened using outright purchases and borrowing on swap lines or repaying.

Member bank borrowing declined also in April. The staff anticipated $2.75 billion in early April, but the weakening economy and the surcharge on borrowing by large banks reduced the total. By the end of April, the staff expected borrowing of $1.25 billion including $600 million to a distressed bank.[55] Staff forecasts of short-term changes were often wrong, and this was particularly true of borrowing. Under the method used to set growth of nonborrowed reserves, forecast errors for borrowing often resulted in large errors in total reserve growth.

At the April 22 meeting, several members recognized that the recession was a test of reserve control. These members wanted to maintain a firm policy. Others wanted to lower interest rates and increase money growth in response to recession. Frank Morris (Boston) stated the case for maintaining a restrictive policy.

> If we abandon, for all practical purposes, our money growth targets at the first occasion we find interest rates that are uncomfortable, then how is the market going to have any confidence that when we require uncomfortable interest rates on the up side we will not then also abandon our money growth targets? We would be right back where we have been. . . . We've simply got to ride it through. (FOMC Minutes, April 22, 1980, 13)

Governor Charles Partee warned of the risk.

---

This addition was very attractive to the large banks (Guenther, 2001, 30–31). To support its position, the Federal Reserve used the bogus argument claiming that non-member deposit institutions hindered its ability to control the monetary aggregates. According to Guenther, the Board's staff believed that they were peddling legislation based on a premise that none of the economists believed in (ibid., 31). Goodfriend and Hargraves (1983) show that the Treasury preferred uniform requirements to provide revenue.

55. The Federal Reserve loaned $600 million to First Pennsylvania Bank & Trust early in April to prevent the bank's failure. This was again a misapplication of Bagehot's principles—protecting the bank not the system. This seems part of the "too big to fail policy" that encouraged risk-taking, mergers and giant size. The Federal Reserve has persisted in avoiding announcement of its policy action in a banking panic. This encourages bailouts because there are always concerns that failure will cause a panic. Bagehot's rule warned them to pre-announce that the Federal Reserve would protect the market, not the distressed bank.

> When we get into a decline, it has always seemed to me extremely difficult to forecast how far it might go because there are dynamics involved. There have been shocks: Chrysler, a major bank that has been referred to, silver, and the possible failure of a brokerage firm. (ibid., 15)

The FOMC voted ten to one to maintain its money growth objective about unchanged at 5 percent annual rate "or somewhat less" for $M_1B$ in the first half of 1980 and a federal funds rate of 13 to 19 percent. Henry Wallich dissented; he wanted slower money growth and a higher federal funds rate. Part of the problem at this meeting and throughout the period was that market participants continued to watch the federal funds rate and other short-term rates. They interpreted a decline in these rates as an easier policy, even if the System insisted that it controlled money growth, not interest rates. The very strong response to credit controls made interpretations more difficult.[56]

For those who watched $M_1$ growth, policy in this period seemed to repeat previous experience. $M_1B$ growth declined sharply in the winter of 1980, then reversed. By summer, this closely watched policy indicator was above the growth rate when the new policy started. Chart 8.6 shows these data. Control problems in spring 1981 are large. During the entire 1979–82 period, money growth varied over a wide range. Control was far from perfect or even adequate.

Many market participants believed that the Federal Reserve had abandoned its anti-inflation program once the unemployment rate reached 7 percent or higher. This had happened before and made observers skeptical. The surge in money growth during and following the recession effectively ended the first phase of the program. Volcker and the FOMC had to start again in the fall.[57]

On April 16, the Board opened the discount window for seasonal borrowing to small non-member banks. Non-members with less than $100 million in deposits could borrow to "meet the credit needs of farmers, small businesses, and other priority users" (Annual Report, 1980, 77).

56. FOMC members disliked the credit control program, made many negative comments, and expressed an interest in repeal beginning in May.

57. Otmar Issing (2005) compared West German and United States experience. Inflation in Germany rose to 6.3 percent in 1981, but this was mainly the one-time effect of oil price increases. The Bundesbank targeted central bank money (the monetary base). It reduced monetary growth targets beginning in 1981, achieved its targets, and promptly reduced inflation. Issing gives credit to Bundesbank policy and its experience with monetary targets. He showed that Germany's long-term interest rates remained far below rates in the United States. The plausible reason was lower expected (and actual) inflation.

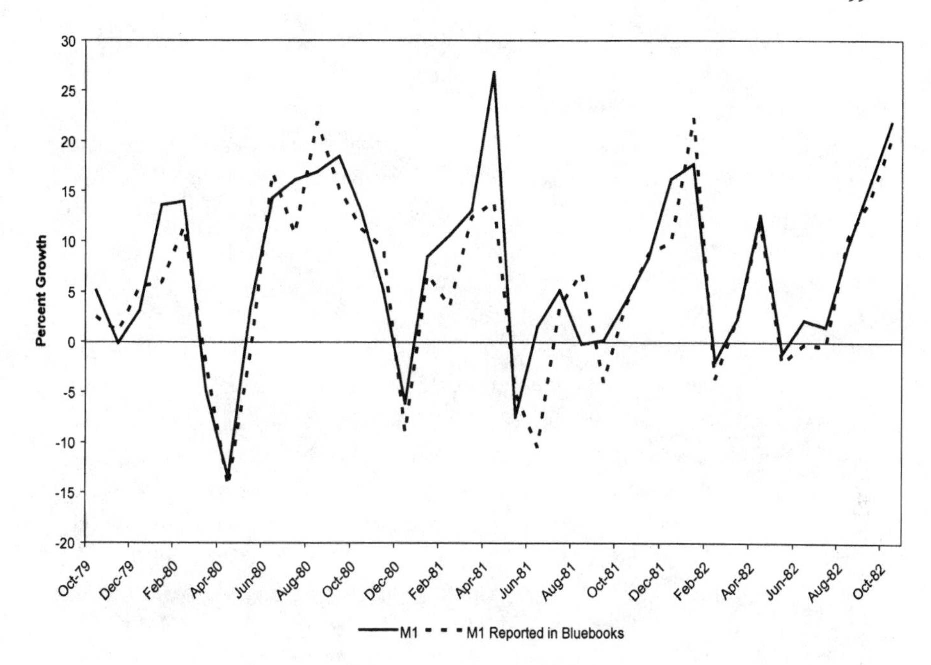


Chart 8.6. $M_1$ versus blue book $M_1$ as reported at FOMC meetings.

Under the Monetary Control Act, these banks would have to hold reserves at Federal Reserve Banks beginning September 1, 1980. This action suggested that the Federal Reserve thought it could influence the allocation of credit, an error it should have learned from Benjamin Strong's writings in the 1920s.

The sharp decline in output was a test of anti-inflation policy. Would the Federal Reserve retreat as it had in the past? Or would it ignore the recession? The market reduced interest rates. The federal funds rate fell below the FOMC's 13 percent lower limit. With the discount rate at 13 percent, and a three percentage point surcharge for large banks, any further decline in demand for reserves would reduce discounts. Excluding the longer-term loan to First Pennsylvania, discounts were $500 million. The staff projected further declines in discounts with downward pressure on the funds rate. Monetary base and money stock growth were negative in April. By a vote of seven to three, the FOMC lowered the lower bound on the funds rate to 10.5 percent. Guffey (Kansas City) and Solomon (New York) voted no because they wanted a smaller reduction in the funds rate. Wallich wanted to maintain the 13 percent rate. In the afternoon, the Board approved removal of the three percentage point surcharge for large borrowers. Wallich voted against because he believed the market would interpret the move as evidence of easier policy that would reduce credibility of the anti-inflation program.

The rapid decline in growth and spending continued. Real GNP fell at a 9 percent annual rate in the second quarter, the most rapid rate of decline in the postwar years before or after. Inflation (deflator) remained high, 9 percent annual rate in the second quarter. The unemployment rate in April rose to 7.0 percent from 6.2 percent in March. By July, it reached a local peak at 7.8 percent, an increase of 2.1 percentage points in a year. It then declined.

The Board's staff had considerable difficulty both in setting and achieving targets for reserve and money growth. With borrowing reduced to low levels, nonborrowed and total reserves moved closely together. Reluctance of the FOMC to allow the funds rate to decline reduced reserve growth. The staff reported that $M_1B$ fell at a 14.5 percent annual rate in April, remained unchanged in May, and rose at a 16.75 percent annual rate in June. For the first six months of 1980, $M_1B$ rose at a 1.75 percent annual rate, far below the FOMC's target.[58] Money growth was again procyclical.

On May 22, the Board moderated credit controls by reducing marginal reserve requirements on managed liabilities of large banks and the special deposit requirement on increases in consumer credit. The new ratios were half the old. But credit controls remained. Chairman Volcker sent a letter to the banks explaining that "bank loans appear to be running comfortably within the 6 to 9 percent guideline" (Board Minutes, May 22, 1980).

A month later, the Board agreed unanimously that the time had come to remove credit controls. Some members wanted to keep controls on growth of money market mutual funds, but the majority rejected this proposal. On July 2, the Board voted to eliminate credit controls effective the next day. The administration agreed.[59] By year-end Congress repealed credit control legislation effective June 30, 1982.

The longer-term effect of credit controls was counterproductive. Despite warnings from several FOMC members, the Federal Reserve responded to high interest rates and rising unemployment by giving up its anti-inflation policy. Monetary base growth rose modestly. By July 1980 the federal funds rate had fallen to 9 percent, almost half its April level, and the SPF expected rate of inflation rose, so real interest rates fell. Whatever

58. The Board's staff, as usual, explained the decline in money growth as a result of shifts in the demand for money. They made no mention of the bound on the federal funds rate as a source of the problem.

59. During July the Board removed special deposits and other parts of the credit control program.

its intentions, the FOMC had again appeared to abandon its anti-inflation policy under administration pressure and to show itself unwilling to pay the cost of disinflation. The episode increased skepticism and further weakened the Federal Reserve's credibility.

*After credit controls.* The Board's staff expected the decline in GNP to continue for the rest of the year. This forecast, too, proved incorrect. Real GNP remained unchanged in the third quarter (0.3) and rose at a 5.2 percent rate in the fourth. Beginning in June, money growth turned strongly positive (see Chart 8.6 above). By August, industrial production began to rise; it increased at a 13 percent average annual rate in the last five months of 1980. The brief, sharp recession was over.

Gradually and for some reluctantly, the FOMC reduced the funds rate. The discussions showed that for several members, control of money growth was one of several objectives, not the most important means of controlling inflation.[60] Roos (St. Louis), supported by Guffey (Kansas City), objected. "We are getting right back to setting interest rate ranges and the stabilization of interest rates. . . . I think we're turning the corner, all for the worse, to right back where we were" (ibid., 42).

Volcker took an eclectic, pragmatic position. "When I look at all these risks, what impresses me is that the greatest risk in the world is not whether we miss our targets or not. I don't want to miss our targets, but we have to put that in perspective of what is going on in the rest of the world. I don't think we can avoid some judgment about what we should do to minimize those risks" (ibid., 28). He also repeated his skepticism about forecasts of money growth and interest rates that he made at almost every meeting. "I yielded to nobody in my skepticism about these things. I am equally skeptical of anyone else's projections—maybe even more so, if that's possible" (ibid., 29). But he did not propose greater emphasis on longer-term projections or improved monetary control.[61]

60. There was not a clear consensus. Henry Wallich expressed the position of several others by describing the policy as an interest rate control policy. "The money supply is a means of getting [desired] interest rates. . . . [I]f we say that we don't want interest rates to move outside a certain range then it seems to me that we've made the judgment that interest rates are to prevail up to a certain point" (FOMC Minutes, May 20, 1980, 12). Earlier in the discussion, Solomon asked Volcker whether the manager increased nonborrowed reserves to compensate for lower borrowing. Volcker replied, "It's possible" (ibid., 11–12). Teeters and Wallich also expressed concern about the depreciation of the dollar, citing criticism of U.S. policy by the IMF.

61. The markets recognized that the Federal Reserve had gone back to managing the funds rate. Henry Wallich said, "I keep hearing about market perceptions that we have moved back to a funds rate objective with a very narrow range." Paul Meek from the desk staff replied, "Yes, I think there has been some feeling in the market to that effect" (FOMC Minutes, July 9, 1980, 8).

Volcker's behavior and his explanation contrasts with what he told Congress the previous February. "The 1979 experience . . . underscores how limited our ability is to project future developments. It reinforces the wisdom of holding firmly to monetary and other economic policies directed toward the evident continuing problems of the economy—of which inflation ranks first—rather than reacting to possibly transitory and misleading movements in the latest statistics or relying too heavily on uncertain economic and financial forecasts" (statement to the Joint Economic Committee, Board Records, February 1, 1980, 2). In a break with tradition, and in an implied criticism of the Carter and Nixon administrations, he rejected the idea that inflation could be reduced by cooperative action by labor unions and businesses. "Experience here and abroad confirms that such programs cannot be the backbone of an anti-inflationary policy. And let us also appreciate, and avoid, the risk that such programs may lull us into thinking that they are a substitute for monetary and budgetary discipline; in that event, the net effect would be counterproductive" (ibid., 15–16). Volcker also proposed letting the oil price increase to reflect its scarcity.[62] Oil had remained under price controls since the Nixon general price controls.

At the July meeting, FOMC members had to reach a first conclusion about the projections of growth, inflation, the unemployment rate, and the monetary aggregates for 1981. They could revise their projection in February, but the initial announcement affected public and market anticipations. Members were more reluctant than usual to announce their views. Nationwide NOW accounts would become effective in January 1981. Payment of interest on household deposits would change some of the monetary aggregates. Non-member banks, thrift associations, and credit unions had to hold reserves equal to member bank reserves, but some could hold their reserves at the Federal Home Loan banks, at the Credit Union National Association, or at member banks. In turn these institutions held larger reserves at the reserve banks. Correctly estimating the effect on reserves was difficult, even impossible. The large decline in money during the second quarter might continue or reverse. In July the Board ended the 2 percent supplementary reserve requirement ratio imposed in November 1978 (Annual Report, 1980, 77–80). In the real economy, the oil shock, productivity growth, and the recession made forecasting unusually difficult. The new operating procedures and the greater weight given to lower inflation af-

62. The administration continued to invoke wage-price policy, but Federal Reserve officials had changed positions. Partee said, "On wage-price control, I would get rid of that program as soon as possible. I think it is totally discredited in the country" (FOMC Minutes, July 9, 1980, 43).

**Table 8.2** Forecasts for 1980 and 1981[c] (per ntages)

| | 1980 | | | 1981 | | |
|---|---|---|---|---|---|---|
| | PRESIDENTS[a] | BOARD STAFF | CEA[b] | PRESIDENTS[a] | BOARD STAFF | CEA[b] |
| 4Q to 4Q | | | | | | |
| GNP | 5.3 | 5.1 | 6.7 | 10.3 | 10.0 | 13.7 |
| Real GNP | −3.8 | −4.0 | −3.1 | 1.5 | 1.1 | 3.7 |
| Deflator | 9.5 | 9.4 | 10.1 | 8.1 | 8.7 | 9.7 |
| Q4 value | | | | | | |
| Unemployment | 8.7 | 8.9 | 8.5 | 9.2 | 9.3 | 8.1 |
| CPI | 8.0 | 7.8 | 9.4 | 8.3 | n.a. | 9.0 |

Source: Board Records, July 7, 1980.
[a] Median value
[b] Mid-year review
[c] Assumes a tax cut in 1981.

fected anticipations, but the members were uncertain about the magnitude and timing of the effect.[63]

The uncertainties that concerned FOMC members and staff were fully justified. By July 1981, the Monetary Control Act added more than 8,000 weekly reporting banks and 8,500 quarterly reporting banks as holders of required reserves. The act included also the Public Sector Adjustment Factor, requiring the reserve banks to price payment services to cover costs and imputed private sector profits. This was the price paid to the large banks for accepting the Monetary Control Act (Guenther, undated, 3). The act also removed state usury ceilings, many of which prevented lending because they did not adjust to inflation. To protect states rights, the states could choose to reenact the ceiling. All depository institutions became subject to a 12 percent reserve requirement ratio for transaction accounts. At institutions with less than $25 million of transaction deposits, the ratio was 3 percent. These changes, too, affected the supply and demand conditions for different deposits.[64]

All of the reserve banks had submitted their forecasts for 1981 with and without a tax cut in 1981. Table 8.2 shows the substantial difference in FOMC forecasts and forecasts by the Council of Economic Advisers.

63. Several members remarked that the past practice of accepting misses in the money growth targets and using the higher level as the base for the next target had greatly reduced the credibility of their announcements and made it imperative to correct excesses and shortfalls. But they didn't change.

64. Following legislation such as the Monetary Control Act and subsequent banking legislation, bank and thrift mergers and failures reduced the number of financial institutions. After several efforts to charter a banking regulatory agency, against the wishes of the Federal Reserve, Congress accepted an agreement between the Treasury and the Federal Reserve giving the Federal Reserve more responsibility.

The table shows that the Board's staff forecast and the median forecast by the presidents were not far apart, but both differed from the CEA. Since the CEA forecast was their last forecast before the presidential election, they may have wanted to show economic recovery and a decline in the unemployment rate; in any case, the CEA showed a much stronger recovery in 1981 than the presidents or the staff.[65] The CEA forecasts were not as optimistic as the forecasts President Carter had received earlier from the CEA.

The Federal Reserve forecast was pessimistic about inflation. It anticipated 8 percent or more. The CEA was even more pessimistic about inflation. These announcements did not add to public confidence in the program.

The FOMC faced a dilemma. If it provided enough money growth to remain consistent with the CEA forecast, money growth targets would have to rise. Raising the target however, would further reduce the credibility of the anti-inflation policy. After extended discussion, the FOMC decided to keep unchanged the targets or objectives for 1980—4 to 6.5 percent for $M_1B$ and 6 to 9 percent for $M_2$—but to stress the uncertainties and avoid specifying numerical values or ranges for 1981. Volcker was aware that members of Congress wanted quantitative estimates, but he was not prepared for their reaction. Senator Proxmire, writing for the Banking Committee, asked the FOMC to reconsider. His letter pointed to the discussion in the Senate committee report prepared at the time the Senate considered Humphrey-Hawkins legislation. The report spoke of "numerical monetary targets for a fixed calendar year" (FOMC Minutes, July 25, 1980, 1). The FOMC agreed to restate its many uncertainties but to announce growth rates 0.5 percentage points below the 1980 targets (ibid., 6–7).[66]

65. By law the Federal Reserve had to explain how its policy would achieve the government's forecast. At about the time of the July meeting, the Board's staff did some computations to estimate the probability that the Board's policy was consistent with the administration's targets for unemployment and inflation. The staff used its econometric model to compute the probability that both unemployment and inflation fell within one percentage point of the 1980 and 1981 targets. The probabilities were 18 and 7 percent for the two years (staff memo, Board Records, July 7, 1980).

66. This excerpt from the FOMC's record suggest some of the uncertainty in the Committee.

> Ms. Teeters. . . . We've been bringing the rate of money supply growth down for the past four years and inflation has been going up. What is a non-inflationary rate of growth in the money supply?
>
> Mr. Roos. There is a lag though, Nancy, isn't there?
>
> Mr. Rice. We don't know. We will keep bringing it down until we find out.
>
> Ms. Teeters. We don't know.
>
> Chairman Volcker. It must be lower than what we've had.
>
> Mr. Partee. Or we have to do it longer. (FOMC Minutes, July 9, 1980, 76)

Some of the difference of opinion at this and other meetings appears to reflect differences in the way members analyzed or thought about inflation. Some, like Governor Teeters, used a Phillips curve, so they believed that lower inflation required higher unemployment, especially in the short-run. Others put greatest weight on expectations and credibility. They believed that once the public and markets became convinced that the System gave priority to reducing inflation, inflation rates would fall and unemployment would fall also. The FOMC never explicitly discussed issues of this kind and, as was typical in the past, made no effort to resolve analytic differences. The big change was that, to greater or lesser extent, emphasis shifted from the unemployment rate to the inflation rate. There was general agreement at last that the Federal Reserve was responsible for inflation. Differences about the cost in unemployment that individual members accepted remained and were never explicitly discussed.

With federal funds trading at 9 percent in July, the Board approved two one percentage point reductions in the discount rate, adding to the belief in financial markets that the anti-inflation policy had ended at least temporarily. By September 2, all banks posted a 10 percent discount rate. Rescinding the two percentage point addition to reserve requirement ratios at large banks also signaled easier policy in July. The reductions weakened the dollar exchange rate; the Federal Reserve and the Treasury sold foreign exchange.

Lyle Gramley took the position vacated by Phillip Coldwell at the July meeting. In August, William Ford (Atlanta) and Gerald Corrigan (Minneapolis) joined the FOMC meeting.[67]

### *End of the Recession*

The National Bureau of Economic Research dated July as the trough of the 1980 recession. In August, the Board's staff recognized that auto sales increased in July and that the rate of economic decline slowed. By mid-September, based on August data, it raised its forecast for the third quarter and anticipated that "the trough in activity will be reached soon, if it hasn't already occurred" (FOMC Briefing, FOMC Minutes, September 16, 1980, appendix). The staff underestimated the strength of the recovery, however.

The Standard & Poor's index of equity prices turned in May. By August, it was 30 percent above its previous year's level, and the index of industrial production rose 14 percent. Treasury bill yields, after reaching a peak at

67. Once again, there was a leak to the press. Volcker threatened to reduce the number permitted to attend, but as on several previous occasions, the threat was reluctant and empty.

15.5 percent in March, declined to about 6.5 percent in June. By late August, these yields had rebounded to near 10 percent.

Despite the decline in interest rates, policy remained procyclical as in past recessions. Growth of money and credit declined; growth of the real monetary base remained negative throughout the recession and did not start a sustained rise until the trough in July. Expected real long-term interest rates are an exception; they declined from April to July. Chart 8.4 above shows some of these data.[68]

Beginning in July, the expected real interest rate began to rise. By year-end it had increased almost three percentage points. Judged by these rates, policy became severely restrictive and, as Chart 8.4 above shows, it became more restrictive in 1981, during the expansion early in the year and the recession that started in July.

Once again, growth of the real base tells a different story, more consistent with events in the economy. Although real base growth remained negative throughout 1981, it reached a trough in April 1980, then started to increase, with one brief setback, until May 1981. It then began a sharp decline foreshadowing the next recession.

The short 1980 recession had, at most, a modest effect on expected inflation. The measured rate of CPI increases reached a peak in March. The twelve-month moving average was 13.7 percent in that month. By August 1980, it was down to 12 percent. Much of the decline in the rate of increase represents the passing through of the one-time oil price increase. Average hourly earnings and the Society of Professional Forecasters' inflation forecast show no evidence of a decline.[69]

Divisions became more pronounced within the FOMC. In the first eight

68. Prodded by Governor Henry Wallich, the staff prepared a number of estimates of real interest rates and after-tax real interest rates. The latter assumed that the corporate tax rate was the relevant tax rate, a very doubtful procedure in view of the many tax-exempt institutions and the growing holdings of U.S. debt by foreign investors. The authors used four measures of expected inflation, including the average of the past three years, current inflation, and the Livingston survey. As in Chart 8.4, they found that real long-term rates were relatively high in 1980 compared to previous recessions (using three-year average inflation). As in the several charts used in the text here, the authors found "no easily discernible pattern in real rates during the initial quarters of an expansion" ("The Behavior of Real Interest Rates in the Postwar U.S. Economy," Board Records, July 2, 1 980, 7). Short-term real interest rates were negative during the 1980 recession in most, but not all, the authors' charts.

69. At the time, the Shadow Open Market Committee expressed considerable skepticism about the Federal Reserve's commitment to its policy of controlling money growth in the first year (policy statement, Shadow Open Market Committee, September 22, 1980). The committee recommended elimination of lagged reserve accounting, prompt adjustment of the discount rates to market rates, and other changes in operating procedures. The House Banking Committee also called on the System to fix the discount rate to a market rate (FOMC Minutes, August 15, 1980, 12).

months, there had been five dissents, three of them by Henry Wallich who often favored a more restrictive policy, and two dissents favoring less restriction at the May meeting. After August, there were dissents at all six regular and telephone meetings. The vote in September and October was eight to four, with all the dissenters favoring tighter policy. The very rapid money growth during the third quarter made it difficult to hit the annual target of 4 to 6.5 percent for $M_1B$. Most of the dissenters wanted more effort to achieve the target; they feared higher inflation and reduced credibility and believed both made it more difficult to reduce inflation. Beginning in November, Nancy Teeters dissented at the next four regular and special meetings. She favored lower interest rates and expressed concern about the recovery.

Volcker tried to find a compromise that would draw a majority. At one point, he expressed the difficulty as he saw it.

> As one market caller put it to me the other day, if the money supply really goes up very sharply for a couple of weeks, we will have big increases in long-term interest rates. I think that is descriptive of the kind of dilemma we are in. I don't know how we get out of that without going through a painful process of deflating the inflationary expectations, which are not deflated yet. And I don't know how they get deflated without deflating the economy more than one would like to see it deflated. I don't have a ready answer to that. (FOMC Minutes, January 8–9, 1980)[70]

In February, Volcker told Congress: "Dealing with inflation has properly been elevated to a position of high national priority. Success will require that policy be consistently and persistently oriented to that end. Vacillation and procrastination, out of fears of recession or otherwise, would run grave risks" (*Federal Reserve Bulletin*, 1980, 214).

His problem was to convince the market and the public that he intended to carry the policy through. First, he had to convince some of his colleagues. Lawrence Roos pointed out that in the first three quarters of 1980, $M_1B$ grew at rates of 6, −2.5, and 12.25 percent with a target of 4.5 to 6 percent. " I don't think these rates of growth in any way reflect any action that this group agreed upon or any policy or directive that we gave" (FOMC Minutes, September 16, 1980, 8). Volcker agreed. "The question

70. Volcker did not take seriously the rational expectations claim that expectations would adjust quickly to his policy actions. The only proponent of rational expectations on the FOMC, Mark Willes (Minneapolis), had left to take a senior management position at General Mills. Both money growth and interest rates were highly variable, so it was difficult to hold firm expectations about future policy. Willes later claimed that a senior staff member warned him not to "shake things too badly or too loudly" (Fogerty, 1992, 4).

is whether we have control in the short-run, and I'm afraid this recent pattern that you point to shows that we don't" (ibid., 8). But he made no suggestions for improving short-run control or giving more emphasis to the long-term.

To all the uncertainties about the economy, the System and the market had to factor in the uncertainties about the meaning of money growth rates at a time of institutional change and redefinition. Lyle Gramley added the usually unspoken concern about what Congress would do if there was another recession. "This country and the Congress may not have the tolerance to let us continue" (ibid., 37). The market's conclusion was that inflation would rise. Between June and December 1980, the yield on ten-year Treasury notes rose 3.7 percentage points to 13.19. Goodfriend (1993, 12) describes this move as evidence of a new inflation scare.

Volcker did not mention Congress, but he was reluctant to "take all the risks on the side of interest rates and the economy. . . . I don't think we can [say] . . . beginning tomorrow or whenever we will go out and in effect force interest rates up. And I would have great reservations about that kind of approach" (ibid., 41). He remained skeptical of forecasts and relied more on actual events. Roos (St. Louis) objected that this was fine-tuning of short-run targets, but he received no support. Much of the discussion was in vain. Money growth remained high in September, borrowing soared far above the staff estimate, and the federal funds rate rose to 12.8 percent for October, up almost four percentage points from July's local low.

Inflationary expectations, reinforced by the policy reversal in the spring, forced more restriction than anyone on the FOMC had anticipated. In late September, the Board approved a 1 percentage point increase in the discount rate to 11 percent. Its announcement explained that it sought to reduce money growth. The Board followed with an increase to 12 percent on November 14, and it restored the 2 percentage point surcharge for large banks that borrowed frequently. St. Louis asked for a 2 percentage point increase, the largest ever, and three banks asked for 1.5 percentage points. Member bank borrowing began to fall. On December 4, the discount rate went to 13 percent, and the surcharge for heavy borrowers rose from 2 to 3 percentage points. Governor Teeters again dissented because she thought interest rates were too high. However, on December 22, the Board rejected requests for a 1 percentage point increase to 14 percent from Richmond and St. Louis and to 15 percent from Cleveland.

## THE 1980 ELECTION

The minutes say very little about the election, and it does not appear to have affected Federal Reserve actions taken in September and October,

**Table 8.3** Government Spending and Budget Deficits, 1979–1982 ($ billions)

| | 1979 | 1980 | 1981 | 1982 |
|---|---|---|---|---|
| Outlays (real)[a] | 660.2 | 699.1 | 726.5 | 745.7 |
| Outlays (nominal) | 503.5 | 590.9 | 678.2 | 745.7 |
| Deficit | −40.1 | −73.8 | −78.9 | −127.9 |

[a] Prices base 100 in 1982
Source: Office of Management and Budget (1990).

although it may have delayed one increase in the discount rate. Ronald Reagan, the Republican candidate, ran on a program to strengthen the military and reduce tax rates and inflation. Reagan's election had little immediate effect on expected inflation. Markets remained skeptical—influenced by the effect on the budget deficit of the promised tax reduction and increased military spending.

The Carter administration increased spending but did not reduce tax rates. Table 8.3 shows Federal government outlays and the budget deficit for the years surrounding the 1980 election. The table shows that government outlays increased more in both real and nominal terms before the election than early in the administration of President Reagan. In a repeat of the shift from President Eisenhower to President Kennedy, President Reagan reduced tax rates after the election, a step that President Carter refused to take. During the campaign, with one exception, Carter did not openly criticize Volcker or Federal Reserve policy. Volcker responded, and the president did not repeat the criticism.[71]

Ronald Reagan won the election. Several of the Board members favored tax reduction to stimulate business investment and increase productivity growth. But just as many expressed concern about higher budget deficits.

About a week after the election, the Board simplified reserve requirement ratios for all depository institutions. The new requirement dispensed with classification into reserve city and country banks, an action the Board had considered since the 1930s. In its place, the Board divided institutions at $25 million in transaction accounts.[72] Small banks and financial

71. In September and October 1980, President Carter complained about the very high interest rates resulting from what he called the Federal Reserve's strict monetary approach. He emphasized Federal Reserve independence and disclaimed responsibility, but he urged the Federal Reserve to give more attention to interest rates. Volcker responded by saying that the Federal Reserve disliked volatile interest rates. He blamed the markets. "According to interviews with a number of key Federal Reserve officials, the Federal Open Market Committee still is paying close attention to interest rates" (Berry, 1980). Schultze (2005, 13) described President Carter in 1980 as "adamant on one thing, no tax cuts." Schultze wanted to have an investment tax credit. "He wouldn't do it. He was a fiscal conservative at heart."

72. Beginning in 1982, the Board adjusted the base upward to reflect inflation. By 1989, the base was $29.8 million in transaction accounts. The base rose 20 percent, about half the rate of consumer price inflation.

institutions paid a three percentage point reserve requirement on transaction accounts; banks with more than $25 million in deposits paid twelve percentage points. For nonpersonal time deposits, the requirement depended on maturity. Under four years, the requirement was three percentage points; over four years, it was zero. The Board allowed eight years to phase in the new requirements. These requirement ratios remained unchanged throughout the 1980s and beyond. In the 1990s, the Board removed the three percentage point reserve requirement ratio for all time deposits.[73] The Board's announcement solicited opinions about a return to contemporary reserve accounting periods. It explained that the change would improve monetary control (Board Minutes, June 4, 1980).

## FINANCIAL DEREGULATION

Remarkable and long-overdue decisions by Congress in the early 1980s repealed several rules adopted in the 1930s and deregulated many financial transactions. The spirit of the 1930s legislation was to limit competition between types of financial institutions with the stated intention of preventing destabilizing competition. Inflation and financial innovation had the opposite effect; as we have seen several times, regulation Q ceilings induced large flows of funds to and from the banking system whenever market rates rose above or fell below ceiling rates.

Of perhaps greater significance for Congress, thrift institutions could issue only fixed rate mortgages. During a time of rising interest rates, the thrifts were profitable. The short-term rates paid to their account holders remained below the long-term rates on their mortgage portfolios. When the Federal Reserve disinflated, short-term interest rates rose above long. To hold their accounts, the thrifts had to pay higher rates. They could only purchase mortgages that yielded lower rates than the rates they paid.

Regulation failed. On March 31, 1980, Congress passed the Depository Institutions Deregulation and Monetary Control Act (DIDMCA). As noted earlier, the act authorized nationwide NOW accounts. It required all depository institutions to hold required reserves either at the Federal Reserve directly or indirectly through other regulatory institutions or in vault cash, made all depository institutions eligible to borrow at the reserve

73. Earlier, the Board's staff prepared a comprehensive report on reserve requirements including elimination of lagged reserve accounting, staggered settlement dates, and other proposals to simplify and smooth adjustment. The staff reported favorably on contemporaneous reserve accounting, but the Board did not adopt any changes. The comprehensive review was mainly the work of David Lindsey and Thomas Simpson. Separately, President William Ford (Atlanta) recommended contemporary reserve accounting in a September letter to the chairman.

banks, and expanded the lending powers of thrift institutions to include business and consumer loans. The thrift institutions gradually lost the competitive benefit of a 0.5 percentage point higher rate that they could pay on liabilities.[74]

The legislation created a Deposit Institutions Deregulation Committee (DIDC) charged with elimination of regulation Q ceilings within six years. The members of DIDC included supervisors of the various institutions—the FDIC, the Federal Home Loan Bank Board, and the National Credit Union Administration—and the Secretary of the Treasury. Paul Volcker became chairman of DIDC. By June 1981, DIDC agreed to a gradual phase-out schedule. In July, a court invalidated the schedule. The DIDC adopted a new schedule in March 1982.[75]

The Federal Reserve had wanted compulsory membership since its inception. Marriner Eccles tried frequently to convince President Roosevelt about its importance, but he did not succeed. Most subsequent chairmen tried. As interest rates rose with inflation, the cost of membership rose and the share of member banks to total banks declined. Between 1970 and 1979, member banks' share of banking offices fell from 71 to 60 percent (Board of Governors, 1981, 470, 488). The number of insured non-member banks rose rapidly. The Board claimed that the relative decline in member banks made monetary policy operations more difficult, although they never presented a cogent argument to support that position, and many of their staff did not believe it.[76] The more plausible but unspoken reason was the desire for political support by bankers willing to accommodate their regulator in the expectation that their requests for mergers, branches, and powers would be treated favorably.

74. The Board gave the banks that withdrew from membership prior to July 1979 eight years to restore required reserves. Many of these banks had invested their reserves in long-term securities that had fallen in value. Institutions with 85 percent of their loans in mortgages remained exempt from the requirements.

75. The legislation authorized the Federal Reserve to price the services it performed for banks such as check clearing, float, provision of currency, etc. The legislation raised the ceiling for deposit insurance from $40,000 to $100,000 (a source of problems later in the decade), broadened the real estate holding powers of national banks, and broadened the range of collateral that the Federal Reserve could hold behind the note issue. DIDMCA passed the House on a vote of 380 to 13 and the Senate by voice vote. The vote suggests the change in sentiment about regulation. To try to hide the failure of savings and loans, the Federal Savings and Loan Insurance Corporation encouraged institutions to include a special certificate of indebtedness among its assets. Congress did not object.

76. "The intellectual argument within the Fed . . . was that we really don't need these reserves to conduct monetary policy anyway. So there was discussion amongst the staff that we were peddling legislation based on a premise that none of the economists believed in" (Guenther, 2001, 31). Guenther was the Board's assistant for political work with the Congress at the time.

DIDMCA did not require membership, but it required financial institutions to hold reserves set by the Board. Burns tried hard to get the legislation but did not succeed because of his poor relationship with Chairman Reuss of the House Banking Committee (Guenther, 2001, 29–30).

After a false start, Miller began negotiations with Reuss.[77] The legislation passed after he moved to the Treasury, but much of the agreement came during his term at the Board.

Although the changes permitted by DIDMCA were long delayed, the timing was far from optimal. National NOW accounts caused shifts in asset portfolios and made the monetary aggregates more difficult to interpret at a time when the Federal Reserve gave more attention to them. Additional legislation, the Garn-St. Germain Bill in 1982, induced larger additional changes.[78]

The difficulties faced by thrift institutions prompted reforms. In 1979, legislation permitted thrifts to make a limited number of variable rate loans, and in 1981 Congress extended that power. Also thrifts could begin to hedge interest rate risk in the futures market. DIDMCA extended their lending powers to commercial and personal loans.[79] The Garn-St. Germain Depository Institutions Act permitted savings and loan associations to issue "net worth certificates" to the regulators in exchange for promissory notes. These gave the appearance of solvency to those who did not look carefully.

Garn-St. Germain authorized banks, saving and loans, and mutual savings banks to issue money market deposit accounts (MMDAs) beginning December 14, 1982. And DIDC authorized a super-NOW account effective January 5, 1983. Banks and thrifts could pay market interest rates on these accounts provided the account balance exceeded $2,500. For the first time, the act permitted out-of-state banks to purchase failing banks and thrifts opening the way to interstate banks.

The response to MMDAs again changed the composition of desired financial assets and obscured the meaning of monetary aggregates. The new instruments had different properties than the old $M_1$. Time and savings deposits and money market funds declined in the first half of 1983, and

77. The Board's lawyers told Chairman Miller that the System could pay interest on bank reserves. This would have reduced the exodus of members. Miller floated the idea, but Reuss threatened to start impeachment proceedings if the System did that (Guenther, 2001, 30). And the Treasury did not want to reduce the revenue it received from the Federal Reserve.

78. Timberlake (1993, 366–70) focused attention on a little-known provision of DIDMCA that permitted the Federal Reserve to use foreign assets as collateral for Federal Reserve notes. He noted that Volcker worked determinedly to get this power after it was removed from the House bill. The conference committee reinstated the provision.

79. DIDMCA was not a completely coherent piece of legislation. The House and Senate produced separate bills that did not mesh. The bill that passed had elements from each.

some of these accounts continued to decline. By 1983, the Federal Reserve had given up control of $M_1$ and $M_2$. The new accounts and uncertainty about the data became the ostensible reason for ending the experiment.[80] Failure to develop successful control of the monetary aggregates and a desire to reduce market rates were at least as important. Congressional pressure seems most important.

Authority to lend to non-bank financial institutions through the discount window promptly attracted attention, especially from mutual savings banks. Most of them suffered losses because their fixed-rate mortgages yielded less than the cost of their deposit liabilities. Failing to renew deposits would force liquidation of mortgages at a loss, impairing their capital. Renewing deposits meant higher interest payments and current losses. Either way, the System's disinflation program threatened their survival. By September 1980, about 90 percent of the New York savings banks operated at a loss.

The Board's position was that it was the lender of last resort. Mutual savings banks and thrifts had to exhaust all other opportunities to borrow. Saving bank representatives disputed this interpretation. At a meeting with Paul Volcker, they "argued that their access to *extended* credit should be on the same terms governing commercial bank access to *short-term* adjustment credit" (memo, Chester Feldberg, Federal Reserve Bank of New York, Box 431.2, September 24, 1980; emphasis added). The Board did not regard the discount window as a source of extended credit. Volcker told them that the Federal Reserve would hold to its traditional position. "He did not believe it was appropriate to apply the same rules to users of both adjustment and extended credit" (ibid.). The intended use of adjustment credit remained temporary shortfalls.

The mutual savings banks and thrifts could not, at first, convince the Federal Reserve, so they appealed to Congress. The result: the Federal Reserve developed a program for long-term loans to "assist depository institutions with longer-term assets when they are confronted with serious prolonged strains on their liquidity arising from an inability to sustain deposit inflows. . . . [A]ssistance for thrift institutions in these circumstances should be available for rather extended periods" (letter, Paul Volcker to Congressman Fernand St. Germain, Board Records, December 22, 1980, 2). This letter at last recognized that the System was the lender of last resort to all solvent financial institutions.

80. $M_1$ rose $15 billion in first quarter 1983. Almost all of the increase was in "other checkable deposits" with little change in demand deposits. MMDAs increased by $280 million (Board of Governors, 1991, 64).

### *Regulation Q*

Congress had at last approved the phase-out of regulation Q ceilings and its discrimination against small savers. The Board's actions in 1980 worked in the opposite direction, limiting competition and imposing ceilings on the interest rates paid to consumers. Money market mutual funds restricted the extent of the harm; these funds bought unregulated large certificates of deposit and paid investors competitive interest rates.

At the start of 1981, the Board authorized banks to issue 2.5-year non-negotiable time deposits at a rate 75 basis points (0.75 percent) below the average yield on a 2.5-year Treasury security. Thrift associations could pay one quarter percent (0.25) more than banks.

On February 27, the Board and regulators of thrift associations limited the return to 12 and 11.75 percent instead of 13.5 and 13.25 percent permitted under the formula. The Board's announcement said that the Board voted unanimously to prevent disruption to financial institutions that held a high proportion of long-term mortgage loans (Board Minutes, February 27, 1980). Opportunities for interest rate regulation of this kind had vanished. The decision increased the outflow to money market accounts and was not renewed in April.[81]

In these and similar decisions, the Board showed greater concern for the financial institutions than for the public. The proposed regulations held the nominal yield below the current rate of increase in consumer prices. Absent the competition from unregulated money market mutual funds, it seems likely that interest rate regulation would have increased. The existence of unregulated accounts, and the public's heightened awareness of the opportunity they presented, had the opposite effect. Competition encouraged more rapid elimination of regulation Q than anticipated in the law.

## A GROWTH INTERLUDE

The economy recovered in late 1980. Fourth-quarter growth at a 5.2 percent annual rate was followed by 8 percent growth in the first quarter. In the next two quarters, output declined modestly then rose modestly, so the level of real output was about the same in first and third quarters of 1981.

81. On March 5, the Board considered a similar restriction on the yield paid on six-month floating-rate time deposits. The Board did not act because regulators of the thrifts would not agree "out of concern over the large deposit drain that could result if depository institutions were unable to offer certificates at rates comparable to those on other market instruments, particularly money market mutual fund shares" (Board Minutes, March 5, 1980, 4).

Industrial production began to rise in August 1980 and began to decline in August 1981.

Reported inflation rates declined. The GNP deflator reached a peak of 12.1 percent annual rate in fourth quarter 1980, then fell back temporarily to 6.7 percent in the second quarter of 1981. This was the lowest reported inflation rate since early 1978. Twelve-month average consumer price inflation declined steadily to 9.1 percent in June 1981. The four-quarter expected rate of inflation (SPF) declined slowly in 1981 from its all time peak at 9.4 percent at the end of 1980.

Most of the reductions in reported inflation resulted from the end of passing through of the oil price increase. It had less to do with the Federal Reserve's disinflation, although it gave the appearance of progress. The market interpreted the fall as an end to the price increase, expected inflation unchanged. Ten-year bond rates remained between 13 and 14 percent in spring 1981. Monthly reported growth of $M_1$ and the monetary base continued to fluctuate over a wide range during this period with no discernible trend at the time. Looking back after the fact, both the nominal and real base declined in the first half of 1981 (Chart 8.5 above). The real base fell at a slower rate.

The trade-weighted dollar exchange rate rose slowly from July to November. The election appears to have strengthened the dollar; the System's exchange rate index rose from 86.59 in October 1980 to 89.31 in November. And it continued to rise. By July 1981, it was 30 percent above its earlier trough. Against the mark, the dollar appreciated from 1.747 to 2.440, nearly 40 percent in the year to July 1981.

The Federal Reserve continued to intervene in 1980. One of the reasons for intervention was to buy marks when they declined in price to use to reduce the swap line and permit the Treasury to pay off the mark-denominated Treasury debt issued by the Carter administration in 1978. By early December, the Carter bonds were fully covered.

The new administration opposed intervention. Treasury Secretary Donald Regan and Undersecretary Beryl Sprinkel announced that the United States would intervene only if markets became turbulent. At its March meeting, the FOMC agreed. Volcker said, "It is extremely difficult to identify any results from intervention per se economically" (FOMC Minutes, March 31, 1981, 15). He noted other reasons, such as acting cooperatively with other central banks.[82] But, he added, "I've never felt eager about inter-

82. The Federal Reserve intervened heavily in 1980. Volcker and several of the FOMC members did not understand exactly how the limits on intervention worked. The manager,

**Table 8.4** Target and Actual Money Growth, 1976–80 (%)

| | TARGET | ACTUAL |
|---|---|---|
| 1976 | 4.5–7.5 | 5.8 |
| 1977 | 4.5–6.5 | 7.9 |
| 1978 | 4.0–6.5 | 7.2 |
| 1979 | 3.0–6.0 | 5.5 |
| 1980 | 4.0–6.5 | 7.1 |

vening anyway" (FOMC Minutes, December 18–19, 1980, 25). This must have come as an unwelcome shock to proponents of intervention at the New York bank.

The Board's staff continued to underestimate the recovery in 1980–81. But member bank borrowing rose above $2 billion. The FOMC decided to raise the funds rate to 18 percent in late November and increase the discount rate. Teeters dissented.

As year-end 1980 approached, it was clear that the Federal Reserve would exceed its annual targets for $M_1$A and $M_1$B. No one proposed taking steps in December required to hit the targets. Many expressed concern about loss of credibility and its effect on expectations, but none favored a further sharp rise in interest rates.[83]

Table 8.4 shows FOMC targets for $M_1$ and actual money growth using data reported at the time. The data for 1980 are for $M_1$B, the closest analogue to old $M_1$. Despite the collapse of money growth during the credit control period, the System exceeded the target. Actual growth was 10 percent above the upper band. As the table shows, this was not an unusual occurrence. The difference was that now many of the members worried about credibility and markets gave more attention to $M_1$ growth.

Scott Pardee, explained that the Federal Reserve had an overall limit and separate limits on the amount of marks and yen that it could hold. There was also a limit on the amount of warehousing (loan to the Treasury). The only limit on the Treasury's Exchange Stabilization Fund was the amount of warehousing it did with the Federal Reserve plus its own limited resources. At the end of 1980, the warehousing limit was $5 billion. The Treasury had used $3 billion. The amount warehoused was a Federal Reserve asset, offset by an off-budget item for the forward contract with the Treasury (FOMC Minutes, December 18, 1980, 2–25).

83. At a telephone conference on December 5, the FOMC voted ten-to-two to raise the upper bound on the funds rate without setting a specific ceiling. Volcker said, "$M_1$B is certainly going to be over [its annual target]. . . . I think we would get a lot of flak from the other direction for having such a big decline in the number in one month" (FOMC Minutes, December 5, 1980). A third inter-meeting telephone conference the following week reaffirmed the absence of a ceiling. Although Volcker emphasized that the interest rate band always changed to control reserve growth, the staff was more candid. Berry (1980) quoted the account manager, Peter Sternlight: "During at least two periods, the level of rates rather than the level of reserves and the money stock became major factors in Fed money market actions." Practice was mixed.

Missing the target soon set off discussion about whether 1981 target money growth should start from the actual value or the 1980 target. In earlier meetings, the consensus claimed that the System contributed to inflation by using actual growth each year as the base for the next target. The implication was that they would not continue that practice. Using the data in Table 8.4, the cumulative difference between the target midpoints and actual growth from 1976 to 1979 was six percentage points. Using the actual values had allowed money to grow at a 6.7 percent average annual rate from 1976 through 1980. The difference in 1980 was nearly two percentage points of money growth above the midpoint.

Views differed. The more aggressive anti-inflationists wanted to use the midpoint of the previous target. Others complained this would be too restrictive in 1981. The members did not reach an agreement at the December meeting. By February 1981, the money stock had declined enough to avoid the issue. The FOMC continued to use the previous actual level as a base.

Everyone at the December meeting expressed confusion and uncertainty about the interpretation of money growth, both retrospective and prospective. Nationwide NOW accounts—in effect, interest-bearing checkable deposits—would soon be available and included in $M_1B$. Also, money market accounts would be included in $M_2$. The System expected large withdrawals from accounts subject to regulation Q ceilings, but it had no reliable way to estimate how much $M_1B$ and $M_2$ would change as a result of the Monetary Control Act. What was the size of the substitution effect? Where would the deposits come from? What should the System announce at the Humphrey-Hawkins hearings in February? How would the announcement affect the System's credibility?

The proposals included use of a reserve target, increased attention to interest rates, and increased support for Henry Wallich's proposal to target the real interest rate. Support for monetary targets had begun to break down. Governor Gramley, for example, had supported monetary targeting. He now favored shifting back to interest rate control using monetary targets "over a longer period" (FOMC Minutes, December 18–19, 1980, 50). Vice Chairman Solomon supported Gramley and Wallich. "I think we have to pay much more attention to real interest rates" (ibid., 56). The proponents of these changes offered no evidence that it would improve inflation control.

For the first time, Governor Partee recognized explicitly that the System had made a major change in policy by shifting emphasis to reducing inflation and away from the unemployment rate. "We no longer care what unemployment is so long as it's plenty low. We now say that in addition to seeing to it that monetary policy doesn't lead to a situation in which demand presses against inflation, we are going to work to reduce inflation through monetary policy" (ibid., 53). Partee inquired rhetorically how weak they would permit the economy to get, and he recognized that the new administration had much in common with the Thatcher administration in Britain in its determination to lower inflation even at the cost of recession.

Chairman Volcker reinforced the point. "An implicit assumption that we are just avoiding excess demand is not the present policy. We have been put in a position or have taken the position . . . that we are going to do something about inflation maybe not regardless of the state of economic activity but certainly more than we did before in looking at it in the form of avoiding excess demand. It is a very important distinction" (ibid., 61).

Here at last was widespread recognition that the Federal Reserve had accepted responsibility for reducing inflation and would pay the near-term social cost to get the long-term benefit. Like former Chairman Martin, Volcker and others complained frequently about lack of support from fiscal policy and being the only agency concerned enough about inflation to work to reduce it. Unlike Martin and Burns, Volcker accepted the responsibility and carried his Committee, some willingly some unwillingly, with him.[84] The Volcker Federal Reserve restored much of the independence within government lost during the Martin and Burns chairmanships.

Despite the sense that the System had to act alone, it "would like to know something a little more definitively about the plans of the new administration" before setting its goal (ibid., 27–28). This was not policy coordination as used in the 1960s. Administration policies would affect economic activity and the System's success in reducing inflation. In this too, the Volcker Federal Reserve broke with the past.[85]

On July 16, 1980, Chairman Volcker had given his Humphrey-Hawkins testimony and the System's forecasts for 1980 and 1981. Table 8.5 shows actual outcomes. Real growth was above the forecast and inflation was within the forecast range. Real wages fell. The recovery came earlier than

84. Volcker also cited the government's assistance to Bache (when threatened by losses on the Hunt's attempt to corner the silver market) as an example of protection from failure. He argued that this protection did far more to reduce credibility than small misses of the monetary targets (FOMC Minutes, December 18–19, 1980, 62–63). He soon had to confront the problem of losses on foreign loans.

85. Again, Volcker expressed skepticism about forecasts. "The economic forecasting ability of the assembled economic wisdom of the United States in the short run has not been notable. And I don't know what the increase in GNP will be in the fourth quarter of the year" (FOMC Minutes, December 18–19, 1980, 63). Note that more than two-thirds of the quarter had passed.

**Table 8.5** Real GNP Growth and Inflation, 1981–82 (%)

| | REAL GNP | DEFLATOR | WAGES[a] |
|---|---|---|---|
| 1981–1 | 8.0 | 10.7 | 9.3 |
| 2 | −1.3 | 6.7 | 7.1 |
| 3 | 1.8 | 9.4 | 8.4 |
| 4 | −5.5 | 7.8 | 3.8 |
| 1982–1 | −5.9 | 6.4 | 6.5 |
| 2 | 1.2 | 5.0 | 4.8 |
| 3 | −3.2 | 5.8 | 4.7 |
| 4 | 0.6 | 3.6 | 4.1 |

[a]quarterly average hourly earnings.

anticipated after a very variable start to 1982. The table shows that by 1982, the Federal Reserve was winning its inflation fight.

Despite Volcker's many speeches affirming the System's determination to reduce inflation, Federal Reserve credibility remained low. The Federal Advisory Council (FAC) politely reminded the governors of that problem. At its February 7–8, 1980, meeting, FAC commented:

> The Council commends the Board's continuing efforts to restrain the rate of growth in the monetary aggregates and bank credit expansion. However because of the disparity between past Fed announcements and actual results . . . there is some skepticism in the marketplace that the Fed is resolved to adhere to its stated policies over the long term. (Board Minutes, February 7–8, 1980, 7)

At its May meeting, the FAC praised the Federal Reserve for hitting its money growth targets and permitting interest rates to rise to unprecedented levels. "The Committee has moved aggressively to dampen expectations about future price increases as well as to establish the groundwork for unwinding existing inflation" (Board Minutes, May 1–2, 1980, 6). The FAC expressed concern that the FOMC would permit another seasonal surge in money growth.

This expression of growing confidence in the Federal Reserve did not last. At its September meeting, the FAC complained about policy implementation. Notably, it did not complain about high interest rates or recession.

> While the Council approves of the intended thrust of monetary policy, it is concerned over the operations designed to achieve the goal. The intent of the October, 1979 initiatives was to control money growth more closely and, consequently, accept greater interest volatility. Fed operations to date have generated both greater volatility in interest rates and in money growth. . . .

> The result of the variability in money growth is a substantial whipsawing of interest rates and also a growing instability in financial markets. High volatility breeds uncertainty, reduces the credibility of Fed policy and raises inflationary expectations. Also, the press reported that the FOMC temporarily shifted from a money growth target to an interest rate target for foreign exchange reasons. (Board Minutes, November 1–2, 1980, 4)

The FAC urged the FOMC to remove all interest rate guidelines and to provide more information about its operations. The FAC repeated this criticism at its December meeting and warned about the Federal Reserve's low credibility.

Faced with the uncertainty about administration policy, measures of the monetary aggregates and oil prices, the preliminary discussion at the December FOMC meeting showed a wider range of opinions than usual. Usually, the members would choose quarterly average rates of growth for the aggregates consistent with their annual targets. Then they would instruct the manager about near-term ranges for the federal funds rate, the monetary aggregates, and the initial level of borrowings. Axilrod and his staff in Washington and Sternlight and his staff in New York would then choose a path for nonborrowed reserves that they thought was consistent with the targets. A major problem was that the staffs did not have a useful model of borrowing; if they missed the level of borrowing, total reserves and money rose or fell more than anticipated.[86] The federal funds rate moved to the top or bottom of its permitted range. The reason for the problem was similar to problems encountered earlier when using a free reserves target because in practice their operation was similar.

The FOMC often had to raise or lower the federal funds rate ceiling or floor, using a telephone conference to change the limit. The range for the federal funds rate was often six percentage points, but interest variability was high, so the FOMC held frequent telephone conferences. And it spent considerable time negotiating ranges for the funds rate.

Unable to get tentative agreement on the annual targets or the short-run targets proposed by the staff, Volcker presented his own proposal at the December meeting. Citing difficulties in making a proper allowance for institutional changes, he proposed to omit targets for $M_1A$ and $M_1B$, and suggested a range of 16 to 20 percent for the federal funds rate until the

86. Roos (St. Louis) objected that "[t]he Committee very carefully chooses aggregate growth targets and fed funds ranges and then the staff with some verbal guidance but no official guidance from this Committee makes the borrowing assumptions. Sometimes the borrowing assumptions are not consistent with the [monetary] aggregates and fed funds decisions we have made" (FOMC Minutes, December 18–19, 1980, 76). Volcker agreed.

next meeting. The FOMC widened the band to 15 to 20 percent. Governors Teeters and Wallich dissented for the same reasons they had earlier.

Volcker had to testify at the Humphrey-Hawkins hearings in late February, so the FOMC had to resolve its doubts, disagreements, and uncertainties. It lowered the range for the $M_1$ variables by 0.5 for the year; that made the target for $M_1B$ 3.5 to 6 percent. $M_2$ and $M_3$ remained unchanged at 6 to 9 and 6.5 to 9.5 percent. These ranges excluded changes arising from the introduction of nationwide NOW accounts. To take account of the overshoot of $M_1$ targets in 1980, Volcker proposed to measure 1981 growth rates from the midpoint of the 1980 target instead of the higher actual value. For the year to December 1981, $M_1B$ rose only 2 percent, well below the target, and $M_2$ rose 9.5 percent, slightly above the target but close to nominal GNP growth. By November–December 1981, the twelve-month moving average of monetary base growth had fallen to about 5 percent annual rate from a peak of 9 percent.

## COULD RESERVE CONTROL WORK BETTER?

The Board's staff and others carried out a large-scale evaluation of the new operating techniques and reported results to the FOMC in twelve papers plus a summary and at a meeting early in February 1981. The staff had at most fifteen months of data; at least four months occurred under the Carter administration's credit control program and the recovery.

Not much could be learned and, despite an intense effort, not much was. One general conclusion was that money had been more variable than in the past but "generally well within the range of foreign experience" ("Overview of Findings and Evaluation," *Study of New Monetary Control Procedure,* microfilm, Federal Reserve Bank of New York, January 22, 1981, 5). Interest rates were more variable on all securities. The staff estimated that the variability in Treasury bill yields doubled, measured on weekly average (ibid., 8).

Increased variability of both money and interest rates suggests inefficiency. The report suggested some improvements in operating procedures, including use of contemporary instead of lagged reserve requirement ratios and changes in rules for discounting.[87]

Although the desk intervened in the foreign exchange market frequently, the staff study found no evidence that "changes in spot exchange

87. A 1976 staff study recommended "moving to a contemporaneous reserve system" (Burns papers, Box B_B77, April 13, 2). The study recognized that bank objections were the main impediment. A 1977 study reached a similar conclusion but added that the change to contemporaneous reserve accounting would be mainly a short-term benefit (ibid., August 30, 1977). Both studies assumed reserve control in place of interest rate control.

rate variability were affected much by changes in intervention" (ibid., 11). The study also found that the new operating procedures did not pose "significant policy problems for other industrial countries, except perhaps for Canada and more recently Germany" (ibid., 12).[88]

The principal conclusion from the studies was that "a monetary targeting procedure is an effective means of communicating to the public the Federal Reserve's objectives for monetary policy" (ibid., 16). However, the relation of monetary aggregates to economic activity is loose. "Unexpected shifts" lead to "undesirable interest rate movements" (ibid., 16). Furthermore, the report concluded that precise monthly control of money "does not seem possible" (ibid., 20).

Turning to operating procedures, the report recognized the difficulty of forecasting borrowing and the consequent slippage in monetary control. It considered, and rejected, several changes in regulation of the discount window. The report dismissed the frequent criticisms of failure to tie the discount rates to market rates. It said doing so would limit flexibility and "raises the danger of upward or downward ratcheting of market rates in the short-run that may be excessive for monetary control needs and unduly disturbing to the functioning of markets" (ibid., 26). This was a familiar System argument; it assumed a highly inelastic demand by banks for loans from reserve banks. Elsewhere, when useful, the System reverted to the argument that borrowing was restrictive because banks were reluctant to borrow. Discussion of borrowing is the weakest part of the report.

The staff report noted, again, that the System could " strengthen the link between required reserves and deposits" by shifting to contemporary reserve accounting. "That advantage has to be weighed against the benefits . . . for reserve management by the banks" (ibid., 27). This very clearly compares the private cost to banks to the social cost to the economy.

One of the principal background studies by David Lindsey found that use of the monetary base net of borrowed reserves as the target in place of nonborrowed reserves would improve control. The FOMC ignored this finding and made no changes in reserve requirement or discount lending procedures to improve control. Chairman Volcker must have been relieved to learn that, under the new procedure, the money stock was not much more erratic, measured weekly or monthly, than before.

88. The reference to Germany differs from the recollection of Dr. Otmar Issing, then on the staff of the Bundesbank. Issing (2005) ignores the short-term fluctuations in the exchange rate that the report discusses and concentrates on the Bundesbank's successful implementation of a medium-term strategy based on monetary targeting. Rich (2005) argues that, despite a floating exchange rate, the Swiss National Bank had difficulty controlling inflation until the Federal Reserve adopted monetary control to reduce inflation.

A review of the report concluded also that short-run control of monetary aggregates could not be tight, but "the results suggest that nonborrowed reserves and the nonborrowed monetary base are the preferred targets—distinctly superior to either total reserves or the total monetary base" (Goldfeld, 1982, 151).[89]

Issues about monetary control received attention in a debate between Federal Reserve's senior staff and members of the Shadow Open Market Committee held at Ohio State University. Robert Rasche proposed a procedure for forecasting the money multiplier connecting the monetary base to the $M_1B$ money stock. Errors in his forecasts of the money multiplier one month ahead were uncorrelated, so he was able to conclude that the "multiplier can be forecast with sufficient accuracy so that the growth rate of $M_1B$ can be maintained within a range of plus or minus 1 percent on an annual average basis" (Rasche in Axilrod et al., 1982, 123). Spokesmen for the Federal Reserve agreed that control could be improved. They did not explain why the Federal Reserve avoided the necessary changes. They had the difficult problem of defending procedures that internal memos now show that they opposed.

Volcker summarized his conclusion. "We get just as good control, according to all these studies, by manipulating the federal funds rate. The operative question is whether we are willing to manipulate the federal funds rate in that way. I think that *the main reason we went to another technique is that we probably are not*" (FOMC Minutes, February 2, 1981, 31; emphasis added). This is, of course, correct up to a point. If the Federal Reserve moved the interest rate target "appropriately," it could achieve control. It left open how it decided when and how much to move the rate. Tieing the discount rate to market rates "would have an explosive short-term situation either up or down that I find impossible to contemplate. The present situation is awkward and is imposed upon us partly, but not entirely, by lagged reserve accounting" (ibid., 38).

About the only decision reached was to adjust the nonborrowed reserve path more rapidly, but nothing more precise was said. As in other discussions, proponents of contemporary reserve accounting made their case but did not change Volcker's views. Often he dismissed their proposals by saying "I wish I thought it worked that way" (ibid., 60).

Missing from the discussion was careful consideration of the horizon

89. Much later, a series of papers on targets and indicators of monetary policy concluded again that short-run control was subject to large errors, mostly random. It showed that all monetary aggregates experienced a large, sharp break in trend growth during the disinflation after 1979. Davis (1990, 75) attributed the break in base velocity growth to the decline in expected inflation.

over which the FOMC's decisions had their main effects. Both the staff report and the FOMC recognized that most of the data they watched were subject to relatively large random errors, but they did not ask: Why pay attention or respond to these noisy short-term data? Why not set a path and adhere to it until it was clearly wrong? Also, changes could be persistent or transitory. There was no way to distinguish promptly which type of change had occurred. Muth (1960) showed that gradual adjustment was the optimal response in the presence of a mix of persistent and transitory changes. The speed of response depended on the relative size of permanent and transitory variances. Further, some of the changes to which they responded were self-reversing. By responding promptly, their actions could increase variability.

A considerable part of the discussion concerned the perceived credibility of announcements. The best way to increase credibility was to announce what the System intended to do and then do it. Although Henry Wallich, especially, urged the FOMC to announce its decisions as the Bundesbank did, the chairman would not consider it. It took almost fifteen more years before the FOMC announced its planned action directly following its meeting.

A large literature considered the new procedures, particularly the positive response of interest rates at different maturities to growth of money above the target or more than anticipated. One study that supported earlier findings found that: (1) unanticipated money growth raised interest rates, especially short-term rates, because markets expected the FOMC to remove some of the excess; and (2) for longer-term rates, the main explanation of the rise was an increase in expected inflation. The market anticipated that some of the unanticipated money growth would remain and that inflation would increase. If correct, this suggests the difficulty the FOMC faced trying to increase credibility and lower expected inflation if it continued its operating procedures.

## POLICY ACTIONS IN 1981–82

Contrary to the original staff forecasts, the economy continued to expand in the new year, and inflation remained high. By late February, the staff forecast for nominal GNP growth rose to 15 percent growth at annual rates in the first quarter.[90] Growth of the monetary aggregates gave different

90. The new administration's forecast created an internal dispute. The supply-siders wanted to forecast a strong response of output to the proposed tax rate reduction. They proposed continued monetary growth to support their forecast. Monetarists wanted slower monetary growth to reduce inflation. The compromise was to let velocity growth increase at an improbable rate (Jordan, 2002, 8).

signals. $M_2$ growth exceeded its target; $M_1$ growth remained below. In late March, the FOMC adjusted the borrowing assumption to slow reserve growth, citing $M_2$, and it permitted the federal funds rate to remain below the 15 percent lower band previously set. Monetary base growth remained variable but slowed on average. Between January and March, the federal funds rate fell from 19 to 14.7 percent.

Most FOMC members did not want to repeat the sharp drop in interest rates in 1980, but some were more concerned by the slower growth of the narrow monetary aggregates. Volcker preferred to let the funds rate decline, and that is what they did. Roos (St. Louis) dissented. The decline proved temporary, and contrary to their tradition they soon reversed their action. By May, the FOMC had a prescribed range of 18 to 22 percent for the federal funds rate, and in June the monthly average rate was again above 19 percent, the highest recorded before or since.

The Board was reluctant to increase the discount rate during the winter of 1981. In January it rejected a request from St. Louis for a 14 percent rate when the federal funds rate averaged 19.1 percent. The Board cited the start of a decline in market rates. By April the funds rate had declined to a 15.7 percent average. The Board rejected requests for a reduction in the surcharge because it did not want the reduction to be misinterpreted as easing policy.

The monetarists in the administration watched the very large changes in money growth during the winter and early spring of 1981. They interpreted the changes as evidence that the Federal Reserve chose to undercut the president's program. President Reagan met with Volcker to urge a more consistent policy. No explicit agreement resulted, but Volcker must have left the meeting assured that the president supported disinflation.[91]

Early in May, the Board approved an increase in the basic discount rate to 14 percent and an increase in the surcharge from 3 to 4 percent. By this time, the funds rate had increased to more than 18 percent. The Board declined subsequent requests for a 15 percent discount rate. Table 8.6 shows these data.

Judged by either the federal funds rate or growth of the real value of the monetary base (Chart 8.5 above), policy tightened sharply in the spring of

91. Jerry Jordan, a member of the Council of Economic Advisers, recalls one discussion between Volcker and President Reagan. "The Treasury supply-siders were screaming in the press about the Federal Reserve undercutting the President. Volcker asked me whether the administration was ready to . . . formally ask him to ease up. I said no, keep at it. He was asked to a private meeting in the White House. President Reagan showed him a chart I had made of money growth and asked Volcker to explain it. Volcker was impressed that the president understood that inflation could not come down until money growth did, and he felt that the president had implied (or said) to stay with it" (Jordan, 2005).

**Table 8.6** Federal Funds, Discounts, and Inflation, 1981

| MONTH | FEDERAL FUNDS RATE (AVERAGE) (PERCENT) | DISCOUNTS ($ BILLIONS) | TWELVE-MONTH CONSUMER PRICES (%) |
|---|---|---|---|
| january | 19.8 | 1.4 | 11.1 |
| February | 15.9 | 1.3 | 10.7 |
| March | 14.7 | 1.0 | 10.0 |
| April | 15.7 | 1.3 | 9.6 |
| May | 18.5 | 2.2 | 9.4 |
| June | 19.1 | 2.0 | 9.1 |

1981. By increasing interest rates in the middle of a recession, the FOMC increased its credibility. This was clearly a change in practice. Never before had the public seen an increase in interest rates with the unemployment rate at 7.5 percent. The first signs of possible success appeared. The twelve-month average increase in consumer prices slowed to less than 10 percent for the first time in two years. Volatile monthly rates of increase declined as low as 7.7 percent in April. Second-quarter expected inflation for the next year fell to 8.7 percent.

After the strong rise in first quarter 1981, output declined in the second, rose modestly in the third, then declined sharply for the next two quarters. Table 8.5 above shows the variable growth of real GNP during this period.

Volcker's testimony to the Joint Economic Committee in February 1981 repeated themes from earlier statements. He stressed the importance of reestablishing credibility, the need for consistency and persistence, and the importance of spending reductions and deregulation. He described the economic situation as unsatisfactory, citing high inflation and "dismal" productivity growth. He emphasized the importance of evidence showing slower inflation and claimed to see changes in public attitudes "which would make things possible now that have not been possible in the past" (Volcker papers, Board of Governors, February 5, 1981, 8).

In a television appearance, Volcker repeated these monetarist themes. Short-run changes were not predictable; reducing inflation and restoring growth required patience and persistence. The right trend would show slower money growth, but there would be more bad news before good results became clear. He suggested progress would be seen by late 1981 or early 1982 (Volcker papers, Board of Governors, *Face the Nation,* March 22, 1981).

By June 1981, the conflict between monetarists and supply-siders broke open within the administration. The chief economist at the Office of Management and Budget, Lawrence Kudlow, and Jerry Jordan at the Council of Economic Advisers foresaw that with the economy slowing, continued monetary tightening and the proposed tax cut would greatly increase the

**Table 8.7** Marginal Tax Rate Reduction, 1982–87

| | MARGINAL TAX RATE[a] | MARGINAL TAX RATE[b] | |
|---|---|---|---|
| *Year* | | *50th Percentile* | *90th Percentile* |
| 1980 | .304 | 28 | 49 |
| 1981 | .303 | 28 | 48 |
| 1982 | .293 | 29 | 44 |
| 1983 | .272 | 26 | 44 |
| 1984 | | 25 | 42 |
| 1987 | | 15 | 35 |

[a] Barro and Sahasakul (1986).
[b] Hakkio, Rush, and Schmidt (1996).

budget deficit. They proposed to revise the winter's "rosy scenario" forecast in the midsummer report.[92] The supply-siders objected strenuously, claiming that Congress would not vote for the tax cuts if faced with the projected deficits (Grieder, 1987, 396–98). The supply-siders won that argument. Tax reduction passed the House by 238 to 195 and 89 to 11 in the Senate.

The reduction in marginal tax rates was an attempt to sustain or increase growth during the disinflation. Table 8.7 shows estimates of the marginal tax rates in 1980 and after the reduction. The table shows a marginal tax rate reduction of 13 to 14 percent using either estimate. For comparison, the 1964 tax cuts reduced marginal rates by 14 percent (Barro and Sahasakul, 1986) or 20 percent (Hakkio et al. 1996) for high-income taxpayers. At the same time, Congress indexed individual tax rates for inflation in 1981, and it reduced corporate tax rates. In 1982, the administration agreed to increase corporate tax payments to respond to criticism of the excessive corporate reduction and the large budget deficit. Chart 8.7 shows marginal tax rates for individual taxpayers. The last two columns include additional tax reduction in 1986.

Once the tax bill passed, Budget Director David Stockman proposed budget reduction to the president. Defense Secretary Caspar Weinberger wanted increased spending on the military. President Reagan chose increased military spending. For the rest of Reagan's presidency, budget deficits fluctuated around $200 billion a year, from 4 to 6 percent of GNP.

The National Bureau includes the 1981–82 recession on its list of se-

92. "Rosy scenario" was the name given to the administration's forecasts when they presented their first budget. The forecasts showed strong growth to satisfy supply-side economists who claimed a strong response of output to the tax cuts. The rosy scenario called for 3 percent growth in 1982 and 5.2 percent in 1983. Actual growth was −1.5 and 7.8 percent in the two years. The 1982 error especially discredited the administration's forecast. Critics ignored the 1983 result. The forecast overestimated inflation in 1982 and 1983 by about two percentage points in each year.

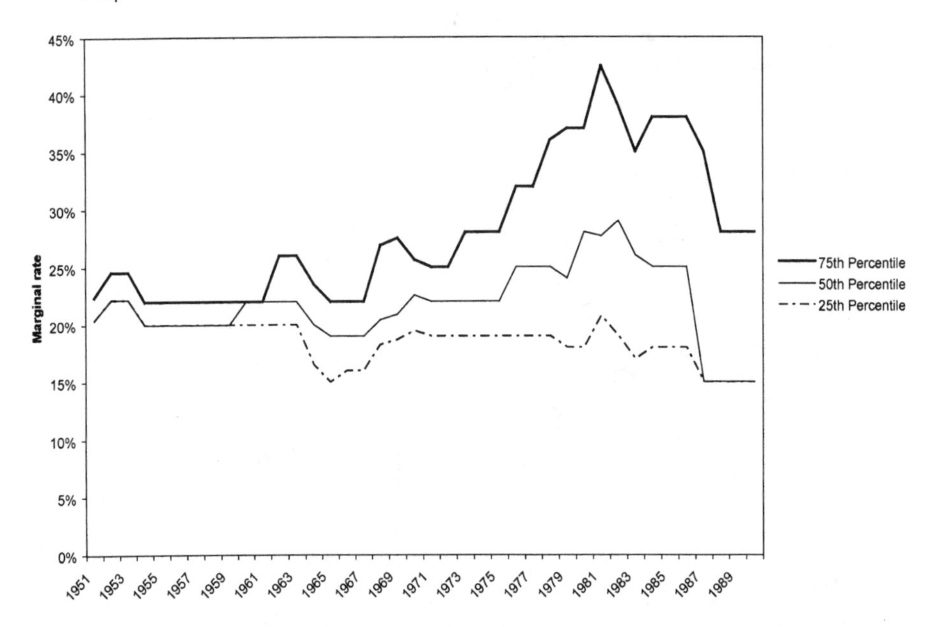


Chart 8.7. Marginal tax rate for assorted percentiles.

vere recessions since 1920, a class that includes the recession of 1923–24, 1948–49, 1953–54, 1957–58, and 1973–75 but excludes depressions. At the time, some commentators and journalists compared 1981–82 to the Great Depression or the 1937–38 depression. This was a typical overstatement by journalists and politicians usually for political effect. The critics did not distinguish between a 3 percent and an 18 percent decline in real GDP. Table 8.8 compares the 1981–82 recession to the 1937–38 depression and to two severe recessions that the National Bureau ranked as more severe than 1981–82. The worst part of the 1981–82 recession came in two quarters, 1981:4 and 1982:1. By the fall of 1982, the S&P index of stock prices began a sustained rise, forecasting the recovery that soon came.

Highly variable output growth added to the uncertainty created by the monetary aggregates. The surge in NOW accounts at the start of the year made it difficult to separate portfolio shifts from policy induced changes in the money growth rate using System procedures.[93]

Growth of the monetary base and the federal funds rate moved over wide ranges in 1981, but both trended down. By December 1981, twelve-

93. The Federal Reserve used the seasonally adjusted money stock in its calculations. There was no reliable basis for seasonally adjusting NOW accounts. The staff considered several alternatives and elected to seasonally adjust $M_1B$ (including NOW accounts) because the seasonal was similar to the former demand deposit seasonal (FOMC Minutes, April 28, 1981, 1). Who could know if that was right given the short history of NOW accounts?

Table 8.8 Comparison of Business Cycles

| DATE | DURATION (MONTHS) | REAL GNP DECLINE | INDUSTRIAL PRODUCTION DECLINE | UNEMPLOYMENT RATE *increase* | *maximum* |
|---|---|---|---|---|---|
| 1981–82 | 16 | −3.0 | −12.3 | 3.6 | 10.8 |
| 1937–38 | 13 | −18.2 | −32.4 | 9.0 | 20.0 |
| 1923–24 | 14 | −4.1 | −17.9 | 2.6 | 5.5 |
| 1973–75 | 16 | −4.9 | −15.3 | 4.4 | 9.0 |

Source: Zarnowitz and Moore (1986).

month moving average base growth was down to 5.26 percent, 2.5 percentage points below the growth rate when reserve control started. The federal funds rate in December 1981 averaged 12.4 percent, 6.5 percentage points below December 1980 and 1.3 percentage points below October 1979. Measures of annual inflation had begun a sustained decline. But ten-year constant-maturity Treasury yields remained at 14 percent. Real interest rates remained high; the public was not convinced that the Great Inflation was about to end permanently.

The System's anti-inflation policy had considerable support in the country. At the Federal Advisory Council's April 30 meeting, the Board heard that the FAC members regarded inflation as the "nation's most serious economic problem" (Board Minutes, supplement, April 30, 1981, 1). Further, the council commended monetary policy actions, specifically citing the "sharp rises in interest rates during the fall . . . to control growth of the monetary aggregates" (ibid., 7). It urged the Board to "stay the anti-inflation course" (ibid.).[94]

Third, the new administration seemed determined to reduce tax rates and increase defense spending. The FOMC members viewed these changes as inflationary. As usual, they thought that they were the only group acting to reduce inflation. The difference—and it was an important change from the past—was that many no longer believed that monetary policy alone would not be effective. They were not helpless; they were responsible for inflation and for ending it.

Relations with the administration had two very different aspects. President Reagan spoke strongly about the importance of ending inflation. In February 1981, the administration issued a statement of its program. The section on monetary policy recognized the central role of the Federal Re-

94. Anecdotal references at the FOMC meeting reinforced the FAC's view. For example, President Balles (San Francisco) commented on discussions with heads of two lumber companies. Both urged the System to complete the disinflation program despite the decline in housing starts and the demand for lumber (FOMC Minutes, May 18, 1981, 11). Other FOMC members told similar stories.

serve and its independence of the administration. It supported the general thrust of System policy, but it called for "stable monetary policy, gradually slowing growth rates of money and credit along a preannounced and predictable path" (Reagan Administration, 1981, 24).[95]

President Reagan's first budget projections called for three years of budget deficits followed by budget surpluses in 1984–86 (ibid., 12). Almost all the spending reductions were listed in "all other" and were not explicitly named. That category fell by $50 billion by 1984, a reduction of more than 25 percent. Of course, Congress approved the spending increases but rejected most of the reductions. Instead of the projected $30 billion surplus in 1986, the federal government ran a budget deficit of $230 billion, 5.7 percent of GNP.[96] Like central banks everywhere, the Federal Reserve considered the deficits inflationary or requiring higher interest rates to avoid financing them.

By early 1981, the twelve-month moving average of consumer prices fell below 10 percent, more than seven percentage points below the peak. In a survey of forecasts based mainly on Keynesian models, Okun (1978) found that the models predicted a 10 percent decline in output for one year for each permanent percentage point reduction of inflation. The early results showed this forecast to be highly inaccurate. As the rational expectationists emphasized, the cost of reducing inflation would fall as the public became convinced that the reductions were permanent. Their predictions did not allow, however, for skepticism about the persistence of policy after years of failed efforts.

The prevailing Keynesian orthodoxy claimed that the tradeoff between inflation and unemployment was socially unsatisfactory unless guidelines or controls held inflation down. Volcker dismissed this claim and substituted another. In late February 1981, he testified as required by Humphrey-Hawkins legislation. Much of his testimony repeated state-

95. The proposal for monetary policy followed the repeated recommendations of the Shadow Open Market Committee. I wrote the first draft for the administration; Beryl Sprinkel served as undersecretary of the Treasury for monetary affairs, and Jerry L. Jordan soon thereafter became a member of the president's Council of Economic Advisers. Both had been members of the Shadow Committee. Both criticized lagged reserve requirements, discount policy, and seasonal adjustment. The draft called for steady reductions in base growth of one percentage point a year until 1986, when base growth would reach 3 percent. Volcker did not like the commitment to a one percentage point reduction in money growth for several years. "I knew that such precision would be impossible to achieve in the real world and, achievable or not, it would look like the administration was trying to order the Fed. I somehow succeeded in talking them out of that kind of language" (Volcker and Gyohten, 1992, 175).

96. Weidenbaum (2005, 9–10) describes the conflict over economic assumptions in the Reagan budget. To reconcile differences, the forecast had a large improbable rise in monetary velocity.

ments he had made to private groups and to Congress. Notable was the shift away from the tradeoff between inflation and real growth. Instead, low inflation was a principal means of ultimately reaching high employment and stable growth. "The rapid rise of prices clearly is the single greatest barrier to the achievement of balanced economic growth, high employment, domestic and international financial stability, and sustained prosperity" (Volcker, 1981, 3). He also stressed the importance of anticipations.

The press and many commentators dismissed the administration forecasts as a rosy scenario. They failed to notice, or comment, that it did not differ greatly from the FOMC consensus. Looking back, it was not wildly inaccurate; it overestimated both inflation and growth. Inflation fell more than projected, and the average unemployment rate in fourth quarter 1981 reached 8.2 percent, 0.5 above the administration's projection.

At the Humphrey-Hawkins hearings and on many other occasions, Volcker supported the administration's tax cuts, but he always warned that their proper size depended on willingness to reduce non-defense spending. Growth of non-defense spending slowed, but defense spending and total outlays increased more. The budget deficit rose above $200 billion in fiscal year 1983. The many who argued that a large deficit would prevent a reduction in inflation or raise interest rates were proved wrong. Foreigners financed a large part of the increased budget deficit. And they continued to do so driven in part by an unwillingness to reduce exports to the United States by permitting their currencies to appreciate against the dollar and in part by the expected return on dollar assets.

Volcker also used the hearing to tell Congress about the staff study of the new control procedures. He blamed the imposition and removal of credit controls for the increased variability of both money and interest rates in 1980. "There was little evidence that alternative operating techniques would improve short-run monetary control" (ibid., 14).

A later study, Gilbert (1994), concluded that the Federal Reserve did not follow its announced procedures consistently. At times, it moved aggressively to adjust its path to achieve its monetary targets, but it did not always do so. Cook and Hahn (1987) reached a similar conclusion. They found that the Federal Reserve frequently returned to interest rate control.

The Federal Reserve found policy discussions with the new administration difficult. "The supply-siders were fighting with the monetarists, and the monetarists were fighting with the Federal Reserve. President Reagan did not understand this area. Once in a while, I was asked to go see him. He would drift off into some Irish jokes" (Volcker, 2001). A more charitable interpretation was that the president accepted the general thrust of Federal Reserve policy and paid little attention to squabbles about policy.

At regular meetings of the Council of Economic Advisers and the Board of Governors, "there was very little discussion of anything of substance" (Jordan, 2002, 3). "It was a tense atmosphere not especially friendly. . . . Occasionally we met jointly with them and with the Treasury staff and Undersecretary Sprinkel and Assistant Secretary [Craig] Roberts which made it a lot more strained" (ibid., 1).[97] President Reagan created a Presidential Economic Policy Advisory Board (PEPAB) of outsiders to counsel on policy. PEPAB, headed by George Shultz before he became secretary of state and later by Walter Wriston, met about four times a year with the president.[98] In 1981, probably in the fall, several members of PEPAB urged the president to persuade Volcker to ease monetary policy and reduce the risk of recession during the 1982 election year. President Reagan rejected that advice. Uncharacteristically, he criticized specific individuals, Arthur Burns, Paul McCracken, and Herbert Stein, for easy money during the 1972 election year under cover of price and wage controls. This made a post-election recession unavoidable. "He said he would not do something to help the chances of Republicans in Congress in 1982 only to have to see the need for restrictive policies afterwards" (Jordan, 2005). At a cabinet meeting about the same time, some cabinet members urged more expansive policies, but the president opposed.[99]

From its low point in July 1980, the index of weighted average exchange value for the dollar rose to a peak in February 1985. The increase on the July 1980 base was 87 percent. Despite the recession in 1981, the index advanced 17 percent. Table 8.9 shows the index value in January and July for 1980 to 1985.[100] The real exchange rate rose also but much less. The

97. I asked Jordan explicitly whether the conflicts between the anti-inflationists and the tax cutters affected President Reagan. "I'm sure it had no effect on him whatsoever. The key elements of what he wanted to do, eliminate inflation and cut tax rates, were in stone as far as he was concerned" (Jordan, 2002, 5). Donald Kohn recalled relationships during the period. Volcker and Treasury Secretary Don Regan did not get along. At meetings, Volcker and Undersecretary Sprinkel discussed fishing, then ignored each other.

98. Most of the members had served in an economic post in a previous Republican administration, but Milton Friedman and Walter Wriston were exceptions. Later, I became a member, but I was not present at the meeting discussed in the text.

99. As part of the budget process, the administration had to produce a forecast of inflation. To make the deficit smaller, James Baker and David Stockman "raised the inflation numbers so they could show more revenue and smaller deficits. Sprinkel, [Lawrence] Kudlow, and I were told by Baker to stay silent" (Jordan, 2005). The supply-siders' concern was that an admission of the true deficit would prevent Congress from approving the tax cut. In fact, Congress increased the size of the tax cut substantially and indexed personal income tax rates to inflation. The tax bill passed the House by 238 to 195, a comfortable margin, and received only 11 negative votes in the Senate.

100. Meltzer (1993) estimated equations for the level and changes in the trade-weighted real exchange rate based on Friedman (1953) using annual data for 1962–91 and 1972–91.

**Table 8.9** Weighted Average Exchange Rate, 1980–85 (base 100 in March 1973)

| | JANUARY | JULY |
|---|---|---|
| 1980 | 85.52 | 84.65 |
| 1981 | 91.38 | 109.87 |
| 1982 | 106.96 | 118.91 |
| 1983 | 117.73 | 126.62 |
| 1984 | 135.07 | 139.30 |
| 1985 | 152.83 | 140.94 |

Source: Board of Governors (1991, 467).

evidence (Meltzer, 1993) suggests that disinflation and rearmament adequately account for the very strong appreciation of the real trade-weighted dollar from 1980 to 1985 and its subsequent depreciation from 1986 to 1988.

Despite the appreciation of the dollar and the rise in oil prices, the United States' current account moved from deficit to surplus. Foreign governments, especially in Europe, complained about the level of U.S. interest rates and dollar appreciation. Since the market quoted oil in dollars, appreciation of the dollar raised the cost to non-dollar countries (Solomon, 1982, 357).

The European response was to establish the European Monetary System (EMS) in 1979. The Bundesbank accepted the new obligations for currency market intervention without abandoning its system of monetary targets. It became the dominant European central bank, and the mark became the anchor currency in the European Monetary System (Baltensperger, 1999, 440).

Faced with a choice between stability of the external and internal value of money, the Bundesbank chose to limit domestic inflation. Between 1978 and 1982, consumer prices in Germany rose by 23 percent; this was half the rate in the United States. Despite Germany's superior control of inflation, however, the dollar appreciated. The Bundesbank did not attempt to prevent currency depreciation although its restrictive monetary policy worked to strengthen the mark against the principal European currencies. Between 1979 and 1981, the Bundesbank raised Germany's money market interest rate from 3 to 12 percent and reduced its monetary target. Its control of money was superior to Federal Reserve control but not so restrictive as to prevent all inflation.

In July, Volcker testified to the Joint Economic Committee on the in-

The estimates suggest that the principal determinants of both levels and changes were the lagged value of the real exchange rate, real money balances, and real government debt (or changes in these variables in the equation for changes).

ternational effects of disinflation in the United States. As always, he emphasized the importance of ending inflation and reminded the committee that market interest rates would not decline until inflation and expected inflation declined permanently. Again, he insisted that the market, not the Federal Reserve, set the interest rate and that slower money growth was necessary to ensure lower inflation and interest rates.

Foreign central bankers, he said, did not question the necessity of reducing U.S. inflation. He insisted that the Federal Reserve did not have an exchange rate policy. The market set the exchange rate, not the Federal Reserve (Volcker papers, Board of Governors, July 15, 1981).

Volcker did not express concern about dollar appreciation, but he also did not go as far as the administration, which cited appreciation as evidence of success. The demand for dollars rose, they said, because markets expected its policies to work. Instead of complaining about job losses, they boasted about the capital inflow and foreign investment in the United States.

At the July meeting, President Anthony Solomon (New York) seemed to urge the Federal Reserve to intervene jointly with the Bundesbank to weaken the dollar. This set off a general discussion of the exchange rate and the response to intervention. Governor Wallich asked whether intervention would affect the exchange rate. Solomon gave a hedged response: "If we had consistent and cooperative intervention both by the Bundesbank and ourselves, yes, they [exchange rates] would be significantly lower because the foreign exchange market would be influenced by that to some degree. And so maybe would corporations. . . . If the psychology is not handled in such a way that the psychology of the traders is influenced by our cooperative intervention, then it's self-defeating" (FOMC Minutes, July 6, 1981, 8). But Solomon never mentioned whether intervention was sterilized or unsterilized. He emphasized cooperative action with the Bundesbank.[101]

Lyle Gramley and Gerald Corrigan supported Solomon, but Volcker again was skeptical about prospects for joint intervention. Solomon replied that the German government favored joint intervention, but the Bundesbank opposed. Reflecting the Treasury's opposition, Gramley asked, "Does

101. Sterilized intervention does not change the monetary base. It substitutes domestic assets for foreign exchange or conversely. The only economic effect is a change in the risk position of the market and the central bank reflecting any differences in risk of domestic and foreign assets. This effect would be very small for countries with large stocks of debt and money outstanding. Unsterilized intervention would change the exchange rate if, and only if, it was perceived as a policy change. If it provided or withdrew reserves as expected, it could change the composition of the monetary base without changing its expected value. See Broaddus and Goodfriend (1996) for a review of the literature and implications for monetary policy. Hutchinson (2003) claims evidence that sterilized intervention has a small, most likely temporary effect on the exchange rate.

it make any difference what we think?" (ibid., 12). Volcker replied, "Of course, we have independent powers. We endeavor to cooperate internally as well as externally" (ibid., 12). Apparently, he believed that the Federal Reserve could pursue its own exchange rate policy, but he was not prepared to do so without strong support from the FOMC. As Wallich put it, the case for intervention depended on shifting the exchange market demand or supply curves by changing psychology, and he did not expect that to happen (ibid., 13).[102] The Board expressed its concern about the effect of United States' interest rates on foreign countries (Board Minutes, July 14, 1981, 2). Usually the Treasury initiated intervention, and the Federal Reserve sterilized the monetary effect. At the time the Treasury opposed intervention.[103]

The FOMC remained divided in 1981. Members expressed more concern about reliance on the monetary aggregates, especially $M_1$, because of institutional changes. Volcker expressed doubts about data accuracy, but he would not change procedures or give up the anti-inflation policy. As the economy returned to recession, Governors Teeters and Partee favored less restraint, but the FOMC continued to vote for monetary restraint and lower inflation. This was a turning point. With the unemployment rate approaching 8 percent in the fall of 1981, the Federal Reserve did not ease. Nothing like that had happened in the postwar years. Market participants and the public recognized the change. Expected inflation rates began to decline slowly. The peak in expected four-quarter inflation shown by the SPF index, 9.4 percent in fourth quarter 1980, fell to 7.5 percent in fourth quarter 1981. A year later, it was 5.6 percent.

At the nine meetings, including inter-meeting telephone conferences in 1981, the minutes record ten dissents, five in favor of less restriction (mainly Teeters and Partee) and four in favor of more (mainly Wallich).[104] The directives continued to specify targets for money growth usually with a six percentage point band on the federal funds rate.

Sprinkel, Regan, and Jordan pressed Volcker and the Federal Reserve to maintain a steady, gradual decline in money. When Volcker spoke publicly,

102. Perhaps because there was now very little to do as manager of foreign transactions, Scott Pardee resigned in July to accept a position at a dealer firm. Sam Cross replaced him.

103. Congress had approved legislation to phase out ceiling rates on deposits, but the Board continued to enforce ceiling rates in 1981. The Comptroller uncovered a blatant example of evasion by Citibank. On July 8 the Board voted unanimously to impose the largest civil penalty ever charged a banking institution, $350 thousand. In addition, the Board voted to publicly announce the fine and the reasons for the decision. The Board's rules permitted banks to offer up to $5 as a premium for a deposit up to $5000 and $10 for larger deposits. The Comptroller found that some Citicorp employees knowingly violated these guidelines.

104. The remaining dissent objected to the "unrealistic sense of precision" in stating money growth rates (Annual Report, 1981, 145–46).

he used similar language, but the Federal Reserve did not adopt any of the procedural changes that would have smoothed money growth, and the monthly money growth numbers varied over a wide range.[105] After slowing in March, money growth surged in April. Despite a rising unemployment rate and slower growth of hourly earnings and consumer prices, the FOMC raised discount rates from 13 to 14 percent on May 4 and increased the ceiling for the federal funds rate at a telephone conference on May 6. Federal funds again traded at 18 to 19 percent. Money growth reached a 14 percent annual rate in April, and ten-year Treasury bonds rose to a local peak at 14.46 percent on May 8.

"Members commented on the considerably greater strength in activity in the first quarter [of 1981] than had been expected, and they continued to stress the difficulties of economic forecasting currently and the importance of adhering to longer-term objectives" (Annual Report, 1981, 110). With the unemployment rate in the neighborhood of 7.5 percent throughout the spring and summer, this was a major step toward increased credibility. But they did not change procedures to reduce forecasting errors, and they made no new effort to focus on longer-term goals. Several members gave much greater attention to current changes in the federal funds rate than to the maintained money growth path. To reduce the very rapid money growth in April, the May 18 meeting set a 3 percent growth rate for $M_1B$ and agreed to accept slower growth, if the federal funds rate remained in the 16 to 22 percent range.[106]

105. Privately, several members were skeptical about the administration's policies. Anthony Solomon (New York) asked rhetorically if the president would abandon his tax reduction and defense increase in the interest of a balanced budget. Vice Chairman Schultz and Governor Partee talked about the upbeat approach taken by the president and the administration.

"Mr. Schultz: If they would talk in a little more practical way, I think it would help.

"Mr. Wallich. I think they believe this. I have heard this now for a week from Beryl Sprinkel. Everything will be easy, if the Fed just keeps the money supply . . .

"Mr. Boehne. . . . If we have problems, it's the Fed's fault.

"Mr. Wallich: That's exactly it" (FOMC Minutes, May 18, 1981, 25).

Roos (St. Louis) reminded them that the monetarists said there was no painless way out of the inflationary excesses, but the others paid no attention.

106. Volcker was clear about his intention. "Suppose we have a happy day and those late May figures come in rather low and it looks as if, indeed, we may come in lower than 1 percent for May and June with interest rates not rising and maybe falling. . . . I myself would be rather happy. And, therefore, I would not want to be pushing out money if the growth rate happened to come in, let's say, at zero in May and June, if interest rates were already stable or declining" (FOMC Minutes, May 18, 1981, 37). When June came, however, he changed his mind. "Up until now, we've reduced the reserve path somewhat to reflect the [3 percent] 'or lower' part of the directive. There is a question of whether we should continue doing that, given the current situation, and I don't think we should" (FOMC Minutes, June 17, 1981, 1). Money growth fell 3 percent in May and rose less than 1 percent in June; the April–June average was 4 percent. The funds rate remained at a 19 percent average in July.

Once again, the contrast between procedures and decisions is apparent. The Federal Reserve continued to act against inflation as it had never acted before. The federal funds rate rose above a 17 percent monthly average for the third (and last) time. Between May and August 1981, it remained between 17.8 and 19.1 percent for four months.[107] Maintaining these extraordinary rates despite 7.5 percent unemployment must have convinced skeptics that policy had changed. Annual growth of the monetary base reached a local peak in April at 8.16 percent. By October, it had fallen below 5 percent, and the annual rate of CPI inflation permanently fell below 10 percent. Federal Reserve policy began to show results.

By July, Volcker cautiously suggested that "there are some signs of progress on inflation and inflationary psychology. . . . [I]t's still in the maybe stage. . . . [H]ard as it is to say, . . . the lesser risk in the long run is taking a chance on more sluggishness in the short run rather than devoting all our efforts to avoiding the sluggishness in the short run" (FOMC Minutes, July 7, 1981, 35). Responding to the recession would put them "back into the kind of situation we were in last fall where we had some retreat [increase] in inflationary psychology and the latent demands in the economy immediately reasserted themselves. Then we would look forward to another prolonged period of high interest rates and strain and face the same dilemmas over and over again" (ibid., 35). Although they were likely to overshoot the annual $M_2$ target, he proposed no change in objective for the year. After much discussion, the FOMC agreed without dissent.

Chart 8.8 supports Volcker's interpretation. Although the GNP deflator is highly variable during this period, its peak at 12.1 percent came in fourth quarter 1980. Growth of hourly compensation also reached a local peak in that quarter. As Chart 8.8 shows, growth of hourly compensation slowed steadily in 1981 and 1982. The twelve-month moving average increase in consumer prices fell below 9 percent for the first time in three years.

The Federal Advisory Council (FAC) supported the policy stance. At its April 30, 1981, meeting, it urged the Board to "avoid a repetition of 1980 when explosive growth of the money supply occurred for five or six months. To allow such an occurrence again would greatly hinder the badly needed restoration of the financial markets' confidence that a proper monetary policy will be carried out" (Board Minutes, April 30, 1981, 6). It urged the Board to de-emphasize the federal funds rate. In November, FAC congratulated the Federal Reserve on its strengthened credibility.

A major difference between 1980 and 1981 was the support of the administration and the Congress. There was not much pressure to change

107. The June 1981 rate of 19.1 percent is the highest in Federal Reserve history.

Chart 8.8. Annual change, nominal compensation per hour, four-quarter moving average, 1971–90.

policy. President Reagan was firmly committed to low inflation and price stability. His main monetary action was appointment of the Gold Commission to satisfy the proponents of a return to gold. Anna J. Schwartz became executive director. The commission members included Federal Reserve governors who opposed the idea, so it was unlikely to conclude that the United States should return to the gold standard.

A surprising feature of the decline in inflation was the speed with which it occurred.[108] Although the Federal Reserve began its anti-inflation program in October 1979, it had to start over again in the fall of 1980. Part of the decline in consumer price inflation resulted from the end of the oil price increase, but compensation was much less affected, so it provides a more accurate measure of progress. See Chart 8.8 above. And with the unemployment rate above the natural rate, it occurred without much change in the unemployment rate—7.5 percent in October 1980 and 7.9 percent in October 1981. Thereafter the unemployment rate continued to rise as the inflation rate fell.

The majority chose to stay the course. Looking forward to 1982, in July

108. Blinder reports an estimate by Otto Eckstein, a leading Keynesian economist and forecaster. Eckstein claimed that lowering inflation by one percentage point would require ten years of high unemployment (Blinder, 2005, 283). This implies that reducing inflation from 8 or 9 percent to 4 or 5 percent would take about forty years!

1981 the Committee lowered the target $M_1$ growth rate to 2.5 to 5.5 percent and kept $M_2$ planned growth at 6 to 9 percent as in 1981. It discarded $M_1A$ and renamed $M_1B$ as $M_1$. Teeters dissented. She objected to the decision to reduce $M_1$ growth.

The Board prepared for a possible financial crisis. In July, it accepted in principle a proposal from the Federal Home Loan Bank Board that the System offer extended credit to members of their system, not including thrift institutions. After rejecting proposals for higher rates for extended credit, the Board on August 20 approved a proposal from Dallas to increase discount rates for borrowing for longer term and to assist thrift institutions with "sustained liquidity problems" (Board Minutes, August 20, 1981, 3).[109]

During the summer, some reserve banks pressed repeatedly for a reduction in the surcharge for large borrowers. The Board did not agree until September 21, when it reduced the surcharge from four to three percentage points. Governor Wallich dissented because the change might be interpreted as easing. To forestall that interpretation, the Board tightened the rule. Originally banks with deposits of $500 million had to pay a surcharge if they borrowed four weeks in a calendar quarter. Thereafter, the surcharge applied to a moving quarter. On October 9, the Board reduced the surcharge to two percentage points. The economy had slowed, and member bank borrowing was 50 percent of its May peak.

As the economy and money growth weakened, several reserve banks continued to urge either eliminating the surcharge or reducing the discount rate. The Board deferred the proposals until October 30, when it reduced the discount rate to 13 percent. Two weeks later, it removed the surcharge, but it voted to keep the discount rate unchanged. The federal funds rate had fallen below the discount rate, and borrowing had fallen from $2 billion in June to $600 million in November. By December 3, the discount rate was at 12 percent.[110]

The National Bureau of Economic Research dates the 1981–82 recession from July 1981 to November 1982. Unemployment rose steadily from

109. The Board set the rules for pricing reserve bank services. The Depository Institutions Deregulation and Monetary Control Act of 1980 (DIDMCA) required the reserve banks to charge for services to member banks. For example, the Board retained control of pricing for automated clearinghouse (ACH) transactions and wire transfers. Later in 1981, it established rules to maintain competitive pricing with the profit-making private sector. To compensate for profits and taxes paid by the private sector, the Board required reserve banks to charge a 16 percent adjustment factor in 1982.

110. Starting in August the Board again discussed a return to contemporary reserve accounting at several meetings. In late October, it agreed to submit a proposal for public comment. It made no change at the time.

**Table 8.10** Real Growth and Inflation, 1981–82 Recession

| QUARTER | REAL GNP GROWTH | INFLATION (DEFLATOR) | INFLATION (CPI)[a] |
|---|---|---|---|
| 1981:3 | 1.8 | 9.4 | 12.1 |
| 4 | −5.5 | 7.8 | 3.4 |
| 1982:1 | −5.9 | 6.4 | −1.3 |
| 2 | 1.2 | 5.0 | 14.5 |
| 3 | −3.2 | 5.8 | 2.0 |

[a]Last month of quarter.

7.2 percent of the labor force at the start to a postwar peak of 10.8 percent in November and December 1982. This was the highest unemployment rate in the postwar years. Although the recession was deep, two of the five quarters show positive real GNP growth. Table 8.10 shows data for real GNP growth and inflation.

Growth of the $M_1$ money supply continued to be variable, but the general direction was toward slower growth. By March 1982, the twelve month moving average was below 6 percent, where it remained until September 1982. The federal funds rate declined very slowly. Despite the recession, it remained 14 percent through the winter and spring of 1982. The Federal Reserve was determined to avoid repeating the 1980 error in anti-inflation policy, so it did not reduce the rate.

The relatively high real interest rate and slow growth of money despite the recession increased the Federal Reserve's policy credibility. Unlike in all recessions since the 1960s, the Federal Reserve gave principal weight to reducing inflation, not to rising unemployment. By December 1981, Vice Chairman Schultz found on a trip to New York that "the credibility of the Federal Reserve is much higher than it has ever been before" (FOMC Minutes, December 21, 1981, 22). But, he reported, if they shifted to a more expansive policy, the market would react strongly, and credibility would be lost.[111]

Volcker gave many speeches during this period emphasizing a few prominent monetarist themes. The fight against inflation had to continue. Previous efforts failed because the Federal Reserve relaxed policy too soon. And the new message: "Inflation is destructive of our economic goals of stronger growth in real incomes, productivity and employment" (Volcker papers, Board Records, September 25, 1981, 2). Inflation was not a "pep

111. Support for reliance on monetary aggregates continued to weaken. Frank Morris, a member of the Maisel Committee on the Directive in the 1960s and 1970s, found the M's hard to interpret. Even Volcker remarked, "I think we have had a problem with interest rates. If anything, we should have paid more attention to them rather than less" (FOMC Minutes, December 21, 1981, 48).

pill" that permanently increased employment and output. "Failure to carry through now in the fight on inflation will only make any subsequent effort still more difficult" (ibid.). His aim was to bring down "excessive growth in money and credit to the point where the supply of our dollars does not outrun the supply of real goods and services" (ibid., 3). He always added the importance of support from fiscal policy. And he recognized the importance of maintaining low inflation once it had been reduced.

The homebuilders were greatly affected by high interest rates and recession. Private housing starts had fallen from 1.8 million in September 1979 to 0.84 million in January 1982 when Volcker spoke to their convention. This was the lowest level since the summer of 1967 that had caused much discomfort and political reaction. It was rare for housing starts to fall below one million; this time it was below a one million rate for six months, and it remained below for several months to come.

Volcker recognized the problem. The year 1981 was "the most depressed in decades" (Volcker papers, Board Records, January 25, 1982, 1). He accepted, and claimed the public accepted, that the job of ending inflation fell to monetary policy. "But I think it is also fair to say that absence of consistent help from other policies can make the job more difficult" (ibid., 2).

Then came a cheerful note. "We can see multiplying and encouraging signs that inflation has begun to subside—that we are turning the corner. . . . Any slackening of our commitment to see the effort through could only jeopardize prospects for full success" (ibid., 3). Changes in expectations and behavior had to occur. These "will work to unwind the inflationary process, perhaps faster than most economists have assumed" (ibid., 4). He was aware of the challenge to avoid a resurgence during the recovery. The key test will be sustaining the gains during a period of recovery and expansion" (ibid., 5).[112] Despite their heavy losses, the homebuilders gave him two standing ovations (Coyne, 2005, 315).

Reported growth of $M_1$ from December 1980 to December 1981, at 2 percent, was far below the target of 3.5 to 6 percent, and $M_2$ growth at 9.5 percent was only 0.5 percentage points above its band. For 1982, the FOMC tentatively agreed again to a target band of 2.5 to 5.5 percent for $M_1$ and 6 to 9 percent for $M_2$.

The economy ended 1981 with the unemployment rate at 8.5 percent and rising. Hourly earnings had fallen from their peak but they rose 7.2 percent in the year to December. The twelve-month moving average of

112. Unlike Burns, Volcker did not blame labor unions for inflation. "Higher wage costs did not spearhead the inflation of the past decade. Labor and management were in large part reflecting inflationary forces originating elsewhere" (Volcker papers, Board Records, January 25, 1982, 5).

consumer prices was down to 8.6 percent, three percentage points below the previous December. Double-digit inflation, it turned out, was over; the expected four-quarter inflation rate was 7.5 percent according to the Society of Professional Forecasters. More disinflation had to occur before the Federal Reserve could claim success.

The year 1982 was a transition year. The FOMC ended targeting nonborrowed reserves. The Board lowered the discount rate from 12 to 8.5 percent. The federal funds rate declined from a 13.22 average in January to 8.95 percent in December. And the twelve-month average consumer price inflation fell from 8.1 in January to 3.8 percent in December. Consumer prices fell in December at a 4.9 percent annual rate.

Early in the year, the Board's staff forecast called for recession to end and recovery to begin in 1982 with continued decline in inflation for the next three years. Unemployment fell slowly in their forecast but would remain above 8 percent with no inflationary money growth. Recovery was expected to start in the spring, but despite progress in reducing inflation, real interest rates remained historically high.

Annualized $M_1$ growth was nearly 12 percent in January. President Balles (San Francisco) asked whether they were "intuitively trying to keep interest rates down" (FOMC Minutes, February 1, 1982, 23). Axilrod evaded the question by commenting on shifts in the demand for money. Gramley pointed out that the January bulge provided most of the $M_1$ required to meet their annual target. He favored abandoning the $M_1$ target. Others proposed to raise the base from which the money growth rate started or widen the band and aim for the top. Volcker reported that Congressman Henry Reuss proposed a 3.5 to 6 percent $M_1$ band, as in 1981. Congressman George Hansen introduced regulation requiring the Federal Reserve to maintain zero inflation.

The policy consensus started to fracture. Balles wanted the Humphrey-Hawkins report to show what the FOMC expected. Roos joined him and added that the FOMC should improve its procedures to better achieve its targets. Teeters wanted to abandon the disinflation policy to increase real growth and reduce the unemployment rate. "If we stick to these targets, we end up with no growth for the fourth year in a row and unemployment of 9 percent or above. I think that's politically very dangerous" (FOMC Minutes, February 1, 1982, 44). Frank Morris wanted to continue disinflation but abandon the $M_1$ target. Members mostly supported either Morris's or Balles's positions.

Volcker recognized the control problem but made a sensible response. "Our credibility will be related more to making the right decision than to worrying too much about what the market says about it in the short-run" (ibid., February 2, 1982, 48–49). He remained convinced that the Federal Reserve had to persist in its anti-inflation policy. He favored rebasing the monetary growth rates and opposed raising the announced growth rates to recognize the January bulge. His argument was that an increase in the growth rate would suggest an easier policy; a lower growth rate from the higher base would not. Much of the problem came from the NOW accounts. In his testimony to the House Banking Committee on February 10, he dismissed arguments based on a tradeoff between unemployment and inflation, insisting that lower inflation would bring lower unemployment rates. He dismissed the Phillips curve as a guide. "More inflation has been accompanied not by less, but by more unemployment and lower growth. We have not 'traded off' one for the other" (Volcker papers, Federal Reserve Bank of New York, Box 97657, February 10, 1982, 9). Then he added that "inflation itself is the greater threat to economic stability" (ibid., 10).

Volcker was not yet ready to abandon an $M_1$ target. He did not think they should put much weight on a month or two of disturbing data. He did not want to eliminate the January bulge immediately, but he wanted "to show some resistance" (ibid., 58). Since the FOMC had no way of knowing whether the January bulge was a permanent or transitory change, that seems the correct approach. But it did not satisfy everyone. Roos, with support from Black, wanted to eliminate the bulge, but Axilrod and Volcker argued that they did not know whether the demand or supply function had shifted and whether they would shift back.[113]

When the Committee turned to short-term policy, they emphasized the uncertainty about short-term projections. The staff explained the high reported growth of $M_1$ as a shift in demand. Under questioning by Roos (St. Louis), Axilrod agreed that it was difficult to forecast the demand for money, and he might have added that it was difficult also to explain what had happened ex post.

To strengthen credibility Volcker proposed letting the federal funds rate rise as high as 14 percent (from 13.2 percent average for January). But there were limits to his concern. After Volcker said "I would worry if the federal funds rate were 16 percent now," Governor Partee, joined by Presidents Black, Ford, and Balles, suggested eliminating the band on the funds rate (ibid., 65–66). Morris, Boehne, and Volcker objected strongly.

The data hint that despite the discussion at the meetings, the System had an interest rate target. Monthly average federal funds rate remained

113. An extended discussion showed that the FOMC did not have a consistent interpretation of the short-term positive relation between higher money growth and a higher funds rate. Most members explained the positive relation as a positive shift in demand for reserves, not an expected reduction to reflect higher expected inflation.

between 14.15 and 14.94 percent from February through June. This is the only period during alleged reserve targeting with so little variation in the interest rate. Monthly $M_1$ growth remained low in these months but varied between −3.5 and 6 percent. With consumer prices rising about 7 percent, the real federal funds rate was about 7 or 7.5 percent.

The vote was unanimous for a near-term 12 to 16 percent federal funds rate, zero $M_1$ growth, and 9 percent $M_2$ growth.[114] The FOMC wanted zero $M_1$ growth in the near term to offset excessive money growth in January.

Discussion of the annual money and credit ranges for the February Humphrey-Hawkins testimony brought out the problems in the economy and the conflicts in the Committee. Teeters urged lower interest rates to prevent failure of many savings and loans, but Volcker opposed because that would require too much ease, and Schultz pointed out that long-term rates were the key to the S&L problem. They depend on the deficit, he said. Voicing the main concern of those who wanted to continue the anti-inflation policy, he said that "[i]f we give up, then the inflation problem is just going to explode again and the economy will be in terrible shape. We have to stay where we are and do our job" (ibid., 88).[115]

Volcker responded by arguing that credibility is a stock that can be used when needed. "We do not build up credibility for the sake of building up more credibility. We build up credibility to get the flexibility to do what we think is necessary.[116] If I were concerned now . . . that this change [rebasing the target] is appropriate I would say the heck with that point. My trouble is that I am not convinced [the bulge] is going to stay" (ibid., 89).

Schultz rarely disagreed with Volcker, but he did now. Political pressure had increased. "The president will not do anything about the deficits. . . . [T]he central bank of the United States has far more responsibility than it ought to have. . . . We have not yet changed those inflationary expectations because everybody thinks that we are going to cave in to the political pressure that is going to be on us" (ibid., 90). The last remark recognized that congressional elections would come that year, and that tax reduction increased the deficit in the short-run. References to elections and political pressures are very rare in the minutes or transcripts, whatever influence these events may have had on discussions at lunch, during coffee breaks, or at other times.

114. Just before the vote, Balles made "a strong plea or caveat as the case may be . . . to avoid the big overshoots" in money growth. Volcker responded with a note of despair: "I wish I knew how to do that" (FOMC Minutes, February 1, 71).

115. Kane (1989) has an excellent study of the savings and loan problem.

116. This is the conclusion in Cukierman and Meltzer (1986) using a formal model.

Once Schultz opened the issue, others commented. The president's counselor, Edwin Meese, had remarked publicly that the president would ask Volcker to discuss current policy. Gramley wanted to act ahead of any meeting with the president to avoid any suggestion that the System responded to political pressure. Nancy Teeters thought the System had to accept responsibility for 9 percent unemployment, but others blamed the administration's fiscal policy for high interest rates and unemployment. Roos reported that he was asked that question frequently: "Are you fellows going to be able to stand the heat from the politicians during an election year?" (ibid., 95).

Volcker took a vote on raising the $M_2$ growth rate but drew only five supporting votes. He chastised the Committee, calling its decision "silly" for putting so much emphasis on recent monthly or quarterly growth rates (ibid., 105). His testimony would stay with the unchanged $M_2$ growth rate but suggest that they may exceed the range. In his February 10 testimony, Volcker said that the announced growth rates would change during the year if conditions changed.

Fearing the loss of political support, the FOMC had to choose between independence and ease. This time the System chose independence but was cautious about raising interest rates. The federal funds rate rose 1.5 percentage points in February to an average of 14.78 percent. By early February St. Louis and San Francisco proposed an increase in the discount rate from 12 to 13 percent. The Board deferred the decision. Other banks joined the request. The Board continued to defer action until March 1, when it disapproved the change.[117] The February meeting was Frederick Schultz's last. He left the Board on February 11. His successor was Preston Martin, who became vice chairman of the Board on March 31. Although this was President Reagan's first appointment, his votes were more like Teeters than Wallich's or Volcker's.[118] Martin's background included long

117. Innovation in financial markets opened new issues about the scope of regulations and new ways of avoiding regulation. The latter included time deposits used to make third party payments avoiding regulation Q. The Board declared such accounts to be transaction accounts. In February, the Kansas City Board of Trade began to offer futures contracts based on the Value Line stock index. The Board discussed margin requirements because it deemed these contracts a substitute for options contracts. The Board of Trade raised its margin requirements, and the Board did not act.

118. Havrilesky and Gildea (1992, 402) classified thirty-two governors who served during 1951 to 1987 based on their "noncontractionary" votes. Preston Martin is fourth from the bottom, more expansionary than Teeters. Other Reagan appointees, such as Martha Seger and at times Wayne Angell, also favored lower interest rates to support supply-side actions. These were not helpful appointments.

association with the California housing industry, often a pressure group favoring lower interest rates.[119]

Following tax reduction and a reduced rate of contraction of the real base, real GNP growth turned positive in the second quarter of 1982, but not in the third. In its economic report written at the beginning of 1982, the administration continued its support of Federal Reserve policy. The report expressed a preference for steadier decline in the $M_1$ growth rate, but it did not criticize the Federal Reserve.

Volcker's short-term gamble succeeded. $M_1$ growth turned negative in February. Quarterly growth was about 6.4 percent as originally reported. At the March 29–30 meeting, April's money growth was a major concern. The staff forecast called for 8 to 10 percent followed by slower growth or decline in May and June. Typically, money growth rose in April because the public paid its income tax, and apparently the seasonal adjustment was inaccurate.

The FOMC divided. About half followed Governor Partee by choosing faster $M_1$ growth. Volcker chose to give more weight to $M_2$ and at one point chose a combination of $M_2$ and $M_1$ growth that were inconsistent based on the staff projections. His chief interest seemed to be avoiding a temporary decline in interest rates and increase in money growth that the FOMC would have to reverse.

The remarkable feature of the discussion was the commitment of many members to continue the disinflationary policy despite a 9 percent unemployment rate and a substantially slower inflation rate. After much discussion, the committee voted nine-to-two to keep the federal funds rate in the 12 to 16 percent range and to aim for a 9 percent annual rate of $M_2$ growth and between 3 and 9 percent $M_1$ growth. The wide range on $M_1$ growth reflected the great uncertainty about both the monthly seasonal adjustment and the degree to which NOW accounts were used for transactions.

Balles asked why market interest rates remained historically high as the inflation rate fell. Axilrod gave three answers. First, "the world isn't yet convinced that the rate of inflation isn't going to get worse when we get out of this rather deep recession" (FOMC Minutes, March 29–30, 1982, 30). Second, variability in short-term rates resulted from efforts to control money. This put a premium in interest rates. Later, Axilrod added that the budget outlook "keeps the public convinced that inflation is not going to

119. Contemporaneous reserve accounting again came up for discussion. Volcker gave a clearer statement of his position. "I do not think it is going to make a lot of difference in and of itself. . . . [T]here is a certain logic just in terms of being consistent with our present techniques. My concern is that people will read into it more than it is worth and we would get more flak rather than less" (FOMC Minutes, February 2, 1982, 91).

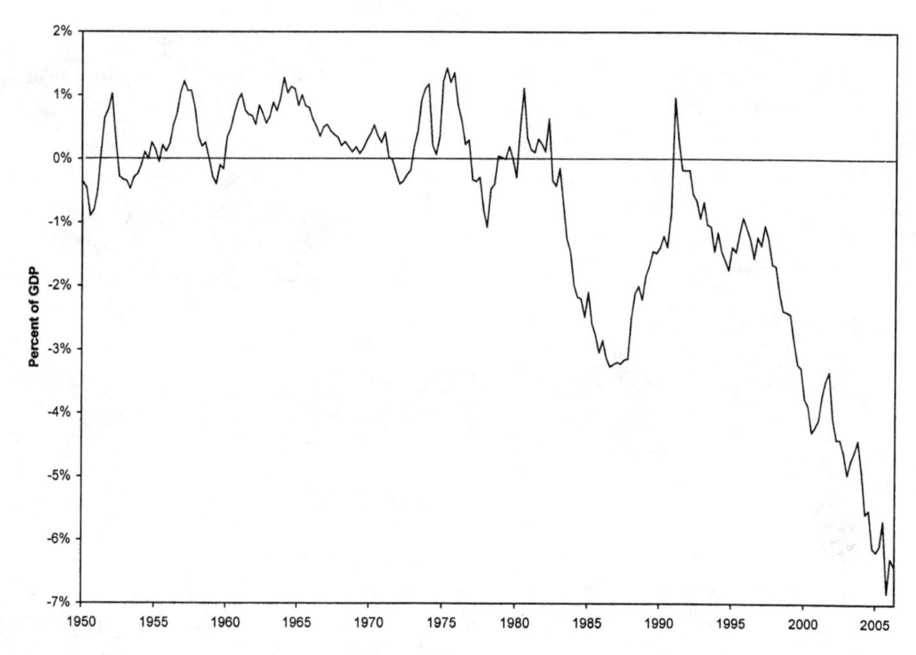


Chart 8.9. U.S. current account in historical perspective.

get better. . . . [T]he odds are that when we get on the up side of the cycle inflation will get worse" (ibid., 31–32).

Evidence soon supported his first answer. The recovery occurred with historically high real interest rates. Later evidence suggested that real interest rates changed very little when the government's fiscal stance shifted from large deficits (relative to GDP) to budget surpluses in the late 1990s and renewed large deficits after 2001. In fact, real interest rates were lower after 2001 than in the earlier period of budget surplus.

What may be true for other countries has not been true for the United States in the past quarter century. A principal reason for the absence of a strong effect of U.S. budget deficits on real interest rates is that foreign purchases of U.S. securities absorb the additional security sales. Chart 8.9 shows the current account deficit. Capital inflow moves in the same direction, rising when the current account deficit rises and becoming highly positive when the current account deficit is highly positive. If foreigners are willing to finance the current account deficit—the excess of investment over saving—at world real interest rates, domestic real interest rates need not change. The desire by governments to increase their exports and domestic employment encouraged them to purchase U.S. securities and sustain the capital inflow to the United States.

The FOMC remained divided about monetary policy. Volcker was not yet ready to change policy openly. Although he had become less certain about targeting reserve growth, seasonal adjustment, and the meaning of the monetary aggregates, he was concerned that letting interest rates fall would provide only temporary relief. With clear understanding of the political pressures, he told the FOMC "I'd love to see them come down and stay down. I wouldn't love to see them come down for a month and then have to go up again. That would kill us for a variety of reasons" (FOMC Minutes, March 29–30, 1982, 49–50).[120] His response was to continue the policy of reducing inflation.

Failures of homebuilders, savings and loan institutions, and other firms was a frequent subject of discussion. The members could only deplore the circumstances, including their policy, that brought this outcome. During the 1970s some farmers had borrowed heavily to expand to take advantage of rising commodity prices. Prevailing interest rates pushed them toward bankruptcy. Corrigan (Minneapolis) proposed special loans for farmers but drew little support.

In May, a small securities firm, Drysdale, was unable to pay interest on the government securities it had sold short. Drysdale had gambled on a decline in interest rate by doing repurchase agreements with banks, especially Chase Manhattan Bank, and selling the securities short. Drysdale had about $20 million in capital, but it had $6.5 billion in securities; it owed $160 million in interest payments to nearly thirty brokerage firms.

The Federal Reserve feared a market panic. The New York bank offered to lend to banks facing payments problems. At first, the Chase bank refused to accept responsibility for the interest payments, claiming that it acted only as an intermediary. Market and Federal Reserve pressure convinced it to change that position. That ended the crisis.

The FOMC voted to broaden the terms on lending government securities from the open market account and relax the financing of short sales of securities. The change was temporary, lasting only eight days. The staff estimated that Chase Manhattan would borrow about $1.25 billion of securities, but others would need much less. As usual, the Board did not adopt a general policy to deal with banking and financial market problems.

### *Beginning of the End*

A series of events, economic, market, international, and political, moved the Federal Reserve toward ending the on-again, off-again experiment in

120. At about this time, March 15, the Shadow Open Market Committee wrote, "The Federal Reserve misleads the public and the Congress by talking as if its main objective were control of bank reserves and money. In practice the Federal Reserve seeks to hold the daily federal funds rate within a narrow range." I served as co-chairman of that committee.

monetary control. No one of these events may have been decisive, but together they added to the growing anxiety about the economy and the Federal Reserve's ability to control it using reserve or money targets.

In our interview, Volcker (2001) cited the difficulties of controlling money, especially in 1982, his reluctance to raise interest rates during a deepening recession, the failure of the recession to end, as predicted, in second quarter 1982, and the developing problem of Mexico's external debt. Axilrod (1997) emphasized the growth of money and the maturing of All Savers Certificates.[121]

There were other events. The failure of Drysdale Securities and a small Oklahoma bank, Penn Square, raised concerns about the solvency of the banking system. Both had large loans outstanding to major banks—Chase, Continental Illinois, Seattle First. Volcker and the FOMC had heightened concerns about financial fragility. Many savings and loans were close to bankruptcy. Large loans to Mexico by money center banks added to these concerns. Prevailing real interest rates heightened the problem.[122]

Volcker was clear about the lender-of-last-resort function. "If it gets bad enough, we can't stay on the side or we'd have a major liquidity crisis. It's a matter of judgment as to when and how strongly to react. We are not here to see the economy destroyed in the interest of not bailing somebody out" (FOMC Minutes, October 5, 1982, 4). Preston Martin rightly stressed that their assistance should go to the market, not to Drysdale.

Penn Square's problem came in late June. It had large loans to oil and gas firms. As oil prices fell in 1982, many of the loans became worthless. The Comptroller's auditors ordered millions of dollars written off. Penn Square was bankrupt.

Penn Square had made more loans than it held in its portfolio. Continental Illinois, Chase Manhattan, Michigan National, and others bought about $2 billion; about $1 billion was sold to Continental. The Federal Reserve made the mistake of lending $20 million to Penn Square to prevent insolvency instead of permitting the failure and defending the market.

121. All Savers Certificates permitted financial institutions to offer one-year tax-exempt certificates. Congress approved when it voted for the Reagan tax reduction. The certificates expired beginning in October 1982. The Board's staff believed that much of the money had come from bank deposits. Neither the staff nor the Committee had any idea how much of the money would again become part of $M_1$. Axilrod also emphasized a change in the interest elasticity of $M_1$.

122. Grieder (1987, 438) pointed out that Volcker did very little to enforce lending standards on international loans. As banks reached 10 percent country limits, the Federal Reserve permitted banks to evade the limits. Grieder (ibid.) quoted William McChesney Martin's comment that "Volcker was 'very good' in conducting monetary policy but 'a complete flop on bank supervision.'"

The assistance was futile; the money was soon gone. William Issac, chairman of the FDIC, would not agree to additional support. He thought Penn Square's failure would be a warning to other banks, a badly needed warning. He favored closing the bank and paying off the depositors. In the end, Treasury Secretary Donald Regan sided with the FDIC, and despite Volcker's concerns, the bank closed.

At the July 1 Board meeting, Volcker got approval of a $700 million loan to Mexico under the swap line. In October, the FOMC renewed the loan. Before that, the System had made overnight swaps to give the appearance that Mexico had sufficient dollar reserves to maintain its payments. "We would transfer the money each month on the day before the reserves were added up, and take it back the next day. . . . [T]he 'window dressing' disguised the full extent of the pressures on Mexico from the bank's lenders and from the Mexicans themselves" (Volcker and Gyohten, 1992, 199).

The $700 million loan had two purposes. Mexico wanted to delay going to the IMF until September 1982, after its election. Also, the Federal Reserve was concerned that a crisis in Mexico would quickly spread to other heavily indebted countries. "Bank loans to developing countries had increased more than 50 percent in three years to more than $362 billion at the end of 1982, one-third of which was held by American banks" (ibid., 198).

The problem arose as part of the recycling of payments to the oil-exporting countries. These countries deposited their receipts in major banks by offering them directly or on the euro-dollar market.[123] The money market banks borrowed the euro-dollars and lent them developing countries. Their loans were for longer term than their euro-dollar deposits, so the banks were at risk. Defaults by the developing countries could wipe out their capital. The world recession slowed the growth of exports, and the high real interest rates increased borrowing costs. The threat of widespread default, perhaps starting in Mexico, added to concerns about financial fragility.

Loans to Mexico by nine major U.S. banks were about $60 billion, about 45 percent of the banks' capital. Loans to all of Latin America equaled about twice the banks' capital (ibid., 198). The Treasury and the Federal Reserve arranged with foreign central banks to join in lending $1.85 billion, about half from the United States. Soon after, the lending banks agreed to a "standstill"; Mexico would not be expected to pay until they arranged an IMF loan, and the banks agreed not to withdraw from Mexico.

On June 14, the French and Italian governments devalued the franc and the lira. The French devaluation was the first of several resulting from the

123. Recall that euro-dollars are U.S. dollar-denominated assets of banks outside the United States.

efforts of President François Mitterrand to pursue an expansive policy with a partly open capital market and a fixed exchange rate against the mark and other European currencies. Following the devaluation, the Saudi king died. The Treasury accepted that markets were disorderly, so the Federal Reserve bought $21 million in marks and $9 billion in yen. Other central banks intervened also, buying $6 billion according to the Federal Reserve report (FOMC Minutes, July 1, 85).

After more than two years, some members of the FOMC wanted to end what remained of the money control experiment. At the May FOMC meeting, Governor Teeters made the strongest statement in opposition to continuing. Pointing to the number of recent failures and the variability of interest rates, she attributed the failure of long-term rates to decline to the risk premium to pay for variability. The economy had not recovered. Unemployment was above 9 percent. "We are in the process of pushing the whole economy not just into recession, but into depression . . . I think we've undertaken an experiment and we have succeeded in our attempt to bring down prices. . . . But as far as I'm concerned, I've had it with the monetary experiment. It's time to put this economy back together again" (FOMC Minutes, May 18, 1982, 27).

Others did not go as far as Teeters, but Gramley, Rice, and Partee wanted to ease policy, and Morris wanted to dispense with an $M_1$ target. Boehne spoke in favor of lowering the funds rate to 10 to 15 percent. Defenders of the disinflation policy—Roos, Black, Ford, and others—argued that the way to get long-term rates down was to persist in the restrictive policy. Ease was what the market expected; it would foster concerns about renewed, higher inflation.

Volcker clearly began to shift to an explicit interest rate target. He no longer favored reliance on $M_1$. NOW accounts made it difficult to interpret. He favored 8 percent growth in $M_2$ because that seemed consistent with nominal GNP growth of 8 percent. "I am not going to [be greatly upset] if $M_2$ growth comes out at 8.5 percent instead of 8 percent or even 9.5 percent . . . or if $M_1$ continues to run somewhat high. . . . I would at this point take the chance of easing the pressures on bank reserve positions. . . . If it turns out that figures are more favorable in terms of restrained growth, we could *move aggressively pretty promptly* (ibid., 34; emphasis added) The FOMC voted eleven-to-one to lower the funds rate to the 10 to 15 percent range.[124]

124. Nancy Teeters voted no. This was Preston Martin's first meeting. He attended the March meeting but could not vote because he had not been sworn in. Volcker described the change years later. "The Mexican crisis was brewing. The economic recovery had not ap-

The problems that drew most comment were the failure of real rates to decline and the economy to improve. Ten-year Treasury rates were 13.5 percent at the time of the meeting. The SPF forecast of inflation was down to 5.9 percent, so using this estimate the real rate was an extraordinary 7.5 percent. Real GNP fell 5.9 percent in the first quarter; it rose a sluggish 1.2 percent in the second quarter and fell 3.2 percent in the third.

Many in Congress supported the disinflation policy, but as the 1982 election approached some became restless. Congressman Henry Reuss sent a letter informing Volcker that the House Budget Committee had adopted a budget resolution urging coordination of monetary and budget policy. Specifically, the resolution called on the Federal Reserve to "reevaluate its monetary targets in order to assure that they are fully complementary" (FOMC Minutes, May 18, 1982, 42). The letter assumed that the proposed deficit reduction was permanent and large and approved by both houses.

Reuss then reminded Volcker that the Constitution gave the monetary power to Congress. The Federal Reserve was the agent of Congress. He wanted assurance that the Federal Reserve would accede to the directive from Congress. Volcker told the FOMC that he saw no reason to vote. "I will tell him that it's clear in the minds of the members of the Open Market Committee that indeed we follow the law" (ibid., 43).

In his letter to Reuss, Volcker did more than accept that the Federal Reserve would follow the law. He advised Reuss that it would be a mistake for Congress "to indicate or direct a specific concern for monetary policy, such as a precise monetary target" (letter, Volcker to Reuss, Board Records, June 8, 1982).

Volcker brought up the resolution at the July 1 meeting. It called for the Federal Reserve to reconsider its monetary targets if Congress made a sizeable, permanent reduction in the deficit. Most of the members argued that permanently reducing the deficit would lower interest rates, but money was neutral so money growth should not increase. Partee argued that the economy was below capacity, so money growth could increase. Volcker was most in favor of increasing money growth, pointing out several times that many economists accepted policy coordination, but Wallich said that coordination meant the Federal Reserve should permit lower interest rates brought about by deficit reduction but should not increase money growth.

A few months later, Congressman Wright Patman sent a letter enclosing proposed legislation that would require the FOMC to send a report

peared. I thought, ahah, here's our chance to ease credibly. So we took the first small step" (Mehrling, 2007, 183).

to Congress within seven days of any decision to change the trend rate of money growth. Volcker had breakfast with Patman, so there is no record of a reply.

Senator Robert Byrd opposed the policy experiment from the start. By spring 1982, he found members concerned about high unemployment and interest rates in an election year. They joined him in proposing that Congress tell the Federal Reserve to target interest rates so as to keep the real rate below 4 percent. In the House, Congressman Jack Kemp called for Volcker's resignation. He and other proponents of a return to the gold standard sponsored Byrd's measure. The possible combination of conservative Republicans and liberal Democrats working to restrict Federal Reserve independence showed the growing resistance in Congress. Fortunately, Chairman Jake Garn and Senator William Proxmire on the Banking Committee did not go along. Senator Howard Baker and others tried to bargain with Volcker. If they reduced the deficit, they wanted the Federal Reserve to lower interest rates.[125]

At the White House, James Baker, a main adviser, worried about the coming election. He dropped hints about legislation reducing System independence. At Treasury, Secretary Donald Regan, a frequent critic, considered legislation restoring the Treasury Secretary to the Board and FOMC, as in the original Federal Reserve Act.[126]

Volcker knew he had support in Congress from the chairmen of the banking committees and many others. And the Federal Advisory Council supported both policy action and the goal of reducing long-term growth of money (Board Minutes, May 21, 1982). Nevertheless, Volcker had to be concerned that James Baker, chief of staff in the White House, had tired of failed forecasts of recovery and was concerned about Republican prospects in November. He wanted lower interest rates. The prospect that the administration might support one of Congress's proposals was a significant threat.

Congressman Reuss mentioned legislation that he would sponsor as part of a bill to raise the debt ceiling. The legislation Reuss proposed would

125. The Federal Reserve remembered 1968. Congress passed a tax increase in an election year to reduce the deficit. The projection claimed that the new taxes would lower the deficit by $100 billion over five years. Actual deficits remained between $185 and $225 billion from 1983 to 1986.

126. Some legislation supported the System's goals. Congressman George Hansen introduced legislation requiring the Federal Reserve to make zero inflation the goal of monetary policy and to prohibit support of interest rates on government securities. Gramley responded, opposing the legislation as a restriction on flexible monetary policy. Unlike the response to similar legislation in the 1920s, Gramley's letter accepted the desirability of a price stability goal.

require the System to follow the resolution calling for coordination with deficit reduction. Legislation was more troublesome than a resolution. "If Congress had a law that told us to do something, we'd have to do it. But a resolution is a much more tricky thing to handle. . . . I would propose to point out in a letter that it would be a very difficult matter if they got very precise in a resolution. It would be a departure, I think, without precedent, if there were really a precise resolution" (ibid., 43). Later Volcker added, "We should not, in my opinion, prejudge precisely what we would do without even knowing what the resolution is" (ibid., 44).[127]

Congress passed the resolution calling for coordination "if Congress acts to restore fiscal responsibility . . . in a substantial and permanent way" (FOMC Minutes, June 30–July 1, 91). The discussion that followed brought out differences in belief about policy coordination and the role of fiscal policy. Volcker, who probably wanted to ease, insisted: "There is a respectable body of economic opinion that says there is some degree of tradeoff between fiscal policy and monetary policy . . . Now, individual members of the Committee may not believe that theory, but it's not a totally unrespectable body of economic doctrine." Wallich, who did not want to ease, argued that in the long run money is neutral. "More money therefore means higher prices not higher output." But, Partee, who wanted to ease, rejected Wallich's argument because "we're so much below an optimal utilization rate" (ibid., 93).

The members then discussed "crowding out" of investment by deficit finance. They did not agree whether it was a current problem or would affect investment only after the economy recovered. Most believed that continued deficits raised long-term interest rates, so rates would fall if Congress reduced the deficit. But they didn't clarify whether the resulting reduction in interest rates constituted an easier monetary policy or whether the Federal Reserve should further reduce interest rates. This issue had troubled the System in 1968. It had not resolved it. Monetary velocity would decline as interest rates declined; there were differences of opinion about whether that would be enough to satisfy Congress or to constitute monetary ease. Political concerns had an important role. Those who favored easier policy argued for increasing money growth. Wallich and Solomon argued against.

The main theme of the policy discussion was to lower interest rates even if money growth exceeded the money targets. The staff reported some signs that the recession was ending, but the unemployment rate at

127. The Board continued to defer decisions calling for a lower discount rate. During February, it deferred increases to 13 percent four times before disapproving an increase on March 1. From March to July, the Board deferred or rejected reductions.

9.6 percent continued to rise. The staff forecast unemployment at 9 percent with real GNP growth at 3 percent in the next six quarters. Actual wage and consumer price increases ran about 6 percent, well below the peak. The dollar continued to appreciate; it rose above its value before August 1971, when President Nixon permitted the dollar to float.

Balles reported concerns about rising bankruptcies. He described bankers in the San Francisco district as "more worried than I've seen them worried in my adult life" (FOMC Minutes, June 30, 1982, 4). He and Boehne wanted to raise the money targets for 1982 and reduce them for 1983. Preston Martin wanted to ease without changing the target.

FOMC members gave many gloomy reports and warnings about possible crises—bank and saving and loan failures, bankruptcies. Partee mentioned that the next stage of tax reduction would release $40 billion, but he cited many offsets. Even Wallich, one of the more optimistic members, favored a cautious increase in the money targets for that year (ibid., 7). Even Roos was willing to let money growth for the year exceed the target.

A main problem was that $M_1$ and $M_2$ grew above the target range in the first half of the year. No one wanted to increase the interest rate to bring them within the target range. The members divided between those who wanted to raise the target for money and those, concerned about loss of credibility at election time, wanted to keep the targets but exceed them. Mexico's problems and its debt to the System added to the pressure on the FOMC.

Solomon described the change that occurred at the meeting. "This is the strangest FOMC meeting that I've attended. There seems to be a whole change or shift in mood. . . . [D]uring the depth of the recession there was a much tougher attitude than I hear today. . . . [I]t seems to me that it's important . . . that there not be an impression in the markets of a sudden reversal or shift toward easing. It would be very *politically* suspect. They see the pressure on us with widespread speculation now that we will ease. And yet at the same time there's a doom and gloom atmosphere out there and very little expectation that interest rates will fall" (ibid., 52; emphasis added).[128]

Caught between the two positions—political pressures, legislator

128. Frank Morris opposed proposals for a cap on the federal funds rate. His statement supports the position taken by those who claim the Federal Reserve targeted reserve growth to avoid taking blame for the increase in interest rates. "One thing we've learned in the last few years is that the presence of an intermediate target . . . has sheltered the central banks—not only ourselves but the Germans said the same thing at that meeting in New York [as did] the British and the Canadians and others—from a direct responsibility for interest rates, and I think that has contributed to a stronger policy posture. . . . And while I think we're following the wrong intermediate target [$M_1$] I believe it would be a big mistake to start doing without one" (FOMC Minutes, July 1, 1982, 56).

threats, and fear of a crisis on one side and concern about their credibility and the need to maintain the appearance of independence on the other—Volcker made a first small change in policy to lower rates.[129] Like most of the others, he wanted lower rates. Like some, he feared a market interpretation that the FOMC had succumbed to political pressure that would end with fears of inflation and higher long-term rates. He moved cautiously. He proposed to keep the same range as before, 10 to 15 percent for the funds rate "without changing the wording but with the knowledge that I would feel very hesitant [to accept it] if in fact the market produced rates of 15 percent continuously for any period of time" (FOMC Minutes, July 1, 1982, 58). But, concerned about a possible financial crisis, he warned, they would "have to respond to it" (ibid., 57). And though he recognized that "we all . . . would love to see interest rates down . . . the question is how much we can do" (ibid.). Credibility of the anti-inflation policy mattered; the market had to accept the change. The $M_1$ target was "about 5 percent" and $M_2$ 9 percent, but higher growth rates were "acceptable" (ibid., 79). The vote was eight to four with Teeters dissenting because she wanted more $M_1$ money growth, 6 to 6.5 percent, and Black, Ford, and Wallich wanted a less expansive policy. Volcker summed up his position. He did not want to reverse a decline in rates. "The problem is not the desirability of getting interest rates down; the question is whether by reaching too fast for that objective we may not be able to keep them down" (ibid., 66).

The same concerns about misinterpretation and permanent versus temporary changes continued in the discussion of the annual targets. Volcker favored keeping them unchanged because "we don't know how to change it without possibly getting ourselves in more difficulty" (ibid., p. 83). The decision warned about difficulties with $M_1$ and did not state a range. The range for $M_2$ remained at 8.5 to 9.5. Volcker's statement warned that the upper part of the range would be acceptable and desirable in a context of declining interest rates. Then the FOMC added that it would accept even more rapid growth of the aggregates if uncertainties continued to increase liquidity demands. The 1983 preliminary targets would continue the 1982 ranges.

Following the meeting, weekly bill rates and the federal funds rate dropped, and long-term rates fell modestly. By July 16, ten-year Treasuries were one-half percentage point lower and bill rates more than one

129. Seeking support for increased money growth, Volcker quoted from Friedman and Schwartz (1963) that uncertainty raises the demand for money (FOMC Minutes, July 1, 1982, 34). President Ford (Atlanta) strongly opposed easier policy, warning that the market would give it a political interpretation. Roos gave him some support, but he voted for easier policy. Wallich warned against easing, and Corrigan called a policy change "totally unappealing."

percentage point lower than at the meeting. On July 19, the Board approved a 0.5 reduction to 11.5 percent in the discount rate followed by a reduction to 11 percent on July 30, 10.5 percent on August 13, and 10 percent on August 26. The two percentage point total reduction followed a long series of deferrals and disapprovals starting in March. The federal funds rate accompanied the discount rate reductions. The monthly average declined from 14.15 percent in May to 10.12 percent in August. By late August, Treasury yields reached 12.5 percent, the lowest value since January 1981. The FOMC signaled to Congress and the market that it wanted lower interest rates. Volcker and the Board believed the market supported the decision to reduce interest rates. The unemployment rate reached 9.8 percent in August. Following the interest rate reductions, monetary base growth rose to 9 percent in July from a 6.5 percent average for the year to that date.

It is an understatement that Volcker was cautious about mentioning the policy change. In his July Humphrey-Hawkins testimony in the Senate, he did not mention the policy change to lower interest rates. He pointed to the decline in inflation, a reason interest rates could decline, but he did not draw that conclusion. He told the committee that "the evidence now seems to me strong that the inflationary tide has turned in a fundamental way" (Volcker papers, Federal Reserve Bank of New York, Box 97657, July 20, 1982, 2). And he suggested cautiously that the recession was ending. But his forecast showed the FOMC much less optimistic than the administration—forecast growth for 1982 was 1 to 4 compared to 5.2 percent.

The market's response emboldened those who favored a policy change. When the FOMC next met on August 24, Mexico was in "financial difficulty." The Treasury advanced $600 million, the Europeans $925 million, and the Federal Reserve voted $325 million in addition to the $700 million, it had approved earlier[130] (FOMC Minutes, August 24, 1982, 5).

Peter Sternlight then reported on some continuing domestic problems. Continental Illinois's certificates of deposit (CDs) were no longer considered top grade because of losses due to Penn Square. Lombard-Wall, a securities dealer, was in bankruptcy, causing problems for Chase Manhattan's CDs. And the $M_1$ money stock fell in July instead of increasing as

130. Governor Partee asked about the collateral behind the loan, citing earlier precedents. He expressed doubt about Mexico's ability to repay. Volcker replied that Mexico would have to undertake a "very draconian adjustment program" that had not been agreed to yet. The System's collateral was an agreement with the IMF that also had not been settled. "Oil revenues are an ultimate backstop" (FOMC Minutes, August 24, 1982, 5). Congress had not approved the Treasury's loan. The FOMC voted unanimously to make the loan.

anticipated. The desk bought $2.9 billion early in the inter-meeting period. Later it sold back some of its purchases, but it added net $2.1 billion to its holdings between meetings (ibid., 4).[131]

The Committee was pleased by the decline in interest rates, concerned about the speed of decline, and uncertain about what to do next. Members agreed on two points. They wanted the decline in interest rates to continue, and they did not want a sharp decline followed by a rise. They found much less agreement on how to do that. As always, some insisted that the right policy was to keep to the money targets, but more members now wanted to control the funds rate directly. Governor Partee expressed what may have been in others' minds. Weak money growth "would risk a second decline in the economy and [perhaps referring to proposed legislation] we *wouldn't survive that as an institution*" (ibid., 26; emphasis added).

Much of the discussion concerned whether $M_1$ growth should be 5.5 or 6.5 percent in September. Actual $M_1$ growth in August and September was 16 and 19 percent. The federal funds rate remained about 10 percent, at the bottom of the range. Member bank borrowing rose to $933 million in September, far outside the range the FOMC set ($300 million).

On August 3, Senator Byrd introduced his bill to restrict Federal Reserve independence by requiring it to lower interest rates and abandon reserve targets. He had thirty-one cosponsors. Volcker continued to push for more spending reductions in his dialogue with members of Congress, and the congressional principals continued to urge lower interest rates.

In part, this was a replay of 1968. Congress and the administration bargained over the fiscal package. Volcker assured them that interest rates would come down if they reduced the deficit, but he did not say whether he would raise money growth. The pressure was considerable. He did not agree to a coordinated effort, but he now moved decisively to lower interest rates.

Volcker and the FOMC had given more attention to interest rates in recent months. Volcker now made the policy changes explicit, but only for internal discussion. "On these money growth targets, in substance, I don't care. I think either of these two sets of numbers [5.5 and 6.5 percent] will make no difference, virtually, in what we actually do. . . . [W]e are within the limits of the growth targets anyway" (ibid., 28). He then proposed an interest rate policy that, as stated, depended on money growth.

131. Several weakened banks borrowed from their reserve banks. Governor Rice asked "whether we want to tell the market why there was a big bulge in such borrowings. . . . Chairman Volcker: This will have to be handled with a certain degree of flexibility" (FOMC Minutes, August 24, 1982, 15).

> I would be totally unable to defend a policy on our part that brought the federal funds rate up to 11 or 12 percent in the coming period. I would be very hard pressed to justify in my mind a pronounced downward shift in the federal funds rate in the near term from where it is. . . .
>
> If money growth comes in distinctly weak, we would ease up by some combination of measures, which would produce a little lower interest rates. If it came in as stronger or stronger than 5 percent, I would suggest that we probably would get some backing up of short-term rates.
>
> I, frankly, cannot live in these circumstances, given what is going on in the money markets, with violent moves in short-term rates in either direction. It would just be so disturbing in terms of expectations, market psychology, and fragility that it's just the wrong policy, period, during this particular period. (ibid., 29)

Prodded by Anthony Solomon, he specified a funds rate range of 7 to 10 percent.[132]

> Robert Black (Richmond). What you're really saying is that on the old procedures you would favor a money market directive. . . .
>
> Chairman Volcker. That is correct. But how we lean would be guided by the money supply, assuming something drastic isn't going on. (ibid., 30)

Governor Partee objected to Volcker's proposal because it gave all the authority to the Chairman. Morris agreed. Both preferred a 7 to 10 percent band on the funds rate.

After a lengthy discussion of the wording in the directive expressing concern about how Volcker's words "unusual volatility" would be interpreted, Volcker reluctantly gave up his wording and accepted a federal funds range of 7 to 11 percent. Money growth targets remained at 5 and 9 percent. The vote was ten-to-one, with Wallich dissenting and Gramley absent. Two days after the meeting, the Board voted to reduce the discount rate to 10 percent.

A month later, the FOMC held a telephone conference. There was no sign of economic expansion. Risks to financial markets seemed smaller, but not by much. Inflation continued to decline.

The purpose of the telephone meeting was to confirm and support Volcker's decision to prevent an increase in the federal funds rate despite

132. It is hard to find support for his comment about violent moves in short-term rates. Weekly three-month Treasury bills in July and August declined every week from July 2 (12.81 percent) to August 27 (7.50 percent). Volcker later responded to a question by saying that he was unhappy with the speed with which rates declined.

the increase in borrowed reserves. "We should not follow—and I would not intend to—a mechanical application of those reserve positions but rather stabilize market conditions somewhere close to where they are presently or even slightly below where they have been in the last couple of weeks" (FOMC Minutes, September 24, 1982, 1).

President Ford (Atlanta) asked for a clarification of the policy change. "Do you want to cap interest rates at 10.25 percent?" (ibid., 2). Volcker denied there was a policy change. He would try to hold borrowings to around $500 to $600 million by moving up the nonborrowed reserve path. "It would be a misguided policy to follow a direction right now that is likely to create a pronounced increase in interest rates" (ibid., 3). In a response to President Roos (St. Louis), Volcker added that he wanted to prevent a rise in interest rates during the two weeks before the next FOMC meeting. He proposed to ignore reserve growth and stabilize money market rates.

Roger Guffey (Kansas City) wanted to vote on the proposal, so there would be a record of their decision. Volcker hesitated and decided not to vote and postponed any announcement.

By deciding to target borrowing, the System returned to the policy target used in the 1920s and the basis for the free reserve target in the 1950s and 1960s. As in the earlier periods, the intent was to have loose control of interest rates without explicitly choosing an interest rate target. At the time, some of the borrowing was for a longer term, made to sustain some of the troubled banks. This borrowing was unresponsive to interest rates and excluded from the definition of borrowed reserves. Other borrowing was sensitive to the interest rate relative to the discount rate, but the relation was not very tight. Inability to project borrowed reserves accurately was one of the main weaknesses in the System's method of targeting money. Several FOMC members expressed these concerns emphasizing uncertainty about the amount of borrowing made by banks facing credit problems. Volcker's concern was to avoid a rise in the funds rate from 10.25 percent at that time. Any concern about financial sector problems was more than matched by concerns about Congress.

The shift to easier money, judged by growth of $M_1$ in September without recourse to higher interest rates, induced a dramatic increase in stock prices. The S&P index rose 4 percent in the first week of September. The index had been rising slowly; prior to the September policy change, it had increased 25 percent in the year to August. Despite the gloomy forecasts and anecdotes at the FOMC, investors and speculators had become more optimistic. The decline in inflation and interest rates and the reluctance to slow money growth added to their optimism.

Weekly Treasury bill rates showed little response to the September

24 meeting, but ten-year Treasury rates continued to fall. By October 1 they were below 12 percent for the first time in two years. A year before these yields reached a peak of 15.68 percent, so the decline was more than 3.75 percentage points in a year.

The rise in stock prices, and the fall in long-term rates and in measures of expected inflation were inconsistent with the predictions of those who opposed policy ease. Volcker must have noticed these responses and was encouraged to continue.

With reserve targeting about to end permanently, the Board approved a return to contemporaneous reserve accounting beginning February 2, 1984. The change applied only to institutions holding $15 million or more in total deposits. Reports remained due on Wednesday with a two-day lag using deposits held during the two weeks ending the previous Monday. The change did not apply to time deposits.

Tentative agreement came on June 28 with Teeters and Gramley opposed. They claimed that eliminating lagged reserve accounting would increase interest rate volatility. One suggestion was to stagger settlement; half the banks would settle each week. After additional staff research, the Board rejected this proposal on the argument that monetary control would be weakened if the settling banks borrowed reserves from the other banks. A minority proposed to try the staggered system, but they did not prevail. On September 29, the proposal for contemporaneous accounting was adopted on a five-to-two vote with Gramley and Teeters still in dissent. Since reserve targeting soon ended, the decision had no effect on monetary control.

The staff forecast put off the recovery to 1983. Then Axilrod discussed the difficulties of forecasting or even interpreting $M_1$. The All Savers Certificates, NOW accounts and other changes created the problem. As Chart 8.4 above shows, these problems did not affect the real monetary base. Growth of the real base turned positive in August. Real output rose slightly in fourth quarter 1982 and more strongly in the first half of 1983. Industrial production surged in January. The recession was over.

The October 5 FOMC meeting was a turning point; the FOMC ended monetary control. Volcker signaled his concern and his intention by speaking first. After noting disappointment at the slow pace of recovery despite lower inflation, he gave his interpretation of world economic problems. The world was in recession with unemployment at record (postwar) levels. "I don't know of any country of any consequence in the world that has an expansion going on" (FOMC Minutes, October 5, 1982, 15). World trade was doing poorly. He then briefly summarized the problems of Mexico, Argentina, Ecuador, Chile, Bolivia, Costa Rica, Peru, Brazil, and Venezuela. “All of these countries are dependent upon sustained borrowing to maintain a semblance of equilibrium during this period” (ibid., 16). These countries depended heavily on loans from U.S. commercial banks, but the banks were “basically unable or unwilling to sell any substantial amount of domestic CDs and are having their lines from other banks cut back” (ibid., 17). Spreads in the euro-dollar market had increased. He suggested that the decline in Treasury yields was, in part, a flight to quality. Some banks tried to withdraw from international lending (ibid., 18). All of these problems increased uncertainty. Appreciation of the dollar added to the world’s problems.

Volcker then reviewed the problems of Latin American countries. He made two groupings. All the main countries, Mexico, Brazil, Argentina, and Chile, had problems with financing their debt. Several others—Ecuador, Peru, Costa Rica, Bolivia, even Venezuela—faced difficulties in financing, and some would likely default. Total external debt for these countries he placed at about $300 billion, much of it owed to banks in the United States.

Next, he reviewed problems at domestic banks. Many faced difficulties when borrowing in the market and had to pay a premium. Euro-dollar market rates had a risk premium over domestic rates “that is not explicable by normal arbitrage calculation” (ibid., 17). One result was that the decline in federal funds and Treasury bill rates had not extended to the rates faced by foreign banks, troubled domestic banks, and sovereign borrowers.

Volcker concluded his survey by emphasizing the uncertainty about domestic and international developments. If the members were not frightened by his summary, he ended by saying, “we haven’t had a parallel to this situation historically except to the extent 1929 was a parallel” (ibid., 19). Other members added to the gloom about problems in Argentina and Brazil. As these countries rolled over debts, they had to pay the real interest rates prevailing at the time. Soon many would default.

At the start of the Committee’s discussion, Volcker made clear that he regarded the situation as extraordinary. “This is not a time . . . for business as usual . . . extraordinary things may have to be done” (ibid., 19). He proposed setting the borrowing target at $200 or $300 million. “The implication is that we would keep the borrowing level more or less the same until something happened to throw us off—in economic activity, in financial markets, or in the actual growth of $M_2$ and $M_3$” (ibid., 52). He made clear several times that he did not want interest rates to increase, and he did not want a target for $M_1$ because the expiration of All Savers Certificates made the numbers meaningless.

Volcker left no doubt that he wanted discretion. In August, he had asked for a directive that permitted him to prevent any increase in interest rates.

He had not convinced the FOMC. Market rates had increased during the month. "I think it was a mistake to have that kind of directive last time. I think it would be more than a mistake this time, and it's not going to be acceptable to me. Beyond that it is desirable to get some easing in this situation" (ibid., 31).

"The central point is that whatever the [monetary variable] is that we are operating on, it is a staff guess, which may or may not be right. I'm saying that I'm not willing to stake my life, so to speak, on that guess being right. The risks are too great. . . . [W]hat this is meant to convey is an operational approach that modestly moves the funds rate down" (ibid., 32).

One reason for resistance was concern about making a policy change to lower interest rates one month before the congressional election. Members rarely mentioned political events as reasons for favoring or opposing policy but Ford was unusually explicit.

> I want to say, respectfully, that I'm flatly opposed to this. If we were to do this, especially now, I think it will consolidate any adverse opinions against us that are already out there about our motives for doing this at this particular time. . . . I have heard from more people than I care to describe to you comments questioning our integrity and our motives in the context of an election campaign. (ibid., 33)

Just three years earlier, Volcker told the members that the proposed change was a temporary move. Now he said they would restore the $M_1$ target once the All Savers Certificate and the new instruments allowed by the Garn-St. Germain legislation permitted transaction accounts to settle down. Later he said to Mehrling (2007, 183) that "we were getting boxed in by the money supply data . . . We came to the conclusion that it was not very reliable . . . so we backed off that approach."

This time, he added a threat and responded to comments about the election.

> It's quite clear in my mind where the risks are. I think I made it quite clear where the risks are. I think I made it quite clear in terms of economic developments around the world. But if one wants to put it in terms of political risk to the institution: If we get this one wrong, we are going to have legislation next year without a doubt. We may get it anyway. . . . I'm not sure how it looks just in strict electoral terms, since that question has been raised, to sit here in some sense artificially doing nothing and then have to make a big move right after the election. I'm not sure that would wash very well in terms of anybody's opinion of our professional competence as an institution. (FOMC Minutes, October 5, 1982, 50–51)

Then he added:

> I wouldn't care where the interest rates were if the economic situation looked a little better—and if we weren't going to have to deal with a succession of sick foreign countries in this time period, if the dollar were not rising into the wild blue yonder right now, and if I thought that all the accumulating problems that we face could wait for a while, we'd have a much easier decision. Under present conditions, four weeks looks like one hell of a long time to me. (ibid., 51)[133]

Volcker was indifferent about whether they specified a range for the funds rate or left it to his judgment. If they wanted a range, he favored 7 to 10 percent. The weekly Treasury bill yield rose in the week of the meeting, but it remained between 7.5 and 7.75 percent for the rest of October. The monthly average federal funds rate declined 0.6 percentage points in October to 9.7 percent. The $M_1$ money stock rose at almost a 14 percent annual rate, but the increase was heavily in NOW accounts. However, the monetary base rose about 10 percent (annual rate) in August and September and 13 percent in October.

The good news was that the CPI rose at annual rates between 2 and 3 percent monthly from August through October; by October the twelve-month moving average was below 5 percent. But the unemployment rate rose above 10 percent for the first time in the postwar years. The S&P index rose strongly in October, probably on evidence that the Federal Reserve would try to prevent a possible crisis.

Discussion turned to whether the System or Volcker would announce the policy change. Volcker seemed hesitant. An announcement would make the change seem "more grandiose" than he intended (ibid., 53). But Ford argued for a more explicit statement "saying that the fed funds rate will not rise above 10.5 percent. Isn't that what we mean? Why not say what we mean?" (FOMC Minutes, October 5, 1981, 67). But Volcker did not accept that description.

Presidents Black, Ford, and Horn were not persuaded. They voted against the directive. Wallich voted in favor, although he had expressed concern during the discussion. The nine-to-three vote expressed a preference for discretionary action and an imprecise directive in the face of pos-

133. Volcker then explained why he was less concerned than some about a negative market reaction. "They have assumed that we moved as alertly . . . as we did during the summer because we were operating against the background of Penn Square and Drysdale and accumulating international problems. This [referring to the FOMC's statement] is in a sense a confession, good for the soul, in making that a little more explicit" (FOMC Minutes, October 5, 1982, 51).

sible crisis. Members' confidence in Volcker's judgment played a decisive role, as several said.[134]

Prior to the meeting, the Board deferred several requests from Chicago to reduce its discount rate to 9.5 percent. After the meeting, New York, Philadelphia, Minneapolis, San Francisco, and Atlanta joined Chicago. The Board approved the 9.5 percent discount rate. It denied Dallas's request for a 9 percent rate. By the end of the year, the discount rate was 8.5 percent everywhere. Following the meeting, the federal funds rate declined from a 10.3 average for September to 9.7 and 9.2 percent for October and November. Long-term Treasury rates fell almost one percentage point by the time of the November FOMC meeting.

A few days after the FOMC meeting, Volcker spoke to the Business Council, made up of CEOs of large corporations, and gave a press conference on recent policy actions.[135] He emphasized no change in policy and pointed to the progress on reducing inflation. He avoided any reference to the problems of foreign governments and financial fragility. He warned the Business Council not to interpret the lower discount and funds rates as evidence of easier policy. "Lower interest rates in an economy in recession are not unusual, and are consistent with the need for recovery. But lower interest rates do not in themselves indicate a change in basic policy approach" (Volcker speeches, Board Records, October 9, 1982, 2). Most of the rest of the speech explained the reasons for reduced attention to changes in $M_1$.

Volcker was not ready to show his hand. In his press conference, Volcker referred to the October 5 decision as "a small, technical matter."

134. The Federal Advisory Council reported at its September 17 meeting with the Board that the Drysdale, Penn Square, Lombard-Wall, and Mexican problems increased caution. Regional banks received CD money that would have gone to money center banks. Markets experienced a "flight to quality" and reduced lending to Latin America. The FAC disagreed with Volcker's assessment of risk. "The failures of Drysdale and Lombard-Wall were not signs of general instability in financial markets. Nor do they threaten to impair the normal, efficient operation of these markets" (Board Minutes, September 17, 1982, 4). They praised the Federal Reserve for supporting the market and taking "no action to rescue the unfortunate participants in the incidents" (ibid.). The FAC agreed with the Federal Reserve policy of allowing money supply growth to exceed the targets and reduce market interest rates. Then they added: "There is concern in the marketplace, as reflected by high real interest rates, about the continuance of the Federal Reserve policy of restraint in the face of political pressures and the unresolved problem of the Federal budget deficits" (ibid., 6). At about the same time, the Shadow Open Market Committee urged a restrictive policy to reduce inflation accompanied by a policy of permitting financial failures but protecting the market from the effects of the failures.

135. The *Wall Street Journal* published a story on the Thursday before the Business Council meeting. Coyne said the story was accurate. "That stirred a lot of interest" (Coyne, 1998, 16).

He again emphasized the unreliability of current data on $M_1$, but as in his talk to the Business Council, he mentioned sluggish real growth, the strong dollar, and evidence of increased demand for liquidity. The Federal Reserve, he said, remained committed to lowering inflation. It would "not force interest rates lower. We welcome declines" (press conference, Board Records, October 9, 1982, 2). He did not say that the System would resist higher interest rates.

Reporters asked if the October 5 decision and the FOMC's statement that it would tolerate growth in $M_2$ above the target reflected concern about bank failures. Volcker was cautious, denied concern about bank failures, and referred to increased liquidity preference. He pointed to the premiums on interest rates as evidence.

The New York staff reported that $M_1$ rose at a 20 percent annual rate in October. "Rapid $M_1$ growth was essentially accommodated through periodic adjustments of the reserve path in line with the Committee's decision at the last meeting" (FOMC Minutes, November 16, 1982, 1).[136] The System explained that expiration of the All Savers Certificate made money growth data unreliable. It accounted for half the growth in M1 (FOMC Minutes, November 16, 1982, 1). There was no reliable way to judge how much of the growth in M1 was temporary and how much represented a permanent increase in transaction balances.[137]

Staff forecasts remained pessimistic about 1982, but the early forecast called for 3 percent growth in 1983. Actual growth for the four quarters was 6.5 percent, double the estimate. Volcker asked if any of the members saw evidence of recovery in November. Most said that there were faint signs especially in housing. The dollar exchange rate against most currencies continued to rise.

Volcker summed up his position. "We will keep the same general framework we had last time [deemphasizing $M_1$] . . . A much more fundamental problem, implicit or explicit in the earlier conversation, is that the business situation doesn't look red hot" (ibid., 20). He then discussed the large shift down in velocity and the uncertainty about whether the shift was temporary or permanent.

Most of the members wanted lower interest rates and were willing to

136. The manager agreed with a criticism by Robert Black (Richmond). "When you ask if it is effective to control $M_2$ via this means, I would have to say I have some real doubts as to how good our control mechanism is on $M_2$" (FOMC Minutes, November 16, 1982, 3). Black was not satisfied. "I don't think we can slow it [$M_2$] down except through affecting $M_1$ and those few assets in $M_2$ that are subject to either reserve requirements or interest rate ceilings" (ibid.).

137. Once again, there was a report of "leaks" from the meeting. Volcker sharply reduced the number of participants.

act to bring that about. Roger Guffey (Kansas City) was most outspoken. "All the talk about targeting reserves and looking at $M_2$ for some information content as to what policy should be I think is a bunch of boloney in the sense that we are targeting interest rates. And we ought to recognize that. . . . I am not suggesting that we do away with or abandon the regime of targeting reserves and money supply, at least for public consumption. But around this table it seems clear to me that [we are on] an interest rate regime and we ought to target on the interest rate we think is appropriate to get the economic recovery started again" (ibid., 23).

Volcker interrupted him. He was not ready to concede that he had abandoned reserve targeting permanently, but his statement partially confirmed Guffey's point. "I don't think that's quite accurate, Roger. . . . I would have lower interest rates if these aggregates weren't rising so darn [fast]" (ibid.). This suggests that growth of the aggregates was no longer the target. It had become a constraint on the interest rate level.

The facts bear out Guffey's comment. The federal funds rate remained in the range specified throughout 1982. All of the monetary aggregates were above the annual range throughout the year.

Volcker's subsequent statement brings out the experimental aspect of the September–October policy change. Ten-year interest rates had declined from 11.8 to 10.5 percent since September. "What we have to balance is how much we think we can get away with, even if we recognize the dangers in the business situation and want to get interest rates lower. . . . I think one would have to conclude from what has happened in the market that people haven't been that upset by what they've seen so far. . . . I suppose that what the market is telling us is that people are not going to get worried about that when they have a sense that the economy, if anything, is still declining" (ibid., 29–30). Most of the other members shared his objective of lowering interest rates.

President Ford (Atlanta) was an exception. He cited the next stage of the tax cuts and the rapid growth in real money balances. "We are sitting here reading each other the gloom and doom report, but unless we are at a historically discontinuous point in our economy . . . we are at a high risk of throwing both of the throttles in our economic airplane fully to the wall and the plane has to take off" (ibid., 33). Governor Partee supported him and urged delay, but Volcker cited the precarious international situation, the very strong dollar, and the world recession to bolster his position. Teeters, however, warned that "our interest rates, the lack of recovery in this country, and the high international value of the dollar are creating a situation in the international field that could lead us into something very similar to the 1930s" (ibid., 23). Although she did not recognize it, the recession was ending; the National Bureau of Economic Research dates the end of the recession in November.

On an eleven-to-one vote, the FOMC approved a directive calling for 9.5 percent $M_2$ growth and a 6 to 10 percent federal funds rate. Ford dissented. The December average funds rate was almost six percentage points below the February value. The ten-year rate stabilized at about 10.5 percent, but the stock price index continued to rise as signs of recovery increased.

Teeters proposed publishing the directive right after the meeting to prevent leaks and provide information. She received considerable support, but Volcker opposed and did not ask for a vote. He argued that if the FOMC released the directive, Congress would schedule a hearing in the afternoon.

With $M_1$ distorted, the committee was at a loss about how to operate. It continued to set a path for nonborrowed reserves, but it recognized that it had little control over $M_2$ growth. Policy had become discretionary, based mainly on Volcker's judgment. Members disliked that arrangement but did not propose another. Volcker explained again that his goal was lower interest rates, but the size of the decline depended on slower money growth in $M_2$ especially. His policy was opportunistic; he would lower interest rates as opportunities appeared.

Several members commented on monetary velocity. It was far below its old trend. No one offered an explanation, and neither the governors nor the staff suggested that velocity growth should decline with expected inflation and interest rates.

The December directive repeated November's. This time, Black joined Ford in dissent, so the vote was ten to two. The discussion brought out market concerns about future inflation, but it did not seem to cause any change in voting or action.

Much of the December meeting commented on a staff report on the choice of target. The main conclusion was that each of the targets had important disadvantages at the time. The staff, however, agreed that $M_1$ was the best target once the economy completed adjustment to new monetary instruments and institutional changes. The staff believed the adjustment would be over by mid-year. Several FOMC members expressed doubt.

The report set off a lengthy but inconclusive discussion. Axilrod proposed using the broader aggregates during the transition. An important reason was to assure the public that the FOMC "is continuing on the anti-inflationary course set earlier, even while taking steps to stimulate economic recovery. This is particularly important at this time in view of the doubts that seem to be emerging, at least in the bond markets, about the Federal Reserve's intentions" (FOMC Minutes, December 20–21, 1982, 11).

Black (Richmond) wanted the FOMC to commit to a return to $M_1$ targets by mid-year 1983. Wallich agreed, but Morris described the proposal as "extremely unrealistic" (ibid., 20). Several members favored $M_2$. There was no agreement. Teeters described the committee as close to "the feel and tone of the market as we've been in thirty years" (ibid., 35).

Volcker's summary noted that Humphrey-Hawkins legislation required the choice of a target. A majority favored $M_2$. "On balance, I think we're left with what would be termed an eclectic, pragmatic approach. It's going to involve some judgment as to which one of these measures we emphasize, or we may shift from time to time. . . .

"There was some question . . . of explicit interest rate targeting. I don't think we have to go to that" (ibid., 39–41).

Volcker accepted the $M_2$ target for the present, but it was "a more qualified target than we've had before" (ibid., 43). Their approach was now "eclectic, pragmatic" (ibid., 41). In response to a question about how they could avoid inflation if they did not follow a rule, Volcker said they had to depend on "internal discipline" (ibid.). He emphasized the difference. The FOMC accepted reserve targeting to bring down inflation. "We were preoccupied with that need for disciplining ourselves and disciplining the economy. . . . The risks have shifted" (ibid.). But he would not admit to targeting interest rates.

### *International Actions*

The first cracks in the international payments system came in May 1982, when Mexico borrowed $600 million under its swap agreement. This was the start of an effort to hide Mexico's financial problem by borrowing on the swap line just before releasing its monthly financial statement, then repaying. It gave the appearance of adequate currency reserves at the Bank of Mexico and may have misled some private lenders.

The Mexican government talked about undertaking an austerity program but wanted to delay until after its July presidential election.[138] Volcker believed that in September President López Portillo would make his farewell speech. "The new president would do something in the beginning of September" (Volcker, 2001, 8). Board members questioned Volcker about risk and repayment. He told them that Mexico planned to go to the IMF after its election, but he did not have a firm commitment.

The Federal Reserve had to choose between two unattractive alternatives. Either they made the Mexican loan or Mexico would default on its

138. Federal Reserve governors were cynical about the promise. Preston Martin said, "I think we're defining austerity as halting construction of four office buildings" (FOMC Minutes, May 18, 1982, 12).

debt. The first put the Federal Reserve at risk, but it postponed and perhaps prevented a crisis. Failure to lend meant heavy losses by large money center banks as well as others. Grieder (1987, 684) puts Mexico's outstanding debt at $80 billion and the share held by the nine largest U.S. banks equal to 44 percent of their capital. Even the prospect of default was likely to reduce or eliminate the money center banks' ability to borrow on certificates of deposits. A scramble for liquidity seemed likely. The Federal Reserve estimated that as many as 1,000 banks had lent to Mexico.

In late June, the Federal Reserve increased its Mexican loan to $700 million. Neither Volcker nor the Mexican government had a long-term plan to prevent default. Even after the election, it did not offer a plan. By lending, it permitted lenders to reduce or eliminate their loans. Most were short-term. As they came due, some lenders withdrew. And the more astute or better-informed Mexicans sold pesos and deposited dollars in U.S. banks. Federal Reserve loans financed these transfers.

The Mexican election did not resolve Mexico's problem. Volcker told the FOMC on August 24 that Mexico needed more assistance to avoid default. Working with others, the Federal Reserve and the Treasury arranged $3.5 billion in additional loans and a willingness of commercial banks to roll over their loans. Some small banks did not go along, pushing the problem on to the money center banks.

Governor Partee questioned the use of the swap line, reminding the members that "we are precisely in the situation the Committee was somewhat concerned we might be in when that swap was first approved some fifteen years ago" (FOMC Minutes, August 24, 1982, 5). Volcker agreed. Repayment would require "a very draconian adjustment program" by Mexico (ibid.). The present swap was "secured . . . by a Fund agreement that doesn't exist yet" (ibid).

Members asked about other countries. Volcker told them that Argentina had the most serious problem after Mexico. It did not have a swap line, and most of its loans were to non-U.S. banks.

The Federal Reserve, and Volcker personally, took an active role in the discussions that followed. All of the problem countries defaulted, but the IMF prevented them from stopping interest payments to the banks. Regulatory rules required the U.S. banks to write down the loans if interest payments stopped. Instead, the banks rolled over the loans, and the IMF made additional loans to the countries. The money did not go to the countries; it went to the banks to pay interest due. The countries' debt rose.

Volcker and the IMF chose to put the solvency of the banks ahead of the debtor countries' growth. For the rest of the decade income in the debtor countries stagnated. Volcker and the IMF never developed a procedure for ending this arrangement by writing down the debt.[139] In 1989, the U.S. Treasury began to resolve the problem by offering the Brady plan, which reduced the debt.

The Volcker policy also put the interest of financial markets and banks ahead of the interests of the developing countries. The latter reduced their exports from the rest of the world. The United States was a major supplier, so much of the burden fell on U.S. farmers and manufacturers. Writing down the debt and lending to sustain the debt market would have been a less costly solution. Once again, the Federal Reserve neglected Bagehot's advice.

## CONCLUSION

Volcker's statements as well as data leave little doubt that monetary policy changed in the summer and fall of 1982, even if Volcker hesitated to say so explicitly. The System's public statements emphasized the difficulties in interpreting money growth, given the changes in regulation and the expiration of All Savers Certificates. Internal discussion gave greater weight to continued recession, rising unemployment (to above 10 percent), risks to money center banks caused by exposure to a Mexican (and other) default, risks to Federal Reserve independence, and the international effects of historically high interest rates. For these reasons, Volcker and others gave priority beginning in June 1982 to lowering interest rates. Internally, Volcker was more forthright. He answered those who thought the policy change mistaken because it reduced credibility just before an election.

> I don't myself perceive that the risks of misinterpretation are as great as some people think. Obviously they are there. . . . [F]ollowing a mechanical operation because we think that's vital to credibility and driving the economy into the ground isn't exactly my version of how to maintain credibility over time. Credibility in some sense is there to be spent when we think it's necessary to spend it and we can carry through a change in approach. . . . We are dealing with the real world and assessing where the risks are. (FOMC Minutes, October 5, 1982, 50; see also Cukierman and Meltzer, 1986)

Volcker then described the risks, including the political risk to the Federal Reserve, if the recession continued or worsened. He acted for a combination of reasons, including political and economic concerns, and domestic and international risks.

139. As an acting member of the President's Council of Economic Advisers, I proposed a writedown of the debt in the 1989 Economic Report of the President. This met strong opposition from the Treasury Department, so only a part of the recommendation remained in the published report. After the 1988 election, the Treasury accepted the writedown.

> If we get this one wrong, we are going to have legislation next year without a doubt.[140] We may get it anyway. . . . I think I know where the risks are. I'm not sure how it looks just in strict electoral terms, since the question has been raised, to sit here in some sense artificially doing nothing and then have to make a big move right after the election. . . . I'd prefer that this problem didn't arise now. If business conditions looked a little better and interest rates were a little lower—and I wouldn't care where the interest rates were if economic conditions looked a little better—and if we weren't going to have to deal with a succession of sick foreign countries in this time period, if the dollar were not rising into the wild blue yonder right now, and if I thought that all these accumulating problems that we face could wait for a while, we'd have a much easier decision. . . . I don't know what is going to happen in a number of directions over the next four weeks. (FOMC Minutes, October 5, 1982, 50–51).

The anti-inflation program became possible because President Reagan and, with the exception of credit controls, President Carter did not interfere. Leading members of Congress supported the policy, and those affected most—the homebuilders—reluctantly accepted the importance of reducing inflation. After three years, facing elections with rising unemployment rates and an incipient international crisis that threatened the United States' financial system, political support wavered and waned. Legislation proposed restricting Federal Reserve independence or requiring it to target and reduce interest rates.

From the 1920s on, the System always responded to the threat of legislation. It was not helpless or without support. But Volcker did not wish to have a test of political strength. Inflation had fallen; the monthly CPI change for November and December 1982 was negative, and the twelve-month moving average fell below 4 percent, nearly ten percentage points below the peak. The December moving average was the lowest since 1973.

Volcker was cautious. He did not want to revive inflation or appear to make obvious policy changes before the November 1982 election. He lowered interest rates beginning in July, and watched the market and public reaction. The Federal Advisory Council told the Board in November that its policy was "appropriate"; it cited the current state of the economy, the level of unemployment, and the rate of inflation. "Moreover, we do not detect any significant loss of credibility on the part of the Fed in its fight on inflation" (Board Minutes, November 5, 1982, 5). However, the FAC warned

140. Volcker talked to Senator Byrd in August. The senator said he would not introduce legislation if interest rates continued to decline (Grieder, 1987, 514).

that "stricter monetary targeting should be resumed in an early stage of a recovering economy" (ibid.).

Although there was talk of inflation, the stock market boomed and long-term interest rates fell. That response encouraged continued ease and continued effort to forestall a banking crisis.

The market reaction has two possible explanations. One interpretation is that expectations of inflation had fallen in step with inflation. An alternative explained the positive market reaction as a response to the lower risk of a domestic and international financial crisis and a cyclical recovery in profits and output together with high, though reduced, inflation expectations.

Evidence supports the second interpretation. The SPF index put expected inflation near 6 percent at the time, a very high rate for peacetime. The ten-year Treasury bond rate remained above 10 percent until November 1985, three years later. In the interim, it remained between 10 and 14 percent, so real interest rates were 6 to 10 percent. These historically high real rates suggest that markets wanted to see sustained recovery without a return of high inflation. Some FOMC members shared the view that real rates would not decline until the recovery was complete without a return to inflation. By 1985, the economy had recovered. The unemployment rate had fallen to 7 percent, while inflation remained below 4 percent.

Goodfriend and King (2005, 982–83) report the wide gap between actual and published Phillips curve estimates of the output loss from disinflation. Okun (1978) summarized six Phillips curve estimates as showing that output would average 9 to 27 percent below capacity each year of the three-year disinflation. The total deviation of output would be 27 to 81 percent. The actual deviation was 20 percent, not small but smaller than even the most optimistic estimate based on published Phillips curves. The Reagan tax rate reduction limited the loss of output. The administration's aggressive response to the air controllers strike helped also by reducing demands for wage growth.

The actual loss was almost certainly larger than required, and the recession probably lasted longer than necessary. The Federal Reserve's control of money was imperfect and often absent. Its signals were hard to read. It did not make any of the institutional changes needed to improve monetary control until after it gave up monetary control. Better control procedures would not have removed all the random fluctuations in reserves and money, but lagged reserve requirements prevented the staff from controlling total reserves, as they reported to the FOMC several times. When reserve requirements had to be met, either the Federal Reserve supplied the reserves by open market operations or the banks borrowed the reserves. By keeping the discount rate often far below open market rates, the System

**Table 8.11** Changes in Real Base Growth and Real Interest Rates, 1979–82

| PERIOD | CHANGE IN REAL BASE GROWTH (%) | CHANGE IN REAL TEN-YEAR RATE (PERCENTAGE POINTS) |
|---|---|---|
| 1979/9–1980/4 | −2.8 | +3.2 |
| 1980/4–1980/10 | +2.7 | −1.1 |
| 1980/10–1981/1 | −1.2 | +0.1 |
| 1981/1–1981/5 | +3.8 | +1.3 |
| 1981/5–1981/9 | −3.3 | +1.4 |
| 1981/9–1982/10 | +7.8 | −3.1 |

favored borrowing. That left decisions about total reserves to the banks and reduced monetary control.

At least as important, institutional changes made it difficult to interpret money growth. Deregulation was long overdue, but its timing made growth of monetary aggregates difficult to interpret. The Federal Reserve was unfortunate in choosing to target money growth just at the time that the financial sector responded to deregulation. And it put too much emphasis on monthly or quarterly changes. As the charts show, growth of the real monetary base is a more reliable indicator during the period. The FOMC did not use it. Academic economists were probably too quick to conclude that the System could not control money. That conclusion puts too much emphasis on short-term changes.

A principal result was that the System made it much more difficult for the market to believe that the Federal Reserve was in control and would continue to reduce money growth until inflation slowed or ended. The System had abandoned anti-inflation policy on several previous occasions. Irregular base and money growth made its policy difficult to interpret. Table 8.11 shows the changes in real base growth and real ten-year Treasury yields dated at turning points in real base growth. Over a three-year period, base growth changed direction five times, often by relatively large amounts. On average, the change in direction occurred about every five months during the first two years. Anyone watching real base growth or real interest rates for evidence that the recession was about to end would have been uncertain until the prolonged increase in real base growth that began in September 1981 continued in 1982. See also Chart 8.5 above.

Although some members at times recognized that transitory changes in reserves, money growth, output growth, and measured inflation distorted current period data, few proposed to center attention on underlying permanent changes. Volcker and many others recognized at times that their goal was a lower trend rate of inflation, but they made no effort to emphasize the permanent trend or to ignore transitory changes. Their most important change was to put little weight on the unemployment rate, a decision that did not have unanimous support.

Despite these impediments, the effort succeeded to a considerable extent. Inflation did not end, but it fell to levels that had not been sustained for a decade. The FOMC and Paul Volcker deserve our praise for this achievement and for sustaining the disinflationary policy until inflation fell. The minutes show that Volcker had support from a few governors and presidents throughout, but he also had opposition much of the time. Success depended on his persistent concern to reduce inflation, and his firm belief that failure would make stability more difficult to achieve.

The 1979–82 disinflation demonstrates the importance of credibility in the implementation of monetary policy. As Goodfriend and King (2005) emphasize, the public did not fully believe that the Federal Reserve would keep its commitment to end inflation.[141] Too many previous attempts were followed by the inflation rate heading to a new peak. The Federal Reserve added to the problem by failing to distinguish between a large one-time increase in the price level, resulting from the 1979–80 oil price increase, and the maintained rate of inflation. Reported rates of inflation would have declined even if the Federal Reserve maintained its earlier policy stance. The Federal Reserve succeeded in reducing the underlying maintained rate of inflation, however.

Continued high real interest rates suggest that more had to be done to convince the public that inflation would not return. Volcker's lasting influence was (1) to increase the weight on inflation and lower the weight on unemployment, in the Federal Reserve's objective function and (2) restore System credibility for controlling inflation. Central bankers in other countries made similar changes at about the same time. Central banks apparently learned that disinflation was costly to society and to them because they were blamed for the surge in unemployment rates and loss of output during disinflation.

The Federal Reserve did not yet have a consistent, transparent means of implementing policy. Procyclicality and excessive attention to near-term changes remained. There was ample reason, therefore, for skepticism about whether the reduction in inflation was permanent.

141. Hardouvelis and Barnhart (1989) used a Kalman filter to measure changes in credibility. They found that the public restored credibility slowly. Apparently, credibility depended on sustained reduction in inflation, not on announcements or the decision to abandon reserve control.

NINE

# Restoring Stability, 1983–86

Mr. Wallich. . . . We have evidence of a very strong monetary expansion. On the other side is a high real interest rate. Which of the two really drives the economy?
—FOMC Minutes, March 28–29, 1983, 43

Chairman Volcker. I don't think we know what GNP is going to be in this quarter.
—FOMC Minutes, November 4–5, 1985, 21

Inflation was greatly reduced but not eliminated by the end of 1982. The GNP deflator for fourth quarter rose at a 3.6 percent annual rate, down from a peak of 12.11 percent two years earlier. Real growth followed money growth, not the real interest rate. A strong recovery had begun.

The years of high inflation were over, but inflation and disinflation left problems behind. Four major problems continued in the 1980s. First, real interest rates remained far above historic norms. Foreign governments and banks that borrowed during the years of negative real interest rates could not earn enough to pay the borrowing cost or retire the debt. Beginning in 1982, borrowers began to default, causing large potential losses at major banks at home and abroad. IMF and Federal Reserve policy protected the banks at the expense of growth in the debtor countries and to a lesser extent at home. Second, domestic banks also faced large losses on loans to real estate and energy companies. Adjustment to reduced oil prices, reduced home building, and historically high real rates on mortgages left many banks facing loan losses. Third, the dollar appreciated in the early 1980s, stimulating imports and reducing exports. Reducing the dollar exchange rate later became a goal of the Treasury, assisted by the Federal Reserve. This involved agreement with other leading countries, especially

West Germany and Japan. This problem occupied the Federal Reserve in the 1980s. Fourth, the FOMC wanted to prevent a return of high inflation. It was uncertain about how to do that. Policy was judgmental, based mainly on Volcker's judgments.

It is not possible to date precisely the end of the inflation. By 1986, long-term interest rates, exchange rates, and changes in wages and other prices no longer incorporated high expected inflation. This evidence of the adjustment of expectations is a good measure of the end of inflation. As Governor Wallich noted above, money growth and real interest rates in 1983 gave very different signals about the future. Base growth had increased from a 5.3 annual rate at the end of 1981 to 8.3 at the end of 1982. By the spring and summer of 1983 twelve-month average base growth was above 10 percent. But yields on ten-year Treasury notes reached 10.6 percent as he spoke and rose further as the year progressed. The SPF expected inflation for the next four quarters fell to 5 percent in first quarter 1983, so the anticipated real yield was about 5.5 percent. It rose with the rise in nominal yields and a further decline in anticipated inflation.

The extraordinary real returns reflected both skepticism about the Federal Reserve's ability or willingness to further reduce inflation or even to keep it from rising and the strong recovery from a deep recession. The high real rate was apparently balanced by an even higher expected return, especially to consumption in the event. The unemployment rate reached 10.8 percent at the end of 1982 and 10.3 percent in March 1983, when Wallich spoke. Experience in the 1960s and 1970s gave ample reason to believe that the Federal Reserve would again respond to the increased unemployment by inflating; hence consumer spending increased in anticipation of higher inflation.

Disinflation was incomplete. The economy was far from stable growth with low inflation. Interest rates reflected pervasive uncertainty and skepticism. The real trade-weighted exchange rate had increased 36 percent between third quarter 1982 and first quarter 1983, so the current account had moved to a large deficit.

The high rate of money growth reflected to an unknown extent the desired increase in real balances following the decline in inflation. Equations for the demand for money could not reliably separate the increase in money balances that the public wished to hold at the lower prevailing and anticipated rate of inflation and the desired reduction in money balances that presaged a return to higher inflation as reflected in the long-term rates.

The FOMC recognized that there was more to be done. It was more uncertain than usual about what to do and how to do it. Memories of the problems with an interest rate target and existing high real rates made an interest rate target unattractive. But the steep decline in monetary velocity and the continuing response to deregulation reduced support for a monetary target.

Wallich doubted that the monetarist predictions would be correct. Rapid money growth implied a strong economic advance followed later by higher inflation. "If I were to follow through the monetary implications of the recent monetary upsurge, I would have to say that the monetarist view is that half a year later the real sector would begin to move strongly. If that were the case, then we'd see something stirring now and certainly have very strong second and third quarters, which we don't seem to expect, and a couple years later prices would begin to expand" (FOMC Minutes, March 28–29, 1983, 43).

His analysis was right, his forecast partly wrong. As in all previous periods since 1920, when real base money growth and real long-term interest rates gave opposite forecasts, the economy followed real base growth. This time was not an exception; it differed only in the unprecedented level of the real interest rate. Despite these rates, real GDP, pushed along by rapid money growth and the permanent tax cuts, rose at an average rate of 8.3 percent in the four quarters starting in second quarter 1983. At the time Wallich spoke, real first-quarter GNP growth was 3.5 percent followed by 9.3 percent in the second quarter. The deflator rose from 3.2 to 4.7 percent between first and fourth quarter 1983.

The Federal Reserve responded by raising the federal funds rate more promptly than in the past. The rate rose from 8.5 percent in February 1983 to 9.6 percent in February 1984, about as much as the deflator. But the funds rate continued to rise, reaching 11.6 percent in August 1984.

This rapid response hides the uncertainty that was a dominant feature of FOMC meetings. The members had a much clearer view of their responsibilities but a murky view of how to achieve them. It took several years to develop an operating procedure that improved their ability to maintain steady growth and low inflation.

Treasury officials during the early (1981–85) Reagan administration opposed exchange market intervention. Many at the Federal Reserve disliked this policy, but the Treasury controlled exchange market operations. Treasury Undersecretary for Monetary Affairs, Beryl Sprinkel, announced that the market would set the exchange rate. He limited intervention to a few periods of market disorder.

A major issue of the period resulted from the large deficits in both the budget and the current account. A popular and widely discussed explanation blamed the latter on the former, the so-called twin deficit problem. It was easy to demonstrate arithmetically that the current account deficit equaled the difference between private saving and investment plus the budget deficit. An increase in the budget deficit, with private saving and investment unchanged, increased the current account deficit. This was true ex post.

The problem with this explanation, as every economist should know, is that both deficits are endogenous variables that are dependent on responses to policy, interest rates, output, and other variables. The same forces that affect the two deficits also affect private saving and investment. For example, an increase in productivity growth increases output, raising tax collections and imports. The budget deficit declines and the current account deficit increases. Other things unchanged, the ex post relation will show that the current account deficit equals the difference between private saving and investment plus the budget deficit. But in this case investment rises, making it possible for the budget deficit to decline while the current account deficit rises. Data for the 1980s and 1990s show that the two deficits often moved in opposite direction. During the productivity surge in the late 1990s, the budget deficit became a surplus, but the current account deficit increased.

Meltzer (1993) studied changes in the trade-weighted real exchange rate using the analysis outlined in Friedman (1953). The principal factors affecting the exchange rate were the increase in military spending and the (lagged) increase in real money balances. Rearmament drew on domestic resources but also foreign resources, and imports substituted for domestic output devoted to rearmament. When the increases in defense spending slowed or reversed, changes in the real exchange rate reversed also.

Chart 9.1 shows the rise and subsequent decline in the real exchange rate. Disinflation and rearmament brought the real exchange rate to a peak in first quarter 1985. In the second quarter, the exchange rate reversed course, declining more than 6.6 percent. The new Treasury secretary, James Baker, reached agreement with other principal countries to intervene, so intervention thereafter reinforced dollar depreciation by the market. By fourth quarter, the rate was back to the level two years earlier, in third quarter 1983. The dollar continued to decline for the next two years. The Louvre agreement early in 1987 attempted to bound the nominal rate, but after a worldwide stock market collapse in October 1987 governments abandoned the effort. Chart 9.1 shows that the exchange rate remained in a narrower range to the end of the decade.

Chart 9.2 shows annual consumer price inflation. The chapter detail discusses the adjustment to reduced inflation and the rise in 1983–84 that sustained concern for a time that high inflation would return. The chart shows that the inflation rate stabilized at 2 to 3 percent only in the 1990s.

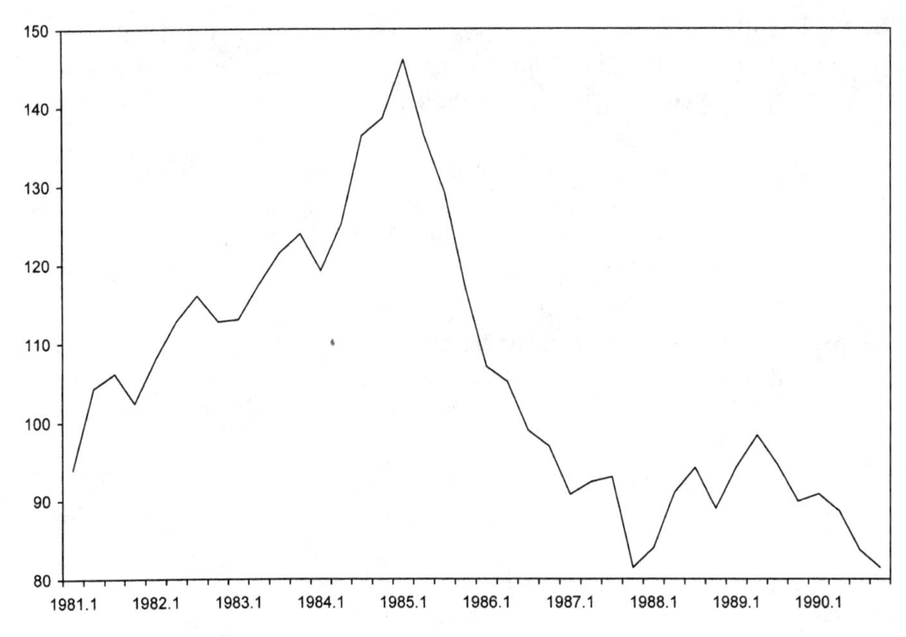


Chart 9.1. Trade-weighted real exchange rate, quarterly, 1981:1–1990:4.

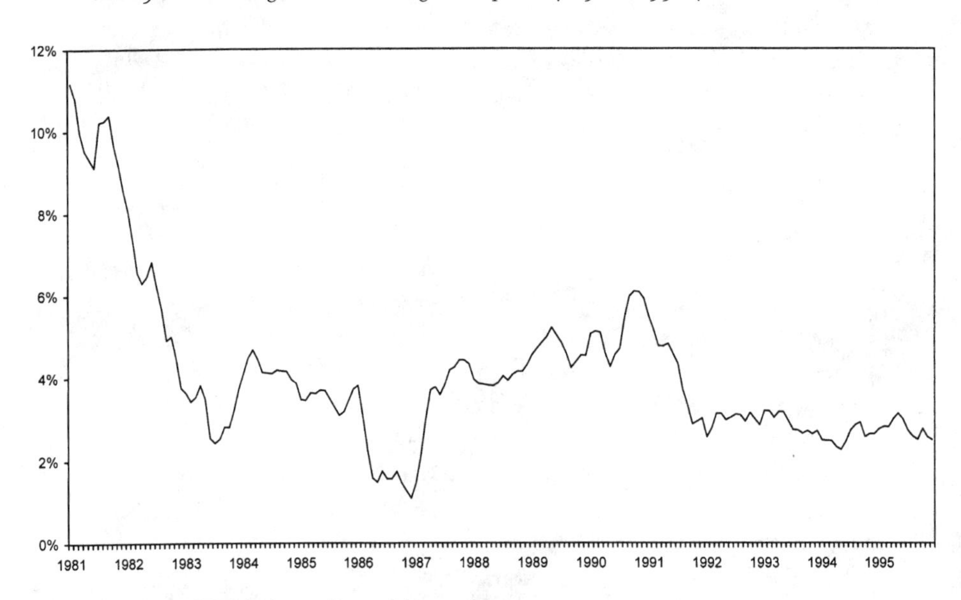


Chart 9.2. CPI inflation, 1981–95. Measured year-over-year.

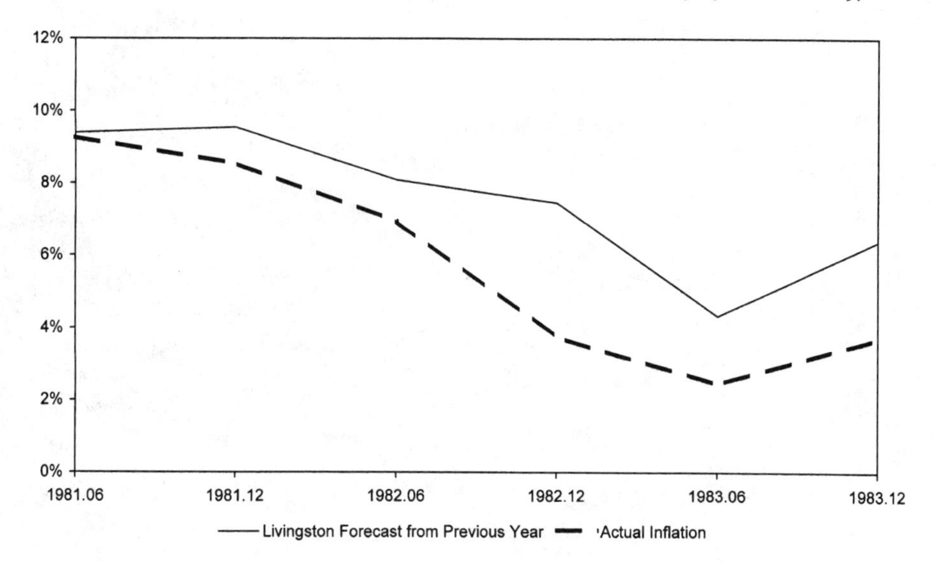


Chart 9.3. Mean inflation forecast from Livingston survey from twelve months prior to actual inflation, June 1981–December 1983.

Chart 9.3 compares a well-known inflation forecast made a year in advance to reported inflation. The forecast consistently overestimated inflation in this period, perhaps reflecting skepticism about the Federal Reserve's willingness or ability to maintain low inflation.

In the 1970s, monetary policy usually reacted quickly and decisively to the unemployment rate. Fortunately, the stronger-than-anticipated recovery in 1983 lowered the unemployment rate by 2.8 percentage points. Thereafter, the rate continued to fall until the end of the decade. Chart 9.4 shows these data. The continued decline in the unemployment rate was one of the factors that eventually reassured the public and the markets that the Federal Reserve was less likely than in the 1970s to increase inflation.

Chart 9.5 shows the response of long- and short-term interest rates to policy and other variables. Long-term rates did not remain below 10 percent until 1985–86. The skepticism noted earlier is especially apparent in the movement of long-term rates in 1983–84. In July 1984, the ten year government bond rate again reached 13.8 percent. As Chart 9.5 shows, this was the beginning of the end of the exceptionally high rates, but two years passed before ten-year rates returned to single digits. The interest rate data confirm the uncertainty that the pubic shared with the Federal Reserve as the latter worked to establish that monetary policy would not repeat past mistakes.

Productivity growth, the rate of change of output per hour, typically

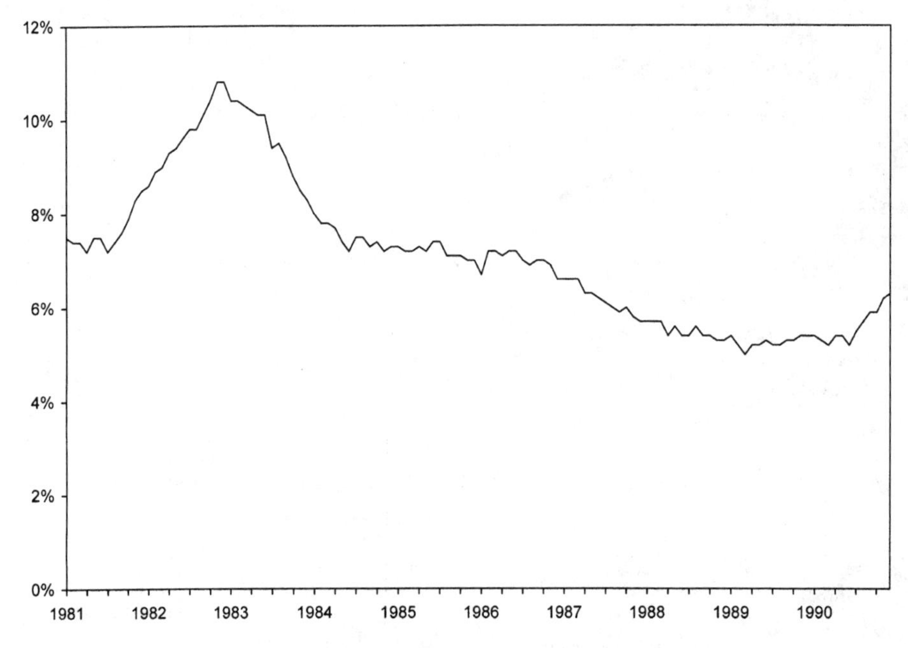


Chart 9.4. Civilian unemployment rate, January 1981–December 1990.

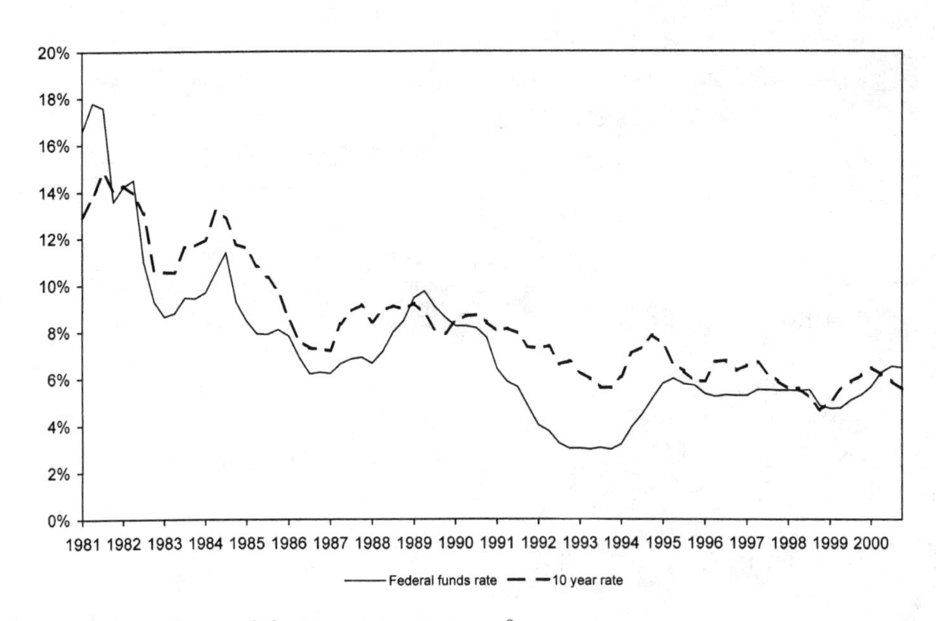


Chart 9.5. Long- and short-term interest rates, 1981:1–2000:4.

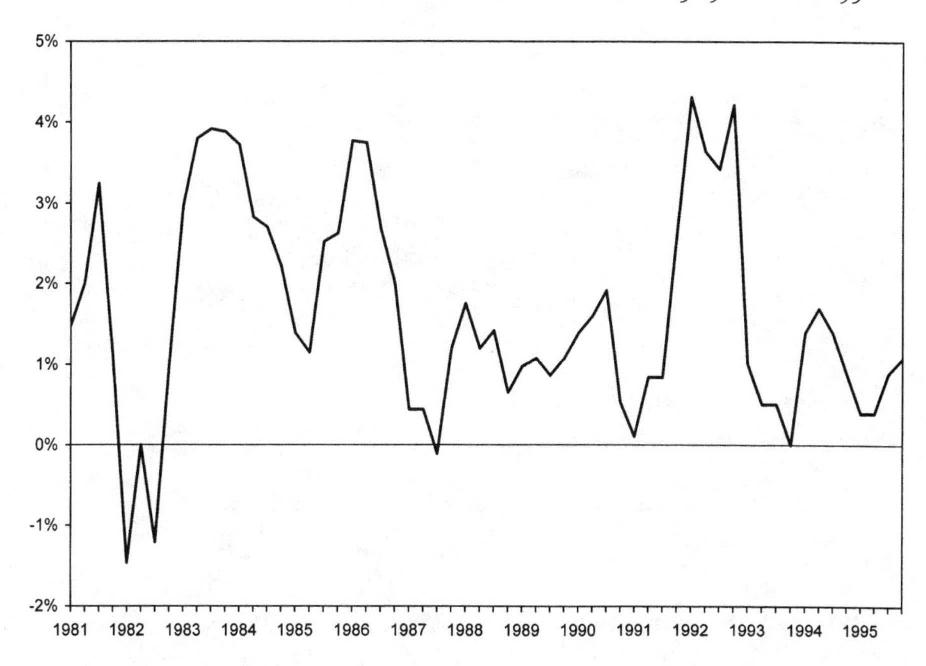


Chart 9.6. Rate of change of output per hour, business sector, 1981–95. Measured year-over-year.

rises following a recession, then falls back to its trend rate. Chart 9.6 shows this pattern, a steep rise in 1983 and 1991. By the late 1980s the average rate outside of recoveries fluctuated around 1 percent. Difficulties in forecasting variable productivity growth are one reason forecasting output growth and inflation is not very accurate.

Chart 9.7 compares two forecasts to actual values of real GNP/GDP growth. The green book forecast is made by the Board's staff, the SPF by private forecasters. The chart shows that the two are broadly similar and both differ much more from actual growth than from each other. The Federal Reserve at first persisted in adjusting its actions to its forecasts despite evidence of frequent, large, and persistent errors. Volcker then adjusted his actions to reports of actual data. The chart shows that errors in forecasts of GDP during the disinflation were exceptionally large, but sizeable errors were not unusual. Errors were exceptionally large in 1983, a period of great uncertainty.

A principal reason for these errors was reliance on a Phillips curve to separate output growth and inflation. The inflation forecasts in Chart 9.8 show again that the forecast error was often much larger than the difference between the two forecasts. The persistence of positive and negative errors in the 1970s or the 1980s is notable. The Federal Reserve and the

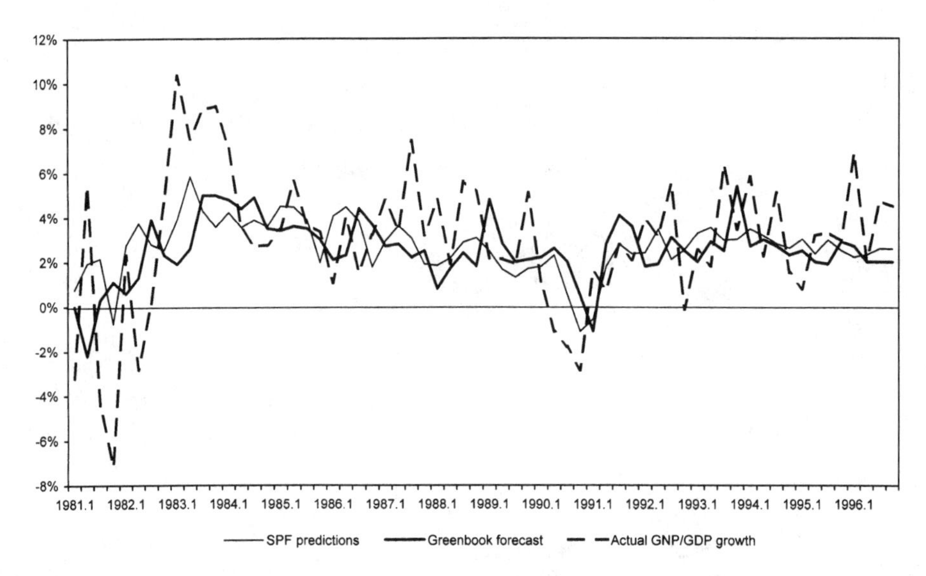


Chart 9.7. SPF vs. green book forecasts of real GNP/GDP annualized quarterly growth, compared with actual GNP/GDP growth, 1981:1–1996:4.

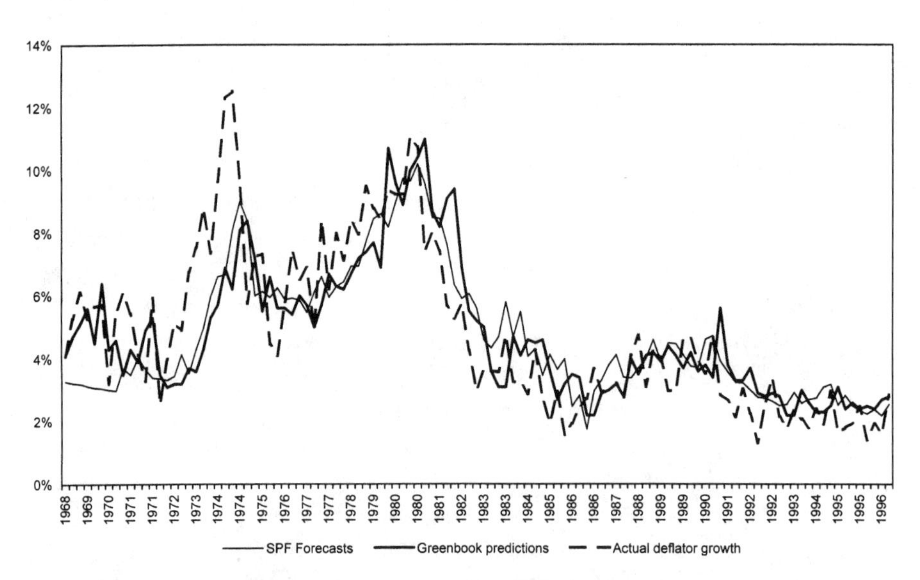


Chart 9.8. SPF vs. green book forecasts of GNP/GDP implicit price deflator annualized quarterly growth, compared with actual deflator growth, 1968:4–1996:4.

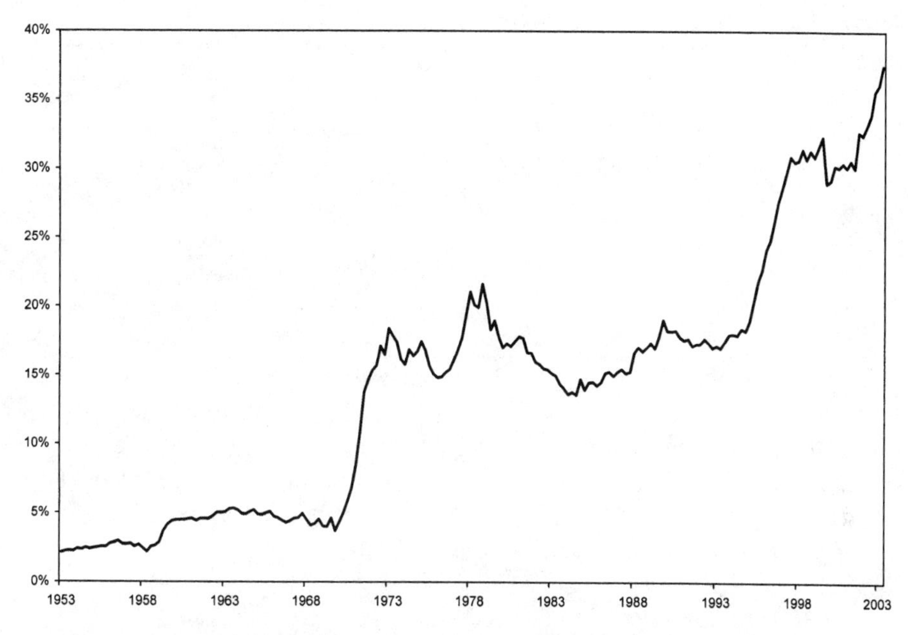


Chart 9.9. Foreign holdings of U.S. Treasury securities as a percentage of total U.S. Treasury securities outstanding.

SPF persistently underestimated the inflation rate when the inflation rate rose in the 1970s, then persistently overestimated inflation as it fell in the 1980s and again in the 1990s.

During the early 1980s foreigners continued to purchase and hold 15 to 20 percent of outstanding Treasury debt. Chart 9.9 shows that foreigners financed a sizeable part of the large Reagan era budget deficits. One of the likely reasons that researchers do not find much of an effect of budget deficits on domestic interest rates is that substantial foreign purchases substitute for increased domestic purchases. The chart shows that foreigners became larger holders in the 1990s and in the new century during years of budget surpluses in the late 1990s and the renewed deficits after 2001.

## PERSONNEL

Two Board members left in the early 1980s. Governor Lyle Gramley resigned after little more than five years of a fourteen-year term. President Reagan appointed Wayne Angell to the position. Angell served from February 1986 to February 1994, then resigned to work in the financial services industry. In July 1984, Martha Seger, a Michigan economist, joined the Board, replacing Nancy Teeters, who resigned to accept an appointment as a corporate economist. Seger resigned in 1991 after more than 6.5 years

**Table 9.1** Personnel Changes, 1983–85

| APPOINTED | REPLACED | START OF TERM | RESERVE BANK |
|---|---|---|---|
| BOARD OF GOVERNORS | | | |
| Wayne Angell | Lyle Gramley | February 1986 | |
| Martha Seger | Nancy Teeters | July 1984 | |
| RESERVE BANKS | | | |
| Robert Forrestal | William Ford | October 1983 | Atlanta |
| Karen Horn | Willis Winn | May 1982 | Cleveland |
| Gary Stern | E. Gerald Corrigan | March 1985 | Minneapolis |
| E. Gerald Corrigan | Anthony Solomon | January 1985 | New York |
| Theodore Roberts | Lawrence Roos | February 1983 | St. Louis |

as a governor. In 1993, Seger paid a civil fine for violating the one-year ban on lobbying after resigning. She arranged and attended a meeting with the Board in August 1991 as a director of Kroger and Co. During his eight years, President Reagan appointed all seven governors, the first president since Franklin Roosevelt to do that. Table 9.1 lists personnel changes from 1983 through 1985.

On June 18, 1983, President Reagan reappointed Paul Volcker to four more years as chairman. This was a surprise. Several of the administration heavyweights—James Baker and Donald Regan especially—found Volcker difficult to work with and insistent on independence. Although Volcker reduced interest rates, he did not agree to ease policy before the 1982 election, responding belatedly from the administration perspective. What would he do in 1984? They were not sure, and they wanted a more agreeable chairman who would at least listen with more understanding of their wishes. But Volcker had support from the bankers, financial markets, and President Reagan for his success in reducing inflation and also from budget director David Stockman. And he was helped by his opponents' inability to agree on an alternative.

Volcker did not request reappointment in 1987. Coyne (1998, 14) said he thought Volcker could have had reappointment if he had asked. "He always said he would never ask for a job." Greenspan (2007, 98–99) reports that James Baker interviewed him for the chairmanship in March 1987, months before Volcker decided to leave. Speculation at the time suggested that Volcker often disagreed with the majority of the Board appointed by President Reagan. Volcker was accustomed to making decisions with advice from the senior staff, not the other governors. The governors could affect the decision made at the meeting. Between meetings, Volcker had authority to act.

Five bank presidents began five-year terms in 1983–85. E. Gerald Corrigan, a Volcker protégé, moved to New York from the Minneapolis bank, and Karen Horn was the first woman appointed as a bank president. Larry Roos and William Ford, two leading monetarists, retired.

## POLICY ACTIONS 1983

The FOMC had given up on monetary targeting without a clear idea about whether the change was permanent. The members recognized that monetary velocity had fallen. They did not have a good explanation of the reasons, and they never mentioned the decline in inflation as a reason for holding more money balances per unit of income, thus lower velocity. The most common explanation was a sense that the new types of deposits now included in $M_1$ had lower velocity, but the staff did not present evidence at the meetings. Nevertheless, they accommodated the increased demand for money.

What should replace the monetary target? The FOMC in 1983 could not agree and was often divided. It did not want to return to an interest rate target. Many expressed concern that an interest rate target would expose them to another surge of inflation. Others expressed concern that the market would interpret return to an interest target as the end of anti-inflation policy.[1] A few members disagreed. They said that in practice the desk used a funds rate target; they urged that the desk make it explicit (FOMC Minutes, February 8–9, 1983, 27). In fact, members proposed different targets and indicators as in the 1950s. Most wanted "flexibility." In practice this meant that they did not want a precise target and would respond to new information. Uncertainty and ambivalence often left the decision to Volcker.

The Humphrey-Hawkins legislation required the FOMC to announce a money growth target. When Volcker testified to the Senate Banking Committee on February 16, 1983, he announced a 4 to 8 percent range for the year to fourth quarter 1983. He did not tell Congress explicitly about flexibility or the uncertainty about the appropriate target. He told them that "some allowance should be made . . . for the uncertainties introduced by the existence of the new deposit accounts" (Monetary Policy Report to Congress, Federal Reserve Bank of New York, Box 97657, February 16, 1983, 27). The Federal Reserve, he said, would watch to see if "velocity behavior is resuming a more predictable pattern" (ibid., 28). He continued to insist,

1. Thornton (2004) summarizes the literature on the choice of target after October 1982. He argues that the Federal Reserve used an interest rate target after October 1982. Others choose later dates, 1987 or 1991. The FOMC chose a band for the federal funds rate in 1982–83 and after, but it had done that in 1979–82. The minutes make clear that the target was borrowed reserves most of the time until the late 1980s. In 1994 and thereafter, the FOMC announced a funds rate target and kept the actual funds rate very close to the target. This was not so in the 1980s, particularly in the first half of the decade.

however, that "inflation requires appropriate restraint on growth of money and liquidity," but he quickly added that the short-term relation between money and spending "may be loose" (Volcker papers, Federal Reserve of New York, Box 97649, May 16, 1983, 14).

Commitment to achieve the money targets was no greater than before. Many on the FOMC did not think they had a role. At the December 1982 meeting, President Black (Richmond) proposed a federal funds rate target. Volcker opposed. He distinguished "between having an explicit interest rate target and having . . . some limits of tolerance on what interest rate change one wants" (FOMC Minutes, December 20–21, 1982, 41).

What was the desk supposed to do? In practice, the Committee's decision at the time was a return to the 1920s program of setting a target for member bank borrowing, very much like the 1950s choice of free reserves. David Lindsey (2005, 15) was responsible for estimating borrowing. Wallich (1984, 11) claimed that after October 1982 the target was borrowed reserves. This acted as a loose target for the federal funds rate. The reason is that to the extent that the staff (Lindsey) had a useful analytic expression for borrowing, borrowing depended on the difference between the federal funds rate and the discount rate plus a random error. The error was often large, and at times the equation was not stable. Nevertheless, it offered a choice. The FOMC could set the funds rate and accept the level of borrowing or set borrowing and allow the funds rate to vary within a wide band.[2]

As was typical in the 1950s, the FOMC did not discuss the relative merits of different choices until much later. The minutes make clear repeatedly that Volcker did not want an interest rate target, mainly out of concern for the likely market interpretation that policy would repeat the errors of the 1970s. Unlike the 1950s, however, there was a thorough discussion of individual preferences at the February FOMC meeting.

The staff opened the discussion of long-run targets, noting the large inflow into new accounts now included in $M_2$. They ruled out $M_2$ as a reliable target for the present mainly because the new bank money market deposit accounts had become a component. Volcker then asked the members whether they needed or wanted monetary targets. At least twelve favored an $M_1$ target with a wide range to increase "flexibility." Partee and several

2. A memo from Donald Kohn to the FOMC discussed the borrowing target. "There is considerable looseness in the relationship between intended borrowing and the federal funds rate especially over the short-run." He went on to describe the several factors that affect the short rate but not borrowing and conversely. An example was the decline in borrowing after Continental Illinois Bank borrowed heavily. Others did not want to appear troubled (Board Records, 1987, July 1, 2).

others said that they no longer targeted reserves. "We just target on net borrowed reserves—that is the funds rate" (FOMC Minutes, February 809, 1983, 28). Teeters and others favored a monetary target primarily for political reasons; it protected the System when it raised interest rates.

The consensus was not complete, and agreement was surrounded by ambiguity, reflecting the uncertainty the members felt. Recovery had started but many doubted its strength and duration. Inflation had fallen, but it might return. Those who did not want to announce a target for $M_1$ offered as alternatives $M_2$ and broader aggregates including $M_3$ and debt (Morris). Corrigan (Minneapolis) favored a GNP target, a position he shared with the Council of Economic Advisers. He did not mention either how that would be done or whether the Federal Reserve could offset all non-monetary influences on GNP, since they could not reliably forecast quarterly velocity.

William Ford (Atlanta) strongly criticized the consensus. "We're generally in favor of leaving $M_1$ in, although with much less emphasis. . . . I don't think it's too much of a stretch of the words to say we want to [fine] tune the economy. . . . We think we can do it. We've all used the word flexibility. . . . and everyone is advocating the wider bands" (ibid, 31). Ford then argued against fine-tuning and urged more consistent adherence to a target "over a long period of time and just let it go in a steady way and the market will know what we're going to do next" (ibid.). Ford concluded that in fact the System had returned to an interest rate target but didn't want to say so. He did not favor that procedure, but he preferred that they state clearly and unambiguously what they were doing.

Volcker agreed that targeting and flexibility were opposites. "The Committee is on two horses. . . . One is targeting and one is flexibility" (ibid., 32). He did not accept that they were targeting interest rates. "We can look at a lot of things in addition to interest rates, which I think is probably what we're doing" (ibid., 32). He did not acknowledge that the manager had to have a target. He continued to use borrowed reserves defined as adjustment plus seasonal borrowing but excluding long-term borrowing used to assist failing banks.[3]

The members agreed on a range of 8 to 9 percent for central tendency

3. Looking back in 1987, staff members David Lindsey and James Glassman concluded that the borrowing target gave "considerable influence over conditions in the federal funds market . . . while still enabling the funds rate to fluctuate" (Board Records, 1987, July 1, 2). They showed that short-term fluctuations in the funds rate often differed considerably from expected values but the differences did not persist. Their econometric estimates showed a standard error for 1982–87 of $230 million (ibid., table 1). This seems large relative to average borrowing.

growth of nominal GNP in 1983 with the deflator rising 4 to 5 percent and real GNP 3.5 to 4.5 percent. Actual values were very different, 10.4 and 6.1 percent. The $M_1$ growth projection was 4 to 8 percent. At the midpoints, these projections assumed 2.5 percent velocity growth. There was general agreement on a cyclical rise in velocity at the start of the recovery.

When choosing the projected ranges, most members forgot their concerns about uncertainty and argued about differences of one-half percent. Volcker did not seem to take the projected ranges very seriously. He cut off discussion of small differences and later told the FOMC: "I don't know how soon I would have . . . any conviction on what the velocity is of $M_1$" (ibid., 72).

The Committee divided eight-to-four on the choice of long-term targets for the aggregates. Governor Wallich and Presidents Black, Ford, and Horn dissented. They wanted a less expansive policy than 4 to 8 for $M_1$ and 7 to 10 for $M_2$.

Choosing a short-term target brought out a wide range of opinions about what was likely to happen.[4] The Committee voted eleven-to-one to "maintain the existing degree of restraint." Although large one-time adjustments occurred, money growth for fourth quarter 1982 reached 13 percent, so restraint on reserves did not correctly describe recent monetary actions. The Committee agreed that "lesser restraint would be acceptable in the context of appreciable slowing of growth in the aggregates" (ibid., 97). The range for the funds rate was put at 6 to 10 percent. President Ford dissented because the Committee made no mention of tightening to slow money growth.

Roger Guffey (Kansas City) took issue with the draft statement. He wanted lower interest rates and proposed a lower discount rate. Ed Boehne (Philadelphia) joined him. Henry Wallich argued that they could not reduce interest rates until money growth slowed. A majority agreed to foreclose any move to tighten policy, without agreeing on what that meant. It seems likely that most wanted an agreement not to increase interest rates. Presidents Ford and Roberts (St. Louis) opposed the decision. Ford reminded the Committee that in the past, they delayed too long before tightening because they based policy on current conditions instead of looking ahead six months or more to the conditions likely to be in place when the policy would impact. This is one of the few clear statements urging less attention to recent events. The Committee ignored it.

The Committee could not agree on whether to include language saying

4. Volcker said, "I think the probabilities are that we are beginning a recovery. But I would not discount at all the [other] possibility" (FOMC Minutes, February 8–9, 1983, 83).

that it would ease if money, credit, or economic conditions justified the change. The vote was five to five, with Volcker and Ford abstaining. The final decision made additional ease depend on money growth falling below the long-run path, a decline from 13 to less than 8 percent. The borrowing target was $200 million. Actual borrowing in February was $582 million. The federal funds rate averaged 8.5 percent, well within the band.

The policy decision was no easier when the FOMC met in March. The staff and several members recognized that real interest rates and money growth had very different implications. Monthly money growth was well above the 4 to 8 percent annual target. Twelve-month average monetary base growth rose to 9.3 percent. But the real interest rate on a ten-year Treasury note remained about 5.5 percent. The FOMC ignored the aggregates. “In that context, the present monetary situation looks relatively restrictive” (FOMC Minutes, March 28–29, 1983, 4).

Sternlight explained that borrowing had greatly exceeded the $200 million target. No one objected. The reserve banks wanted lower interest rates, so several requested a reduction of the discount rate to 8 percent. The Board deferred action on the requests from at least six banks on eight different dates in January and February, citing growth of the aggregates. On March 7, the Board disapproved the reduction. The following week, Richmond proposed an increase to 9 percent. The Board at first deferred action, then rejected the request on March 21. Banks reduced the prime rate by 0.5 percentage points to 10.5 percent.

The staff described the recovery as “well underway” and raised its growth forecast for the first quarter to 4.1 percent (from 3.5). The earlier forecast proved correct. Inflation remained low. Several members remained skeptical about the duration of the recovery. Despite high real rates, the strongest sector was the housing sector with 1.6 million starts. Guffey (Kansas City) expressed concern that higher interest rates would terminate the recovery in housing. Gramley said that recoveries tend to cumulate initially. Greater strength seemed likely. Volcker again expressed concern about more defaults on international debt, and Partee added concern that export growth would remain low.

Robert Black reminded the members that “most of the time the majority has been wrong. . . . I have less and less sympathy for discretionary monetary policy” (ibid., 32–33). No one commented. Preston Martin expressed concern that banks and thrifts continued to buy fixed rate mortgages.

The FOMC had to combine these diverse views into a short-term policy statement. The members did not agree on whether to adopt a money market or aggregate objective. Volcker favored the aggregates. “If we stop targeting them, we’ve got to tell the Congress we are going to stop targeting them" (ibid., 45). But he again expressed concern about velocity, so he did not want strict monetary targeting. Banks and markets watched $M_1$ growth. This was a main factor driving members back to monetary targets.

Volcker urged a cautious approach, and the FOMC concurred. They set $M_1$ growth at 6 to 7 percent, a borrowing target of $250 million believed consistent with an 8.5 percent funds rate. The FOMC agreed to maintain about the existing restraint. Volcker continued to act as he wished. Actual borrowing in April was $1 billion, and the average funds rate was 8.8 percent. The monetary base increased at almost a 12 percent annual rate. $M_1$ growth declined slightly in April, but the staff projected 24 percent annual growth in May (FOMC Minutes, April 29, 1983, 1).

Nevertheless, at a telephone conference on April 29, Solomon (New York) and Guffey (Kansas City) urged lower interest rates. Others objected, and Volcker agreed that it was not appropriate to act on data for one month. Discount rate decisions at the banks show difference of opinions and confusion. In a rare, open display of differences in outlook, Richmond, later joined by Atlanta, Dallas, and Cleveland, proposed to increase the discount rate by 0.5 to 9 percent; Boston, Chicago, Kansas City, San Francisco, and Minneapolis voted for reductions of 0.25 or 0.5 percentage points Later Philadelphia and New York joined them. At one time or another during the spring and early summer seven banks requested a reduction. The Board deferred or disapproved all the requests. By late June it too divided. Some governors wanted to approve an increase but others feared that the economy would slow. Governor Teeters dissented from the decision to defer action because she wanted to reject any increase.

Division of opinion declined in July. Five banks requested an increase. The others voted to keep the discount rate unchanged. Despite the strong recovery and the large (nearly one percentage point) spread between the federal funds rate and the discount rate, the Board kept discount rates unchanged.

The Board began to repeat the mistakes of the 1970s. The unemployment rate in May and June was 10.1 percent, and the twelve-month rate of CPI inflation fell to 2.5 percent. They disregarded growth of the aggregates and delayed responding to the increase in nominal and real long-term interest rates. By the new year, twelve-month CPI inflation was above 4 percent, nominal ten-year Treasury bonds yielded 11.8 percent, and SPF inflation expectations had increased. The staff based its inflation forecasts on the short-run Phillips curve; with a 10 percent unemployment rate, they did not anticipate the increase.

At the May meeting, Governor Wallich asked the account manager for his impression of what the market thought the Federal Reserve used as a target. Sternlight replied it was free or borrowed reserves. This surprised President Black, who asked why market participants did not believe they used a funds rate target. Sternlight replied:

> I think they would feel, with some reason, that if we were aiming at free reserves or borrowing we are aiming at something that has a likely range of variation in the federal funds rate but not a federal funds rate target in the very narrow sense where the Desk pinpointed within 0.12 points or so a particular funds level and intervened every time there was ever so little a variation from that. (FOMC Minutes, May 24, 1983, 2–3)

Later Volcker added that "$M_1$ is getting relatively less emphasis; that does not mean no emphasis. I suppose we remain someplace in the vague area" (ibid., 18). He did not mention how the free reserve or borrowing level reflected that emphasis. It seems clear that he did not fully trust any single measure and made discretionary judgments based on his interpretation of accruing data. The members could discuss and vote, but he decided between meetings and influenced decisions at meetings.

Despite historically high real interest rates, most of the members thought the economy would be stronger than the staff forecast of 5 percent annual growth. Those who disagreed cited the negative effect of high real interest rates on recovery abroad (Solomon), the budget deficit (Corrigan), and inflation (Balles and Ford). Ford also mentioned possible banking failures in Tennessee following the failure of banks controlled by the Butcher family.[5]

The Committee could not agree on a policy. The FOMC in 1983 had little common sense of direction or agreement on action. In May, some wanted to increase the borrowing target from $250 to $350 million. They described that as more restrictive, a sign that the free reserve interpretation remained strong. Guffey thought that was dishonest because actual borrowing was above $350 million. No one agreed. Gramley wanted $400. The vote was six to six, with Solomon, Guffey, Morris, Rice, Roberts, and Teeters voting no. Some wanted higher borrowing, some lower. Some non-voting members accused Roberts (St. Louis) of fine-tuning. He "reluctantly" voted for $350, although he wanted $400, a level he considered more restrictive. After a seven-to-five vote, the FOMC adjourned.

The final directive called for a slight increase in restraint. It mentioned that "lesser restraint would be appropriate in the context of more pro-

5. Beginning in April, the Board began to remove regulation Q ceilings on interest rates by reducing the maximum maturity subject to ceilings. At the same time, it reduced the maximum maturity of time deposits subject to reserve requirements. By October 1, 1983, the Board had eliminated all ceiling rates.

nounced slowing of growth of the broader monetary aggregates relative to the paths implied by the long-term ranges and deceleration or $M_1$" (ibid., 57). Earlier, Morris and Solomon had objected to mentioning $M_1$.

> Vice Chairman Solomon. What you're saying is that even though we have deemphasized $M_1$, when it's large we have to take it into consideration.
>
> Chairman Volcker. I think that's precisely what we're saying.
>
> Vice Chairman Solomon. I don't agree with that. (ibid., 51)

Once again the staff underestimated the strength of the expansion. The FOMC held a conference call on June 23 at which the staff reported that the Commerce Department expected real growth of 6.6 percent annual rate in the second quarter. Expected $M_1$ growth was 11.5 percent in June. From March to June, $M_1$ rose at a 12 percent annual rate, twice the rate forecast at the March meeting. Twelve-month growth of the monetary base rose to 10.4 percent. Long-term interest rates rose by ten to twenty basis points to 10.9 percent at the meeting date. Borrowing reached $600 to $700 million, twice the target level. The federal funds rate rose to 9 percent. Sternlight said the market was uncertain whether the Federal Reserve wanted more restraint.

Volcker started the discussion at the June meeting by saying that borrowing was between $400 and $500 million. This excluded almost $1 billion of extended borrowing. He wanted to keep it there. He proposed raising the funds rate to 9 percent. No one objected, and all interpreted the higher borrowing level as a modest move toward restraint.

July brought the last reduction in tax rates voted in 1981. The economy continued to expand, and the staff again raised its forecast. The Board's inflation forecast for 1984 was 4 percent. Most private forecasters predicted 5 to 6 percent inflation. Based on its inflation forecast, the staff predicted a decline in long-term interest rates by late 1984. That proved to be early.

At the July 12–13 meeting, discussion began about why the interest rate remained at 11 percent when inflation had fallen to about 4 percent or less. Axilrod blamed fear of additional policy tightening. The market expected short rates to rise, as they later did. The Treasury had prepared a paper claiming that there was no necessary association between budget deficits and interest rates. This was received with considerable skepticism. Gramley quoted a survey of bond buyers showing expected inflation for five to ten years had increased and was now 6.5 to 7 percent. The one-year SPF forecast called for 4.95 percent.

Axilrod reported that staff research showed that $M_1$ growth was not distorted by deregulation and new types of accounts. Deregulation produced both inflows and outflows, but on balance the two were about the same. $M_1$ now had a larger saving component and was more interest sensitive, but it was not distorted. He proposed that they raise the annual target from 4 to 8 percent to 7 to 11 percent. And he remarked that high money growth was one main factor leading to the strong recovery.

The July meeting revised the projections for money growth in 1983 and gave preliminary indications for 1984.[6] Despite $M_1$ growth far above the projected range for the year, no one considered reducing it. The FOMC discussed three options: raising the growth rate to incorporate the high first half, rebasing the growth rate, and keeping the same projection and ignoring $M_1$. Volcker spoke against rebasing, but most of the Committee favored that choice. Most of the discussion emphasized appearance, interpretation, and political issues. No one thought they would conduct policy to achieve the announced money growth rate, although some proposed doing so. Partee warned that the funds rate target was too slow to change in expansions (FOMC Minutes, July 12–13, 1983, 46).

The Committee split on the choice of $M_1$ growth rates. A majority favored rebasing and setting the growth range at 5 to 9 percent for the rest of 1983 and for 1984. The central tendency forecast for nominal GNP growth, 9.75 percent, allowed monetary velocity to remain unchanged or rise about 4 percent.[7]

The FOMC did not consider explicitly how their borrowing or free reserve target related to the monetary projection. Although they argued over the choice of borrowing target, the actual level of borrowing was generally above the target during this period. The difference was $400 million or more during July and August; extended credit borrowing was $578 and $491 in July and August. The federal funds rate was more nearly constant from month to month. Between July and December, the monthly average remained between 9.37 and 9.56. Monthly growth of the monetary base ranged from 3.5 to 13.9 percent.

The FOMC's concern about inflation brought an early response. Real base growth reached a peak in July. It fell for the next two years. Real interest rates rose from 4 to 6.9 percent. Both measures show a more restrictive policy. CPI inflation rose above 6 percent in second quarter 1983. The funds rate rose modestly. By November, the twelve-month moving average of S&P 500 prices fell. Growth of industrial production began to slow in the spring of 1984. Chart 9.10 shows the real base growth and the

6. Volcker began the meeting by warning about leaks. The policy discussion was held in executive session and most staff had to leave.

7. The members' nominal GNP forecasts ranged from 7 to 11.25 percent. The staff forecast 8.3 percent.

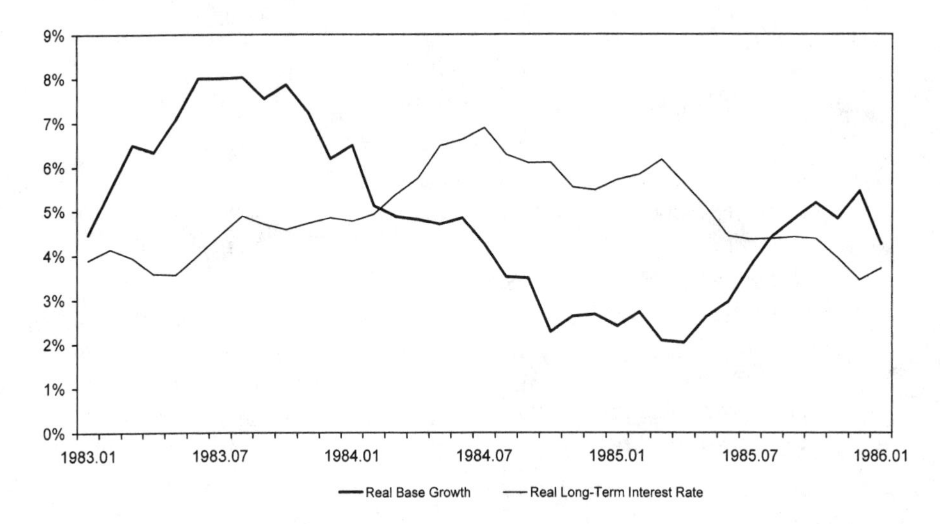


Chart 9.10. Real base growth vs. real long-term interest rate, January 1983–January 1986. Real base growth measured year-over-year; long-term interest rate measured as yield on ten-year Treasury bonds.

real interest rate. Both show a decisive move to tighten in 1983 and ease in 1985. By acting early, the FOMC showed the market the 1970s would not return.

In August, Volcker had the FOMC spend part of a day discussing forecasts and policy objectives. This was a rare event, and it showed again the different opinions held by the members. They used different frameworks and did not have the same objectives. Anthony Solomon pointed out that they did not have a common view of the effects of fiscal policy. In fact, they differed on basic points. Balles said the long-run effect of monetary policy is on the price level; fiscal policy affects real growth, productivity, and other real variables. Teeters disagreed. "She believed that the Federal Reserve affects real output in the long-run as well as the short-run" (FOMC Minutes, August 22, 1983, 14). Guffey thought the objectives in the Employment Act were "inconsistent" (ibid., 14). No one suggested making an effort to resolve differences.

Volcker took a vote on whether their long-run objective should be zero inflation. Most of the governors voted no; most of the presidents voted yes. President Boehne was an exception. He found the idea of the long run not useful, a theoretical concept without much relevance to the real world (ibid., 15). Ford and Roberts argued that the Federal Reserve should give more attention to the long-run consequences of its actions.

Board Vice Chairman Preston Martin opposed a zero-inflation goal. "If we were indeed to bend our efforts to achieve zero cpi inflation, however measured, we would have a resultant unemployment level that would be destructive to the social fabric of their country" (ibid., 17). He wanted 2 percent inflation as a goal. Solomon said: "We'd be laughed at if we said our only legitimate objective is price stability" (ibid., 21).

John Balles persisted. To those who argued that there was a short-run tradeoff between inflation and growth, he replied that "the cost of trying to exploit that tradeoff may well be a procyclical monetary policy" (ibid., 22).

There was very little agreement and no convergence. Volcker cut off the discussion by asking what implications fiscal policy had for monetary policy. Specifically, if Congress raised tax rates, would the Federal Reserve commit to lower interest rates?

Wallich favored a one-year increase in money growth to offset some of the effects of a tax increase. He warned that the monetary increase must not be permanent, but he did not suggest how to prevent it. Partee reminded him that the Federal Reserve made that mistake in 1968. Gramley added, "We ended up with the worst of all possible worlds" (ibid., 34).

No one spoke in favor of coordination. That was an improvement. Volcker, mindful of his 1982 experience, reminded them that Congress would likely not agree to raise tax rates if they would not coordinate. Senator Byrd's bill in 1982 had thirty-one cosponsors. It required the Federal Reserve to abandon money targets and adopt an interest rate target that kept real interest rates within their historic range. Congressman Jack Kemp proposed to introduce similar legislation in the House at the time. The majority leader, Senator Howard Baker, opposed the legislation but used the threat to urge Volcker to agree to lower interest rates if Congress reduced the budget deficit. Volcker did not make an explicit commitment, but he reduced the funds rate. Congress passed a bill raising revenues by about $100 billion. Volcker was less committed to policy coordination than William McChesney Martin had been in 1968, perhaps because he remembered that experience.

The discussion ended without reaching a conclusion. Most members who spoke opposed coordination in principle. Volcker did not think that was a politically acceptable answer. No issue of this kind was currently pending. He recognized limits to Federal Reserve independence.

At the October 1983 FOMC meeting, the staff reported that $M_1$, $M_2$, and $M_3$ remained within their projected ranges for the first time since 1980. Volcker lowered the target for borrowed reserves on a conference call in early September. Total actual borrowing averaged $1 billion, confirming for President Guffey and others that their borrowing decisions had little or no importance; the desk and the chairman used an interest rate target. Average monthly borrowing from October through December ranged from \$774 to \$906 million. By November, extended credit borrowing had become negligible. The federal funds rate remained in a narrow range—between 9.34 and 9.48 percent. Monetary base growth declined.

The October meeting had a lengthy discussion of monetary velocity. Axilrod opened the discussion by noting that the cyclical behavior of $M_1$ velocity in 1982 and 1983 was not "unusual enough to have warranted downplaying the role of that aggregate in policy" (FOMC Minutes, October 4, 1983, 8). He remained cautious, however, citing the increased interest elasticity of $M_1$.

Balles (San Francisco) pointed out that research at his bank showed no relation between $M_2$ or $M_3$ and nominal GNP. By this standard $M_1$ "may be far from perfect but the alternatives are even worse" (ibid., 25). Wallich pointed out that the demand function for $M_1$ may be stable even if the simple $M_1$-to-GNP relation is unstable.

The discussion ended there. The Committee did not reach a consensus and did not decide to maintain or disregard its $M_1$ target. Volcker continued to make the operating decisions with support from Axilrod and Sternlight. The desk attempted to hit the borrowing target.

The November 14–15 meeting opened with a discussion of inflation. The staff first described three approaches—based on monetarism, the Phillips curve, and rational expectations. The staff dismissed rational expectations. The public is "not as sophisticated in forming their expectations as the rational expectations theory assumes" (FOMC Minutes, November 14–15, 1983, 5). This statement neglects the role of arbitrage in the markets on which the Federal Reserve relied for information. Open market rates can fully reflect information even if everyone does not know all the information.

The Board's staff preferred the Phillips curve approach for analyzing inflation. It did not mention the errors made earlier. The staff recognized, however, that the natural rate of unemployment was not constant. Equilibrium unemployment at full use of resources had increased to between 6 and 7 percent, they estimated, because of reduced labor productivity growth and the relative growth in numbers of less experienced workers. Volcker did not share their view. "The Phillips curve that looked so persuasive when based on historical data without a long-term inflationary trend turned out to be less stable over time when policy was heavily influenced by the implied premise that we could 'buy' prosperity with a 'little' inflation" (Volcker, speech to American Economic Association, 1983, Board Records, December 28, 6).

The staff forecast called for "a small acceleration of prices in 1984." It gave four reasons including rapid real growth in 1983 and dollar depreciation. It did not include rapid money growth.

Volcker criticized the omission of the deficit as a factor affecting inflation. He did not appeal to economic theory. "A hundred and eighty million people out there . . . think there is some relationship" (ibid., 6). But he ended the discussion by challenging the members. "You have to come up with a better model or a different model if you don't like these results" (ibid., 22). There was no response at the time. The staff continued to use the Phillips curve, but members did not commit to act on the staff forecast. Although the Federal Reserve was seventy years old, it did not have a common explanation of the causes of inflation or the role of money growth.[8]

By November, most members expected growth to persist, so they favored a slightly tighter policy. Money growth had slowed from the early part of the year, but the staff predicted it would increase in 1984. The members proposed an increase in the funds rate from about 9 percent to 9.5 percent. One member asked for 10 percent. The more monetarist contingent—Balles, Black, and Horn—urged more attention to money growth and wanted to increase it. The majority favored no change.

The Committee voted to reduce the September-to-December target for $M_1$ growth from 7 percent to 5 to 6 percent. The general view was that this was a message for the market, not a policy proposal on which they would act. Borrowing remained at $650 million.

The Federal Reserve then made the odd decision to implement the 1982 decision to return to contemporary reserve accounting effective February 4, 1984. They no longer tried to control money, so there was no reason for the change. They had resisted the change when it hindered their ability to control reserves or meet their reserve targets. In 1997 they reversed the decision and restored lagged reserve requirements.

Not all agreed that the change was constructive. Several expected increased volatility of the funds rate. President Black (Richmond) urged more "automaticity" in policy actions. "The Committee is really out of it once it chooses its initial borrowing target unless we have another meeting." Roberts (St. Louis) agreed (FOMC Minutes, December 19–20, 1983, 6). When it was uncertain about how to implement policy, the FOMC agreed to have more "flexibility." In practice, this gave discretion to Volcker. Several wanted reduced flexibility, but Volcker did not bring the issue to a vote.

8. Ted Truman briefed the FOMC on emerging market debt. Volcker told them that the creditor banks would soon be asked to increase reserves for losses by $300 million. He believed that many of the banks would write down loan values. He did not ask their opinion or consent to the increase in reserves (FOMC Minutes, November 14–15, 1983, 34–35).

Much of the discussion expressed concern about higher inflation in 1984. In his December 1983 speech to the American Economic Association, Volcker defined price stability as a situation in which decisions do not depend on expectations of inflation. Confidence had returned. In February, the Committee forecast real growth and inflation for 1983 at 3.5 and 3.9 percent respectively. The unemployment rate forecast for the fourth quarter was 10.6 percent. The actual values for growth and inflation were 6.5 and 3.6 with the fourth quarter unemployment rate at 8.5 percent. Reported inflation rose in the fourth quarter to 4.7 percent, but CPI inflation remained low, 1.6 percent in December. Those few who watched monetary base growth noted that it had started to decline, as shown in Chart 9.10 above. The SPF forecast for the next four quarters put inflation at 5 percent, 4.5 percentage points below the 1980 peak and the lowest value in a decade.[9]

Axilrod recommended 4 to 8 percent as the range for $M_1$ growth. He forecast a 2 percent rise in velocity and 9 percent growth of nominal GNP. Morris and Solomon objected to the emphasis on $M_1$ growth. They preferred credit or $M_3$. Horn and Black disagreed. Balles, Roberts, Keehn, and Partee joined them in seeking greater emphasis on $M_1$. Several members commented on the risks of inflation rising in 1985. Teeters reminded them that when they analyzed forecast accuracy, they found that they did well one or two quarters ahead. After that the errors were large. "By the time we get to a year-and-a half or two years out, the econometric models give us almost random numbers" (ibid., 41).

The FOMC did not vote on a growth rate for 1984 at this meeting. They turned instead to the near-term targets. Volcker began by proposing that the FOMC maintain existing restraint with an intention of tightening if the monetary aggregates and economy expanded rapidly. Most of the discussion proposed values for borrowing. Proposals ranged from $650 to $850 million. Volcker summarized the consensus as preferring to wait to tighten. He favored borrowing of $650 million in January. If the report on the December unemployment rate and $M_1$ growth showed strength, he favored a slight move to restraint in early January.

The vote was six to four to keep the funds rate range at 6 to 10 percent. The four dissenters preferred 7 to 11 percent.

Looking back on the use of a borrowing target, senior staff wrote that "the relationship of borrowing objectives and the federal funds rate has not been very precise or stable. Moreover, for a variety of reasons, borrowing

9. Volcker said, "My ideal forecast always has a declining inflation rate" (FOMC Minutes, December 19–20, 1983, 32).

objectives can not be achieved with great precision in a given two-week maintenance period. . . . [T]he federal funds rate can vary as much as a half percentage point for a given borrowing objective" (Kohn and Sternlight to FOMC, 1987. Board Records, December 11, 2).

## REGULATION AND SUPERVISION

The Board made regulatory changes reflecting changes in banking and financial institutions after deregulation and the phasing out of regulation Q. It adjusted the components of $M_1$ by including NOW accounts and tax-exempt money funds. Money market deposit accounts, the banks' substitute for money market funds, became part of $M_2$. Also, the Board exempted time deposits with more than eighteen months maturity from some reserve requirements. On October 1, 1983, regulation Q ceilings ended.

Board members, including the chairman, testified several times on regulatory matters. Most of the Board favored payment of interest on demand deposits but wanted to defer payment of interest on bank reserve balances until a later time. It singled out reserves against deposits that are directly competitive with money market funds, on grounds that it wanted to discourage growth of deposits outside the banking system. The main argument against paying interest on all reserve balances was to avoid a sizeable reduction in payments to the Treasury during a period of large budget deficits (letter, Volcker to Walter Fountroy, Board Minutes, May 16, 1983). Later, Congress approved interest payments on reserves.

The November 1983 meeting of the Federal Advisory Council (FAC) made an unusual report. The FAC criticized the Federal Reserve's regulatory activities. These responsibilities "have not always been executed in a positive and constructive way. In a period of very rapid change in the financial services area, the Fed has been relatively slow in adapting to the competitive pressures that have confronted the banking industry. Its active support of legislation intended to strengthen the competitive environment has often been disappointing to bankers" (Federal Advisory Council, Board Minutes, November 4, 1983, 1–2). The bankers on FAC said the Federal Reserve's regulation of bank holding companies did not encourage innovation. Also, the Federal Reserve had not eliminated all reserve requirements on nonpersonal time deposit accounts, putting banks at a disadvantage with corporate customers. The Board made the change in the 1990s.

The Federal Reserve relied on banks for support in Congress. The criticism came at a time of considerable deregulation but also a time of congressional activity to adopt and revise legislation affecting all financial institutions. Once again the Reagan administration's task force, headed by Vice President Bush, proposed a consolidation of banking regulation in a single banking agency. That proposal had a long history. The Federal Reserve usually opposed reduction in its regulatory and supervisory role by claiming that these responsibilities facilitated monetary policy. A more likely reason was that regulation, especially regulation of bank holding companies and authority to approve mergers and branches, sustained a powerful constituency that supported the Federal Reserve in its dealings with Congress. Proponents of a separate banking agency usually pointed out that many countries with successful monetary policy actions, such as West Germany, separated banking regulation and monetary policy.

The Board discussed the Bush task force's proposals on November 22 and compared them to the proposals that Congress considered. The Board did not object strongly to letting the Justice Department handle anti-trust issues, particularly if Congress permitted interstate branching. No one objected to transferring decisions about stock market margin requirements to the Securities and Exchange Commission.

Regulation of banks and holding companies received the most attention. One member suggested that the Federal Reserve assume all supervisory and regulatory functions, but others said that was politically unattainable. Proposing it would reduce the ability to affect the legislation. "Board members were unanimous in the view that under any restructuring format, the Federal Reserve must continue to be involved in bank supervision in order to ensure the effectiveness of its monetary policy and other central banking functions" (Board Minutes, November 22, 1983, 2).

Board members agreed to communicate their views to the Bush task force, but they did not vote. They decided to wait until the task force sent its proposals to Congress. They agreed that "the draft proposals were not a substantial improvement over the existing system" (ibid., 5).

By March 1984, Congress approached the end of year-long hearings on revision of financial regulation. Several possible and actual conflicts arose about the proposed changes—small versus large banks, banks versus non-bank financial institutions, holding companies versus ordinary banks, national versus international concerns, especially concerns about risk. Issues arose about risk, equity, and conflicts of interest. Surprisingly, problems of growing size and the corresponding importance of "too big to fail" received little attention.[10]

10. "Too big to fail" means that the consequence of failure by a "large" bank could not be accepted, so the Federal Reserve, the FDIC, or the government had to arrange financing to sustain the bank. Large was not defined. "Too big to fail" encouraged banks to expand their size. It violated Bagehot's well-established principle that an insolvent bank should be allowed to fail and policy agencies should confine their efforts to preventing secondary consequences

On March 27, Paul Volcker testified on legislation under consideration in the Senate. He divided his testimony into five sections: (1) new definition of a bank, (2) definition of a qualified thrift, (3) procedures to streamline holding company applications, (4) powers of holding companies, and (5) statutory guidelines governing division of authority between state and federal government.

Volcker expressed concern about growth in the size and number of "nonbank banks" that took deposits but did not offer loans.[11] He had proposed earlier that a bank was an entity eligible for FDIC insurance that took deposits and made loans. He now excluded (1) industrial banks that were not federally insured and did not offer deposit accounts with checking privileges, (2) state-chartered thrift institutions, and (3) non–federally insured thrifts and industrial banks that would not be covered by the Bank Holding Company Act (Paul A. Volcker statement, Banking Legislation, Federal Reserve Bank of New York, Box 97645, March 27, 1984, 5–6). He proposed that consumer banks should be included with other banks and that securities companies and others be required to divest non-bank banks.

The main concern about the regulation of thrifts was to regulate thrifts that engaged in banking activities as if they came under the Bank Holding Company Act. These were "qualified thrifts." Thrifts that engaged entirely or mainly in mortgage lending would be exempt from banking rules. Volcker proposed 65 percent of the portfolio in mortgages as the cutoff.

Volcker favored extension of holding company powers to permit holding companies to sponsor and distribute mutual funds, underwrite and distribute revenue bonds and mortgage backed securities, engage in real estate and insurance brokerage, own thrift institutions, and offer other financial services (ibid., 14). Congress considered these additional powers in the legislation before the Senate.

Beginning in 1982 the Federal Reserve began to permit banks to invest across state lines. Congress was not willing to permit interstate banking or able to resolve conflicts between banks, investment banks, and insurance companies. Solvent existing banks were a principal source of capital, so the rules changed to permit acquisition of troubled banks by out-of-state

in markets. The problem was that regulators preferred to use public money rather than accept the risk of (usually unspecified) disastrous consequences, if failure occurred. Failure did not require that the bank disappear; bank equity had to pay for losses, and bank management had to be replaced. Later, Congress restricted lending to weak and failing institutions.

11. Sears Roebuck and other retailers started to take deposits in the 1980s. The Federal Reserve disliked unregulated competition.

banks. Resolving conflicts between banks and others and legislation to permit interstate banking came in 1994. The Depository Institutions Act of 1982 permitted adjustable rate mortgages and eliminated interest rate ceilings for savings and loans.

Reform of regulation faced two major obstacles. Institutions and their trade associations supported regulations that favored them or put their competitors at a disadvantage. They fought to keep their advantages. Although the history of regulation showed that regulation often stimulated innovation to circumvent a regulation, regulators (usually lawyers) preferred prohibition to incentives as a regulatory procedure. Eventually, Congress adopted rules, such as structured early intervention, that increased incentives for prudent behavior.[12]

## POLICY ACTIONS IN 1984

Inflation continued to slow in 1984 and the unemployment rate fell a bit. It remained below the expected value. Real growth slowed markedly. Table 9.2 shows the principal measures for 1984. The twelve-month average of monetary base growth ending in December slowed steadily from 10 to 6.8 percent. Ten-year Treasury yields ranged between 12 and 14 percent until the fourth quarter. By December the ten-year rate reached 11.4 percent. Using these data, the real yield remained at an extraordinary 7 percent or higher during the year.[13]

The Federal Reserve raised the federal funds rate from 9.6 in January to a local peak of 11.6 percent in August. By December the funds rate was back to 8.4 percent, an unusual reversal in a short period. Member bank borrowing followed a similar path, rising until August, then falling. Borrowing reached more than $7 billion in August, much of it lent to Continental Illinois Bank as extended borrowing to prevent failure. The FOMC excluded extended borrowing from the measure it monitored.

The Board approved an increase in the discount rate to 9 percent at seven banks on April 6 to more closely align discount and market rates and to reduce borrowing. This was the first change since 1982. It came after the Board dismissed two earlier requests in March and early April and two proposed reductions in January. Between April 6 and September 17, the Board dismissed or deferred fourteen requests for an increase in the discount rate to 9.5 percent. Beginning November 13, it received requests for reductions to 8.5 percent. It accepted a decrease on November 21. It approved a second

12. Benston (1997) is a thorough discussion of reasons for financial regulation and a proposal calling for increased use of incentives.

13. The Bureau of Labor Statistics revised computation of the CPI by replacing measures of rental cost by measures of "rental equivalency." This raised reported CPI growth.

**Table 9.2** Inflation, Output, and Interest Rates, 1984 (%)

| PERIOD | DEFLATOR | SPF EXPECTED | OUTPUT GROWTH | UNEMPLOYMENT |
|---|---|---|---|---|
| Q1 | 4.2 | 5.0 | 10.7 | 7.8 |
| Q2 | 3.0 | 5.4 | 5.5 | 7.2 |
| Q3 | 3.4 | 4.8 | 2.6 | 7.3 |
| Q4 | 3.0 | 4.4 | 1.3 | 7.3 |

decrease to 8.25 percent on December 21. The discount rate lagged behind market rates throughout the year. The Board changed the rate to align it more closely with market rates. This required a change in the level of the borrowing target; otherwise, borrowing was not expected to change.

Much of the discussion in the first six months of 1984 repeated 1983. The members distinguished "flexibility" and "automaticity." Flexibility meant discretion. The FOMC permitted Volcker to modify its instructions when he thought he should. Sometimes, but not always, the FOMC had a telephone conference. A minority opposed substantial discretion and urged automaticity—hitting the agreed target, especially the money growth target.

Volcker and the staff included in the directive three money growth rates—$M_1$, $M_2$, and $M_3$—a borrowing objective, and a range for the federal funds rate. Modest efforts to relate borrowing and the federal funds rate target did not succeed very well. Volcker and the desk concentrated on different targets at different times. This also gave Volcker considerable discretion. The FOMC members did not agree on whether they faced higher inflation, recession, or both in the near-term. Also, bank failures and financial fragility made most members hesitant to propose major changes. Some expressed concern about the effects of higher interest rates on emerging market debtors and therefore on lending banks in the United States.

Volcker expressed his uncertainty frequently. For example, at the May meeting, he said:

> My bottom line is that we've run out of room for the time being for any tightening. . . . I don't know for how long. I don't know what is going to happen in the weeks or months down the road, either to the economy or to the aggregates or these other things. I don't have any sense here that we should be easing. But I do think we have to be concerned about a very potentially volatile and actually volatile set of attitudes here and elsewhere. (FOMC Minutes, May 21–22, 1984, 27–28)

No one suggested that the lack of consistency in their actions added to uncertainty and volatility. There are, however, frequent statements about market anticipations of higher inflation. The lack of an accepted procedure increased attention to current data, often with large random elements and subject to subsequent revisions. This increased volatility also.

Board Vice Chairman Preston Martin cited political factors as a constraint on independent action especially in a quadrennial election year. "In order to add an element to the discussion that we have all been a little too polite to enunciate, I will say that we are in such an intense political environment at the moment, with so much scrutiny from the Hill and elsewhere about what we are alleged to be doing, that holding to the course . . . is called for both for economy and political considerations" (ibid., 34). The reference to politics made the comment unusual. FOMC members maintained the fiction that they ignored politics. The federal funds rate was above 10 percent with the unemployment rate at 7.4 percent. Also, the Continental Illinois failure and failure of other banks and savings and loans were major concerns at the time.

Henry Wallich disagreed with Martin. "One ought to hesitate a little before one takes for granted that financial fragility was necessarily a cause for relenting. The rule about a lender-of-last-resort operation is to lend freely but at a high rate" (ibid., 34). Volcker responded that his concern was not Continental Illinois; it was the effect of higher interest rates on the debtor countries and therefore on the lending banks. In practice this meant that the Federal Reserve supported the banks and did not make them show their losses on international loans. The market certainly recognized the losses at money center banks; the banks' market values declined. Federal Reserve policy, however, provided a guarantee against failure but placed a restriction on its policy by making members more reluctant to raise interest rates if called for.

FOMC members had several concerns about financial fragility at this time. The savings and loan or thrift industry had many insolvent institutions kept from failure by public policy. Higher market interest rates would have widened the spread between the rates paid by the thrifts and market certificates that were now deregulated. A mark-to-market policy for emerging market debt would reveal insolvency at many banks, especially money market banks. Higher interest rates would worsen the position of the debtor countries and thus the creditor banks. The domestic agricultural sector was hurt by the appreciation of the dollar and by the interest payments required by farmers who had borrowed to buy farms during the period of high inflation and high nominal interest rates. Keehn (Chicago) reported that 15 percent of the farms were heavily indebted (FOMC Minutes, March 26–27, 1984, 36–37). And, as always, the members expressed concern repeatedly about the budget deficit. Raising interest rates increased cost to the Treasury.

The recurrent problem of "leaks" arose again. Volcker summarized a report by the General Accounting Office that suggested that the leaks came from Congress (ibid., January 30–31, 1984, 1). He appointed a committee to propose new procedures and later barred many bank staff from the part of the meeting that discussed current policy. Not until 1994 did the FOMC publish its decisions following the meetings. That ended the principal problem of policy leaks by reducing the amount of information that remained confidential.

Axilrod warned in January that money growth was too high in 1983 to reach price stability. He proposed a reduction in $M_1$ growth for the 1984 Humphrey-Hawkins hearing to a range of 4 to 7 percent from 4 to 8 percent. He proposed $M_2$ growth at 6 to 9 percent in place of 7 to 10 percent. Balles, Wallich, Forrestal, Horn, Roberts, and Black urged more emphasis on $M_1$ growth to control inflation. This led to a discussion of $M_1$. Wallich acknowledged that in practice the desk managed the federal funds rate. This led to the following exchange that shows that the members of FOMC lacked a clear idea about how Volcker implemented policy action and that Volcker acted on his own.

> Vice Chairman Solomon. . . . "What you're really saying is that we allow significant movements in $M_1$ to influence our management of the funds rate gradually. . . .
>
> Chairman Volcker. Manage our reserve position.
>
> Vice Chairman Solomon. Well, in managing our reserve position we're guided by the fed funds rate.
>
> Chairman Volcker. Who is?
>
> Vice Chairman Solomon. It shows the accuracy of our reserve calculations, right?
>
> Chairman Volcker. Seldom. (ibid., 26)[14]

About a week after the March meeting, Henry Wallich spoke to an economic conference about operating procedures. He denied that the System had returned to pre-1979 interest rate control. The main evidence he cited was that the funds rate was more variable, especially at the end of each quarter. He then explained more fully:

> If the interest rate established by this technique is not consistent with a stable rate of inflation, it will have an increasingly disequilibrating effect, causing inflation to accelerate or decelerate. . . . Thus, letting the market set

14. That the New York Fed president was one of the ill-informed suggests the extent to which Volcker and the Board's senior staff controlled decisions. It shows, also, the extent to which control had shifted away from New York.

the interest rate for a given money-growth target is a safer way of achieving an equilibrium interest rate rather than trying to set it directly. (Wallich, speech to Midwest Finance Association, Board Records, April 5, 1984, 6)

Decisions at this time favored "flexibility." This meant acting with discretion, in practice not achieving the growth rates or borrowing levels they announced if new information changed their minds or, more often, changed Volcker's mind.[15] As in the 1970s, the emphasis given to interest rates or borrowing led to an unplanned decline in the growth rate of the monetary base from a twelve-month average of 10.7 to 5.8 percent between January 1984 and May 1985 followed by a sharp fall in real growth.[16]

By late March, the funds rate reached 10.25 percent. Sternlight explained that the market anticipated an increase in the discount rate to 9 percent. On April 6, the Board approved the increase. The staff forecast that it expected inflation of 5.5 to 6 percent in 1985. SPF forecast put one-year expected inflation at 5.4 percent in third quarter 1984. This was a small rise from 5 percent in the second quarter, but it shows continued concern about the Federal Reserve's actions.

The FOMC had a lengthy discussion about its proposed policy actions. Some wanted to slow money growth or raise interest rates. Morris (Boston) pointed to the two percentage point difference between the funds rate and the discount rate. Borrowing reached $1 billion. He proposed a one percentage point increase in the discount rate. Conscious of congressional reactions, Volcker replied that even half a point would see "an explosion" in Washington (ibid., 85). An "independent" Federal Reserve had to be aware of congressional attitudes.

Gramley reflected the unhappiness of many of the members who feared a return of inflation. "I think we're pussy-footing. I think we've been sitting here for some months now looking at an economy that continues to exceed everybody's expectations. This is going to come back to haunt us if we don't decide to act" (ibid., 91–92). Wallich agreed. But Volcker expressed satisfaction with the modest changes he proposed and seemed more concerned by political response to a funds rate above 11 percent then to Gramley and Wallich's concerns about inflation. Twelve-month average CPI inflation remained about 3.5 percent.

At the March meeting, the vote was nine to three for a funds rate of 7.5

15. Earlier, Kydland and Prescott (1977) showed that this was a poor choice of tactics.

16. At the March meeting, the FOMC agreed to discontinue repurchase agreements in banker's acceptances. Authority to do the transactions remained. A memo from Peter Sternlight discussed the pros and cons. The main argument against ending operations was that System operations allowed some smaller banks to participate (memo, Sternlight to Board, Board Records, March 12, 1984).

to 11.5 percent and $M_1$, $M_2$, and $M_3$ growth of 6.5, 8, and 8.5 from March to June. Gramley and Wallich dissented because policy was not sufficiently restrictive and Martin because he wanted less restraint. In a speech at the end of April, Volcker recognized the progress against high inflation but added, "We haven't passed the test of maintaining control over inflation during a period of prosperity" (speech to Wharton Entrepreneurial Center, Board Records, April 30, 1984, 2).

Between March and August the funds rate increased from an average 9.9 to an 11.6 percent rate. The operating target for adjustment plus seasonal borrowing remained at $1 billion during this period, but in order to avoid the appearance of internal problems, fewer banks were borrowing. Growth of the monetary base and money slowed. The unemployment rate remained above 7 percent; the market could see that policy had tightened. Although Volcker had expressed political concern about an 11 percent funds rate, and this was an election year, the average remained above 11 percent between June and September. This action was strikingly different from the actions in the 1970s, so it contributed to the credibility of the Federal Reserve's commitment to low inflation.[17] Criticism of Federal Reserve policy declined after President Reagan defended the Federal Reserve at a news conference.

In May, borrowing from the Federal Reserve surged as Continental Illinois Bank (Chicago) tried to avoid failure. Gramley asked whether the desk offset some or all of the borrowing by removing reserves. The manager replied that interest rates were high at the time and the desk was reluctant to drain reserves but he was now beginning to drain excess reserves.[18] For the FOMC, Continental's problems and the problems at other banks and thrifts added to concerns about international lending and to reluctance to raise interest rates. Volcker made this explicit by speaking before the policy discussion. He recognized that "it might take somewhat more aggressive action than we've taken before to bring the economy to a suitable path. . . . But, unfortunately, I don't think that course of action is open to us. . . . My bottom line is that we've run out of room for the time being for any tightening" (FOMC Minutes, May 21–22, 27). Like previous chairmen, Volcker felt independence was constrained at the time.

Members of FOMC again as in the 1950s used different measures to express their policy preferences. Some used $M_1$; Wallich commented on the

17. At about this time Congressman Jack Kemp organized some Republican members to propose legislation to limit Federal Reserve independence, including returning the Secretary of the Treasury as an ex officio member of the Board. The legislation did not advance, but the threat of congressional action always alarmed the Board.

18. Federal Reserve response to Continental Illinois's problems is discussed below.

return of free reserves; he preferred gross borrowing, the measure used by the manager. The FOMC could agree only on a directive that named different measures but they did not know whether they were consistent. The vote was ten to one. Boykin (Dallas) favored tighter policy. Nancy Teeters had left the Board, and her successor was not confirmed. Martha Seger joined the Board in July.

Despite the decision to make no change, the federal funds rate rose in June and July. The average July rate, 11.23 percent, was 0.91 percentage points above May. Actual and anticipated inflation continued to fall slowly. The ten-year Treasury rate at 13.4 percent had not begun to reflect lower inflation. The S&P 500 fell sharply in July and several subsequent months as the economy began to grow more slowly and investors worried about widespread financial fragility. The staff forecast anticipated modest interest rate increases, but predicted a 15 percent decline in the exchange rate.

The July 1984 meeting had to decide on the projections for growth and inflation announced to Congress and the public. This time Board members' median expected growth for 1985 fell to 3.75 percent from 6.75 in 1984; median predicted inflation was 3.75 rising to 5 percent in 1985. The medians for the presidents were similar. The precise meaning was unclear because the members made different assumptions about dollar depreciation. Expected dollar depreciation added up to one percentage point to the 1985 median inflation forecast. The members agreed to keep projected $M_1$ and $M_2$ growth for 1985 about unchanged at 4 to 7 and 6 to 8.5 percent. This represents a slight reduction for the upper end of the $M_1$ and $M_2$ growth rates.[19]

Heightened uncertainty about growth and inflation, signs of slower growth, and increased banking problems made it difficult to reach agreement on proper action in August. Volcker took charge. After announcing ranges for the monetary aggregates, borrowing, and the funds rate, he told the Committee:

> If we get a weaker employment number, weaker this number or that number—broadly lower than expectations, yes. If we have financial problems that are great enough, we would provide some liquidity. I don't know how one judges that in advance. I think we have to play it by ear. (FOMC Minutes, August 21, 1984, 38)

19. Volcker's testimony in the Senate blamed high interest rates on the budget deficit, not for the first time. He urged again that Congress reduce the budget deficit both as a way of achieving macroeconomic balance and to lower the size of the capital inflow. He warned about the inability to sustain the capital inflow and the risk of rising protection (statement, Paul Volcker to Senate Committee on Banking, Box 97645, Federal Reserve Bank of New York, July 25, 1984, 4).

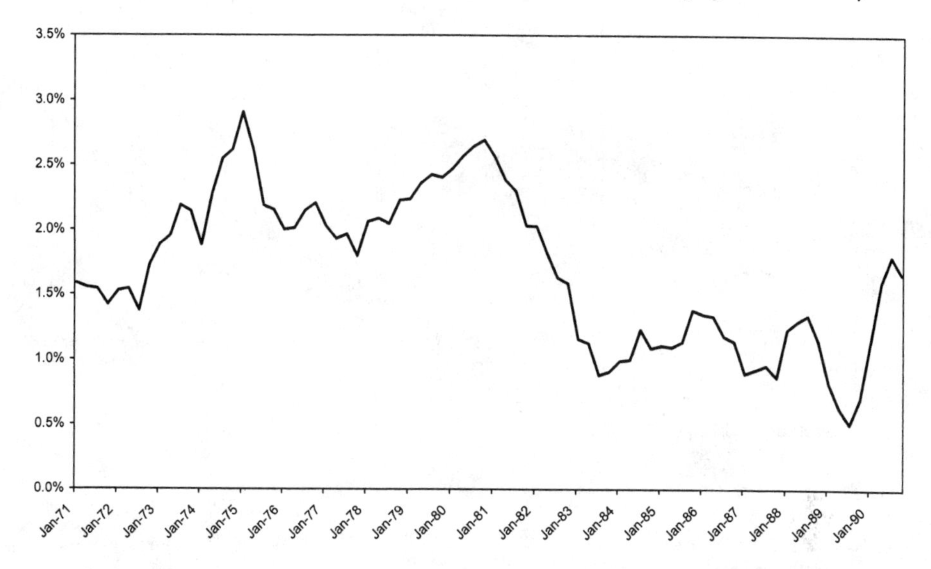


Chart 9.11. Quarterly change, nominal compensation per hour, fourquarter moving average, 1971–90.

Two years had passed since the end of the explicit disinflation policy. Measures of actual and anticipated inflation remained about 3 to 4 percent. Unemployment rates had declined from more than 10 to about 7.5 percent. But nominal interest rates had not returned to the pre-1979 ranges. In September, the federal funds rate averaged 11.3 percent, and the ten-year Treasury note yielded 12.5 percent, only one percentage point below its local peak. The ten-year rate remained almost two percentage points above the level in October 1982. Apparently, the public regarded the risk of inflation as very high. The FOMC had no plan for lowering these rates. Several of its members shared the concern that inflation would return.

Volcker stated their puzzle. "It's a very strange period. Every indicator normally would be associated with lower interest rates" (FOMC Minutes, October 2, 1984, 6). Chart 9.10 above shows that the real interest rate remained in the 6 to 7 percent range. The real value of monetary base growth fell persistently during this period. In October, the staff began to reduce its forecast.

Though unremarked at FOMC, nominal wage growth had declined steadily from its peak in the early 1980s. By 1984, the nominal rate of change was about 4 to 5 percent at annual rates. Chart 9.11 shows these data at quarterly rates. This proved to be a harbinger of lower real and nominal interest rates. It is difficult to reconcile the expectations reflected in interest rates and nominal wage growth.

During the summer and early fall, St. Louis voted regularly to raise its

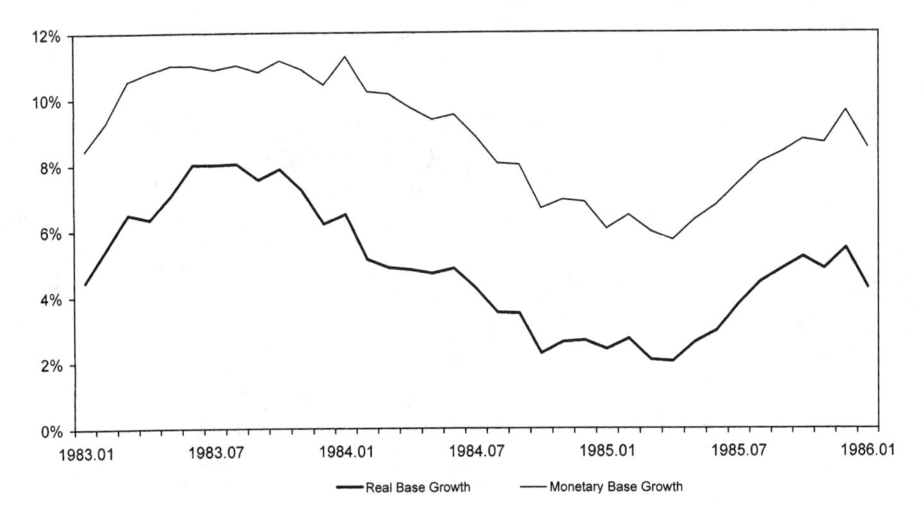


Chart 9.12. Monetary base growth versus real base growth, January 1983–January 1986. Growth measured year-over-year.

discount rate to 9.5 percent. No other banks agreed with them. The Board recognized the large spread between the discount and the funds rate, but it rejected the requests because borrowing had declined and the economy showed evidence of slower growth. By mid-November evidence of slower growth prompted Chicago, St. Louis, Dallas, and San Francisco to ask for a reduction to 8.5 percent. New York, Philadelphia, and Kansas City joined them a bit later. The Board deferred the requests until November 21, when it approved 8.5 percent. The Board cited the slowing economy, the spread between the funds and discount rate, and slowing growth of $M_1$ and $M_2$.

By mid-December, three banks requested an additional reduction. The Board deferred the request but recognized that it might be appropriate after the FOMC meeting. On December 21, the Board voted for an 8 percent rate, citing the same factors as in November. Governor Gramley dissented because he thought that slower growth was temporary.

Monetary policy continued to lack a consistent approach during the last six months of 1984. In the usual procyclical patterns, the FOMC permitted base and $M_1$ growth to decline as the economy slowed. Twelve-month base growth fell to 6.8 percent, two percentage points less than in July. Falling nominal base growth did not change the inflation rate. Inflation remained about 4 percent as shown by the difference between nominal and real base growth in Chart 9.12. The SPF predicted that 4 percent inflation would continue.

The federal funds rate declined also. Its December 1984 average, 8.4 percent, was almost three percentage points below July. By November, the ten-year Treasury rate was below 12 percent. Real long-term rates began to decline slightly as inflation fell.

For the July Humphrey-Hawkins hearings, the Board forecast a rise in inflation to 5 percent in 1985; the presidents forecast a 5.25 percent median with an outlier at 6.5 percent. The staff forecast 4.75 percent. Members expressed concern about a rapid decline in the dollar exchange rate, a credit binge, wage increases, and always the budget deficit.[20] Most of all, the members expressed uncertainty about the future and the difficulty of making forecasts. No one expressed sentiment for following a long-run policy path, although some of the remarks about more "automaticity" could be interpreted that way.

Volcker favored reducing slightly the 1985 $M_1$ range from 4 to 8 percent to 4 to 7 percent. Boehne (Philadelphia) objected that would make an increase difficult in February 1985. Volcker responded:

> Well what would happen next February? None of us knows. Let's suppose we're running above that [range] . . . ; that must mean we've worried about something—interest rates or something in the economy. In that kind of scenario we would go [to Congress] and say "Look you haven't done anything about the budget. We can't hold it by monetary policy alone without running undue risks. We're going to have to raise the target." (FOMC Minutes, July 16–17, 45)

Volcker told the FOMC that his concerns about the banking system kept policy from tightening. Martin showed that he was in the wrong job. He said that the FOMC had a bias toward tightening. He quoted people who called the FOMC "knee jerk inflation fighters" (ibid., 67). Volcker replied that it's a good reputation to have, and Solomon said, "[T]hat's what central bankers are supposed to have" (ibid., 68).

With Martin dissenting, the Committee voted to tighten policy slightly to slow economic growth. The exchanges at this meeting suggest the major change that had occurred since the 1960s and 1970s. Volcker's analysis of inflation and the deficit was much the same as William McChesney Martin's. The difference was that he didn't coordinate, emphasized the importance of controlling inflation, and was willing to act within the limits set by political concern about the banking system and the international debt.[21]

Lyle Gramley continued to express concern about inflation. He warned

20. Volcker noted, "All FOMC members are expecting a big decline in the dollar" (FOMC Minutes, July 16–17, 1984, 30).

21. In August the Committee expressed concern about the large volume of collateralized borrowing by Continental Illinois. The loans pressed against the rates on collateral for Federal Reserve loans because the loans were secured by government securities.

his colleagues not to repeat the two mistakes made by the Carter administration, where he had served. He described the mistakes as (1) underestimating the natural rate of employment as 5.5 percent, when it was higher, and (2) overestimating productivity growth. "So I think we ought to be very, very careful in looking at recent productivity statistics and not to get overly optimistic" (ibid., August 21, 1984, 26).

By November, the Treasury had started to intervene in the exchange market as part of a consortium that wanted to depreciate the dollar. The Federal Reserve always sterilized intervention, usually including Treasury intervention, so the actions had no more than a brief effect. The dollar continued to appreciate.

By October, slowing activity and declining growth rates for $M_1$ and $M_2$ prompted an early move toward easier policy action. The federal funds rate declined on average in both months. Axilrod said that money demand had shifted downward, but he offered no explanation of the alleged shift. Several members began to emphasize $M_1$ growth. Roberts (St. Louis) explained that $M_1$ had not grown for five months. He blamed the use of borrowing and free reserve targets, and the decision to slow the decline in the funds rate. Morris (Boston) also blamed use of a borrowing target, citing the large increase in borrowing to support Continental Illinois.

Volcker then asked, "Do you want to target the federal funds rate? . . . I wouldn't recommend it" (FOMC Minutes, November 7, 1984, 30). He defended FOMC actions, pointing out that higher-than-expected interest rates had occurred for several months without objection from the members. Others also objected to the control mechanism, but there were no agreement on what to do differently and no discussion of the reasons for their differences.

The discussion resumed in December. Axilrod prepared a paper on two problems with using a target for borrowing. One arose because the relation between borrowing, interest rates, and money changed at different levels of economic activity. At lower levels, he claimed that banks were less willing to borrow, so interest rates remained higher. The banks did not want to show large borrowing on their balance sheets, a version of the old "reluctance" theory from the 1920s. Second, higher interest rates reduced the quantity of money demanded. Axilrod also suggested using the monetary base as a target because the market focused on $M_1$. He proposed more automaticity in their procedures.

This set off a discussion of the use of rules and discretion that was a rare event for the FOMC. The discussion also brought out criticisms of their procedures. Frank Morris described their procedure. The staff estimated required reserves, added an estimate of excess reserves, and subtracted expected borrowing to get nonborrowed reserves. The error in estimating borrowed reserves reduced total reserve growth because the desk aimed for nonborrowed reserves.

Volcker objected that the FOMC had seen the result of these procedures at meetings from July to October without responding. Why change procedures?

John Balles favored introducing more rule-like behavior. He claimed that the more basic problem came from the use of borrowing or free reserves as a target. "Any given level of borrowing or any given level of free reserves is compatible with a wide range of interest rates, a wide range of economic outcomes, and a wide range of growth in the monetary aggregates." He reminded them that the same problem arose in the 1950s, when free reserves were the target. He preferred nonborrowed reserves because it was more closely related to money.

Robert Black supported his proposal for a semi-automatic response to unforeseen changes in nonborrowed reserves. He urged a penalty discount rate also. Corrigan, Forrestal, and Gramley opposed Axilrod's proposal.

Henry Wallich said "good judgment is always bound to be better than a mechanical rule. The question is whether good judgment is more likely than not" (ibid., 15). He thought judgment had been correct recently, so they should not change.

It is striking that this discussion took place seventy years after the Federal Reserve began and fifty years after abandoning the gold standard rule. No consensus had formed about correct procedures. No less striking was the lack of agreement about the use of rules and absence of any reference to the Kydland and Prescott (1977) paper showing the superiority of rules over single-period discretionary choices. The members may not have been aware of the paper, but the staff certainly was.

Volcker then turned the discussion to the use of an $M_1$ target to the exclusion of everything else. He summarized: "I see a few hands go up weakly and then they go down again" (ibid., 20). In his view the main problems came from the difficulty of forecasting accurately. "You can't project the economy quarter-to-quarter or half-year to half-year with a degree of sensitivity that is required ex post to make everybody happy. That's another way of saying that you can't fine-tune on the basis of economic projections" (ibid., 21).

This statement could have started a discussion of aiming at a target more than one quarter or half year ahead with less attention to short-term changes. But Volcker did not choose that path. Instead, he emphasized using information in "other indicators of what is happening" (ibid.). He mentioned the exchange rate and commodity prices, but he did not suggest how to interpret the information without a more comprehensive and accurate model than they had or were likely to develop.

After the discussion, the FOMC considered its policy for early 1985. The only sign of the preceding discussion was the increased number of references to the exchange rate. Governor Gramley emphasized that their concern should be the real exchange rate and that he did not know how monetary policy could change the real exchange rate.

The staff forecast growth of 2.9 percent in 1985. The Committee returned to business as usual, some wanting faster growth, some anticipating faster growth, and some favoring more attention to inflation. Preston Martin again introduced a political element by citing congressional response to a forecast of 2.9 percent growth when the unemployment rate remained above 7 percent. His concern was that there would be efforts to restrict independence.

The discussion, as so many others, turned on a narrow issue—a proposed borrowing target of $250 or $300 million. The issue was whether the funds rate would ease or remain about 8.5 percent. The vote was ten to two with Solomon favoring higher borrowing and Gramley favoring more attention to inflation. The FOMC did nothing to resolve their differences about long-term policy.

## BANKING PROBLEMS

Persistence of high real interest rates and disinflation brought problems in the global financial system to attention. There were two distinct types of problems and solutions. Large-scale borrowing by developing countries during the 1970s became very expensive to service in the 1980s, when real interest rates rose. Beginning with Mexico in 1982, countries defaulted. Many of the debts were owed to large U.S. banks, especially New York banks, but European and Japanese banks faced similar problems. The Federal Reserve's strategy was to use international loans, especially IMF loans, to pay the interest to keep the countries from defaulting. The countries' debt increased but the new money went to the creditor banks. A later section discusses this problem.

Regulators treated domestic banking problems very differently. Mergers and closing of failed banks and thrifts or massive loans to restore solvency became standard practice. Among the failures was the Continental Illinois Bank, the largest Chicago bank. But it was not alone. The rise in oil prices had induced a real estate boom in Texas and Oklahoma. When oil prices fell and the boom collapsed, home prices followed. Many home mortgages went into default. If no local owners offered to buy failed or failing banks, out-of-state banks could buy them. Later, interstate banking became an accepted outcome even if the acquired bank remained solvent. This was a major change for the better in U.S. banking practice. It permitted much greater portfolio diversification and reduced the risk that difficult local economic conditions would result in bank failures or systemic financial fragility.

Volcker was on vacation in early August, when he received a visit from the chairman of Continental Illinois Bank, who told him the bank would require federal assistance to avoid failure (Volcker and Gyohten, 1992, 200). Continental had purchased many of its energy loans from Penn Square. When Penn Square Bank in Oklahoma failed, news of Continental's problems spread through the financial markets. It faced a risk premium in the market for the large purchased deposits that it used to finance its activities. The bank could not replace the deposits that holders withdrew as they matured. By the end of the week, the Federal Reserve Bank of Chicago made $3.6 billion in loans to keep Continental Illinois operating. This was an unprecedented loan for the System. In July, the FDIC assumed $3.5 billion of debt.

The Board, the Comptroller, and the FDIC acted to provide permanent capital. This replaced a $2 billion subordinated loan by the FDIC and a group of banks. The regulators removed the management and appointed two outside managers to run the bank (Permanent Assistance Program for Continental Illinois National Bank, Board Minutes, July 25, 1984). The FDIC committed to protect all depositors, insured and uninsured, in any solution. The bank paid one percentage point above the discount rate for its extended borrowing. When market rates rose above the discount rate in August, the Board set the rate at 11.75 percent to be adjusted as market rates changed (Board Minutes, August 10, 1984, 8).

These actions had no precedent in United States experience. Instead of liquidating the bank and paying off insured depositors, regulators assumed responsibility for all deposits and provided capital to keep the bank solvent. Two arguments at the time cited the loss of banking services threatening bank customers and the fear of contagion that threatened other, solvent banks (Stern and Feldman, 2004, 48). Also, the size of the bank, seventh largest in the country at the time, and the very large share of purchased foreign deposits heightened concern about a run on domestic banks.[22]

Stern and Feldman (ibid., 13–14) point out that the Continental bailout was not the first use of "too big to fail," but it expanded use of that term. By protecting a large bank, government agencies encouraged "giantism"

22. The Federal Reserve advanced $3.5 billion repaid over five years by the FDIC. That was the largest loan for the longest term in its history.

and increased moral hazard—the willingness of banks to increase risks in the knowledge that if the risks pay off, they gain, and if losses increase, the taxpayers absorb the losses. Moral hazard had long been present in deposit insurance protection, but extending protection to uninsured depositors increased the problem.

The source of the problem lies in the choice that a regulator has to make under uncertainty at a time of banking crisis. One option is to let the bank fail but lend freely to the market at a penalty rate to protect solvent banks from a possible run. This is the Bagehot rule. Let the stockholders bear the loss and replace the management, but allow the bank to continue operating. The other option is to bail out the failing bank. The second course always gains from fear that the crisis will spread and become a large panic with many failures. Faced with the choice under these conditions, few regulators choose the first course.[23]

Knowing that large banks will not fail encourages mergers and acquisitions to become sufficiently large to be too big to fail. And it encourages excessive risk taking. At hearings on the Continental Illinois failure, the Comptroller of the Currency announced that "too big to fail" applied to eleven U.S. national banks. Many observers concluded that the list was longer or would be enlarged in a crisis (ibid., 155).

Congress responded to "too big to fail" and regulatory decisions in the 1980s by passing the Federal Deposit Insurance Corporation Improvement Act of 1991 (FDICIA). The act tried to restrict discretion and limit bailout of uninsured depositors. It required regulators to choose the least costly means of resolving banking problems while showing concern for adverse effects on the financial system.[24] It made clear that Congress had a continuing oversight interest and would require ex post explanations of actions. This was not new, but there is some evidence that FDICIA worked to reduce bailouts to uninsured depositors (Stern and Feldman, 2004, 153).[25] In FDICIA Congress acted to restrict the Federal Reserve and the FDIC from protecting bankers and uninsured depositors. The act prohib-

23. Stern and Feldman (2004, 48) cite studies showing that failure of Continental Illinois "would not have wiped out the entire financial capital of any respondent banks . . . and therefore would not have led many of them to fail."

24. FDICIA shifted the cost of bank failures from taxpayers to banks by requiring FDIC to maintain a minimum ratio of reserves to insured deposits (1.25 percent). If the ratio fell below the target, FDIC had to increase premiums paid by solvent banks. FDICIA also introduced "structured early intervention," a requirement that regulators act promptly to restrict a failing bank's actions before it became insolvent.

25. Large borrowing by Continental Illinois contributed to slower growth of the monetary base and money. The Federal Reserve chose to target nonborrowed reserves but included large borrowing with nonborrowed reserves, so it supplied fewer reserves through open market operations.

ited the FDIC from paying off more than the insured depositors, but other sections of the act weakened the prohibition. And FDICIA restricted the Federal Reserve from lending large sums to failing banks, thereby shifting the cost to the FDIC.

The July assistance to Continental did not end its borrowing. A month later, Peter Sternlight reported that Continental's borrowing increased to around $7.5 billion from $5 billion in mid-July (FOMC Minutes, August 21, 1984, 2). A month later, Sternlight appended a report from his staff showing additional problems; large money center banks became more reluctant to borrow from the Federal Reserve and held larger excess reserves. He said this increased the federal funds rate for any level of borrowing (ibid., September 28, 1984).

Volcker conducted monetary policy forcefully, but he was less forceful and less successful as a bank supervisor. He told a Senate committee that he urged Continental to take drastic action in 1982 after Penn Square failed, but he did not require them to do so. The bank continued to pay dividends to shareholders. With hindsight he recognized his mistake (Grieder, 1987, 626).

Continental was the largest failure but far from the only one. During the first half of 1984, forty-three banks failed. Most suffered from falling crop and land prices, an event with many precedents. The FDIC paid off the insured depositors and usually merged the failing bank with another local bank.

Large banks experienced losses especially on agriculture, energy, and real estate lending. Bank of America and Manufacturers Hanover had to pay a premium to borrow on CDs after the collapse of Continental Illinois.

The Financial Corporation of America, a holding company, was the largest operator of thrift associations in the country. Its principal holding, American Savings and Loan Association (Los Angeles) experienced deposit losses. These increased following a decision by the Securities and Exchange Commission requiring American Savings to restate its earnings using generally accepted accounting in place of regulatory accounting permitted by the Home Loan banks. The ruling converted a reported profit into a loss.[26]

The Board of Governors could approve collateralized loans to American if requested by the Federal Home Loan Bank. The Board discussed the loan and collateral available. It decided to authorize long-term loans at an

26. Barth, Bartholomew, and Labich (1989, 41) examined the available evidence on failures of thrift institutions to conclude that "insufficient capital and the lack of a timely closure rule were major causes of the thrift crisis." Moral hazard and regulators' forbearance made serious contributions to the losses.

above-market rate. The holding company had only $6 billion dollars in collateral and was unlikely to get more. Deposit losses increased as rumors spread that the Federal Savings and Loan Insurance Corporation (FSLIC), the government's deposit insurance company for thrift institutions, was unlikely to be able to meet all of the claims from failing savings and loan associations (Board Minutes, August 17, 1984, 7).

Ohio had several problems with savings and loans that were not members of FSLIC. The Federal Reserve helped to close the failing associations. At the May FOMC meeting, President Horn (Cleveland) commented on the moral hazard problem. The position of some failing thrifts is so bad that "there is nothing to keep them from trying to take a big bet and trying to hit a home run in real estate development kinds of projects. Because if they fail to hit the home run, have they really worsened their condition?" (FOMC Minutes, May 21–22, 1984, 10). The moral hazard problem, recognized when deposit insurance started, had finally become a major problem.[27] Regulatory forbearance aggravated the problem.

The Board took an important step in January, when it approved the sale of two failing thrifts in Florida to a major New York bank, Citicorp. The Board fully discussed its concerns about allowing Citicorp to expand when it had large holdings of foreign debt in countries such as Mexico and Brazil that had defaulted. Unwilling to permit the failures in Florida, the Board permitted the acquisitions, thereby introducing interstate banking in Florida. The vote was four to two with Governor Wallich abstaining and Governors Rice and Teeters dissenting mainly out of concern for problems in Citicorp's portfolio (Board Minutes, January 19 and 20, 1984).

During the year, the Board considered major mergers and acquisitions to prevent failures by banks and thrifts. Out-of-state banks acquired most of the large Texas banks. Chase Manhattan acquired Lincoln First Bank in New York State, permitting it to expand out of New York City for the first time. Selin Corporation, a one-bank holding company in Chicago, acquired four banks in Illinois, a major break in the Illinois unit banking law that did not permit branching until that time.

These actions changed the nature of the financial system. They could occur because legislation permitted acquisition of a failing thrift association by an out-of-state bank holding company as a last resort.[28] After 195

27. In the midst of the series of problems in summer 1984, Volcker recognized lax regulation and supervision, noting that he was not proud of regulatory policy in general and by the Federal Reserve. He announced that the Federal Reserve would soon require members to increase capital (FOMC Minutes, July 16–17, 1984, 56).

28. In June, the Board rejected acquisition of a solvent North Carolina thrift by a Rhode

years, the United States had interstate banking. Banks could now diversify more readily, a step that particularly helped smaller, rural banks.[29]

### *Regulatory Changes*

The large number of failures and losses to the deposit insurance funds and regulatory forbearance stimulated interest in reform of the deposit insurance system. The public became aware of political pressures to avoid closing failing banks and the difference in treatment of small and medium banks versus "too big to fail" for large banks. The Treasury Department proposed to adjust deposit insurance premiums for the risk undertaken by the bank. In principle, this would increase incentives for reducing risk and penalize high risk. The Treasury also proposed to permit the FDIC to withdraw insurance for certain classes of risky depositors.

The Board recognized the need for change, but it did not endorse the Treasury proposal. It argued that the proposals were inadequate in part because insurance premiums were too small to affect the desired outcome. Also, the Board wanted to require banks to increase capital (letter, Volcker to Thomas J. Healey, Board Minutes, May 4, 1984).

To its discredit, Congress concentrated most of its attention on finding malefactors and charging them in public. It largely ignored structural problems in financial regulation, lax regulation, the pressures it put on regulators, and flaws in the deposit insurance system. This delayed reform for several years. In 1991, it corrected these errors by passing FDICIA, as noted earlier.

When foreign banks began to purchase domestic banks, the Board considered the capital requirements of the foreign banks. At the time, the requirement for domestic banks was 5 percent of assets. The Board could not agree on how this standard could be applied to foreign banks that used different accounting and regulatory conventions. It did not set a standard for foreign banks.

As Japanese banks became active in the domestic financial system, the Board decided to consider each acquisition on its merits. For example, although the Board members believed that the capital ratio of Mitsubishi Banks was inadequate, the Board voted five to two to permit Mitsubishi to acquire a California bank. Governors Martin and Rice dissented on grounds that foreign banks should meet the same standards as domestic banks.

---

Island bank. It had previously permitted the Rhode Island bank to acquire a failing North Carolina thrift (Board Minutes, June 4, 1984, 7).

29. The first and second banks of the United States had branch banking systems in the years that these banks operated, 1791 to 1811 and 1816 to 1836.

The Board set or recommended bank capital requirements, but it was slow to change them. In July, the FDIC and the Comptroller proposed new capital standards. The Board's concern was that the proposed standards raised the standards for most banks, but the proposed level was lower than the standards at smaller community banks. Although the Board was reluctant to lower any standards, it joined in the proposal but issued the standards as guidelines for banks and not as a regulation. All member banks and holding companies were asked to have minimum primary capital equal to 5.5 percent of total assets and total capital equal to 6 percent of adjusted assets.[30] The Board continued to use "zones" for capital. Institutions with a 7 percent capital-to-asset ratio were considered "adequately capitalized." Below 6 percent, the bank was "undercapitalized" (press release, Board Minutes, July 26, 1984).[31]

### *Other Regulations*

The Board in January also adjusted reserve requirements as required by the Monetary Control Act of 1980. In January, it reset to $29.8 million the amount of transaction balances subject to the 3 percent reserve requirement. Under the Garn-St. Germain Depository Institutions Act, it reset the aggregate amount of deposits subject to zero percent reserve requirement from $2.2 to $2.4 million.

In February, the Board issued a statement opposing the growing practice of making payments from accounts at banks located far from the payee to capture additional days of float. The Board objected that the practice reduced the efficiency of the payments system.

### *Litigation*

Several court cases approved Board actions extending opportunities for bank holding companies to own and operate brokerages, insurance agencies, and industrial banks, and to expand across state lines. Affected parties often sued to challenge the expansion of banking powers. The relative positions of banks, investment banks, and insurance companies had been limited by rules and legislation adopted in the 1930s. Another decade passed before Congress could agree to change these rules and increase competition in financial services. Some examples of the 1984 cases follow (Annual Report, 1984, 161–88).

30. The Board excluded intangible assets from primary capital. Reserves for loans and leases were included as primary capital.

31. In May, the New York bank announced capital adequacy guidelines for dealers in the government securities market. The guidelines were voluntary and proposed after a number of defaults (statement of Edward J. Ging, Board Records, May 31, 1984).

In 1983, the Board approved Bank of America's acquisition of a discount brokerage, Charles Schwab, for its holding company. The Securities Industry Association sued to reverse the acquisition. The Supreme Court upheld the order.

Also in 1983, the Board approved an application by three Missouri banks to sell property and casualty insurance directly related to financial services. On June 13, 1984, the court upheld the Board's decision.

First Tennessee National Corporation sued to require the Board to reverse its decision permitting Citicorp to acquire an industrial bank in Tennessee. The case was dismissed.

The Board amended its regulation of bank holding companies to permit new powers. These included commodity trading services, check guaranty services, financial counseling, armored car services, tax planning and preparation, and operating a credit agency (ibid., 189).

## INTERNATIONAL DEBT AND EXCHANGE RATES

During the spring and summer of 1982, Mexico had borrowed overnight from Treasury and Federal Reserve swap lines to show more reserves on its monthly statement in the hope that holders of Mexican dollar securities would roll over their loans. This made it difficult for lenders to know the extent of Mexico's problem, but they knew there was a problem. Mexicans had more dollar liabilities than it was likely to repay and service. Wary foreign lenders withdrew their loans, and informed Mexicans sent money abroad, draining foreign reserves. The games played by the Bank of Mexico and the Federal Reserve made it difficult to know the magnitude of the problem, but that did not stop the capital outflow.

Mexico would not act before its July election, and outgoing president López Portillo would not act after the election during his last months. He left the problem to two able officials, Jesús Silva Herzog and Ángel Gurría, assisted by Miguel Mancera, president of the Bank of Mexico. López Portillo would not permit negotiations with the IMF, so Silva Herzog and Gurría had to find an interim solution that would keep Mexico from defaulting before the new administration took control in December.

By mid-August Mexico's foreign exchange reserve had fallen to about $200 million. It lost $100 million a day in capital outflow. Without support from abroad, Mexico could not avoid default. Whatever concern the United States had for Mexico, its first concern was the effect of a default on domestic banks and financial institutions with loans to Mexico. Other debtor countries would soon follow Mexico, adding to the financial problem. British, Swiss, and Japanese banks also faced substantial losses, so the governments of these countries participated in the lending program.

The central banks agreed to provide $1.85 billion in swap credits, half from the United States. Also, agricultural credit and advance payment for oil shipments added about $2 billion. The private sector banks agreed to a "standstill," i.e., a "hidden" default; Mexico would not pay and the banks would not declare a default (Volcker and Gyohten, 1992, 200–202). The banks agreed also to advance more loans.

Although the Mexican banks tried to defer payments to foreign banks, the capital outflow continued, so much of the money advanced by the central banks leaked out as payments for capital outflow. The Mexican government would not float the exchange rate or devalue. Foreign banks may have been willing to defer payments, but individuals and other financial institutions took advantage of the fixed exchange rate to withdraw their loans. Holding the exchange rate fixed became a means for the Mexican taxpayers to protect their creditors' assets. This eliminated or reduced the creditors' incentives to limit risky lending. In this instance, lenders received interest rates of 15 percent or more on some loans as compensation for risk bearing. When the risk came due, the governments and the IMF prevented most of the creditors' losses, an example of socialism for the creditors.

Mexico's problem could not be solved without a substantial reduction in the country's budget deficit and in the growth of the monetary base. The problem worsened while Silva Herzog and Gurría were at the Toronto meeting of the IMF. President López Portillo surprised them and everyone else by announcing that Mexico would nationalize its banks to penalize them for paying out foreign exchange. The government had fixed the exchange rate; it penalized the banks for following the policy. López Portillo also announced that he had imposed exchange controls. Capital outflow increased.[32] The crisis worsened.

Finally, in December, the new government began serious negotiation. In exchange for IMF-proposed loans, it devalued and accepted the long-delayed austerity program. The resolution that Mexico adopted became the pattern for subsequent defaults. Foreign lending declined after the Mexican crisis, so other countries were unable to service international debts. Brazil, Argentina, Venezuela, much of the rest of Latin America, and parts of Africa had to go to the IMF and agree to austerity programs. This began the period known in Latin America as the lost decade. Economies stagnated or declined. The IMF required the commercial banks to commit to additional lending used mainly to pay the interest to themselves

32. I am grateful to Ángel Gurría, vice minister in the Mexican Treasury at the time, for helpful discussion of this period.

on outstanding debt. The Federal Reserve agreed to not criticize the new loans as imprudent (ibid., 212).

The rationale for this policy was to prevent domestic banking failures. Unlike Continental Illinois, regulators did not replace managements, insert capital, and mark the bad debt to market. Instead, the IMF and the banks loaned money to the debtors to pay the interest as it came due. The new loans did not go to the countries; they just increased the countries' debts. Most calculations at the time showed that few of the debtor countries could expect to increase exports enough to repay the debt. The decline in world commodity prices added to their problem.[33]

Toyoo Gyohten (Volcker and Gyohten, 1992, 220) reported that the current account deficits of the principal debtors increased from $31 to $49 billion and the ratio of their outstanding debt to their exports rose from 165 to 204 percent.[34] The problem worsened. Instead of receiving a net capital inflow, debtors had a net capital outflow that reached $24 billion in 1986. The IMF and central bank program was not helping the debtors to move toward a resolution. For their part, most of the debtor countries were slow to adopt the austerity programs agreed to as part of the IMF program. Tax increases and spending reductions were not politically acceptable in stagnant economies.

The program did not work. As early as May 1984, Volcker told the FOMC that "the biggest sign we have of something not working at the margin . . . is the LDC situation (less developed countries)" (FOMC Minutes, May 21–22, 1984, 27). This was his main reason for opposing an increase in interest rates. Later he added that "the sense of knife's edge or fragility is going to be with us for a while" (ibid., 37).

There was surprisingly little discussion of the debt problem and the policy of sustaining the banks. Volcker was involved actively but did not say much at the meetings. The other FOMC members left the problem to him.

Volcker recognized by 1985 that the program would not reduce the size of the debt. "It was obvious that the fundamental problems from the borrowers' perspective had not been resolved and a certain fatigue had set in

33. Volcker testified in February 1983 on the actions necessary for resolution. These included determined action by borrowing countries to reduce budget deficits and inflation and to increase productivity growth, additional loans from foreign banks, and management by the IMF (Volcker papers, Federal Reserve Bank of New York, Box 97649, February 2, 1983, 2–4). Resolution did not come until banks began to write down debt values and the U.S. Treasury agreed to the writedown.

34. U.S. banks held 37 percent of Latin American loans. Other shares were Japan 15 percent, Britain 14, France 10, Germany 9, Canada 8, and Switzerland 3.

among the lenders" (Volcker and Gyohten, 1992, 212). The banks received more in interest payments than they lent to the debtors. He recognized that the U.S. banks were less willing, or even unwilling, unlike the Europeans, to increase reserves against the loans. "It was all very frustrating. The logic of the situation seemed to require that the banks at least volunteer some significant concessions on interest rates while building their reserves. But as regulators, we did not feel that we could in effect impose losses on the banks by forcing below-market interest rates or large reserves without jeopardizing their willingness to lend" (ibid., 213).[35] Once again, concern for the banks dominated decisions.

Attitudes changed in several ways. James Baker, who became Secretary of the Treasury in President Reagan's second term, offered a plan that recognized at last that the debt could not be repaid without resuming economic growth in the debtor countries. The Baker plan called for increased lending by the IMF, the development banks, and the commercial banks. It was a start but it did not last as a program. The next important step was a bold move by Citicorp to increase reserves against Citicorp's holdings by $3 billion. This was, at last, recognition by a major creditor that the debt was not worth its face value, a judgment the market reached much earlier. Following this step, some debt-equity exchanges and other approaches reduced the outstanding debt. Final resolution did not begin until 1989, when officials at the New York Federal Reserve developed plans named for Secretary Nicholas Brady, who replaced Baker at the Treasury. Under the Brady plans, debtor countries issued "Brady bonds," collateralized debt, to the creditor banks. The bonds could be sold. Each debtor country negotiated when it was ready to agree to an IMF medium-term austerity program. The commercial banks had to agree to reduce the value of their claims but they were not required to make additional loans.[36] Over the next few years, the principal debtors made Brady agreements. By the early 1990s, most U.S. banks had finally allocated to reserves 50 to 100 percent of the value of their international debt.

About 50 percent of the creditor banks chose to reduce their claims, mainly by reducing interest rates. Only 10 percent agreed to provide new

35. In 1983, I wrote that a solution to the debt problem required the acceptance by the creditors of a reduction in their claims just as in a bankruptcy. I tried to explain this to Volcker at the time, but he dismissed it (Meltzer, 1983). I published my proposal in a popular magazine to give it wide circulation.

36. Terence Checki at the New York bank did much of the preparation. The Treasury was not at first agreeable, as I learned when serving as an acting member of the Council of Economic Advisers in 1988. The council's 1989 report, written only a few months before Brady's announcement, called for reductions in principal, a watered-down recommendation to satisfy strong resistance from Treasury.

**Table 9.3** Nominal Exchange Rates (selected dates)

| | WEIGHTED AVERAGE | GERMAN MARKS | JAPANESE YEN |
|---|---|---|---|
| July 1980 | 84.6 | 1.75 | 221.1 |
| February 1985 | 158.4 | 3.30 | 260.5 |
| July 1985 | 140.9 | 3.06 | 241.1 |
| May 1987 | 96.0 | 1.79 | 140.6 |

Source: Board of Governors (1991).

loans; 40 percent agreed to cancel part of their debt. Governments and multilateral banks provided most of the new loans.

Volcker explained his reluctance to propose debt reductions by commercial banks. "I was concerned that countries that still had adequate means to pay would demand similar treatment" (Volcker and Gyohten, 1992, 217). This does not explain, however, the difference in treatment of domestic and international debt problems.

The Brady plans gradually ended this carryover from the 1970s and the Great Inflation and disinflation. As countries adopted stabilizing economic policies and greater openness, capital returned to the developing countries and investment increased.

*Depreciating the Dollar*

Appreciation of the dollar exchange was another issue left over from the Great Inflation and disinflation. Chart 9.1 earlier in this chapter shows the sustained appreciation from 1981 to 1985 and the subsequent depreciation of the real exchange rate from 1985 to 1987. Most of these changes mirror changes in the nominal exchange rate. Table 9.3 shows the appreciation from July 1980 to the peak in February 1985 followed by depreciation through July 1985 prior to the Plaza agreement (discussed below). May 1987 is the end of the depreciation.

The table brings out that for the period as a whole, the weighted average appreciated 13 percent, the mark barely changed, and the yen appreciated 36 percent against the dollar. But the swings within and between periods were large.

Critics of these swings made much of the current account deficit, the low saving rate, the budget deficit, and the dependence on foreign capital to finance investment and the budget deficit. Critics pointed out frequently that the United States was no longer a world creditor. Its net investment position fell from a peak surplus of $392 billion in 1979 to a deficit of $270 billion by the end of the decade. The deficit increased steadily in later years.

During President Reagan's first term, the Treasury opposed exchange rate intervention. Official rhetoric welcomed appreciation and irritated foreign governments by citing appreciation as evidence of economic strength. Foreigners complained about the budget deficit and the unwillingness or inability to reduce it. Appreciation of the dollar increased foreigners' exports but it also raised the domestic prices of their imports, including oil and other commodities priced in dollars. West Germany intervened frequently, at times by large amounts, to limit the depreciation of the mark. By 1984, the United States occasionally intervened but by lesser amounts.[37]

Germany faced two main problems. It announced an annual target for money growth keyed to the inflation rate it wished to maintain. Unsterilized intervention prevented the Bundesbank from reaching its target; it chose to accept more policy flexibility than it wanted. Also, Germany's exchange rate was a central rate for other European countries. Appreciation or depreciation of the mark-dollar exchange rate increased the difficulty of maintaining relatively stable exchange rates with its partners in western Europe. Dudler (1989) discussed the problems of Bundesbank policy during the period.[38] He insisted correctly that the Bundesbank authorities remained unconvinced that mostly sterilized intervention could "exert a lasting impact on the exchange rate or break underlying market trends" (ibid., 11).

On paper, United States international economic policy is mainly a responsibility of the Treasury Department. The Treasury can decide to fix the nominal exchange rate. Short of a decision to do so, the exchange rate is determined in the market in response to current and prospective economic conditions at home and in other principal countries. Federal Reserve policy—misleadingly called domestic policy—is a major factor influencing market views about future economic activity and inflation. The Federal Reserve's dominant role in setting monetary policy gives it a major influence on the exchange rate. Therefore, Treasury decisions to intervene in the exchange market are usually discussed with the Federal Reserve in advance.

At the start of President Reagan's second term, his chief of staff, James Baker, and his Secretary of the Treasury, Donald Regan, agreed to change places. Baker did not share Regan's views about exchange rates. He recognized and wanted to respond to the political pressures from manufacturers, farmers, and especially members of Congress. Exporting manufac-

37. For example, with the dollar at a local peak 3.17 marks per dollar, the Bundesbank sold $450 million and foreign central banks sold $1.5 billion in the last two weeks of September 1984. The Federal Reserve sold $135 million during that period (FOMC Minutes, October 2, 1984, 3). Volcker mentioned that there was informal coordination.

38. Hermann-Joseph Dudler was head of the Bundesbank's research department during this period.

turers complained about the value of the dollar that, they said, made it difficult for them to compete. Farmers could see that their products' prices in dollars were more expensive than foreign competitors'. Members of Congress reflected these complaints and responded by introducing bills to restrict imports and protect domestic markets.[39] Japan's trade surplus was their principal concern.

Volcker did not want to expand. He agreed that dollar appreciation had become a problem. "We could have gone out and eased policy, more than policy already was eased. I didn't want to do that, because I didn't think we had won the game yet, expectations were so fragile" (Mehrling, 2007, 183).

By the end of 1984, the United States' current account deficit—essentially the excess of imports over exports—reached $100 billion. Responding to these pressures and concerns, Baker and his deputy, Richard Darman, began discussions with the Japanese that ended at the Plaza Hotel in New York on September 21, 1984. At first, the discussions focused on both macroeconomic policies and exchange rates, but agreement was difficult to achieve. At the Plaza, five finance ministers and central bank governors agreed to attempt an orderly depreciation of the dollar.[40] As Table 9.3 shows, the dollar had depreciated substantially during the first half of 1985, before the agreement. The aim was to coordinate intervention policy and further depreciate the dollar. Volcker said, "The Plaza was basically a Treasury-inspired operation, which I was not terribly keen about" (Mehrling, 2007, 185). He described it as a "get-the-dollar-down operation" (ibid.).

The agreement created excitement in the press and financial markets and its implementation required frequent meetings and official consultations with press attention. Proponents of intervention and currency "zones" were delighted. And at the end of the intervention period, the dollar was lower particularly against the yen. The precise effect of the Plaza agreement and subsequent agreements is difficult to separate from other influences. One reason is that intervention was limited. Also, monetary policy changed in a way consistent with depreciation of the dollar.

Coordinated intervention appeals to many, as it did to Baker.[41] The

39. Gyohten (Volcker and Gyohten, 1992, 235) claims that Congress had 400 bills to restrict imports or to place surcharges on Japanese exports to the United States. Many of these actions pointed to Japan's restrictions on imports, including especially beef, tobacco, and rice. The Japanese claimed the problem was the large United States budget deficit. Volcker claimed that Prime Minister Thatcher told President Reagan that he had to do something about the dollar. The pound was close to $1 (Mehrling, 2007, 184).

40. Those of Britain, France, West Germany, Japan, and the United States.

41. Humpage (1991) is an excellent introduction to issues about the effectiveness of sterilized intervention. Balbach (1978) provides a detailed analysis of many alternatives.

Plaza agreement illustrates some of the problems. First, the Plaza meeting did not agree on changes in fiscal and monetary policies. Although the United States wanted Germany and Japan to increase aggregate demand, and they wanted the United States to reduce its budget deficit, the agreement did nothing of the kind. As in the 1977–78 discussions, Germany especially was unwilling to adopt coordinated macro-policies. The idea of coordinated policies has a superficial appeal that vanishes when a government has to tell its parliament that it wants to increase tax rates or reduce spending to help foreigners. Or, a government is reluctant to ask for more fiscal stimulus and risk inflation to accommodate another country. Germany had finally agreed reluctantly to fiscal stimulus in 1978. They did not believe the coordinated intervention produced the promised results. And they worried about the "clear risk that the authorities could miss their ultimate medium-term objectives for non-inflationary growth" (Dudler, 1989, 9). They remembered that although the July 1978 agreement was advanced as a means of keeping exchange rates stable, by November 1978 the Carter government had to intervene to defend the dollar.

Second, within the United States policy coordination often appeared to mean using monetary policy to finance fiscal deficits. Volcker was familiar with the coordination in the 1960s that began the Great Inflation. He did not want to sacrifice Federal Reserve independence to the Treasury and was wary of Treasury efforts to influence monetary policy. He expressed concern about the risk of inflation following rapid depreciation of the dollar.

Third, behind the bold talk about coordinated policy, there was little consensus about the aim of policy and about who would intervene and how much each would spend. The Germans claimed that the problem was mainly a U.S.-Japan problem. Dudler (1989, 11) reports the internal view. The Bundesbank "was determined, however, to reject binding exchange rate commitments which would have forced major central banks to indefinitely defend narrowly perceived target ranges for the biggest currencies." It favored inflation control over exchange rate management. The Germans wanted much greater appreciation of the yen than the mark. The United States did not want the agreement to call for depreciation of the dollar, so it referred to appreciation of other currencies. Volcker insisted on inserting "orderly" before "appreciation." He did not want to commit to a large change (Funabashi, 1989, 15).[42] However, a paper circulated at the meeting stated that "a 10 to 12 percent downward adjustment of the dollar

42. Funabashi was a Japanese journalist who interviewed most of the principals in these agreements.

from present levels would be manageable over near term" (ibid., 17). It is not clear how those who objected to dollar depreciation could agree to that statement. The depreciation reached these objectives before the end of 1985.[43]

Fourth, reports of the discussion did not mention real exchange rates. All of the discussion was about nominal rates. A discussion of real exchange rates would have brought economic policy to their attention. This did not happen. Ministers did complain to their counterparts about their policies, but they never agreed on what should or could be done. This is a weak link in any coordination effort.

Fifth, the meetings did not discuss the difference between sterilized and unsterilized intervention. This is surprising because the G-7 had authorized and read a report by an international committee, the Jurgensen report, that emphasized this distinction. The report concluded that sterilized intervention has little if any effect. Volcker and Funabashi suggest the probable reason for neglecting the distinction was that finance ministers and central bankers thought the distinction was "academic." That was an error. Sterilized intervention does not change the monetary base or the money stock, so it does not change the expected rate of inflation, interest rates, or the exchange rate. Coordinated intervention, even if sterilized, signals that the governments or central bankers may think exchange rates are misaligned. Markets may go along with them for a while, particularly as in 1985, when the dollar had depreciated substantially prior to the agreement.

In the 1980s, the Federal Reserve and the Bundesbank always sterilized their intervention. Both were independent and suspicious of efforts by the government to influence monetary policy. The Bank of Japan was not independent at the time and did not sterilize all of its sales of dollars. For that reason alone the yen appreciated more than other currencies. The Japanese government expressed concern frequently about the risk of controls on trade by the United States Congress.[44]

The Plaza meeting talked about $18 billion of intervention but did not set a target for the next few weeks to the end of October. The United States spent $3.2 billion. Other central banks in the G-10 spent $7 billion (ibid.,

43. Baltensperger (1999) discussed this period in the Bundesbank's history. He does not give much attention to the agreement as an influence on Bundesbank policy.

44. During the fall of 1984 and the winter of 1985, I was a visiting scholar at the Bank of Japan. Policy officials expressed concern about the risk of trade restrictions. They were concerned also that the strong dollar encouraged their export industries, such as automobile and consumer electronics, but other parts of their economy were less dependent on export markets. They expressed concern about distortions.

**Table 9.4** Current Account Deficits, 1983–89 ($ millions)

| | |
|---|---|
| 1983 | 9,956 |
| 1984 | 12,621 |
| 1985 | 15,473 |
| 1986 | 16,009 |
| 1987 | 14,575 |
| 1988 | 15,005 |
| 1989 | 14,720 |

Source: CEA (1991).

23). The Plaza agreement did not include an agreement on interest rates. West German rates moved very little in 1985, but short-term Japanese rates rose by one percentage point to 7.36 percent by the end of the year. The federal funds rate rose modestly, from 7.9 in September to 8.27 in December. The Board was reluctant to reduce the discount rate. Mainly it followed market rates. In Germany, the Bundesbank announced a monetary target, so it could adjust its exchange rate only by departing from its announced target. At times, it did.

When the Federal Reserve met in early October, Sam Cross of the New York bank reported on events following the Plaza agreement. The agreement was a surprise, but the ministers' statement was vague. At first the dollar fell 3 to 4 percent without any central bank intervention. Since there was no stated objective, the dollar began to appreciate. Heavy intervention, particularly in Japan, persuaded the speculators that the yen would appreciate. By October 1, official intervention by the central banks reached $2.5 billion, of which the United States contributed 15 percent. Germany remained more reluctant to intervene because changes in the mark's value disrupted its relations with the European currencies that had pegged to it.

What did intervention achieve? The dollar declined as shown in Chart 9.1 above. It is not clear if much can be attributed to exchange rate policies. Unsterilized Japanese intervention appreciated the yen. Baker's aim had been to reduce the current account deficit. Table 9.4 shows that the current account deficit rose through 1986 before declining modestly. The deficit was about the same in 1988 as in 1985. By 1988, the exchange rate policy had ended. Possibly lagged effects of the agreement had some influence on the deficit.

In February 1986, the Federal Reserve asked the regional banks to report on the effects of dollar depreciation. The overall summary states: "All of the summaries [by each reserve bank] of these reports began with a sentence like that from Boston. 'First District businesses have seen little, if any, impact from the decline in the value of the dollar, with respect to either input prices or, in the case of manufacturers, their firm's ability to compete in domestic and foreign markets'" (Board Records, February 4, 1986, 1). The most common explanation of the lack of response was delay. Some did not think the depreciation was permanent. A main reason for the lack of change was concentration on the exchange rate and failure to coordinate interest rate policy to achieve a reduction in the real value of the current account deficit.

The failure to agree on fiscal coordination, the absence of improvement in the current account deficit, and the decline in oil prices led Baker to make new efforts to coordinate. At the start of 1986, he urged countries to reduce their interest rates. The central bankers opposed (Funabashi, 1989, 45). As the economies slowed in early 1986, the Board received multiple requests to reduce the discount rate from 7.5 to 7.25 or 7 percent. The Board deferred action eight times, usually citing conditions in the foreign exchange market as one reason.

Oil prices declined from a peak of $26 a barrel to $12 at the end of 1985. The Saudis contributed by increasing production. The rate of increase in consumer prices followed, reflecting the fall in oil prices. But banking problems in the southwest increased as oil companies failed and homeowners defaulted on their mortgages. Soon thereafter, the Soviet Union defaulted on its debts.

Bordo and Schwartz (1991, table 1) report intervention by the United States for 1985–89. They show large purchases of marks in mid-October 1985 and no purchases from November 1985 to March 1989. The United States neither purchased nor sold during 1986 but sold marks and yen in 1987 and 1988. January 1987 was the peak month ($20 billion) for intervention done mainly by Germany and Japan to slow the depreciation of the dollar (ibid., table 3).

The more important change during the period was the increase in growth of the monetary base and money. The increase was greater in the United States than in Germany and Japan in 1985–86, so the dollar depreciated relative to the mark and the yen. More rapid expansion of the United States base began in May 1985 and continued until 1987. Twelve-month growth rose from 5.8 to 10.7 percent; the monthly average federal funds rate declined. A decline in oil prices contributed to the reported decline in measured inflation.

### *Discount Rate Action*

In February 1986, Charles Partee completed his term. President Reagan appointed Manuel Johnson to replace Partee and Wayne Angell to replace Lyle Gramley, who left in September 1985. Both began service early in February. Reagan appointees—Johnson, Angell, Martin, and Seger—now made up a majority. The weights they gave to inflation and expansion differed from Volcker's at times. This was true especially of Preston Martin.

With the economy slowing, the Board voted four to three on February 24 to reduce the discount rate to 7 percent. Volcker was in the minority. His concern was the belief that unilateral action by the Federal Reserve would cause the dollar to plunge and bring back inflation. The only previous time that the Board outvoted the chairman was in 1978, when Miller served as chair.

Volcker was angry. He was not accustomed to strong opposition and did not like it. Rumors spread that he would resign. Wayne Angell and Preston Martin were not prepared to continue a conflict, so they reversed their votes. The Board agreed to delay the discount rate action up to ten days while Volcker tried to obtain coordinated reductions in Japan and Germany.

The Board's action and reversal did not remain secret. Market commentary sided mainly with Volcker. The White House staff wanted the reduction mainly for domestic reasons in a year with a congressional election. Many stories at the time suggested that the Treasury encouraged the four members of the Board.

A few days later, February 27, Volcker reported on his conversations with foreign central bankers.[45] No one agreed to cut, but he believed they would do so. On March 6, the Board believed that other central banks would coordinate their actions. It voted unanimously to reduce the discount rate to 7 percent. Germany reduced to 3.5 percent and Japan to 4 percent. The press release cited the common action and the decline in market interest rates. At 7 percent, the discount rate was temporarily above the federal funds rate.

The economy continued to slow in April. Three banks proposed to reduce the discount rate to 6.5 percent. The Board deferred action, citing the desirability of international coordination. Concern about accelerating the decline in the dollar overcame concern about the economy. The delay was only four days. On April 18, the Board reduced the discount rate to 6.5 percent. It cited the decline in market rates, the weakening economy, and probable action by foreign governments. Governor Rice dissented.

On March 21, Preston Martin resigned to return to California. He had requested assurance that he would replace Volcker as chairman, when Volcker's term ended in August 1987. Secretary Baker would not make

45. On February 19, Volcker testified to the House Banking Committee. "A sharp depreciation in the external value of a currency carries pervasive inflationary threats" (quoted in Funabashi, 1989, 48). The dollar had fallen to 180 yen, about 25 percent in a year.

the commitment. In August, Manuel Johnson became vice chairman and Robert Heller replaced Martin as a member of the Board.

### *The Louvre Agreement*

Baker was dissatisfied with the progress toward closing the current account deficit. There was no immediate progress. At a series of meetings at the IMF, with the G-7 finance ministers, and with the West Germans and Japanese, he pressed the finance ministers to adopt expansive policies in the expectation that more growth abroad would increase United States' exports. As Volcker wrote, Baker seemed to want further dollar depreciation. "Whether that reflected frustration over the inability or unwillingness of Germany and Japan to take more aggressive expansionary action, or was an aggressive means of attempting to force such a response, was never really clear to me. In any case, by the middle of 1986 and early in 1987, the limits to this approach seemed increasingly evident" (Volcker and Gyohten, 1992, 260).

Gyohten gave the Japanese perspective (which the German government shared). "The surplus countries were obsessed by a deep suspicion that in introducing policy coordination and exchange rate management, the United States was trying to impose on them a system that would benefit only itself" (ibid., 263). This was the flaw in pleas and claims for policy coordination. It required countries to act in the interests of others, at times against their own perceived interest and when suspicious of Baker's motives. The result was an increasingly acrimonious relation between officials of the countries, particularly between Germany and the United States. Japan made more effort to cooperate with Baker. Kiichi Miyazawa, as minister of finance, persuaded the Bank of Japan to reduce its discount rate to 3 percent in October 1986, but other ministry officials were concerned about Japan's fiscal deficit and would not support fiscal expansion to satisfy Baker and Miyazawa.

Baker also faced opposition from the Federal Reserve. He may not have understood that a central bank that targets an exchange rate cannot control money stock growth or domestic interest rates, but Volcker did. Volcker was reluctant to relinquish central bank independence that he had worked so diligently to restore. As the dollar fell against the mark and the yen in 1986, resistance to further depreciation rose abroad. Governments accused the United States of talking down the dollar to gain economic advantage. In a sense, their discussion was back to the early 1970s. They wanted the United States to close its current account deficit without harming their exports. But now they could point to the U.S. budget deficit and urge fiscal restraint.

In January 1987, intervention reached a peak, more than $20 billion for the month, done almost entirely by Germany and Japan. The weighted average value of the dollar had declined more than 20 percent in a year (Board of Governors, 1991, 467). Complaints about Baker's policy reached a new peak. Baker responded to their complaints by adopting a new approach. He had become "intrigued by the target zones" (Mehrling, 2007, 185). He offered to agree to fix target zones for principal bilateral exchange rates in exchange for foreigners' commitment to more expansive policies. In February 1987, the G-7 finance ministers met at the Louvre in Paris to agree on the new approach. Like many other agreements reached by politicians, agreement required statements that could be interpreted in different ways. In this case, both Volcker and Hans Tietmeyer, president of the Bundesbank, were unwilling to sacrifice their independence. The agreement on target zones said that policy would "seek to maintain exchange rates around current levels for the time being" (Volcker and Gyohten, 1992, 267). "No effort was made to formalize the agreement and to obtain firm commitments. . . . The Germans felt they had made no clear commitment, and while the Japanese were willing to stop the rise of the yen, they were reluctant to support it from falling" (ibid., 268).[46]

The agreement did not work as planned. Gyohten explained that at the time of the agreement, the yen was 153.5 and the mark 1.825 to the dollar. The discussion mentioned maintaining a band of ±2.5 percent around these values. The ministers agreed to allocate $12 billion to defend the bands for the next three months. These values were not recorded in a document, and the details were not published or announced. By the end of April 1987, the yen had appreciated a further 10 percent. The mark appreciated within its band.[47]

The other part of the agreement called for greater efforts to expand by the surplus countries. Expansion in the United States slowed in 1986, and the agreement looked to the surplus countries to contribute more to world growth. Baker pointedly reminded the Germans of the agreement he thought they had made. They did not agree and did not act.

46. Volcker said, "I was much more in sympathy with [the Louvre] than the Plaza, not so much in the technical details but the general philosophy. . . . [Y]ou've got to worry about who is going to act if the ranges are threatened, and how" (Mehrling, 2007, 185).

47. Funabashi (1989, 188) reports that the Bank of Japan added $16 billion to its dollar reserves in the spring of 1987. The Federal Reserve sold about $3 billion in yen. At the April G-7 meeting of finance ministers, Miyazawa wanted intervention to push the yen back within the Louvre baseline. Instead, the ministers rebased the yen at 146 to the dollar ± 2.5 percent. Two days later, the yen appreciated to 144.2 to the dollar. The Bank of Japan intervened heavily, but the Germans were inactive (ibid., 190–91). It should have been clear that the Louvre had not adopted equilibrium real rates.

Volcker left the Federal Reserve in August 1987, when his second four-year term as chairman ended. Different stories are told about his departure. It is clear that Volcker and James Baker were not in agreement about co-ordination. Donald Regan was also not supportive. Both Baker and Regan were uncertain whether they could depend on Volcker to run an expansive policy in 1988. By 1987, Volcker had a Board appointed entirely by Reagan with many supply-siders with whom he did not agree. Baker secretly interviewed Alan Greenspan but waited for Volcker's decision. Volcker insisted in our interview that he had decided to leave. In June 1987, the president announced that Alan Greenspan would replace Volcker in August 1987.

The coordination policy ended abruptly after stock markets fell sharply all over the world in October 1987. Exchange rate policy had forced an increase in interest rates during the year. Concerns about a possible recession rose. At a meeting with President Reagan and James Baker, Beryl Sprinkel and others made a strong case for letting the dollar float.[48] It fell as the interest rate declined. Between October and December, the dollar depreciated from 1.80 to 1.63 marks per dollar.

Freed of concern about the exchange rate, the Federal Reserve assumed its stance as lender of last resort. Markets did not function smoothly in the aftermath of the stock market decline. There was a scramble for liquid assets. The Federal Reserve satisfied the demand, helped markets to settle transactions, and prevented the devastating secondary effects of the 1929 stock market drop. Economic growth resumed after a brief pause.[49]

### *Summary on Coordinated Policy*

Toyoo Gyohten described the results of three years of policy coordination as "not very satisfactory . . . because all our efforts in aligning exchange rates and coordinating macroeconomic policy had failed to produce tangible, clear results. The external imbalances . . . did not improve despite the major changes in exchange rate relationships" (Volcker and Gyohten, 1992, 269). If Baker's objective was to remove trade imbalances, it certainly failed. An alternative interpretation of his program emphasizes reducing congressional protectionist pressures. Though he did not eliminate those pressures, he managed to reduce them.

The objective was never clear; the ministers did not announce clear objectives or, in the Louvre agreement, announce the targeted rates. Lack of clarity contributed to the wrangling that went on at the time. Many Ger-

48. This recollection is based on a conversation with Sprinkel in 1988. Greenspan (2007) fails to mention this decision in his book.

49. For months newspapers printed a chart comparing the 1929 and 1987 stock market declines. The difference in policy ended the point of the comparison after a few months.

mans and Japanese thought that the principal objective was to improve the competitive position of the United States at their expense. They thought that the United States could show its commitment by reducing its budget deficit. The budget deficit declined for a few years beginning in 1987 but remained above $150 billion. If deficit reduction had received higher priority, perhaps cooperation would have increased.

Lack of an agreed objective and a commitment to achieve it was a major problem.[50] Previous experience with coordinated policies suggests the importance of a common objective and adequate means of achieving it. The gold standard from the 1870s to the start of World War I is an example of effective coordination through markets. Participants accepted a common objective—to keep exchange rates fixed—and a means of achieving the objective—buying and selling gold at a fixed price. Countries accepted primacy of the external value of their currency and permitted money stocks, interest rates, employment, and prices to vary as required by the exchange rate. The nations that agreed to stabilize exchange rates at the Louvre were not willing to relinquish control of interest rates and employment. The agreement had to break down, as it did in October 1987.

Other attempts at policy coordination through the gold exchange standard of the 1920s, the tripartite agreement of the 1930s, and the Bretton Woods Agreement lacked the commitment to a mutually agreed objective and full reliance on markets to achieve the objective. As earlier chapters show, the United States in practice did not respect the commitment to a fixed exchange rate under Bretton Woods, and surplus countries would not adjust their exchange rates enough to remove payments imbalances.

Proponents of target zones in the 1980s pointed to the virtues of increased exchange rate stability but said little or nothing about domestic consequences of maintaining permanently misaligned real exchange rates. Discussion was mainly about nominal, not the more important real, exchange rates.[51] Baker's program incorporated this weakness and Baker was either unwilling or unable to get agreement on the objective of policy coordination. As Volcker and Tietmeyer recognized at the time, successful coordination required monetary policy to achieve nominal exchange rate stability by forgoing use of monetary instruments to achieve low domestic

50. Even when finance ministers agreed to maintain exchange rate bands, they were reluctant to make them precise. Funabashi quotes Baker as saying, "Don't let us be too precise," a position that echoed German concerns. Nigel Lawson reaffirmed the position (Funabashi, 1989, 183).

51. The dollar depreciated 40 percent nominally and 30 percent in real terms in the two years after the Plaza (Volcker and Gyohten, 1992, 269).

inflation and stable growth. They never agreed to do that, so the program did not succeed.

After the experience with intervention, Henry Gonzales, chairman of House Banking, proposed that the General Accounting Office audit the Exchange Stabilization Fund (ESF) and the Federal Reserve's foreign currency operations. The report would remain confidential, but Congress would know how much intervention occurred and how much the account gained or lost.

Gonzales questioned the large purchases, a 165 percent increase in the ESF in two years. He recognized that the Federal Reserve enabled large purchases by "warehousing" for the Treasury. But Gonzales understood that "warehousing" was a thinly disguised loan and that the ESF purchases were expenditures made without congressional approval. He recognized also that there was not much evidence that the exchange operations stabilized exchange rates. Congress declined to act, however.

## END OF DISINFLATION

By spring 1986, the twelve-month average rate of consumer price increase had fallen to about 1.5 percent, the lowest rate since the early 1960s. These rates included the one-time decline in the level of oil prices, so they overstate the sustained decline. SPF forecasts of annual inflation fell to 2.5 to 3.5 percent in 1986. The unemployment rate continued to fall until it was below 6 percent by 1987. When Paul Volcker left the Board in August 1987, the unemployment rate was 6 percent, and twelve-month consumer price inflation was 4.2 percent.

Other adjustments to the end of high inflation included the end of regulation Q. Oil prices fell to less than $10 a barrel in 1986 contributing to the decline in measured inflation. The decline in long-term nominal and real interest rates began. Ten-year Treasury yields fell below 11 percent in May 1985 and below 10 percent in November 1985. From summer 1986 to spring 1987, ten-year nominal rates remained between 7 and 8 percent, with real yields about 3.5 percent.

The Great Inflation was over, and markets recognized that it was over. Although sustained inflation did not fall below 2 percent until 1997, the market acted on the belief that the high inflation of the late 1970s would not soon return.

The Federal Reserve had renewed its credibility as an anti-inflation central bank. It took a significant step in that direction in 1986, when the economy experienced slow growth in the last three quarters of that year. It lowered the federal funds rate and increased money growth, but inflation did not increase. Concerns that high inflation would return dissipated as the dollar declined without restoring inflation.

Problems remained. Financial fragility, bank failures, and problems in agriculture continued. Inflation remained above its long-term average and the unemployment rate remained above the consensus estimate of full employment. The imbalance between saving and investment maintained the large current account deficit. Restoring steady growth with low inflation left much to do, but markets began to reflect belief that the Federal Reserve could continue on that path. It had taken three years to lower the inflation rate to about 4 percent. It took an additional four years, to about 1986, to see expected low inflation incorporated in wages, interest rates, and the exchange rate.

## MONETARY POLICY IN 1985–86

The FOMC remained uncertain about the proper way to conduct policy. It did not want to remind the public about its flawed policies in the 1970s, so it did not set a federal funds rate target. It did not find monetary targets reliable in the short term, so it set them as the law required but did not adjust to meet them. That left borrowing, a return to the 1920s policy procedure of affecting interest rates indirectly. But the desk found that achieving that target was difficult. These procedures remained until after Alan Greenspan replaced Paul Volcker as chairman in August 1987. The Greenspan FOMC eventually set a narrow band around a federal funds rate target, but it adjusted the target as needed to maintain low inflation and relatively stable growth. Labor and product markets rewarded its success by reducing variability of inflation and growth.

Discussion of policy operations returned several times in the 1980s. President Robert Black and Vice President J. Alfred Broaddus Jr. of the Richmond bank proposed an explicit inflation target to "maintain the credibility of the Committee's longer run program to reduce inflation" (note, Black to FOMC, Board Records, February 6, 1987, 1). An inflation target would direct attention to the longer-term consequences of policy actions. That did not fit well with Volcker's operating tactics.

A memo from Michael Prell to the Board discussed the staff's use of the Phillips curve to forecast inflation. The memo recognized that "[i]n the long-run, money growth is the key determinant of inflation" (memo, Prell to the Board, Board Records, July 1876,1, 1). His memo distinguished one-time price level changes and persistent inflation. A chart comparing price acceleration and the unemployment rate showed a negative relation for the period 1954–85. The points are scattered over the page; the unemployment rate explains only 30 percent of price increases.

Despite Prell's memo, the staff continued to rely on the Phillips curve. Many FOMC members, including Volcker and later Greenspan, did not find the forecasts useful.

The FOMC remained divided. A lengthy discussion of operating procedures at the March 29, 1988, meeting considered a memo from Donald Kohn and Peter Sternlight (Board Records, March 25, 1987). The memo cited the loose relation between the funds rate and borrowing as the principal disadvantage. Since a main purpose was to manage the federal funds rate indirectly this problem seemed large in part because the market misread the System's intentions. Also, when the funds rate remained in its expected range, there was "little scope for market forces to show through."[52]

As usual, the discussion at the meeting was divided and inconclusive. A majority favored continued use of borrowing as their target. In late 1989, they decided to target the federal funds rate, and that decision remained.

Uncertainty about the economic future often dominated discussion during these years, reinforcing uncertainties about the policy instruments. "I don't attach a lot of weight to small changes in this forecast, whether it's prices or GNP within the ranges that are set. I don't think we know what GNP is going to be in this quarter. Things have less than an ebullient tone to them so I think: 'Fair enough: one might think of easing slightly if the dollar gave one room to do that.' I am not sure it does right at the moment" (Paul Volcker, FOMC Minutes, November 4–5, 1985, 21).

Policy actions tried to balance objectives for growth, employment, inflation, and the exchange rate without clear understanding of their interaction. Henry Wallich, after years on the Board, recognized that reliance on short-run changes was a source of error including procyclical actions that deepened inflations and recessions. "We have always leaned toward fine-tuning. When the economy is going down, immediately one sees what one could do by monetary policy if one doesn't think too much about the long lags. . . . What we do now in May may have effects early next year, at which time the problems we face may look quite different. There has been a proclivity at the Federal Reserve to push harder later in the cycle. . . . [O]ne tries hard to postpone the evil day and push back the moment when the economy flattens out so that we do not have to go into recession. . . . [I]nstead of a mild growth recession, one may get a real recession a little later" (FOMC Minutes, May 21, 1985, 14–15).

Wallich's statement might have started a discussion of the best way to

52. An attached memo by Anne-Marie Meulendyke from the New York operating staff reviewed the history of different targets used from the 1950s to the 1980s. It pointed to the need for procedures that controlled reserves or money over a longer period. But it pointed to the usual criticism that such procedures required large changes in the federal funds rate.

conduct monetary policy in a highly uncertain environment. A possible conclusion might have been that it was better to give priority to low and stable inflation and limit responses to short-run changes by setting long-term objectives and directing actions to that end. That didn't happen. The only response to Wallich's statement was a question from Volcker about what price Wallich would propose currently to pay for lower inflation. He and others ignored the more basic point. As usual, the members did not discuss their longer-term objectives or how to achieve them.

Concern about dollar appreciation produced an agreement among five countries—Germany, Japan, U.K., France, and the United States—to act in concert to hinder further appreciation. In mid-January, Secretary Regan warned the markets that intervention policy had changed from neglect to greater activism. At a telephone conference, Volcker discussed the Federal Reserve's responsibilities under the changed policy. He expected intervention to increase. Purchases of foreign currencies would be shared with the Exchange Stabilization Fund as in the past.

Apparently, the FOMC's role was to set limits on aggregate holding of international reserves and quotas for principal currencies—marks, yen, pounds sterling. Existing limits seemed adequate, so the FOMC did not vote. No one objected. Governor Partee usually opposed intervention, but he thought the situation was extreme. For the rest of the year, the FOMC received reports of intervention, but there was little discussion. At times the manager, Sam Cross, reported that foreign central banks complained that they intervened more heavily than the Federal Reserve.

The dollar continued to appreciate. In the three days from February 27 to March 1, 1985, the European central banks led by the Bundesbank sold $4.1 billion of dollars. The Federal Reserve bought $257.5 million of marks jointly with the Treasury. Cross reported that "the results were first judged to be inconclusive. On the one hand, the momentum of the dollar's rise was broken . . . On the other hand, many were impressed that the dollar did not fall precipitously under the pressure of heavy intervention" (FOMC Minutes, March 26, 1985, 2). Later, as evidence increased that economic growth was slowing, and financial failures in Ohio and later Maryland became known, the dollar resumed its long depreciation.[53] From a peak around 3.5 marks per dollar in early March the dollar reached 3.2 marks in mid-March. This was about the level in January, when the finance ministers agreed to intervene.

53. In the two months from mid-January to late March, central banks intervened with $10 billion. They considered this massive, but the exchange markets traded hundreds of billions a day at the time.

The most contentious issue about targets for monetary aggregates in 1985 was the extent to which the FOMC wanted to reduce inflation below 4 percent. Wallich and Gramley were in favor, but the proposal lacked general support. One problem was that the members had little confidence in the implicit forecast of monetary velocity. Frank Morris (Boston) said, "It seems to me that all we can do is assume that we're going to get trend velocity, anything else is pure speculation." Volcker responded, "The trouble is that we don't know what the trend is" (FOMC Minutes, February 12–13, 1985, 48). Volcker remained humble about how much could be known about the future.

### *Financial Fragility*

Financial problems worsened during the winter. On March 1, 1985, the Board issued regulations to increase capital standards first proposed in July 1984. At the same time, it authorized the director of the Board's Division of Banking Supervision and Regulation to issue preliminary notices if a state member bank or holding company had insufficient capital. The final notice required Board action (Board Minutes, March 1, 1985, 3–7).

In January, the Board became concerned about the solvency of deposit insurance agencies. The Federal Savings and Loan Insurance Corporation (FSLIC) eventually had to close as claims for payments rose. The Federal Deposit Insurance Corporation (FDIC) remained open, but insurance premiums increased. In January, the Board considered and approved increases in net worth for FSLIC-insured institutions proposed by the Federal Home Loan Bank Board (FHLBB). But both Boards were late in taking action. Part of the problem arose from the long-term portfolios of most savings and loans. Net worth would be slow to improve. In its letter to FHLBB, the Board commented that "we strongly support your efforts to tighten the capital requirements for FSLIC-insured depositories, and our questions concern whether the actions specifically proposed go far enough" (letter, Volcker to Edwin J. Gray, Board Minutes, January 2, 1985, 12).[54]

The FHLBB proposal revived interest in risk-related deposit insurance. Risk-taking institutions paid the same insurance charges as others. The incentive to take on risky investments increased as net worth declined. FHLBB proposed increased capital, improved and standardized accounting procedures, and better examination and supervision. Available resources limited examinations. The Board considered using private audits.

54. "Aggressive growth, even when capital is low is, of course, facilitated by the explicit and implicit protections afforded by FSLIC insurance and Home Loan Bank membership" (letter, Volcker to Edwin Gray, Board Minutes, January 2, 1985). Clear recognition did not lead to strong actions to protect taxpayers.

One member commented that the public now believed that the regulators accepted "too big to fail." The main decision called for increased capital including use of subordinated debt, but the Board delayed implementation.

In February, the FDIC proposed to send a letter to directors of all member banks urging strong action and threatening loss of membership. The Board's concern was that banks in agricultural areas would be subject to the threat because of their condition (Board Minutes, February 11, 1985, 6).

Failures and threats of failure increased beginning in March. A Florida securities dealer, ESM, suffered large withdrawals. The state of Florida could not quickly provide assistance. ESM applied to the Federal Reserve. Although some members expressed concern that ESM was certain to fail, and that loans would not save it, the Board approved the loans (Board Minutes, March 7, 1985, 2).

The next day the Board learned that the collapse of ESM hurt several Ohio savings banks. All had deposit insurance with the Ohio Deposit Guarantee Fund, a private insurance fund that insured 81 state chartered savings institutions. The report advised that the fund could not pay the losses and would fail. News of the problems at one of the banks, Home State, led to a run on others similarly insured. In the next two months, the problem spread to banks in Maryland, Massachusetts, and North Carolina that had private insurance.

The Board worked diligently to prevent failures. When the governor of Ohio closed the banks and allowed limited deposit withdrawals, the Federal Reserve agreed to lend enough to permit the withdrawals. Out-of-state banks acquired many of the failing institutions.

The Board did not follow the classical position set out by Bagehot more than a century earlier. He advised the central bank to lend freely to the market, against collateral at a penalty rate. The Board lent at standard rates to prevent banks from failing. Later many of the institutions were sold or merged. To its credit, the Board took an active role and did not repeat the errors made in the Great Depression.

The Board asked the Federal Advisory Council (FAC) to discuss regulation and supervision at its September meeting. FAC was critical of existing procedures. Regulators' responsibilities overlapped. Their rules differed. Capital standards differed. No single rule applied to all institutions. The rule should be conditional on portfolio risk and problem assets. Off–balance sheet risks should be included. Also, regulators should concentrate on safety and soundness and reduce emphasis on social and political issues. FAC proposed improved quality of examiners (Board Minutes, September 6, 1985, Supplement 1–2).

The FAC proposed reform of deposit insurance that introduced more market discipline. It favored risk adjusted premiums with rebates for conservative institutions. It criticized recent actions. "Greater market discipline can be accomplished by a very clear statement that absolutely no deposits above the statutory limit (currently $100,000) will be paid from the insurance funds in the event of failure" (ibid., 4). Then the FAC added, "Free market discipline will be effective only if a decision is made and explicitly communicated that depository institutions will be allowed to fail except where systemic risk prevails in the opinion of the regulators or other public interest factors are overriding" (ibid.).

Despite the proviso at the end, the FAC statement puts bankers in favor of failure and against bailouts. Within a few years, Congress adopted two significant changes in rules to reduce risk and give a larger role to market disciplines.

In 1989, Congress approved FIRREA, the Financial Institutions Reform, Recovery, and Enforcement Act. This act embodied congressional efforts to attribute problems in the thrift industry to malevolent owners and operators. There were such operators, but their contribution to the problem was much smaller than the press and members of Congress claimed. Regulation Q, inflation and disinflation, and the undiversified portfolios of most mortgage lenders played a much larger role. Like a depository institution, thrifts borrowed at short-term to lend at long-term, so periods of stress were inevitable. Reflecting congressional beliefs, FIRREA increased the number of individuals subject to enforcement actions. But it also lowered the "standard of harm" needed to support issuance of cease-and-desist orders. And it increased penalties for violations, thereby increasing incentives for responsible behavior (Brunmeier and Willardson, 2006, 24).

Two years later, Congress passed the Federal Deposit Insurance Corporation Improvement Act (FDICIA). FDICIA represented a major change in regulatory policy toward market incentives and market discipline in place of prohibitions and requirements. The main new feature called for structured early intervention. Instead of waiting for failures to happen, regulators could require an end to dividend payments or closure of the institution before net worth disappeared. This provision watered down the proposal by George Benston and George Kaufman leaving many decisions to policymakers' judgment instead of mandating a response. Congress talked about restricting "too big to fail," but many observers believe it did not succeed (Broaddus, 2000; Stern and Feldman, 2004). Stern and Feldman conclude that FDICIA made only a small change in policymakers' incentives (Stern and Feldman, 2004, 157). In the next banking crisis, 2007–9, the Federal Reserve and FDIC did not invoke FDICIA. Stern and Feldman's prediction was correct.

### *Watching and Worrying*

During most of 1985, the FOMC expressed concerns about uncertainty and did almost nothing. $M_1$ grew rapidly during much of the year, a source of worry and reinforcement of concern about inflation. The FOMC kept the federal funds rate between 7.5 and 8.5 percent, allowing a modest decline as the economy slowed in the spring. As usual, nominal base growth declined with the funds rate. Judged by monetary base growth, policy remained slightly procyclical.

At the July meeting, President Edward Boehne (Philadelphia) addressed the uncertainty that concerned most of the members. "One prudent way to move forward, if we really don't know quite what to do, is to go forward staying about where we are, keeping a very open mind about what we do three, four, five weeks from now, depending on how the economy comes in and the money numbers come in" (FOMC Minutes, July 9–10, 1985, 31).

Volcker replied, "That's about the way I would read it, yes" (ibid.). Several others supported the proposal. No one suggested setting a medium-term target. Almost everyone agreed to ignore rapid money growth. The main issue in contention was whether to rebase the annual target for $M_1$ growth to accept earlier growth. By 1987, the annual increase in the CPI reached 4.25 percent.

Volcker frequently expressed concern about the effect of dollar depreciation on the price level and the measured rate of inflation, but he and others also noted rising protectionist pressures. Like Secretary Baker, they favored depreciation to improve the trade balance and reduce protectionist pressures. The dollar had fallen 17 percent in three months to July 1985, so the concern was immediate. If they recognized that depreciation would at most affect the price level not the maintained rate of inflation, they did not say so.[55] Thus, they missed an opportunity to make clear their objective to themselves and others. Did they want to prevent the price level from rising? Or was their concern mainly with the sustained rate of inflation? Did they let the price effects of depreciation remain, or did they force other prices down to offset the price level effects of a rise in import prices?

Robert Black (Richmond) remarked that "the relationship between the level of borrowed reserves and the growth of $M_1$ is very tenuous and we keep getting fooled by that. . . . I would like to see us insert in our operating

55. Volcker: "Well, if I could blink my eyes and wake up tomorrow with a lower dollar and no accompanying change in attitudes . . . I might argue that that is a good thing. But that is an impossible scenario. The question is: How do we get a lower dollar if that is what we inevitably have to get over time without throwing inflation off course, interest rates off course, and without overshooting on the down side" (FOMC Minutes, August 20, 1985, 37).

**Table 9.5** Ranges and Results for Money Growth, 1986

| | RANGE | RESULT |
|---|---|---|
| $M_1$ | 3–8 | 15.0 |
| $M_2$ | 6–9 | 8.9 |
| $M_3$ | 6–9 | 8.7 |

instructions to the Desk something more explicit" (ibid., August 20, 1985, 26). His proposal did not fit with Volcker's eclecticism, and the Committee ignored it. Gerald Corrigan described their approach: "We've advanced from pragmatic monetarism to full-blown eclecticism" (FOMC Minutes, October 1, 1985, 33).

Eclecticism did not lead to any firm conclusion about what to do. Volcker summarized his judgment at the time as "no great desire to change things aggressively. . . . I don't know where we are on the economy; it's not looking very good. I do know the exchange rate is awfully high and I surely wouldn't want to push it any higher. I would rather do the reverse. I don't know what's going on with $M_1$ or $M_2$ or $M_3$. I know they are giving out different signals, but I don't feel very religious about $M_1$ at this point" (FOMC Minutes, May 21, 1985, 34).[56]

For the year 1986, $M_1$ far exceeded its pre-announced range, but $M_2$ and $M_3$ remained within their ranges, though near the top. Table 9.5 shows these ranges and the results recorded at the time.

In practice, no one paid attention to $M_3$. Members commented on $M_1$ and $M_2$ during the year, but those aggregates had minimal effect on policy actions. The models used by the staff to forecast the aggregates underestimated the size of changes. The velocities of each of the aggregates continued to decrease from 1981 to 1986 as expected inflation declined (memo, Donald Kohn to FOMC, December 10, 1986, chart 1).

The steady annual increase in velocity so apparent in data for the 1970s disappeared in the 1980s. The Board's staff (and many others) tried to explain the change by considering the redefinition of the various aggregates following deregulation. $M_1$ now included a large proportion of interest-earning deposits, and these deposits grew most rapidly in the 1980s. Staff estimates suggested that the response to interest rates increased in the 1980s. The spread between the rates for deposits and open market rates rose markedly in the 1980s; in 1986 open market rates declined by 200

56. Volcker chose a borrowing target. Roger Guffey (Kansas City) asked what the federal funds rate would be. Volcker responded with irritation, "[Y]ou ask this question every time, Roger, and I'm not a prophet" (FOMC Minutes, May 21, 1985, 42). Lyle Gramley suggested a target for the federal funds rate. Preston Martin responded, "Shame on you, Governor Gramley!" (ibid., 43).

basis points while rates offered by banks on NOW accounts declined only 60 basis points (ibid., 3).

Surprisingly, the staff did not consider the effect of the change in inflation. Rising inflation in the 1970s reduced desired cash balances, increasing monetary velocity. Lower inflation in the 1980s did the opposite. The change was a one-time change spread over time as the public learned or believed that the decline in inflation was likely to persist. Over the fifteen years beginning in 1990, $M_1$ velocity declined on average at a much lower rate than in the early 1980s, about 1.6 percent a year; $M_2$ velocity was about unchanged.

Even the most persistent advocates of targets for monetary aggregates could not explain their behavior or forecast the size and growth of the new components. The FOMC lowered the federal funds rate when real growth was negative (−0.8). The funds rate declined from 8.14 percent in January to 6.56 percent in July. Growth turned positive in the third and fourth quarters but remained below 1.5 percent annual rate. The funds rate continued to decline, reaching 5.85 percent in October. Although Volcker claimed that his target was borrowed reserves, these do not show a comparable pattern. By early 1987, the growth slowdown ended, and the federal funds rate was back to about 6.5 percent. It remained between 6.5 and 7 percent until Volcker left in August 1987.

The Board reduced the discount rate four times in 1986, from 7.5 to 5.5 percent. The first reduction was the now famous decision in March to coordinate the reduction with Germany and Japan. The vote was four to three, with Volcker in the minority. Volcker wrote out his resignation, but Governors Angell and Martin agreed to delay the reduction as noted earlier (Coyne, 1998, 11–12).[57] The second reduction, coordinated with the Bank of Japan, came on April 18, after deferring a reduction four days earlier. The remaining reductions on July 10 and August 20 were made without coordination. All four changes followed prior reductions in open market rates. Some reserve banks proposed an additional reduction to 5 percent after July 10, but the Board did not agree. Dallas, hurt by the oil price decline and agricultural distress, usually led these efforts, sometimes joined by other reserve banks. At 5.5 percent, discount rates reflected the decline in inflation and market interest rates.

The decline in interest rates came too late for troubled banks mainly

57. Coyne (1998, 14) thought that "[t]hings were never the same." Volcker left eighteen months later. "The four votes came from President Reagan's appointees and were prompted by White House staff" (ibid.).

in agricultural and oil producing areas. In 1986, 189 banks ceased operations. Most of them were non-member banks. This compares to an average of 8 a year from 1980 through 1984 (Board of Governors, 1991, 527–28). Problems at the banks also affected thrift institutions. The problems continued for several years.

### *Long-Term Securities*

At the end of the bills-only policy in 1960, the Federal Reserve portfolio held $24 billion of coupon securities, 89 percent of its portfolio. Over time, the amount held increased, but the proportion declined. At the end of 1985, system holdings reached $92 billion, 48.6 percent of the portfolio (memo, Normand Bernard to FOMC, Board Records, August 13, 1986, 9).

Paul Volcker asked why the System continued to purchase coupon securities. The account manager prepared a memo giving pros and cons. The principal advantages claimed were the information the desk received about the market and the enhanced market liquidity resulting from System purchases. (The latter is unlikely.) The main disadvantage arose because the System did not sell coupon issues. Their portfolio was, therefore, less liquid. Members' opinions divided, but no one strongly supported either position. The account manager wanted to continue, and no one objected strenuously. Pressure from Congress was probably the most important reason for buying and not selling.

## OTHER REGULATORY MATTERS

Financial fragility, legislative changes, and innovation continued to force regulatory change. The 1980s were very different from the 1930s. Deregulation became more attractive and tight regulation less attractive. Gradually the regulators recognized that every regulation offered an opportunity to profit from circumvention. Although regulators and Congress were not ready to repeal the Glass-Steagall Act, they began to move in that direction.

The Depository Institutions Deregulation Act mandated that ceiling rates for time deposits end on March 31, 1986. After that date, only the prohibition of interest payments on demand deposits and reserves remained of deposit interest rate regulation. The Board removed reserve requirements on some savings and money market deposit accounts at banks. It removed a $150,000 ceiling for business savings accounts, provided there were no more than three telephone transfers a month.

In June, the Board expanded the list of activities permitted to bank holding companies. The list now included consumer finance counseling, tax preparation, commodity trading, credit bureau and collection services, and appraisal of personal property. The Board also granted a limited amount of insurance activity to the holding company. Later, this authority expanded.

The Board expanded the definition of primary bank capital to include perpetual debt. A bank could use preferred stock and perpetual debt as primary capital up to one-third of capital.

The Board recommended that Congress revise the Bank Holding Company Act to broaden holding company powers and reduce regulatory burden. It asked Congress to permit holding companies to underwrite municipal revenue bonds, mortgage-backed securities, commercial paper, and mutual funds. It suggested also that Congress consider insurance and real estate brokerage and insurance underwriting. These proposals were a first step toward ending the separation of investment and commercial banking required by the Glass-Steagall Act.

The Garn-St. Germain Act of 1982 permitted banks to make interstate mergers and acquisitions of financially troubled thrift institutions and failed commercial banks. The Board asked for amendments that reduced some restrictions and permitted acquisition of failing as well as failed banks. In a letter to Senator Riegle, chairman of Senate Banking, Volcker urged legislation to alter or remove Glass-Steagall restrictions.

> Proceeding piecemeal within the context of a statute written in quite different circumstances can not assure results that are consistent with the public interest in promoting competition, serving consumer needs, and protecting the banking and financial systems.
>
> Because of these concerns, all of the members of the Board join in expressing our strong recommendation that the Congress act on these and other banking issues as early as possible in the next Congress. (letter, Volcker to Riegle, Board Minutes, December 24, 1986)

## CONCLUSION: WHY INFLATION DID NOT RETURN

A main, at times *the* main, objective in the years 1983–86 was to prevent the return of high inflation while maintaining expansion. There were two inflation "scares." The System successfully reversed the first in 1983–84, thereby contributing to its credibility and the subsequent decline in long rates. The second in 1987 occurred in Germany and Japan as well. It appears related to the effort to coordinate expansion while maintaining a fixed exchange rate.

Two main changes occurred. First, the Volcker FOMC, Volcker himself, and his successor Alan Greenspan put greater weight on inflation control. Interest rates increased at times during recessions or periods of rising unemployment if needed to control inflation. By 1994 the Federal Reserve finally accepted monetarist criticism and adopted counter-cyclical policies by reducing money growth during expansions and raising it during contractions. The Federal Reserve was less influenced by the idea that low interest rates always meant policy was expansive. No less important, FOMC members said repeatedly that low inflation encouraged and even facilitated high employment and economic growth. The facts supported them; the economy had three expansions of above average length in the twenty-five years after 1982. And the volatility of output and inflation declined, contributing to the belief that monetary policy had at last succeeded in restoring and maintaining economic stability.

Since the passage of the 1946 Employment Act, the Federal Reserve operated under some version of the "dual mandate" that after passage of the Humphrey-Hawkins Act became an explicit concern for both unemployment and inflation. Spokesmen for the Federal Reserve continued to accept the dual mandate, but the mandate was not precisely stated. In the early years, unemployment received most weight. Inflation became an objective when the inflation rate rose but only as long as the unemployment rate did not rise above 6 or 7 percent. After Humphrey-Hawkins and the disinflation, the Federal Reserve and other central banks recognized that the policy of abandoning inflation control to seek lower unemployment had brought more of both. The policy change sought to lower both by reducing inflation, keeping it low, and relying on clearer signals from relative prices and real returns to maintain growth and employment.

Second, market participants responded to excessive stimulus or perceived inflation by selling bonds, raising long-term interest rates, and bringing on an "inflation scare." The Federal Reserve responded to the scares. In this way, market behavior reinforced Federal Reserve actions and conversely (Goodfriend, 1993). By 1994, the FOMC was confident enough about its operations and secure in its ability to resist pressure to lower interest rates to announce its interest rate decisions as they made them. This required agreement on process—that they targeted the federal funds rate. It showed also that there was much greater understanding that the FOMC's success could continue if the market understood its actions, as rational expectations implied. With that recognition came heightened interest in communications, transparency, and rejection of the old idea that fooling the market was important or useful.

For an economist, it would be ideal to conclude that the Federal Reserve successfully applied modern economic theory to control inflation. Alas, it was not truc. Members of FOMC did not have a systematic approach based on analysis and evidence. Much of the time, members did not know what the operating target was. They voted for a target, but Volcker was eclectic. He did what seemed to him right at the time.

After Greenspan replaced Volcker, actions became more systematic at least as to choice of target. Greenspan's FOMC used a federal funds rate target after late 1989, but the choice depended more heavily on Greenspan's analysis of events than on any systematic economic model. The staff continued to use a Phillips curve to forecast inflation, but both chairmen did not.

The Federal Reserve in the 1980s and beyond accepted and relied on some monetarist propositions. It no longer denied that it was responsible for control of inflation; some accepted that money growth in excess of output growth caused inflation, and it asserted that low inflation was important for getting low and stable unemployment. Also it accepted that high interest rates reflected high expected inflation. It continued to insist that budget deficits caused inflation (memo, Volcker, Board Records, April 30, 1984, 2) and it did not develop successful procedures for controlling money growth.

Volcker expressed doubt about forecast accuracy. He relied on actual data, neglecting to say that revisions reduced data accuracy. At one point, November 1984, he recognized that imprecise forecasts made "fine tuning" impossible. But he did not take the next step—setting a medium-term target. Probably he did not accept that medium-term projections were reliable. The FOMC continued to respond to noisy current data.

The Federal Reserve staff continued to explain many of its forecast errors by claiming that the demand for money shifted. The staff, most members of the FOMC, and large parts of the academic and financial market community concluded that instability of the demand for money made control of money infeasible and undesirable. In 1988, the Federal Reserve staff reported on their research concerning monetary base control. The FOMC concluded that monetary base velocity fluctuated unpredictably in the short-run and required large changes in interest rates

At the time, Robert Rasche (1988) estimated the equations for velocity shown in the appendix to this chapter. His results, using monthly data for the St. Louis base (Appendix Table 1) and the Board's version (Appendix Table 2) show that the response of base velocity growth to changes in personal income, prices, and interest rates changed very little in the 1980s from experience from the 1950s through the 1970s. The principal and only important change was a decline in trend growth from 2.5 percent a year to zero.

In 1986, the staff reported on its ability to forecast money growth. The results showed that average absolute quarterly errors were large, almost two percentage points at annual rates in 1985–86. Annual forecasts for

**Table 9.6** Predicted and Actual $M_1$ Growth 1974–86

| YEAR | ACTUAL | PREDICTED | ERROR |
|---|---|---|---|
| 1974 | 4.8 | 5.0 | −0.2 |
| 1975 | 5.0 | 5.6 | −0.6 |
| 1976 | 6.1 | 6.5 | −0.4 |
| 1977 | 8.1 | 6.2 | 1.9 |
| 1978 | 8.2 | 7.6 | 0.6 |
| 1979 | 7.5 | 7.6 | −0.1 |
| 1980 | 7.3 | 9.7 | −2.3 |
| 1981 | 5.1 | 4.0 | 1.2 |
| 1982 | 8.8 | 8.8 | 0 |
| 1983 | 10.4 | 11.8 | −1.4 |
| 1984 | 5.4 | 5.7 | −0.2 |
| 1985 | 12.0 | 11.2 | 0.8 |
| 1986 | 13.0 | 11.6 | 1.4 |

Source: "Econometric Money Demand Analysis," Board Records, August 14, 1986, 4.

1974 to 1986 had an average absolute error of 0.8 percent. Years of policy change have large errors. Table 9.6 shows the forecasts and errors. The data suggest that control of inflation by controlling money growth is feasible if the Federal Reserve decided to pursue a medium-term strategy. And control of the monetary base requires the Federal Reserve to control only the size of its balance sheet. It can continue to set interest rate targets, but it must adjust the target at least quarterly to respond to the base.

It is impossible to date the end of the Great Inflation precisely. I have used 1986. The years 1983 to 1986 saw the unwinding of some main effects of the Great Inflation. Interest rate ceilings ended, and the preferred composition of portfolios changed. One main result was uncertainty about the reasons for growth in monetary aggregates, particularly $M_1$. Another was bankruptcy and merger of a large part of the thrift industry.

The anti-inflation policy and the enlarged defense spending that increased aggregate demand caused an appreciation of the dollar against most or all foreign currencies not pegged to the dollar. Pressure from foreigners, domestic exporters, and members of Congress brought a change in policy. By March 1985, the dollar began to depreciate. The new Treasury secretary, James Baker, wanted to demonstrate concern for the rising current account deficit and the strong dollar. He obtained agreement from Germany and Japan in September 1985 on coordinated efforts to depreciate the dollar. The agreement did not specify the policy changes to be made on either side, and it did not decide on appropriate exchange rates or policies. Most importantly, the agreement did not distinguish between real and nominal exchange rates or between sterilized and unsterilized intervention. The dollar depreciated in real and nominal value against the yen. Both the Bundesbank and the Federal Reserve sterilized most or all of their intervention, but the Federal Reserve increased base growth. Faster base growth contributed to depreciation. There was little effect on the current account deficit.

In retrospect, the action appears motivated more by politics than by consistent economic policy. It succeeded in preventing Congress from considering trade restrictions at the time. The dollar depreciated in real terms by the end of the decade.

Perhaps the most enduring lesson for central bankers from the Great Inflation and subsequent disinflation was that the responsibility for stopping inflation fell on them. Although Volcker and others pleaded frequently for reducing government spending and smaller deficits, their pleas did not produce the assistance they wanted. The experience of disinflation was painful for the economy and for them. They learned to avoid a repetition. The weights they gave to inflation and unemployment did not shift back to their earlier values and sustained high inflation did not return in the next two decades.

Experience in the 1970s convinced many that inflation was costly and undesirable. Disinflation in 1979–82 had public support that persisted as a desire for low inflation. The fact that the economy expanded in the 1980s and 1990s, that expansions were long and recessions mild, sustained the policy's popular support. Unemployment and interest rates eventually returned to the range experienced before the Great Inflation. Pressures to expand more or lower interest rates are always present, but the pressures were muted. The Federal Reserve learned that its policies could count on public, congressional, and administration support for low inflation by providing reasonably stable growth and low inflation. This support remained until the credit crisis that started in 2007.

## APPENDIX TO CHAPTER 9

Recent Behavior of Monetary Base Velocity[58]

Robert H. Rasche
Department of Economics
Michigan State University
East Lansing, Michigan 48824-1038

At the last meeting of the Shadow Committee I reported on research then underway concerning demand functions for the monetary base. In the

58. Prepared for meeting of the Shadow Open Market Committee in 1989.

interim, the staff of the Board of Governors has investigated the question of using the monetary base as target for monetary policy. A summary of that research is published as an appendix to the July, 1988 Monetary Policy Report to Congress [*Federal Reserve Bulletin,* August, 1988, pp. 530–33].

Apparently on the basis of this latter research, the FOMC has dismissed the possibility of any role for the monetary base in the implementation of monetary policy at the present time. "The Committee decided against establishing a range for the monetary base because it seemed unlikely to provide a more reliable guide for policy than the aggregates for which ranges already are established. Although the base has been less variable in relation to economic activity than M1, its velocity nonetheless has fluctuated appreciably and rather unpredictably from year to year." [Monetary Policy Report to Congress, July 13, 1988; *Federal Reserve Bulletin,* August, 1988, p. 519].

Unfortunately the staff research that is the basis for this conclusion is classified FOMC material at the present time, so we apparently have to wait at least five years before there is an opportunity to review the studies in detail. At the present time all that is available is the published appendix to the monetary policy report. Approximately 1/3 of that appendix is devoted to describing the differences between the Board measure of the monetary base and the St. Louis Federal Reserve Bank measure of the monetary base (Adjusted Monetary Base). The remainder of the appendix states four major conclusions:

> 1) [Statistical] technique that allow for a break in behavior (of base velocity) in the early 1980s . . . make somewhat smaller but still large errors in the 1980s and leave unanswered questions about the potential for additional shifts in the relationships.
>
> 2) The demand for the base has substantial interest sensitivity. . . . The base probably is less interest sensitive than are the other monetary aggregates.
>
> 3) Over long periods of time, the demand for the base appears to be fairly predictable, especially compared with M1-A and M1.
>
> 4) It is likely that the base, or for that matter any of the broader aggregates, could be controlled reasonably well over a span of several quarters—a period that would be meaningful in terms of the effects of monetary policy. However, the degree of interest rate volatility under base targeting could be quite substantial, especially in the short-to-intermediate run.

The remainder of this report will examine these major conclusions, particularly in light of our own research into the demand for the monetary base. The data presented here use both the Board and St. Louis Federal Reserve Bank monetary base concepts, and personal income. Since personal income is available on a monthly basis, this gives a substantial number of observations during the controversial 1980s period. Results available elsewhere [Rasche, 1988] suggest that the conclusions drawn from these data are consistent with those derived from other measures of aggregate economic activity such as GNP or final sales to domestic purchasers, and with other levels of time aggregation.

Any analysis of the demand for the monetary base, or monetary base velocity, has to recognize that while the experience of 1980s is not identical to that of the previous three decades, the similarities far exceed the differences. Emphasizing the similarities is more productive than emphasizing the differences. The primary lesson from the 50s–70s is that base velocity behaves like a random walk. That characterization of base velocity, and its implication for monetary policy, has been discussed many times by this committee. That fundamental property of base velocity *has not* changed in the 1980s.

Past changes of base velocity are of little, if any use, in predicting future changes in base velocity. The only significant difference in the behavior of base velocity between the 1980s and the previous three decades is the average month-to-month percentage change, or drift. Through 1981 the drift in the random walk of velocity was around 2.5 percent at annual rates; during the 1980s it is zero. After allowing for this break in the drift of base velocity, there is no evidence of increased variability in the 1980s compared with the previous experience.

Thus the first of the conclusions cited above is somewhat misleading. To my knowledge it is correct that no one has a convincing explanation for the shift in the drift of base (and M1) velocity that occurred abruptly in late 1981. This leaves us uncertain as to when, if ever, such a change might occur in the future. It would be nice to live without such uncertainty. Unfortunately this is beyond our present understanding. Yet this does not have to be a matter of major concern to monetary policymakers. First, the fact that over 80 months have passed with no reoccurrence of such a shift suggests that such shifts are not an everyday phenomenon but rather low probability events. Second, even if such shifts occur from time to time, base growth rules that incorporate feedbacks such as proposed by Meltzer (1986) or McCallum (1988), insulate the growth of nominal income from their effects. Thus, the occurrence of infrequent and unpredictable shifts in the drift of base velocity are not a basis for dismissing the monetary base as an operating guide for monetary policy.

The second and third conclusions cited above are consistent with our own research into the demand for the monetary base. As reported at the last Shadow meeting, our preferred specification for the demand for the monetary base is:

$$[\Delta\ln B_t - \Delta\ln Y_t] = \alpha + \beta^* \sum_{i=0}^{n} \Delta RTB_{t-i}/(n+1) + \vartheta^* \Delta\ln(Y/P)_t - \vartheta^* \sum_{i=0}^{n} \Delta\ln(Y/P)_{t-i}/n + \vartheta^* DINFU_t + \varphi^* D82_t + \varepsilon_t \quad (1)$$

where B is the monetary base, Y is nominal personal income, P is the deflator for personal income, RTB is the Treasury bill rate. DINFU is a measure on unexpected inflation and D82 is a dummy variable that is zero through 1981, 12 and 1.0 thereafter. Estimates of the parameters of equation (1) for the St. Louis Adjusted Monetary Base are presented in Table 9A.1 and for the Board Monetary Base are presented in Table 9A.2. Estimates are presented for a full sample period, and for sample periods through and subsequent to December, 1981.

The estimates for the Adjusted Monetary Base in Table 9A.1 indicate that, aside from the shift in the drift at the end of 1981, there is absolutely no difference in the estimated parameters or the standard error of the residuals, regardless of the sample period that is used in the estimation. In particular, the interest sensitivity and short-run real income elasticity parameter estimates from the 1982–88 sample for all practical purposes reproduce the estimates from the 50s–70s.

The results from the estimation for the Monetary Base in Table 9A.2 are quite similar to the results for the Adjusted Monetary Base. In this case there is some slight variation in the estimated parameter values from the pre-82 to the post-81 sample periods, and the standard error of the residuals is somewhat higher in the latter sample period. These differences are far too small to have any significance.

The residual standard errors in both of these tables are considerably smaller than those from the corresponding specifications in terms of M1 or M1-A, which provides support for the conclusion that monetary base velocity is more predictable than that of either measure of transactions money.

At first glance, the long-run interest elasticity of the demand for the monetary base, computed as β times the level of the Treasury bill rate, appears quite small in absolute value. This is an inference that should be treated with great caution. It may not be appropriate to construct an estimate of the long-run interest elasticity with such a calculation from this type of specification. The issues involved in the appropriate measurement of the interest elasticity of the monetary base, given the random walk nature of velocity are complex and highly technical. The highly preliminary results of other research that is currently underway into this question sug-

**Table 9A.1** Estimates of Adjusted Monetary Base Demand Equations Monthly Seasonally Adjusted Data at Annual Rates
[Dependent variable = $\delta \ln B_t - \delta \ln Y_t$]
Semi-Log Specification

| Sample | | 53,1–88,4 | 53,1–81,12 | 82,1–88,4 |
|---|---|---|---|---|
| α | | −2.4499 | −2.5128 | 0.0000 |
| | | (.2184) | (.2129) | |
| β | | −.0080 | −.0080 | −.0077 |
| | | (.0010) | (.0012) | (.0017) |
| θ | | −.8835 | −.8813 | −.8993 |
| | | (.0342) | (.0362) | (.0849) |
| Ø | | −2.4499 | na | na |
| | $\bar{R}^2$ | .65 | .65 | .62 |
| | se | 3.97 | 3.86 | 3.91 |
| | d-w | 1.86 | 1.91 | 1.72 |

**Table 9A.2** Estimates of Monetary Base Demand Equations Monthly Seasonally Adjusted Data at Annual Rates
[Dependent Variable = $\delta \ln B_t - \delta \ln Y_t$]
Semi-Log Specification

| Sample | | 59,2–88,4 | 59,2–81,12 | 82,1–88,4 |
|---|---|---|---|---|
| α | | −2.4787 | −2.5721 | 0.0000 |
| | | (.1943) | (.1908) | |
| β | | −.0054 | −.0045 | −.0067 |
| | | (.0008) | (.0010) | (.0015) |
| θ | | −.8445 | −.8374 | −.8683 |
| | | (.0297) | (.0322) | (.0732) |
| ø | | −2.4787 | na | na |
| | $\bar{R}^2$ | .73 | .72 | .66 |
| | se | 3.12 | 3.04 | 3.37 |
| | d-w | 1.62 | 1.67 | 1.50 |

gest a long-run interest elasticity of the monetary base of the order of −.3 to −.5. The corresponding long-run interest elasticities of M1 demand are somewhat larger in absolute value.

It is not at all clear that the demand for the monetary base is less interest sensitive than the demand for broader monetary aggregates such as M2 or M3. In the case of the broad aggregates, it is not possible to reject the hypothesis that the long-run interest elasticity is zero, computed under the assumption that own rates of return on deposits are fully adjusted to changes in market rates of interest. The size of the short-run interest elasticity of the broader aggregates is critically dependent upon how fast deposit rates are adjusted to changes in market rates of interest. Given regulation Q controls into 1985 on at least some types of deposit rates, there is very little experience from which to infer how unregulated deposit rates adjust to changes in market rates of interest.

When all the dust settles, the ultimate reason for the rejection by the FOMC of either measure of the monetary base as an operating instrument or target for monetary policy is the fourth conclusion above, namely that such an operating instrument would produce intolerable interest rate fluctuations. This is the historical basis of objections by the Federal Reserve to any monetary aggregate that has been proposed as a target or operating instrument for monetary policy. The substantive basis for this position is extremely weak. The experience with the New Operating Procedures in 1979–82 is typically cited as support. However, the experience of 1979–80 is contaminated by (1) the uncertainty of market participants (and perhaps also Federal Reserve officials) in the fall of 1979 about exactly how the New Operating Procedures would be implemented and (2) the credit controls fiasco in the spring of 1980. Analysis of the experience in 1981 and 1982 under the New Operating Procedures suggests that interest rate variability during this period was no greater than prior to 1979 or subsequent to 1982.

TEN

# Past Problems and Future Opportunities

Don't try tricks, don't try to be too clever; keep steady, keep committed to your mandate, even in exceptional circumstances; say as much as you can about what you are going to do: announce a "strategy"; don't be dogmatic, but follow a policy which is always in line with your strategy. (Issing, 2003)

Otmar Issing, a distinguished central banker, showed in his years spent guiding the European Central Bank how to operate successfully in the space between rules and discretion. He rejected both commitment to a fixed rule and no rule at all. He called it rule-like behavior. Central banks' policy should announce and implement a clear strategy that market participants understand and from which they can predict central bank responses. In the normal course of events, it should follow that strategy.

Central banks operate in an uncertain world. They have lender-of-last-resort responsibility in addition to their macroeconomic responsibility. Serving as lender of last resort requires departing from the normal operating rule or strategy. To prevent liquidity problems from becoming crises, the central bank must not follow a fixed strategy. The rule for crises should be known in advance, as Bagehot (1873) first stated clearly. It then becomes part of rule-like behavior.

The Federal Reserve's authority is delegated; the U.S. Constitution gives Congress the power over money. In 1913 Congress chose to appoint an agent to carry out these tasks. It granted independence, but it always retained the right to withdraw or restrict it. Members of the Board of Governors hesitate to act in ways that arouse public and congressional ire. This alone makes the Federal Reserve a political as well as an economic institution and weakens independence, as the preceding chapters show.

Political pressures also come, at times, from the administration. The Federal Reserve is not part of the administration, but its actions affect the degree of public support that an administration receives. The modern public holds the administration responsible for the state of the economy and its current and expected well-being. The administration can not sanction the Federal Reserve. Public complaints are usually counterproductive. There is a gap between responsibility and authority. The administration and Congress are held responsible for economic shortcomings; most people are unaware that the shortcomings often result from Federal Reserve actions and decisions.

A central bank is better able to resist political pressures if it has public support. The German Bundesbank and the Swiss National Bank established firm reputations as opponents of inflation that earned the respect and support of their countrymen. One way to gain and hold support is to operate in a known and predictable way, as Issing prescribed at the head of this chapter. Being successful is important.

Federal Reserve history has two major crises—the Great Depression of the 1930s, and the Great Inflation of the 1960s and 1970s and subsequent 1980s disinflation. Together these events occupy more than thirty years of the seventy-three-year history to 1986 considered in these volumes. The years of relatively stable growth and low inflation were many fewer until recently; 1923 to 1928 and 1952 to 1964 stand out. From the end of the Great Inflation to 2007, the United States experienced three of its longest expansions interrupted by relatively mild, brief recessions. Federal Reserve policy contributed to the change sometimes called "the great moderation." This chapter looks at some major past errors and some changes that contributed to better outcomes. Then it suggests some further changes, many of which FOMC members proposed on occasion.

The two principal sources of policy errors resulted from political interferences or pressure and mistaken beliefs. Volume 1 of the history made the case for mistaken beliefs or incorrect theory—mainly the real bills doctrine as a decisive cause of the failure to take effective action to limit, prevent, and end the Great Depression. A different set of beliefs and failure to resist political pressures caused the Federal Reserve to start and continue the Great Inflation. To end high inflation, Paul Volcker made two major changes. He increased Federal Reserve independence, and he gave greater weight to reducing inflation and permitted the unemployment rate and interest rates to rise as required to control inflation.[1]

1. Federal Reserve officials in the 1970s often gave concern about interest rate changes as a reason for failure to control money growth. This may have been a statement about perceived

At its founding in 1913–14, the Federal Reserve was a system of semi-autonomous regional banks with a supervisory board in Washington.[2] This arrangement was a compromise that reconciled populist fears that bankers would run the new system for their benefit with bankers' fears that the political authorities would run it for theirs. The compromise set off a struggle for control mainly between the Board in Washington and the New York reserve bank. Autonomy contributed to the Federal Reserve's failure in the early 1930s. The Banking Acts of 1933 and especially 1935 greatly reduced Reserve bank autonomy, greatly reduced the role of the bank's outside directors, and centralized control in Washington. The Banking Act of 1935 created the legal structure of the central bank that remains today.

The Board remained under the guidance of the Treasury from 1934 to 1951. It did not begin to exercise control until after the 1951 Accord. In the early years of the Martin era, 1951–54, the System agreed to the changes necessary to consolidate the Board's control and weaken the authority of the banks, especially New York.

External events made inevitable this change from a semi-autonomous system of banks to a central bank. In 1913, the United States was emerging as one of several world or regional powers. Financial markets had not consolidated. It was possible to have interest rates set regionally. London was the global center of finance, and European powers such as Britain, France, and Germany struggled for international dominance. Existence of the Federal Reserve created a national market in the United States that later brought regional interest rates closer together.

Occasionally, members of Congress question the role of the reserve bank presidents as members of FOMC, the presence of member bank directors on the boards of the reserve banks, and the fact that reserve bank presidents vote on national monetary policy but are not confirmed by the Senate. The usual response to comments of this kind stresses the importance of local information in interpreting national policy and the value of having different opinions voiced at FOMC meetings. The Federal Reserve has not committed to a single analytic model. At times, differences in approach gradually changed policy analysis and operations. Examples are the emphasis the St. Louis bank president gave to money growth and the Minneapolis bank gave to rational expectations. Also, the presidents and

---

political constraints or a complaint that inflation could not be controlled when government ran budget deficits. Perhaps both. Some recognized also that they failed to develop a medium-term strategy or the means of implementing it.

2. McAfee (2004, 29) wrote, "Our formal legislated structure still describes 12 unaffiliated specialized national banks run by their directors." He points out that practice strayed far from original intent and legislation.

their staff use anecdotal information acquired in discussions with local leaders to modify their forecasts or judgments.

In a country as large and diverse as the United States, differences in interpretation of events and their future implications are both inevitable and useful. If the members of FOMC accepted a precise model or a common rule, regional and analytic differences would be of lesser importance. That has not happened and is unlikely. The advantages of having the regional banks express differences of opinion should not be forsaken. Mark Willes, an effective and outspoken member of FOMC as president of the Minneapolis bank, emphasized the importance of independent research departments at the reserve banks as a major source of strength in the system (Willes, 1992, 8). Also, St. Louis, aided at times by Richmond and San Francisco, was an early proponent of an effective anti-inflation policy. President Ford (Atlanta) raised pertinent issues at many meetings in the 1980s, and Presidents Stern and Hoenig urged an end to too big to fail.

By 1950, and in the years that followed, the United States was a superpower of unparalleled strength. It proposed and brought to fruition an international order built upon the International Monetary Fund, the General Agreement on Tariffs and Trade, the World Bank, and, in the political sphere, the United Nations. The central financial markets had moved to New York or developed there. Monetary actions by the Federal Reserve influenced conditions at home and abroad. The original design would not have survived in the new conditions.

The Federal Reserve in 1951 was not well equipped to manage either the domestic or the international economy. Congress had approved the Employment Act of 1946 and the Bretton Woods Enabling Act of 1944. The former committed the government to preventing a return of the Great Depression by promising "maximum employment and purchasing power" but did not define either. The latter tied the dollar to gold and made the dollar the central currency in the international monetary system. No one mentioned that a central bank could not expect to realize both commitments unless it maintained low inflation or price stability.

The Federal Reserve resolved the conflict by accepting domestic concerns as its responsibility. The Banking Act of 1933 had restricted its international role; the Treasury took responsibility, although it relied on Federal Reserve members and staff for advice, recommendations, and assistance in financing currency support operations.

Volume 2, books 1 and 2, summarizes the main developments and actions in the years 1951 to 1986. It considers three main topics: the relation of Federal Reserve policy to monetary theory; the independence of the Federal Reserve; and inflation and disinflation. The Federal Reserve made many errors, as the text notes. Some of the principal errors reflected prevailing beliefs in the academic profession and elsewhere in society. These contributed to the weakening of independence and the persistence of inflation.

In addition to its two central banking functions—monetary policy and lender of last resort—the Federal Reserve regulates and supervises financial institutions. During the years discussed in this volume, there were several banking regulators. The Comptroller of the Currency, part of the Treasury, supervised and examined national banks. In the early 1960s, the Comptroller pushed deregulation, putting pressure on an often reluctant Federal Reserve to follow.

Regulations are often written by lawyers who approach problems and crises by introducing new prohibitions and restrictions. They have been slow to recognize that markets often respond to regulation by innovating to circumvent the regulation. Government securities funds and money market funds circumvented restrictions on rules that prohibited small buyers from purchasing Treasury bills and certificates of deposit that paid market interest rates. Protection of large banks as "too big to fail" encouraged mergers and giantism. One justification for deposit rate regulation was protection of thrift institutions that lent on home mortgages. This was a costly error. Markets developed money market funds to circumvent ceiling rates at banks and thrift institutions. Inflation and regulation combined to eliminate most thrift institutions and to force removal of most interest rate restrictions. Taxpayers paid between $120 and $150 billion to cover the losses of failed thrift institutions.

Central bankers spent several years developing risk-based standards. This raised the cost to banks of risky loans. In the current, internationally competitive, open financial system, to circumvent regulation banks removed risky assets from their balance sheets. Risk did not disappear. Risk shifted from the regulated, supervised, and monitored banks to many places. We learn where the risks have moved when failures arise. This policy is inconsistent with a proper lender-of-last-resort function. More regulation cannot solve this problem. Risky assets will gravitate to less regulated markets and institutions.

Time will pass before lawyers recognize that they must rely more on incentives and less on regulations that prohibit or require action. Market discipline—which often means failures—is a costly way to teach prudent and effective risk management. The principal alternative is effective internationally agreed incentives. Experience with recent efforts to agree on common rules for risk management that create incentives for stabilizing behavior suggest two major impediments. Lawyers have a large role in regulation; they emphasize command and control. Devising incentives for stability in a global economy is a challenge that economists have not accepted.[3]

Bagehot (1873) is famous for proposing a crisis rule: lend freely at a penalty rate against acceptable collateral. Central bankers who cite this rule often neglect another main message. Bagehot did not criticize the Bank of England for failing to lend. He insisted that the Bank announce its policy in advance and follow it. In more than ninety years, the Federal Reserve failed to announce its strategy for responding to crises. Sometimes it lends against collateral; sometimes it supports failing institutions with help from other agencies like the Federal Deposit Insurance Corporation. Past practice provides no guide to future conduct. By failing to announce a strategy, the Federal Reserve encourages failing institutions to press for assistance, urging help to avoid calamity. Absence of an explicit policy increases uncertainty. As Bagehot emphasized, market chaos continues until policy is known and implemented.

## SOME PRINCIPAL ERRORS

In the years 1951 to 1986 the Federal Open Market Committee never formulated or accepted a theory relating its actions to economic outcomes. Under the convention known as the "Riefler rule," the Board's staff did not make explicit forecasts until the mid-1960s. The staff then began to build an econometric model of the economy and to revise it from time to time. But judgmental forecasts coexisted with econometric forecasts, and the staff adjusted the econometric forecasts using judgment and new information. By the 1980s the Board's staff and the staffs of several reserve banks used econometric models to forecast and brief their principals. There was neither a common model nor general agreement on what it should contain. More importantly, the members of FOMC and its chairman remained appropriately skeptical about the relevance or accuracy of their staffs' models.

In the 1960s, many in the economics profession believed, or perhaps hoped, that large econometric models would provide consistently reliable forecasts of economic variables. In the 1970s, Robert Lucas (1976) showed why these hopes would not be realized. Economic outcomes depend on expectations. Responses adjust; people learn from observation and experience. Often large changes occur after forecasts have been made.

3. The Shadow Financial Regulatory Committee and several similar groups are exceptions to this statement. A main incentive is the compensation arrangement. Investment banks pay large bonuses. This encourages purchases and sales of highly risky assets that pay large commissions.

At the start of the period, in the 1950s, the Federal Reserve relied mainly on judgments about market conditions. Chairman Martin had no interest in economic or monetary explanations of events. Winfield Riefler, his main staff adviser, used a simple rule of thumb to guide policy actions—on average keep the sustained growth of money about equal to output growth. The FOMC met every three weeks to make a decision for the next three weeks. It did not follow Riefler's rule or any other. Members used several different policy indicators ranging from explicit values of free reserves, borrowing, or interest rates to color, tone, and feel or money market conditions. No one reconciled the members' statements, and no one could because the members did not have an agreed framework. That left decisions to the account manager and perhaps to Martin.

The 1950s were atheoretical and procyclical. Members interpreted interest rate increases or reductions in free reserves as tighter (more restrictive) policy and increased free reserves as easier (less restrictive) policy much as they had used borrowing in the 1920s. Often the main reason for the direction of change in free reserves was a change in member bank borrowing. In a slowing economy the public borrowed less, and the member banks repaid borrowing from the Federal Reserve. The Federal Reserve interpreted the increase in free reserves as evidence of easier policy mainly because free reserves rose and short-term interest rates declined. But fewer reserves meant a decline of the monetary base and money; to a monetary economist, the decline meant that policy was more restrictive. In recovery and expansion the opposite occurred. The mistaken interpretation of borrowing and interest rates contributed to procyclicality of monetary policy.

The System's standard explanation reasoned that banks were reluctant to borrow. When they repaid, they reduced their assets; they contracted, reducing aggregate reserves. But with fewer aggregate reserves, other banks borrowed, expanding money and credit. The Federal Reserve continued to hold this mistaken interpretation of borrowing even after it became clear that borrowing increased when it became profitable to borrow. Eventually the staff model made borrowing depend on the profitability of borrowing, but the FOMC was slow to accept that idea.

Although recessions occurred in 1953–54, in 1957–58, and in 1960–61, the Federal Reserve successfully maintained prosperity and low inflation to the mid-1960s. Despite the deficiencies and errors of its framework, policy was more successful than in the late 1960s and 1970s. Under its 1951 Accord with the Treasury, the Federal Reserve regained much of its independence, but it retained responsibility with the Treasury for successful debt management. Its role was to maintain unchanged money market conditions, called even keel, when the Treasury sold securities. During the

Eisenhower years, the administration favored balanced budgets except during recessions. Consequently, fiscal actions and deficit finance put much less pressure on interest rates than in later years, so money growth and interest rates remained generally moderate, and inflation was generally low. President Eisenhower expressed concern about unfavorable long-term consequences of anti-recession policy. After the deep 1957–58 recession, the Eisenhower administration promptly reduced its large budget deficit and rejected tax reduction because of its long-term budget consequences. The Federal Reserve moved to reduce inflation, reestablishing price stability by 1961. This was one of the rare occasions when policy acted to achieve long-term stability. This policy decision did not prevent tax reduction. The new administration reduced tax rates in 1964. More than thirty years later, President Clinton rejected proposals for tax reduction. The second Bush administration implemented them soon after taking office.

President Eisenhower started holding regular meetings to discuss economic policy that included Chairman Martin, but he did not pressure Martin and respected central bank independence. Principal members of Congress criticized the Federal Reserve's "bills only" policy. With support from many academic economists, they blamed the increase in long-term interest rates for slow growth. This was an analytic error; it claimed that the Federal Reserve could change the shape of the yield curve.

This claim became the basis of policy in 1961. The Federal Reserve accepted administration urging to buy long-term and sell short-term debt. Evidence suggests that the policy failed to achieve its objective of twisting the yield curve.

A major change occurred in the 1960s. The new administration gradually introduced activist Keynesian policies.[4] In addition to "twisting the yield curve," it urged the Federal Reserve to coordinate its operations with administration fiscal actions, called policy coordination. Many academic economists favored coordination. In practice, this meant financing more of the budget deficit by monetary expansion. This reduced central bank independence but did little harm as long as deficits remained small.

Deficits to finance the Vietnam War spending and for the so-called Great Society increased the size of deficits. Chairman Martin often said that the Federal Reserve was independent within government. In practice, this meant that the Federal Reserve was free to raise interest rates enough to stop a private spending boom. But Congress approved government spending without increasing taxes, so the Federal Reserve was obligated

4. Congress took a strong Keynesian approach in the report called *Employment, Growth and Price Levels* (Joint Economic Committee, 1960b, 6). The Federal Reserve demurred.

to help finance the deficit. Martin's beliefs about independence and policy coordination meant that money growth and inflation began to rise. Chairman Martin was strongly opposed to inflation, but his decisions started the Great Inflation. The Federal Reserve made the mistake of sacrificing its independence to coordinate. Many years passed before it restored independence. It learned that coordination worked only one way. The Federal Reserve supported administration actions, but there was no reciprocity.

The simple Keynesian models used at the time encouraged the belief that economists could control short-term changes in such principal economic variables as economic growth, inflation, employment, and investment. This was hubris. The models at the time did not recognize anticipations and uncertainty, did not distinguish temporary and persistent changes, or distinguish real output and inflation, or real and nominal values of interest rates and exchange rates. As the text notes, some FOMC members pointed to these errors or omissions at times, but the comments did not influence either theory or policy.

Perhaps the two most costly errors in the 1960s were the sacrifice of Federal Reserve independence and reliance on belief that economists could improve welfare by trading a little more inflation for a lower unemployment rate. At his meetings with Presidents Kennedy and Johnson, Chairman Martin rarely made explicit commitments, but he was slow to raise interest rates despite recognizing the start of inflation after 1964.[5] In 1968, he agreed that the administration's tax surcharge would lower interest rates. He did not promise to lower them by Federal Reserve action, but he responded to pressure to do so. By year-end he acknowledged that he had made a mistake.

Early versions of the Phillips curve implied that increased inflation would permanently lower the unemployment rate. This was based on an error—failure to distinguish nominal and real responses. Friedman (1968b) pointed out the error; he explained that persistent inflation would increase expected inflation and restore equilibrium employment. Any reduction in unemployment would be temporary, but the increase in inflation would persist.

Policy actions in the 1960s were based on two mistaken beliefs that persisted until disinflation policy began in 1979–80. First was the claim that in a modern market economy like the United States, inflation started to increase before the economy reached full employment. The policy solution called for government intervention in the wage and price process to

5. In 1962, he committed to keeping free reserves within a range. He did not tell the FOMC.

encourage non-inflationary settlements. In practice, the policy failed in the United States and abroad. It did not distinguish between price levels and rates of price change.

Second was dismissal of the role of money in monetary policy. For many years, the Federal Reserve gave most attention to money market conditions[6] and to credit and interest rates. Later, it introduced a "proviso clause" that called on the manager to raise market rates if some measure of bank credit, reserves, or money grew faster or slower than a specified rate. The manager rarely acted on the proviso. The Board staff often explained the failures by claiming that the demand for money shifted. They never provided evidence, not even when challenged to do so. Another explanation was that responding to money growth required large changes and much greater variability of market rates. A solution adopted by the German Bundesbank and later the European Central Bank ignored short-term variations but responded to medium-term growth of a principal monetary variable.

Nelson (2003a, 1054) argues that money "serves as a proxy for a variety of yields that matter for aggregate demand." As he notes, this is the implication of studies of the demand for money by Friedman, Schwartz, Brunner, and Meltzer. In periods when markets function well, short-term rates may summarize financial information. In periods when expectations are changing, other relative prices remain important.

Additional support comes from an exhaustive study of 1,000 demand functions for money. Knell and Stix (2004, 20) conclude in part, "In cases where a short rate is included with a long rate the short rate acts as an own rate (positive sign) for broad money but not for narrow money (negative sign). Concerning the size of the impact it is found that the sensitivity of money demand with respect to long rates is higher than with respect to short rates."

A reason often given for neglecting money in policy analyses is that monetary velocity is highly variable. Chart 10.1 relates base velocity to a long-term interest rate. Two notable features of these data are: (1) when interest rates in the 1960s returned to the levels reached in the 1920s, velocity returned to those levels also; (2) during the disinflation of the 1980s, velocity and the interest rate declined along the path on which it rose during the peak years of the Great Inflation.

A possible third error mentioned in the text was the often stated idea

6. In Chapter 4, I quote Stephen Axilrod, a principal staff member, expressing frustration about money market conditions. He noted that emphasis shifted from borrowing to free reserves, to color, tone, and feel, and other indicators. Money market conditions were often vague and loose and not closely related to inflation and growth.

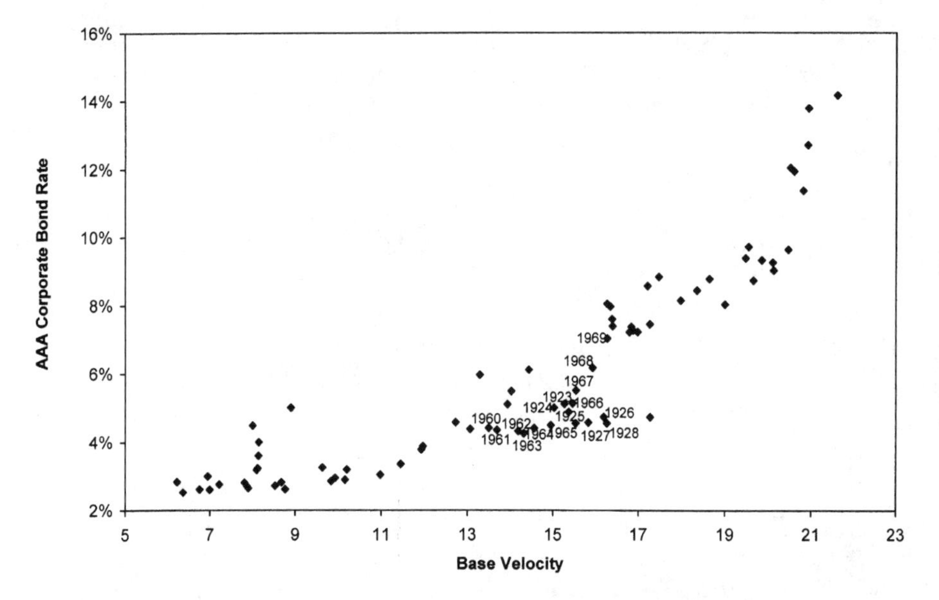


Chart 10.1. Velocity and interest rate, base velocity versus AAA corporate bond rate, 1919–97.

that the Federal Reserve should create uncertainty. Rational expectations implies the opposite. It took time for the Federal Reserve to recognize that it depends on market responses, so it has a strong interest in informing markets about its policy and its intentions, beliefs, and interpretations. There are, of course, limits to what it can say because it is necessarily uncertain about the future. By letting the public know about the rule or quasi-rule that it follows, it permits the market to interpret incoming data more accurately.

Chapter 3 shows that several members of the FOMC, led by Sherman Maisel, recognized some of the principal problems with operating procedures in the 1960s. Members mentioned uncertainty, the problem of distinguishing permanent and temporary changes, and absence of agreement on how Federal Reserve actions should be judged and how they affected the economy. Vice Chairman Balderston at times commented on the absence of procedures to achieve long-term objectives. Chairman Martin showed little interest and made few changes.

The new Nixon administration in 1969 brought a different team of economists to give advice and, after a year, a new chairman of the Board of Governors. The new team accepted that excessive money growth was the principal cause of inflation and that the long-run Phillips curve was vertical. Higher inflation could not permanently reduce the unemployment rate.

The new Federal Reserve chairman, Arthur Burns, opposed administration efforts to influence Federal Reserve policy, but he did not hesitate to instruct the administration. He continued to give greater weight to reducing the unemployment rate than to reducing inflation. And he proposed repeatedly that the government adopt wage and price guidelines to keep prices from rising. After repeatedly opposing wage-price policy, President Nixon changed course, imposing price and wage controls in 1971. Later, he eased controls. The efforts, both more and less restrictive, failed. Reported inflation rose especially after controls ended.

Burns and other advocates never made a convincing argument showing why controls of prices would work to control rates of price change. One of their mistakes was to mix control of one or more relative prices with control of the sustained rate of price change. Suppose controls prevented a rise in steel prices. Unless the change somehow reduced total spending and increased saving, buyers would have more money to spend elsewhere. The lower relative price of steel might change a price index, but it would not change the (correctly measured) rate of price change.

By suppressing the rise in the price level, controls encouraged the government to choose expansive policies to reduce unemployment. Unemployment was President Nixon's main political concern, lest it deny him reelection. Controls were a political success; he was reelected. But inflation rose.

The Federal Reserve sacrificed much of its remaining independence to lower unemployment in time for the 1972 election. Burns met frequently with President Nixon, who urged him repeatedly to increase money growth. Burns agreed, but he could not do it alone. The other members of the Board had been appointed by Presidents Kennedy and Johnson. They had no reason to support President Nixon's reelection. They acted on the belief that it was more important to reduce the unemployment rate than to control inflation. Like other members of the FOMC and principal members of Congress, they supported inflationary actions based on their beliefs about relative social costs. In some cases, FOMC members believed either that they would reduce inflation later or that inflation would not occur as long as price controls or slack remained. They were misled by their economic analysis and beliefs.

Failure to distinguish one-time price level changes from sustained rates of change became a more serious problem following oil price increases in 1973 and after. The Federal Reserve and many others did not separate the two reasons for higher prices. Both were taken as evidence of inflation. There was a difference, however. The one-time change in oil prices was a change in a relative price. Once it passed through the economy, the reported rate of price change would fall. If policy, especially monetary policy, remained unchanged, the reported rate of inflation would return to the rate preceding the oil price increase. The Federal Reserve's actions and public statements would work to prevent the public from anticipating a persistent increase in the rate of price change.

Slowing money growth in response to the oil price increase reduced aggregate demand in the mistaken belief that lower aggregate demand could offset the effect of reduced aggregate supply. Since the first effect of reduced money growth is on output, the unemployment rate rose to the highest level since the 1937–38 depression. Predictably, the Federal Reserve responded to increased unemployment by increasing money growth, thereby converting some of the one-time price level change into persistent inflation.

This was an analytic error. The oil price increase reduced wealth. The wealth loss had to be borne by reductions in real wages and profits. By mistaking the wealth loss for a recession, the Federal Reserve postponed the loss and increased inflation

Economic theory does not give a firm answer to the question, Should the central bank stabilize the price level or the rate of price change? The former gives the public an opportunity to plan on stable prices, a valuable contribution to those planning investments and allocating wealth over time. This benefit carries a cost. It requires the central bank to reverse any increase or decline in the price level. The classical gold standard produced such a result. Over long periods, the price level remained approximately constant. The costs of achieving stable prices under the gold standard proved higher than the modern public is willing to bear. In democratic countries especially, the public expected the state to respond to unemployment. We do not have the gold standard not because we do not know about the gold standard; it is because we know about its costs.

Inflation control, unlike price level control, does not promise to keep the price level stable. The price level becomes a random walk around the constant (perhaps zero) average inflation rate. Positive oil shocks cause the reported price level to rise and negative oil shocks cause it to fall. Once the shocks pass through, the reported rate of inflation returns to its previous zero or perhaps 2 percent per annum. Currency devaluations or revaluations, excise tax changes, and changes in productivity similarly affect the price level but not the maintained rate of inflation. Sustained changes in the productivity growth rate would change the sustained rate of inflation unless money growth adjusted.

The Federal Reserve is in the money business. It is responsible for growth of the money stock and its consequences. By controlling money growth it influences growth of aggregate demand. It has no direct influence on aggregate supply, so it can respond to positive aggregate supply shocks only by introducing an unanticipated reduction in aggregate demand, reducing spending to lower prices. Such action complicates unnecessarily the consumer's problem of determining expected future inflation and adds a monetary disturbance to the one-time reduction in measured output growth from the supply disturbance. Better to let the disturbance pass through. If government response is unavoidable, the supply shock should be seen as an increased tax paid to oil producers; offset it by lowering domestic tax rates.

The Federal Reserve treated the 1973 and 1979 supply shocks as inflationary. In 2006, they allowed the oil price increase to pass through and did not try to force other prices to offset it. They concentrated attention on preventing other prices from rising. This was a step forward. The Federal Reserve should complete the policy change by informing the public that they seek to control the maintained rate of price change, not the price level.

After 1979, "practical monetarism" replaced what remained of Keynesian analysis. In practice, practical monetarism suffered from three principal problems. First, monetarism is a medium- to long-term theory of inflation. Second, short-term money growth rates are relatively variable and difficult to forecast. Third, timing was poor. The Federal Reserve tried practical monetarism just at the time that Congress reduced financial regulation. This made it difficult to estimate how much money growth to permit. In 1982 the Federal Reserve gave up whatever remained of the policy of monetary control.

Paul Volcker recognized that monetary policy could not succeed based on quarterly or semiannual forecasts. At the policy discussion in December 1985 and elsewhere, he explicitly rejected short-term forecasts and fine tuning.[7] In contrast, some FOMC members describe policy as "data driven," suggesting that they change decisions based on noisy current data (Yellen, 2006, 3). That problem continues. Chairman Bernanke claimed that policy action should change only if new data change the outlook, and he has responded to noisy data in practice.

7. See Chapter 9 for the discussion and quotation. Stern and Feldman (2004, 2) reject the short-term focus that dominates policy decisions. "We conclude that current procedures put too much emphasis on short-term countercyclical policy and too little emphasis on long-term inflation control. We argue that these shortcomings could lead to significant monetary policy mistakes." At the time this is written, May 2009, the FOMC has responded again to market and congressional pressures by giving main weight to recession and unemployment and little weight to longer-term inflation.

The staff continued to use a Phillips curve to forecast inflation. Research has shown that a key input to the forecast, the full employment level or natural rate of unemployment, has not been estimated accurately (Stock and Watson 1999). Orphanides and van Orden (2004) showed that main errors in forecasting inflation resulted from the use of contemporary data. These data differed substantially from the later revised data. Atkeson and Ohanian (2001, 10) concluded that "for the last 15 years, economists have not produced a version of the Phillips curve that makes more accurate inflation forecasts than those from a naïve model." A principal reason is variability of the natural rate of unemployment or NAIRU.[8]

The text of Chapters 8 and 9 has many comments by Paul Volcker that praise the staff but dismiss their forecasts as inaccurate and unreliable. Alan Greenspan (2007, 170) also did not find staff inflation forecasts useful. "The 'natural rate,' while unambiguous in a model, and useful for historical analyses, has always proved elusive when estimated in real time. The number was continually revised and did not offer a stable platform for inflation forecasting or monetary policy." I believe economists and central bankers should take seriously this rejection of Phillips curve forecasts by the two most successful chairmen of the Board of Governors.

Orphanides and van Orden (2004) compared alternative inflation forecasts using information available to policymakers at the time of the forecast. They found that using information about unemployment, as in the standard Phillips curve, was less accurate and less reliable than other models they studied.

Current academic researchers and many central bank staffs work within the analytic framework developed in Woodford (2003). Michael Woodford's work is carefully and elegantly presented.[9] It uses the rational expectations paradigm. Two equations determine output and inflation. The central bank sets the only interest rate in the model. All other rates and relative prices depend on the model and rational expectations.

The money stock, bank credit, and other financial variables have no independent role. Setting the interest rate determines the money stock from the demand function. Long-term interest rates depend only on current and expected future short rates. The model cannot analyze the financial failures that were a main concern in 2007.

8. Dennis (2007, 3) has surveyed recent Phillips curves and concluded that they were useful pedagogically but were not useful for practical policymaking. Arthur Okun (1980, 818), who relied on Phillips curve forecasts as a presidential adviser, described the work as "seriously undermined when that empirical generalization collapsed."

9. The model builds on earlier work by Goodfriend and King (1997) and Clarida, Gertler, and Gali (1999).

A central bank that used the Woodford model to set the interest rate would have to judge whether the policy was correct by observing output and inflation. These respond with a lag to interest rate changes so in practice central bankers rely on other measures, including money and credit growth, housing starts, industrial production, employment and unemployment, and many other variables, including anecdotal reports from their districts. They believe that these variables provide relevant, independent information.

Alan Greenspan's interpretation of wage and profit data to infer a change in the productivity growth rate is a now famous example of data-based judgment improving on and replacing model-based forecasts. Model forecasts at the time called for higher interest rates. Greenspan resisted. Several years passed before the models confirmed the productivity increase.

Further, the Woodford model is not the first to dismiss the role of money. In the history of economics, money has been dismissed many times, only to return. The early Keynesian era and Chairman Martin's tenure are examples; the nineteenth-century Banking School is another. The high variability of short-period money growth makes money an unreliable indicator at this frequency. Long ago, the Federal Reserve learned that, using the St. Louis equation, quarterly changes in money did not promptly affect the rate of inflation, but persistent changes did. The European Central Bank ignores short-period changes but pays attention to maintained growth rates. The many charts in the text showing the relation of real base growth to real GDP growth before each recession is evidence of a reliable influence but not a constant lead. Researchers at the Bank of England wrote, "Understanding the role of money in the economy has always been an important issue for policymakers. . . . Monetary data can potentially provide important corroborative or incremental information about the outlook for inflation" (Berry et al., 2007, abstract). Earlier, Nelson (2002) showed that the monetary base growth had a significant effect on inflation in the United Kingdom.

A common result of research on the term structure of interest rates rejects the theory that explains long-term rates as dependent only on current short rates and expectations.[10] Rudebusch, Sack, and Swanson (2007) studied changes in the term premium. They found that the premium changes by amounts too large to ignore (Federal Reserve Bank of San Francisco, 2004).[11] Litterman and Scheinkman (1991) concluded that changes

10. A simple regression of current and lagged changes in the short-term rate on the change in the long-term rate using monthly data explains about 25 percent of the long-rate change in the period 1951–66 and 45 percent for 1967–81.

11. Many studies show a significant relation between recessions and the term structure of interest rates. These studies have two deficiencies. They relate two endogenous variables,

in longer-term bond yields reflect three factors: changes in the level of all interest rates, changes in the slope of the yield curve that raise or lower longer-term rates relative to short-term rates, and changes in the curvature of the yield curve. For example, an increase in energy prices that is expected to persist but not increase further raises short-term rates relative to long rates. An increase in anticipated inflation that is expected to persist raises all rates in a parallel shift. To interpret changes in level slope and curvature require more than a single short-term rate.

Feldstein (2003, 376) concluded that "the models are far too limited. . . . to be an operational guide to policy. The models inevitably give inadequate attention to financial conditions, to changing institutions, to international markets, and to many other things."

Lucas (2007, 168) concluded in his usual succinct way that neglect of money was a mistake. "Events since 1999 have not tested the importance of the [ECB's] second monetary pillar. . . . I am concerned that this encouraging but brief period of success will foster the opinion, already widely held, that the monetary pillar is superfluous and lead monetary policy analysis back to the kind of muddled eclecticisms that brought us the 1970s inflation."

This rejects the use of models with only one interest rate and no role for money. It suggests a role for asset markets including credit and money, and it supports the distinction between price level changes and maintained inflation (Brunner and Meltzer 1989, 1993). Svensson (2002–3, 9) accepts part of this view. "Any realistic model of the economy requires more variables than just inflation and the output gap to describe the state of the economy."

Mistaken models of the economy contributed to policy mistakes.[12] It is an unfortunate fact, nonetheless a fact, that the Federal Reserve produced better results for the economy in the atheoretical 1950s and the eclectic 1980s and 1990s. I believe that part of the problem in the 1960s and 1970s was that there was too much emphasis on quarterly forecasts and

usually an unreliable procedure. And they seek to explain real output using differences in nominal interest rates.

12. A recent costly error based on faulty judgment was the concern with deflation in 2003. An economy with a very large budget deficit and a depreciating currency is extremely unlikely to experience deflation. The Federal Reserve did not accept this argument. Its concern for deflation delayed the increase in the federal funds rate, contributing to the subsequent housing price increase and substantial expansion of housing credit at low introductory rates. Federal Reserve history shows that concerns about a zero bound for a single short-term rate are misplaced. There are many non-zero interest rates and relative prices. Sellon (2003) supports the analyses in Brunner and Meltzer (1968) rejecting the standard liquidity trap and zero bound.

too little attention to medium- and long-term policy implications. Economics is not the science that gives reliable quarterly forecasts. Currently, there is no such science. Federal Reserve policy will do better at achieving stable growth and low inflation if it directs more attention to medium- or longer-term results.

International monetary policy varied from the classical gold standard at the start in 1913 to fluctuating exchange rates after 1973. Efforts to coordinate international policy in the 1920s under the gold exchange standard reflected the strong public belief in the gold standard at that time. In the 1930s, Britain, France, and the United States attempted limited coordination under the Tripartite Agreement. In the postwar period from 1945 to 1973, most countries adopted the Bretton Woods system. Later, the 1978 and 1985–86 agreements to coordinate broke down. All such efforts failed.

Two related reasons dominate. First, the public and policy typically give greater weight to avoiding recession and perhaps inflation than to maintaining fixed exchange rates. Second, governments take responsibility for social problems, including but not limited to unemployment, and use budget expenditure or tax changes that produce budget deficits. Third, governments have little interest in adjusting policies for the benefit of other countries. Given these conditions, international coordination or fixed exchange rates are unlikely to return to the United States.

In nearly a century of experience with financial failures, the Federal Reserve never developed and announced a lender-of-last-resort policy. Sometimes it lets the institution fail; sometimes it lends to keep it solvent. Failure to announce and follow an explicit strategy increases uncertainty and encourages troubled institutions to press for bailouts at taxpayers' expense. The credit crisis after 2007 is the latest example.

Many of the faults and errors arise for three principal reasons. First, the FOMC gives excessive weight to current and near-term events over which it has little control. Longer-term consequences that could be prevented or achieved receive little attention. Much of the discussion at FOMC meetings is about whether to change the federal funds rate by 0.25 percentage points. Forecasts that look ahead a year or more have little observable effect on current or future actions. The Federal Reserve has not developed procedures that adjust its actions to achieve its medium- or longer-term objectives.

Second, economic data are subject to permanent and temporary changes. Oil price changes are examples of permanent or persistent changes that are usually unforeseen. Bank failures, especially failure of a large bank or financial firm, can occur without prior warning. Most changes in productivity growth are of this kind. Wars, major political events, and currency devaluations or revaluations are other examples. Permanent or persistent changes alter wealth and income. Adjustment to persistent changes in the environment can cause temporary changes in consumption investment, employment, and measured rates of price change. Most of these changes are real, not monetary. The Federal Reserve has to learn to make the distinction.

Third, the Federal Reserve frequently confuses private and public interest. This occurs especially in its response to banking and financial problems. Preventing financial failures protects stockholders often at the expense of taxpayers. The Federal Reserve's public responsibility requires maintenance of the payments system. Depositors are insured.

The Federal Reserve makes mistakes. No readers of these volumes should have any doubt about that. Many of the mistaken actions result from errors, but not all. During the Great Inflation, Board members and the FOMC often failed to distinguish between nominal and real values. Some errors reflect uncertainty about the future. Also, the Federal Reserve is the agent of Congress. Too many of its actions respond to actual or perceived congressional pressure. To protect its independence from congressional legislation, it accedes to political pressure.

Not all chairmen are intimidated. In August 1982 Paul Volcker refused to commit to reduce interest rates if Congress voted to reduce the budget. His decision came despite his efforts to reduce interest rates at the time. This was unusual.

Offsetting some of the errors are some notable achievements. These include developing the payments system, maintaining a reputation for integrity and the absence of corruption, abetting development of an efficient financial system, managing a complex domestic and international monetary system under changing external conditions, and recognizing that it is lender of last resort to the entire financial system.

A strong, independent chairman can overcome the emphasis on the short term. The Federal Reserve, and its then chairman, deserve praise and respect for reducing inflation after fifteen years of increasing inflation amid widespread skepticism. This remarkable period in Federal Reserve history brought in the period known as "the great moderation." The next chairman maintained low inflation and relatively stable growth. Success of this kind increases public confidence and reduces congressional and administration pressures. The country experienced three of the longest periods of growth punctuated with mild recessions.

## TOWARD BETTER RESULTS

In more than twenty countries, central banks have now (2009) adopted some type of inflation target as the policy goal. Usually the goal is a dual mandate—stable growth and low inflation. The European Central Bank has a legally stated objective to maintain price stability. But it does not ignore unemployment. A principal benefit of a stated objective for inflation is that it directs attention toward a medium-term objective and away from the excessive concentration on current and near-term changes. The Federal Reserve greatly needs to give more attention to the medium-term consequences of its action.

The earlier chapters show that some FOMC members recognized at times the need to direct more attention to the medium term. Proposals of this kind had no effect on policy action or decisions. Although it has not adopted an explicit inflation target, the FOMC has encouraged the belief that it has a 1 to 2 percent target. There is, as yet, little evidence that the possible target consistently affects FOMC decisions.

Four reasons bolster the case for directing more attention to the medium term. First, quarterly values of several of the variables FOMC members watch can be described as near random walks. Output or real GDP is one of those variables. Short-term movements are dominated by random movements that cannot be predicted reliably or controlled effectively.

Second, Federal Reserve quarterly forecasts have smaller errors in the recent more stable years than the errors that I summarized in my presidential address to the Western Economic Association (Meltzer, 1987). Forecast errors are still large. McNees (1995, table 7) reported mean absolute forecast errors by private and FOMC forecasters for the years 1983 to 1994. Table 10.1 shows these errors.[13] The table shows that most FOMC forecasts are about as accurate as the average of private forecasts. Inflation forecasts for eighteen months ahead were better than other forecasts.

One striking conclusion is that short-term forecasts are not substantially more accurate than forecasts one-and-a-half years ahead. Also, forecast errors for near-term real GDP growth of about 1 percent are a large fraction of average growth—2.5 to 3 percent. This suggests that aiming at a longer term would not greatly reduce accuracy. And by concentrating on longer-term results, accuracy might improve.

Chart 10.2 shows the difference between forecast and reported values of real output from 1971 through 1999.[14] There seems little benefit to be gained from continued reliance on short-term forecasts. The Federal Reserve should not ignore current data. It should reduce the weight given to

13. Blue chip forecasts are the median value of a large number of professional forecasters. FOMC forecasts were made semiannually by members of FOMC. The data show the range and central tendency for these forecasts. Many other summaries of forecast errors yield similar results. In 2008, the FOMC members started to publish quarterly forecasts.

14. SPF forecasts are similar to Board of Governors staff forecasts.

**Table 10.1** Forecast Errors, Blue Chip, and Midpoints of the Range and Central Tendency of FOMC Forecasts, 1983–94

| HALF YEAR | REAL GDP | INFLATION | UNEMPLOYMENT RATE |
|---|---|---|---|
| Blue Chip | 1.0 | 0.6 | 0.3 |
| FOMC Range | 1.0 | 0.6 | 0.3 |
| FOMC Central Tend. | 0.9 | 0.6 | 0.3 |
| ONE YEAR | | | |
| Blue Chip | 1.2 | 0.8 | 0.5 |
| FOMC Range | 1.2 | 0.7 | 0.4 |
| FOMC Central Tend. | 1.3 | 0.6 | 0.5 |
| ONE-AND-A-HALF YEARS | | | |
| Blue Chip | 1.0 | 1.2 | 0.7 |
| FOMC Range | 1.2 | 0.9 | 0.7 |
| FOMC Central Tend. | 1.0 | 0.8 | 0.7 |

Source: McNees (1995).

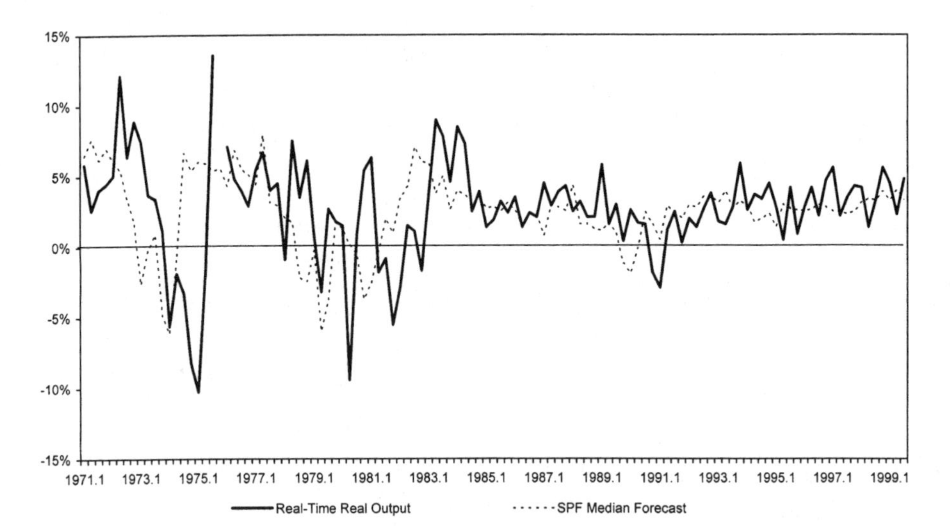


Chart 10.2. Median forecast of real output from survey of professional forecasters versus "real time" real output, 1971:1–1999:3. Real output measured as GNP through 1991, as GDP thereafter.

these data using the method explained in Muth (1960) that extracts the persistent component in the data. Muth showed that the weights attached to transitory and permanent changes should reflect the relative variances of the two types of change.

Third, data revisions are a second source of error. Although data revisions are large at times and capable of misleading policymakers, revisions are less troublesome than forecast errors. Chart 10.3 shows the size of data revisions. In the relatively stable 1990s, data revisions became less trouble-

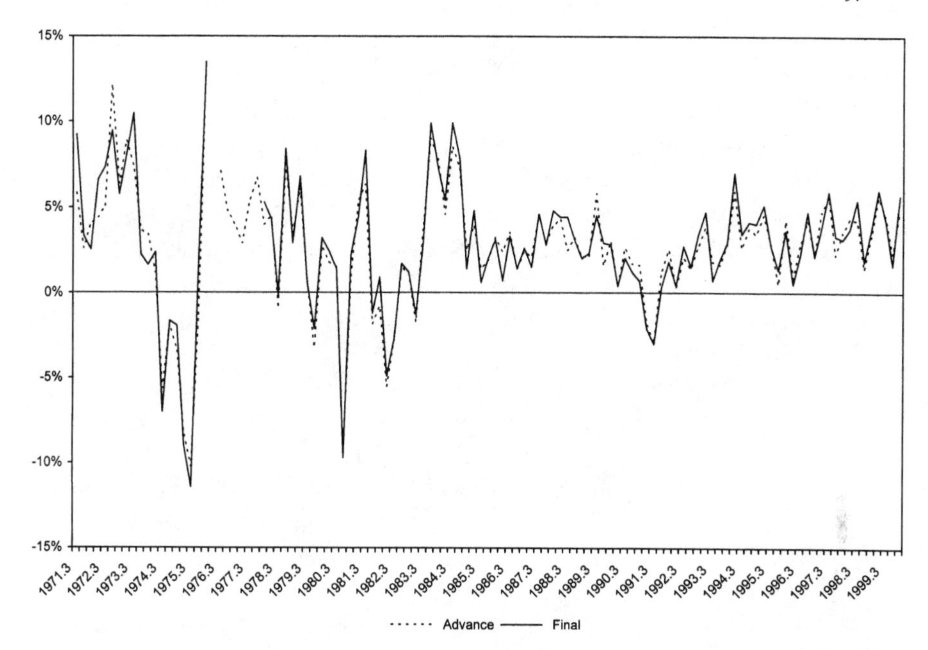


Chart 10.3. Revised real output versus "real time" real output, 1971:1–1999:3. Real output measured as GNP through 1991, as GDP thereafter.

some.[15] However, the July 2005 revision of national income accounts (not shown on Chart 10.3) raised the 2004 inflation rate from 1.6 to 2.2 percent.

Fourth, central banks make their judgments under considerable uncertainty about the evolution of the economy, the public's behavior, financial innovation, and a host of other events, including errors in reported data. One source of uncertainty is the persistence of observed changes and failure to separate persistent and temporary changes. Some of the latter reverse promptly.

To reduce the influence of temporary or one-time changes the Federal Reserve relies on a measure of inflation that excludes volatile food and energy prices. This moves in the right direction. As noted above, Muth (1960) proposed a better alternative. If the transitory variance is relatively large, the reported change is considered transitory, so the best response is to do nothing. If the permanent variance is relatively large, the change is likely to

15. Here is an example: The Bureau of Labor Statistics (BLS) reports payroll employment and unemployment on the first Friday of the next month. Employment is close to 140 million. BLS tries to hold its estimate within 1 percent of total employment. It fails frequently. Small changes in the seasonal factor can produce large errors (Furchgott-Roth, 2007). The Federal Reserve pays considerable attention to the announced unemployment rate despite frequent large revisions.

persist, so policy should respond. In intermediate cases, the proper size of the response depends on the degree to which it appears to be persistent.

Adhering to an explicit inflation target can overcome the problem of giving excessive attention to recent events and reports that are frequently revised. Some FOMC members have recognized these problems, but until recently they did not offer an alternative. Flexible inflation targeting that seeks to control inflation and minimize loss of output is an alternative. But it should not be adopted without congressional acceptance of the proposal. Congress could require a target for the unemployment rate as in Humphrey-Hawkins legislation. Congressional authority over money stems from the Constitution. The Federal Reserve is its agent. If principal members of Congress concerned with monetary policy do not accept or acquiesce in the proposal, it is unlikely to succeed or remain.

Inflation targeting introduces rule-like behavior, the type of behavior Otmar Issing suggested in the epigraph to this chapter. It provides a solution that is neither fully discretionary nor a rigid rule. Under the dual mandate, the public knows that the central bank aims to achieve both a low rate of inflation and sustained growth, so it can develop its plans with less fear of unanticipated disturbances. Of course unforeseen events do occur. Financial distress is one of the most important: The Federal Reserve is the lender of last resort. To carry out this function, it departs temporarily from its rule-like stance for monetary policy. Former Chief of Staff Stephen Axilrod concluded after years of experience that the best course for monetary policy is somewhere between discretion and a rule.

Since the 1970s, the Federal Reserve has improved its operation as lender of last resort. It recognized that this function requires response to the financial system, not just banks. But in its more than ninety years, it has never announced a strategy or rule, and it has not been consistent. It helped First Pennsylvania and Franklin National to survive. It allowed Drexel, Burnham to fail, but it helped in the rescue of Long-Term Capital Management. These and many other examples create uncertainty that contributes to the virulence of the market's reaction to crises and to pressures for assistance and bailouts. Recent credit problems show much evidence of changing actions and inconsistent responses.

Significant changes in policymaking occurred in the 1980s and thereafter. The Federal Reserve now distinguishes real and nominal interest rates and exchange rates. It recognizes that policy should not be made one meeting at a time, although it is not always willing to give longer-term objectives greater weight than short-term, possibly transitory or random, events. It gave up regulation Q interest rate ceilings. In 1994 and 2001, it successfully implemented counter-cyclical policy actions. In 1994 it began to announce the current interest rate target and some clues to what it planned for the next meeting.

The Federal Reserve did not adopt a rule, but it encouraged the belief that it aimed at a 1 to 2 percent inflation rate, presumably in the deflator for personal consumption expenditure net of food and fuel prices.[16] Economists then opened discussion of what in addition a central bank should announce. Some proposed announcing a path for expected interest rates or policy actions. Others proposed publication of quarterly forecasts for output and inflation or financial market risk.[17] Some smaller central banks publish their interest rate projections. They are price takers in the interest rate market. The Federal Reserve is a price setter; its announcements carry weight in world markets, so it must be cautious about what it announces. A possible rule of thumb is to release information that it believes will not mislead the public and the market. The information should enhance, or at least not diminish, Federal Reserve credibility.

Many central banks make explicit their objective of controlling inflation, and they recognize the central role of inflationary expectations in the inflationary process. This, also, could be a major change for the Federal Reserve.

The Federal Reserve has not tried to agree on a common framework for analyzing the economy and its actions. The best that it can expect to do is agree on a rule such as the Taylor (1993) interest rate rule or the Meltzer (1987) and McCallum (1988) rule for monetary base growth. These rules are compatible with several different models or frameworks. FOMC members with different views can base their decisions on a rule without trying to agree on the model that determines the economy's path. These rules are relatively simple, an advantage in communicating them.

Fischer (1994) and Blinder (1998) proposed that the political authority should choose the central bank's objective, leaving the central bank freedom to choose how to achieve the objective. Few countries go as far as the Europeans who set the objective—price stability—in law. The United States law in 1946 called for maximum employment and purchasing power and left to officials to decide on the interpretation. In 1977, Congress amended the Federal Reserve Act to make the objective maximum employment, stable

16. This measure is subject to larger revisions than the consumer price index. As noted above, for "rule" one should read "rule-like behavior." Blinder (1998, 37) objected to treating rules based on outcomes as rules because central bankers had to make judgments to adapt to changing circumstances. Announcing the "rule" informs the public about the bank's medium-term objectives. In November 2007, it brought back overall price inflation in addition to "core" measures.

17. FOMC has announced and published forecasts semiannually for thirty years. In November 2007, it changed to quarterly frequency and extended the range of its forecasts to three years ahead.

prices, and moderate long-term interest rates. In practice, the Federal Reserve chooses its objective aware that congressional committees and the public have to be informed. This procedure permits the Federal Reserve, as in 1979–82, to take unpopular action to achieve a popular medium-term goal. Independent choice of objectives can be valuable. Congress can, if it chooses, demand a different objective, as some members started to do in 1982.

One of the lessons of Federal Reserve history is that coordination agreements with other central banks fail and are abandoned. The basic reason is that the primary objective of modern central banks in principal countries is domestic. International coordination introduces a conflicting objective, usually the nominal exchange rate. The gold exchange standard, the Tripartite Agreement, Bretton Woods, and the Louvre agreement all failed. One or more countries was unwilling to put exchange rate stability ahead of domestic employment and price stability.

It is well-known that no country can achieve internal and external stability acting alone. To achieve some of the advantages of international coordination while pursuing domestic goals, the major central banks—the Federal Reserve, the European Central Bank, and the Bank of Japan—can announce a domestic inflation target, preferably a common target. The common target would gradually remove or reduce changes in expected inflation as a source of exchange rate adjustment, leaving real exchange rate adjustment as the principal reason for change. Each country would manage its policy without active coordination (Meltzer, 1987).

This system permits small and medium-sized countries to fix their exchange rate to one or more of the large countries. They benefit by having a fixed exchange rate and importing low, or preferably zero, inflation. The three major countries benefit by facing fixed exchange rates at small and medium-sized countries while permitting real and nominal exchange rate adjustment to changes in productivity, tastes, and demands.

In recent years, some economists have proposed that central banks should respond to asset price changes as well as output and inflation. In many papers, Karl Brunner and I introduce asset prices and expected returns to capital as variables important in the transmission of monetary policy. These models separated markets for money and credit. The underlying structure had three assets: base money, government debt, and real capital. Recent work by Goodfriend and McCallum (2007) brings a modern version of money and credit market interaction.[18]

18. Earlier Bernanke and Blinder (1988) introduced a "credit channel." They add bank lending as a distinct asset market and implicitly combine bonds and real capital, so assets consist of money, credit, and a mix of bonds and real capital.

Empirical estimates from these models provide information about the response of reported inflation and output to asset prices. A major problem for central banks and others is to determine whether asset price changes reveal inflationary pressures, productivity changes, or changes in the expected return to capital that raise or reduce the real value of assets. Central banks should not respond to asset price changes. If they can identify the inflationary component, central banks should respond to expected inflation from this source as from any other. That is, they should follow rule-like behavior.

The Federal Reserve should increase its effort to develop a common framework for analyzing the economy and the transmission path by which policy and other changes influence its objectives. Currently, there are three approaches. First is an elaborated version of the IS-LM model supplemented by a Phillips curve and some expectations model. This has been used and modified for decades. It was the source of persistent, large errors in forecasting inflation. Second is the analytic model developed by Woodford (2003), which emphasizes the role of rational expectations as the link between a short-term interest rate and other relative prices. Third is the relative price transmission mechanism (Brunner and Meltzer, 1993 and elsewhere). It highlights the central role of asset prices and the expected return to real capital in the transmission of policy and other impulses. In this model, monetary policy changes the relative price of current and future consumption and the relative price of new and existing capital.

## CONCLUSION

This chapter summarizes some of the main lessons learned by the Federal Reserve and other central banks from experience and actions. Central banks are much more professional and, as a consequence, better equipped to avoid major mistakes of the past. Through much of the last half of the twentieth century, central banks struggled to find an alternative to the gold standard rule and the rule for balanced budgets. Economists pointed out that the gold standard was procyclical and that discretionary monetary and fiscal actions could produce well-timed policy changes that would improve welfare. They ignored the discipline that the two rules maintained. The result was a large inflation lasting many years and reaching many countries. One result of the Great Inflation was renewed effort to develop stabilizing rules for the conduct of monetary policy. Following the German Bundesbank's relatively successful results, the Maastricht Treaty adopted the Bundesbank's objective—price stability—as the policy objective.

Progress can continue. Useful steps include more attention to rule-like behavior, more attention to medium-term consequences, less attention to noisy quarterly or monthly data, and a common international inflation rule that increases nominal exchange rate stability. Reliance on the Taylor rule as a medium-term guide is a good place to start. In conducting its function as regulator of financial firms and lender of last resort, the Federal Reserve should give more attention to incentives, and less to command and control, and it should announce and follow a rule or strategy for crises. Lawyers and bureaucrats write most regulations. Markets decide how and whether to circumvent them. Regulation will be more effective if it takes account of the incentives it creates and adjusts its rule to give incentives for improved behavior.

Large future budget deficits to pay for promised social security and health care benefits will likely challenge the Federal Reserve in the future. Inflation is one way of reducing the real value of these promises. If Congress is unwilling to reduce promised benefits or raise tax rates, the Federal Reserve will be pressed to expand money growth to finance deficits. Adopting a non-inflationary rule may help to reduce pressures to inflate.

Experience in the twenty years following the Great Inflation suggests the size of the welfare gain from avoiding inflation and disinflation. The economy experienced three of the longest periods of growth with only two relatively mild recessions. Per capita disposable income increased 33 percent, an average of 1.6 percent a year. Real aggregate personal consumption rose from $4.2 trillion to $8.2 trillion, $200 billion per year. Inflation remained low. This is an enviable record that monetary policy should seek to repeat regularly.

To end this history, it is useful to repeat from the start of Volume 1 the advice Henry Thornton ([1802] 1962, 259) gave independent central bankers two hundred years ago. The policy should be

> to limit the total amount of paper issued, and to resort for this purpose, whenever the temptation to borrow is strong, to some effectual principle of restriction; in no case, however, materially to diminish the sum in circulation, but to let it vibrate only within certain limits; to allow a slow and cautious extension of it, as the general trade of the kingdom enlarges itself . . . To suffer the solicitations of the merchants, or the wishes of government, to determine the measure of bank issues, is unquestionably to adopt a very false principle of conduct.

# EPILOGUE: THE UNITED STATES IN THE GLOBAL FINANCIAL CRISIS OF 2007–9

Events following the start of the housing, mortgage, and credit market crises in summer 2007 opened a new chapter in Federal Reserve history. Never before had it taken responsibility as lender of last resort to the entire financial system, never before had it expanded its balance sheet by hundreds of billions of dollars or more over a short period, and never before had it willingly purchased so many illiquid assets that it must hope will become liquid assets as the economy improves. Chairman Ben Bernanke seemed willing to sacrifice much of the independence that Paul Volcker restored in the 1980s. He worked closely with the Treasury and yielded to pressures from the chairs of the House and Senate Banking Committees and others in Congress.

Events highlighted several of the flaws in Federal Reserve policy discussed in this volume. Current pressures dominated longer-term objectives. The Board had never developed or enunciated a lender-of-last-resort policy. Markets had to observe its actions and interpret the statements as always in the past. Instead of reducing uncertainty by offering and following an explicit lending policy rule, it continued to prevent some failures while permitting others. It failed to give a believable explanation of its reasons and reasoning.

One of the main failings of monetary policy in 1970s was the neglect of longer-term consequences of near-time actions. Whenever the unemployment rate rose to about 7 percent, the members abandoned any concern about the inflationary consequences of their actions. Preventing inflation

Marvin Goodfriend, Alan Greenspan, Robert Hetzel, Andrew Levin, John Taylor, and Peter Wallison provided helpful comments. Fallout from the crisis continues as this is written.

had to wait. When the right time came, it didn't remain long enough to end inflation. Raising interest rates and slowing money growth raised the unemployment rate, so policy became expansive again. The result: inflation and unemployment both rose.

We seem likely to repeat these mistaken actions. In 2008, the Federal Reserve increased its balance sheet from about $800 billion to more than $2.2 trillion. Many of the assets it acquired are illiquid. The market's demand for reserves rose because participants were frightened and uncertain, and lacked confidence that financial fragility and failure would end. Once confidence begins to return, the Federal Reserve will have to absorb a large volume of reserves. The 1970s problem will return in an exaggerated form.

Economists and central bankers have discussed policy discretion for many years. Discretion enabled the Federal Reserve to make the many mistakes discussed in this volume and to facilitate the risky loans that are the source of credit and economic problems after August 2007. The main lesson of these experiences should be that monetary policy should remain consistent with a rule, not a rigid rule but rule-like behavior that responds both to short-term fluctuations in output and employment and to maintaining low inflation. Discretion has made too many errors.

In 2008 Congress approved $700 billion for the Treasury to use to support banks and financial institutions. The Treasury lacked a coherent plan and frequently allowed its actions to differ from its statement, adding to uncertainty and lack of confidence in policy. By year-end the Treasury had helped 206 banks, and the Federal Reserve had lent $100 billion to support a large failed insurance company. At year-end, President Bush advanced loans to prevent bankruptcy by General Motors and Chrysler, and the Federal Reserve accepted GMAC as a bank so that GMAC could borrow at the discount rate. GMAC immediately offered zero percent interest rate loans to borrowers with less than median credit ratings, precisely the type of loans that caused the crisis.

Financial problems spread to many other countries. Asset owners ran to the dollar and U.S. Treasury securities for safety. This pushed Treasury bill rates to zero or slightly above and lowered longer-term rates. Managing the reversal of these flows will be a major challenge for the Federal Reserve in the future.

Current housing and credit market problems gave rise to expected new claims blaming financial deregulation and hailing the end of American-style capitalism or, in more extreme instances, the end of capitalism. It is hard to ignore such comments, but it is just as hard not to laugh. Despite active criticism and frequent condemnation, capitalism in one form or another has become the dominant form of economic organization throughout the world because only capitalism provides freedom, improved living standards, and an ability to adapt to cultural and institutional differences.

Those who blame recent deregulation are careful not to cite examples. The most recent major change in 1999 repealed the Glass-Steagall prohibition of combined investment and commercial banking. No other country adopted that rule or had a crisis caused by failure to do so. Many years ago, George Benston (1990) showed that proponents of the rule did not make a substantive case when they claimed that combined investment and commercial banking was a cause of the Great Depression.

Members of Congress, as usual, looked for scapegoats to blame for financial failures. Others proposed new regulations to increase governmental control of financial firms. Most proposals of this kind presuppose the reason for the financial failures. In this essay, I discuss seven sources of current problems and how systemic problems can be reduced. Bear in mind that most financial firms borrow short to lend long. That arrangement means that crises will occur when there are sudden changes in the economic environment or expectations. Not all crises can be avoided. Risks will remain, but they can be reduced.

## SEVEN CAUSES

Repairing the weaknesses of the U.S. financial system that contributed to the crisis requires changes in the practices of the Congress, the administration, the Federal Reserve, and managers of financial institutions. To succeed, changes must recognize the incentives they create. This section discusses seven problems that contributed to make the crisis severe. It suggests changes to reduce risk and uncertainty.

### *Congress and the Administration*

Homeownership has long been regarded as a source of social stability, a public good that Congress and administrations of both parties encourage. Intervention takes several forms. Mortgage interest has remained tax deductible through several tax reforms including 1986, when most other interest payments lost that benefit. The Community Reinvestment Act (1977) encouraged home ownership by lower-income groups. The act gave citizen groups the opportunity to pressure banks to increase inner city lending by rating banks according to how much credit they supplied to low-income borrowers. The ratings influenced decisions to permit mergers and branches. In 1995, Congress strengthened the act. The American Dream Downpayment Act (2003) subsidized credit for low-income individuals. When that act passed, President Bush said that it was in the national interest to have more people own their home. He neglected to add "if they invested in them." In 1999, the Federal Housing Administration introduced the down payment assistance program that permitted no-down-payment loans.

In 1931, Congress urged the Federal Reserve to help the mortgage and housing markets by buying mortgages. The Federal Reserve declined, saying that was not its responsibility. Congress then established the Home Loan Bank System and followed with other agencies to support housing and the mortgage market. The Federal National Mortgage Association (FNMA, called "Fannie Mae") opened in 1937. Its mandate was to increase liquidity of the mortgage market by buying mortgages. It expanded in the 1960s and became a privately held entity in the late 1960s. The market treated its debt as subject to a federal government guarantee, although the guarantee did not become explicit until the Treasury replaced the management and took control in 2007. The Home Loan Banks chartered the Federal Home Loan Mortgage Corporation (FHLMC, called "Freddie Mac") to operate like Fannie Mae. It too lacked explicit guarantee of its debt until the Treasury assumed control. In addition, the Government National Mortgage Association (GNMA) is a government corporation that guarantees mortgage securities backed by federally insured or guaranteed loans issued by government agencies such as the Federal Housing Administration (FHA) and other agencies. Unlike Fannie Mae and Freddie Mac, GNMA does not own mortgages or mortgage-backed securities. Its guarantee subsidizes homeownership by lowering the interest rate on the mortgage.

With all the subsidies and assistance, expansion of mortgages and housing should not surprise anyone. Between 1980 and 2007, the volume of mortgages backed or supported by the three government-chartered agencies rose from $200 million to $4 trillion, an unsustainable compound growth rate of 36 percent a year. As the volume rose, the quality of mortgages declined. Government encouraged this development; in 1999 the FHA introduced a zero down payment loan, as noted above. Lenders expanded subprime mortgages, mortgages to buyers with relatively poor credit histories. Soon afterward, mortgage lenders began to offer mortgages that did not require a down payment. Then they eliminated credit checks on some mortgages. Such mortgages are called Alt-A.

Purchases and support for these subprime and Alt-A mortgages put Fannie Mae and Freddie Mac at much greater risk than in the past. In December 2008 congressional testimony, the heads of three agencies explained that they were aware of the increased risk but believed it necessary to compete with the private market. They did not add that the Federal

Home Loan Banks supplied almost half the funding for two large private lenders, Countrywide and Indy Mac, that later failed. Nor did they add that Fannie Mae and Freddie Mac owned $1.5 billion in assets related to subprime and Alt-A mortgages, about half the total outstanding. Prodded by members of Congress and the Clinton and Bush administrations, they lowered the quality of their portfolios to promote home ownership. With the failure of Fannie Mae, Freddie Mac, Countrywide, and Indy Mac, taxpayers will bear a considerable loss.

Edmund Gramlich, a member of the Federal Reserve's Board of Governors, reported on the problem but did not formally warn the Board about the deterioration of loan quality. William Poole, president of the Federal Reserve Bank of St. Louis, spoke publicly about the taxpayer's risk and urged remedial action. Alan Greenspan warned Congress about growth of Fannie Mae and Freddie Mac. There were many other warnings including from Senator Shelby, a senior member of the Banking Committee. Congress declined to act and several members denied that there was a problem. Congressional inaction increased the incentive for Fannie Mae and Freddie Mac to accept very risky loans.

There are homebuilders, mortgage lenders, and real estate agents in every congressional district. This alone encourages support for mortgage and housing subsidies and delays corrective action. It is very likely that the government will continue to subsidize homeownership. Reform should seek to put the subsidy on the budget and subject it to the appropriation process. Government mortgage market operations were a means of hiding the subsidy and often denying it. The subsidy took the form of a reduced interest rate on Fannie Mae and Freddie Mac borrowing, and did not require off-budget finance.

Fannie Mae and Freddie Mac are in receivership and under government control. They should be liquidated and terminated. Congress should vote the subsidy directly.

After much hesitation and policy change, the Treasury used most of the money in the first half of the Troubled Asset Relief Program (TARP) to supply capital to banks and other financial institutions. No large bank was allowed to fail. Once the banks received this assistance, many in Congress wanted to influence the banks' lending. Congress urged them to lend even if it meant acquiring risky loans with substandard repayment prospects.

A better alternative would have required bankers to borrow part, perhaps one-half, of the additional capital in the market. That would have increased a bank's cost, but it would deter some banks from borrowing from TARP and identify banks that the market considered insolvent. Those banks should fail. Failure means that shareholders lose their investment and management loses its job. The reorganized bank should be sold or merged.

The government and Federal Reserve treat all large banks as "too big to fail." That encourages gigantism. Instead, policy should impose a different standard: if a bank is too big to fail, it is too big. The social cost of losses to taxpayers exceeds the social benefit of large banks. The new standard would increase the incentive for bankers to be prudent.

### *Role of the Federal Reserve*

Many politicians, bankers, and journalists blamed the housing and mortgage crisis on the Federal Reserve. The basis of their complaint was that from 2003 to 2005 the Federal Reserve held the federal funds rate at one percent. This permitted credit expansion, much of which concentrated in the mortgage market.

During these years, Chairman Alan Greenspan believed and said that the country faced risk of deflation. That was a mistake. Deflation is very unlikely to occur in a country with a relatively large budget deficit, a long-term depreciating currency, and positive money growth. Critics are correct about this part of their criticism. Federal Reserve policy was too expansive as judged by the Taylor rule or the 1 percent Federal funds rate that held the real short-term interest rate negative in an expanding economy.

The next part is wrong. The Federal Reserve did not force or urge bankers and others to buy mortgage debt. That was the bankers' decision. Prudent bankers avoided excessive accumulation of low-quality mortgages. Bankers could have purchased Treasury bills or other assets with lower risk. They decided to overinvest in very risky assets and to lower quality standards. They share responsibility.

One plausible explanation of the errors that many made was the so-called "Greenspan put." Whether such a put was available, the belief was widespread that the Federal Reserve would prevent large losses, especially for large banks. Several bankers and investment bankers raised the leverage they accepted and invested in risky assets. Whether or not there was a Greenspan put, prior actions that prevented financial failures, for example protecting Long-Term Capital Management (LTCM), created moral hazard and reduced concerns for risk. Arranging the rescue of LTCM is the most recent example in a long history of preventing failures. Notable examples include First Pennsylvania Bank, Continental Illinois, and most of the New York money market banks during the Latin American debt crisis. Bankers had reason to believe that the Federal Reserve would prevent failures.

One of the criticisms earlier in this history of the Federal Reserve is that the Federal Reserve has not announced its lender-of-last-resort strategy in its ninety-five-year history. Sometimes institutions fail, sometimes the Federal Reserve supports them, and sometimes it arranges a takeover by others. There is no clear policy, no policy that one can discern. But there was a firm belief that failure was unlikely at large banks.

The absence of a policy has three unfortunate consequences. First, uncertainty increases. No one can know what will be done. Second, troubled firms have a stronger incentive to seek a political solution. They ask Congress or the administration for support or to pressure the Federal Reserve or other agencies to save them from failure. Third, repeated rescues encourage banks to take greater risk and increase leverage. This is the well-known moral hazard problem.

As financial problems spread in 2008, pressure built on Bear Stearns. The Treasury and the Federal Reserve arranged a takeover. The Federal Reserve contributed by buying—not lending—$29 billion of risky assets. Markets improved. Many bankers claimed the worst was over. A few months later Lehman Brothers failed. Without prior warning, the Federal Reserve and the Treasury announced that they would not prevent the failure, a major policy change. Next the Federal Reserve prevented the bankruptcy of American International Group by replacing management and providing up to $80 billion in credit.

What conclusion could a portfolio manager draw? There was no clear pattern, no consistency in the decisions. Uncertainty increased. Portfolio managers all over the world rushed for the safety of Treasury bills. A classic panic of the kind described by Walter Bagehot followed. Officials did not announce or follow a clear strategy, as Bagehot urged. Regulators reacted to each subsequent rush for safety by guaranteeing in turn bank deposits, money market funds, commercial paper, and other instruments.

Influenced by Bagehot's (1873) criticism, the Bank of England announced the lender-of-last-resort policy that it had followed in past crises and successfully followed the policy into the twentieth century. Panics and failures occurred, but they did not spread or accumulate. The policy called for lending without hesitation in a crisis at a penalty rate against acceptable, marketable collateral. That policy induced prudent bankers to hold collateral, and it reduced uncertainty.

By guaranteeing deposits, money market liabilities, and other instruments, the Federal Reserve prevented bank runs and further breakdown of the payments system. Unlike response during the Great Depression, depositors could not demand gold from banks, but they could demand currency and use deposits to buy gold or Treasury bills with the same effect. Because banks and other financial firms were unwilling to lend to other firms, they too bought Treasury bills and held idle reserves. The Treasury and the Federal Reserve supported these demands by paying interest on idle reserves and by exchanging Treasury bills for less liquid assets.

The Federal Reserve acted creatively to establish new lending facilities to accommodate market demands. They put off to the future any consideration of how and when they can reverse these overly expansive actions.

One lesson from the current crisis is that the Federal Reserve should announce a lender-of-last-resort strategy and follow it without exception. A second lesson is that Congress should dispense with "too big to fail." Banks and financial firms should not have incentives to become so large that they cannot fail. "Too big to fail" encourages excessive risk taking and imposes costs on the taxpayers. If banks considered too big to fail are not reduced in size, they should have substantially higher capital requirements including subordinated debt. The very high leverage ratios at large financial institutions responded to the incentives created by earlier rescues and belief in a Greenspan put.

One of the Treasury's proposed reforms gives the Federal Reserve responsibility for maintaining financial stability. This is a poor choice. The Federal Reserve did nothing about growing savings and loan failures in the 1980s. Ending that crisis cost the taxpayers about $150 billion. The Federal Reserve worked with the International Monetary Fund to protect lending banks during the Latin American debt crisis. The crisis began to end when Citicorp's chairman decided to recognize the losses by writing down the debt's value. Others followed. Soon thereafter, the Treasury began a systematic program to write down the debt. The Federal Reserve did nothing.

Although Alan Greenspan warned publicly in 1996 about irrational exuberance in the equities market, neither the Federal Reserve or the Securities and Exchange Commission tried to prevent rampant stock market speculation. And it followed by doing nothing to prevent the large expansion of subprime, Alt-A, and other mortgage loans and the rise in housing prices. This error will cost taxpayers much more than the savings and loan failures.

Reading transcripts of Federal Open Market Committee meetings, one finds very little discussion of regulatory and supervisory credit problems. The Federal Reserve's record does not support a proposal to increase its responsibility for financial stability. More important, regulation of this kind can succeed only if the regulator makes better judgments about risk than those whose wealth is at risk. A better change would make risk takers bear the risks they take. Failure should remove management and cost stockholders as in the FDICIA rule. Companies would not disappear. They would get new management and stockholders.

## *FDICIA*

In 1991, Congress passed the Federal Deposit Insurance Corporation Improvement Act (FDICIA). A main reason for the act was to reduce Federal Reserve lending to failing banks, thereby reducing losses paid by the FDIC. FDICIA gave regulators authority to intervene in solvent banks when losses reduced capital below required limits and to assume control before a bank's capital was entirely gone. The bank could then be sold or merged. Stockholders would take the loss and managers would be replaced. The regulators did not apply FDICIA standards to failing financial firms in this crisis. FDICIA should be extended to apply to all financial institutions. It is an explicit rule that, if enforced, is known to all interested parties. Prudent bankers will act to avoid failure and the loss of their jobs.

## *Regulation*

The financial crisis brought many demands for increased regulation. Few recognize that regulation works best if it takes account of the incentives it fosters. The Basel Accords agreed to by developed countries are a timely example. The accords required banks to hold more capital if they acquired more risk. The rationale seems clear and unassailable. The practice was very different.

Instead of increasing capital, banks chartered new entities to hold the risky assets. The intent was to keep the risk off their balance sheets. When the mortgage crisis occurred, the banks had to assume the risk and responsibility for losses. Regulation failed, and so did circumvention. The cost to the public is very large. This experience shows again that lawyers and bureaucrats choose regulations, but markets circumvent costly regulations.

Successful regulation recognizes that it creates incentives for avoidance or circumvention. Successful regulation aligns the interests of the regulated with socially desirable outcomes. Successful regulation induces market action to eliminate externalities. Successful regulation recognizes that market participants respond to regulation by changing their actions to find a new optimum.

Regulators rarely respond to this dynamic process by adopting regulations in response to market outcomes. Because all countries have some type of deposit insurance, either de jure or de facto, regulation must limit risk taking. FDICIA provides an incentive to avoid excessive risk. Capital requirements also help to align incentives and avoid excessive risk taking. Regulations such as the Basel Accords do not meet this standard.

After the Treasury supported General Motors and Chrysler with what will be a growing bailout of automobile companies, the Federal Reserve accepted General Motors Acceptance Corporation (GMAC) as a bank, enabling GMAC to borrow at the discount window. GMAC at once began to offer zero interest rate loans for up to five years to borrowers with below median credit ratings. This appears to be a response to pressure from prominent members of Congress, a further sacrifice of independence. Many members of Congress want the Federal Reserve to allocate credit to borrowers that they favor. This avoids the legislative and budget process just as Fannie Mae and Freddy Mac did. It subverts the principles of an independent central bank.

Independence is not just important. It is a critical part of the institutionalization of a low-inflation policy. It prevents Congress and the administration from financing deficits by printing money. And it avoids pressures for credit allocation to politically favored groups.

### *Compensation and Incentives*

MBAs who graduated from the world's leading business schools purchased and sold mortgages that carried a high degree of risk. In many cases they accepted the credit ratings supplied by others without investigating accuracy. At many banks, traders were well rewarded for doing the transactions and likely fired if they failed to do so. Compensation systems at many firms rewarded short-term increases in revenue without regard for long-term losses. Compensation systems of this kind encourage excessive risk taking.

Not all firms behaved alike. We know now that J.P. Morgan Chase, Bank of America, and some others limited risk taking much more than Citigroup, Merrill Lynch, Bear Stearns, and other failures.

Setting compensation schedules is management's responsibility. Congress cannot establish rules that managements cannot circumvent, if they choose to do so. An improved compensation system would spread rewards over time to permit losses to be recognized. This can be done in many ways. Regulators should encourage and monitor the actions that managements take, but should leave the choice of compensation schedule to management.

### *Rating Agencies*

The mix of incentives facing rating agencies are well-known as a contributor to the credit crisis. The agencies applied a rating system that had worked for decades in rating corporate bonds. This may have misled users. More seriously, rating agencies at times adjusted their ratings to satisfy client demands.

Not all of the fault falls on the rating agencies, but they share the blame. The clients did not look at the underlying securities or question the ratings except to ask for more favorable ratings. They too share the blame.

Rating agencies must develop compensation and incentive programs that reward accuracy of rating achieved over time. The aim is to give the agency and its personnel incentives for diligence and accuracy.

### *Transparency and Risk*

More information improves decisions and reduces risk. But transparency and increased information are most useful when interpretation is clear. Better reporting of asset and liability positions is most useful when risk models permit users to interpret the information correctly.

Risk models contributed to the credit crisis. These models use standard distributions. They make no distinction between permanent or persistent and transitory changes. Deciding whether risk spreads had permanently fallen before the crash or would return toward historic averages played a role in the crisis. Similarly, risk models were not useful for deciding whether the increase in house prices, or the decline in 2007, would persist. Improving ability to judge persistence can improve judgments and economic performance. Using rating agencies' judgments without due diligence is a mistake.

## RECOMMENDATIONS OF THE ISSING COMMITTEE

After the November meeting of the international grouping known as the G-20, the German government appointed a committee chaired by Professor Dr. Otmar Issing to recommend changes in policies, regulations, and supervision that would reduce the chance of future crises. The Issing committee identified three major causes of incentive misalignment: structured finance, rating agencies, and management compensation. It found that the crisis was a consequence of "massive liquidity and low interest rates" (Issing, 2008, 2) in an "environment of inadequate regulation and important gaps in supervisory oversight [and] inappropriate incentive structures" (ibid.). Unlike most comments on regulation, the report of the Issing committee emphasized incentives. This section summarizes some of its main proposals.

The committee recommended that the accuracy of rating agencies should be monitored and reported to the public. Rating fees should be linked to the accuracy of past ratings.

Many of the main proposals concern increases in transparency by specifying rules of disclosure that improve incentives by buyers and sellers of financial instruments. Securitization transactions should disclose the allocation of loss to the tranche that receives the first loss. Disclosure should be mandatory to permit the market to price risk more accurately.

The Issing committee did not propose legal limits on compensation as such rules "are expected to backfire" (ibid., 3). Instead they favored full disclosure and the development by rating agencies and auditors of a metric that reports on management incentives.

The committee also proposed a global credit register to show exposure by lenders and their counterparties. The report recognized that the register would be incomplete in real time.

## CONCLUSION

The credit crisis should be used to recognize and correct errors on several sides, not to look for scapegoats and evildoers. This is a first step to market reforms that reduce the risk of repetition. We cannot avoid all risk and should not try. We can reduce risk by better policy choices.

Public and private actions contributed to the crisis. Congress and several administrations encouraged public agencies to accept much greater risk to promote home ownership. The Federal Reserve failed to develop a lender-of-last-resort policy. This failure increased uncertainty. Many banks and financial institutions reward risk taking, thereby increasing incentives for actions that later produced losses. Rating agencies erred.

This epilogue suggests some changes to respond to these failings. Unlike the claim that more regulation is needed, I argue that regulation works well only if it takes account of the incentives it induces. Good regulation aligns public and private interests where there is evidence of market failure. Bad regulation usually requires strong enforcement.

To prevent future crises, Treasury Secretary Geithner proposed creation of a new super-regulator responsible for monitoring risk throughout the financial system. His proposal has major problems. First, there is no evidence that anyone can succeed at that task. The Federal Reserve's record in the savings and loan, Latin American debt, and recent mortgage and banking crises strongly suggests that they would fail. The Securities and Exchange Commission failed totally to prevent the Madoff scandal despite receiving evidence of Madoff's fraud. Also, the proposal ignores the pressures from Congress and others to support failing institutions important to the members. Second, the proposal increases regulators' responsibility with errors being paid for by taxpayers. A much better alternative is to strengthen bankers' responsibility by ending too big to fail and making managements and stockholders responsible for losses. This encourages bankers to hold collateral, monitor risks, and remain vigilant about the risks they accept. And it removes the risk of losses falling on taxpayers and the public.

One consequence of the credit and economic crisis is the aggressive response by governments and central banks to restore stability and growth. Eventually the excessive liquidity they created must be eliminated, a task that will not be easily accomplished. The Federal Reserve has not given much thought to how it will avoid inflation after the recovery is under way. And the greatly expanded role of governments and central banks must not become a precedent. A main lesson of this crisis is that societies must reinvent individual responsibility for avoiding excessive risk. This will be neither easy nor popular with many, but the survival and prosperity of a free society requires greater acceptance of individual responsibility for mistakes. We cannot expect a private system to survive if the profits go to the bankers and the losses go to the taxpayers.

We cannot know what the future consequence of the crisis and the policy response will be. We should recognize, however, that despite the severity of the crisis, regulators have not announced a policy or encouraged financial markets to believe that they have abandoned "too big to fail." In fact, mergers have made the largest firms larger.

The broader lesson of this experience should be that policy misjudgments by Congress and the Federal Reserve helped to bring on the crisis. Discretionary policy failed in 1929–33, in 1965–80, and now. The Federal Reserve should announce and follow a rule for its lender-of-last-resort actions. For monetary policy, the lesson should be less discretion and more rule-like behavior. For several years, I have proposed a multilateral arrangement under which major currencies—the dollar, the euro, and the yen—would agree to maintain a common rate of inflation. That would work to increase both expected price stability and greater nominal exchange rate stability. To implement the policy, the Federal Reserve should commit to the Taylor rule. For the monetary policy to work well, the Congress and the Treasury should agree to limit the budget deficit to a narrow range. A rule of this kind increases stability of both domestic and global economies. And Congress should put its housing subsidies on budget and close Fannie Mae and Freddie Mac. As the Issing committee showed, the route to less risky financial markets starts with stabilizing incentives.

The current crisis calls for reopening long-settled issues about Federal Reserve governance and independence. The 1913 Federal Reserve Act and all subsequent legislation made the Federal Reserve independent but never defined independence. Under the gold standard, that was not much of a problem, but this history shows that Federal Reserve chairs often gave up independence. The Volcker and Greenspan eras restored independence, but Chairman Bernanke has acted frequently as a financing arm of the Treasury.

The purpose of independence is to prevent government from using the central bank to finance its spending and budget deficit. Independence should not be left to the decision of the chair or the members of the Board of Governors. To protect the public, it should be defined in law. At the same time, the position of the presidents of the reserve banks should be clearly defined. Questions about their role arose many times in the past, and it has come up again. The presidents have an important role. They talk to people in their districts, and they have been a source of valid criticism of the Board's procedures for controlling inflation or analyzing the economy. Also, as the system developed, the Board chair became the dominant spokesperson. This too seems an unwise development.

# REFERENCES


Abel, Andrew B. (1997). "Comment on Feldstein," in Christina D. Romer and David H. Romer (eds.), *Reducing Inflation: Motivation and Strategy*. Chicago: University of Chicago Press for the National Bureau of Economic Research, 156–86.

Abrams, Burton A. (2006). "How Richard Nixon Pressured Arthur Burns: Evidence from the Nixon Tapes." *Journal of Economic Perspectives*, 20 (Fall), 177–88.

Ackley, Gardiner (1961). *Macroeconomic Theory*. New York: Macmillan.

Aliber, Robert Z. (1993). "Comment," in M. Bordo and B. Eichengreen (eds.), *A Retrospective on the Bretton Woods System*. Chicago: University of Chicago Press for the National Bureau of Economic Research, 257–64.

Andersen, Leonall C., and Jordan, Jerry L. (1968). "Monetary and Fiscal Actions: A Test of Their Relative Importance in Economic Stabilization." *Review*, Federal Reserve Bank of St. Louis, 50, 11–24.

Anderson, Richard G., and Rasche, Robert H. (1999). "Eighty Years of Observations on the Adjusted Monetary Base." *Review*, Federal Reserve Bank of St. Louis, 81 (January–February), 3–22.

Annual Report. *See* Board of Governors of the Federal Reserve System (various years). *Annual Report*.

Atkeson, Andrew, and Ohanian, Lee E. (2001). "Are Phillips Curves Useful for Forecasting Inflation?" *Quarterly Review*, Federal Reserve Bank of Minneapolis, winter, 2–11.

Auerbach, Robert (2006). "The Painful History of Fed Transparency." www.Marketwatch.com, May 18.

Axilrod, Stephen H. (1969). "An Empirical View of Even Keel." Board of Governors, April 22. Unpublished.

Axilrod, Stephen H. (1970a). "The FOMC Directive as Structured in the Late 1960s: Theory and Appraisal." Board of Governors, January 28, 1–63. Unpublished.

Axilrod, Stephen H. (1970b). "Formulation and Implementation of Federal Reserve Open Market Policy." Board of Governors. Unpublished draft.

Axilrod, Stephen H. (1997). Interview, June 26.

Axilrod, Stephen H. (2005). "Commentary." *Review*, Federal Reserve Bank of St. Louis, 87 (March–April), 237–42.

Axilrod, Stephen H., Meltzer, Allan H., Rasche, Robert H., and Sternlight, Peter D. (1982). Money, Credit and Banking Debate. *Journal of Money, Credit and Banking*, 14 (February), 118–47.

Bach, George L. (1971). *Making Monetary and Fiscal Policy*. Washington: Brookings.

Bagehot, Walter ([1873] 1962). *Lombard Street*. Homewood, IL: Richard D. Irwin.

Balbach, Anatol B. (1978). "The Mechanics of Intervention in the Foreign Exchange Market." *Review*, Federal Reserve Bank of St. Louis, 60, 2 (February), 2–7.

Ball, Laurence (1991). "The Genesis of Inflation and the Costs of Disinflation," *Journal of Money, Credit and Banking*, 23 (3, Part 2), 439–52.

Ball, Laurence (2002). "Short-Run Money Demand." National Bureau of Economic Research, Working Paper 9235 (October).

Ball, Laurence, and Mankiw, N. Gregory (1994). "A Sticky Price Manifesto." *Carnegie-Rochester Conference Series on Public Policy*, 41 (December), 127–51.

Baltensperger, Ernst (1999). "Monetary Policy under Conditions of Increasing Integration," in Deutsche Bundesbank (ed.), *Fifty Years of the Deutsche Mark*. New York: Oxford University Press, 439–523.

Barger, Harold (1964). *The Management of Money*. Chicago: Rand McNally.

Barro, Robert J., and Gordon, David B. (1983). "A Positive Theory of Monetary Policy in a Natural Rate Model." *Journal of Political Economy*, 91, 589–610.

Barro, Robert J., and Sahasakul, Chaipat (1986). "Average Marginal Tax Rates from Social Security and the Individual Income Tax." *Journal of Business*, 59 (October), 555–66.

Barsky, Robert B., and Killian, Lutz (2004). "Oil and the Macroeconomy Since the 1970s." *Journal of Economic Perspectives*, 18 (Fall), 115–134.

Barth, James R., Bartholomew, Philip F., and Labich, Carol J. (1989). "Moral Hazard and the Thrift Crisis: An Analysis of 1988 Resolutions." Washington: Federal Home Loan Bank Board, May.

Benston, George J. (1964). "Interest Payments on Demand Deposits and Bank Investment Behavior." *Journal of Political Economy*, 72 (October), 431–49.

Benston, George J. (1990). *The Separation of Investment and Commercial Banking*. London: Macmillan.

Benston, George J. (1997). *Government Regulation of Financial Services and Markets: An Overview and Critique*. Atlanta: Emory University Press.

Benston, George J. (2007). "Looking Back Twenty Years: What Changed, What We Wrote, and What We Did and Did Not Accomplish." *Economic Review*, Federal Reserve Bank of Atlanta, 120–23.

Bernanke, Ben (2004). "Fedspeak." www.centralbanknet.com, January 6, 1–13.

Bernanke, Ben S., and Blinder, Alan S. (1988). "Credit, Money, and Aggregate Demand." *American Economic Review*, 78 (May), 435–39.

Bernstein, Edward M. (1960). *International Effects of U.S. Economic Policy*. Study Paper 16, Study of Employment, Growth and Price Levels. Washington: U.S. Congress, Joint Economic Committee, January 25.

Bernstein, Edward M. (1972). "Discussion," in F. Machlup, A. Gutowski, and F. A. Lutz (eds.), *International Monetary Problems*. Washington: American Enterprise Institute, 37–40.

Bernstein, Irving (1996). *Guns or Butter: The Presidency of Lyndon Johnson*. New York: Oxford University Press.

Berry, John M. (1980). "Policymaking at the Fed." *Washington Post*, October 12.

Berry, Stuart, Harrison, Richard, Thomas, Ryland, and de Weymaon, Iain (2007). "Interpreting Movements in Broad Money." ERN Monetary Abstracts, October 2.

Biven, W. Carl (2002). *Jimmy Carter's Economy*. Chapel Hill: University of North Carolina Press.

Black, Robert (2005). "Reflections on the October 6, 1979 Meeting of the FOMC." *Review*, Federal Reserve Bank of St. Louis, 307–9.

Blinder, Alan S. (1997). "What Central Bankers Could Learn from Academics and Vice Versa." *Journal of Economic Perspectives*, 11 (Spring), 3–19.

Blinder, Alan S. (1998). *The Quiet Revolution: Central Banking Goes Modern*. New Haven: Yale University Press.

Blinder, Alan S. (2004). *Central Banking in Theory and Practice.* Cambridge, MA: MIT Press.

Blinder, Alan S. (2005). "What Have We Learned Since October 1979?" *Review,* Federal Reserve Bank of St. Louis, 87 (March–April), 283–86.

Board Minutes. *See* Board of Governors of the Federal Reserve System (various dates). Minutes of the Board of Governors.

Board of Governors of the Federal Reserve System (various years). *Annual Report.* Cited in text as Annual Report.

Board of Governors of the Federal Reserve System (various dates). *Minutes of the Board of Governors.* Unpublished. Cited in text as Board Minutes.

Board of Governors of the Federal Reserve System (various dates). *Minutes of the Federal Open Market Committee.* Washington. Unpublished. Cited in text as FOMC Minutes.

Board of Governors of the Federal Reserve System (various dates). Records. Cited in text as Board Records.

Board of Governors of the Federal Reserve System (1913–54). Central Subject Files, 1913–54. National Archives. Unpublished. Cited in text as Central Subject Files.

Board of Governors of the Federal Reserve System (1954). *The Federal Reserve System: Purposes and Functions,* 3rd ed. Washington: Board of Governors.

Board of Governors of the Federal Reserve System (1955). *Flow of Funds in the United States, 1939–53.* Washington: Board of Governors.

Board of Governors of the Federal Reserve System (1959). *The Federal Funds Market.* Washington: Board of Governors.

Board of Governors of the Federal Reserve System (1961). *The Federal Reserve System: Purposes and Functions,* 4th ed. Washington: Board of Governors.

Board of Governors of the Federal Reserve System and the United States Treasury Department (1963). *The Federal Reserve and the Treasury: Answers to Questions from the Commission on Money and Credit.* Englewood Cliffs, NJ: Prentice Hall for the Commission on Money and Credit. Cited in text as Commission on Money and Credit (1963).

Board of Governors of the Federal Reserve System (1971). *Reappraisal of the Federal Reserve Discount Mechanism.* Washington: Board of Governors, August.

Board of Governors of the Federal Reserve System (1976). *Banking and Monetary Statistics, 1941–1970.* Washington: Board of Governors.

Board of Governors of the Federal Reserve System (1981). *Annual Statistical Digest 1970–79.* Washington: Federal Reserve System.

Board Records. *See* Board of Governors of the Federal Reserve System (various years). Records.

Bopp, Karl A. (1965). "Confessions of a Central Banker," in P. C. Walker (ed.), *Essays in Monetary Policy in Honor of Elmer Wood.* Columbia: University of Missouri Press, 3–17.

Bordo, Michael (1993). "The Bretton Woods International Monetary System: A Historical Overview," in M. Bordo and B. Eichengreen (eds.), *A Retrospective on the Bretton Woods System.* Chicago: University of Chicago Press for the National Bureau of Economic Research, 3–98.

Bordo, Michael, and Eichengreen, Barry (1993). *A Retrospective on the Bretton Woods System.* Chicago: University of Chicago Press for the National Bureau of Economic Research.

Bordo, Michael, and Schwartz, Anna J. (1979). "Clark Warburton Pioneer Monetarist." *Journal of Monetary Economics,* 5 (January), 43–66.

Bordo, Michael, and Schwartz, Anna J. (1991). "What Has Foreign Exchange Intervention Since the Plaza Agreement Accomplished?" *Open Economies Review,* 2, 39–64.

Bordo, Michael, and Schwartz, Anna J. (1999). "Monetary Policy Regimes and Economic Performance: The Historical Record," in John B. Taylor and Michael Woodford (eds.), *Handbook of Macroeconomics,* v. 1A. Amsterdam: North-Holland.

Bordo, Michael, Simard, Dominique, and White, Eugene (1995). "France and the Bretton Woods International Monetary System, 1960 to 1968," in J. Reis (ed.), *The History of International Monetary Arrangements.* London, Macmillan.

Borio, Claudio, and Toniolo, Gianni (2006). "One Hundred Thirty Years of Central Bank Cooperation: A BIS Perspective." BIS Papers 27. Basel: Bank for International Settlements, February.

Boschen, John F., and Mills, Leonard O. (1992). "The Relation between Narrative and Money Market Indicators of Monetary Policy." *Economic Inquiry*, 33 (January), 24–44.

Bremner, Robert P. (2004). *Chairman of the Fed*. New Haven: Yale University Press.

Brimmer, Andrew (2002). Interview, February 26.

Broaddus, J. Alfred (2000). "Market Discipline and Fed Lending." *Proceedings of the Federal Reserve Bank of Chicago's 36th Annual Conference on Bank Structure and Competition*. May.

Broaddus, J. Alfred, and Goodfriend, Marvin (1984). "Base Drift and Longer Run Growth of $M_1$: Experience from a Decade of Monetary Targeting." *Economic Review*, Federal Reserve Bank of Richmond, November–December, 3–14.

Broaddus, J. Alfred, and Goodfriend, Marvin (1996). "Foreign Exchange Operations and the Federal Reserve." *Economic Quarterly*, Federal Reserve Bank of Richmond, 82, 1, 1–19.

Brunner, Karl (1961). "A Schema for the Supply Theory of Money." *International Economic Review*, 2 (January), 79–109.

Brunner, Karl (1961). "The Report of the Commission on Money and Credit." *Journal of Political Economy*, 69 (December), 605–20.

Brunner, Karl (1986). "Fiscal Policy in Macro Theory: A Survey and Evaluation," in R. W. Hafer (ed.), *The Monetary versus Fiscal Policy Debate: Lessons from Two Decades*. Totowa, NJ: Roman and Allanheld, 33–116.

Brunner, Karl, Cukierman, Alex, and Meltzer, Allan H. (1980). "Stagflation, Persistent Unemployment, and the Permanence of Economic Shocks." *Journal of Monetary Economics*, October, 467–92.

Brunner, Karl, and Meltzer, Allan H. (1964). *The Federal Reserve's Attachment to the Free Reserve Concept*. Washington: House Committee on Banking and Currency. Reprinted in K. Brunner and A. H. Meltzer (eds.), *Monetary Economics*. London: Blackwell (1989).

Brunner, Karl, and Meltzer, Allan H. (1967). "The Meaning of Monetary Indicators," in George Horwich (ed.), *Monetary Process and Policy*. Homewood, IL: Irwin, 187–217.

Brunner, Karl, and Meltzer, Allan H. (1968). "Liquidity Traps for Money, Bank Credit, and Interest Rates." *Journal of Political Economy*, 76 (January–February), 1–37.

Brunner, Karl, and Meltzer, Allan H. (1983). "Strategies and Tactics for Monetary Control." *Carnegie-Rochester Conference Series on Public Policy*, 18 (Spring), 59–103.

Brunner, Karl, and Meltzer, Allan H. (1989). *Monetary Economics*. Oxford and New York: Basil Blackwell.

Brunner, Karl, and Meltzer, Allan H. (1993). *Money and the Economy: Issues in Monetary Analysis*. Cambridge: Cambridge University Press for the Raffaele Mattioli Foundation.

Brunmeier, Jackie, and Willardson, Neil (2006). *The Region*. Minneapolis: Federal Reserve Bank of Minneapolis, September, 23–27, 38–43.

Burgess, W. Randolph (1927). *The Reserve Banks and the Money Market*. New York: Harper and Bros.

Burns, Arthur F. (1965). "Wages and Prices by Formula?" *Harvard Business Review*, 43, 2 (March–April), 55–64.

Burns, Arthur F. (1970). *The Business Cycle in a Changing World*. New York: National Bureau of Economic Research.

Burns, Arthur F. (1974). Statement before House Committee on Banking and Currency. Board Records, June 30.

Burns, Arthur F. (1978). *Reflections of an Economic Policymaker*. Speeches and Congressional Statements: 1969–1978. Washington: American Enterprise Institute.

Burns, Arthur F. (1987). "The Anguish of Central Banking." *Federal Reserve Bulletin*, September, 687–98.

Burns, Arthur F. (1988). "Ford and the Federal Reserve," in Kenneth W. Thompson (ed.), *The Ford Presidency*. Charlottesville: Millar Center, University of Virginia, 135–140.

Burns, Arthur F. (various dates). Papers. Gerald R. Ford Library. Cited in text as Burns papers.

Burns, Arthur F., and Samuelson, Paul A. (1967). *Full Employment Guideposts, and Economic Stability*. Washington: American Enterprise Institute.

Burns, Joseph M. (2004). "Monetary Policy Wasn't Manipulated for Nixon." *Wall Street Journal,* April 26, A15.

Burns papers. *See* Burns, Arthur F. (various dates). Papers.

Cagan, Phillip (1978a). "Monetarism in Historical Perspective," in T. Mayer (ed.), *The Structure of Monetarism*. New York: Norton.

Cagan, Phillip (1978b). "The Reduction of Inflation by Slack Demand," in W. Fellner (ed.), *Contemporary Economic Problems in 1978*. Washington: American Enterprise Institute.

Califano, Joseph A., Jr. (2000). *The Triumph and Tragedy of Lyndon Johnson*. College Station: Texas A&M University Press.

Calomiris, Charles (1994). "Is the Discount Window Necessary? A Penn Central Perspective." *Review,* Federal Reserve Bank of St. Louis, 76 (May–June), 31–55.

Calomiris, Charles (2002). "Safety Nets, Bailouts and Market Discipline." *Financial Regulator,* 7 (1), 16–23.

Carter, James E. (1982). Interview. Carter Presidency Project, Millar Center, University of Virginia, November 29.

Carter, James E. (various). Papers of President Carter. Atlanta: Jimmy Carter Presidential Library.

Central Subject Files. *See* Board of Governors of the Federal Reserve System (1913–54).

Chappell, Henry W., Jr., McGregor, Rob Roy, and Vermilyea, Todd A. (2005). *Committee Decisions on Monetary Policy: Evidence from Historical Records of the Federal Open Market Committee*. Cambridge: MIT Press.

Clarida, Richard, Gali, Jordi, and Gertler, Mark (1999). "The Science of Monetary Policy: A New Keynesian Perspective." *Journal of Economic Literature,* 37 (December), 1661–1707.

Clarida, Richard, Gali, Jordi, and Gertler, Mark (2000). "Monetary Policy Rules and Macroeconomic Stability: Evidence and Some Theory." *Quarterly Journal of Economics,* 115 (1), 147–80.

Clark, Lindley H. (1980). *Wall Street Journal,* December 9, p. 26.

Clarke, S. V. O. (1970). "The Interest Rate Policy Changes of 1947 and 1951." Sproul papers, office correspondence, January 19.

Collard, Fabrice and Dellas, Harris (2004). "The Great Inflation of the 1970s." European Central Bank, Working Paper 336 (April).

Comment (2004). "Role of Regional Development Banks," in N. Birdsall and L. Rojas-Suarez (eds.), *Financing Development*. Washington: Center for Global Development, 216–20.

Commission on Money and Credit (1961). *Money and Credit: Their Influence on Jobs, Prices, and Growth*. Englewood Cliffs, NJ: Prentice Hall.

Commission on Money and Credit (1963). *See* Board of Governors of the Federal Reserve System and the United States Treasury Department (1963).

Committee on the Working of the Monetary System (1959). *Report*. London: Her Majesty's Stationery Office.

Committee to Fight Inflation (1980). *A Policy Statement*. Washington: American Enterprise Institute, June 23.

Comptroller of the Currency (1966). *102nd Annual Report*. Reprinted in James J. Saxon (ed.), *Studies in Banking Competition and the Banking Structure*. Washington: Comptroller of the Currency.

*Congressional Record* (1971). Washington: Government Printing Office.

Cook, Timothy (1984). "Determinants of the Federal Funds Rate: 1979–82." *Economic Review,* Federal Reserve Bank of Richmond, January/February, 3–19.

Cook, Timothy, and Hahn, Thomas (1987). "The Effect of Changes in the Federal Funds Rate Target on Market Interest Rates in the 1970s." Federal Reserve Bank of Richmond, Working Paper 87-7.

Coombs, Charles A. (1962). "Treasury and Federal Reserve Foreign Exchange Operations." *Federal Reserve Bulletin,* September, 1138–53.

Coombs, Charles A. (1976). *The Arena of International Finance.* New York: Wiley.

Cooper, Richard N. (1993). "Comment," in Michael Bordo and Barry Eichengreen (eds.), *A Retrospective on the Bretton Woods System.* Chicago: University of Chicago Press for the National Bureau of Economic Research, 104–07.

Corden, W. Max (1993). "Why Did the Bretton Woods System Break Down?" in M. Bordo and B. Eichengreen (eds.), *A Retrospective on the Bretton Woods System.* Chicago: University of Chicago Press for the National Bureau of Economic Research, 504–9.

Council of Economic Advisers (various years). *Economic Report of the President.* Washington: Government Printing Office.

Coyne, Joseph R. (1998). Interview, April 7.

Coyne, Joseph R. (2005). "Reflections on the FOMC Meeting of October 6, 1979." *Review,* Federal Reserve Bank of St. Louis, 87 (March–April), 313–15.

Croushore, Dean (1997). "The Livingston Survey: Still Useful After All These Years." *Business Review,* Federal Reserve Bank of Philadelphia, March–April, 1–12.

Cukierman, Alex (1984). *Inflation, Stagflation, Relative Prices, and Imperfect Information.* Cambridge: Cambridge University Press.

Cukierman, Alex (1992). *Central Bank Strategy, Credibility, and Independence: Theory and Evidence.* Cambridge: MIT Press.

Cukierman, Alex (2006). "Central Bank Independence and Policy Results: Theory and Evidence," in Guillermo Ortiz (ed.), *Stability and Economic Growth: The Role of the Central Bank.* Mexico City: Banco de Mexico.

Cukierman, Alex, and Meltzer, Allan H. (1986). "A Theory of Ambiguity, Credibility and Inflation under Discretion and Asymmetric Information." *Econometrica,* 54 (September), 1099–1128.

Cukierman, Alex, and Wachtel, Paul (1979). "Differential Inflationary Expectations and the Variability of the Rate of Inflation: Theory and Evidence." *American Economic Review,* 69 (September), 595–609.

Cukierman, Alex, Webb, Steven, and Neyapati, Rilin (1992). "Measuring the Independence of Central Banks and Its Effect on Policy Outcomes." *World Bank Economic Review,* 6 (September), 353–98.

Currie, Lauchlin (1968). *The Supply and Control of Money in the United States.* With *A Proposed Revision of the Monetary System of the United States.* Submitted to the Secretary of the Treasury, September 1934. New York: Russell and Russell.

Darby, Michael, Lothian, James, Gandolfi, Arthur, Schwartz, Anna, and Stockman, Alan (1983). *The International Transmission of Inflation.* Chicago: University of Chicago Press.

Davis, Richard G. (1990). "Intermediate Targets and Indicators for Monetary Policy: An Introduction to the Issues." *Quarterly Review,* Federal Reserve Bank of New York, 15 (Summer), 71–82.

deLeeuw, Frank, and Kalchbrenner, John (1969). "Monetary and Fiscal Actions: A Test of their Relative Importance in Economic Stability." *Review,* Federal Reserve Bank of St. Louis (March), 6–11.

Dennis, Richard (2007). "Fixing the New Keynesian Phillips Curve." *FRBSF Economic Letter,* Federal Reserve Bank of San Francisco, November 30.

Department of Commerce (1988). *Business Conditions Digest.* Washington: Government Printing Office.

Department of Commerce (1989). *Business Conditions Digest,* November.

Department of State (various dates). *Foreign Relations of the United States, 1964–68.* Volume VIII. www.state.gov.

Dewald, William G. (1963). "Free Reserves, Total Reserves, and Monetary Control." *Journal of Political Economy,* 71 (April), 141–53.

Dillon, Douglas (various dates). Papers. JFK Library, Boston.
Dominguez, Kathryn, and Frankel, Jeffrey (1993). "Foreign Exchange Intervention: An Empirical Assessment," in Jeffrey Frankel (ed.), *On Exchange Rates*. Cambridge: MIT Press.
Dudler, Hermann-Joseph (1989). "Monetary Control and Exchange Market Management: German Policy Experience from the 1985 Plaza Agreement to the 1989 Summit of the ARCH." Tel-Aviv: Horowitz Institute, January 3–5.
Eastburn, David P (ed.) (1970). *Men, Money, and Policy*. Philadelphia: Federal Reserve Bank of Philadelphia.
Ehrlichman, John D. (various dates). Notes of meetings. White House Special Files, Nixon Presidential Materials. College Park, MD: National Archives II. Cited in text as Ehrlichman notes.
Ehrlichman notes. *See* Ehrlichman, John D. (various dates). Notes of meetings.
Eichengreen, Barry (1996). *Globalizing Capital: A History of the International Monetary System*. Princeton: Princeton University Press.
Eichengreen, Barry (2000). "From Benign Neglect to Malignant Preoccupation: US Balance of Payments Policy in the 1960s," in G. Perry and J. Tobin (eds.), *Economic Events, Ideas and Policies: The 1960s and After*. Washington: Brookings, 185–229.
Eichengreen, Barry (2004). "Global Imbalances and the Lessons of Bretton Woods." National Bureau of Economic Research, Working Paper 10497 (May).
Eisenhower, Dwight D. (1963). *Mandate for Change, 1953–1956*. Garden City, NY: Doubleday.
Eizenstat, Stuart (1982). Interview. Carter Presidency Project, Millar Center, University of Virginia, January 29–30.
Emminger, Otmar (1967). "Practical Aspects of the Problem of Balance-of-Payments Adjustment." *Journal of Political Economy*, 75, 4, part 2 (August), 512–22.
Ewald, William B., Jr. (1981). *Eisenhower the President*. Englewood Cliffs, NJ: Prentice-Hall.
Federal Credit (1963). *See* Report of the Committee on Federal Credit Programs (1963).
*Federal Reserve Bulletin* (1959). August, 5.
Federal Reserve Bank of New York (various dates). Archives.
Federal Reserve Bank of New York (various dates). Correspondence.
Federal Reserve Bank of St. Louis (various dates). *Rates of Change in Economic Data for Ten Industrial Countries*. St. Louis: Federal Reserve Bank of St. Louis.
Federal Reserve Bank of San Francisco (2004). "US Monetary Policy: An Introduction." *FRBSF Economic Letter*, January 30.
Feldstein, Martin (1982). "Inflation, Tax Rules, and Investment: Some Econometric Evidence." *Econometrica*, 50 (July), 825–62.
Feldstein, Martin (1993). "Lessons of the Bretton Woods Experience," in M. Bordo and B. Eichengreen, (eds.), *A Retrospective on the Bretton Woods System*. Chicago: University of Chicago Press for the National Bureau of Economic Research.
Feldstein, Martin (1997). "The Costs and Benefits of Going from Low Inflation to Price Stability," in Christina D. Romer and David H. Romer (eds.), *Reducing Inflation: Motivation and Strategy*. Chicago: University of Chicago Press for the National Bureau of Economic Research, 123–56.
Feldstein, Martin (2003). "Monetary Policy in an Uncertain Environment." *Monetary Policy and Uncertainty*. Federal Reserve Bank of Kansas City, September, 373–81.
Ferrell, Robert H. (ed.) (1981). *The Eisenhower Diaries*. New York: Norton.
Fieleke, Norman (1969). "The Buy-America Policy of the United States Government: Its Balance of Payments and Welfare Effects," *New England Economic Review*, July, 2–18.
Financial Institutions (1963). *See* Report of the Committee on Financial Institutions (1963).
Fischer, Stanley (1981). "Towards an Understanding of the Costs of Inflation: II." *Carnegie-Rochester Conference Series on Public Policy*, 15, 5–41.
Fischer, Stanley (1983). "Comment," in J. Tobin (ed.), *Macroeconomics, Prices, and Quantities*. Washington, Brookings Institution, 267–76.

Fischer, Stanley (1984). "The Benefits of Price Stability," in *Price Stability and Public Policy.* Federal Reserve Bank of Kansas City, 33–49.

Fischer, Stanley (1994). "Modern Central Banking," in F. Capie (ed.), *The Future of Central Banking.* Cambridge: Cambridge University Press.

Fisher, Irving (1920). *The Purchasing Power of Money* (rev. ed.) New York: Macmillan.

Fogerty, James E. (1992). Interview with Mark H. Willes. Website, Federal Reserve Bank of Minneapolis.

FOMC Minutes (various dates). *See* Board of Governors of the Federal Reserve System (various dates). *Minutes of the Federal Open Market Committee.*

Friedman, Milton (1951). "The Effects of a Full Employment Policy of Economic Stability: A Formal Analysis." *Economie Applequé,* 4 (July), reprinted in M. Friedman (ed.) (1953), *Essays in Positive Economics.* Chicago: University of Chicago Press, 117–32.

Friedman, Milton (1953). "The Case for Flexible Exchange Rates," in M. Friedman (ed.), *Essays in Positive Economics.* Chicago: University of Chicago Press, 157–203.

Friedman, Milton (ed.) (1956). *Studies in the Quantity Theory of Money.* Chicago: University of Chicago Press.

Friedman, Milton (1957). *A Theory of the Consumption Function.* Princeton: Princeton University Press for the National Bureau of Economic Research.

Friedman, Milton (1960). *A Program for Monetary Stability.* New York: Fordham University Press.

Friedman, Milton (1961). "The Lag in Effect of Monetary Policy." *Journal of Political Economy,* 69 (October), 447–66.

Friedman, Milton (1968a). "A Proposal for Resolving the U.S. Balance of Payments Problem." Unpublished memo to President-elect Richard Nixon.

Friedman, Milton (1968b). "The Role of Monetary Policy," *American Economic Review,* 58 (March), 1–17.

Friedman, Milton (1970). "Controls on Interest Rates Paid by Banks." *Journal of Money, Credit and Banking,* 2 (February), 15–32.

Friedman, Milton (1982). "Monetary Policy: Theory and Practice," The Money, Credit and Banking Lecture. *Journal of Money, Credit and Banking,* 14, 1, February, 98–118.

Friedman, Milton, and Heller, Walter, W. (1969). *Monetary vs. Fiscal Policy: A Dialogue.* New York: W. W. Norton for the Graduate School of Business, New York University.

Friedman, Milton, and Roosa, Robert V. (1967). *The Balance of Payments: Free versus Fixed Exchange Rates.* Washington: American Enterprise Institute.

Friedman, Milton, and Schwartz, Anna J. (1963). *A Monetary History of the United States, 1867–1960.* Princeton: Princeton University Press for the National Bureau of Economic Research.

Fuhrer, Jeffrey C. (1994). "Goals, Guidelines, and Constraints Facing Monetary Policymakers: An Overview." *New England Economic Review,* September/October, 3–14.

Funabashi, Yoichi (1989). *Managing the Dollar: From the Plaza to the Louvre,* 2nd ed. Washington: Institute for International Economics.

Furchgott-Roth, Diana (2007). "An Unnecessary Flab," email, October 8.

Furlong, Frederick T., and Kwan, Simon H. (2007). "Safe and Sound Banking Twenty Years Later: What Was Proposed and What Has Been Adopted." *Economic Review,* Federal Reserve Bank of Atlanta, 1–22.

Garbade, Kenneth D. (2004). "The Institutionalization of Treasury Note and Bond Auctions, 1970–75." *Economic Policy Review,* 10 (May), Federal Reserve Bank of New York, 29–45.

Garvy, George (1959). *Deposit Velocity and Its Significance.* New York: Federal Reserve Bank of New York.

Gavin, Francis J., and Mahan, Erin (undated). "Hegemony or Vulnerability: Giscard, Ball, and the 1962 Gold Standard Proposal." Unpublished. University of Virginia, Millar Center for Public Affairs.

Gilbert, R. Alton (1994). "A Case Study in Monetary Control, 1980–82." *Review,* Federal Reserve Bank of St. Louis, 76 (September–October), 35–55.

Goldfeld, Stephen M. (1976). "The Case of the Missing Money." *Brookings Papers on Economic Activity,* 3, 683–739.

Goldfeld, Stephen M. (1982). "Review: New Monetary Control Procedures." *Journal of Money, Credit and Banking,* 14, February, 148–55.

Goodfriend, Marvin (1986). "Secrecy and Central Banking." *Journal of Monetary Economics,* 17 (January), 63–92.

Goodfriend, Marvin (1991). "Interest Rates and the Conduct of Monetary Policy." *Carnegie-Rochester Conference Series on Public Policy,* 34 (Spring), 7–30.

Goodfriend, Marvin (1993). "Interest Rate Policy and the Inflation Scare Problem." *Economic Quarterly,* Federal Reserve Bank of Richmond, 79 (Winter), 1–23.

Goodfriend, Marvin (2005). "The Monetary Policy Debate since October 1979: Lessons for Theory and Practice." *Review,* Federal Reserve Bank of St. Louis, 87 (March–April), 243–62.

Goodfriend, Marvin, and Broaddus, J. Alfred (1996). *Economic Quarterly,* Federal Reserve Bank of Richmond, 82 (1), 1–19.

Goodfriend, Marvin, and Hargraves, Monica (1983). "A Historical Assessment of the Rationales and Functions of Reserve Requirements." *Economic Review,* Federal Reserve Bank of Richmond, March–April, 3–21.

Goodfriend, Marvin, and King, Robert G. (1997). "The New Neoclassical Synthesis and the Role of Monetary Policy." *NBER Macroeconomics Annual,* 12, 231–83.

Goodfriend, Marvin, and King, Robert G. (2005). "The Incredible Volcker Disinflation." *Journal of Monetary Economics,* 52 (July), 981–1015.

Goodfriend, Marvin, and McCallum, Bennett T. (2007). "Banking and Interest Rates in Monetary Policy Analysis: A Quantitative Exploration." *Journal of Monetary Economics,* 54 (July), 1480–1507.

Goodhart, Charles (1984). *Monetary Theory and Practice: The U.K. Experience.* London: Macmillan.

Goodwin, Doris K. (1991). *Lyndon Johnson and the American Dream.* New York: St. Martin's.

Gordon, Robert A., and Klein, Lawrence R. (eds.) (1965). *Readings in Business Cycles.* Homewood, IL: R. D. Irwin.

Gordon, Robert J. (1973). "The Response of Wages and Prices to the First Two Years of Controls." *Brookings Papers on Economic Activity,* 3, 765–78.

Gordon, Robert J. (1977). "Can the Inflation of the 1970s Be Explained?" *Brookings Papers on Economic Activity,* 1, 253–77.

Gowa, Joanne (1983). *Closing the Gold Window.* Ithaca: Cornell University Press.

Greene, John R. (1995). *The Presidency of Gerald R. Ford.* Lawrence: University Press of Kansas.

Greenspan, Alan (1989). "Statement Before the Subcommittee on Domestic Monetary Policy." October 25, 1–23, Board Records.

Greenspan, Alan (2003). *Monetary Policy Under Uncertainty.* Kansas City: Federal Reserve Bank of Kansas City.

Greenspan, Alan (2007). *The Age of Turbulence: Adventures in a New World.* New York: Penguin Press.

Grieder, William (1987). *Secrets of the Temple: How the Federal Reserve Runs the Country.* New York: Simon and Schuster.

Guenther, Kenneth (2001). Interview, July 10.

Guenther, Kenneth (undated). "Some Thoughts on Chairman Henry Reuss." Personal correspondence.

Gurley, John G., and Shaw, Edward S. (1960). *Money in a Theory of Finance.* Washington: Brookings.

Haberler, Gottfried (1965). *Money in the International Economy.* Cambridge: Harvard University Press.

Haberler, Gottfried (1990). "The International Monetary System, and a Single European Currency in a Single European Market," in W. S. Haraf and T. D. Willett (eds.), *Monetary Policy for a Volatile Global Economy.* Washington: American Enterprise Institute, 156–67.

Haberler, Gottfried, and Willett, Thomas D. (1971). "A Strategy for the U.S. Balance of Payments Policy." Washington: American Enterprise Institute. Reprinted in *Selected Essays of Gottfried Haberler,* Anthony Koo (ed.), Cambridge: MIT Press, 1985, 175–206.

Hackley, Howard (1972). "The Status of the Federal Reserve System in the Federal Government." Unpublished.

Hackley, Howard (1983). "Abbreviated Appendix of Legislation and Hearings Relating to the Federal Reserve's Status as a Non-Appropriated, and Financially Independent Agency." Board Records, February.

Hafer, R. W. (1999). "Against the Tide: Malcolm Bryan and the Introduction of Monetary Aggregate Targets." *Economic Review,* Federal Reserve Bank of Atlanta, 84 (first quarter), 20–37.

Hakkio, Craig S., Rush, Mark, and Schmidt, Timothy J. (1993). "The Marginal Income Tax Rate Schedule from 1930 to 1990." Federal Reserve Bank of Kansas City. Unpublished.

Hakkio, Craig S., Rush, Mark, and Schmidt, Timothy J. (1996). "The Marginal Income Tax Rate Schedule from 1930 to 1990." *Journal of Monetary Economics,* 38, 1 (August), 117–38.

Haldeman, H. R. (1994). *The Haldeman Diaries.* New York: G. P. Putnam's Sons.

Hamdani, Kavsar, and Peristiani, Stavros (1991). "A Disaggregate Analysis of Discount Window Borrowing." *Quarterly Review,* Federal Reserve Bank of New York, 16 (Summer), 52–62.

Hardouvelis, Gikas, and Barnhart, Scott (1989). "The Evolution of Federal Reserve Credibility: 1978–84." *Review of Economics and Statistics,* 71, 3 (August), 385–93.

Hargrove, Erwin C., and Morley, Samuel A. (eds.) (1984). *The President and the Council of Economic Advisers, Interviews with CEA Chairmen.* Boulder, CO: Westview Press.

Hartmann, Robert T. (various dates). Papers. Gerald R. Ford Library.

Havrilesky, Thomas, and Gildea, John (1990). "Packing the Board of Governors." *Challenge,* March–April, 52–55.

Havrilesky, Thomas, and Gildea, John (1992). "Reliable and Unreliable Partisan Appointees to the Board of Governors" *Public Choice,* 73: 397–417.

Hayami, Masaru (2002). "Opening Speech." Tenth International Conference, Bank of Japan, July 1.

Heller, Walter (various dates). Oral history. Lyndon Baines Johnson Library, Austin.

Heller, Walter W. (1966). *New Dimensions of Political Economy.* Cambridge: Harvard University Press.

Heller, Walter (various dates). Papers. JFK Library, Boston. Cited in text as Heller papers.

Heller papers. *See* Heller, Walter (various dates). Papers.

Hetzel, Robert L. (1996). "Sterilized Foreign Exchange Intervention: The Fed Debate in the 1960s." *Economic Quarterly,* Federal Reserve Bank of Richmond, 82 (Spring), 21–46.

Hetzel, Robert L. (1998). "Arthur Burns and Inflation." *Economic Quarterly,* Federal Reserve Bank of Richmond, 84 (Winter), 21–44.

Hetzel, Robert (2003). *The Monetary Policy of the Federal Reserve System: Analytics and History.* Federal Reserve Bank of Richmond. Unpublished.

Hetzel, Robert, and Leach, Ralph (2001). "The Fiftieth Anniversary of the Treasury-Fed Accord" Federal Reserve Bank of Richmond. Unpublished.

Hoffman, Dennis L., and Rasche, Robert H. (1991). "Long-Run Income and Interest Elasticities of Money Demand in the United States." *Review of Economics and Statistics,* 73, 665–74.

Holmes, Alan R. (1969). "Operational Constraints on the Stabilization of Money Supply

Growth," in *Controlling Monetary Aggregates*. Boston: Federal Reserve Bank of Boston, June, 65–77.

Holmes, Alan R. (1975). "Monetary Policy in a Changing Financial Environment." *Federal Reserve Bulletin*, April, 197–208.

Holmes, Alan R. (1976). "The Strategy of Monetary Control." *Federal Reserve Bulletin*, May, 411–21.

Holtfrerich, Carl-Ludwig (1999). "Monetary Policy under Fixed Exchange Rates," in Deutsche Bundesbank (ed.), *Fifty Years of the Deutsche Mark*. Oxford: Oxford University Press, 307–401.

House Committee on Banking and Currency (1962). "Bretton Woods Agreement Act Amendment." Washington: Government Printing Office, February 27.

House Committee on Banking and Currency (1966). Hearings on H.R. 14026, 89th Congress, 2nd session. Washington: Government Printing Office.

House Committee on Banking and Currency (1974). *Federal Reserve Policy and Inflation and High Interest Rates*. 93rd Congress, 2nd session, July and August. Washington: Government Printing Office.

House of Representatives, U.S. Congress (1977). *Report, Federal Reserve Reform Act*. 95th Congress, 1st session, August 2.

Humpage, Owen F. (1991). "Central Bank Intervention: Recent Literature, Continuing Controversy." *Economic Review*. Federal Reserve Bank of Cleveland, 27 (second quarter), 12–26.

Humpage, Owen F. (1994). "Institutional Aspects of U.S. Intervention." *Economic Review*, Federal Reserve Bank of Cleveland, 30 (first quarter), 2–19.

Hutchinson, Michael (2003). "Is Official Foreign Exchange Intervention Effective?" *Federal Reserve Bank of San Francisco Economic Letter*, 20 (July 18), 1–4.

IMF (1971). *Annual Report*. Washington: International Monetary Fund.

IMF (1990). *Annual Report*. Washington: International Monetary Fund.

Issing, Otmar (2003). "Monetary Policy in Uncharted Territory." Stone Lecture, London, November 3.

Issing, Otmar (2005). "Why Did the Great Inflation Not Happen In Germany?" *Review*, Federal Reserve Bank of St. Louis, 87 (March–April), 329–35.

Issing, Otmar (2008). "New Financial Order, Recommendations by the Issing Committee." Washington: G-20, November 15.

James, Harold (1996). *International Monetary Cooperation Since Bretton Woods*. Washington: International Monetary Fund; New York and Oxford: Oxford University Press.

Johannes, J. M., and Rasche, Robert H. (1979). "Predicting the Money Multiplier." *Journal of Monetary Economics*, 5 (July), 301–25.

Johnson, Harry G. (1966). "Balance of Payments Controls and Guidelines for Trade and Investment," in George P. Shultz and Robert Aliber (eds.), *Guidelines, Informal Controls, and the Market Place*. Chicago: University of Chicago Press, 165–182.

Johnson, Harry G. (1970). "The Case for Flexible Exchange Rates, 1969," in G. H. Halm (ed.), *Approaches to Greater Flexibility of Exchange Rates*. Princeton: Princeton University Press, 91–111.

Johnson, Lyndon B. (various dates). Recordings of telephone conversations—White House series. Lyndon Baines Johnson Library, Austin.

Johnson, Lyndon B. (various dates). Papers. Lyndon Baines Johnson Library, Austin.

Johnson, Lyndon B. (1971). *The Vantage Point*. New York: Holt, Rinehart and Winston.

Johnson tapes. *See* Recordings and Transcripts of Conversations and Meetings, Lyndon Baines Johnson Library (various dates).

Joint Economic Committee (various years). *Hearings on the [Year] Economic Report of the President*. Washington: Government Printing Office.

Joint Economic Committee (1952). *Monetary Policy and Management of the Public Debt*. Washington: Government Printing Office.

Joint Economic Committee (1956a). *Conflicting Official Views on Monetary Policy*. 84th Congress, 2nd session. Washington: Government Printing Office.

Joint Economic Committee (1956b). Hearings on Monetary Policy, 1955–56. 84th Congress, 2nd session. Washington: Government Printing Office.

Joint Economic Committee (1957). Hearings. Washington: Government Printing Office, February 5.

Joint Economic Committee (1959a). *Staff Report on Employment, Growth, and Price Levels*. Washington: Government Printing Office.

Joint Economic Committee (1959b). *Employment, Growth and Price Levels*. Hearings. Washington: Government Printing Office.

Joint Economic Committee (1960a). Report on the January 1960 Report of the President. 86th Congress, 2nd session. Washington: Government Printing Office.

Joint Economic Committee (1960b). *Employment, Growth and Price Levels, Report*. 86th Congress, 2nd session. Washington: Government Printing Office.

Joint Economic Committee (1960c). *A Study of the Dealer Market for Government Securities*. 86th Congress, 2nd session. Washington: Government Printing Office.

Joint Economic Committee (1962). *State of the Economy and Policies for Full Employment*. Washington: Government Printing Office, August 15–16, 1962.

Joint Economic Committee (1963). *Hearings on Economic Growth and Monetary Policy*. Washington: Government Printing Office, February 1, 1963.

Joint Economic Committee (1966). *Twentieth Anniversary of the Employment Act of 1946*, Washington, February 23. Washington: Government Printing Office.

Joint Economic Committee (1967). Hearings on the Economic Report of the President. Washington: Government Printing Office.

Joint Economic Committee (1968a). Report on the January 1968 Economic Report of the President. Washington: Government Printing Office.

Joint Economic Committee (1968b). *Federal Reserve Discount Mechanism*. Hearings before the Joint Economic Committee, September 11 and 17. Washington: U.S. Government Printing Office.

Joint Economic Committee (1968c). *Standards for Guiding Monetary Action*. Washington: Government Printing Office, May.

Joint Economic Committee (1968d). *Compendium on Monetary Policy Guidelines and Federal Reserve Structure*. Washington: Government Printing Office, December.

Joint Economic Committee (1969). *Federal Reserve Discount Mechanism: System Proposals for Change*. Report, Washington: Government Printing Office, February 6.

Joint Economic Committee (1976). *Thirtieth Anniversary of the Employment Act of 1946—A National Conference on Full Employment*. Washington: Government Printing Office, March 18 and 19.

Joint Committee on the Economic Report (1954). *United States Monetary Policy*. 83rd Congress, 2nd session. Washington: Government Printing Office.

Joint Committee on the Economic Report, Subcommittee on Economic Stabilization (1954). United States Monetary Policy: Recent Thinking and Experience. Hearings, 83rd Congress, 2nd sess. Washington: Government Printing Office.

Joint Economic Committee, Subcommittee on Economic Stabilization (1958). Economic Policy Questionnaire, 85th Congress, 2nd Session. Washington: Government Printing Office.

Jordan, Jerry L. (1978). "Two Histories of International Monetary Developments." *Journal of Monetary Economics*, 4, 415–24.

Jordan, Jerry L. (2002). Interview, December 16.

Jordan, Jerry L. (2005). Email message, May 18.

Kaldor, Nicholas (1982). *The Scourge of Monetarism*. London: Oxford.

Kane, Edward (1989). *The S&L Insurance Mess: How Did It Happen?* Washington: Urban Institute Press.

Katz, Bernard, S. (ed.) (1992). *Biographical Dictionary of the Board of Governors of the Federal Reserve System.* New York: Greenwood.

Kaufman, George G. (1980). "The Depository Institutions Deregulation and Control Act of 1980: What Has Congress Wrought?" *Economic Review, Conference Supplement,* Federal Reserve Bank of San Francisco (Autumn), 199–236.

Kearns, Doris (1976). *Lyndon Johnson and the American Dream.* New York: St. Martins.

Kennedy, John F. (various dates). Oval Office tape recordings, transcribed by Francis J. Gavin. Millar Center, University of Virginia.

Kennedy, John F. (1963). President's Special Message on the Balance of Payments. Washington, July 18.

Kennedy, John F. (2001a). *The Presidential Recordings: The Great Crises, Volume 1.* T. Naftali (ed.). New York: Norton.

Kennedy, John F. (2001b). *The Presidential Recordings: The Great Crises, Volume 2.* T. Naftali and P. Zelikow (eds.), New York: Norton.

Kennedy tapes. *See* Recordings and Transcripts of Conversations and Meetings, Kennedy White House (various dates).

Kettl, Donald F. (1986). *Leadership at the Fed.* New Haven: Yale University Press.

Keynes, John Maynard (1924). *Monetary Reform.* New York: Harcourt, Bruce.

Keynes, John Maynard (1930). *A Treatise on Money.* New York: Harcourt, Brace.

Keynes, John Maynard (1936). *The General Theory of Employment, Interest and Money.* London: Macmillan.

King, Mervyn (2004). "The Institutions of Monetary Policy." www.centralbanknet.com, January 6, 1–2.

Kitterer, Wolfgang (1999). "Public Finance and the Central Bank," in Deutsche Bundesbank (ed.), *Fifty Years of the Deutsche Mark.* Oxford: Oxford University Press.

Knell, Markus, and Stix, Helmut (2004). "Three Decades of Money Demand Studies, Some Differences and Remarkable Similarities." Österreichische Nationalbank, Working Paper 88.

Knipe, James L. (1965). *The Federal Reserve and the American Dollar.* Chapel Hill: University of North Carolina Press.

Kosters, Marvin H., with J. Dawson Ahalt (1975). *Controls and Inflation: The Economic Stabilization Program in Retrospect.* Washington: American Enterprise Institute.

Kramer, Gerald (1971). "Short-Term Fluctuations in U.S. Voting Behavior." *American Political Science Review,* 65 (March), 131–43.

Krooss, Herman (1969). *Documentary History of Banking and Currency in the United States.* New York: Chelsea House in Association with McGraw Hill.

Kydland, Finn, and Prescott, Edward C. (1977). "Rules Rather than Discretion: The Inconsistency of Optimal Plans." *Journal of Political Economy,* 85 (June), 473–92.

Laderman, Liz (2004). "Has the CRA Increased Lending for Low-Income Home Purchases?" *Federal Reserve Bank of San Francisco Economic Letter,* June 25.

Laidler, David E. W. (2004). *Macroeconomics in Retrospect: The Selected Essays of David Laidler.* Cheltenham, UK, Edward Elgar Publisher.

Laidler, David, and Parkin, Michael (1975). "Inflation: A Survey." *Economic Journal,* 85 (December), 741–809.

Lansing, Kevin J. (2002). "Can the Phillips Curve Help Forecast Inflation?" *Federal Reserve Bank of San Francisco Economic Letter,* 29 (October 4), 1–4.

Laumas, G. S., and Spencer, David E. (1980). "The Stability of the Demand for Money: Evidence from the Post-1973 Period." *Review of Economics and Statistics,* 62 (August), 455–59.

Lindsey, David (2005). Interview, January 3.

Lindsey, David, Orphanides, Athanasios, and Rasche, Robert (2005). "The Reform of October 1979: How It Happened and Why." *Review,* Federal Reserve Bank of St. Louis, 87 (March–April), 187–236.

Litterman, Robert, and Scheinkman, Jose (1991). "Common Factors Affecting Bond Returns." *Journal of Fixed Income*, 1 (1), 54–61.
Livingston, Joseph (1965). "The Business Outlook." *Philadelphia Bulletin*, May–June.
Lombra, Raymond, and Moran, Michael (1980). "Policy Advice and Policymaking at the Federal Reserve." *Carnegie-Rochester Conference Series on Public Policy*, 13 (Autumn), 9–68.
Lucas, Robert E., Jr. (1972). "Expectations and the Neutrality of Money." *Journal of Economic Theory*, 4(2), 103–24.
Lucas, Robert E., Jr. (1976). "Econometric Policy Evaluation: A Critique." *Carnegie-Rochester Conference Series on Public Policy*, 1, 19–46s.
Lucas, Robert E., Jr. (1988). "Money Demand in the United States: A Quantitative Review." *Carnegie-Rochester Conference Series on Public Policy*, 29 (Autumn), 137–68.
Lucas, Robert E., Jr. (2007). "Central Banking: Is Science Replacing Art?" in European Central Bank (ed.), *Monetary Policy: A Journey from Theory to Practice*, 168–71.
Lynn, James T., and Schultze, Charles L. (1976). *The Federal Budget: What Are the Nation's Priorities?* Washington: American Enterprise Institute.
MacAvoy, Paul W. (2003). "'Don't Just Stand There' . . . Treasury Secretary William E. Simon and Fiscal Policy During Stagflation 1975–76." *Atlantic Economic Journal*, 31 (September), 213–18.
Maisel, Sherman J. (various dates). Maisel's diary. Board of Governors of the Federal Reserve System. Unpublished. Cited in text as Maisel diary.
Maisel, Sherman J. (1973). *Managing the Dollar.* New York: Norton.
Maisel, Sherman J. (2003). Interview, November 10.
Maisel diary. *See* Maisel, Sherman J. (various dates). Maisel's diary.
Makin, John (1974). *Capital Flows and Exchange-Rate Flexibility in the Post-Bretton Woods Era.* Princeton: Essays in International Finance, 103, February.
Marshall, Alfred (1890). *Principles of Economics*, 8th ed. New York: Macmillan.
Martin, William McC., Jr. (various dates). Testimony before congressional committees, Board of Governors of the Federal Reserve System. Board Records. Cited in text as Martin testimony.
Martin, William McC., Jr. (various dates). Speeches of William McC. Martin, Jr. Board Records. Cited in text as Martin speeches.
Martin, William McC., Jr. (various dates). Papers. Missouri Historical Society. Cited in text as Martin papers.
Martin, William McC., Jr. (1959). "The Government Securities Market and Economic Growth." *Federal Reserve Bulletin*, August, 17–22.
Martin, William McC., Jr. (no date). Oral history. Missouri Historical Society. Cited in text as Martin oral history.
Martin, William McC., Jr. (1968). "The Price of Gold Is Not the Problem." Speech to the National Industrial Conference Board, February 14. Washington: Board of Governors.
Martin, William McC., Jr. (1985). "In Remembrance of Real Money." *New York Times*, December 10, B6.
Martin oral history. *See* Martin, William McC., Jr. (no date). Oral history.
Martin papers. *See* Martin, William McC., Jr. (various dates). Papers.
Martin speeches. *See* Martin, William McC., Jr. (various dates). Speeches of William McC. Martin, Jr.
Martin testimony. *See* Martin, William McC., Jr. (various dates). Testimony before congressional committees.
Matusow, Allen J. (1998). *Nixon's Economy: Booms, Busts, Dollars, and Votes.* Lawrence: University Press of Kansas.
Mayer, Thomas (1999). *Monetary Policy and the Great Inflation in the United States: The Federal Reserve and the Failure of Macroeconomic Policy, 1965–79.* Cheltenham: Edward Elgar.
McAfee, James (2004). "Historical Perspectives: Form and Function." *The Region*, Federal Reserve Bank of Minneapolis, September, 24–29.

McCallum, Bennett T. (1986). "Monetary Versus Fiscal Policy Effects: A Review of the Debate," in R. W. Hafer (ed.), *The Monetary and Fiscal Policy Debate: Lessons from Two Decades*. Totowa, NJ: Roman and Allanheld.

McCallum, Bennett T. (1988). "Robustness Properties of a Rule for Monetary Policy." *Carnegie-Rochester Conference Series on Public Policy*, 29 (Autumn), 173–204.

McCallum, Bennett T. (1999). "Recent Developments in Monetary Policy Analysis: The Roles of Theory and Evidence." *Journal of Economic Methodology*, 62, 171–198.

McGuire, Timothy W. (1976). "On Estimating the Effects of Controls." *Carnegie-Rochester Conference Series on Public Policy*, 2, 115–56.

McKinnon, Ronald (1993). "Bretton Woods, the Marshall Plan, and the Postwar Dollar Standard," in M. Bordo and B. Eichengreen (eds.), *A Retrospective on the Bretton Woods System*. Chicago: University of Chicago Press for the National Bureau of Economic Research, 597–604.

McNees, Stephen K. (1995). "An Assessment of the 'Official' Economic Forecasts." *Review*, Federal Reserve Bank of Boston, July–August, 13–23.

McWhinney, Madeline (1952). "Member Bank Borrowing from Federal Reserve Banks," in *Money Market Essays*. New York: Federal Reserve Bank, 8–12.

Meese, Richard A., and Rogoff, Kenneth (1983). "Empirical Exchange Rate Models of the Seventies: Do They Fit Out of Sample?" *Journal of International Economics*, 14 (February), 3–24.

Mehrling, Perry (2007). "An Interview with Paul A. Volcker," in Paul Samuelson and William Barnett, eds., *Inside the Economist's Mind*. Malden, MA: Blackwell, 165–91.

Meigs, A. James (1962). *Free Reserves and the Money Supply*. Chicago: University of Chicago Press.

Meiselman, David (1962). *The Term Structure of Interest Rates*. Englewood Cliffs, NJ: Prentice Hall.

Meltzer, Allan H. (1964). "Public and Private Financial Institutions: A Review of the Reports from Two Presidential Commissions." *Review of Economics and Statistics*, 46 (August), 269–77.

Meltzer, Allan H. (1974). "Credit Availability and Economic Decisions: Some Evidence from the Mortgage and Housing Markets." *Journal of Finance*, 29 (June), 763–78.

Meltzer, Allan H. (1983). "A Way to Defuse the World Debt Bomb." *Fortune*, November 28, 137–41.

Meltzer, Allan H. (1986). "Comment on Increasing Indebtedness and Financial Stability in the United States." In *Debt, Financial Stability, and Public Policy*. Kansas City: Federal Reserve Bank of Kansas City, 55–61.

Meltzer, Allan H. (1987). "Limits of Short-Run Stabilization Policy: Presidential Address to the Western Economic Association." *Economic Inquiry*, 25 (January), 1–13.

Meltzer, Allan H. (1991). "U.S. Policy in the Bretton Woods Era." The Homer Jones Lecture. *Review*, Federal Reserve Bank of St. Louis, 73 (May–June), 54–83.

Meltzer, Allan H. (1993). "Milton, Money, and Mischief: Symposium and Articles in Honor of Milton Friedman's 80th Birthday," J. L. Jordan (ed.), *Economic Inquiry*, 31 (April), 197–212.

Meltzer, Allan H. (1998). "Monetarism: The Issues and the Outcomes." *Atlantic Economic Journal*, 26 (March), 8–31.

Meltzer, Allan H. (2003). *A History of the Federal Reserve, Volume 1: 1913–1951*. Chicago: University of Chicago Press.

Meltzer, Allan H. (2005). "Origins of the Great Inflation." *Review*, Federal Reserve Bank of St. Louis, 145–76.

Meyer, Laurence H. (2004). *A Term at the Fed: An Insider's View*. New York: Harper Business.

Miller, G. William (2002). Interview, April 10.

Modigliani, Franco (1977). "The Monetarist Controversy, or Should We Forsake Stabilization Policies?" *American Economic Review*, 67 (March), 1–19.

Morris, John D. (1951). "Treasury Settles Rift with Reserve over Bond Policy." *New York Times,* March 4.

Mundell, Robert A. (1962). "The Appropriate Use of Monetary and Fiscal Policy for Internal and External Stability." *International Monetary Fund, Staff Papers,* 9 (March), 70–79.

Mundell, Robert A. (2000). "A Reconsideration of the Twentieth Century." *American Economic Review,* 90 (June), 327–40.

Mussa, Michael (1986). "Nominal Exchange Rate Regimes and the Behavior of Real Exchange Rates: Evidence and Implications." *Carnegie-Rochester Conference Series on Public Policy,* 25, 117–213.

Muth, John F. (1960). "Optimal Properties of Exponentially Weighted Forecasts." *Journal of the American Statistical Association,* 55 (June), 299–306.

Nelson, Edward (2002). "Direct Effects of Base Money on Aggregate Demand: Theory and Evidence." *Journal of Monetary Economics,* 49 (4), 687–708.

Nelson, Edward (2003a). "The Future of Monetary Aggregates in Monetary Policy Analysis." *Journal of Monetary Economics,* 50, 1029–59.

Nelson, Edward (2003b). "The Great Inflation of the Seventies: What Really Happened?" Unpublished. St. Louis: Federal Reserve Bank of St. Louis.

Neumann, Manfred J. M. (1999). "Monetary Stability: Threat and Proven Response," in Deutsche Bundesbank (ed.), *Fifty Years of the Deutsche Mark.* Oxford: Oxford University Press, 269–306.

Nixon, Richard M. (various dates). Papers. College Park, MD: National Archives II. Cited in text as Nixon papers.

Nixon, Richard M. (various dates). White House tapes. College Park, MD: National Archives II. Cited in text as White House tapes.

Nixon, Richard M. (1962). *Six Crises.* Garden City, NY: Doubleday.

Nixon, Richard (1978). *The Memoirs of Richard Nixon.* New York: Grosset and Dunlap.

Nixon papers. *See* Nixon, Richard M. (various dates). Papers.

Nordhaus, William D. (1975). "The Political Business Cycle." *Review of Economic Studies,* 42 (April).

Nordhaus, William D. (1983). "Macroconfusion: The Dilemmas of Economic Policy," in J. Tobin (ed.), *Macroeconomics, Prices, and Quantities.* Washington: Brookings Institution, 247–67.

Nordhaus, William D. (2004). "Retrospective on the 1970s Productivity Slowdown." National Bureau of Economic Research, Working Paper W10950 (December).

Nurkse, Ragnar (1944). *International Currency Experience.* Geneva: League of Nations.

O'Brien, Frank (1989). "Working at the Board, 1930s–1970s." In Eleanor Stockwell (ed.), *Working at the Board, 1920–1970.* Washington: Board of Governors of the Federal Reserve System, chapter 7.

Obstfeld, Maurice, and Rogoff, Kenneth (1995). "The Mirage of Fixed Exchange Rates." *Journal of Economic Perspectives,* 9 (Fall), 73–96.

OECD. (1990). Leading Economic Indicators. http://www.oecd.org.

Office of Management and Budget (1990). *Historical Tables.* Washington: Government Printing Office.

Oi, Walter Y. (1976). "On Measuring the Impact of Wage Price Controls." *Carnegie-Rochester Conference Series on Public Policy,* 2, 7–64.

Okun, Arthur (various dates). Oral history. Lyndon Baines Johnson Library, Austin. Cited in text as Okun oral history.

Okun, Arthur M. (1970). *The Political Economy of Prosperity.* Washington: Brookings Institution.

Okun, Arthur M. (1978). "Efficient Disinflation Policies." *American Economic Review,* 68, 2 (May), 348–52.

Okun, Arthur M. (1980). "Rational-Expectations-with-Misperceptions As a Theory of the Business Cycle." *Journal of Money, Credit and Banking,* 12, Part 2 (November), 817–25.

Okun oral history. *See* Okun, Arthur (various dates). Oral history.

Oral History Interview (1964). Walter Heller, Kermit Gordon, James Tobin, Gardner Ackley, and Paul Samuelson interviewed by Joseph Pechman, August 1 and 2. Boston: JFK Library, oral history program.

Orphanides, Athanasios (2001). "Monetary Policy Rules Based on Real-Time Data." *American Economic Review,* 91 (September), 964–85.

Orphanides, Athanasios (2002). "Monetary Policy Rules and the Great Inflation." *American Economic Review,* 92 (May), 115–20.

Orphanides, Athanasios (2003a). "The Quest for Prosperity without Inflation." *Journal of Monetary Economics,* 50, 633–63.

Orphanides, Athanasios (2003b). "Historical Monetary Analysis and the Taylor Rule." *Journal of Monetary Economics,* 50, 5 (July), 983–1022.

Orphanides, Athanasios (2004). "Monetary Policy Rules, Macroeconomic Stability and Inflation: A View from the Trenches." *Journal of Money, Credit and Banking,* 36 (April), 151–75.

Orphanides, Athanasios (2005). "Comment on: The Incredible Volcker Disinflation." *Journal of Monetary Economics,* 52 (July), 1017–23.

Orphanides, Athanasios, Porter, Richard, Reifschneider, David, Tetlow, Robert, and Finan, Frederico (2000). "Errors in the Measurement of the Output Gap and the Design of Monetary Policy." *Journal of Economics and Business,* 52 (January–April), 117–41.

Orphanides, Athanasios, and Van Orden, Simon (2004). "The Reliability of Inflation Forecasts Based on Output Gap Measures in Real Time." Finance and Economic Discussion Papers 68, Board of Governors of the Federal Reserve System.

Owens, Raymond E., and Schreft, Stacey L. (1992). "Identifying Credit Crunches." Federal Reserve Bank of Richmond, Working Paper 92-1.

Pauls, B. Dianne (1990). "U.S. Exchange Rate Policy: Bretton Woods to the Present." *Federal Reserve Bulletin,* November, 891–908.

Pierce, James L. (1970). "The Trade-Off Between Short- and Long-Term Policy Goals." Board of Governors. Unpublished. March.

Pierce, James L. (1978). "The Myth of Congressional Supervision of Monetary Policy." *Journal of Monetary Economics,* 4, 363–70.

Pierce, James L. (1979a). "A Case for Monetary Reform." *American Economic Review,* 69 (May), 246–50.

Pierce, James L. (1979b). "The Political Economy of Arthur Burns." *Journal of Finance,* 34 (May), 485–96.

Pierce, James L. (1980). "Comments on the Lombra-Moran Paper." *Carnegie-Rochester Conference Series on Public Policy,* 13 (Autumn), 79–85.

Pierce, James L. (1998). Interview, September 26.

Pierce, James L., and Enzler, Jared J. (1974). "The Effects of External Inflationary Shocks." *Brookings Papers on Economic Activity,* 1, 13–54.

Poole, William (1970). "Optimal Choice of Monetary Policy in a Simple Stochastic Macro Model." *Quarterly Journal of Economics,* 84 (May), 197–216.

Poole, William (1979). "Burnesian Monetary Policy: Eight Years of Progress?" *Journal of Finance,* 34 (May), 473–84.

Poole, William (2005). "Tracking Inflation." Speech, Kentucky State University, November 17.

Rasche, Robert (1988). "Demand Functions for U.S. Money and Credit Measures." Michigan State University, Department of Economics, Working Paper.

Rasche, Robert, and Johannes, James (1987). *Controlling the Growth of Monetary Aggregates.* Boston: Kluwer Academic Publishers.

Reagan Administration (1981). *America's New Beginning: A Program for Economic Recovery.* Washington: White House, February 18.

Recordings and Transcripts of Conversations and Meetings, Kennedy White House (various dates). Cited in text as Kennedy tapes.

Recordings and Transcripts of Conversations and Meetings, Lyndon Baines Johnson Library (various dates). Cited in text as Johnson tapes.

Reifschneider, David L., Stockton, David J., and Wilcox, David W. (1996). "Econometric Models and the Monetary Policy Process." Board of Governors. Unpublished. October.

Report of the Committee on Federal Credit Programs (1963). Washington: Government Printing Office, February. Cited in text as Federal Credit (1963).

Report of the Committee on Financial Institutions (1963). Washington: Government Printing Office, April. Cited in text as Financial Institutions (1963).

Rich, Georg (2005). "The International Consequences of the 1979 U.S. Monetary Policy Switch: The Case of Switzerland." *Review,* Federal Reserve Bank of St. Louis, 87 (March–April), 337–41.

Riefler, W. W. (1930). *Money Rates and Money Markets in the United States.* New York: Harper and Bros.

Riefler, W. W. (1958a). "Should the Federal Reserve Buy Long-Term Securities?" Unpublished. Board of Governors, May.

Riefler, W. W. (1958b). "Open Market Operations in Long-Term Securities." *Federal Reserve Bulletin,* November, 1260–74.

Robertson, Dennis H. (1956). *Economic Commentaries,* London: Staples Press.

Robinson, Joan, and Wilkinson, Frank (1985). "Ideology and Logic," in Fausto Vicarelli (ed.), *Keynes's Relevance Today* (Philadelphia: University of Pennsylvania Press), 73–98.

Roelse, Harold (1952). "The Money Market," in *Money Market Essays.* New York: Federal Reserve Bank.

Rogoff, Kenneth (1985). "The Optimal Degree of Commitment to an Intermediate Monetary Target." *Quarterly Journal of Economics,* 100 (November), 1169–89.

Romer, Christina D., and Romer, David H. (1994). "What Ends Recessions?" in Stanley Fischer and Julio Rotemberg (eds.), *Macroeconomics Annual,* 9, 13–57.

Romer, Christina D., and Romer, David H. (2002a). "A Rehabilitation of Monetary Policy in the 1950s." National Bureau of Economic Research, Working Paper W8800 (February).

Romer, Christina D., and Romer, David H. (2002b). "The Evolution of Economic Understanding and Postwar Stabilization Policy," in *Rethinking Stabilization Policy.* Kansas City: Federal Reserve Bank of Kansas City, 11–78.

Romer, Christina D., and Romer, David H. (2003). "Choosing the Federal Reserve Chair: Lessons from History." University of California, Berkeley, Department of Economics. Unpublished.

Roosa, Robert V. (1951). "Interest Rates and the Central Bank," in *Money, Trade and Economic Growth: Essays in Honor of John H. Williams.* New York: Macmillan, 270–95.

Roosa, Robert V. (1965). *Monetary Reform for the World Economy.* The Elihu Root Lectures. New York: Harper and Row for the Council on Foreign Relations.

Rose, Sanford (1974). "The Agony of the Federal Reserve." *Fortune,* July, 90–93, 180–88.

Rowan, Hobart (1978). "Farewell from Fed Chairman." *Washington Post,* April 1.

Rowe, James L., Jr. (1978). "Miller Warns of Harsh Inflation Curbs." *Washington Post,* March 23, D10.

Rudebusch, Glenn D., Sack, Brian P., and Swanson, Eric T. (2007). "Macroeconomic Implications of Changes in the Term Premium." *Review,* Federal Reserve Bank of St. Louis 89 (July–August), 241–70.

Runkle, David E. (1998). "Revisionist History: How Data Revisions Distort Economic Policy Research." *Quarterly Review,* Federal Reserve Bank of Minneapolis, 22 (Fall), 3–12.

Safire, William (1975). *Before the Fall: An Insider View of the Pre-Watergate White House.* New York: Doubleday.

Samuelson, Paul A. (1973). *Economics: An Introductory Text.* New York: McGraw Hill.

Samuelson, Paul A. (2001). Letter to the author. Unpublished. January 24.

Samuelson, Paul, and Solow, Robert (1960). "Analytical Aspects of Anti-Inflation Policy." *American Economic Review,* May, 177–94.

Samuelson, Robert J. (2004). "Unsung Triumph." *Washington Post,* June 9, 21.

Sargent, Thomas J. (1999). *The Conquest of American Inflation.* Princeton: Princeton University Press.

Sargent, Thomas J. (2002). "Commentary: The Evolution of Economic Understanding and Postwar Stabilization Policy." *Rethinking Stabilization Policy.* Kansas City: Federal Reserve Bank of Kansas City, 79–90.

Sarno, Lucio, and Taylor, Mark P. (2001). "Official Intervention in the Foreign Exchange Market: Is It Effective and, If So, How Does It Work?" *Journal of Economic Literature,* 39 (September), 839–68.

Saulnier, Raymond J. (1991). *The Constructive Years: The U.S. Economy under Eisenhower.* Lanham, MD: University Press of America.

Schlesinger, Arthur (1965). *A Thousand Days: John F. Kennedy in the White House.* Boston: Houghton Mifflin.

Schreft, Stacy L. (1990). "Credit Controls: 1980." *Economic Review,* Federal Reserve Bank of Richmond, 76 (November–December), 25–55.

Schultz, Frederick H. (2005). "The Changing Role of the Federal Reserve." *Review,* Federal Reserve Bank of St. Louis, 87 (March–April), 343–51.

Schultze, Charles (various dates). Papers. Carter Library, Atlanta.

Schultze, Charles (2005). Interview.

Schwartz, Anna J. (1987a). *Money in Historical Perspective,* with an introduction by Michael D. Bordo and Milton Friedman. Chicago: University of Chicago Press for the National Bureau of Economic Research.

Schwartz, Anna J. (1987b). "The Postwar Institutional Evolution of the International Monetary System," in A. Schwartz (ed.), *Money in Historical Perspective.* Chicago: University of Chicago Press for the National Bureau of Economic Research, 333–63.

Schwartz, Anna J. (1997). "From Obscurity to Notoriety: A Biography of the Exchange Stabilization Fund." *Journal of Money, Credit and Banking,* 29 (May), 135–53.

Sellon, Gordon H., Jr. (2003). "Monetary Policy and the Zero Bound: Policy Options When Short-Term Rates Reach Zero." *Economic Review,* Federal Reserve Bank of Kansas City, 88 (fourth quarter), 5–43.

Senate Committee on Banking and Currency (1951). Nomination of William McC. Martin, Jr. 84th Congress, 1st session. Washington: Government Printing Office.

Senate Committee on Banking and Currency (1953). Nomination of Arthur F. Burns (to Council of Economic Advisers), March 11. Washington: Government Printing Office.

Senate Committee on Banking and Currency (1969). *Nomination of Dr. Arthur F. Burns.* Washington: Government Printing Office, December 18.

Senate Committee on Banking, Housing, and Urban Affairs (1976a). Hearings, Full Employment and Balanced Growth Act of 1976, May 20. Washington: Government Printing Office.

Senate Committee on Banking, Housing, and Urban Affairs (1976b). Hearings, Third Meeting on the Conduct of Monetary Policy, May 3–5. Washington: Government Printing Office.

Senate Committee on Banking, Housing, and Urban Affairs (1978). Hearings, Full Employment and Balanced Growth Act of 1978, May 8–10. Washington: Government Printing Office.

Senate Committee on Banking, Housing, and Urban Affairs (1979). Nomination of Paul A. Volcker, July 30. Washington: Government Printing Office.

Senate Committee on Finance (1957). *Investigation of the Financial Condition of the United States.* 85th Congress, 1st session. Washington: Government Printing Office.

Shadow Open Market Committee (various dates). Semi-annual Policy Statement. Unpublished. Carnegie Mellon University and the University of Rochester, March and September.

Sheehan, John E. (2002). Interview with Mark Fischer and Sam Rushay. College Park, Maryland, August 19. Unpublished.

Sherman, Merritt (1983). "Economic Developments and Monetary Policy, 1963–1969." Board of Governors of the Federal Reserve System, 25–47. Unpublished.

Shouse, Aimee D. (2002). *Presidents from Nixon Through Carter, 1969–1981*. Westport, CT: Greenwood Press.

Shultz, George P. (various dates). Records of Secretary of the Treasury George P. Shultz, 1971–74, National Archives.

Shultz, George P. (1975). Foreword to Marvin H. Kosters, with J. Dawson Ahalt, *Controls and Inflation: The Economic Stabilization Program in Retrospect*. Washington: American Enterprise Institute, 1975, 1–4.

Shultz, George P. (2003). Interview. November 10.

Shultz, George P., and Aliber, Robert Z. (eds.) (1966). *Guidelines, Informal Controls, and the Market Place*. Chicago: University of Chicago Press.

Shultz, George P., and Dam, Kenneth W. (1998). *Economic Policy Beyond the Headlines*. 2nd ed. Chicago: University of Chicago Press.

Small, David H., and Clouse, James A. (2004). "The Scope of Monetary Policy Actions Authorized under the Federal Reserve Act." Finance and Economic Discussion Series, Board of Governors of the Federal Reserve System.

Smith, Warren L. (1956). "On the Effectiveness of Monetary Policy." *American Economic Review*, 46 (September), 588–606.

Smith, Warren L. (1969). "A Neo-Keynesian View of Monetary Policy," in *Controlling Monetary Aggregates*. Boston: Federal Reserve Bank of Boston, June, 105–126.

Solomon, Robert (1977). *The International Monetary System, 1945–76*. New York: Harper & Row.

Solomon, Robert (1982). *The International Monetary System, 1945–1981*. Rev. ed. New York: Harper & Row.

Sproul, Allan (various dates). Papers. Federal Reserve Bank of New York. Unpublished. Cited in text as Sproul papers.

Sproul, Allan (1964). "The Accord--A Landmark of the First Fifty Years of the Federal Reserve System." *Monthly Review, Federal Reserve Bank of New York*, November, 227–36.

Sproul, Allan (1980). *Selected Papers of Allan Sproul*. Lawrence Ritter (ed.). New York: Federal Reserve Bank of New York.

Sproul papers. *See* Sproul, Allan (various dates). Papers.

Staiger, Douglas, Stock, James H., and Watson, Mark W. (1997). "How Precise Are Estimates of the Natural Rate of Unemployment?" in Christina D. Romer and David H. Romer (eds.), *Reducing Inflation: Motivation and Strategy*. Chicago: University of Chicago Press for the National Bureau of Economic Research, 195–242.

Stein, Herbert (1988). *Presidential Economics: The Making of Economic Policy from Roosevelt to Reagan and Beyond*. Washington: American Enterprise Institute.

Stein, Herbert (1990). *Presidential Economics*, 2nd ed. Washington: American Enterprise Institute.

Stein, Herbert (1994). "Lessons from Living with Economic Policy." American Enterprise Institute, June 1. Unpublished.

Stern, Gary H., and Feldman, Ron J. (2004). *Too Big to Fail*. Washington: Brookings Institution.

Stock, James H., and Watson, Mark W. (1999). "Forecasting Inflation." *Journal of Monetary Economics*, 44, 293–355.

Stockwell, Eleanor (ed.) (1989). *Working at the Board, 1920–1970*. Washington: Board of Governors of the Federal Reserve System.

Strongin, Steven, and Tarhan, Vefa (1990). "Money Supply Announcements and the Market's

Perception of Federal Reserve Policy." *Journal of Money, Credit and Banking,* 22 (May), 135–53.

Subcommittee on Monetary, Credit, and Fiscal Policies (1950). *Monetary Credit and Fiscal Policies.* Joint Committee on the Economic Report. 81st Congress, 2nd session (November–December). Washington: Government Printing Office.

Subcommittee on Domestic Finance (1964). *The Federal Reserve System After Fifty Years.* Hearings before the Subcommittee on Domestic Finance, House Committee on Banking and Currency, 88th Congress, 2nd session. Washington: Government Printing Office.

Svensson, Lars E. O. (2002–3). "Liquidity Traps, Policy Rules for Inflation Targetting, and Eurosystem Monetary-Policy Strategy." *NBER Reporter,* Winter, 8–12.

Tamagna, Frank, and Garber, Margaret (1954). "The Private Demand for Gold, 1931–53." *Federal Reserve Bulletin,* September, 1–10.

Taylor, Alan M. (2000). "A Century of Purchasing Power Parity." National Bureau of Economic Research, Working Paper 8012 (November).

Taylor, John B. (1993). "Discretion versus Policy Rules in Practice." *Carnegie-Rochester Conference Series on Public Policy,* 39 (December), 195–214.

Taylor, John B. (1999). "A Historical Analysis of Monetary Policy Rules," in John B. Taylor (ed.), *Monetary Policy Rules.* Chicago for the National Bureau of Economic Research, 319–41.

Teeters, Nancy H. (1995). *The Region,* Federal Reserve Bank of Minneapolis, 9 (September), 36–37.

Thornton, Daniel, L. (1988). "The Borrowed Reserves Operating Procedure: Theory and Evidence." *Review,* Federal Reserve Bank of St. Louis, 70, 1 (January–February), 30–54.

Thornton, David L. (2004). "When Did the FOMC Begin Targeting the Federal Funds Rate? What the Verbatim Transcripts Tell Us." Unpublished. Federal Reserve Bank of St. Louis, March.

Thornton, Henry (1802). *An Inquiry into the Nature and Effects of the Paper Credit of Great Britain.* Reprint New York: Kelley, 1962.

Timberlake, Richard H. (1993). *Monetary Policy in the United States.* Chicago: University of Chicago Press.

Tobin, James (1956). "The Interest Elasticity of the Transactions Demand for Money." *Review of Economic and Statistics,* 38 (August), 241–47.

Tobin, James (1970). "Deposit Interest Ceilings as a Monetary Control." *Journal of Money, Credit and Banking,* 2 (February), 4–14.

Tobin, James (1980a). "The Monetarist Counter-Revolution Today--An Appraisal." *Economic Journal,* 91 (March), 29–42.

Tobin, James (1980b). "Stabilization Policy Ten Years After." *Brookings Papers on Economic Activity* (1), 19–71.

Tobin, James (1983). "Okun on Macroeconomic Policy: A Final Comment," in J. Tobin (ed.). *Macroeconomics, Prices, and Quantities.* Washington: Brookings Institution, 297–300.

Tobin, James (1987). *Policies for Prosperity: Essays in a Keynesian Mode.* P. M. Jackson (ed.) Cambridge: MIT Press.

Triffin, Robert (1947). "National Central Banking and the International Economy." *Postwar Economic Studies,* 7, 46–81.

Triffin, Robert (1960). *Gold and the Dollar Crisis.* New Haven: Yale University Press.

Tufte, Edward R. (1978). *Political Control of the Economy.* Princeton: Princeton University Press.

U.S. Department of Commerce (various years). *Business Conditions Digest.*

U.S. Department of State (2001). "Foreign Relations of the United States," volume 3. Washington: U.S. Government Printing Office.

Velde, Francois R. (2004). "Poor Hand or Poor Play? The Rise and Fall of Inflation in the U.S." *Economic Perspectives,* Federal Reserve Bank of Chicago, 1st quarter, 34–51.

Villard, Henry (1948). "Monetary Theory," in H. S. Ellis (ed.), *A Survey of Contemporary Economics*. Blakiston for the American Economic Association, 314–51.

Volcker, Paul A. (various dates). Volcker papers. General Records of the Department of the Treasury, RG 56, National Archives of the United States, College Park, MD.

Volcker, Paul A. (various dates). Papers. Board of Governors, Federal Reserve System, Washington.

Volcker, Paul A. (various dates). Papers. Federal Reserve Bank of New York.

Volcker, Paul A. (1970). Contingency Planning Paper, U.S. Treasury Department. National Records Center, Washington.

Volcker, Paul A. (1979). "Statement to Congress." *Federal Reserve Bulletin*, September, 738–42.

Volcker, Paul A. (1981). *Monetary Policy in 1981*. Washington: Board of Governors, Federal Reserve System, February 25–26.

Volcker, Paul A. (2001). Interview. October 31.

Volcker, Paul A. (2006). "Comments." BIS Papers 27. Basel: Bank for International Settlements, 17–19.

Volcker, Paul A., and Gyohten, Toyoo (1992). *Changing Fortunes*. New York: Times Books.

vonHagen, Jurgen (1999). "A New Approach to Monetary Policy," in Deutsche Bundesbank (ed.), *Fifty Years of the Deutsche Mark*. New York: Oxford, 403–38.

Wallich, Henry (1984). Speech to the Midwest Finance Association, Board Records, April 5.

Washington Post (1978). "Humphrey Hawkins Vote Set for Today." October 13, A9.

Weber, Arnold, and Mitchell, Daniel (1978). *The Pay Board's Progress: Wage Controls in Phase II*. Washington: Brookings Institution.

Weidenbaum, Murray (2005). *Advising Reagan: Making Economic Policy 1981–82*. St. Louis: Washington University.

Weintraub, Robert (1978). "Congressional Supervision of Monetary Policy." *Journal of Monetary Economics*, 4 (April), 341–62.

Wells, Wyatt C. (1994). *Economist in an Uncertain World*. New York: Columbia University Press.

White House tapes. *See* Nixon, Richard M. (various dates). White House tapes.

Willes, Mark H. (1992). "Interview with Mark H. Willes." Federal Reserve Bank of Minneapolis, December 8, 1–12.

Woodford, Michael (2001). "Fiscal Requirements and Price Stability." *Journal of Money, Credit and Banking*, 33 (August), 669–728.

Woodford, Michael (2003). *Interest and Prices: Foundations of a Theory of Monetary Policy*. Princeton: Princeton University Press.

Woodford, Michael (2005). "Comment on: Using a Long-Term Interest Rate as the Monetary Policy Instrument." *Journal of Monetary Economics*, 52 (5), 881–87.

Wooley, John T. (1984). *Monetary Politics: The Federal Reserve and the Politics of Monetary Policy*. Cambridge: Cambridge University Press.

Wooley, John T. (1995). "Nixon, Burns, 1972, and Independence in Practice." Unpublished. University of California, Santa Barbara, Department of Political Science, May.

Yellen, Janel L. (2006). "Prospects for the Economy." *Economic Letter*, Federal Reserve Bank of San Francisco, April 28, 1–3.

Yohe, William P. (1967). Letter to A. Meltzer. August 8.

Young, Ralph, and Yager, Charles (1960). "The Economics of 'Bills Preferably'." *Quarterly Journal of Economics*, 74 (August), 341–73.

Zarnowitz, Victor, and Moore, Geoffrey (1986). "Major Changes in Cyclical Behavior," in R. J. Gordon (ed.), *The American Business Cycles*. Chicago: University of Chicago Press for the National Bureau of Economic Research, 519–72.

# INDEX

*Page numbers in italics refer to tables or charts.*